Handbook of Accounting for Insurance Companies

ACCOUNTING AND FINANCE PRACTICE SERIES

Handbook of Accounting for Insurance Companies

Clair J. Galloway
Joseph M. Galloway

PRENTICE HALL
Englewood Cliffs, New Jersey 07632

Prentice-Hall International, Inc. *London*
Prentice-Hall of Australia, Pty. Ltd., *Sydney*
Prentice-Hall of Canada, Inc., *Toronto*
Prentice-Hall of India Private Ltd., *New Delhi*
Prentice-Hall of Japan, Inc. *Tokyo*
Prentice-Hall of Southeast Asia Pte., Ltd., *Singapore*
Whitehall Books, Ltd., *Wellington, New Zealand*
Editora Prentice-Hall do Brasil Ltda., *Rio de Janeiro*
Prentice-Hall Hispanoamericana, S.A., *Mexico*

10 9 8 7 6 5 4 3 2

Library of Congress Cataloging in Publication Data

Galloway, Clair J.
Handbook of accounting for insurance companies.

Includes index.
1. Insurance—Accounting—Handbooks, manuals, etc. I. Galloway, Joseph M. (Joseph Morris), 1957— . II. Title.
HG8077.G35 1986 657'.836 85-23082

ISBN 0-13-376013-8

PRENTICE HALL
BUSINESS & PROFESSIONAL DIVISION
A division of Simon & Schuster
Englewood Cliffs, New Jersey 07632

PRINTED IN THE UNITED STATES OF AMERICA

CONTENTS

PREFACE

While providing service over a period of years to all types of insurance companies, the authors became aware that there was no comprehensive handbook available covering accounting and financial reporting for both statutory insurance company reporting requirements and generally accepted accounting principles of public reporting companies. Books previously available have usually been limited to either statutory or public reporting needs, and even then they cover only one segment of the insurance industry. We believe there is a need for a single reference source that, first, includes both accounting and financial reporting used for all types of insurance companies, and second, provides useful information for a broad spectrum of professional people who work for or with insurance companies—directors, executive managers, accountants, actuaries, lawyers, investment advisers—as well as for educators and for students who are preparing for insurance accounting careers.

In this book, as in other accounting books, much of the subject matter is interrelated and cannot be fully described in a single chapter. Where this occurs, we have provided cross references to applicable material in other chapters. In addition, the Appendix includes illustrative filled-in annual statement forms for both property and life insurance companies. Throughout the text, references are made to the relevant sections of these annual statement forms.

Generally accepted accounting principles and statutory accounting practices are often equally applicable to all types of insurance companies. For this reason, most of the chapters cover a single accounting subject, which is subdivided by type of company only where the accounting treatment differs. Examples of bookkeeping entries are usually omitted since most readers will be more interested in an explanation of the theory and accounting rules than in their mechanical application.

Many accounting handbooks are written by a large number of authors, each responsible for a single chapter. Recognizing that this approach does have advantages, we nevertheless decided to write the entire book ourselves, believing that two authors could provide a more organized, integrated, and practical handbook.

We wish to especially thank Esther M. Galloway, wife and mother of the authors, for her encouragement and for her loving forbearance about the late evenings and weekends consumed by the authors in writing this book. We also wish to thank the accounting firms of Ernst & Whinney (Clair J. Galloway, partner, retired) and Deloitte Haskins & Sells (Joseph M. Galloway, former manager). These companies gave us, during our tenure with them, opportunities to provide a variety of services to the insurance industry.

Handbook of Accounting for Insurance Companies

1

THE BUSINESS OF INSURANCE

The material covered in this handbook is about accounting that is peculiar to insurance companies. The broad principles of accounting followed by commercial companies are equally applicable to insurance companies; the unique aspects of insurance accounting arise because the business activities and financial reporting of insurance companies are highly regulated and because the products they sell are valued on estimates of future revenues and costs. To better understand insurance company accounting principles and practices, it will be useful to review their organizational structures and some of their insurance products. Bearing in mind that there are textbooks covering the many facets of accounting that are related to the operation of insurance companies, it should be sufficient here to review the insurance organizations and their products in order to relate them to the rules governing insurance accounting and reporting.

Insurance companies—life, property and liability, and special risks—qualify for incorporation under specific state statutes. Unlike most commercial companies, which are qualified under general corporate statutes and can begin operations immediately, insurance companies must have their products approved before they can be sold.

Insurance companies organized as capital stock companies can, after providing for all their contractual liabilities and required reserves, retain any excess earnings and pay dividends to their stockholders. On the other hand, insurance companies organized on the mutual plan must return the excess surplus to their policyholders.

Life insurance companies may sell life insurance, annuities, accident and health insurances, and disability income protection. They are not permitted to issue insurance policies covering property damage, personal liability, natural calamities, or title guarantees.

Property and liability insurance companies are permitted to sell insurance policies to protect against loss from fire and windstorms, automobile accidents, injury of workers, hospital confinement and loss of wages, loss of business, failure to perform specifically, and hail, flood, and other casualties. Some companies sell only one type of policy, such as title or mortgage guarantee insurance. Property and liability companies may offer life insurance protection covering credit risks but may not issue long-term policies containing life contingencies.

In addition to specific statutes governing the organization and operation of insurance companies, the insurance departments of the various states have broad powers to regulate insurance activities, including approval of insurance policies and premium rates.

The general types of insurance products that these companies may sell are described below.

LIFE INSURANCE AND ACCIDENT AND HEALTH INSURANCE

Life Insurance

Life insurance is based on the principle that the prior loss experience of a large group is a reasonable basis for predicting the life expectancy of a new policyholder from the date on which the insurance policy is issued. The premiums paid by each policyholder are expected to cover the cost of issuing the policy, the expenses of continuing the policy in force, and the liabilites for the benefits promised. Current benefit costs are funded by the amounts held for policy liabilities plus the current premiums and investment earnings. Excess funds over the amounts required to pay these benefits are held to fund unexpected losses, company growth, and policyholder or stockholder dividends.

Life insurance is written in several forms. The two most common forms are term life and whole life insurance. Most other coverages, including those with current interest yields, are variations of term life and whole life policies.

Term life insurance policies are written for a limited period and are usually renewable until a specified age. The premiums charged for term insurance cover the risk that the insured will not survive the policy period, the expenses of issuing and maintaining the policy in force, and the expected profits or margins for the services provided by the company, discounted for the time value of money received in advance. The premiums are expressed as a unit cost per $1000 of coverage. The following factors are considered in determining term life insurance premiums:

- The expected mortality for a policyholder at current age, assuming normal health and occupational activities
- An interest assumption that reflects expected yields on the company's investment
- A loading factor for the costs of acquiring and servicing the business and for profits or margins

The latter costs include the agents' commissions and the underwriting, issuance, maintenance, and termination costs. Margins or profits can be included specifically in the calculation or can be an implicit part of other estimates. If the estimates of mortality, withdrawals, and expenses are conservative, the profits will emerge implicitly when the actual costs and expenses are paid.

Whole life insurance contains all the elements of term life insurance except that the premium is calculated to be paid over the lifetime of the policyowner and includes a larger investment element. A mature whole life policy provides for the payment of cash value upon surrender of the policy. *Endowment life insurance*, a form of whole life, requires premium payments to a fixed date, when the policy matures and the face amount becomes payable even though the insured is surviving.

The premium-collections method may cause a policy to be classified as *ordinary life insurance*, which is an individual life policy sold by an insurance agent with subsequent premiums billed by the insurance company. Or it can be classified as *industrial life insurance* if the premiums are collected directly by the agent. *Credit life insurance* is written for a limited period of time to cover the policyholder's financed purchases. Even though there are numerous variations to the premium-collection provisions, they will generally be classified under one of the subtitles mentioned above.

Accident and Health Insurance

The insurance protection offered for economic losses due to injury or poor health is classified as accident and health insurance. This policy is written for a short period of time and is generally renewable on an annual basis. If the policy contains a noncancelable clause, the policyowner has the right to renew the policy without any modifications in either the terms of coverage or the premiums charged. Alternatively, a policy with a guaranteed renewable clause may be renewed each term, subject to the insurance company's right to modify the premiums for all policyholders in that class. The premiums for accident and health policies are calculated by using morbidity tables that estimate the expected claims for individuals or groups of policyholders having common age and health experience. Other premium-determining factors include an expected lapsing of policies for nonpayment of premiums, an anticipated investment income, and expected margins or profits.

Disability Income Insurance

This insurance provides income benefits for a period of years or life should the policyholder become disabled. Most policies have a waiting period after the onset of disability or sickness before the benefit begins. Disability income protection is often purchased in connection with a wage continuation plan. The premiums are based on the claim costs incurred by the company for individuals at various age and occupational levels, the expected earnings rate on unexpended premiums, and the costs of acquiring and maintaining the policies in force. Profits and margins may be included separately or as an implicit part of the assumptions.

Annuities

Annuities are classified as immediate and deferred. An *immediate annuity* is issued for a single premium that provides a monthly or annual benefit over a definite future period or for life. Premiums for a *life annuity* are calculated much like premiums for a whole life insurance policy. Life annuity benefits terminate when the policyholder dies. In contrast, an *annuity certain* will pay to the policyholder or his or her estate a certain sum that is guaranteed at the inception of the policy.

A *deferred annuity* is similar to a savings account until converted to either a life annuity or an annuity certain. Deferred annuity premiums are collected on a periodic basis to accumulate funds that will provide benefits at some time in the future, often at retirement. Annuity policies may guarantee specific benefits or a variable benefit based on the performance of investments. Deferred variable annuity policy benefits may become fixed at the annuity starting date.

Life, annuity, accident and health, and disability income protection are the primary coverages offered by a life insurance company. Policies may be issued to individuals or in group plans. They may be sold separately or combined with other policies, such as life insurance and annuities. Many new life insurance policies provide substantial investment earnings as well as life protection. These newer policies permit flexibility in premium payments in order to accommodate the current needs of the policyholders. Many of these new policies are referred to as "variable life," "universal life," and "indeterminate premium whole life" insurance. All the traditional life protection elements are present in such products even though the policy provisions and premium payment methods are quite different than for traditional life and annuity policies.

PROPERTY AND LIABILITY INSURANCE

While life insurance coverages are subject to the long-term risks of mortality and investments, property and liability coverages are more subject to the risks of short-term losses. Property and liability insurance is generally written on a year-to-year basis. Consequently, the risk element in property and liability insurance is not as certain as it is in life insurance, which is based upon a rather reliable mortality history. Rather, property and liability insurance is subject to a greater risk of loss from natural occurrences and calamities as well as from carelessness and abuse by policyowners of insured property.

The determination of these risks is more difficult than is the determination of losses in the case of life insurance. Property and liability risks are relatively more volatile, given unexpected occurrences and the underwriting practices of the writing company. In addition, similar coverages develop different loss experiences in diverse geographic areas because the hazards are different. For example, the northeastern and central regions of the United States are far more subject to the hazards of cold and freezing temperatures which create unsafe driving conditions. The driving attitudes and enforcement practices in large metropolitan areas may create an atmosphere that causes the risk of property damage to be much greater than in areas that have smaller populations, wider streets, and a more strict enforcement of traffic rules. Similar analogies can be drawn for fire, wind, liability, crop hail, and other insurance.

Property and liability insurance covers risks not involving life contingencies. These risks include fire, water damage, burglary and theft, boiler and machinery, collision, personal injury liability, elevator, glass, property damage, workers' compensation and employers' liability, credit, fidelity and surety, aircraft, marine, mortgage guarantee, lightning, windstorms and tornadoes, earthquakes, crop, electrical disturbances, vandalism or malicious damage, collapse of buildings, explosion, and other risks. Most such policies may be included in the following categories:

Fire and Wind Insurance

The risk of loss to real and personal property from fire or windstorm is an immediate or deferred cost that must be borne by property owners. The risk is absolute. If an owner of property is willing to assume the immediate risk, there is no purpose in paying insurance premiums. For the most part, however, property owners choose to purchase insurance to provide indemnity against the risk of such losses.

Fire hazards can arise from a failure of heating, electrical, and power-generating systems and from lightning, inflammable liquids, explosions, carelessness with matches, and a multitude of other risks. Many of these hazards arise from physical sources over which the property owner has no control. They can also arise from negligence or deliberate destruction.

The premiums charged for fire and windstorm insurance are based on prior loss experience and on an analysis of current risk factors. For example, the risk of fire loss is greatly diminished if the property owner provides fire alarm systems, fire-resistant building materials, and fire extinguisher systems. In addition, the risk of loss is affected by the property location. In urban areas where there is quick response by fire-fighting equipment, the risk of loss is reduced. Also, property located in a well-developed industrial area that has adequate space between buildings and requires fire-resistant construction will be less subject to fire hazards than are buildings crowded in an older area. Homeowner properties are affected in a similar way. The risk of loss is generally greater in rural areas, especially if they do not have first-class fire-fighting facilities.

Windstorms are the result of nature's forces, and these losses are less predictable than fire losses. Certain geographic regions are subject to severe windstorm occurrences and require special construction methods and materials to reduce the risk of loss. These and other factors are considered in the determination of windstorm premiums.

Companies writing fire and windstorm policies obtain risk and rate data from various rate-making organizations. The organizations compile industry loss experience by geographic regions and consider available fire-fighting protection, neighborhood characteristics, and other factors to determine rates. Whether an insurance policy is issued depends on the company's assessment of these factors and of the physical condition of the property. The premium charged for this protection is loaded to cover the costs incurred in operating the company and a contingency factor for unexpected losses and for profit. The insurance policy describes the property covered, the maximum indemnity paid in the event of loss, and the expiration date. All covered losses occurring within the policy period will be indemnified. Payments of fire and windstorm losses are usually made promptly.

Most properties, personal or business, are insured by a licensed property and liability insurance company against loss from fire and windstorm. If such coverage is denied, property owners may request coverage through a separately operated insurance facility. The availability and amount of coverage is determined by state Fair Access to Insurance Requirement (FAIR) plans created to promote an equitable distribution and placement of responsible risk among insurers.

Property and Casualty Insurance

For some users, the term "property and casualty insurance" includes fire and windstorm coverage. More often, the term describes insurance that pays for losses arising from accidental occurrences. Losses from intentional occurrences are also covered unless they are prepetrated against the policyholder's own property.

Property and casualty losses arise from such diverse causes as collisions, explosions, dishonesty, theft, personal accidents, water leakage, faulty machinery, burglary or robbery, lost articles, and similar adversities. If these adversities involve property, the losses are determined in a manner similar to that for fire and windstorm losses. The determination of a personal loss involves judgments made by the claimant, the company, and an independent arbitrator or a jury.

Property and casualty insurance is written for a relatively short period of time. Property damage claims are usually settled promptly during or shortly after the expiration of the policy term. Personal injury, workers' compensation, and employers' liability claims that occur during the term of the policy may not be settled until long after the losses are first reported. Claims may be made after the policy expires if it can be established that the loss was incurred or aggravated during the policy term.

The process of estimating losses for property and casualty coverages requires considerable skill and experience to determine the nature of the losses and their expected cost.

Surety Insurance

Surety insurance involves a guarantee that a policyholder will perform certain obligations. These policies or bonds involve the principal who promises to perform in a certain way, a third party who is the beneficiary of these promises, and the surety company which obligates itself to indemnify the third party should the principal fail to perform as promised. In some respects, surety coverage does not fit the historical insurance concept since no protection is provided for the principal in the event of loss. It is the third party who is the potential beneficiary.

In addition, surety insurance has a theoretical zero loss ratio. The premiums charged for this coverage are really in the nature of service fees for the use of the surety bonding company's guarantee, and principals must demonstrate that they possess adequate surplus to assure performance or must deposit in escrow amounts equal to the potential losses. Unlike the premiums for other property and liability insurance, these premiums are calculated to include a high percentage of expenses and a low percentage of losses.

Surety insurance is usually required in connection with construction and similar types of contracts, and most state and municipal authorities require surety insurance in connection with all performance contracts. The agency letting the contract usually requires surety bonds that guarantee timely performance. Losses to the insurer, if any, arise from the contractor's insolvency or the failure of the amounts held in escrow to cover potential losses.

Surety insurance may be written by a multiline company or by one specializing in this type of insurance.

Crop Hail Insurance

Protecting against the hazards of hail damage to growing farm crops is a specialized field of property and casualty insurance and is especially significant to the farming economy. While the growing crops are subject to damage from other hazards, the greatest risk of loss arises from hailstorms. The coverage is not unlike that offered for windstorm damage, except that the ascertainment of losses is somewhat more difficult. A hailstorm during the early growing season may destroy the entire farm crop; if the hailstorm occurs in more mature farm crops, the expected yields at harvest are substantially reduced. Because of the limited market for crop hail insurance, it tends to be underwritten by specialty companies or by those offering farm risk policies. Unlike other insurance, the incurred losses are usually ascertainable by the end of the harvesting season and are paid before the year's end. The policy benefits are usually limited to a certain amount for each acre planted and may contain deductible features for each of the insured amounts.

Title Insurance

This is a specific risk insurance that protects owners of real property against the hazard of holding a title inferior to others. It is written by a specialty company having extensive property records (title plants) for the geographic area it serves. These records include official maps of townships and counties, copies of prior title insurance contracts, and other ownership documents and records affecting titles to properties. Title plants must be kept up to date by continuous searches of title exchanges.

The title to property that is being passed by warranty deed is usually confirmed by a lawyer after searching the deed and abstract to determine that the title is free and clear. In some instances, there may be a cloud on the title, and legal action to prove property ownership may become costly. To avoid this risk, a property owner or the mortgage loan company may choose to purchase title insurance to indemnify against the loss of property from superior title claims made by others. A single premium is paid and the policy continues in force so long as the property is owned by the same person.

Mortgage Guarantee Insurance

This is another specialized insurance that protects the mortgage lender from losses arising from the owner's default on mortgage repayments. Since mortgages are secured by real property, the insurance seldom exceeds 20 to 30 percent of the loan amount. By obtaining mortgage guarantee insurance, lenders are able to sell these loans to other investors.

The insurance may continue in force for the term of the mortgage or may be for a specified period. The insurance expires when the mortgage obligation is paid. This insurance also may be used in connection with mortgage revenue bonds covering low-income housing, mortgage pass-through certificates collaterized by individual mortgages issued by financial institutions, and other mortgage-backed investments. The premium charged for this coverage is contemplated to cover losses and expenses as incurred. A single premium plan continues the insurance in force for the term of the policy. Annual premium-paying policies are guaranteed renewable and may provide for level annual premium payments.

Professional Malpractice Insurance

This insurance offers protections to physicians, attorneys, accountants, and other licensed professionals from claims of negligence in providing services. Claims for negligence asserting failure to exercise the required standard of care by licensed professionals are often subject to jury trials to determine the value of the losses incurred. The insurance is written by multiline companies and to a more limited extent by professional cooperative associations; the latter organizations specialize in writing insurance for a single profession, such as for medical malpractice liability. The policies often provide for significant deductible amounts, and maximum policy limits are fixed. Because claims arising from professional liability are often not reported in a timely fashion and may require lengthy periods to settle, many current policies are written to cover only claims made during the policy term. The premiums for this insurance are calculated to cover losses and expenses; however, the changing claims experience makes it difficult to project future losses, and thus the premiums include significant amounts for contingencies. In states where professional liability insurance is difficult to obtain, the legislatures have often authorized the creation of joint underwriting associations requiring insurers to participate in the underwriting of malpractice insurance.

OTHER INSURANCE ARRANGEMENTS

Most insurance is written by companies offering standard insurance policies to the public. In a few instances, separate companies or accounts are created to fund special insurance needs. Many insurance arrangements are constructed to operate as a trust, following the normal corporate form. The following arrangements are some of the other insurance forms commonly encountered:

Captive Insurers

These are regularly organized insurance companies that serve one or a limited number of policyholders. The companies operate similarly to those serving the general public; however, the risks are shared by a limited number of policyholders, sometimes only one. For companies serving one or a very limited number of policyholders, the arrangement is a form of self-insurance. For those serving a wider range of policyholders, the arrangement represents a specialty company providing insurance for specific industrial or service companies.

Fair Access to Insurance Requirement (FAIR) Plans

These plans are authorized in a number of jurisdictions and operate as an association, a pool, or a syndicate to make property insurance available to owners who are denied coverage from regularly organized property and liability insurance companies. The insurers participating in the arrangement share in the losses and expenses in proportion to the property insurance premiums written within the state. The premiums charged for such insurance are based on the normal risk elements and are likely higher than for property owners not participating in the plan. These plans do not guarantee insurance for uninsurable risks; rather, they offer an opportunity for such property owners to obtain coverage if they comply with the plan's underwriting rules. The policies are generally "fronted" by the insurance companies participating in the plan, with the FAIR plan acting as the principal underwriter and claims adjuster. These FAIR plan facilities may be operated separately or in conjunction with other established rating organizations or other types of organizations.

Insurance Guarantee Associations

To protect policyholders who suffer from the insolvency of an insurer, many states have enacted guarantee plans for property and liability, life, and accident and health insurance companies. Under the plans, assessments are made against companies authorized to do business in the state whenever insolvency occurs and all policyholders benefits cannot be paid. Since the plans are designed to protect only policyholders, once all policyholder rights have been satisfied, no further support is provided to the insolvent company.

Lloyd's and Other Underwriters and Exchanges

The Lloyd's operates as a syndicate of underwriters through a single agent or manager. Those desiring insurance from Lloyd's submit their request through brokers who write the policies and submit them to the underwriters for their participation. Lloyd's does not function as an insurance company but offers significant reinsurance protection to operating companies. The coverages offered are often indistinguishable from those offered by other insurance carriers.

Some states permit the formation of an insurance exchange which functions in a manner similar to that of the Lloyd's underwriters. However, the members of the exchanges are generally regularly authorized insurance companies and brokers who choose to participate in insurance pool arrangements.

Reciprocal Insurers

For most policyowners, a reciprocal exchange company is indistiguishable from other forms of insurance companies. The basic difference is that reciprocal companies appoint, either in the policies or by contract, attorneys-in-fact to operate the companies. Consequently, a policyholder is usually considered a subscriber and the attorney-in-fact may be a separately elected individual or a management corporation responsible for the operation of the reciprocal company. The reciprocal insurer may act as a specialty company operating in a single field, such as malpractice insurance, or it may operate as a standard insurance company; it is usually subject to all the rules and regulations imposed on other insurers.

Fraternal Benefit Societies

Organizations operating under a society or lodge system and insuring only their own members are classified as fraternal benefit societies. These companies operate in a manner very similar to that of mutual insurance companies but are subject to separate regulations and are often taxed differently than ordinary life insurance companies.

Nonprofit Medical and Dental Indemnity Companies

The most prominent organizations operating under this type of plan are the Blue Cross and Blue Shield plans. The companies are subject to regulation and reporting requirements similar to those for all other insurance companies but are often exempt from state premium and other taxes.

Life Insurance Separate Accounts

Most life insurers are permitted to organize segregated investment accounts for the purpose of allocating investment income directly to contract holders participating in the account. The account forms a part of the insurance company but is separately administered and is often subject to securities regulations. If it were organized outside of a life insurance company, it would likely be classified as an investment company.

There are a number of other underwriting programs, trust funds, special risk companies, and similar facilities or organizations which may be required to operate under specific state statutes.

REINSURANCE

An insurance company accepts the risk of losses for persons or property insured by the policyowner. This protects the policyowner from the burden of losses and expenses that he or she would otherwise have to bear. When the insurance company's risk from hazard of loss increases beyond its reserves and surplus capacity, it looks for another company to share its risks. This risk sharing of original insurance contracts is called "reinsurance." Under reinsurance, the originating company remains responsible for the losses incurred but has the right to claim reimbursement from the other companies with whom it has shared the insurance premiums.

The company that issues the policy is called the "ceding"company (reinsured) and the accepting company the "assuming" company (reinsurer). If the reinsurer passes some of its risk to a third party, the transaction is called a "retrocession." Reinsurance transactions are often a significant part of the operation of any direct writing insurance company. A reinsurer may specialize in reinsurance or be a direct writing company.

There is a similarity between the reinsurance transactions of life, accident and health, and property and liability insurance companies. The reinsured first determines the amount of risk it will accept and the amount it will retain. The availability of reinsurers to participate in the risk has a significant effect on these two issues. Generally, a direct writing company will choose to retain a significant part of the risk since, if the business is profitable, any reinsurance arrangement will require the company to give up part of the profits it would otherwise earn on the business. However, the cost of reinsurance can also be viewed as a premium paid to avoid exposure to losses that could adversely affect the company's financial condition.

The following reinsurance concepts apply to life, accident and health, and property and liability insurance companies:

Life Insurance and Accident and Health Insurance Companies

Reinsurance for these companies is often written on an automatic basis whereby the reinsurer will accept the amounts in excess of the writing company's retention limits up to a predetermined maximum. Automatic reinsurance arrangements place the burden of underwriting on the reinsured, and so long as there are not significant underwriting changes, the reinsurer accepts all risks ceded to it.

Facultative reinsurance is a form of risk sharing in which each of the policies written is handled on a separate basis. The direct writing company negotiates with the reinsurer for the transfer of a part of each risk. Under this type of arrangement, the reinsurer often requires the company to conform to specific underwriting practices or may impose the use of its own standards for acceptance.

Life reinsurance is written in the following two basic forms:

Yearly Renewable Term (YRT). Under this arrangement, the writing company transfers to the reinsurer the net amount of insurance at risk and pays a 1-year term premium. The net amount at risk represents the excess of the insurance coverage over the amount of reserves held by the writing company. The reserves may be ignored, in which case the reinsurance applies to the face amount of the policy. This coverage is written on a year-to-year basis and usually expires exactly at the end of the year. If a policy is surrendered, cash values must be paid by the reinsured since these amounts are not included in the agreement.

Coinsurance. This type of reinsurance requires the writing company and the reinsurer to share losses at an agreed percentage of the total risk. The reinsured pays a proportional part of each premium to the reinsurer and charges the reinsurer for the reinsurer's share of expenses, death claims, and other benefits. The reinsurer establishes reserves for the policies assumed, thereby relieving the reinsured from providing for these amounts. Coinsurance permits a direct writing company to recover part of the first-year costs and avoids some of the new business strain on surplus.

Coinsurance may also be written on a modified basis which provides that the reinsured will retain all life reserves. Instead of transferring a portion of each policy benefit, the reinsurer pays to the reinsured the amount of increase in reserves for the year less an agreed interest rate computed on the reserves at the end of the prior year. The reinsured also receives an agreed amount covering commissions and other allowances previously paid. Using modified coinsurance, the companies avoid some of the details that are required for coinsurance in which each company must account for its proportionate share of all the benefits provided in each policy.

Property and Liability Insurance Companies

Property and liability companies are exposed to calamities of natural and human origin which could severely impair the companies' ability to continue in business. For that reason, property and liability reinsurance contracts, in addition to providing relief from new business surplus drain, also provide protection for the large unexpected losses that can occur from such calamities.

Property and liability reinsurance is classified in the following categories:

Facultative Reinsurance. This reinsurance is similar to that described above for life insurance companies. Individual risks are offered to the reinsurer on a pro rata or excess-of-loss basis. Pro rata binds the reinsurer for a predetermined percentage of each new risk, while excess of loss covers a risk in excess of amounts retained up to a specified limit.

Treaty Reinsurance. These contracts provide an arrangement whereby a certain class or type of business written is covered on an automatic basis. It is written on the following bases:

Pro Rata Reinsurance. This provides for an agreed splitting of business written on a fixed percentage of each policy loss. It may also be written on a quota share basis which automatically includes an agreed percentage of each outstanding policy.

Excess-of-Loss Reinsurance. This requires the reinsurer to reimburse the ceding company for 100 percent of the loss above a specified limit on each policy. Aggregate excess-of-loss reinsurance arrangements are similar; they provide reimbursement for amounts by which the total loss incurred during a specified period exceeds a predetermined dollar amount or a predetermined loss ratio.

Catastrophic Reinsurance. This reinsurance provides for the reimbursement of losses in excess of specified amounts arising from a single calamity of natural or human origin.

All reinsurance is based on the principle of trust. That is, the writing company is responsible for accurately recording the contracts and dividing the risks between itself and the reinsurer. The reinsurer has a right to inspect the books of the writing company but may seldom do so. In many instances, reinsurance contracts are brokered by companies that specialize in placing reinsurance. These brokers are paid a fee and are responsible for collecting and paying the reinsurance premiums and losses.

There are many variations in reinsurance contracts which arise from the diverse financial needs of the ceding and assuming companies. These contracts may also contain sharing arrangements which may affect each company's income tax provisions. The details of reinsurance contracts are covered in greater detail in Chapter 16, Reinsurance Ceded and Assumed.

2

REGULATION OF INSURANCE COMPANIES

In October 1894, in the case Commonwealth vs. Vrooman, *Mr. Justice Williams of the Pennsylvania Supreme Court made the following statement, which fairly summarizes the necessity for regulating the insurance industry:*

> *In view of the magnitude and the nature of insurance business, it is apparent that the public is largely interested in all that relates to it. The security of policyholders requires, first, permanency in the custodian of the funds gathered from them and on which their indemnity in case of loss depends; second, an honest and competent administration of these funds; third, restraint against the division of the profits of the business whenever such division would injuriously affect the security of the policyholders. How are these safeguards to be obtained? There is but one way in which they can be obtained and that is by means of general laws regulating the insurance business.*

This view of regulating the insurance business is incorporated in most current insurance laws and regulations. Legislators have generally viewed the security of policyholder funds as a public trust—and hence as an obligation superior to the security funds loaned to a commercial enterprise for a fee. In the latter instance, it is the responsibility of the lender, whether an individual or a corporation, to assess the financial stability of the borrower properly before executing the loan. But insurance transactions are not as simple as loan transactions. The insurance company has far more knowledge of the risk of loss on its policy than does the purchaser. Consequently, insurance companies are required to furnish the policy form and provide explanations about policy benefits and exclusions before the policy is issued. The agent who sells insurance coverage is also subject to state licensing requirements attesting to the agent's knowledge about the law of insurance contracts.

Policyholders seldom feel compelled to review the financial condition of the insurance company before purchasing protection, since regular state insurance examinations are made each 3 to 5 years. For commercial companies on the one hand, a review of a company's financial conditions to assess its ability to pay is considered a prerequisite to investing. On the other hand, the public buys insurance protection with confidence that the insurance company will pay according to promises made in the policies. This confidence about the financial stability of an insurance company is steeped in the history and tradition of insurance business operations.

STATE INSURANCE REGULATION

The operations of insurance companies are regulated nearly exclusively by the individual states. The federal Congress has generally deferred to state regulation as the preferable method of compelling insurance companies to operate in a responsible manner. States have responded with a reasonably consistent pattern of regulation to achieve the following purposes:

- It is in the long-range good of the public interest for insurance companies to be limited in the scope of their corporate activities.
- Laws and regulations should have as a primary objective the continuing solvency of the company.
- Insurance should be sold and funded in a manner that protects third-party beneficiaries.
- Competition should be controlled to preclude the use of unfair trade practices.

These objectives are achieved in a number of complementary ways.

Insurance Organization Laws

Insurance companies are organized or permitted to do business as domestic, foreign, or alien companies.

Domestic Companies. These companies have been incorporated in a state and have complied with all the licensing requirements for doing business in that state. The company may be organized as a capital stock company having a minimum capital stock and surplus requirement ranging from $25,000 to $3 million, depending upon the individual state capital requirement. The company may also be incorporated as a mutual policyholder company, a fraternal benefit association, or other membership-type insurance company when it has acquired the necessary policyholders and has met minimum surplus-funding requirements. A domestic company complying with state laws and regulations is permitted to operate freely as a licensed insurer within the state of incorporation.

Foreign Companies. Companies incorporated in a state and choosing to do business in another state are considered to be foreign (nondomestic) insurance companies. The rules applicable to domestic companies are usually imposed upon foreign companies seeking to do business in another state, even though such rules may be more liberal in the state of incorporation. For example, a foreign corporation may have a minimum capital requirement of $1 million in the state of domicile but is required to have one of $2 million in another state having that minimum requirement.

Alien Companies. An alien insurance company is one that is incorporated outside of the United States and seeks to do business in one or more of the several states. Because it is often difficult for alien companies to comply with state laws and regulations, these insurers usually operate as reinsurance companies.

The scope of state insurance laws covers the organization and operations of insurance companies, including life, accident and health, property and liability, medical malpractice, mutual hospital service, health maintenance organizations, township and county fire insurance associations, prearranged funeral plans, and other types of insurance organizations. It also provides for rules governing group insurance, pension plans, public employees' insurance, variable annuities, variable life insurance, and other specialized forms of insurance. In addition, the state insurance statutes usually provide for regulations of agents and brokers, insurance holding company systems, mergers, consolidation and reinsurance, social insurance, and industry-related activities.

These state laws are often specific about such items as permissible investments, required reserves for policies issued, periodic financial and other reporting, trade practices, examinations of companies, insurance policies and contracts, advertising, agents' contracts, cancellation of policies, and other operating practices.

Administrative Rules

Most states authorize the appointment or election of a commissioner or superintendent of insurance to be the state's chief insurance administrator. This state officer has broad powers to control and regulate the activities of all domestic, foreign, and alien insurers. His or her interpretations and rulings about a company's compliance with state laws and regulations are usually subject only to judicial review. Rules and regulations issued by the insurance commissioner usually need only comply with the reasonable requirement that they are necessary to assure the proper operation of insurance companies. The individual state insurance departments vary in size and scope of operation depending upon the number of domestic and foreign insurers doing business in that state. Most state insurance departments are responsible for the following functions:

Company Organization. Companies are not permitted to organize or sell securities without the prior approval of the commissioner's office. Unless the plan and similar details have been specified in state law, the commissioner must usually review the plan of organization, approve the funding plan (including determining maximum promotional expense allowances), investigate the organizers, and assure compliance with the applicable securities laws.

License Requirements. A company organized to conduct insurance operations must be licensed to issue life, accident and health, property and liability, or other forms of insurance. To receive such licenses, the company must have complied fully with the laws and regulations of each state in which it chooses to transact such business. The licenses are usually issued annually and are a precondition for all insurance sales. In addition to licensing companies, the commissioner also issues licenses for agents and brokers to sell company-approved policies.

Policies and Forms. Each policy or contract issued by a licensed insurance company must be approved in advance by the commissioner of insurance. Many state laws and regulations stipulate the standard wording that must be included in the insurance contract. Also, where future benefits are dependent upon policy accumulations, the minimum valuation standards and loan and surrender values must be specified. Often, grace periods, renewal options, and similar provisions must be provided on a uniform basis. Separate divisions in the insurance department are created to approve contracts for life insurance and property and liability insurance. Policies and contracts with standard coverages are usually approved promptly. Those with new and novel provisions may be subject to a more thorough investigation to ascertain that the forms comply with existing regulations and that the promises are achievable.

Insurance Rates. The regulation of insurance rates, an important function of the state insurance department, is intended not to prohibit competition but to ensure that standards established in the rate law are complied with. These standards, whether specified in the law or by administrative ruling, are established to preclude unlimited competition which can be injurious to the public welfare. In addition, rate regulation is intended to ensure that insurance companies charge adequate rates, sufficient to pay losses when due.

Most state insurance departments require that the rates be reasonable and adequate. This means that there should be no unfair rate discrimination between risks having similar hazards and costs. To ascertain the rate adequacy, companies must use their past and projected experience to prepare demonstrations that such rates comply with regulatory expectations. Rate demonstrations include estimates of losses, expenses, and policy services to provide the basis for premiums charged.

For property and liability coverages, companies often participate in rate-making organizations that file statistical data with the state insurance department. For life and other similar coverages, the demonstration must include reasonable estimates for losses, expenses, dividends, and other benefits.

Premium rates for credit life insurance and credit accident and health insurance are often subject to a maximum per $100 of credit life and a maximum loss/premium ratio for credit accident and health insurance. These policies are directed toward consumer group insurance, are issued on a franchise plan, and are more subject to regulatory control than most other types of insurance, to ensure that the rates are not excessive, inadequate, or unfairly discriminatory.

Premium rate concessions to special classes are usually not permitted since it is contrary to public policy to permit the return of premiums or the payment of dividends on any basis other than for an entire class of policies. The assumptions made for losses in rate applications may not be directly related to the statutory requirements used to determine legal reserves for financial reporting. Individual states often have different programs to determine whether rates are excessive or unfairly discriminatory. Some require prior approval before rate changes are made, some permit companies to use new rates as soon as filings are made, and others permit open competition which does not require rate filings.

Marketing and Trade Practices

A state insurance department has broad powers to investigate and control the marketing and trade practices of insurance companies and their agents. This regulatory activity involves preapproval for policies and forms and after-the-sale review of agent and company market conduct.

A state insurance department first determines that the agents and brokers are competent and trustworthy representatives of an insurance company before issuing them a license to do business. Insurance agents are specifically prohibited from engaging in the following unfair trade practices:

Rebating. A licensed agent is not permitted to pay or offer to pay or otherwise give an allowance which amounts to returning part of the insurance premium as an inducement to accept an insurance policy.

Twisting. Agents and brokers are precluded from misrepresenting premiums or policy benefits for the purpose of inducing a policyholder to lapse, forfeit, or convert an existing insurance policy for a new policy.

Misleading Advertising. An agent or broker may not by means of public advertising misrepresent the benefits, terms, or conditions of an insurance policy or of potential policy benefits, such as dividends. Insurance policies or classes of policies cannot be combined in a manner that will misrepresent the true nature of each policy.

Misappropriation and Comingling. Laws and regulations generally provide for penalties in connection with the misappropriation of funds belonging to others and the comingling of policyholder premiums with other funds of the agent or broker.

The commissioner's office also regulates the activities of the insurance companies to prevent unfair methods of competition or unfair and deceptive acts or practices. The following are some of the more significant areas reviewed by the commissioner's office:

Sales and Advertising. All promotional materials must be presented in a manner that does not misrepresent the policy benefits and terms and that provides adequate disclosure of exclusions, limitations, or reductions. The companies are also precluded from making misleading or disparaging references about competitors' financial conditions.

Underwriting Practices. The accuracy of underwriting practices is reviewed to determine that proper forms and ratings are used in the selection of risk and that there is compliance with all underwriting rules in order to avoid unfairly discriminating, canceling, or refusing to renew policy coverage.

Rate Application. Since rates must be approved by the commissioner's office, a market conduct review is made to determine that rates are appropriately applied to each risk.

Claims Practice. Claims files must indicate that established procedures are followed in examining loss history and that timely payments are made for claims incurred. Denial of claims reimbursement for covered losses is considered an unfair trade practice unless the files fully disclose the basis for denying payment.

Financial Examination. It is the responsibility of the commissioner of insurance to ensure that insurance companies are well managed and financially sound. The commissioner's department has free access to insurance company books and records and conducts periodic financial examinations at least every 3 to 5 years. For companies having marginal solvency, the commissioner may conduct an annual examination until the financial condition improves.

Financial examinations may be conducted on a "zone" basis, requiring the participation of several states, which avoids unnecessary duplication of examinations by the various state insurance departments. Under the terms of a reciprocal agreement, the states agree to accept a zone examination to satisfy most financial examination requirements. Some states also require that insurance companies provide annual financial audits conducted by certified public accountants.

All states require the filing of an annual financial statement which includes details about assets, liabilities, and operations. These annual statements are prepared on a form that is universally accepted and which reflects the admitted value of assets and the minimum reserve requirements of the domicile state. The annual statements are prepared on a basis that emphasizes the solvency of the company and its ability to pay policyholder benefits when due. These statements are also available for public inspection. The financial examination conducted by insurance departments ensures that companies are adhering to statutory investment policies, that loss reserves are provided in an amount to satisfy legal reserve requirements, that premiums collected in advance are held for future policy cancellation, and that premiums and expenses are recorded in accordance with established regulatory practices.

Other Regulatory Functions. The commissioner or superintendent of insurance usually has broad powers to investigate the financial or operating condition of any company doing business in the state and may hold hearings on rate violations and unfair trade practices. Companies not satisfying the financial solvency requirements may be declared insolvent, in which case they are subject to rehabilitation or liquidation plans prepared by the insurance commissioner.

The insurance commissioner's office also issues administrative rulings or advisory opinions about the conduct of insurance business. These rulings and opinions generally have the force of law. The rulings and opinions may be in response to interpreting current law, implementing trade practices, or limiting investments and establishing reserve requirements. As the state's chief insurance enforcement officer, the commissioner's primary responsibility is to control risk selection, ensure efficient operations and financial solvency, and control investment policies, all for the purpose of protecting policyholders and claimants.

NATIONAL ASSOCIATION OF INSURANCE COMMISSIONERS

This is a voluntary association of the top insurance administrators of each state. The association promotes the uniform administration of insurance companies through its development of programs designed to provide fair administration of insurance companies operating in several states and uniform financial and marketing examinations.

Because of its general acceptance in most states, the association is recognized as a quasi-legal authority for annual reporting and financial examination requirements. All states require or permit the filing of an annual statement prepared from annual report blanks developed by the association. These report blanks provide detailed information about the assets, reserves and liabilities, surplus, and revenue and expenses of all insurance companies. While some states may require additional filings, the annual report blanks provide the basic information about all insurance companies and are filed separately in each state in which the company is licensed to do business.

The association also develops model insurance laws covering all aspects of the regulation of insurance companies. Other important publications include the examiner's handbook for financial and market examinations, accounting handbooks, and other insurance-related references.

An important service provided by the association is the valuation of securities, which is published annually for the purpose of determining admitted asset values for public and private investment securities. This ensures that investment securities are uniformly valued by all companies. Companies holding securities not registered or regularly traded may request a separate valuation by submitting the necessary financial and operating data for companies issuing the investment securities.

The association's activities are funded by membership assessments through a central office. The organization meets regularly and acts upon the recommendations made by its various committees.

VOLUNTARY ASSOCIATIONS

To a great extent, insurance companies voluntarily regulate their activities by membership in industry organizations. Most property and liability insurance companies participate in rate-making organizations that file countrywide rates for most lines of business. These companies conform to the rates or file modifications or deviations to establish their individual premium rates.

There are a number of other voluntary associations that provide marketing programs, research, public relations, and education. Most of these associations impose membership requirements that are intended to assist in the proper business conduct of their members.

3

RELATIONSHIP OF GENERALLY ACCEPTED ACCOUNTING PRINCIPLES AND STATUTORY ACCOUNTING PRACTICES

Accounting principles are intended to provide established methods of recording and reporting upon the activities of a business enterprise and to value the cumulative results in terms of financial strength at a given period of time. Accounting technicians have long applied a set of standards that will achieve these goals. However, the goals of the accounting technician, the needs of management, and other uses of financial statements have not always been in full agreement. One group may look for consistency, another group may look at asset valuation that measures current value, and still another group may emphasize liquidity and the ability to pay all debts in cash. Therefore, when comparing the generally accepted method of accounting to statutory accounting practices, it is important to understand that neither lays claims to a perfect system. Rather, each emphasizes a group of principles or practices that best serves a group of users of financial statements.

FINANCIAL STATEMENT USERS

Generally accepted accounting principles presume that all users of financial statements will require similar classification and valuation processes for reporting the financial results of a business enterprise. It is at this reporting point that a distinction between the use of generally accepted accounting principles and of statutory accounting practices emerges, particularly in terms of the reporting needs that they serve.

The regulators of insurance companies require financial data that is based on a set of accounting practices that emphasize *liquidity* as the primary measurement of the reporting process. Their goal is to ascertain that sufficient funds will exist to pay the insurance and other liabilities incurred by companies from the insurance products they sell. For example, insurance accounting practices require the immediate expensing of product acquisition costs. This accounting practice varies significantly from generally acccepted accounting principles, in which there is an underlying assumption that the best financial measurement is the matching of costs and expenses with revenue in the current accounting period. This difference in the two systems of accounting is based on the user's perceived need of financial information: To one, the accounting effect on liquid assets is more important; to the other, the measurement of results of operations is more important. Underlying this basic difference is the question of who the users of financial statements for insurance enterprises are.

If the company is owned by stockholders, there is a natural presumption that they will require the use of generally accepted accounting principles since this seems to be the best measurement of current operating results. Stockholders are generally more interested in emphasizing return on invested funds than in determining underlying book value. For these users, the consistency in matching revenues and expense is of paramount importance to the financial statements.

Insurance company regulators are financial statement users and as a group place more emphasis on the liquidity of company assets than on operating results. Their view of the need for financial statements does not give great weight to the needs of stockholders, who benefit from the success of the enterprise only after all insurance liabilities are fully provided for. The funds of the stockholders and policyholders are considered together to determine solvency. If a balance remains in the capital and surplus account after all the insurance and other liabilities are fully provided for, the matter is incidental in the preparation of the statutory financial statements. That is not to say that insurance regulators are disinterested in how stockholders may be treated. Rather, it is to emphasize that insurance regulators are responsible to see that the promises made by the insurance enterprise to policyholders are kept and fully funded.

Other potential users of financial statements of insurance enterprises are the individual policyowners. They have a right to receive financial information, and it may be in their best interest to investigate the financial strength of the company insuring their risk. It is rather doubtful that, as a group, they have a great interest in the details of the financial statements. A policyholder generally takes comfort in the knowledge that the insurance company is required by law to maintain adequate reserves for the payment of policyholders' claims or to indemnify on behalf of the policyowner the party injured. Policyowners' interests in financial statements are presumed to be satisfied by following statutory accounting practices, and the board of directors of a stock or mutual insurance company has a fiduciary responsibility to ensure that the interests of policyholders are provided for.

COMPLIANCE REPORTING

Insurance companies may generally be classified as capital stock insurance companies, which are organized and owned by stockholders; mutual insurance companies, which are organized and owned by the policyholders; and reciprocal exchanges, which are organized and funded by attorneys-in-fact. In many respects, all of these companies are subject to similar compliance reporting. However, capital stock companies may be subject to special reporting under the securities law of the state of which they are organized or under the Securities and Exchange Commission (SEC), which is governed by provisions of the federal code and regulations. These agencies ensure that investors receive adequate information about the activities of the company, including its results of operations and financial condition. For the most part, these reporting requirements follow generally accepted accounting principles.

Insurance companies are also subject to some statistical reporting for purposes of determining premium rates. For property and liability companies, the statistical data includes the geographic location of losses and the type of coverage provided. For life insurance companies, the data is not so voluminous and may often include industry tables of experience rather than the company's own experience, which may be somewhat limited. Statistical reporting is intended to provide a basis for consistency in the approved rate structure for similar types of risk.

Annual Statement Blank

The most significant and universally required reporting that is peculiar to insurance companies is included in the statutory annual statement. The ability of a company to continue in the business of insurance is dependent upon the results that are obtained in these annual statements. The statement blanks are uniform for all states and result from the recommendations made by the National Association of Insurance Commissioners (NAIC). Most state codes and regulations set out the detailed information that must be included in the annual statement; however, these requirements are deemed to be met if the NAIC blank is used. While some states may require additional reporting, the basic data that discloses the strength or weakness of an insurance company is found in this blank. The annual statement blanks are different for life insurance companies and property and liability insurance companies; however, each consists of a series of financial statements supported by parts, exhibits, and schedules. The annual statement is prepared in great detail and is cross-referenced to the basic financial statements and their supporting parts, and exhibits, and schedules. The reported financial data includes the following:

Ledger Amounts. These represent amounts recorded in the general ledger of the insurance company and for the most part reflect the results of cash transactions. Ledger amounts consist of investments and other assets, premiums and investment income received, and paid claim costs and expenses. Property and liability companies also record amounts due from agents and policyholders for premiums that have not yet been received but which are included in income.

Non-Ledger Amounts. These amounts represent accruals and valuation items not included in the general ledger. Accrual items include amounts recoverable from reinsurance companies, investment income due and accrued, and valuations applied to the common stock portfolio for the purpose of stating these investments at market. Other non-ledger amounts include estimated liabilities for policy reserves, claims outstanding, unpaid dividends and expenses, unearned premiums and investment income, and, for life insurance companies, a valuation account for securities.

Assets Not Admitted. A number of ledger and non-ledger items are excluded from reported assets. These items are excluded because they are not recognized by law or regulation as meeting the requirements for liquidity. Non-admitted assets include furniture, equipment, automobiles, accounts receivable not taken for premiums, and investments not meeting return requirements or made in excess of permissible limits. The exclusion of such items from the annual statement reflects the emphasis on liquidity of assets.

The financial statements appearing in the annual statement are similar to the financial statements required for generally accepted accounting principles; a balance sheet, a summary of operations, changes in capital and surplus, and a statement of changes in financial position. The detailed parts, exhibits, and schedules that support these financial statements are included in much greater detail than is required for most commercial reporting. For example, certain schedules include details of all invested assets, significant insurance liabilities, and premium income. In addition, there are a number of parts, exhibits, and schedules that display significant operating results of the company. These include details of investment income, capital gains and losses, premiums, costs and expenses, analysis of insurance reserves, and numerous other schedules.

The annual statement is constructed from the general ledger, from subsidiary detail records that represent non-ledger amounts, and from statistical data derived from the company's own experience during the period.

Financial details are collected from several operating areas within the company. While it is not necessary here to review the details of each item appearing in the annual statement, the following significant financial statements and supporting parts, exhibits, and schedules are covered in summary form; the material in the following two sections covers annual statements for life, accident and health, and property and liability insurance.

LIFE INSURANCE AND ACCIDENT AND HEALTH INSURANCE

Statement of Assets, Liabilities, and Surplus

Assets. This statement includes all the ledger assets, which for the most part comprise the invested assets of the company. Other amounts include non-ledger assets and are comprised of common and preferred stock values in excess of or less than cost, amounts due from reinsurers, federal income taxes recoverable, accrued investment income, net deferred or uncollected premiums on life insurance and accident and health insurance contracts, and miscellaneous other assets. The significant nonadmitted assets are comprised of investments which are not in good standing, amounts in excess of the cost of investments over the values placed on the securities by the NAIC subcommittee on valuation of securities, furniture, equipment and automobiles, and amounts receivable from agents and employees. The details of ledger assets, non-ledger assets, and non-admitted assets which comprise "admitted assets" are included in Exhibit 13.

The details of the company's investments and securities are included in Schedule D. This schedule lists each investment, showing the acquisition date, cost and market value, amortization of premium and discounts, and investment income received or receivable. Schedule D is divided into parts to show the securities owned, the securities purchased during the period, and the disposition of the securities during the year.

Other net admitted assets are further supported by Schedule A, which includes the details of home office real estate and investment real estate; Schedule B, a summary of mortgage loans on real estate outstanding; Schedule BA, other long-term invested assets; Schedule C, a summary of collateral loans outstanding; Schedule E, a listing of bank accounts and deposits; and Schedule S, the details of reinsurance receivable.

Exhibit 12, which is a reconciliation of ledger assets, does not support detailed asset balances but rather reconciles the total of ledger assets at the beginning and end of the year with the transaction during the year.

Liabilities, Surplus, and Other Funds. With the exception of a few items such as amounts withheld from payroll, agents' credit balances, and premiums and other items received but not yet allocated to income accounts, most liability amounts are not recorded in the general ledger. The largest liabilities are for insurance reserves. Life insurance reserves are summarized in Exhibit 8 as life insurance, annuities, supplementary contracts with life contingencies, accidental death benefits, disability-active lives, disability-disabled lives, and miscellaneous reserves. Reserves are further classified as industrial, ordinary, credit, and group insurance. These aggregate reserves are reduced for reinsurance-ceded credits, which are detailed by èach reinsurance company in Schedule S. Like the aggregate reserves for life policies and contracts themselves, which do not require an outlay of cash funds, the reinsurance-ceded credit likewise does not produce an inflow of funds until a policy claim is made. The details of these reserves are covered in Chapter 16, Reinsurance Ceded and Assumed.

Accident and health policy reserves are summarized in Exhibit 9, which is composed of two sections. Section A contains the detail of active life reserves, which has two parts. The first part represents the unearned premium reserve for premiums received in advance; the unearned premium reserve is based on the pro rata unexpired portion of the premiums. The other component of Section A is the additional reserves that are required. These reserves are calculated by using valuation standards for morbidity and interest that are required or permitted by law or regulation. The totals in Section A are reduced by the amount of unearned premium that applies to reinsurance ceded.

Section B of Exhibit 9 includes the value of claim reserves. This reserve consists of the gross value of claims which have been incurred, discounted to their present value. Expected credits for reinsurance ceded are used to reduce the Section B claim reserves. Accident and health reserves are classified between group, credit, and individual health and accident insurance. The latter classification is further summarized by noncancelable, guaranteed renewable, and other policy features.

Supplementary contracts without life contingencies and dividend accumulations represent, for the most part, policy proceeds which have been left with the company to accumulate at interest and which are subject to periodic withdrawals under various option plans. Supplementary contracts without life contingencies outstanding at the end of the year are summarized in Exhibit 10 by the guaranteed contract and current interest valuation rates. These reserves are further summarized by the present value of amounts not yet due and of amounts left on deposit to accumulate at interest. These reserves do not contain life contingencies, as do other reserves for life insurance policies and contracts.

Policy and contract claims are identified in liabilities, surplus, and other funds between life insurance and accident and health insurance. These claims are summarized in Exhibit 11, Part 1, and are divided between those claims that are resisted as of the end of the year, those claims not resisted but in the process of settlement, and an estimate of the claims that have been incurred but not reported to the company. Claims included in due and unpaid or in the course of settlement, resisted and other, are divided between direct claims, reinsurance claims assumed, and reinsurance claims ceded. Incurred but not reported claims are reported as a single net-of-reinsurance amount. Exhibit 11, Part 1, claims are further separated into industrial and ordinary life insurance, individual annuities, supplementary contracts, credit life insurance, group life insurance and annuities, accident and health group insurance, credit insurance, and all other accident and health insurance.

Other liabilities include policyholder dividends that have been left on deposit with the company to accumulate at interest, policyholder dividends which are due but not paid, and a statutory required liability for policyholder dividends that will be payable in the following calendar year. Coupon policies that require guaranteed future income payments are reported in the annual statement like policyholders' dividends.

Some policyholders choose to pay premiums in advance. These unapplied premiums are discounted to their present value and are reported separately in the annual statement. The discounted premiums and accumulated interest are used to pay premiums on contracts when due. Life insurance companies may also receive other deposit funds which are accumulated at a contractual interest rate and carried as a liability at their current principal and interest accumulation.

Operating liabilities are provided for in much the same manner that is required for commercial companies. These amounts include accrued commissions due to agents and reinsurers, general insurance expenses, insurance taxes, license and fees, federal income taxes, payroll and other taxes, and miscellaneous accrued liabilities.

There are two other liabilities that are peculiar to life insurance companies. At the end of an accounting period, there are a number of cash items (such as premium and investment income) which have been remitted to the company but which have not been allocated to an insurance account. Since these amounts have not been processed through the daily accounting cycle, they appear as a separate liability; however, most amounts have previously been accrued into premium and investment accounts receivable, and thus the income amounts are correctly stated. The other liability peculiar to life insurance accounting is the mandatory securities valuation reserve. In commercial accounting, this amount would be considered an allocation of surplus. The reserve is calculated from a prescribed formula that is intended to smooth out some of the fluctuations that occur from applying current valuations to the investment portfolio and from realized capital gains or losses. The reserve is composed of two parts; a bond and preferred stock reserve component and a common stock reserve component. The detailed calculation of this reserve is included with Schedule D. The operation of this reserve causes the increase or decrease in capital gains and capital losses to be offset by additions or deductions to the reserves. Capital losses are charged to this account so long as there is a positive reserve balance.

Separate account liabilities are exactly offset by an asset account. The transactions occurring in separate accounts are discussed in Chapter 21, Variable Annuities and Life Insurance.

Summary of Operations

Like the statement of income for commercial companies that bridges the results of operations from the beginning to the end of the year, the summary of operations portrays the insurance operating results except for items that are required or permitted to be charged or credited to surplus. This statement is supported by many exhibits and schedules.

Premium income, which is usually the largest revenue source, is detailed in Exhibit 1. Part 1 classifies premiums by ordinary life and individual annuities, credit life, group life and annuities, and group, credit, and other accident and health. Premiums are classified as first-year, renewal, and single premium amounts net of reinsurance ceded and assumed. While the total premiums received come directly from the general ledger, the details provided in Exhibit 1 are derived from supplementary records.

Net investment income is supported by Exhibit 2, which is a summary of investment income and expense items, and by Exhibit 3, which provides the details of sources of gross investment income. Exhibit 3 includes the sources of investment income, the amount collected during the year, as well as the due and unearned amounts for the current and preceding year, and self-rent for company-owned and -occupied real estate.

Revenue derived from commissions and allowances on reinsurance ceded is reported in Exhibit 1, Part 2.

Many insurance costs and expense items are taken directly from the general ledger. Some are further detailed in exhibits. Commissions paid to agents and brokers and commissions paid to reinsurers for business ceded are included in Exhibit 1, Part 2, as first-year, renewal, and single premium amounts. Commissions are identified by ordinary and group life and annuity, credit life, and accident and health group, credit, and other. General insurance expenses—such as salary and employee benefits, space and equipment rentals, agency expense allowances, traveling, advertising, printing, and similar expenses—are reported separately in Exhibit 5. These expenses are directly charged to or allocated among insurance costs related to life and annuity insurance, accident and health insurance, and investment operations. Exhibit 5 is prepared on an accrual basis and reconciled to the ledger on a cash basis. Expenses incurred to pay taxes, license, and fees are reported in Exhibit 6. These include real estate taxes, insurance department license and fees, state taxes on premiums, employment taxes, and other taxes. Federal taxes on income are included in the summary of operations as a separate item.

Dividends paid or payable to policyowners are reported in Exhibit 7 by amounts applied to pay renewal premiums, applied to shorten the premium-paying period, applied to paid-up additions, paid in cash, or left on deposit with the company at interest. Dividends are classified between life and annuity and accident and health insurance. Policy coupon benefits are reported and classified in a similar manner. The analysis of operations by line of business parallels the reporting in the summary of operations for ordinary life and annuities, supplementary contracts, credit life, group life and annuity contracts, and accident and health insurance. Line items for premium income and other considerations, benefits paid or provided for, commissions paid to agents and others, premium taxes, some salary costs, and related benefits can be directly assigned. Other revenue items such as net investment income and other costs and expenses, including general insurance expenses, are allocated to lines of business on the basis of premiums, salary costs, or other formula methods.

Capital and Surplus Account

This account reconciles current-year transactions with the aggregate capital and surplus account at the beginning and the end of the year. No distinction is made in the beginning and ending balances between invested capital and retained earnings. Reportable transactions include the following items:

- Net gain as reported in the summary of operations.
- Net capital gains from Exhibit 4, which include realized and unrealized amounts. Exhibit 4 includes realized capital gains and losses, the net change in unrealized gains or losses between the beginning- and end-of-the year valuations, and any adjustments to book value made during the year. These amounts are reported for government and other bonds, common stocks of both affiliated and unaffiliated companies, and other invested assets such as mortgage loans, real estate, policy loans, and short-term investments.
- The net change in non admitted assets is reported in Exhibit 14. Included are supplies and stationery, furniture and equipment, discounted commissions, agents' balances, notes and other accounts receivable not fully collaterized, automobiles, and similar items. If the company capitalizes furniture and equipment, the difference between the beginning- and end-of-year net balances are nonadmitted and the depreciation expense is reported in Exhibit 5. If the company expenses these items as they are acquired, the total annual cost incurred is reported in Exhibit 5.
- Changes made in the insurance reserve accounts that arise from using new valuation bases are separated between the change for the current year, which is included in the summary of operations, and the change for prior years, which is charged directly to surplus.
- Changes made in the mandatory securities valuation reserve are charged or credited directly to surplus.
- Stock life insurance companies report additions to common stock and paid-in capital and amounts of cash dividends paid to stockholders.
- Prior-period surplus adjustments are permitted for income taxes, correction of errors, contingency reserves, and other amounts clearly identified with prior years' operations.

Statement of Changes in Financial Position

This statement reconciles the transactions for the year with the beginning- and end-of-year cash balances and is prepared on a basis similar to statements for commercial companies. However, the statement contains significantly more detailed entries than would be required for most commercial companies.

PROPERTY AND LIABILITY INSURANCE

Statement of Assets, Liabilities, and Surplus

Assets. This statement includes all the ledger assets of the insurance company, which for the most part comprise the invested assets, home office building properties, and premiums and agents' balances in course of collection. Other amounts included are non-ledger assets, which are comprised of federal income taxes recoverable, accrued interest, dividends and real estate income, and miscellaneous other assets. The detailed summary of ledger assets, non-ledger assets, and nonadmitted assets is included in Exhibit 1.

Significant nonadmitted assets are comprised of investments which are not in good standing, amounts in excess of the cost of investments over the values placed on the securities by the NAIC Subcommittee on Valuation of Securities, premiums and agents' balances in the course of collection over 3 months due, furniture, fixtures and automobiles, and loans and other accounts receivable. Common stock values in excess of cost are included in the non-ledger assets and increase the admitted value of such investments. That amount plus the nonadmitted values of bonds, common or preferred stocks, mortgage loans, and other invested assets included in Exhibit 1 are reported in Part 1A as capital gains and losses on investments. All other nonadmitted assets are reported in Exhibit 2.

The details of the company's individual investments in securities are listed in Schedule D and include the historical cost, market value, and investment income received or receivable. Schedule D is divided into parts to show the securities owned (Parts 1 and 2), the securities purchased during the year (Parts 3 and 5), and the disposition of securities during the year (Parts 4 and 5).

Other assets are supported by Schedule A, which includes the details of home office and branch office real estate; Schedule B, a summary of mortgage loans on real estate outstanding; Schedule C, a summary of collateral loans outstanding; Schedule F, a summary of reinsurance recoverable on incurred losses; and Schedule N, a detail of cash on deposit.

Exhibit 3 does not support specific asset balances; rather, it reconciles the total of ledger assets at the beginning and at the end of the year with the ledger transactions for the year.

Liabilities, Surplus, and Other Funds. With the exception of a few items—such as amounts withheld from payroll accounts, premiums and other items received but not yet allocated to income accounts, and ceded reinsurance balances payable—most liabilities of a property and liability company are non-ledger amounts.

The largest liabilities are reserves for outstanding losses, loss adjustment expenses, and unearned premiums. The liabilities for losses are determined individually from claim files or are determined by using an average cost of prior losses, or a combination of both. Reserves for losses and adjusting expenses are summarized in Part 3A and arise from settled but unpaid claims, from unsettled claims made on behalf of or to indemnify policyholders, and from unreported claims. These reserves are reported by line of business for fire, allied lines, farmowners' and homeowners' multiple peril, commercial multiple peril, ocean and inland marine, medical malpractice, accident and health, workers' compensation, liability for automobile and other, automobile physical damage, and other property and liability insurance coverages. The reserves are separated by losses (both direct and reinsurance-assumed) adjusted or in the process of adjustment, by reinsurance recoverable on losses paid, and by estimated reserves for losses incurred but not reported for both direct and reinsurance-assumed losses. Reinsurance amounts are included in Schedule F, which is divided into Part 1A, Section 1, covering ceded reinsurance, and Part 1A, Section 2, covering assumed reinsurance.

The company's experience with net unpaid losses and loss adjustment expenses for fire, allied lines, group and credit accident and health, automobile physical damage, fidelity and surety, and similar lines are included in Schedule O, Part 3. This schedule summarizes the amounts of unpaid losses and loss adjustment expenses by the years in which the premiums were earned and the losses incurred. Schedule P covers unpaid losses and loss adjustment expenses for automobile liability, other liability, workers' compensation, homeowners' and commercial multiple peril, and ocean and inland marine. Schedule P provides a historical demonstration of the adequacy of these insurance reserves. Reserving practices are covered in Chapter 13, Property and Liability Loss Reserves.

If a company writes accident and health policies, it must also complete Schedule H. Part 2 of this schedule summarizes reserves for unearned premium amounts, additional policy reserves, and reported claim reserves. Unearned amounts include the pro rata unearned premiums, advance premiums, and any reserves arising from rate credits. Additional reserves include amounts necessary to provide for expected losses and for future contingent benefits such as deferred maturity benefits. Reported claim reserves include a provision for claims that have been adjusted, for those in process of adjustment, and for incurred but not reported claims. Accident and health reserves are reported in Schedule H by ordinary group, credit group and individual, noncancelable and guaranteed renewable policy, and other accident coverage. All accident and health insurance reserves are adjusted for credits expected from reinsurers.

A special Schedule P reserve is required for the excess of statutory over statement-basis reserves. Statutory reserves are computed on a formula basis and include automobile liability (Part 1A), other liability (Part 1B), medical malpractice (Part 1C), and workers' compensation (Part 1D). This computation is made to ascertain that the total incurred losses and loss expenses for the current year, including unpaid amounts, are at least equal to the company's prior years' loss experience for these coverages or to a minimum statutory amount. Statutory reserves are determined by comparing the premiums earned for each of these coverages with the company's loss percentage for the current and prior years. If the company's loss ratio is less than 60 percent for automobile liability, other liability, and medical malpractice, the company is required to use an assumed loss ratio of 60 percent. For workers' compensation, the minimum statutory loss ratio is 65 percent. If any of the company's loss ratio is in excess of 75 percent, then the statutory loss ratio is 75 percent. The company's own experience is used when the loss ratio falls between the minimum and maximum statutory loss ratios. If the total loss and loss expense incurred is less than the Schedule P statutory reserve, the excess must be reported as a separate liability.

Unearned premium reserves represent another significant liability of a property and liability insurance company. The premiums received are taken into income on a pro rata basis over the policy period. Policy periods may be as short as 3 months or may be for periods covering 3 to 5 years. Unearned premiums are included in Part 2B for fire, allied lines, farmowners' and homeowners' multiple peril, commercial multiple peril, ocean and inland marine, medical malpractice, accident and health, workers' compensation, automobile and other liability, automobile physical damage, and a number of other insured perils. Premiums are also divided between those running 1 year or less and those running more than 1 year. Premiums received in advance are included in the reserves for unearned premiums at gross amounts.

Reinsurance liabilities include amounts payable for reinsurance ceded and other reinsurance funds and are reported as a separate liability. Amounts due from companies which are not licensed in the ceding company's domicile state are usually considered to be from unauthorized companies and require separate reporting. Amounts recoverable from such companies for paid and unpaid losses must be recorded as a liability. The liability can be reduced by unearned premiums on reinsurance ceded to them and by other funds held for their account. To the extent that these latter two items exceed the recoverable amounts for paid and unpaid losses, the liability can be ignored.

Other operating liabilities are provided for in much the same manner required for most commercial companies. These include agents' commissions, general operating expenses, taxes, license and fees, federal and foreign income taxes, payroll and other taxes, and miscellaneous other accrued liabilities. Agents' commissions may include contingent amounts based on policyholders' loss experience. Where the loss experience is less than a stipulated amount, a contingent commission is payable to the agent. The liability for unpaid dividends includes amounts due to stockholders and policyholders.

The section on surplus and other funds include paid-in and contributed capital, special surplus from guaranteed certificates, special perils insured, and unassigned funds. Paid-in and contributed surplus is reported at the gross amount paid in by stockholders, and the cost of the stock issued and related expenses are charged to unassigned funds. Except for guaranteed fund certificates or special funds, all surplus funds of a mutual company are included in unassigned funds.

Summary of Operations

Like the statement of income for commercial companies that bridges the results of operations from the beginning to the end of the year, this summary of operations portrays the insurance operating results except for items that are required or permitted to be charged or credited to surplus. This statement is supported by several exhibits and schedules.

The premiums earned (usually the largest revenue source) are detailed in Part 2. Part 2 classifies premiums by fire, allied lines, farmowners' and homeowners' and commercial multiple peril, ocean and inland marine, workers' compensation, automobile and other liability, automobile physical damage, and other insured perils. The premiums are classified as net premiums written and assumed, unearned premiums at the beginning and end of the year, and premiums earned during the year, all net of reinsurance ceded. The premiums are summarized in Part 2C; they include direct premiums written during the year, reinsurance premiums assumed and ceded, and net written premiums. Unearned premiums at the end of the current year are supported by Part 2B, which (as earlier described) is computed from premiums in force by type of peril insured. Premiums in force are detailed in Part 2A by premiums written or renewed and by expiration and return premiums for the current year. Schedule T provides premium information allocated by states and territories. While the total premiums received come directly from the general ledger, the details provided in Part 2, Part 2A, Part 2B, Part 2C, and Schedule T are derived from the statistical records maintained by the company.

Other significant income items include the following:

- Net investment income is reported in Part 1, which separates interest, dividends, and real estate income by source: United States government bonds, state and municipal bonds, corporate bonds, bonds of affiliates, preferred and common stock both affiliated and unaffiliated, mortgage and collateral loans, and real estate. These amounts are summarized by amounts collected, paid in advance, due and accrued, and earned for the year. Real estate income includes amounts for self-rent of company-owned and -occupied real estate and is offset by a rent expense included in expenses (Part 4). Earned investment income is reported net of investment expenses and depreciation on real estate. Investment expenses are detailed in Part 4 and include direct charges and allocated general expenses.
- Net realized capital gains and losses are reported in Part 1A and are separated by United States government bonds, state and municipal bonds, corporate bonds, bonds of affiliates, preferred and common stock both affiliated and unaffiliated, mortgage and collateral loans, and real estate. Profits or losses on sales or maturity are reported separately. Unlike life insurance companies, which include net realized capital gains and losses directly in surplus, property and liability insurance companies include these amounts in the statement of income.
- Other income, which may be combined, include recovery from agents or premium balances charged off, finance and service charges not included in premiums, and similar items.

Deductions from income are summarized below. They include losses, loss expenses, and other underwriting expenses.

- Losses incurred are summarized in Part 3 and are separated by fire, allied lines, farmowners' and homeowners' and commercial multiple peril, ocean and inland marine, workers' compensation, automobile and other liability, automobile physical damage, and other miscellaneous coverages. Losses are classified as direct business written, reinsurance-assumed, and reinsurance-recovered. These items are all reduced for the amount of salvage or subrogation received in settling losses. The total losses paid are increased by the net loss unpaid at the end of the current year and decreased by the net loss unpaid at the end of the previous year.

- Loss adjustment expenses incurred are summarized in Part 4 for direct claim adjustment services on business written, reinsurance-assumed, and reinsurance-ceded losses. Other expenses allocated to loss adjustment expenses include all other expenses except commissions and brokerage to agents, direct underwriting expenses, taxes, license and fees imposed by state and local insurance authorities, and miscellaneous other nonallocable underwriting and investment expenses.
- The details of other underwriting expenses are reported in Part 4 and include commissions and allowances to agents, brokers, and managers, advertising costs, boards, bureaus and associations, surveys and underwriting reports, salaries, employee benefits, travel expenses, rent (including self-rent for the company's home office), equipment, printing and stationery, utilities, taxes, license and fees, and others.

Capital and Surplus Account

This account reconciles beginning and ending capital and surplus with the transactions for the year. For purposes of this reconciliation, no distinction is made between invested capital and unassigned surplus.

Net income from operations is included from the statement of income and net unrealized capital gains or losses from Part 1A. Part 1A includes adjustments to book value and unrealized gains or losses for investments, including bonds by source of origin, common stocks both affiliated and unaffiliated, mortgage loans, real estate, and other. Unrealized gains or losses are determined from information in Schedule D. Part 1 includes state, municipal, and other bonds, including affiliates; Part 2, Section 1, preferred stocks; and Part 2, Section 2, common stocks, including parent, subsidiaries, and affiliates. Unrealized gains and losses arise from the difference between the amortized cost of bonds and the statutory bond valuation, the excess cost of preferred stock over current market value, the difference between the cost and market value of publicly traded common stock, and the cost of common stocks of affiliates and the net asset value or other statutory values for these companies.

The net change in nonadmitted assets is reported in Exhibit 2. Included are agents' balances or uncollected premiums over 3 months due, accounts receivable not taken for premiums, personal loans, furniture and supplies, and other assets. If the company capitalizes furniture and equipment, the difference between the beginning- and end-of-year net balances is nonadmitted and the depreciation expense is reported in Part 4. If the company expenses these items as they are acquired, the total annual costs incurred are reported in Part 4.

A change in the liability for unauthorized reinsurance is charged or credited directly to surplus.

The year-to-year change in excess of statutory reserves over statement reserves is charged or credited directly to surplus rather than being included in the statement of income.

Stock property and liability insurance companies also report the additions to common stock and paid-in capital and the amounts of cash dividends paid to stockholders.

Mutual property and liability insurance companies may issue surplus notes which bear interest at a fixed rate and which may have an indefinite maturity date. Such interest is charged directly to surplus. Generally, the surplus notes cannot be redeemed without the prior approval of the commissioner of insurance.

Prior-period surplus adjustments such as income taxes, correction of errors, and contingency reserves are permitted if they are clearly identified with prior years' operations.

Statement of Changes in Financial Position

This statement, which reconciles the transactions for the year with the beginning and ending cash balances, is prepared on a basis similar to that for commercial companies. However, the statement provides for significantly more detail than would be required for a commercial company because of the many estimates used to determine underwriting gains, such as losses and loss adjustment expenses, unearned premiums, reinsurance balances, and nonadmitted assets.

OTHER REGULATORY REPORTS

Insurance companies may be required to file an insurance expense exhibit, a statement separating operating results (which is filed by companies writing both participating and nonparticipating business), statistical reports on premiums and losses, and investment reports. In certain circumstances, reports may be required for the following:

Subsidiary, Controlled, or Affiliated Companies

Insurance companies owning subsidiaries or having the ability to exercise control over other companies through stock ownership, a board of directors, or other controlling arrangements are required to file Form SUB-1 with the NAIC Subcommittee on Valuation of Securities within 30 days after the acquisition or formation of a subsidiary, controlled, or affiliated company. Thereafter, each company must file Form SUB-2 annually, no later than April 1. The purpose of these filings is to supply the information that will support the valuation basis of each subsidiary, controlled, or affiliated company.

Stockholders' Information Supplement

Publicly held stock companies are usually required to file annual proxy statements and to furnish annual reports to stockholders, both of which are prepared in accordance with the rules and regulations of the Securities and

Exchange Commission (SEC). Insurance companies complying with state reporting requirements are usually exempt from other proxy and annual statement report rules if they file the Stockholders' Information Supplement (SIS).

The Stockholders' Information Supplement is a uniform reporting form promulgated by the NAIC and to a great extent parallels the SEC requirement for proxies and annual reports. While only statutory financial statements are required, most companies also furnish annual reports based on generally accepted accounting principles. This annual report may be incorporated into Form 10-K, provided that it also complies with the SEC requirements.

SOURCES OF ACCOUNTING RULES

A distinction is made between accounting principle rules that are generally accepted for most business enterprises and accounting practices that are specifically applicable to insurance companies. This distinction is presented in professional literature as that between generally accepted accounting principles and statutory accounting practices.

Generally Accepted Accounting Principles

Accounting principles can be described as a body of accounting rules selected for the purpose of best recording and reporting the effects of the transactions conducted by a business enterprise. Accounting principles are derived both from the theoretical review of accounting practices and from conceptual notions. The body of accounting principles is evolutionary and is underscored with numerous objectives, the bases of which are the matching of costs and revenues and the valuation of assets on the basis of costs. These objectives are satisfied by choosing from among a number of accepted accounting methods.

Generally accepted accounting principles have been developed to narrow the gap for alternative selection of accounting methods. The use of the term "generally accepted" should not imply that these principles arise from the exercise of a democratic process. The wide use of an accounting method does not of itself make an accounting principle generally accepted. Rather, accounting principles receive their authoritative support from organizations which have been delegated the responsibility for determining generally accepted accounting principles. These groups set the standards for determining the principles and thereby bind the professional accounting group to their uses. To use as generally accepted other principles which are in conflict with these accounting principles and which have not been granted recognition by these authoritative bodies would require considerable justification on the part of the users—but accounting principles that have received recognition as generally accepted may be used without fear of question or contradiction.

Where no specific accounting principle has been approved to describe a business transaction or activity, then precedent for the use of nonapproved accounting principles must be established from sources that are considered to be authoritative. For the most part, the use of accounting principles other than those which have been officially granted general acceptance is limited to those rare occasions when peculiar transactions or activities occur that are not common or expected in most business enterprises.

The use of generally accepted accounting principles (GAAP) is incumbent upon every public reporting company and most other business enterprises that are required to furnish financial information to lenders or others. This almost universal application of GAAP makes the use of any other accounting practice subject to considerable scrutiny. The source of authoritative support for generally accepted accounting principles presently resides with the Financial Accounting Standards Board; previously, the Accounting Principles Board and its predecessor committees of the American Institute of Certified Public Accountants gave authoritative recognition to accounting principles. In the case of reporting companies, the SEC's rulings on accounting principles are also considered to be generally accepted accounting principles for those companies.

Statutory Accounting Practices

The accounting practices which are required to be used by insurance companies do have authoritative support. However, this authoritative recognition does not extend to these accounting practices the status of GAAP. *Statutory accounting practices* are those practices which are prescribed for use in reporting accounting transactions for insurance companies. In many instances, the statutory accounting practices and GAAP are in agreement; that is, there is no perceptible difference between the two. In other instances, however, the statutory accounting practices are not based on accounting theory, but rather are determined to produce a desired result. The exclusion of some items from the assets in the balance sheet of an insurance company is an example of a statutory accounting practice. This practice arises from a perceived need by insurance regulators to ensure that most assets will be realized in cash in the normal course of business operations and will be available to pay the benefits or claims of policyholders.

It should not be presumed that all nonadmitted assets are automatically reinstated when the statements are translated to generally accepted accounting principles. For property and liability companies, for example, agents' balances over 90 days past due are considered to be nonadmitted. The criteria for determining whether such assets are includable in the balance sheet of an insurance company prepared on the basis of generally accepted accounting principles is based on the estimated collectibility of such balances. If a reserve against such balances is deemed necessary, the reserves will reduce the amount of nonadmitted assets that can be restored. In a similar manner, life insurance companies are required to provide a mandatory securities valuation reserve, which is determined in a prescribed manner; fixed amounts are set aside in this reserve to cushion the impact of realized and unrealized capital gains and losses. Restoring this statutory reserve to the surplus of an insurance company does not eliminate the need to provide for the possibility that all investments may not be fully realizable at maturity.

The remaining chapters of this book will more fully cover the effect on financial statements that occur from following statutory accounting practices. Statutory accounting practices arise from state laws and from rules adopted by state insurance commissioners. Many state commissioners adopt most of the accounting practices promulgated by the NAIC, and in some instances the use of these practices is expressly permitted by statute. In other instances, the use of these practices is considered an acceptable alternative to following other state requirements. While there is diversity between states, the use of statutory accounting practices to comply with the annual reporting requirements of insurance companies is usually satisfied by using the annual statement blank adopted by the NAIC. The instructions accompanying the blank provide some explanations for some accounting classifications and expense allocation methods. In the absence of accounting rules covering the reporting of an unusual item, the insurance commissioners usually issue letter rulings specifying how such items are to be reported.

GENERAL-PURPOSE FINANCIAL STATEMENTS

Whether financial statements are prepared on the basis of statutory accounting practices or on the GAAP basis, there are some required disclosures that must accompany the statements. The disclosures that are peculiar to insurance companies will be covered in Chapter 20, Financial Statements. The disclosure requirements covered here are for general-purpose financial statements, whether prepared for commercial or insurance enterprises. Other disclosures may be required for financial statements filed with the SEC.

A number of available references cover nearly all the possible disclosures required in most general-purpose financial statements. A good rule to follow in determining the adequacy of disclosures is that an explanation should be provided for the following: the method used to account for an item, information about the collectibility of assets or the payment of liabilities, the restrictions on assets or capital, the treatment of unusual income or expense items, and the significance of off-ledger items, such as contingencies, unused tax benefits, lease arrangements, and unfunded pension costs.

Disclosure items may be separated between those usually appearing in the financial statements and those included in the footnotes. Some of the more significant items are described below.

1. Items which should be disclosed in the financial statements:
   - □ Valuation allowances applicable to specific assets should be shown separately and deducted from the assets to which they apply. Examples of such allowances are for estimated losses on receivables, unearned finance charges and interest, and depreciation.
   - □ Amounts due from officers or affiliated companies, if significant, should be shown separately.

- The carrying value of investments should be reported at the aggregate cost or market value, with the alternative values shown parenthetically.
- Stockholders' equity should include: the title of each security issue; the number of shares authorized, issued, and outstanding; the number of treasury shares; and the dollar amount for each class of capital shares authorized. The cost of treasury shares should be deducted from the stockholders' equity.
- Elements of surplus that are allocated or restricted for specific purposes should be reported separately from unrestricted amounts.
- Depreciation and interest expense, if significant, should be reported separately. Earnings per share should be distinguished for income from continuing operations, cumulative effect of a change in accounting principles, extraordinary items, and net income.

2. Items which should be disclosed in the notes to financial statements:

- Significant accounting policies should describe items such as valuation of investment securities, subsidiary consolidation policies, investments carried on the equity method of accounting, and other similar accounting policies.
- The amount of interest costs capitalized should be disclosed separately from other interest costs.
- Lease arrangements should disclose significant terms, including arrangements with related parties, future minimum rentals on noncancelable leases for each of the next 5 fiscal years, and the amount of contingent rentals included in the income statements.
- Reported business combinations should include a description of the combined companies, the method of accounting used, the acquisition costs, and details relating to revenue, extraordinary items, net income, and dividends for each of the combining companies. Pro forma results of operations should be reported as though the combination occurred at the beginning of the period.
- Income tax disclosures include the amount and expiration dates of net operating loss carryforwards, the reasons for significant variations in customary relationships between income tax expense and pretax accounting income, and the method of accounting for investment tax credits.
- Pension plan disclosures should identify employee groups covered, the accounting and funding policies followed by the company, the amount of pension plan costs for the period, and the treatment of actuarial gains and losses. For defined benefit pension plans, the actuarial present value of vested benefits, nonvested plan benefits, and the net assets available for all benefits should be reported.
- Capital stock warrants or rights outstanding during the period—including exercise price, dividend restrictions, and other restrictions on capital—should be disclosed.
- Unaccrued contingencies should include a description of the contingency, the range of the loss, and outstanding guarantees made for others. Com-

mitments for significant long-term financing, commitments for purchase of property or equipment, and other binding commitments should be described.

- Significant events occurring subsequent to the balance sheet date—such as sale of securities, issuing of bonds, business combinations, and settlement of litigation—should be fully described.
- Changes made in previously issued financial statements, including reclassifications, should be explained.

The preceding items, although neither a complete nor a detailed listing of all necessary disclosure items, are presented to indicate some of the significant disclosure requirements for financial statements prepared on a statutory or a GAAP basis.

4

REVENUE RECOGNITION

The method by which revenues are determined is essential to the accounting process for all business enterprises. Revenue can be recorded on the cash or accrual basis. Using the cash method, revenue is earned and reportable when it is received in cash. Cash-basis revenue is easy to recognize: If it is collected, it is revenue; if it is not collected, it is not revenue. The cash basis is not an acceptable accounting method for most business enterprises. It may, however, be appropriate for not-for-profit organizations and for some governmental or related types of entities.

Even though the cash basis is not an acceptable method for most business enterprises, it nevertheless has a preciseness in its revenue recognition method. The accrual-basis method also has a precise moment to begin the revenue recognition process. For commercial companies, revenue is usually recognized when a sale is made. The point of sale is determined by using customary terms or specific contractual arrangements; it may be when a contract is signed, when an agreement is made to deliver, or when the products are received by the buyer. Revenue from services is usually recognized in proportion to the amount of services performed as compared to the total services to be rendered. Payments received at the point of sale or the performance of services are reported as collection on open accounts, since the revenues are already recorded. Payments made in advance are reported as customer deposits.

Timing revenue recognition is important for an insurance enterprise since it determines which matching costs should be recognized in the financial statements. This matching process emphasizes the importance of operating results over the determination of capital and surplus. Product or service pricing policies determine the gross revenue for most commercial enterprises. Pricing is determined by accumulating the costs incurred to produce the product or service and adding a margin to cover the selling and administrative costs and profits. For commercial companies, all production, selling, and administrative costs are usually incurred before the product or service is sold. Insurance company pricing policies, on the other hand, must also consider estimated costs to be incurred in the future. Future costs are estimated by using the past experience of a company or a group of companies. For life insurance, annuities, and acci-

dent and health insurance, future benefit costs can be estimated by using recognized mortality or morbidity tables. For property and liability insurance, future costs are determined by using a company's or industry's prior experience with similar products. If the estimates of future benefit costs are inadequate, it is possible that future revenues will be insufficient to cover policy costs.

Pricing insurance products would appear to consist of a series of calculations using current and anticipated losses, costs, expenses, and investment earnings. However, the insurance industry is confronted with the same sales pressure as a commercial company, and product pricing thus often involves an element of optimism. If the product is priced above competition, there is a risk that it may not sell. Consequently, estimated selling prices are adjusted for anticipated improvement in cost or volumes in sales.

Even though insurance products are often sold on a deferred premium basis requiring monthly, quarterly, semiannual, annual, or flexible payments, they should be recognized in revenue on an accrual basis. The preferred method for recognizing premium revenues is over the period of time that benefits are provided. For the most part, this is the method followed in the annual statement blank filed with the insurance commissioner. For the purposes of annual statement reporting, however, the premiums for life insurance, annuities, and accident and health insurance are increased or decreased by the deferred premiums at the beginning and end of the year. Deferred premiums arise in the determination of life, annuity, and accident and health reserves and offset an overstatement (assuming that all premiums will be paid through the next policy anniversary date). Gross deferred premiums are included in premium income with an offsetting amount representing the net premium included as an asset and the balance as a charge to expenses. Property and liability insurance premiums are recognized as revenue on a pro rata basis over the policy term.

The following material summarizes premium accounting for the most common insured risk and the basis upon which it is recognized in revenue.

LIFE INSURANCE PREMIUMS

Life insurance costs are based on the company's own mortality experience or on mortality tables derived from the experience of a segment of the general population. If the company imposes a higher standard of health examination before accepting life insurance risks, the experience data may be modified for the expected improvement in mortality during the early years of the policy.

Other factors affecting life insurance premium determination are: earnings on investments from accumulated premiums; the cost of policies lapsing for nonpayment of premiums; sales, administrative, and maintenance costs to continue the policy in force; and profit. A mutual life insurance company may not include a profit element but will likely include higher cost estimates for mortality risk and expenses.

Premiums are calculated by assuming annual installments; however, where options are offered to pay premiums semiannually, quarterly, or monthly, a small margin is added to reflect the increased handling costs and reduced earnings. Preauthorized or postdated check payment methods permit the company to collect installment premiums directly from the policyholder's bank. These installment premiums may be the same as annual premiums or have a reduced expense loading since the mailing and handling costs are reduced.

Life insurance premiums are calculated separately for each product and may be classified under one of the following policy forms:

Term Life Insurance

This protection underlies all life insurance products. Term policies are written to provide life insurance protection for 1 year at a time or for a fixed number of years. Term insurance offered on an annual basis is classified as annual renewable term. This insurance protection is provided at a specified dollar amount for the annual premiums, which increase with age.

The premiums for extended term insurance covering a fixed number of years are aggregated and charged at a level amount over the term of the policy. The premium cost is determined for each insured group, taking into account their attained age and expected mortality in the following year. Expected mortality is the principal cost element in the determination of term insurance premiums. Other costs include expected distribution and administrative costs and profits, or margins for contingencies.

Annual renewable term premiums contain only minimum estimates for investment income and policy lapse. Policies written for longer periods and charged on a level annual basis include reasonable estimates of expected investment earnings and policy lapse costs. Policies written on a participating basis have more conservatively priced premiums, and the savings, if any, are returned to policyowners in the form of dividends.

Term life insurance may also be written to provide decreasing protection over a specified policy term. This is often referred to as "mortgage protection insurance" since the coverage decreases as the mortgage principal is reduced. It may also be written as credit life or group life or written in connection with annuity products.

Annual renewable and level term premiums should be included in revenue when they become due. Reducing term premiums should be aggregated and recognized on a pro rata basis, taking into account the amount of insurance protection over the policy term.

Whole Life Policies

These types of policies have a fixed amount of insurance protection for the lifetime of the policyowner. The fixed benefit requires a level annual premium that is payable for life. Generally, these policies are considered to be fully paid at age 95.

In contrast to term life insurance, which provides life insurance protection only, a whole life insurance policy contains a series of options and benefits. Whole life policies usually develop a cash value after being in force for 1 or 2 years. Cash value benefits, besides providing a fixed surrender value, underwrite a number of other benefits. The cash value can be borrowed by the policyowner at terms fixed in the policy, used as collateral for a loan, or used to provide funds for other policy benefits, such as paid-up additions and extended insurance. The paid-up benefit is equal to the amount of fully paid-up insurance that the cash value will purchase, using the guaranteed mortality and interest assumptions contained in the policy. The extended term benefit continues the original amount of life insurance protection for a specified future period.

Whole life premiums include the cost of insurance, the cash value, marketing and administrative costs, earnings on investment funds held to pay future benefits, the cost of policy lapse for nonpayment of premium, and expected profits. Mutual life companies will not likely include profits, but they provide somewhat more conservative assumptions, returning actual favorable experience to policyholders in the form of dividends. Premiums for whole life policies are usually payable over the life of the policyholder and should be included in revenues as they become due. This results in the recognition of premiums in proportion to the benefits that are provided in the policy.

Other traditional variations to whole life policies include the following:

Limited Payment Policies

The premiums for these policies are determined in a manner similar to that for annual premium whole life policies. However, to provide the fixed lifetime benefits, the premiums are modified to include an additional amount to fund these benefits when the premiums are no longer payable. The higher premiums on these policies are invested and the related earnings used to fund future benefits when the premiums cease.

The premiums for this type of policy are usually payable for a period of 20 to 30 years. These premiums are recognized in revenue in proportion to the benefits provided. This results in a limited policy payment premium being recognized when due, since most policy costs and expenses are incurred during the premium-paying period and since the benefits extended beyond that time are funded by earnings on accumulated funds.

Endowment Policies

An endowment policy is a whole life policy that also funds benefits at a fixed maturity date. Endowment policies can be for a specific number of years, such as 20 or 30 years, or to a fixed date in the future, such as age 60 or 65.

The premiums on policies covering a fixed number of years or for a fixed maturity date are calculated in a manner similar to that for limited payment policies, except that the premiums are loaded so that there will be an accumulation of funds sufficient to pay the face amount of the policy at maturity. In either instance, the expected mortality cost differs from that required for a whole life policy. For whole life policies, the expected mortality costs include the period from inception to policy maturity, which covers a lifetime. For endowment policies, mortality costs are incurred for a shorter period, since the policy matures at the endowment date. Investment earnings on endowment funds are calculated to provide a fully funded policy at the maturity date. Other premium costs include a provision for marketing, administrative and overhead, and profits, except that mutual companies usually include extra margins for contingencies and provide for policyholder dividends.

The premiums on endowment policies are recognized as revenue when due, resulting in revenues in proportion to benefits provided.

Policies with Variable Premiums and Benefits

These policies provide unique benefits not offered in traditional life insurance policies. The benefits include nonlevel premium modes, level benefits with saving elements, nonlevel benefits with savings elements, nonlevel premium and nonlevel benefits, and larger cash benefits.

Although these enhanced-benefit policies differ in many respects from traditional life policies, the premiums are determined by using similar factors for the following: expected mortality; investment earnings; lapsing of policies for nonpayment of premium; loading for marketing, administrative, and overhead costs; and profits. Mutual companies usually exclude a profit factor and use more conservative assumptions about mortality and investment earnings, returning the margins, if any, in the form of dividends. Premium recognition for these types of policies is governed by the same accounting rules that apply to traditional life insurance policies. Because these policies are in a current development stage, it may not be as easy to categorize premiums as for traditional fixed-premium–type policies.

While these policies may have distinct individual features, most can be grouped in the following categories:

Policies with Fixed Benefits and Variable Premiums. These plans are often described as "indeterminate premium," "universal life," and "vanishing premium" policies. Premium assumptions contemplate favorable mortality and investment experience and lower unit expenses because of larger premiums. These assumptions are usually reasonable since the risk premiums can be increased if the actual losses are greater than estimated. These policies differ from level-premium policies, which are loaded to provide for possible unfavorable results from mortality losses, investment earnings, and operating expenses.

Indeterminate-type premium policies usually provide for a fixed-level premium for a limited period, which may then be adjusted up to a maximum fixed amount guaranteed in the policy. The premium calculations for an indeterminate-type policy are not unlike those of a traditional participating type, except that the cushion for the risk elements is reversed. Participating policy premiums are loaded for the risk that the company's experience will be less favorable than projected, and unused margins will be returned to policyholders as dividends.

Indeterminate-type premium policies assume that current or improved experience for mortality costs, investment income, and expenses will persist during the term of the policy and that unfavorable results will be corrected by increasing premiums. A unique feature of the indeterminate-type premium policy is that it permits policyholders to share in the company's favorable operating results currently.

Universal life–type and vanishing-type premium policies tend to produce some of the same benefits to policyholders. However, these policies may place greater emphasis on the benefits of cash value accumulations resulting from larger premiums and high current interest rates.

Experience with persistency for these types of policies is not fully developed since many are of recent issue, making it more difficult to estimate future policyholder premium payments. In the absence of circumstances that preclude an assumption that minimum policy premiums will be paid as provided in the policy, such premiums are recognized when due, and any amounts in excess of minimum premiums are recognized when collected.

Policies with Level Benefits and Savings Elements. This is a universal life–type policy that permits fixed or variable benefits. *Fixed benefits* provide a single policy amount that includes cash value. A *variable benefit* is a fixed policy amount in excess of cash value. The premiums may be required on a level, nonlevel, or flexible basis. The distinguishing feature of this type of policy is the current benefit earned on the accumulated cash value. Level-premium policies are similar to whole life policies and usually require minimum or target premiums.

Policies having nonlevel or flexible premium provisions are more like a combined term and deferred annuity policy, requiring a single premium to initiate the policy. The initial premium is based on expected mortality, current investment earnings, policy persistency, and immediate cash value. The initial premiums for nonlevel or flexible premium policies often require a significant savings element to fund the term costs of life insurance benefits over the life of the policyholder. Current earnings on the cash value are used to pay annual term life premiums and administrative costs. These costs will not equal or exceed the cash value so long as the earnings on the cash funds exceed the costs of administration and of term life insurance premiums.

The premiums for this type of policy should be considered separately as expected and other amounts. In the absence of circumstances that preclude an assumption that the expected premiums will be paid as provided in the policy, such premiums should be recognized when due; and other amounts, in excess of expected premiums, should be recognized when collected.

Increasing-Benefit Policies. Some policies issued on a whole life basis guarantee excess interest earnings on a month-to-month basis or for several years in the future. Increasing-benefit policies apply excess interest to increase the face amount of the life insurance protection.

Most such policies require a level premium payment to keep the policy in force. For most policies, the increasing benefits are automatic and the policyholder has no option to change that feature. However, this type of policy may be issued under another form which provides for level annual premiums to fund benefits that may be increased or decreased at the election of the policyholder.

Participating policies that permit the use of policyholder dividends to purchase paid-up additions are not considered to be an increasing-benefit policy, although the effect of electing to purchase paid-up additions with dividends does result in increasing the policy benefits.

Revenues from increasing-benefit policies should be recognized in a manner similar to that of a whole life insurance policy, for which the premiums are recognized as revenue when due. If the level annual premium for a policy is loaded to provide for increasing or decreasing benefits in the future, the premiums should be recognized in proportion to the benefits that are offered for each period to the sum of all policy benefits.

ACCIDENT AND HEALTH PREMIUMS

Life insurance provides survivor benefits for the risk that a policyholder will not survive to the policy maturity date. Accident and health insurance, on the other hand, provides insured benefits for the temporary or permanent incapacity of policyholders to pursue their customary activities in their business and professional lives. The insured benefits may pay the direct cost incurred for medical expenses or for loss of wages during the disability period. Accident and health risks are affected by the insured's circumstances, such as personal health history, type of employment, and current age. Aggregate loss exposure also varies with the types of benefits, deductibles, and policy limitations.

These policies are written either on a cancellable basis (that is, they are renewable at the option of the company and the rates are adjusted to reflect the company's experience with claim costs) or on a guaranteed renewable or noncancelable basis. The guaranteed renewable provision allows the policyholder to continue the policy in force by paying the current premium, and the noncancelable basis guarantees that neither the premium nor the policy will be changed so long as each premium is paid when due.

Most accident and health policies offer coverages for the following two categories:

Medical Expense Insurance

The most common form of accident and health insurance provides reimbursement for the costs and expenses incurred in connection with medical treatment and rehabilitation. This type of insurance is offered in a wide variety of forms and covers nearly all segments of the population. It provides coverage not only for the cost of hospitalization, but also for medication, medical tests, and surgical fees. It may be written in a broad form, covering nearly all medical services and fees, or it may be limited to specific fees for specified services. Reimbursement is made either to the policyowner or to the healthcare provider and may be calculated on actual charges or on a fixed dollar amount for each service. Deductible provisions may require the policyholder to pay a fixed amount or to share pro rata in the total cost; the deductible provision applies to many hospitalization-type policies. A coinsurance provision is more common in major medical–type policies, which pay an umbrella-type benefit for the costs incurred from long-term illnesses and accidents.

Other available policy benefits cover the costs incurred for dental care, mental and emotional ailments, and eye glasses. Some policies reimburse for accidents only, for certain illnesses only, or for the deductible provisions of ordinary or government-sponsored insurance programs.

The premiums for medical expense insurance are calculated to cover morbidity costs (that is, those related to the risk of illness or accident), the costs of underwriting and maintaining the policies in force, investment earnings on premiums held to pay future claims, and profits. Mutual companies generally follow the same pricing practice as do stock companies, holding the profits, if any, to finance future programs, although some margins may be returned to policyholders as dividends. The premiums for medical expense insurance should be recognized as revenue on a pro rata basis over the premium-paying period.

Disability Insurance

This type of policy provides insurance for loss of time due to disabling accidents or illness. If policyowners are unable to pursue their usual occupational duties, they will likely suffer from a loss of income, which can be protected by a disability income–type policy. Disability benefits reimburse the policyholder for a specified dollar amount payable over a specific period of time or for life. The risks insured are similar to those insured in a medical expense insurance policy, and the claim costs incurred by the company provide the basis for determining the premiums.

Unlike medical expense insurance, disability income insurance does not require that the policyowner be hospitalized. Rather, disability benefits are payable if the policyowner is unable to perform usual and customary occupational duties. Because of the diverse demands upon various occupations, the claim costs in a particular group may be higher than those in other groups. Occupations with a history of high disability occurrences will be charged larger premiums than will those in less hazardous groups.

Premium determination for disability insurance coverage includes estimates of the claim costs, the costs of maintaining the policy in force, investment earnings, and profit. There is no significant difference between policies written by mutual or stock companies except for possible policy dividends. Premiums for disability insurance should be recognized as revenue on a pro rata basis over the term of the policy.

ANNUITY PREMIUMS

Unlike life insurance contracts, which utilize estimates to determine the premiums that must be paid to provide life insurance protection, the annuity contract is fully funded before benefits begin. Deferred annuities are those in the accumulation period before benefits begin. Benefits may be payable over the life of the annuitant or for a fixed period of time. These benefits are payable from funds held and accumulated at interest.

In some respects, an annuity contract works like a savings account; in other respects, it works like a life insurance policy. In the former instance, the annuity contract is much like a savings account during the accumulation (or deferred) period, since the benefits are usually equal to the cash values. In the latter instance, the annuity is like life insurance, since it takes into account the life expectancy of policyowners in determining lifetime payments.

Annuity policies provide benefits, accumulation, and cash values under the following options:

Refunding Annuities

A refunding annuity provides for repayment of the total amount of the fund to the policyowner or the policyowner's beneficiary. Periodic payment refunds include interest earned on the unpaid balance of the annuity fund. The payments are usually fixed and continue until the entire annuity amount is paid out. If the policyowner dies before all payments are made, the remaining payments will continue to be made to a beneficiary. Some policies may provide for payment of a lump-sum amount at the death of the annuitant. However paid, the total refunding payment cannot exceed the cost of the annuity plus interest and other earnings accumulations.

Life Annuities

A life annuity terminates upon the death of the annuitant. The amount of the annuity fund, the life expectancy of the annuitant, and the expected interest earnings on the annuity fund, less the costs and expenses of administering the policy, determine the period payment benefits. Since benefit payments are guaranteed for life, accumulated contract funds not paid because the annuitant dies early are not refunded but are used to provide benefits for annuitants that live beyond their expected payout period.

Life Annuities Including a Period Certain

These annuities combine some of the elements of a refunding annuity and of a life annuity. Since these annuities guarantee benefit payments for a certain period even if the annuitant dies, the periodic benefit payments for life must be reduced because of the costs of providing annuity benefit payments for a certain period. Likewise, the certain period payments cannot be the same as refunding annuity payments since the costs of providing a life annuity must be taken into account.

Joint and Survivorship Annuities

This type of annuity differs from a life annuity because the expected payments include the cost of providing a life payment for the annuitant's survivor. Survivor benefit payments may be equal to the amount payable to the annuitant or may be a constant percentage, such as 50 or 75 percent of the amount paid to the annuitant. Periodic benefit payments paid to the joint annuitant are reduced by the cost of the survivorship annuity benefits.

Variable Annuities

A variable annuity is one that is invested in a segregated investment account created by an insurance company. Accumulated funds are increased or decreased by the investment performance in the account. Annuity benefits may vary by the investment performance of this account or may be fixed at maturity date as are other annuities. Periodic payments based on variable values are not guaranteed as to amount. A refunding annuity is usually limited to the balance in the policyholder's account, not to the amounts that have been paid in.

Annuity premiums, whether ordinary or variable, may be paid in a single lump-sum amount or over a specified period of time. Variable annuity premiums are reported separately, although some companies may also include these amounts in the general account with offsetting provisions for benefits, expenses, and reserves. The premiums for ordinary and variable annuities should be recognized as revenue when they become due.

Annuity with Current Investment Yields

Traditional annuities offer a guaranteed rate of interest and, in some instances, policy dividends over the life of the annuity. When investment rates are at a low level, the guaranteed rate is more attractive than when investment rates are increasing. A distinctive feature of annuities with current investment yields is that the amount credited to the accumulated annuity value is a "new-money" rate. These rates usually are not guaranteed over an extended period of time, often being on a year-to-year basis. New-money rates may reflect returns based on third-party investment indexes or current treasury bill rates. Companies offering these rates expect that they will be able to realize higher yield rates on their investments.

These types of annuities provide for fixed or flexible periodic benefit payments. The former requires sufficient deposits that will accumulate at interest to produce a specified periodic or lump-sum benefit. The latter permits the policyowner to choose the amount and timing of premiums during the accumulation period. Single premium policies are offered either for immediate benefit payout or on a deferred basis providing benefits sometime in the future.

Another distinctive feature of many current investment yield annuities is that there is either no front-end or a reduced front-end load which permits crediting new-money rates to larger gross premium amounts. Withdrawals are usually subject to surrender charges that are reduced over a period of time, often 10 years. This permits the company to recover some of the acquisition cost incurred in issuing the policy. For later years, it is assumed that the excess earnings over policy requirements will be sufficient to cover future servicing costs. There may be annual administrative charges assessed to the accumulated funds for the costs of maintaining and updating the annuity values.

The premiums received on these policies for fixed annuities should be recognized in a manner similar to that for traditional annuity contracts when due. The revenue from flexible premiums should be recognized as revenue when collected, except that minimum or target premium amounts should be recorded when due.

GROUP INSURANCE POLICIES

Group insurance plans cover life insurance, accident and health insurance, and annuities. Group annuity plans involving pension plans are covered under the pension plan caption. Group life and group accident and health insurance are common forms of protection provided by employers as a fringe benefit and may also be issued through associations or other common-interest organizations.

Group life insurance may be funded entirely by an employer, or the cost may be shared between the employer and employee. Life insurance offered to associations and other common-interest groups generally provides that the excess premiums over the group experience cost will be returned. Some group policies do not require individual underwriting if the group is large enough and the health standards for new participants are reasonable. For smaller association groups, it is often necessary for the participant to qualify under a normal health profile. Premium rates are usually guaranteed, although some may be adjusted based on prior claims experience and may also provide for future premium credits or dividends.

Group accident and health insurance covers either medical indemnity or loss of wages from disability. Medical indemnity policy premiums are based on past medical costs incurred by the group, adjusted to reflect expected changes in benefit costs. Many group policies are guaranteed renewable so long as current premiums are paid or may be issued for a specified term. Disability income insurance is usually individually underwritten and is subject to an occupational rating. The premiums may be guaranteed, but even if they are not, they are much less subject to change than are medical indemnity premiums. Policies with guaranteed premium rates are subject to the same risk as individual policies in that future premiums may be inadequate to cover future benefits.

Premiums for group life insurance should be recognized when they are due. Premiums for group accident and health insurance providing medical expense indemnity should be recognized on a pro rata basis over the policy period. Group premiums on accident and health policies covering disability income should be recognized when due.

PENSION PLAN PREMIUMS

Premiums paid by employers to fund pension plans are generally classified as qualified premium products. Qualified plans are distinguished from all other types of life and annuity insurance which are classified as nonqualified and reflect the income tax treatment accorded each plan. If an insurance product is qualified, the premiums may be deducted from gross income by the employer, subject to a maximum deduction, and the insurance company is allowed a special reserve deduction to offset the premiums. Except for the income tax treatment, qualified and nonqualified insurance products are accounted for in a similar fashion.

Some of the more common insured-type pension plans are covered below.

Individual Retirement Annuities

These annuities are similar to the regular annuity described earlier and may be in the traditional guaranteed-interest form, the current-yield annuity form, or the variable annuity form. Premiums on individual retirement annuities are usually not fixed or required in the policy and are recognized in revenue when collected.

Self-Employed Retirement Savings (Keogh Plans)

Self-employed individuals and partnerships may establish a pension plan that includes benefits for the owner and employees. Plans of this type are distinguished from other retirement plans in that there is a fixed limitation on the amount of contributions for an individual, irrespective of earnings. These are defined contribution plans, and the retirement benefit is based on planned contributions made over the working career of the individual. The premiums paid into the plan, plus the interest and other credits earned, minus the administrative and other costs of maintaining the plans, produce a fund that is available to pay retirement benefits. The premiums on these types of retirement plans are not fixed or required in the policy and are recognized as revenue when collected.

Group Deferred Annuities

This is a defined benefit plan that requires current funding of an annuity for each qualifying employee. Premiums are calculated on attained age and salary levels to provide a specified benefit at retirement age for each employee qualified in the plan. The sum of all individual annuity calculations is the single annual premium paid by the employer. Employees may be permitted to contribute fixed amounts to fund additional retirement benefits. Annuity purchase rates are usually guaranteed for a fixed period and may then be changed based on company annuity expenses. Premiums for group deferred annuities are recognized in revenue as they become due.

Deposit Administration Plans

Rather than fund currently the cost of each individual annuity in the retirement plan, an employer may fund the aggregate benefit on an installment basis. Contributions are not allocated to individual accounts; rather, the annuities are purchased from the fund when employees retire. Contributions to the fund are subject to a minimum and a maximum amount and are increased by interest earnings and reduced by administrative expenses. Participating plans also receive additional credits as dividend distributions are made. These plans usually offer excess interest above the amounts guaranteed and annuity purchase rates for a specified period. Premiums from deposit administration plans are included in revenue as they become due.

Deposit administration plans are sometimes modified to provide for immediate participation guarantee (IPG). These plans differ from deposit administration plans in that no annuities are purchased for retired employees. Rather, retired employees receive pension benefits directly from the fund. The fund reflects the net investment result of plan assets and the mortality experience of participating employees. While a minimum interest rate is guaranteed, the actual rate usually reflects current investment experience.

For either deposit administration or immediate participation guarantee plans, some or all of the funds may be invested in an insurance company "separate account." These accounts are established for specific investment programs such as equity growth, maximum current interest, and real estate participation funds. Separate accounts have small management and investment fees and the net investment return is often greater than for general account plans. Favorable investment experience results in smaller deposit requirements to fund the plan.

Other group pension plans provide funding for retirement benefits by the purchase of life insurance contracts or may combine life insurance benefits with retirement annuities. Also, the Internal Revenue Code permits certain governmental and not-for-profit employees to defer portions of their earnings in what is commonly referred to as a "tax shelter annuity."

Premiums received for deposit administration and other group pension plans are recognized in revenue when they are due.

OTHER PREMIUMS

Supplementary Contracts

These contracts arise from options available to policyholders or their dependents, using proceeds from death, maturity, or surrender benefits. When periodic payments are elected, a supplementary contract is issued in the gross amount of the proceeds. A stipulated interest earning rate is offered for specific periods and the guaranteed rate is offered for the term of the contract. The accumulated balance, including interest, is paid to the policyowner or beneficiaries over a specified period of time or for life. Benefits payable over a fixed period of time are *supplementary contracts without life contingencies* and pay benefits similar to a refund annuity. If benefits are payable for life, a *supplementary contract with life contingencies* pays benefits similar to a life annuity with a guaranteed fixed-period option.

Proceeds from matured or surrendered policies used to purchase supplementary contracts are accounted for separately as current costs. Supplementary contracts are issued for a single payment and should be recognized in revenue when due.

Dividend Accumulation

Participating policyholders qualify to receive additional benefits in the form of dividends, representing a return of excess premium margins. Dividend benefits are more common for life or annuity products issued by mutual insurance companies, although some stock insurance companies have similar plans. A policyholder has the option to receive the dividends in cash, to apply them to reduce premiums or to increase policy coverage, or to deposit them with the company to accumulate at interest. The margins for accident and health products are smaller, and the dividend payments for these plans are also smaller and paid less frequently. Dividends left to accumulate at interest provide additional investment funds for life insurance company operations. Policy dividends left with the company to accumulate at interest are included in revenues when due.

Advanced Premiums and Deposits

Certain premiums and other funds received by a life insurance company and not included in current revenue are described below.

Advanced Premiums. Policyowners may remit premiums in advance of the due date or in excess of the periodic policy premium. Some advanced premiums arise because they are paid as soon as premium notices are received, which may be up to 30 days prior to the premium due date. Some arise because policyowners choose to pay future premiums before they are due. All advanced premiums are recorded as liabilities until the premium due date and are not subject to discounting or other interest credits. As premium due dates occur, advanced premiums are applied to pay current premiums due. Advanced premiums are not included in revenue until the due date of the policy premium.

Discounted Premiums. Most life insurance companies offer policyowners the opportunity to pay the present value of future discounted premiums. Policyowners may pay a fixed amount for future premiums or may pay an amount for a fixed number of future premiums. Discounted premiums are held and accumulated at interest so that at future premium due dates amounts can be withdrawn to pay the premiums then due. Discounted premiums are recorded as a liability and are not recognized in revenue until the premium due date.

Other Deposit Funds. These funds are usually received in connection with the sale of other life insurance products and are reported as a liability. These amounts are held and accumulated at interest but not recognized in revenue unless the funds are converted to an insurance product.

PROPERTY AND LIABILITY PREMIUMS

Property and liability insurance premiums are calculated to insure risks over a shorter period of time than is required for most life insurance policies. While title and some fire insurance companies have issued long-term property protection, most other property and liability insurance coverages are from 3 months to 5 years. Currently, a typical policy will provide coverage on an annual renewable basis. While policies may insure a risk for a shorter period, such as 6 months or even 3 months, the underlying adequacy of premiums is more often determined on an annual basis.

Property and liability insurance is offered in many forms and can provide nearly universal protection for individuals and business enterprises. There is hardly a risk that cannot be insured. While there are some specialized insurance products that insure unusual risks, most policies can be neatly categorized under traditional property and liability lines of insurance. Fully collaterized risks, such as bailment and certain performance bonds, offer minimal protection for a small premium to cover losses and administrative services. All other property and liability insurance premiums include estimates for the risk of loss, marketing and administrative expenses, and margins or profits. Policy dividends, if any, usually result from favorable claims experience and, unlike life insurance dividends, are more in the nature of experience refunds.

Property and liability insurance policies do not develop cash surrender values as do life insurance policies. Losses from property and liability policies arise from many perils, including fire, collision, hail and windstorms, earthquakes, floods, negligence, crimes, dishonesty, sickness, and loss of time and income. Many hazards contribute to the possible loss from these perils. For example, driving an automobile with faulty brakes greatly increases the peril of collision and the consequences of a resulting loss. Correcting the hazards can reduce the risk of possible loss. However, some perils cause losses even though no risks are taken. The windstorm that blows the roof off is a type of peril that is beyond the insured's control. Property and liability insurance provides protection to a policyowner in the form of indemnity payments for the monetary loss from most perils.

Two principles underlie the property and liability policy insurance protection. First, there must be an insurable interest in the property or an exposure to a loss. For example, it is against the public interest to issue a fire insurance policy on a building for which the insured has no insurable interest. Second, the insurance coverage is limited to a fixed amount or to actual cash value (replacement cost less depreciation). Liability claims are also insured for actual cash value even though such losses are often intangible and subject to negotiations or litigation. Most insured losses are limited to the policy amount and may be adjusted for other insurance, for deductibles, and for coinsurance provisions.

Revenue from property and liability insurance premiums is generally recognized over the policy period in proportion to the risk assumed. Premiums are usually paid in advance and result in the recording of a liability for unearned premiums. Revenue is recognized on a pro rata basis as earned even though the premiums are paid monthly, quarterly, semiannually, or annually. Unpaid premiums are recognized as revenue so long as the amounts outstanding are deemed to be collectible. For statutory accounting purposes, the deemed collectible period is generally limited to accounts that are less than 90 days past due.

The major categories of property and liability insurance premiums are covered below.

Property Insurance

Fire and Extended Insurance. Fire insurance is available to protect against losses for buildings and for the contents of retail establishments, manufacturing companies, public buildings, and dwellings. The largest unknown costs in determining premium rates are the risk of loss from fire or other perils and the cost of adjusting such losses. Premium rates are affected by the method of construction, the materials used, and the physical location of the risk. Other cost elements for selling, administration, overhead expenses, contingencies and profits are more fixed and are easily estimated. These premiums are based on long-term loss experience, with allowances for current construction methods and for municipal and other fire code requirements.

Structures built of good fireproof materials, with sprinklers or other fire-retardant protection, and located in an area with first-class fire protection will have the most favorable fire premium rates. Buildings of poor construction, old buildings with dry timber and siding, buildings without sprinklers or other fire-retardant protection, and buildings located in areas with insufficient fire fighting equipment will have the most unfavorable fire premium rates. Although each building in a given area may not be given the benefit of a separate rating, the rating structure does give credit for each of the elements that tend to reduce or control fire losses.

Extended insurance covers other losses, such as building contents, extra expense for temporary quarters after a loss, and business interruption insurance to cover losses of profits and fixed charges that continue during nonoperating periods. A personal dwelling policy covers living costs for the insured incurred away from the damaged dwelling. Other extended insurance includes loss of rent, demolition, damage to business stock and inventory by temperature changes, and extra expenses incurred to retain business.

Fire and extended insurance premiums are recognized in revenue on a pro rata basis over the term of the policy.

Allied Lines. Perils can be insured on a specific basis or may be included in a multiple-peril policy. Two of the more common forms of allied line policies are crop hail insurance and windstorm insurance, both of which are subject to sudden losses. The determination of premiums for these policies is based on calculations similar to those made for fire and extended insurance. The long-term history with hail and windstorm losses provides the basis for determining that current premiums are adequate to fund losses in the years when hail and windstorm losses are severe. Unlike the risks of loss from fire insurance, which decrease when the hazards are reduced, the losses from hail and windstorms result from natural hazards, which are difficult to predict.

Two other common specific property losses covered are sprinkler leakage and loss from water damage other than floods. Sprinkler leakage coverage provides protection for damage caused by the faulty operation of automatic sprinkler systems. Other water damage usually results from faulty roofs or plumbing. Other less common coverages include earthquakes, floods, and rain.

Allied lines insurance premiums are recognized in revenue on a pro rata basis over the policy term.

Ocean and Inland Marine. This type of insurance has been closely related to the business of navigation and trade. Ocean marine policies insure ships and cargoes. Inland marine policies, on the other hand, insure domestic transportion shipments, bridges, tunnels, radio towers, pipelines, and in-transit property. Ocean marine insurance is so specialized that few companies underwrite these risks. Inland marine insurance is a common coverage for both business and personal risks.

Business floater policies for property risks provide insurance for goods that are in transit. For example, a contractor's equipment floater policy insures a contractor's equipment, regardless of where it is located, against loss from fire, windstorm, theft, and damage while in transit. Other floater policies cover salespeople's samples, rental equipment, and livestock in transit.

Personal floater policies insure personal property kept inside or outside the home, including bicycles, wedding presents, power boats, and unscheduled property such as jewelry, furs, and silver. Premiums for floater policies are calculated in a manner similar to that for other property coverages and include expected losses, loss adjustment expenses, marketing and administrative expenses, and profits.

Ocean and inland marine insurance premiums are recognized in revenue on a pro rata basis over the policy term.

Automobile Physical Damage. This coverage pays the insured, irrespective of fault, for accidental losses to an owned automobile. The policyholder's attention to potential hazards relating to automobile damage greatly affects the cost of this insurance. Carelessness, inattention to necessary maintenance of mechanical parts, inattention to hazardous road conditions, and general negligence may cause the premiums for this insurance to increase significantly. To determine equitable premium cost distribution, the insurer classifies individual drivers by their age, occupation, and driving habits when estimating future losses.

Premiums for automobile physical damage insurance include provisions for estimated losses, agency and marketing expenses, the cost of maintaining the coverage in force, and margins for profits. Even though there may be adequate historical statistics for the company and the industry, estimates of future losses and loss expenses for a policy period are extremely difficult to determine. Losses are caused by collisions, upsets, falling objects, theft or larceny, windstorms, hail, water and floods, civil commotions, glass breakage from flying objects, and other perils which often cannot be avoided. If the estimates of losses and loss expenses are made on an optimistic basis, there is a likelihood that the losses and the related operating expenses incurred in the future will exceed the premiums charged for the coverage. On the other hand, if the estimates of losses and loss expenses are made on a pessimistic basis, the resulting premiums will likely not be competitive and new business opportunities will be reduced. Because the premiums are fixed for a short period, corrections can be made when the estimates of losses and loss adjustment expenses vary too far from actual experience.

Physical damage insurance also includes towing and labor costs, temporary automobile rental, medical payments, bodily injury from uninsured motorists, and damages other than by collision. Premiums for automobile physical damage are generally determined on an annual basis. However, when the policies are sold for short periods, the premiums can be adjusted on each policy renewal date.

Irrespective of the policy or premium-paying period, premiums for automobile physical damage insurance are recognized in revenue on a pro rata basis over the policy period.

Specific Property Insurance. Besides providing insurance against loss for fire, allied lines, ocean and inland marine, and automobile physical damage, many companies insure the following risks:

Burglary and Theft. This type of coverage is often called "crime insurance." It offers protection against losses from burglary, theft, robbery, embezzlement, forgery, and other dishonesties and is available to both businesses and individuals. It can be purchased on an all-inclusive peril basis or for a single peril. Businesses purchase this insurance to protect against loss of money, furniture and fixtures, securities, and merchandise stock. Specialized crime insurance is available for such businesses as banks and other financial institutions having a significant amount of cash or cash-convertible assets. Personal theft and robbery policies cover both dwellings and off-dwelling risks and include damage caused by a theft or theft attempt.

Premiums for this insurance are recognized in revenue on a pro rata basis similar to that for other property insurance premiums.

Fidelity Bonds. This insurance, while in actuality not a bond, guarantees to reimburse the insured for losses that are incurred from dishonest acts of employees or officers. Losses from individual dishonesty acts are difficult to predict. However, by using the experience of a large company or an industry, a reasonable estimate of potential losses can be determined and included in the premiums. Fidelity bonds contain a maximum coverage for each occurrence and often have significant deductible amounts for each loss. These bonds may be written on an individual position basis or may provide blanket protection for all employee positions. Government officials and others having fiduciary capacities are often required to qualify for a position fidelity bond. The premium for these bonds covers a short term and may be changed at each policy renewal date.

Premiums from fidelity bonds are recognized ratably over the policy period.

Surety Bonds. These are often referred to as "performance bonds." They guarantee that an insured will perform specific contractual obligations. Unlike most other insurance coverages, surety bond premiums require a smaller provision for losses. They have a theoretical zero loss ratio and are more in the nature of service fees for use of the company's name. Surety bonds should provide for deposits of adequate collateral to pay for possible claims. These bonds are normally required for construction contracts and are mandatory for most government construction.

Premiums on surety bonds should be recognized ratably over the expected construction period.

Other Property Insurance. This includes credit risk, valuable papers, license and sales tax permits, accounts receivable records, judicial and litigation bonds, boiler insurance, and other specialized coverage.

Premiums from these specialized risks are recognized on a pro rata basis in revenue, much as is all other property insurance.

Liability Insurance

Liabilities attributable to organizations or individuals arise from an action or inaction by them that causes a loss to third parties. Liability insurance, which pays for such losses, is classified as automobile and other liability.

Liabilities arise from several causes. Some arise because intentional wrong is committed against another person or property. Others arise because it is in the public interest to protect persons and properties from losses arising from negligence or from activities that have dangerous tendencies. The types of liability insurance that cover these risks are described below.

Automobile Liability. This insurance limits loss protection for individual or aggregate occurrences to a fixed amount stated in the policy. Except for specific perils, the liability protection is determined by the policyowner. When policy limits are restricted or coverage is declined, the insured is classified in a single risk pool and companies are required to insure some of these risks with minimum liability insurance.

To estimate the losses included in the premiums, it is probably easier to determine the accident frequency than it is to determine the maximum exposure of each occurrence. For a broad base of policies, the incurrences will not significantly change for a group of insured drivers that is identified by age, occupation, and driving habits. However, the maximum liability of each incurrence is subject to a number of unknown circumstances, such as state and local laws, the attitudes of local judges and juries, and regional customs.

An automobile liability insurance policy covers payments to third parties for bodily injury or property damage caused by the insured while operating his or her motor vehicle. These policies require the insurance company to settle or defend, within policy limits, the liability for losses incurred. Automobile liability insurance applies to all accidents, irrespective of the policyowner's unintentional actions or neglect. It may also pay the insured when the third party is an uninsured driver. Premium calculations must take into account the frequency and severity of long-term exposures as well as the cost of expenses to settle the losses, marketing and administrative expenses, and profits.

Premiums for automobile liability insurance are recognized in revenue on a pro rata basis over the term of the policy.

Other Liabilities. Other liability insurance provides protection against monetary losses to the policyowner arising from third-party claims not involving automobiles. It does not cover criminal proceedings if a business enterprise or an individual deliberately violates the law.

Other liability insurance may cover only specific risks or may be on an all-risk basis. Like automobile liability policies, this insurance contains a maximum benefit for individual occurrences or aggregate exposures. Losses in excess of these limits, unless provided for by excess coverage, are the responsibility of the policyowner. Liability for personal injury or property damage includes medical expenses, the cost of claims investigations, legal counsel, and intangible losses.

Some of the more common forms of other liability insurance cover storekeepers, general business, manufacturers and contractors, aircraft, garage keepers, commercial vehicles, insurance agents and brokers, dramshops for taverns, personal liability insurance, and owners, landlords, and tenants.

Premiums on these policies are recognized in revenue on a pro rata basis over the term of the policy.

Other Property and Liability Insurance

Property and liability insurance is also available for nearly any business risk, including such specialized coverages as rain insurance for athletic events. Property and liability insurance companies may also underwrite group accident and health insurance and credit accident and health insurance on a group or individual basis.

Premiums for accident and health insurance and other specialized insurance are recognized in revenue on a pro rata basis over the policy term.

Medical malpractice insurance and professional liability insurance is usually written by a company specializing in those products and may be written on an incurred or claims-made basis. Premiums for an incurred-basis policy must contain allowances for long-term risk exposures. For claims-made policies, the allowance may be less, since the protection is limited to the losses reported during the current policy term.

Irrespective of how the claims are paid, the premiums on these policies are recognized in revenue ratably over the policy term.

Other more common forms of liability insurance are covered below.

Workers' Compensation. This is a required business insurance that pays employee disability benefits under a uniform program, except for employers exempted because of the size or nature of their operations. Some states administer a workers' compensation fund. Others permit employers to purchase this protection from authorized companies. This insurance pays medical benefits for employment injuries, cash benefits for loss of time, and rehabilitation benefits when employees do not fully recover from their disabilities. Premiums for these benefits are determined by using the company or industry experience for similar occupational activities for losses, loss adjustment expenses, marketing and administrative costs, and profits. Workers' benefits are payable after a limited waiting period and can extend for the lifetime of the employee.

Workers' compensation premiums should be recognized in revenue on a pro rata basis over the term of the policy.

Multiple-Peril Policies. Most of the policies previously discussed are limited to specific risks. However, a significant part of property and liability insurance protection is written to cover the policyholder on an all-risk basis. These policies package all-lines risks and permit policyowners to purchase a single policy to protect their property or business. Most such policies are written as commercial, homeowners, and farmowners multiple-peril policies. The risks covered include losses from fire, windstorm, hail, malicious damage and theft, and third-party liability claims. The multiple-risk policy provides the same insurance protection as do the individual policy forms, but the premiums are combined into a single amount. Premium expenses for marketing and administration are also combined, usually resulting in a smaller aggregate policy premium.

Multiple-peril premiums are recognized in revenue on a pro rata basis over the term of the policy.

TITLE INSURANCE

Title insurance is a form of property and liability insurance offering protection to a buyer of property. Instead of providing reimbursement for property and losses, title insurance protects the current property owner from future claims by prior titleholders. A title insurance policy remains in force as long as the property is owned by the insured or the insured's heirs, and it protects against loss from forgeries, mistakes in public records, wills that are not probated, and undisclosed or missing heirs. Title companies own detailed records that disclose prior title ownership, transfers, and liens reported in the public records. Before issuing a title insurance policy, the title company makes a search of the title plant and public records to determine the current title status.

Title insurance premiums are due at the time the policy is issued and are usually not refundable. Some states require title insurance companies to maintain an unearned premium reserve. While this results in statutory recognition of premiums over an extended period of time, the transaction is more in the nature of a reserve for future unaccrued losses.

Title insurance premiums are recognized in revenue as a single amount when they are due.

Some title insurance companies may receive fees for services such as closing costs, escrow agent fees, and mortgage lender fees. These fees are recognized in revenue when they are due.

MORTGAGE GUARANTEE INSURANCE

This is third-party insurance that protects the mortgage lender against losses when the mortgagor does not pay as agreed and the proceeds from foreclosure are less than the outstanding amount of the loan. The amount of protection can range up to 100 percent of the loan but is usually in the range of 10 to 30 percent. With mortgage guarantee insurance, a lender is more able to sell loans in the secondary market. Lenders with good underwriting practices can usually obtain this insurance without a detailed review of borrower files by the mortgage guaranty company, although other lenders may be separately underwritten by the company.

The policies may be issued for the term of the mortgage, but subsequent sales and attrition reduce the average policy term. The premiums are estimated by using company or industry loss experience, sales and administrative expenses, and profit. The lender may usually pay the premiums on an annual level or reducing term basis or in a single amount.

Premiums for mortgage guarantee insurance are recognized in revenue on a pro rata basis over the term of the policy.

INVESTMENT AND OTHER INCOME

In the recording of investment income, there is very little difference between generally accepted accounting principles and statutory accounting practices. Both are maintained on an accrual basis of accounting. The major differences relate to the treatment of certain investment income being excluded from revenue and to recording as revenue self-charged rent for home office occupancy. For nearly all other investment income, the treatments under both accounting methods are parallel. Additionally, there is virtually no distinction between the accounting for investment income between life insurance companies and property and liability companies even though some investments are different, such as policy loans in life insurance companies.

The following is a summary of accrual accounting for investment income and of special rules for statutory accounting practices:

Bonds

The earnings rate for these investments is usually fixed and guaranteed in the bonds. Bond investments include: United States government issues; state, municipal, and other bonds which are exempt from federal income taxes; and bonds issued by corporations and affiliated companies. Interest collected during the year is recorded on a cash basis, and due and unpaid interest is accrued between interest-paying dates. In addition, bond discounts or premiums are amortized over the term of the bond to reflect a level annual yield. For statutory accounting, such amounts are amortized to the earliest call date, and the interest due on bonds delinquent as to principal or interest is nonadmitted and deducted from the gross interest earnings.

Preferred and Common Stocks

Dividends are recorded in revenue when they are collected and accrued amounts when due between dividend-paying dates. Common stock dividends are generally accrued on the ex-dividend date. For statutory accounting, dividends on cumulative preferred stock in arrears or on non-cumulative preferred stock for which sinking fund payments are in arrears are considered nonadmitted and deducted from gross preferred stock dividends for the year.

Mortgage Loans

Mortgage loan interest is recognized on a ratable basis over the term of the loan. Interest on mortgage loans for the year includes the interest due and not paid, the accrual of discounts and the amortization of premiums, and accrued amounts between payment dates. Interest received in advance is recorded as unearned and not included in revenue until due. For statutory accounting, interest in arrears for a specified certain period is treated as nonadmitted and deducted from the interest revenue for the year. For statutory reporting, mortgage interest is usually nonadmitted if not paid for 12 months or when a mortgage is in foreclosure.

Real Estate

Rental income is recorded in revenue as it becomes due. Rental amounts received in advance are recorded as unearned until the payment due date. For statutory accounting purposes, if the real estate is subject to a mortgage, the interest paid on the mortgage is deducted from real estate income. Additionally, insurance companies that occupy their own buildings are required to report self-charged rent on a comparable basis to that for rent received from others, with an offset to rent expense.

Policy Loans

Life insurance companies usually have policy loans outstanding for which policyholders are required to pay interest. In some instances, interest is charged in advance; these amounts are unearned and included in revenues when due. In other instances, interest is charged annually but accrued when due or ratable between interest payment dates. For statutory purposes, there should not be any nonadmitted interest on policy loans, since unpaid interest amounts are added to the loan. If loan amounts exceed cash value, the policy is surrendered.

Other Investments

Insurance companies are permitted to invest in a number of other assets, including items such as lease arrangements and real estate joint ventures. Income from these investments is recorded in revenue when it is due, except that real estate joint-venture income is generally recorded as distributions are made.

Realized Capital Gains and Losses

These gains and losses are recognized when a sale, other transactions, or a maturity date occurs. There is no significant difference in reporting for generally accepted accounting principles (GAAP) or statutory accounting practices, except that in some instances the statutory basis used to determine gain or loss may be different than for the GAAP basis. This usually occurs because of required write-downs of assets for statutory purposes. For life insurance companies, statutory reporting requires that these amounts be charged or credited to surplus, with an offsetting amount charged or credited to the mandatory securities valuation reserve.

All other items of income are recorded in revenues when they become due. Other income items are usually not significant in amount for insurance companies but may include items such as finance and service charges not included in premiums and vending machine income. For statutory reporting, other income may also include recoveries made on assets previously charged off; for life insurance companies, some items related to reinsurance contract settlements are recorded in revenue. Reinsurance accounting is discussed in Chapter 16, Reinsurance Ceded and Assumed.

5

INVESTMENTS IN SECURITIES

The funds received by an insurance company are paid in by policyowners to secure protection against loss from property and liability exposures, sickness and accidents, untimely deaths, and the like. Unlike the funds received by investment companies for the sole purpose of investment opportunities, the funds received by insurance companies are for liabilities assumed and expenses incurred in providing protection. To provide this protection, insurance companies calculate premium charges that will result in an accumulation of funds sufficient to pay the benefits when they become due. Without this premium concept, insurance benefits could only be paid by means of an assessment on policyholders after the loss.

In determining premiums charged for protection, the time value of money is considered. If premiums were calculated on the basis of expected losses and not discounted for the time value of money that accumulates to pay those losses, the premiums charged for insurance policies would be significantly higher. The time value of money for this purpose may be different than that determined by lending institutions. This is true since insurance companies are not "borrowing" funds from the individual policyowner. Rather, insurance companies pool the funds paid in by policyowners. This pool of funds, when appropriately invested, should provide the amount necessary to pay benefits. To state it another way, the needed amount of earnings on the pooled fund should be available in liquid form *at the actuarially expected loss date. These circumstances require insurance companies to view the investment of their funds in a significantly different manner than do investment companies or other financial institutions.*

INVESTMENT OBJECTIVES OF INSURANCE COMPANIES

Except for investments made with funds received from stockholders or lenders, insurance companies plan their investment purchases and maturity dates to meet the future expected cash payments of policy benefits. If benefits are expected to be payable within a short period of time, it would not be prudent to buy bonds that mature many years in the future. Conversely, short-term investments would not be prudent to fund benefits that are expected to be payable many years away. At times, this program of investing prevents the insurance company from taking advantage of current high-yield opportunities. On the other hand, this approach to investing does not expose the insurance company to many of the normal risks related to the decline of yields on current investments. In many respects, the investment objective of insurance companies that relates to policyholder funds is like buying a "put" option on the portfolio. In other words, it is more important for the insurance company to be protected against a declining yield rate than it is to participate in increasing yield rates. To a very great extent, the investment restrictions imposed upon insurance companies are directed towards creating a "safe" investment portfolio to ensure the future availability of funds to pay benefits.

Another objective of insurance companies is to maximize the return on investments. Within the general constraints discussed in the preceding paragraph, insurance companies seek to maximize their investment return for several reasons. Since most insurance products are priced to produce the lowest cost and maximum benefit to the policyowner, only a small profit element, if any, is included in the premium payments. Yet an insurance company's need for additional profit is the same as the need for additional profits by commercial companies. For insurance companies, profits are needed to fund stockholders' and policyholders' dividends and to provide capital for expansion. While some of these additional profits may arise from having a more favorable loss experience than was anticipated in calculating the premium, a major share of additional profits must be earned by managing the investment portfolio to produce a higher return on investments than was estimated in developing the premium calculation. Consequently, by utilizing their discretionary investment authority, insurance companies may invest in a wide range of investment securities. Their investment portfolio will always reflect the first objective of safety mentioned above; however, the investment portfolio is also likely to contain nearly all types of securities.

A third influence on investment objectives arises from the requirement of state regulators and the fiduciary responsibilities of directors and officers that are unique to the insurance business.

The material covered here reflects the accounting treatment for investments in securities from both the regulatory point of view and the view of management and directors.

An insurance company's investment securities are grouped in a manner that classifies the investment portfolio from the most secure to the least secure. Other commercial and investment companies may group securities by industry classification. The traditional insurance classification is required for financial statements filed with state insurance regulatory authorities. The investments and securities covered below are classified in the manner required for reporting by most insurance companies.

BONDS

United States Government Bonds

This classification includes United States treasury bills, bonds, and notes issued directly by the United States government. In addition, it includes securities issued by instrumentalities of the U.S. government, such as the Farmers Home Administration, the Federal Land Bank Corporation, and the General Services Administration. These securities are generally considered to be the most secure form of investment. For this reason, the yield on these investments may not be as high as that on other bonds and notes. For the most part, insurance companies have unlimited authority to invest in U.S. government securities. Indeed, a company may, but likely will not, invest its entire portfolio in them. Companies that derive investment income from U.S. government bonds have little cause to be concerned about their ultimate yield. A typical insurance company would not expect to dispose of the bonds prior to maturity and therefore would not be affected by fluctuations in market prices that occur when interest rates are increasing or decreasing. These investments protect some of the long-term guarantees made by insurance companies to their policyholders.

Investments in U.S. government bonds are reported at the cost of acquiring the bonds adjusted for the amortization of premium or discount. No other adjustments are made to the carrying basis of these bonds.

Bonds guaranteed by the Dominion of Canada or other foreign governments are also reported under this caption. The financial reporting for these bonds is the same as for U.S. government securities unless there is a loss that must be recognized because of foreign currency fluctuations. For statutory purposes, these foreign currency adjustments are prescribed by the Valuation Committee of the National Association of Insurance Commissioners (NAIC) on an annual basis. For financial reporting of public companies, any such loss is reported as a realized loss in the income statement. In the statutory statement for a life insurance company, the loss is charged directly to surplus. While insurance companies usually have unlimited authority to invest in Canadian bonds, each other foreign investment is generally limited to 5 percent or less of invested assets.

Bonds of States, Territories, Possessions, and Local Governments

Insurance companies may generally invest in direct obligations of any state without limitation. The bonds must be guaranteed by the state and be subject to repayment of principal and interest out of the state's general revenues. However, no more than a certain percentage of an insurance company's total assets may be invested in the bonds of any single political subdivision (generally a city, county, or school district). The limitation on these investments is related to the type of guarantee and to the revenues that underlie repayment. Direct obligations funded from the general revenues of a political subdivision are subject to less restriction than are obligations guaranteed only by specific revenues or special assessments. Bonds issued by state or municipal public utilities and other revenue bonds are generally limited both as to the amount that can be invested in any one bond obligation and the total investment in this class of obligations.

As a group, these bonds are often tax-exempt since the interest paid on them is generally excluded in computing federal income taxes. As will be pointed out later, the peculiarities of life insurance company taxation may cause some of this interest to be taxed.

These bonds are valued for financial reporting at cost adjusted for the amortization of premium and discount. It is rare when bonds in this classification would be valued on any other basis. For annual reports filed with the insurance commissioner, these bonds are separated between (1) states, territories, and possessions; (2) political subdivisions of states, territories, and possessions; and (3) special revenue and special assessment obligations and all nonguaranteed obligations of agencies and authorities of government and their political subdivisions.

Railroad and Public Utility Bonds

Bonds of regulated industries such as railroads and public utilities have traditionally been classified separately from other corporate obligations. The regulations that govern these companies include specific provisions about debt retirement and about net income requirements to fund fixed charges. The investment authority for these two types of bonds is usually greater than for other corporate issuers. These bonds are valued at cost adjusted for amortization of premium or discount but are subject to the same valuation test, which is more fully described just below under "Industrial and Miscellaneous Bonds." Adjustments to the carrying value other than amortization of premiums and discounts are treated as valuation allowances and charged to operations. For statutory reporting, valuation allowances are treated as nonadmitted assets.

Industrial and Miscellaneous Bonds

All bonds other than those described above and other than bonds of affiliates and subsidiaries are included in this category. These bonds, for the most part, are those issued by industrial corporations. Bonds issued by medical facilities, religious organizations, and the like are also included. Generally, these bonds can be grouped as follows:

Marketable Bonds. Bonds subject to federal and state registration are usually freely traded and their price reflects a current market yield. These bonds can usually be acquired or disposed of without limitation. Since the investment objectives of insurance companies are influenced by factors other than market conditions, the market price of these bonds has little impact on their carrying value. It is only when bonds are impaired as to payment of interest or principal that market valuations are used.

Corporate bond yields are affected by the credit ratings received from brokers and other rating agencies. A significant drop in such a rating may be cause to reconsider the carrying value of the bonds. A write-down in the bond valuation is included in an allowance account and charged to current operations. For purposes of valuing bonds in the annual report filed with the insurance commissioner, there is a separate system of valuation that is followed in most jurisdictions.

The NAIC annually publishes the *Valuation of Securities Manual,* which contains uniform reporting values for marketable securities. These values are determined by the NAIC Subcommittee on Valuation of Securities and take into account the current status of the bonds with respect to payment of principal and interest and other valuation factors. The bonds are classified between those which qualify for using the amortized cost basis and those which are given a separate valuation. If the payment of interest or principal is impaired, if sinking fund requirements are being violated, or if the issuing company's credit rating is reduced, then the bonds are classified as "No" bonds. This means that an adjustment may have to be made to the valuation basis of the bonds. Some "No" bonds owned by life insurance companies will not require an adjustment to the valuation basis, since these companies maintain the required investment reserve. The components of this reserve are discussed in Chapter 15, Capital and Surplus.

The adjustment to the valuation basis of these bonds is included as a nonadmitted asset or as an unrealized capital loss. The book value for these bonds is not changed, and the nonadmitted adjustment can be reduced or eliminated in the future if the bond impairments are removed.

Private Placement Bonds. There is no significant difference between the nature of a marketable bond and that of a private placement bond, except that one is freely traded and the other is not. Private placement bonds comprise a significant part of total insurance company portfolios, especially those of life insurance companies. Private placement bonds are generally limited to purchases by the informed institutional investor. Financial and operating data is provided to investors, but registration with federal or state regulatory authorities is usually not required. Since the cost of placing these bonds is significantly less than the cost of placing marketable bonds, the yield on private placement bonds is usually higher. Reporting obligations for private placement bonds is considered separately when negotiating the bonds' sales.

Unlike marketable bonds, private placement bond valuations must be individually determined. Bonds that qualify because of the financial strength of the issuer are carried at cost adjusted for the amortization of premium or discount. Bonds impaired as to payment of principal or interest are adjusted to estimated realizable value through an allowance account which is charged against operations.

For reporting on the statutory statement, a value provided by the NAIC Subcommittee on Valuation of Securities is used. Insurance companies owning private placement bonds are required to furnish financial and operating data on such companies in order to receive a valuation basis. If the bonds are deemed to qualify, they may be carried at amortized cost value. If another value is provided, the adjustment to the valuation basis is treated as a nonadmitted asset and reported as an unrealized capital loss.

Bonds of Subsidiary and Affiliated Companies

Bonds issued by subsidiaries or affiliates can be either marketable or private placement bonds. These are classified between those which can be properly valued at amortized cost and those which are subject to a separate valuation basis. For the most part, bonds of subsidiaries and affiliates are valued in the same manner as are other industrial and miscellaneous bonds. For statutory purposes, the amount that can be owned may be subject to a separate investment limitation, which is discussed in Chapter 23, Subsidiary Companies.

PREFERRED STOCKS

In many respects, preferred stocks are similar to bonds. The main distinction between the two is that preferred stocks have a lesser claim on the issuer's net assets than do bonds. This is true since bonds are a liability of the company, whereas preferred stock represents part of the capital structure.

Preferred stock stands ahead of common stock, but behind all creditors of the company. Consequently, preferred stocks are less secure as to their ultimate redemption value. This does not mean that preferred stocks are poor investments for insurance companies. In fact, there are a number of reasons why preferred stocks might enhance an insurance company's portfolio. Not the least of these is the income tax consideration. Most preferred stocks are eligible for the 85 percent dividend-received deduction. For an insurance company paying a significant amount of income tax on its investment portfolio, the benefit of this deduction might be such that the preferred dividends will produce an after-tax return greater than that for some other investment.

Preferred stocks may have a number of special investment features. Most preferred stocks provide for dividends that are a fixed percentage of the issue price. Some preferred stocks also provide for additional participation in the earnings of the company. Generally, most preferred stocks in an insurance company's portfolio will provide for cumulative dividend rights. Preferred stocks that are noncumulative as to the dividend payment often do not provide the capital growth or investment return needed for insurance company operations.

Another significant feature of preferred stock is the redemption right. Preferred stocks with early redemption rights or sinking fund requirements are rated as a more secure investment than issues without these provisions. For the most part, preferred stocks do not have voting rights on corporate matters.

All preferred stocks, except those redeemable at the option of the owner or the issuer, are classified as marketable equity securities and carried at market value. The annual change in total market value should be reported net of deferred income taxes in the stockholders' equity section. Permanent declines in market values should be recognized in the determination of net income. Redeemable preferred stock, on the other hand, should be valued at its amortized cost basis.

For statutory accounting purposes, preferred stocks are classified into two broad groups. Preferred stock is considered to be in "good standing" if (1) dividends are not in arrears (noncumulative stock must have paid dividends in each of the last 3 years), (2) sinking fund payments, where required, are on a current basis, and (3) the issuer's net earnings over the past 3 years are equal to 125 percent of its aggregate fixed charges. Preferred stock "not in good standing" is one that does not meet each of these requirements. All insurance companies other than life insurance companies and others that maintain a mandatory securities valuation reserve are required to value preferred stock at amounts determined by the NAIC Subcommittee on Valuation of Securities. These are generally market or comparable values, except that preferred stock which provides for a mandatory sinking fund may be valued at cost. For life insurance companies and other companies maintaining a mandatory securities valuation reserve, preferred stock in good standing may be carried at cost. Preferred stock not in good standing is valued at market or other values furnished by the Subcommittee on Valuation of Securities. Preferred stock in good standing that was purchased prior to December 1964 may be valued at the statement values as of that date, which may be other than a cost basis. For life insurance companies and other companies maintaining a mandatory securities valuation reserve, the classification of preferred stock in one of these two groups will require a different allowance to be provided for each group in the determination of that reserve.

For statutory statement purposes, each issue of preferred stock must be grouped by issuers into the following categories: railroads; public utilities; banks; bank, trust, and insurance companies; industrial and miscellaneous; and parent, subsidiary, and affiliated companies.

COMMON STOCKS

Unlike preferred stock, common stock contains no stated dividend rate. Of course, some common stocks have traditionally paid dividends, thereby creating an expectation that dividends will continue. Other companies have paid little if any dividends on their common stock and have reserved their capital for future use, which, hopefully, will cause the stock to appreciate. Some insurance companies may wish to take advantage of potential appreciation in the value of common stock as opposed to realizing the current returns on their investments, which are generally taxable on a current basis. Common stocks offer the opportunity to participate in future operations and, conversely, create circumstances in which unsuccessful operations of the company will be reflected in the loss of market value. For this and other reasons, the portfolio of an insurance company will not have a large proportion of its total investment in common stocks. In fact, regulatory provisions limit the percentage that may be so invested.

For the most part, common stocks have a current indicator of their value in the public trading market. The change in this value can significantly affect the amount of surplus available for company operations. Investments in common stocks are valued similarly in financial statements prepared either on the basis of generally accepted accounting principles or statutory accounting practices. The end result is that the surplus is increased when the market prices in common stocks are on the rise and, conversely, that the surplus is decreased when there is a decline in the market price of common stocks that are held.

Also, unlike preferred stock, there is no classification of common stocks between companies which pay dividends and those which do not. However, there is a valuation method that may be used in different circumstances. For example, common stocks that are not regularly traded and do not have a market price at the valuation date receive a value based on the latest bid and ask prices. While these are not true market values for accounting purposes, they are acceptable when valuing common stock. The difference between the aggregate market value at the beginning and end of the period is included in a valuation allowance for unrealized gains or losses and charged or credited directly to stockholders' or policyholders' equity, net of applicable income taxes. Since the balance sheet of an insurance company is not classified between current and noncurrent items, only realized gains or losses are reported directly in the income statement.

For reporting common stocks in the statutory statement, publicly traded stocks are valued at market as of the statement date. For stocks not publicly traded, other than insurance company stock, the value is set by the NAIC Subcommittee on Valuation of Securities. To a great extent, these values are determined based on information provided by the insurance company about the financial condition and operating results of such companies. For insurance company stock that is not publicly traded, the value is equal to the statutory book value per share. While all insurance companies record unrealized gains and losses directly in the surplus account, only property and liability companies record realized gains and losses in the Statement of Income as a component of investment income. Life insurance and accident and health insurance companies, on the other hand, include both realized and unrealized gains and losses, net of federal income tax, as a surplus adjustment. In addition, life insurance and accident and health insurance companies are required to include these amounts in the calculation of their mandatory securities valuation reserve.

Warrants and options to purchase common stocks are valued at their market price in a manner similar to that for common stocks. Where securities are loaned under a collateral agreement, the stock continues to be reported at market value so long as the collateral is at least equal to the market price. Some jurisdictions permit insurance companies to invest in call options. These are reported at their current market price, and gains or losses occurring from their sale or expiration are reported as realized gains or losses. If the call option is exercised, the option price is added to the cost of the common stock acquired. Where an insurance company sells a call option, the common stock to which the option applies is reported at the lower of current market price or exercise price.

On the statutory statement, common stocks are grouped into the following categories by the issuer: railroad; public utility; bank, trust, and insurance company; industrial and miscellaneous; and parent, subsidiary, and affiliate.

POLICY LOANS

Policy loans usually are not thought of as an investment, but rather as a policyholder benefit. From an investment standpoint, most companies would prefer to avoid policy loans, since the returns are generally less than the company would realize on other investments. Policy loans are allowed only because sales of insurance would not be as attractive without that benefit provision.

Policy loans are discussed at this point since they can greatly restrict the ability of life insurance companies to achieve their investment objectives. To begin with, the company must structure its investment program so that sufficient liquid funds will be on hand to meet the expected level of policy loan requests (which tend to fluctuate with interest rates and economic conditions). Furthermore, the company must plan its premium level, as well as its investment program, to take into account the potential investment income that will be lost when a policy loan is made. Including the discussion of policy loans here should help explain yet another investment restriction encountered by life insurance companies.

Policy loans are included in most life insurance products that provide for cash accumulation benefits. Policy loans do not exist for term life policies, accident and health policies, and property and liability policies. In order for a policy loan provision to become effective, there must be a buildup of funds from premiums that have been paid. For periodic premiums, the cash buildup is related to the timing and amount of premiums. For single premium policies, the cash buildup is immediate.

In a sense, policy loans are merely a collateralized advance against the cash value fund that has been accumulated. In another sense, they are not loans at all since there is no promise to repay. Rather, where policy loans are not repaid, the ultimate death or endowment benefits are reduced by the loan amount. While interest is charged to the policyowner, there is no requirement that interest be paid on a current basis. If not paid, the interest charged is simply added to the policy loan balance.

A distinguishing feature of whole life policies, whether written in the traditional fixed-benefit form or the flexible premium and benefit form, is that the premiums are calculated to include a savings element, in addition to provisions for mortality, the time value of money, adjustments for possible policy lapse, and other factors. The savings element may not necessarily compare with that of a bank or other financial institution. The latter programs are a pure function of dollars paid plus accumulated investment earnings. In the usual savings program of a financial institution, the charge for administration is "hidden"; that is, the interest rate offered by a bank or other financial institutions is lower to take into account the cost of the institution's administrative services. The charge for the administrative services of a life insurance company with respect to the savings element is handled differently.

Unlike savings received by a bank or financial institution, which are immediately credited to the depositor's account, the premiums paid in the early years of an insurance policy are often used for the payment of marketing and administrative expenses and the establishment of life insurance reserves. Banks and other financial institutions provide investors with a single savings service and therefore will not incur a large first-year cost in setting up an account. The life insurance company, on the other hand, offers a package of services for which the first-year costs are quite large. To pay these costs and still provide the package of services, very little of the earlier premiums can be used to provide a cash buildup in the policy. Normally, depending on the policy's provisions, cash values may not begin to accumulate until after the first, second, or third year. The delay in the buildup of cash values is not viewed as a detriment since the life insurance policy offers other significant benefits over a long period of time as opposed to investment earnings only, as in the case of savings accounts.

A policyowner can surrender a whole life policy and receive the cash value that has accumulated. By surrendering the policy, the policyowner forfeits all rights to future life insurance benefits. To avoid losing these life insurance benefits, whole life policies contain a standard provision allowing for policy loans as an alternative to surrender. The life insurance company will loan substantially all the cash value, except for a minimal amount retained so that the policy loan does not exceed the guaranteed cash value as of the next policy anniversary date. The amount of interest charged for the policy loan is specified in the policy. If the interest on a loan is not paid when due, it is, by terms of the cash value provision of the policy, added to the outstanding loan balance. This total amount will then be subject to interest at the same policy rate.

An important aspect of cash value buildup in a life insurance policy is that there is no current tax on the interest accumulation so long as the policy remains in force. This fact may make the cash buildup more attractive on a long-term basis and is another incentive for selecting an endowment-type policy.

Policy loans can be classified into two groups: cash loans and automatic premium loans.

Cash Loans

A policyowner may request a cash loan directly from the life insurance company or its agent. Technically, this request is usually required to be accompanied by a signed loan agreement. However, to provide prompt policyowner service, most life insurance companies will accept a telephone request for a policy loan. If the policy has been assigned or pledged, the assignee may request a policy loan. Policy loan procedures are subject to a number of control features to ensure that the loan is received by the correct person. In many instances, a special endorsement is included on the loan check to serve as a loan agreement.

Interest is charged on policy loans at either the beginning or the end of the loan period. When charged at the beginning of the period, the first-year interest is deducted from the policy loan proceeds. In other words, the net loan proceeds equal the amount requested less the interest charged for the first year. Where interest is charged in advance, it is necessary to provide an unearned interest reserve, which is amortized over the months during the year that the loan is outstanding. Where interest is charged at the end of the year, it may be necessary to accrue the interest earned through the year-end. These interest adjustments are accounted for separately and are not included with the balance of policy loans outstanding.

Automatic Premium Loans

Another feature found in a whole life policy is the provision for automatic premium loans. Again, this is not a loan that requires repayment. Rather, it is a provision for continuing the policy by subtracting the amount of unpaid current premiums from the cash value.

Unlike a cash loan which originates with the policyowner's request, an automatic premium loan is made because the policyholder has previously elected that option. Where an automatic premium loan is not elected, a policy will lapse for nonpayment of premiums and will be converted into paid-up life insurance, extended term insurance, or another form of benefit as directed in the policy nonforfeiture provisions.

The automatic premium loan is a special policy provision intended to avoid the lapse of the policy for inadvertent nonpayment of periodic payments or because the policyowner did not wish to pay the current premium. By utilizing the automatic premium loan provision, the policy is kept in force by drawing on the cash value to pay current premiums. If automatic premium loans were not in effect and the policy lapsed, it would be necessary for the policyowner to comply with the policy reinstatement provisions, which usually include showing evidence of insurability. Automatic premium loans can continue to be made so long as there is a cash value in the policy.

While policy loans were traditionally not viewed as investments, new policies often permit charging a higher interest rate or a variable rate to make policy loans more competitive with other investment instruments. Under many old policies, the interest rates were quite low (often 5 or 6 percent), which hindered the insurance company's investment program.

Policy loans are reported at their unpaid balance. In this respect, policy loans are carried on a cost basis. This valuation method is the same for statutory reporting purposes. However, if the policy loan exceeds the cash surrender value of the policy, the excess is a nonadmitted asset.

COST BASIS OF INVESTMENTS

Many times the terms "cost" and "book value" are used interchangeably. *Cost,* the more readily understood term, represents an amount of money that is expended for goods or services acquired. The distinctive feature of cost is that it requires little or no measurement of the value of the acquired goods or services. It is a measurement that is rather precise. The amount paid, whether in cash, property, capital stock, or personal services, can usually be identified easily and measured. Cost in this sense eliminates any need to otherwise determine value for the purchase of goods or services. If the amount was expended, the total measure of the expenditure is the cost.

Book value, on the other hand, is not always the same as cost (although sometimes it may be the same). Where book value describes an amount measured by cost, then the terms have similar meanings. Often, however, book value merely describes the value at which assets, liabilities, and surplus are reported under a particular accounting method. In other words, book value can have a different meaning depending on whether one is following generally accepted accounting principles or statutory accounting practices.

These distinctions are important since the cost basis of securities in the investment account may differ between generally accepted accounting principles, statutory accounting practices, and the Internal Revenue Code. To reflect income and gains or losses arising from security transactions properly, it is necessary to maintain records that can be used for any of the three reporting purposes.

For all reporting purposes, cost generally represents the initial value of securities. Although the cost paid for a particular security may be in excess of or less than a traded market value, there is nevertheless an underlying assumption that the price paid is a fair determination of current economic value.

Since cost is the beginning amount against which future gains or losses are measured, common cost elements should be identified. For all reporting purposes, the cost of securities includes the initial amount paid plus the cost of brokerage services, bank charges, transfer and recording fees, transfer taxes, and the like. Indirect expenses such as those arising from the operation of an investment department are excluded from the initial cost. In other words, only the initial costs directly expended for purchasing the investment security should be included. Amounts paid for accrued interest and dividends declared but unpaid are excluded from the cost. These are recorded as debits in the interest and dividend accounts that will be offset when the interest and dividends are actually received.

The *par value* for bonds and redeemable preferred stock is the face amount of the security. For common stock and nonredeemable preferred stock, par value is a nominal value given to each share. In the former instance, par value represents the ultimate redemption value of the security. In the latter instance, par value is usually meaningless. For common stock, the only significance is that the shareholders may be liable for corporate debts to the extent that the full par value is not paid for the stock when issued. For nonredeemable preferred stock, par value is the amount that would be received in liquidation, if corporate assets were sufficient.

The significance of par value for bonds and redeemable preferred stock is that yield rates are determined by reference to this amount. Where bonds and redeemable preferred stocks are purchased exactly at par, the yield is equal to the stated interest or dividend rate. Where the purchase price is greater or less than par value, the difference must be amortized to the maturity date. Several amortization methods are acceptable; however, the level-yield method is preferred. For statutory reporting, many states require the use of a level-yield method.

Premiums

The excess of the purchase price over the par or maturity value is amortized to the maturity date, unless options are reserved by the issuer to redeem the securities at an earlier period and it appears that the issuer will do so. In the latter instance, the amortization period would be to the expected redemption date. For statutory reporting purposes, all premiums are amortized to the earliest possible redemption date. For income tax reporting, premiums paid on tax-exempt bonds are amortized to the maturity date, and premiums paid on taxable bonds are amortizable at the option of the taxpayer. As a practical matter, following the statutory rules for premium amortization will satisfy most other reporting requirements.

Discounts

Where the purchase price is less than the face amount of the security, the difference is accounted for over the remaining period to maturity. The accrual of the discount can be prorated by periods or preferably will be allocated to reflect a level yield on the security. For statutory reporting purposes, the level-yield method is required. For income tax reporting, the treatment of the discount depends on whether it is original issue discount or market discount.

Original issue discount is the difference between the issuing price and the face amount of the bond. The original issue discount must be accrued for income tax reporting and included in income over the life of the bond. This results in adjusting the cost basis of the bond so that at maturity no gain or loss is recognized. If the bonds are disposed of before maturity and the amount received is greater or lesser than the adjusted basis, a gain or loss will result. Original issue discount must be amortized for both taxable and nontaxable bonds. *Market discount,* on the other hand, is not amortized for income tax reporting and the cost basis is not adjusted. Consequently, at maturity a gain will be recognized. If the bond is disposed of before maturity and the amount received is greater or lesser than the cost basis, a gain or loss will also be recognized.

Premiums on Convertible Bonds

Where bonds have a conversion feature which permits the owner to convert them into another type of security, the premium paid on such bonds must be allocated between the convertible feature and the investment feature. Generally, the value of the convertible feature is the difference between the market values of bonds with and without convertible features. Where the market value difference cannot be determined in this manner, the premium can be estimated based on the expected yield of the bond without convertible features. This accounting treatment should be used whether following generally accepted accounting principles or statutory accounting practices. However, such an allocation is not necessary for income tax reporting.

Stock Dividends and Splits

A corporation issuing dividends in the form of stock will determine whether there is a stock dividend or a stock split. If the distribution of new stock is more than 20 to 25 percent of the previous outstanding number of shares, it is considered a *stock split.* Stock distributions of lesser amounts are considered *stock dividends.* From the issuer's standpoint, the distinction between the two is that a stock dividend is treated much as a cash dividend. That is, the stock dividend is viewed as "bonus" stock and retained earnings of the issuing company are decreased and capital stock is increased to the extent of the fair market value of the dividend. On the other hand, a stock split is merely an increase in the number of shares outstanding without capitalizing additional retained earnings.

From the shareholders' standpoint, the accounting treatment for a stock dividend or a stock split is not materially different. In either instance, it is necessary to reallocate the cost of the old shares to the old and new shares on a pro rata basis. Where lots of stock are accounted for separately, it is necessary to reallocate the cost to the new shares by identifiable lots. Where an average cost basis is used, the reallocation of cost to the new shares can be on an aggregate basis. For income tax reporting, the shareholder can elect not to allocate the basis where the stock dividend is less than 15 percent.

Common Stock Rights and Common Stock Warrants

These have a zero cost basis unless a premium is paid to receive the rights or warrants or unless they are purchased on the open market. If they are acquired as a part of a package including the security, the accounting treatment is the same as described above for premiums on convertible bonds.

Other Cost Adjustments

1. The initial cost assumption used should be consistently followed. The specific identification cost basis and the average cost basis often do not produce significantly different results. Where there are numerous lots of the same securities, the average cost basis is preferable.
2. Cash dividends received in the nature of liquidating dividends are used to reduce the cost basis of securities.
3. Proceeds received from sinking fund payments are used to reduce the cost basis, except that amounts attributable to premiums are recognized in income when received.
4. The discount on a short-term investment is accrued ratably to maturity, except that for income tax reporting the cost basis is not adjusted.
5. For federal income tax reporting, a loss is not allowed on securities sold if like securities are acquired within 30 days before or after the sale. This is true even though for accounting purposes a loss may have been realized on the disposition. This transaction is referred to as a "wash sale," and the basis of the securities is the same as that of those sold.
6. Securities may be partially or entirely written off by an insurance company and included in Schedule X. For income tax reporting, there is no change in the cost basis until the securities become entirely worthless.

COST FOR EXCHANGED SECURITIES

Where securities are acquired other than by cash purchase, it is necessary to determine the cost basis of such securities by alternative means. Securities can be acquired in a number of noncash transactions. Where such transactions occur, each security acquisition must be carefully analyzed to determine its proper cost basis.

Transactions for other than cash are generally referred to as "nonmonetary transactions." These transactions can arise from a number of sources. One of the most common is an exchange of assets between two entities to satisfy outstanding debt. These transactions can also arise when assets are exchanged to accomplish a business purpose, or when assets are contributed to strengthen the capital or surplus of the transferee. These transactions create some uncertainty as to the cost that should attach to the assets that are exchanged, transferred, or contributed.

Nonmonetary Transactions

The accounting treatment that applies to nonmonetary amounts should be based on the fair value of the assets used in the transaction. As a general rule, the fair value of an asset given in an exchange represents the new cost of the asset acquired. However, if the fair value of the asset acquired is more clearly evident than the fair value of the asset given, then the former amount should be used as the cost of the new asset.

Where there is cash or cash equivalency involved in an otherwise nonmonetary transaction, the accounting treatment does not change, unless the sum of the cash or cash equivalent and the fair value of the assets received exceeds the fair value of the assets surrendered. The excess amount received in such a transaction is recognized as a gain. However, where there is a transfer of nonmonetary assets between related entities, the transaction should be recorded at the underlying book value of the assets distributed.

Some of the more common nonmonetary types of transactions that may occur in the investment securities of an insurance company are set forth below.

Spin-Off. This occurs when a corporation transfers stock of a subsidiary to its shareholders, often in connection with a plan of corporate reorganization or liquidation. It may also occur when there is a disposal of a significant segment of the total business.

When a spin-off occurs, the shareholders receive the stock being distributed without surrendering any of their stock in the parent corporation. In effect, this transaction makes the shareholders direct owners of a new corporation, whereas before they had only been indirect owners of the subsidiary whose stock is being distributed.

After the spin-off, the shareholders are owners of securities in two or more corporations for which they had previously recorded a single cost amount. The cost basis of the previously owned stock must therefore be distributed between the old stock and the newly acquired stock on the basis of the relative values of the old and new shares. Where both the old and the new stock have a public trading value, the proration can be based on these values. Where the old stock has an established trading value and the new stock does not, the cost can be prorated based on the reduction in the traded value of the old stock immediately after the new stock is distributed. Where neither stock has a publicly traded value, the cost should be prorated based on appraisals, on the fair value of the net assets of the separate entities, or on similar measures that fairly reflect the underlying value of each entity. The accounting treatment is essentially the same for generally accepted accounting principles, statutory accounting practices, and income tax reporting.

Split-Off. This exchange differs from a spin-off because some or all of the shareowners surrender old stock in exchange for the stock of the subsidiary corporation. The transaction is one which essentially reduces the shareowner's underlying interest in the old corporation and at the same time gives the shareowner a like amount in the value of the corporation being distributed. While the split-off transaction is constructed differently than the spin-off transaction, the accounting for the cost basis is essentially the same.

Split-Up. A split-up occurs when all the assets in the parent corporation are transferred to a pair of other corporations (which may be subsidiaries or newly created corporations). The shareowners surrender their original stock in exchange for shares of the subsidiary or new corporations. This transaction results in a complete liquidation of the original corporation but does not change the shareholder's relative interest in the surviving corporations. While this transaction results in a separation of the business activities in distinctively new corporations that were previously operated by a single corporation, the cost of the original stock is allocated among the new shares received in a manner similar to that of a spin-off.

Business Combinations

Business combinations can take a number of forms. One form is a *merger,* which results in one corporation being absorbed by another. The acquired corporation is liquidated and the surviving corporation succeeds to all the property and liabilities of the liquidated entity. A business combination can also take the form of a *consolidation,* which results in the liquidation of both corporations into a new corporation. For income tax purposes, these transactions are generally referred to as "reorganizations."

A business combination is classified for accounting purposes as being either a pooling of interests or a purchase. A *pooling of interests* occurs when substantially all the equity owners of the combining corporations become the owners of a single new corporation that owns all the assets of the combined companies. A pooling of interests is sometimes described as a consolidation. On the other hand, where a significant number of the equity owners of the combined corporation sell their interest for cash or consideration other than common stock, the transaction is described as a *purchase.* Following such a purchase, only some of the equity owners of both corporations continue to own stock of the surviving corporation.

When either a purchase or a pooling occurs, there is no change in the basis of the stock held by the owners of the surviving corporation. In the case of a purchase, this is because the assets of the acquiring corporations are used to buy the assets of the corporation being merged. In the case of a pooling, it is because the equity interest of each shareholder remains the same in terms of value. The percentage held by each shareholder is diluted, but the value of each share is increased by an equivalent amount since the corporation is larger after the pooling.

For income tax purposes, business combinations that occur solely from an exchange of stock in another corporation are referred to as "tax-free exchanges." If certain requirements are met, no income tax is assessed as a result of the reorganization of two or more companies into a single corporation, and likewise there is no change in the cost basis as a result of the exchange of stock. The receipt of promissory notes or similar obligations in exchange for common stock will not

in exchange for common stock will not be considered a tax-free exchange. For accounting purposes, if any consideration is received which reduces the pro rata interest of any equity owner, the cost basis of the former equity securities is reduced in proportion to the gain that is recognized.

Securities Exchanged in a Reinsurance Transaction

The consideration received in a reinsurance transaction for assuming insurance liabilities can be cash or other assets. Where other assets are given, the cost basis is determined by the fair value of the assets received. The liabilities assumed are measured by the unearned premium reserve that is transferred by a property liability company, or in the case of a life insurance company, by the reserves required to be carried for the transferred insurance. This measure of the cost of liabilities assumed may not be the fair measure of assets received upon assuming these liabilities. The general rule in accounting is that cost is determined by the fair value of the consideration given up unless the fair value of the property received is more clearly evident. However, in a reinsurance transaction, a fixed liability is assumed in consideration of property received. Under these circumstances, the liabilities received are not a fair value of the cost of property acquired unless the fair value of all property acquired is equal to the fair value of the liabilities assumed.

Generally, the securities or other property received in a reinsurance transaction are valued at their current market price. If the fair value of the securities received is less than the liability assumed, the balance is a current charge to operations. If the fair value of the assets received is greater than the fair value of the liabilities assumed, the balance is deferred and amortized during the period that the liabilities will be retired. For securities received with a fixed maturity value, a current value based on yield may be less than the maturity value. In these instances, the difference is accrued ratably to the maturity date by periodic credits to investment income. The accounting treatment is essentially the same for generally accepted accounting principles, statutory accounting practices, and income tax reporting.

Investment Securities Received in a Business Purchase

Where one entity is acquired by another entity in a purchase transaction, the assets acquired receive a new cost equal to their fair value. This means that investment securities acquired receive a cost equal to their current market price. Any excess of the total purchase price over the fair value of all assets is accounted for as an intangible asset. Conversely, where the fair value of the assets received exceeds the cash or the fair value of the assets given in exchange, the difference, after all noncurrent assets are reduced to zero, is accounted for as a negative intangible asset. Such intangible amounts are amortized over their expected life or over 40 years, if shorter.

For statutory accounting, the difference between the fair value of the assets received and the fair value of the property given up is charged or credited directly to surplus. For income tax reporting, the fair value of the assets given are cost. Where the fair value of assets received in exchange is less, these amounts are increased to cost. Likewise, where the fair value of the assets received in exchange is greater, these amounts are reduced to cost.

Cost for Transactions between Affiliates

For accounting purposes, two companies are *affiliated* if they are directly or indirectly controlled by common owners. This control can exist through stock ownership or it can arise as a result of the ability to control business enterprises through some other means. For purposes of determining the cost basis, control needs to be direct—and the definition is more restrictive where there is stock ownership.

Control for accounting purposes is presumed to occur where one entity owns 20 percent or more of the voting stock of another company. This presumption is rebuttable since control may or may not actually exist, depending on the composition of the board of directors, significant intercompany transactions, intermingling of management personnel, and the like. Thus, control may exist where there is less than a 20 percent ownership of voting stock, or it may not exist even though there is more than a 20 percent ownership of voting stock. In the latter instance, opposition by the subsidiary corporation or regulation by the government may overcome the presumption of control. When more than 50 percent of the voting stock of another corporation is owned, control actually exists in a parent-subsidiary relationship and the investment must be accounted for on a consolidated basis.

For statutory reporting, the presumption of control is often triggered by a 10 percent ownership of voting stock. For income tax reporting, more than 80 percent of the voting stock of another corporation must be owned to have any effect on intercorporate investments. Even then, if the controlled companies are not included in a consolidated tax return, the actual voting control of another corporation may not affect the cost basis used to account for intercompany transactions involving investment securities.

For accounting purposes, no gain or loss is recognized on transactions between controlled entities. This accounting rule is significant since it precludes manipulating gains or losses by the exchange of investment securities. Without such a rule, controlled companies could generate significant gains or losses merely by transferring investment securities at their current value and recognizing the difference between the value and cost basis as a gain or loss. Such accounting would result in what is essentially a surplus of appraised value, since an ultimate gain or loss would not occur until the investment securities were disposed of to a third party.

Where no gain or loss is recognized because of the above rule, the investment securities that are transferred continue to retain the same cost basis.

For statutory reporting purposes, the accounting is usually different. Generally, investment securities received in a liquidation, merger, consolidation, or similar transaction are accounted for on a fair market value basis. The transferring company recognizes a gain or loss from the transaction measured by the difference between the current value and its cost basis in the securities. The receiving company records a new cost basis equal to the current market value.

For income tax purposes, the exchange of investment securities between controlled corporations included within a consolidated return is accounted for at cost. Any gain or loss is deferred until the securities are sold outside the consolidated group, or until the selling corporation leaves the consolidated group, if earlier. However, transactions in investment securities between controlled entities that are not included in a consolidated return will result in a gain for tax purposes if the value exceeds cost. Losses will also be recognized, unless the two corporations are more than 50 percent controlled by common owners.

6

MORTGAGE LOANS

A mortgage *is a legal instrument which represents the lender's collateralized position in property or real estate. The instrument is drafted in such a fashion that, when properly recorded, it becomes a lien on the property or chattel. A mortgage given for machinery, equipment, and other personal property is described as a "chattel mortgage." A mortgage given for land and buildings is described as a "real estate mortgage." For accounting purposes, this distinction has more to do with the investing practices of insurance companies than it does with the legal distinction between the two. Generally, chattel mortgages are not utilized by insurance companies in their investment portfolios. To a great extent, the investment restrictions placed on insurance companies do not allow significant commitments to mortgages other than real estate mortgages.*

Real estate mortgages, even while they are a permissible investment for all insurance companies, are usually a more significant part of the investment portfolio for life insurance companies than for the others, which have different investment objectives. Property and liability companies, for example, have a greater need for liquidity in their investments since the claim costs under policies issued by these companies are incurred over a relatively short period of time. On the other hand, claims for benefits under life insurance policies occur over an extended period of time and funds available for investment can be committed to a much longer term. Therefore, the material in this chapter applies most to the operations of a life insurance company.

Real estate mortgage loans may be classified into residential loans, farm loans, commercial and industrial loans, development loans, and purchase money loans. Residential and farm loans may be further classified into loans which are guaranteed or supported by governmental agencies and those which are considered to be conventional loans. The distinctive features of real estate mortgage loans are covered in this chapter.

RESIDENTIAL LOANS

The most common type of real estate mortgage is that attached to residential property. Mortgages of this type are given by debtors (i.e., buyers) to secure all or part of the funds needed to acquire residential real estate. The transaction usually occurs in connection with the sale of residential real estate that is not purchased for cash. The buyer who has agreed to purchase real estate may fund the purchase price partly with cash and partly with borrowed funds. The title to real estate, having a current value in the marketplace, is used to collateralize the loan that is needed to complete the purchase price. Since land and residential buildings are considered excellent collateral, insurance companies (especially life insurance companies) find long-term residential mortgage loans a very secure investment. Most residential real estate mortgages are scheduled for repayment over 15 to 30 years. A good feature of residential mortgage loans is that the payment terms and due dates are well defined, which greatly simplifies administration and the maintenance of accounting records.

A typical mortgage loan requires a significant amount of review and underwriting before the loan is granted. The creditworthiness of the borrower and the marketability of the collateral are of great importance to the lender. If the borrower proved not to be creditworthy, then in the event of foreclosure the lender could find itself in the position of a landlord or real estate dealer, neither of which usually comes within the scope of an insurance company's investment operations. On the other hand, without the ready marketability of the collateral, the lender would not enjoy a secured position—which is a fundamental necessity for an insurance company.

The details that support the creditworthiness of the borrower are found in numerous documents. The initial loan application includes the financial history of the borrower and a summary of current resources. This application is supported by credit reports, financial statements, employment verifications, and confirmations of checking and savings accounts. The loan application also summarizes current liabilities and life insurance coverages. Every one of these supporting details is significant in determining the borrower's creditworthiness.

The adequacy of the collateral for the mortgage is generally supported by a current appraisal of the property. Appraisals are prepared on a number of bases, and each type of appraisal may be useful in different circumstances for granting mortgage loans.

A common approach to appraising is called the *cost approach.* This approach involves estimating the current value of the property based on reproduction costs. When the reproduction costs have been determined, the current cost is reduced by an estimated depreciation factor. This depreciation factor is not the same as accounting depreciation; the latter represents a systematic amortization of the original costs so that the total cost can be recognized over the estimated useful life of the property. Rather, the depreciation factor used in the cost approach is an estimate of the physical deterioration of the building. It may also involve recognition of obsolescence because of current economic conditions or changes in the functional use of the building. The cost approach to appraising property is useful in establishing the value of purchased property, but it is not the preferable method of determining values for mortgage collateral.

Another approach to determining appraisal values, used more in connection with income-producing properties, is referred to as the *income approach.* It is based on the capitalized earning power of the property. The property's annual earning power is used by the appraiser to determine a value of future earnings.

These future earnings are capitalized to determine a reasonable return on investment.

A third approach, the one more appropriate for residential property, is the *market approach*. This method of determining values is based on recent sales of comparable property. "Comparable properties" are sometimes difficult to define, but usually they are considered to be properties with the same relative construction and characteristics and in comparable residential areas. This value tends more nearly to reflect the current marketability of the property and is therefore more often used in connection with residential property.

Performing appraisals is often complicated. While a recognized appraiser will follow a normal appraisal process, there are no uniform standards by which appraisals can be made. Some investment departments may place higher loan values on the property location, some may tend to emphasize the type of building construction, and others may place greater emphasis on the manner in which maintenance is performed. Regardless of the approach to the appraisal process, a current market type of appraisal is required in order to issue a loan and may be required from time to time in order to continue to carry the loan at its amortized value.

In addition to obtaining the data about creditworthiness and the property's current value, it is necessary that a number of other factors be considered. Many states require a title policy, to ensure the integrity of the current ownership of the property. Also, it may be necessary to have the property surveyed, to update the abstract of title, and to record any deed of trust. Generally, the closing of a mortgage loan involves signing an original note, a mortgage contract with scheduled repayments, a proof of property insurance, and an assignment of life insurance.

Escrow Agreements

Quite often, in connection with the execution of a residential mortgage loan, an escrow agreement is required which provides for periodic deposits along with the principal and interest payment. These periodic deposits are scheduled to provide enough funds for property insurance premiums and property taxes. Typically, the premium on property insurance is payable on a semiannual or annual basis. Property taxes are usually payable in two installments. The escrow amounts that are accumulated prior to the payment date may provide some additional investment earnings for the company.

Conventional Mortgage Loans

A significant percentage of mortgage loans are of the "conventional" variety, in which the lender has no government guarantees and is willing to look solely to the creditworthiness of the borrower and the current value of the property to secure the loan.

Conventional mortgage loans are subject to the standards imposed by each individual lender. Generally, lenders are willing to furnish mortgage funds up to a fixed percentage of current market value; since they have no other recourse in the event of nonpayment, their evaluation of the property's current value and the borrower's ability to repay will determine the extent of their commitment. It is not unusual for conventional loans to be issued for up to 90 percent of the current market value of the property to be mortgaged. In some states, however, the regulations may impose a maximum loan value on each property; often, this loan value may not exceed 75 percent of the current appraisal price.

Lending companies may impose a number of restrictions and conditions that must be met before the loan is granted. Typical of such requirements is that they be furnished with an assignment of life insurance or with a mortgage guarantee insurance policy. These requirements are intended to protect the lender further by ensuring future payment of the mortgage loan. Aside from the conditions or restrictions that may be required to complete the mortgage loan, the lender has no guarantee for repayment except through foreclosure procedures. Thus, the standards for determining creditworthiness and appraisal values are determined solely by the lender.

Government-Backed Mortgage Loans

There are certain loans for which the lender may receive further guarantees of repayment. The most common of these loans are those which are insured or guaranteed by government agencies. The underwriting standards for these loans are dictated by the agency that insures or guarantees them. The lender must abide by these standards in order to execute the mortgage.

Two government agencies are active in the residential mortgage market. These agencies are authorized by Congress to insure or guarantee mortgages that require smaller downpayments or are issued on behalf of those qualifying for special loan guarantees.

Federal Housing Administration Loans. Most conventional mortgage loans require a significant downpayment. Mortgage loans backed by the Federal Housing Administration (FHA) are issued with a smaller downpayment requirement. The FHA does not issue mortgage loans, but rather insures loans that are made in accordance with its standards. The agency specifies the standard for properties which may be insured, determines the maximum interest rate that can be charged, and establishes the terms and amount of the loan. To fund the insurance, the borrower is required to pay a premium equal to one-half of one percent of the current balance of the loan along with the principal and interest payment. In the event of default on the loan, the lender has the option of assigning the defaulted loan to the FHA for cash or securities equal to the current loan balance. Alternatively, the insurance company may retain the loan, foreclose on the mortgaged property, and satisfy the current balance of the loan out of a subsequent resale of the property. Because of the insured status of loans backed by the FHA, the interest rate on such loans is usually less than on conventional loans.

Veterans Administration Loans. In contrast to an insured loan as described above, Veterans Administration loans are issued with a guarantee for a portion of the loan. The Veterans Administration (VA) imposes its underwriting policy upon the lender by specifying maximum interest rates, appraisal standards, and repayment terms. These loans require only a small downpayment and, in some instances, no downpayment. VA loans are available to all veterans who qualify by their term of military service as specified by federal law. There is no deadline by which veterans may obtain these loans; however, a new loan cannot be granted until any previous VA loan made to the veteran has been satisfied. When defaults occur, the VA will reimburse the lender for losses to the extent of the maximum guaranteed amount. If the lender suffers a loss in excess of the VA guarantee, that portion of the loss is not recoverable.

Lien Satisfaction

The mortgage holder enjoys a secured position with respect to the property that is the collateral for the loan. This is true whether the mortgage is issued by the seller (a *purchase money loan*) or is issued to finance the purchase of third-party property. The relative security of the position is determined by the priority of the lien and the record date. The most secure loan is a first mortgage loan, which has first claim on the property to satisfy any unpaid balance. Mortgages issued subsequently are classified as second, third, fourth, etc., in the order of their priority. Any mortgage holder has the option to foreclose on a property to satisfy an unpaid mortgage balance; however, only first mortgage holders may foreclose without regard to the collateral rights of subsequent mortgage holders that are issued on the same property. If holders of subsequent mortgages foreclose on the property, they must satisfy all prior liens before applying any of the proceeds from foreclosure to their own outstanding loan. Holders of loans with lesser priorities may, in fact, be in a secured position. However, in most states, insurance companies are precluded from investing in mortgage loans that do not represent first liens. In any circumstances, the maximum value that may be reported for other than first mortgage loans would be the difference between the amount of the prior outstanding liens and the maximum loan value of the property determined on a current market basis.

Direct Loans

Mortgage loans can be acquired by an insurance company in a number of ways. Where an insurance company has its own mortgage loan department, loans may be acquired on a direct basis; this is likely to occur in a company which has a broad operating base and is able to make loans in a number of geographic areas. Obtaining loans on a direct basis may not be desirable for a company which does not have this ability, since limiting its loan activities to a few areas may result in an undesirable concentration of lending risks. Were this to occur, local economic conditions could cause the insurance company to have significantly more foreclosures. If the economic events resulted only in increased foreclosures, the security position of the insurance company would probably not be impaired. However, if the economic conditions in an area where loans were concentrated resulted in a general decline in the market value underlying the mortgage loan, then the insurance company could experience a significant write-off of uncollected balances.

The operation of a mortgage loan department usually requires a significant commitment on the part of the insurance company not only to process the loans but also to create detailed individual mortgage loan records. Mortgage loans are solicited from real estate agents and brokers, commercial banks, and others involved in the sale of real estate. Operating a mortgage loan department also requires the establishment of an underwriting process. New applications must be carefully screened to determine whether the mortgage loan should be given. This process includes completion of a loan application form, review of the borrower's credit history, review of the borrower's current financial condition, verification of the borrower's employment or business activities, and appraisal of the property being mortgaged. In addition, the legal validity of the title to the property must be confirmed, and usually the abstract of title must be brought up to date.

In addition to underwriting the loan, the mortgage loan department must maintain detailed records of the loan payments and the allocation of funds received between principal, interest, and escrow deposits. Overpayments and underpayments of principal and interest must be accounted for and the proper credits or charges applied to the borrower's account. In addition, the records must provide for the handling of advance payments, late payments, prepayment penalties, and other items.

Accounting for mortgage loans acquired by an insurance company on a direct basis is not significantly different from the accounting treatment for loans acquired through a correspondent mortgage banker. One difference may occur in connection with capitalizing the cost to originate the loan. Whereas the fees charged by a mortgage banker to originate a loan are easily identified, the cost of originating a mortgage loan on a direct basis is more difficult to determine. If the cost of originating a direct loan can be properly identified, it may be deferred and amortized over a reasonable period. For statutory accounting, however, this option is usually not available and the cost of acquiring loans directly is generally expensed through operations.

MORTGAGE BANKERS

The majority of insurance companies that invest in mortgage loans acquire these loans through a mortgage banker. Even for those companies which operate their own mortgage loan department, some loans will be acquired through mortgage bankers to achieve a greater geographic dispersal of loans held.

Mortgage bankers are sometimes referred to as "mortgage companies" or "correspondent bankers." Since there are often no legal qualifications or limitations for engaging in mortgage banking activities, these companies may be engaged in several other activities—such as real estate sales, general insurance agency operations, and real estate management. For purposes of this discussion, however, *mortgage banking* covers only those activities involved in originating, marketing, and servicing real estate mortgage loans for others.

Mortgage bankers usually have large loan portfolios, some of which are owned directly and some of which are held as agent for others. The better to understand mortgage loans, which may be a significant part of an insurance company's investment program, it is necessary to look at the operations of the mortgage banker:

Acquisition of Loans

The mortgage banker may operate as an agent for the insurance company and acquire loans directly from real estate brokers. In this situation the mortgage banker processes the loans in accordance with investment restrictions imposed by the insurance company. These restrictions are general in nature and may specify the type of property that will be accepted as collateral, the minimum and maximum balances that will be extended to borrowers, the interest rates that will be charged, and the repayment schedule. To the extent that the mortgage banker can locate such loans, they will be placed with an insurance company up to the maximum lending limit. Under this arrangement, the mortgage banker does not own the loans and acts only on behalf of the insurance company. Consequently, there is no acquisition fee. Rather, the mortgage banker is paid for services rendered, which cost is often charged to the borrower. These amounts are income to the mortgage banker and are not accounted for by the insurance company. Consequently, the original loans are equal to the amounts disbursed to the borrowers.

Mortgage bankers also acquire mortgage loans for their own account and resell them. Under these circumstances, the mortgage banker must not only locate the borrower and underwrite the loans but must also disburse its own funds. The loans are held in inventory until they can be resold. When the mortgage banker locates a permanent investor, such as an insurance company, the loans are sold in bulk to that company. Or instead of underwriting new loans, the mortgage banker may purchase existing ones from agencies such as the Federal Housing Administration or Veterans Administration and then resell them to permanent investors. Loans acquired by an insurance company in a bulk transaction from a mortgage banker are usually purchased at a premium or discount. This is due to the difference between the specified interest rate in the mortgage loan contract and the current interest rate available for new loans. These premiums and discounts are amortized ratably over the life of the loan, except that for statutory accounting purposes the amortization period is 3 to 5 years.

The mortgage banker may charge a loan origination fee, which is computed to cover the underwriting and other costs incurred in acquiring the loan as well as to include a profit margin. Such fees paid by an insurance company can be deferred and amortized over the life of the loan as an adjustment to the interest return on the investment. For statutory purposes, these fees may be accounted for as a current expense and charged to the income statement. An alternate statutory accounting practice permits the capitalization of these fees if they are amortized over a 3- to 5-year period in a manner similar to that for the premiums or discounts previously described.

Servicing Costs

An important part of a mortgage banker's operation is the mortgage loan service provided to insurance companies. The original loan file, which contains the application, credit report, confirmation with employers and financial institutions, abstract, and the like, is sent to the insurance company; however, the actual servicing of periodic payments and escrow accounts is performed by the mortgage banker. The servicing fee is usually expressed as a percentage of amounts collected for principal and interest. A servicing fee is usually not assessed against escrow funds since these funds technically belong to the borrower; however, the loan service agreement may provide that the mortgage banker will retain investment earnings on these funds.

The servicing agreement may provide that the insurance company will create a monthly loan due list that will be used by the mortgage banker to process payments. In other instances, the mortgage banker may provide these listings as a service to the insurance company. Collecting mortgage payments is an important servicing responsibility of the mortgage banker. This may involve sending periodic notices to the borrower and providing facilities for receiving payments.

Other services provided by mortgage bankers include maintaining records for escrow funds. The escrow deposits are calculated so that sufficient cash will be accumulated to pay property taxes and insurance premiums as they become due. The required amount of the periodic escrow payment is periodically recomputed to take into account increases that may occur in property taxes and property insurance premiums. If the servicing agreement provides for taxes and premiums to be paid by the mortgage banker, records must be maintained to ensure that these amounts are paid on a timely basis. But if the servicing agreement provides for remitting escrow amounts to the insurance company, the mortgage banker will not usually be responsible for the payment of property taxes and property insurance premiums.

Under some circumstances, the mortgage banker may act as a collector only and will remit all principal, interest, and escrow payments directly to the insurance company. Some servicing agreements require the mortgage banker to assume responsibility for reviewing loan delinquencies and initiating follow-up collection efforts. Additionally, the servicing agreement may provide for complete management of the loan portfolio, including handling foreclosures and renting or selling the foreclosed property.

The servicing fees charged by the mortgage banker can be paid by the insurance company periodically, or the mortgage banker may deduct them from principal and interest collections. The fees paid can be accounted for on a gross basis, whereby the total interest is recorded as income and the service fees are expensed when incurred, or the fees can be netted against interest collected, which results in a reduction in the interest income received on the loans. The former method is the preferred accounting treatment; however, for statutory accounting purposes and income tax reporting, either method may be used.

Unexpended escrow accounts balances held by the insurance company are shown twice on the annual statutory blank: once as a cash asset and once as an offsetting escrow liability account. If the funds are held by the mortgage banker, they are still recorded in the same manner if the insurance company shares in the investment income generated by the escrow funds. But if the mortgage banker retains all such investment income, then the escrow account balances need not be recorded on the statutory statement.

The statutory accounting treatment of escrow accounts has resulted in an income tax controversy for some life insurance companies which compute their income taxes based on investment income. The computation of this income tax liability requires that assets held by the company be used as the denominator to determine the investment yield which is set aside for policyholders.

Loan Administration

Insurance companies that arrange for mortgage bankers to collect and process payments from the borrowers should have, in-house, complete mortgage loan files. Some additional monitoring of the activities of mortgage bankers may be required. The mortgage bankers should provide periodic financial audits that include the Uniform Single Audit Program for mortgage bankers. This program requires that the reporting auditor examine at least 10 percent of the mortgage loans that are being serviced by the mortgage banker. This program is intended to provide additional assurance to the insurance company, and others, that the loans being serviced are handled in accordance with the servicing agreement. The mortgage banker may be required to have a fidelity bond in a specified amount and to provide insurance coverage for possible errors and omissions.

Even though the loans are being serviced by a mortgage banker, many companies will monitor all cash remittances, loan delinquencies, and escrow disbursements for taxes and insurance. Since the real estate securing the loan is subject to the risk of loss by fire or other hazards, or to foreclosure to pay delinquent property taxes, many insurance companies will implement these and other auditing procedures.

FARM LOANS

Farm loans are made on improved land used for crop raising or pasture. For the most part, the terms and conditions of farm loans are not greatly different from residential loans. However, unlike residential loans, which are noncommercial in nature, farm loans are dependent upon the income-producing ability of the land. For that reason, unimproved land, which is not used for crops or livestock raising, usually does not qualify for a farm loan. The repayment terms of farm loans generally provide for fewer payments during the year, and these payments tend to coincide with crop harvesting periods.

For statutory reporting purposes, loans on unimproved land are not recognized, except to the extent allowed under the permissive investment clauses of the various states. The amount of such nonpermitted loans must be aggregated with all other nonpermitted investments. If the total of these nonpermitted investments exceeds the statutory limit, the excess balance is treated as a nonadmitted asset.

REAL ESTATE FORECLOSURES

A mortgage loan is a priority claim. Thus, when repayments are delinquent or have been discontinued, a foreclosure process is begun which results in the insurance company obtaining the real estate for payment of the debt. This process varies among the states, and foreclosures must be completed in accordance with local laws. As discussed in the following, a number of accounting considerations arise in connection with foreclosure proceedings.

Foreclosures in Process

Between the time of the mortgage default and the acquisition of the foreclosed property by the insurance company, the accounting process is not significantly changed. That is, until the foreclosure has been completed, the loan continues to be accounted for as a mortgage loan investment.

During the foreclosure process, payments are not received for principal and interest, and consequently the income expected from the loan ceases to be accounted for. The amortization of premiums and discounts is also discontinued while the foreclosure is in process, since it may not be known whether the property will be resold or redeemed by the borrower or whether the mortgage will be reinstated. Because of these uncertainties, no gain or loss is recognized.

A mortgage subject to foreclosure proceedings is accounted for as a non-interest-bearing investment. Following statutory accounting practices, the interest that is accrued on these mortgages may be either charged to expense or shown as a nonadmitted asset. For income tax reporting, such interest is not written off until its uncollectibility is clear. Delinquent interest may be recovered from the proceeds of eventual resale or from reinstating the mortgage loan.

Where the principal, accrued interest, and costs relating to the foreclosure (such as insurance premiums, property taxes, and legal fees) are probably not recoverable in full, a reserve should be established. The reserve should be equal to the excess of the loan principal, accrued interest, and related costs over the fair market value of the property. This reserve is also required or permitted when following statutory accounting practices, but it is not recognized for income tax reporting.

Foreclosures Transferred to Real Estate

When foreclosure proceedings have been completed and title to the property is obtained, the investment should be reclassified from mortgage loans to real estate in foreclosure. The property is held in this account until resold or otherwise disposed of.

During the time the property is held in this account, it may be rented; when this occurs, the real estate costs are charged to operations. If the property is not rented but is held for resale, the continuing costs of holding the property are usually capitalized. This accounting treatment is essentially the same for generally accepted accounting principles, statutory accounting practices, and income tax reporting. While the property is being held for resale, if the recorded costs exceed the fair market value, a reserve should be provided for the difference. For income tax reporting, this reserve is not recognized.

A mortgage which has been foreclosed and for which title to the property has been received by the insurance company is classified separately on the annual statement blank from all other real estate properties. The carrying value of this property consists of the unpaid principal, plus items such as interest, taxes, and foreclosure costs, and is adjusted for the value of the reserve when the market value is less than the carrying amount. This separate classification is necessary in order to distinguish between (1) properties received in foreclosure and (2) home office and other investment properties. The analysis of the carrying value for properties transferred from mortgage loans to real estate during the current year is included in Schedule B, Part 3, in the annual statement blank.

COMMERCIAL AND INDUSTRIAL MORTGAGE LOANS

Mortgage loans given in connection with commercial and industrial activities often comprise a significant part of the mortgage loan portfolio of an insurance company. This is partly due to the need for an insurance company to invest significant amounts of the funds which it is holding for insurance reserves. An additional consideration is that commercial and industrial mortgage loans entail fewer administrative costs than do residential mortgage loans, which tend to be much smaller; that is, an investment in 50, 100, or more residential mortgage loans would be required in order to provide the same amount as a single investment in a $5 million or $10 million commercial mortgage loan.

Another important consideration in making commercial and industrial loans is that these provide an opportunity for higher investment returns and for participation in the future earnings of such undertakings. Some insurance companies do not invest in the commercial and industrial mortgage market because to do so would require more investment skills and staffing than they have. On the other hand, the larger insurance companies which have the investment staff available to pursue these loans may realize a higher net return by investing in this market.

Commercial and industrial mortgage loans, even while they usually provide a greater potential for return on investment than do residential mortgage loans, nevertheless pose greater risks. Because commercial and industrial loans depend upon a successful business operation to generate net income, they arise from income-producing properties (as distinct from residential loans, which arise from owner-occupied dwellings or in some cases from multiple-family dwellings). The risks associated with commercial and industrial loans vary in terms of the property's source of income. The properties that are security for these loans may be single-purpose property or may be held for leasing to others. In the former instance, the risk associated with a mortgage loan is greater since the property must generally be used by its present owners or by others engaged in similar business undertakings. Properties held for leasing to others may have a lesser risk since there are usually multiple tenants and since the leases are subject to renegotiation with current users and potential users.

The way in which the terms are negotiated for commercial and industrial loans also pose an element of risk. On the one hand, the rate of return available on residential mortgage loans is more readily determinable since there are many financial institutions in this market; consequently, the mortgage rate on these loans is developed in an atmosphere of competition with other investors. On the other hand, commercial and industrial loans may arise under circumstances such that only a limited number of companies may want to accept the investment. These circumstances and the potential for additional participation in future earnings will result in separate negotiations for each loan. The commitment of resources to such projects by the buyer will greatly influence the ultimate interest rate and the participation terms that will be required to make the loan funds available.

Commercial and industrial loans can be classified into three broad categories:

Existing Real Estate Projects

Loans on existing real estate projects arise from the operation of office buildings, local and regional shopping centers, buildings used in industrial activities, and the like. These loans are given in a more traditional mortgage loan program; that is, the property has been constructed and is in use, a fair market value has been determined, and the creditworthiness of the borrower has been ascertained. Given these circumstances, a mortgage loan on existing income-producing real estate will be handled in much the same manner as a residential mortgage loan, except that the amount will be significantly larger. Normally, these mortgage loans will carry a competitive interest rate that is usually less than the current open-market borrowing rate because of the security provided by the real estate. For the insurance company, the rate of return on such mortgage loans is equal to or greater than that for residential mortgage loans, and these loans are also easier to administer. The accounting considerations for such loans, including the determination of the carrying amount, the recognition of interest income, and the treatment of premium and discount, are the same as for residential mortgage loans.

Construction Loans

These loans are made when the real estate is not in operation but is under construction. Such loans may be made for either residential or commercial property developments. Construction-type loans are for a shorter term since the income-producing property is not yet in service. These loans are made on a periodic basis as the construction progresses and are usually not made until the costs are incurred by the borrower. The lender will closely examine the evidence of the costs incurred and make advances against the total loan commitment. This reviewing process ensures that construction loan funds are used solely for the completion of these real estate projects.

Generally, insurance companies will not make construction loans unless there has been an arrangement for the long-term financing of the property; this long-term financing arrangement may be undertaken by the insurance company or by others. The interest rate on construction loans is usually higher than for long-term mortgage loans. Many insurance companies will not make construction loans unless they also participate in the long-term financing; other insurance companies will not make construction loans at all and will only make commitments for long-term financing after construction loans have been obtained from others. The construction loan is paid off from the proceeds of the long-term financing. During the construction period, the security for the loan is the uncompleted structure; for this reason, an investigation is made of the proposed construction project and the creditworthiness of the borrower so that there is reasonable assurance that the construction project will be completed as proposed. More often than not, the incentive for making construction loans is to create an opportunity for long-term financing of good real estate projects.

There are no unusual accounting requirements relating to the granting of a construction loan, except that the level of detail required to monitor such loans is greater than for other commercial mortgage loans.

Development Loans

Many times the construction of residential real estate is preceded by a land development program. Such a development program requires the construction of streets, sewer lines, water lines, utility lines, and the like before any building construction begins. Development loans differ from construction loans in that the construction loan is made on a specific structure where the property is already developed; development loans, on the other hand, are made for land improvements that do not produce income. Not until the residential construction is undertaken will there be an opportunity for a return on investment to the borrower.

Land development loans are usually made by financial institutions other than insurance companies. The insurance company may participate in such programs, but its primary interest would be in the residential structures.

The accounting for development loans is more difficult than for loans on existing real estate or for construction loans, since there are several indeterminate factors which must be resolved before the loans can be made. For example, development loans may be proposed for property that is subsequently determined to be unsuitable for its proposed ultimate use. Such loans will not be income-producing and will not support the long-term funds required to carry insurance contracts. Because there are no current earnings on such loans, they are often accounted for as being within the unrestricted lending authority of the company, or they may be classified as a nonadmitted asset.

Commitment Letters

Commitment letters usually arise in connection with commercial and industrial mortgage loans. This is true since the funds required to complete such projects are not always available unless arranged for in advance. In addition, the insurance company must plan its investment program over an extended period of time and must therefore take into account new funds that come into the company from premiums, investment earnings, and the maturing of previous investments. For these reasons, the commitment letter is useful to both the potential borrower and the lender. The borrower usually cannot proceed until such a letter is obtained, thus ensuring that the loan funds will be available at a specified time in the future. Conversely, the letter is useful to the insurance company because it is thus able to plan for the investment of future funds at a specified rate. A commitment letter tends to "lock in" the final loan arrangements even though no funds have been advanced. Sometimes commitment letters are referred to as "take-out" or "standby" commitments.

There is no accounting effect when a commitment letter is issued, except that these letters will be grouped with other similar items to determine the future financial commitments of the insurance company which may have to be disclosed. The accounting for fees received in connection with commitment letters is discussed in the following section, "Revenue and Expense Recognition."

REVENUE AND EXPENSE RECOGNITION

The majority of revenue and expense items have been covered previously in this handbook. Many are reported the same for generally accepted accounting principles, statutory accounting practices, and income tax reporting. Where differences exist in accounting treatment, they will be discussed separately.

Interest

Interest income from mortgage loans is accounted for on an accrual basis. For statutory accounting, the amounts are usually classified as nonadmitted when the interest is due and unpaid beyond 1 year. An alternative statutory accounting practice is to discontinue the accrual of interest that is in default or to establish a reserve for the uncollectible amount and charge it against operations. For income tax reporting, such amounts are restored to income and not written off until they become uncollectible. For generally accepted accounting principles, a middle ground is chosen and amounts deemed uncollectible are reserved or written off.

Premiums and Discounts

When mortgage loans are acquired at amounts other than par value, the difference between the face amount of the loan and the acquisition price is accounted for as a premium or discount. Premiums or discounts should be amortized over the estimated period that the loan will be outstanding, which is generally significantly shorter than the original loan period. These amounts should be amortized in a manner that will result in a level yield while the mortgage loan is outstanding.

For statutory reporting, the maximum amortization period ranges from 3 to 5 years. For income tax reporting, the amortization period should reflect the company's prior experience with other mortgage loans.

Closing Costs

Closing costs can represent either expense or revenue. Closing items such as insurance costs, appraisal costs, legal costs, and abstracting costs should generally be charged to expense as incurred. The revenue aspect of these amounts arises from the specific reimbursement received from the borrower. The reimbursement payments may be offset against the related costs incurred or they may be recognized as other income.

Closing costs other than those enumerated above are generally difficult to determine exactly. These include in-house underwriting, interviewing, and review time. To provide the company with some reimbursement for these other costs, borrowers may be charged a flat fee or some percentage of the loan amount. The difference between the actual cost and the reimbursement is difficult to ascertain and usually not significant in size; therefore, both the cost and the reimbursement are allowed to flow through the income statement and nothing is capitalized. However, if the difference can be determined with reasonable accuracy, it may be possible to capitalize this amount and amortize it to produce a level yield over the life of the mortgage loan.

Late Payments

Penalties charged to borrowers when mortgage loan payments are late are usually accounted for as other income.

Prepayment Penalties

Many mortgage loan agreements provide for penalties (expressed as a fixed amount or as a percentage of the contract balance) if the loan is paid off prior to the normal termination date. These charges are made to compensate the insurance company for an unexpected loss in future earnings resulting from the liquidation of the loan. Since the funds of an insurance company must be invested on a planned schedule, an interruption of that schedule will produce additional costs in placing another loan; moreover, this other loan may not currently have a rate as favorable as had been expected.

Prepayment penalties are generally recognized as other income when received. For statutory reporting, they may be recognized as capital gains. For income tax reporting, it is generally held that such amounts are income when received.

Commitment Fees

These fees are charged for issuing a commitment letter in connection with a future mortgage loan. In some instances, the commitment fee may be refundable if the loan is not closed in accordance with the commitment letter; in other instances, the commitment fee may be nonrefundable. If refundable, the commitment fee is deferred and not recognized as income until the loan has been made; otherwise, the commitment fee is recognized as income when received. For income tax reporting, commitment fees have been held to constitute investment income.

Mortgage Buy-Back Agreements

When current interest rates for mortgage loans are high, a mortgagor may be offered the opportunity to buy back the mortgage at a discount. The amount of the discount represents a current cost to the insurance company and is usually recognized as an ordinary loss. If a partial buy-back is arranged, only the discount that applies to the canceled part of the loan is included in the loss.

Loan Assumption Fees

Where a new buyer is charged a fee to assume the mortgage loan of a previous property owner, this fee is recognized as income currently. Generally, the face amount of the outstanding loan and the loan conditions do not change. However, the interest rate may be adjusted to reflect current market conditions. If so, the periodic payments will be adjusted to reflect this new rate. The payments will be adjusted to liquidate the loan at its normal retirement date.

Loan Extension Fees

These fees can arise under at least two circumstances. When a mortgage is in default, the lender and borrower will sometimes negotiate a settlement. One method of settling the delinquency is to extend the term of the loan and thereby reduce the periodic payments. This will most often occur when the mortgaged real estate has a market value considerably in excess of the loan balance. The process of making a mortgage loan extension is similar to that for an original loan. However, since the mortgage loan file already contains the basic documentation underlying the loan, it is usually only necessary to reestablish the creditworthiness of the borrower and to update the abstract of title.

A second circumstance that could result in a loan extension occurs when a "balloon" payment is required at the end of the loan term. A balloon arrangement is usually made with the intention that the mortgage loan will be paid in full or refinanced when the balloon becomes due. In many circumstances, the lender will agree to refinance a balloon payment by offering a new loan with a current interest rate and new schedule of payments.

These extension arrangements are often referred to as "refunded" mortgages. They usually occur during periods when interest rates are high and expected to decline in the near future. Upon refunding these mortgages, the lender generally requires an extension fee. This fee is calculated to reimburse the lender for the cost of refinancing and to include a reasonable profit margin for such services. The fee should be included in income when the extension is granted, unless a portion of the fee is considered "points," in which case it will be treated as described below under "Mortgage Loan Points."

Mortgage Loan Points

When mortgage loans are granted, the specified interest rate may be lower than the expected yield required by the lender. This is especially true with loans insured by the Federal Housing Administration or guaranteed by the Veterans Administration. In these instances, the lender will calculate the additional amount required to produce the expected yield and will charge that amount at the origination of the loan. The amount is usually expressed as a percentage of loan principal. Usually, the points will be assessed against the seller.

The accounting effect of such arrangements is that the points effectively reduce the amounts that must be funded to provide the mortgage loan. The present value of this reduction, when added to the interest received over the term of the loan, will result in a yield that is higher than the interest rate stated in the mortgage loan. The amount of the funds received as points should be amortized ratably over the term of the loan. For income tax reporting, this amount is generally income when received.

Contingent Interests

Some mortgage loan agreements contain a participation agreement. That is, in addition to the stated interest rate in the mortgage loan agreement, there may be a provision for sharing in the gross or net earnings of a project funded by the loan. The amount of the sharing and the basis for the calculations are specified in the loan agreement. Amounts due under these agreements should be recognized on an accrual basis as soon as they can be determined. For statutory reporting, the amounts accrued for contingent interests must be realized on a current basis and are subject to the nonadmitted treatment given to delinquent interest on mortgages.

Prepaid Installments

When periodic payments on mortgage loans are paid in advance, the interest element as well as the principal amount is deferred, and the interest is not recognized in income until it becomes due. When prepaid amounts are applied to reduce the outstanding mortgage loan principal, the interest element must be included in investment income.

Imputed Interest

For loans that have no stated interest rate or for which the interest rates are unrealistic when compared to market rates, it is necessary to discount the loan by a rate of interest that is at or near the current market rate. Principal payments are accounted for as being part principal and part imputed interest. These transactions usually arise in connection with the exchange of properties, mergers, or reinsurance transactions. For income tax reporting, a statutory minimum interest rate is prescribed for all transactions that qualify for capital gains treatment. Loans between related corporations are subject to a maximum and minimum rate for tax purposes.

OTHER MORTGAGE LOAN CONSIDERATIONS

In addition to the foregoing, there are a number of mortgage loan transactions that may give rise to other accounting considerations. Some of the more common circumstances are described below.

Mortgage Loan Participation Agreements

Often, in connection with underwriting large commercial and industrial loans, the principal underwriter will seek to share the loan with others. This sharing of the single loan among several lenders is accomplished by a participation agreement. In this situation, the principal underwriter will investigate and grant the loan and provide the details of the loan to companies that wish to participate. By executing a participation agreement, the individual companies will fund their share of the loan and receive their pro rate participation in subsequent principal and interest payments. They will also share in any other benefits and risks associated with the loan. The borrower may or may not be aware that the loan was made on a participating basis. The servicing fees charged to the participants by the principal underwriter are treated in a manner similar to that for the servicing fees charged by mortgage bankers.

Wraparound Mortgages

A *wraparound mortgage* transaction is one in which the buyer gives a second mortgage note and the seller continues to be liable for payments on the original mortgage. This transaction results in a conditional sale, since the seller cannot deliver a title free and clear of all liens. The periodic payments made by the buyer are usually equal to the periodic payments made by the seller to the mortgagee. The profit on the transaction usually arises from the cash or property transferred by the buyer at the inception of the second mortgage note. There is no income effect from the periodic payments since the principal and interest payments made by the buyer are used by the seller to reduce the original mortgage loan debt. For statutory accounting, the original mortgage loan balance is carried as a liability. The amount receivable from the second mortgage note is carried as an asset. However, unless this balance is further collateralized, it would be a nonadmitted asset.

Mortgage Loan Pools

Participation in residential mortgage loan pools is not unlike the participation in commercial loans previously described. A group of residential mortgage loans is pooled by a single issuer, and participation certificates are offered to others. Residential mortgage loan participation certificates arise from two sources:

Conventional Mortgage Loan Participation Certificates. A pool of conventional mortgage loans is accumulated by a single issuer and offered to others by what is referred to as a "pass-through" certificate. A *pass-through* means that the principal, interest, and other funds received on these loans are passed through to the participants. The issuer is responsible for collecting the periodic payments and is usually paid a servicing fee, which is deducted from the amounts passed through to the certificate holder. These loans are accounted for in a manner similar to that for other conventional mortgage loans.

Government National Mortgage Association Participation Certificates. These certificates represent a fraction of the pool of mortgage loans made available under the Government National Mortgage Association Program. Two different kinds of participation certificates are issued. The first is a straight pass-through certificate similar to the conventional mortgage loan pass-through certificate, except that the principal and interest payments are guaranteed by the Government National Mortgage Association. The second type of straight pass-through certificate is somewhat different in that the Government National Mortgage Association guarantees only that the mortgage servicing company will perform in accordance with the servicing agreement. In other words, there is no guarantee against loss due to nonpayment by borrowers. The only guarantees are that the servicing company will actually possess the mortgages set forth in the servicing agreement and that certificate holders will be protected against loss due to fraud or nonperformance by the servicing company.

On these straight pass-through certificates, most insurance companies record the principal and interest payments in a manner similar to that for the amounts received on regular mortgage loans. However, on the first type of fully guaranteed Government National Mortgage Association pass-through certificates, some companies account for them like a corporate or government bond. Under these circumstances, discounts on the pass-through certificates are not amortized, and realized gain or loss is recognized when the certificate is liquidated. For income tax reporting, this latter treatment has been challenged.

Other Collateral Assignments

In connection with commercial and industrial mortgage loans, there may be collateral that is taken in addition to the underlying real estate. Often, assignments are taken for life insurance policies. If the mortgage property is income-producing, assignments may be taken for tenant rentals. Assignments and liens of this nature are non-ledger items that do not result in accounting entries.

7

REAL ESTATE INVESTMENTS

Insurance companies require a significant amount of office space to conduct their activities of marketing, underwriting, claims review, settlement, investing, financing, administration, and the like. Because of their need for office space, most insurance companies invest in real estate to accommodate these home office operations. Of course, an insurance company may lease the space from others rather than owning it; however, in addition to providing the necessary office space at the lowest possible cost, the home office building may provide a distinct identification symbol for an insurance company. A large, impressive building provides tangible evidence of the company's financial strength and stability.

This is not to say that a company will be unsuccessful if it does not invest in real estate for its home office operations; rather, by owning such real estate, the insurance company attains a visibility comparable with other financial institutions. Some of the best-constructed buildings in the community often belong to insurance companies.

There are a number of other reasons why insurance companies invest in real estate. One reason is that real estate has, over time, appreciated in value and is usually considered an excellent investment. Another is that, while home office properties will be used by the insurance company in its own operations, space in them may also be leased to others.

For the most part, property and liability insurance companies invest in real estate that will be used almost exclusively for home office operations. If a property and liability insurance company has significant operations in other locations, it may also invest in real estate that will be used for branch office functions such as marketing, underwriting, and claims settlement. On the other hand, a life insurance company home office building often has excess space that is leased to others; this is because the long-term nature of life insurance contracts makes funds available that can be committed to long-term investments.

Because property and liability insurance companies have more current needs for their funds, they may not be able to utilize real estate investments to achieve a satisfactory level of current earnings and liquidity. The various state laws and regulations reflect these facts. As a general rule, property and liability insurance companies may invest only in home office and branch office real estate, although some state laws permit other real estate investments.

Life and accident and health insurance companies, on the other hand, usually have a broader statutory authority to acquire real estate. However, even these companies are limited to an amount they can invest in real estate. These restrictions are generally expressed as a percentage of the company's total assets, often 10 percent. In the case of smaller companies, the investment authority may be further restricted by capital and surplus levels.

For property and liability insurance companies, real estate investments are classified between properties occupied by the company and other investment properties. For life insurance companies, real estate investments are classified between properties occupied by the company, properties acquired in satisfaction of debt, and other investment real estate. Properties acquired in satisfaction of debt usually have been received through mortgage loan foreclosures. This real estate is generally held on a temporary basis. Investments in other real estate properties are made on a long-term basis to realize a reasonable current yield and the benefits from long-term appreciation.

There are very few differences between the various types of insurance enterprises with respect to real estate accounting.

HOME OFFICE PROPERTIES

Land Cost

Traditionally, the cost of land is established at the date of acquisition and no further adjustments are made to that amount while it is held by the insurance company. Land costs are usually easy to identify since they are generally paid for in cash. However, where land is acquired with a building already on it, an allocation for the cost of land must be made. The allocation process is discussed below in this chapter under "Allocation of Acquisition Cost."

If land is purchased for cash, the cost basis is equal to the amount paid. This includes the purchase price of the land, fees paid to real estate agents, fees for title examination, and similar closing costs. The cost of surveying the land should also be included. Other land costs may be incurred where it is necessary to clear the land of unwanted buildings, timber, and the like before construction can begin. Legal fees and related costs are also capitalized as part of the land cost, if incurred in connection with the property's title or zoning rights. The land costs should be carefully detailed and, once established, should not be adjusted for depreciation or amortization. Any amounts received as salvage value in connection with the clearing and landscaping of the property should be used to reduce the original cost.

Land Improvements

Expenditures for land improvements can arise from a number of sources. If the land is undeveloped, it is often necessary to provide drainage, streets, sanitary sewer lines, water systems, and the like. Generally, these types of land improvements are accounted for in a manner similar to land costs and are not subject to depreciation or amortization. However, to the extent that these expenditures are considered "connecting" costs—that is, costs that begin at the property boundary and extend up to the building—they can be depreciated. Other improvements made in the nature of landscaping, garden development, tree planting, parking facilities, boundary fences, connecting walkways, rest and recreational areas, and similar expenditures should also be depreciated.

Local assessments made for public improvements such as street paving, overhead lighting, utility improvements, and related expenditures are usually nondepreciable. For income tax reporting, these special-purpose assessments are neither depreciable nor deductible.

Buildings

The cost assigned to buildings may be related to new construction or to the acquisition of existing buildings. If the buildings are acquired for cash, the costs are easily measured. However, it is necessary to distinguish between costs that should be capitalized and costs that should be expensed:

Cost of New Construction. The cost of constructing a new building is usually specified in a construction contract. The type and quantities of materials to be used in the building are set out in detail along with the aggregate cost for the total project. While expenditures to prepare the land for construction are accounted for as mentioned above, there are a number of other expenditures that should be considered in arriving at a final building cost.

For example, acceleration payments made to terminate existing leases should be included in building costs, not land costs. Likewise, the cost of excavating land to accommodate the building substructure should also be included in building costs. Architectural, construction management, building permit, and license fees are likewise included in building costs. The cost of temporary structures used for construction offices, storage for tools and materials, and the like should be capitalized if these are paid for separately.

There are other expenditures that should be included in building costs. The cost of insurance coverage during the construction period should be capitalized. Likewise, if noninsured claims are paid in settlement of injuries or accidents, these should also be included if they are incurred because of medical claims. However, other payments made in connection with long-term disabilities, fatalities, punitive damages, and the like should not be capitalized in building costs, but should be expensed.

Another significant period cost that should be capitalized is the interest cost on money borrowed during the construction period. Once the building is ready for occupancy, of course, further accruals of interest should be expensed. If part of the building is occupied while other parts are under construction, an allocation of the interest costs should be made. If funds are borrowed for the specific purpose of providing the construction funds, the interest charged on those borrowings is the amount that should be capitalized. If the funds required to complete the construction are in excess of the amounts specifically borrowed for that purpose, and the company has other debt outstanding, the interest rate that applies to the excess should be the weighted average of the rates for all other borrowing. For purposes of arriving at an appropriate interest rate, the premium or discount associated with the debt should be considered. If borrowed funds are received in advance of paying for the construction costs and invested on a temporary basis, the interest income on these temporary investments should be recorded as investment income and not offset against the interest expense that is capitalized.

In accumulating the building costs, care should be exercised to exclude unusual or abnormal costs. For example, if part of the building collapses during construction and is not covered by insurance, the cost of rebuilding the collapsed part should not be capitalized. Likewise, if there are extended delays in the construction so that significant unanticipated costs occur (owing to strikes, for instance), these costs should not be included in building costs. However, the wages of company personnel performing functions in connection with the building construction should be capitalized.

Purchase of an Existing Building. The purchase price of an existing building is the basic component of building cost. However, there may be additional costs that should be included, such as repairs and improvements to make the building serviceable for the company's operations.

Other costs that should be considered are building permits and licenses, architects' fees, construction management fees, insurance premiums, interest related to borrowing during the renovation period, and the like. To a great extent, the cost incurred in the purchase and renovation of an existing building contains many of the same elements as the cost incurred for new construction.

Additions and Improvements. Where costs are incurred to enlarge or extend the life of a building, the additions and improvements should be capitalized and made a part of the building cost:

Additions. The costs of additions to existing structures are accounted for in a manner similar to that for new building construction. However, where alterations are made to enlarge the structure, some additional cost considerations arise. In extending existing structures, it is usually necessary to remove old walls that separate the addition from the old building. Likewise, where new floors are added to the building, it may be necessary to remove the existing roof. Or the enlargement may require additions to the heating, plumbing, or electrical facilities of the old building. Also, where the existing structure does not comply with current building codes, the permit needed to construct the addition may require that all existing deficiencies be corrected.

If the expenditures to remove old parts of the building to accommodate the addition can be identified, these costs (and accumulated depreciation) can be eliminated from the asset account and expensed. If the original costs are not available, an estimate of the original cost and the accumulated depreciation should be made. However, if to do so involves a significant amount of engineering and accounting time to detail these costs accurately, the practical approach may be to ignore these amounts and simply account for all construction expenses as costs of the building addition.

Improvements. Improvements may be made to a building which do not represent additions but rather make the building more usable or enduring. Replacing old lighting fixtures with new, more efficient lighting may be in the nature of an improvement. Likewise, the lowering of ceilings, the replacement of windows, the insulation of walls, and the like would normally be classified as improvements. For accounting purposes, improvements are much like additions, except that improvements do not increase the quantity of working space, while additions do.

Major expenditures are usually required for either additions or improvements. Where major improvements are made, the new cost should be capitalized and the cost of old property which is removed should be eliminated along with the accumulated depreciation on those items. If the original costs were not separated and the amounts related to the replaced property cannot be determined, an estimate of the original cost and the accumulated depreciation should be made. The costs of minor additions or improvements are usually charged to expense.

Replacements and Repairs. There is a fine line between replacements, on the one hand, and repairs or maintenance, on the other. The treatment of these items for book and tax purposes is basically the same. While the differences between replacements, repairs, and maintenance are often not significant, it may be useful to define the three items:

Replacement Expenditures. Often it is necessary to substitute a new unit for an existing unit. For example, where an existing air conditioning system is dismantled and replaced by a new air conditioning system, it is clear that a replacement has occurred. In those circumstances, the cost and accumulated depreciation of the old system should be removed from the property and equipment account. The cost of the new system should be added to the property and equipment account. Again, where the original cost has not been properly separated so that it is difficult to determine, an estimate should be made. The total replacement of property occurs because the cost of placing it in an operable condition is uneconomical. From an accounting point of view, a replacement is viewed as something more than an incidental expenditure to maintain the property in workable order.

A more difficult accounting distinction occurs when parts of a whole unit are replaced. An example of this might occur when a motor is replaced in an existing auxiliary electrical system. To a great extent, the amount of the expenditure in this circumstance may indicate that a replacement has occurred. On the other hand, if the cost of replacing the engine is no greater than the cost of repairing it, it likely would not be classified as a replacement, but as a repair.

Repair Expenditures. Repairs can be thought of as expenditures to put the property in usable condition. For example, if water pipes are broken, the cost of replacing the broken section of pipe is usually considered to be a repair.

Ordinarily, the amounts expended for repairs involve small sums for each project. However, in the instance previously cited for a broken water pipe, if on inspection it is determined that all the pipe (not just a section) must be repaired, then the repair may be classified as a replacement. The distinctive feature of repairs is that they do not add to the value of the property or in any way prolong its life.

Where there are numerous repairs that otherwise would be classified as improvements or replacements, it is possible to avoid a significant amount of accounting for these items if a dollar threshold is established that must be exceeded before the items are considered for capitalization. For example, if a threshold of $500 was established, no expenditure of less than this amount would be considered an improvement or replacement. The actual dollar threshold should be established based on the company's own experience with its repair program. This treatment is especially important as a building becomes older and requires more upkeep.

Maintenance Expenditures. Maintenance expenses are never capitalized. These are incurred to maintain the property in good condition. A useful life is placed upon a building acquired either by original construction or by purchase. Implicit in this estimate is an expected level of maintenance; without proper maintenance, the expected useful life of properties would be greatly shortened.

For that reason, expenditures for maintenance are a key consideration in preventing the property from deteriorating at a rate faster than was originally estimated.

All these expenditures have a common element. They are not incurred to cure a defect in the building, but rather to maintain it in a usable condition over its expected life. For example, wooden casement windows must be caulked and painted to keep them usable; without this maintenance, they would deteriorate and require replacement during the lifetime of the building's use. Generally, the cost of these and similar maintenance programs will always be expensed, irrespective of the size of the expenditure. It is only when there are multiple expenditures, some of which are maintenance and some of which are repairs or replacements, that a clear distinction must be made between the expenditures. If the accounting descriptions are carefully made, the maintenance expenditures will always be easy to distinguish.

The distinction between repairs and maintenance is made for the purpose of describing the accounting process. The practical implication of the classification may not be significant for financial reporting purposes, although it may be for operational reports, and maintenance may then be combined with repairs.

Allocation of Acquisition Cost

Where an existing building is purchased, it is necessary to allocate the total cost of the property between the amounts that apply to the land and to the building.

There are a number of approaches to the cost allocation process. A common approach is to allocate the total cost between land and building based on independent appraisals. One of the drawbacks to this approach is that the purchaser may place a higher relative value on the building or on the land based on its intended use. For example, a market data approach to the allocation may result in an unrealistic value being placed on the land. The value given to home office properties which are used in the operations of the insurance company will not be the same values given to that property if it was acquired for rental purposes. Estimating the values based on reproducing the property may also result in an unrealistic allocation.

The best accounting approach is to combine the market and reproduction appraisal methods to arrive at a basic value which then can be modified, based on the intended use of the property. This approach to valuing properties should also be satisfactory for statutory and income tax reporting.

If the price paid for the property is greater or lesser than the sum of the appraised land and building values, the purchase price should be allocated in proportion to the relative values. If the property is acquired for a combination of cash and other assets, the fair value of the other assets should be added to the cash to arrive at the total purchase price. (Exception—a like-kind exchange for tax purposes.)

Depreciation Charges

In some respects it is easiest to think of the accounting for depreciation as being an amortization process. The cost of assets acquired is amortized systematically over their estimated useful life. Depreciation provides no fund for replacement and in fact may not reflect the actual deterioration that takes place in the building; nevertheless, amortizing the cost of the property over its estimated useful life is required by both generally accepted accounting principles and statutory accounting practices. It is a permissible charge for income tax reporting.

There are no hard-and-fast rules governing the depreciation computation, except for income tax purposes. For accounting purposes, the amount of depreciation should fairly reflect a systematic method of amortizing the original cost. The straight-line method is the most easily understood method for amortizing this original cost. It is a simple division process that takes into account the estimated useful life of the property and spreads the cost evenly over that period on a monthly or annual basis. The advantages of the straight-line method are that it is simple to apply and may not be materially different in result from more accurate methods.

A number of other methods have been developed which result in faster depreciation than the straight-line computation. The theoretical support for these methods, such as the sum-of-the-years' digits and declining-balance methods, is found in the conservative attitude of accounting for fixed assets. That is, these methods recognize the depreciation charge to a greater extent in the early years of use and consequently reduce the carrying value of the asset. If the amortized amounts represented the economic factors that occur in the deterioration process, then the methods would probably be reversed; however, the amortization of the cost of the property ratably over its useful life is an accounting concept that does not necessarily reflect economic deterioration. For that reason, many insurance companies will endeavor to use a single method of recording depreciation charges for generally accepted accounting principles, statutory accounting practices, and income tax reporting. However, with the introduction of the accelerated cost recovery system in the Internal Revenue Code, it usually will not be possible to use the same depreciation amounts for all three reporting purposes. The differences between tax and book depreciation must be separately maintained since this may affect the calculation of deferred income taxes.

OTHER INVESTMENT REAL ESTATE

The accounting principles described above with respect to the recording of land costs, land improvements, newly constructed or purchased buildings, and additions and improvements apply equally to other investment properties acquired by insurance companies. The basic distinction between home office property investments and other real estate investments is in the use made of the properties. It was previously suggested that home office properties are acquired essentially to provide working space for the insurance company. Investment properties, on the other hand, are acquired for the purpose of earning income; for this reason, the investment in other real estate is more like investments in securities and mortgage loans. The other investment real estate probably will not be used in insurance company operations.

For the most part, property and liability insurance companies are not permitted to invest in urban real estate, except to the extent made under the general permissive rules of each state for nonauthorized investments. Life insurance companies, on the other hand, may commit a significant amount of their available funds for investment in urban real estate.

Besides limiting the total amount that an insurance company may commit to these investments, the statutes generally provide that investments in other real estate must be income-producing properties. Some states further limit these investments to exclude properties used for agriculture, mining, ranching, and the like. As a general rule, the statutory test for permitted investments is that there should be an expectation of recovering the cost of the investment over the useful life of the property. For this reason, it is difficult for an insurance company to invest in such items as land held for speculation. This is not to say that each real estate investment is required to produce net income every year. Rather, it is to emphasize that there should be an expectation of a fair return on investments of these types.

Land Investments

While insurance companies are not permitted to acquire land for the purpose of speculating on its future value, they are permitted to invest in land on which they do not own the buildings or other improvements. A typical investment in land is for the purpose of leasing it to someone else for the erection of a rental building. For example, land leased in an urban area on which an income-producing building has been constructed will usually represent a qualified investment in land. Under these circumstances, income produced by leasing the building is available for paying the lease on the land. If the land does not contain an income-producing structure but is leased to an organization that can demonstrate its ability to pay the rent, the investment in land will likewise be a qualified investment. There are few if any costs connected with these leases, except for property taxes.

Another type of land investment qualifying for the income-producing requirement is land used for parking facilities. This investment may be made in two different ways: The insurance company may (1) lease the bare land to an operator who makes the necessary improvements and operates the parking facility or may (2) improve the land so that it is usable for parking and then contract with an outside business to operate the lot. In the first instance, there probably will be no cost related to the lease except for property taxes. In the second instance, the insurance company usually bears all costs except those for personnel and receives all the income less a fee charged by the parking lot operator.

Building Investments

Nearly any type of income-producing building will qualify as investment real estate. However, certain types of buildings are generally more suitable than others for insurance company investments. A general characteristic of these investments is that no individual investment represents a significant concentration in any geographic area; this precludes the risk of unusual losses from natural disasters or local economic problems. Some of the more common investments are as follows:

Industrial Warehouse Buildings. These are service structures that do not require significant maintenance and upkeep. They usually have multiple tenants, which tends to reduce the possibility of significant vacancies; yet even when such a building is leased to one tenant at a time, it does not require extensive refurbishing when tenants change. These facilities are often leased on a net basis which requires the tenant to pay all operating expenses, including property taxes. The leases may also provide that the tenant will maintain the building, while the landlord assumes responsibility for additions and permanent improvements. Where the net lease method is used, there is very little accounting related to the investment. Since many industrial warehouse facilities are constructed in newly developed areas, the buildings are usually in very good condition and provide an excellent investment for the insurance company. The most significant operating charges against income from the building consist of depreciation, repairs, property taxes, and the like, where they are not paid for by the tenant. Amounts expended for additions and improvements to the building are capitalized and depreciated over the remaining life of the building, unless the life of the improvement is less.

Office Buildings. Because these buildings are often built in prime urban areas, they make excellent investments for an insurance company. Many insurance companies provide only mortgage loans for such office buildings; however, that type of investment seldom provides the opportunity to realize appreciation on the property. On the other hand, by investing in an office building, an insurance company can receive a significant amount of current income from tenants and at the same time be able to realize the long-term appreciation that usually occurs with these buildings. Many times the insurance company will invest in these buildings as a partner; under these circumstances, another partner usually manages the building. Depreciation expense is usually the most significant charge against operating income, unless a net lease is not used. Amounts expended for additions and improvements are amortized over the lease term rather than over the life of the building.

Retail Establishments. Many retail businesses operate in numerous geographic areas and need facilities for each location. Their store facilities are usually leased from others on a net lease basis and provide the insurance company with a good long-term investment opportunity. Since the retail establishments are widely dispersed, they are relatively free from the risk of a single disaster. Most of these leases make the tenant responsible for all improvements, repairs, and expenses.

Retail Shopping Centers. These are often found in new areas undergoing significant development. The centers become an integral part of the development and provide the opportunity for insurance companies to realize long-term appreciation. In addition to leasing these facilities for fixed rent, there are usually participation agreements which provide for additional contingent rent based on total sales. Consequently, as the areas develop and the retail sales grow, the rentals received by the insurance company increase proportionately.

Other investment real estate includes motels and hotels, apartment houses, manufacturing facilities, and the like. For statutory purposes, each such investment property is individually reported in Schedule A, Part 1, of the annual statement blank. The properties are described as to type, location, date acquired, cost and book value, and yearly costs of additions and improvements. The amount of rentals, taxes, repairs, depreciation, and other expenses are also shown for each property. Appraisal adjustments are not recognized unless the market value is less than book value.

RENTAL OPERATIONS

This part of the insurance company's operation has two aspects. The first consists of leasing activities, and the second consists of gains or losses on the sale of investment real estate.

Rental and Leasing Income

The income derived from real estate operations is accounted for on an accrual basis; that is, the amounts collected are adjusted for rentals received in advance and unearned, and for rentals accrued but unpaid. The unearned amounts represent advance payments made by tenants. The accrued amounts include the contractual rent payments and contingent amounts. Contingent rental income may be more difficult to ascertain since the period for calculating the contingent amounts may not coincide with the year-end of the insurance company; however, it is necessary to make an estimate of these contingent amounts. If based on sales, an interim calculation of contingent amounts should reflect a proportionate increase in the rental payments based on year-to-date sales. The contingent amount accrued should equal the contingent amount due at year-end, plus collections during the year, less the amount accrued at the end of the prior year.

For statutory reporting purposes, space occupied by the insurance company for its operations is accounted for as if it were rented from an outside entity; in other words, the insurance company is required to charge itself rent on properties it owns and occupies. The amount charged for rent is considered to be the fair rental value the company would otherwise be required to pay others. This is included in Exhibit 3 (Life) and Part 1 (Property) of the annual statement, along with other gross investment income. The amount of rent for the company's own occupancy is shown in a footnote; this same amount is included in general expenses in Exhibit 5 (Life) and Part 4 (Property) of the annual statement. The purpose of this self-charged rent is to recognize the investment value of the home office real estate. There is, of course, no effect on net income since the entries for rent income and rent expense are offsetting. Many companies determine the fair value of self-rent based on the rent charged to tenants of their home office building.

Realized and Unrealized Gains and Losses

Where real estate is sold during the year, the realized gain or loss is measured by the difference between the recorded book value and the selling price, less sales commissions, closing costs, and the like. Book value for an insurance company is the cost of the property, less encumbrances, depreciation, and market value write-downs. These gains or losses are aggregated and reported net of income taxes as a separate item on the income statement. For statutory reporting, the realized gains or losses of a property liability insurance company are reported as a separate component of investment income. For life insurance companies, the realized gains or losses are reported as an adjustment to the capital and surplus account. For income tax reporting, the book value is not adjusted for changes in market value; consequently, the realized gain or loss reported for income tax purposes may vary from the amounts reported for generally accepted accounting principles or statutory accounting practices.

Unrealized gains or losses are not taken into account on the income statement unless a downward market value adjustment is considered to be a permanent impairment to the real estate investment, in which case the amount reserved or written off is charged directly to income. The statutory reporting of unrealized gains or losses is the same for property and liability insurance companies and life insurance companies. These amounts are reported as adjustments to the capital and surplus account. For income tax reporting, the unrealized amounts will be eliminated in determining the gain or loss arising from the sale of the real estate.

REAL ESTATE EXPENSES

Real estate expenses are separately accounted for and include the cost incurred in the operation of home office property as well as the costs incurred in connection with other investment real estate. These expenses can be classified into three separate categories:

Real Estate Taxes

Probably the largest single cash expense in the real estate operation is property taxes. These are accounted for on an accrual basis and are based on the assessed value of the property and a lien date. A *lien date* is the point that an absolute liability for the property taxes becomes fixed. This date may be the basis that some companies use for accruing real estate property taxes. If the lien date coincides with the fiscal year-end of the insurance company, a proper liability will be recorded. On the other hand, if the lien date occurs at another time during the year, a proper liability will not be reflected unless the real estate taxes are ratably accrued.

The preferred accounting treatment is to record property taxes on a pro rata basis to reflect the expected amounts that will be payable when future liens occur. Unless the pro rata method of accruing real estate taxes is used, the taxes may not be deductible for income tax reporting until the lien date. For statutory accounting practices, real estate taxes are included in Exhibit 6 (Life) and Part 4 (Property) of the annual statement.

Depreciation Expense

Depreciation methods were described in the preceding materials. However, for statutory reporting, depreciation may be computed by using the leasehold period instead of the useful life of the building. This use of the lease period is not appropriate for generally accepted accounting principles unless the expected useful life and the leasehold period cover approximately the same term. Real estate depreciation expense is included as a separate item in the determination of net investment income and for statutory reporting is included in Exhibit 2 of the annual statement blank.

Other Real Estate Expenses

When insurance companies operate real estate projects such as their home office properties, the real estate expenses include salaries and benefits of employees engaged in maintenance, building cleaning, engineering, painting, carpentry, and the like. For all real estate investment properties, expenses are likely to include property and liability insurance, agents' fees, inspection costs, advertising for tenants, and similar items. For statutory reporting, these are included as a single item of investment expense in Exhibit 5 (Life) and Part 4 (Property) of the annual statement blank.

8

OTHER ASSETS

Most of an insurance company's assets are invested in bonds, stocks, mortgage loans, real estate, and other income-producing assets. This investment program is to a great extent the result of requirements imposed on these companies by state laws and regulations. The earnings on investments provide some of the cash needed to pay current costs, liquidate liabilities, and provide additional surplus.

While insurance companies are not required to invest all their funds in income-producing assets, most of their "other assets" are related to the operation of an insurance business. For example, amounts due for premiums that have been invoiced and are not paid represent a type of other asset. Many of these other assets are similar both for property and liability insurance companies and for life insurance and accident and health insurance companies. Where there are differences, they will be covered separately.

Some of the most common other assets are described below.

UNCOLLECTED PREMIUMS: PROPERTY AND LIABILITY INSURANCE

These amounts are similar to customer accounts receivable for commercial and industrial enterprises. However, they also represent uncollected premiums for services yet to be provided. This is because insurance premiums are always billed in advance, generally on an annual, semiannual, quarterly, or monthly basis. Most of the outstanding premiums can be classified into the following groups:

Uncollected Premiums

Many property and liability companies offer insurance protection through their agency representatives on a direct billing basis. This means that the agent sells the insurance policy and the insurance company sends the billing directly to the customer. These premiums are usually payable on an annual, semiannual, or quarterly basis; a few companies may bill on a monthly basis. The initial premium payment must accompany the application for insurance; thereafter, premiums are billed in advance of the due date, and if not paid by that date are carried as uncollected premiums. Thus, even though the premium has not been paid, the insured has insurance protection for a limited period.

The policy will state when the coverage will lapse if the premiums are not paid in a timely fashion. The termination provisions are approved by state regulators when the policy is submitted for the insurance department's initial approval. Even though the policy will terminate automatically, the insurance company may be required to notify the insured of the lapsed condition and the period of time permitted to correct that condition.

In addition to billing customers, the insurance company also sends follow-up notices for premiums that are not paid when due. The writing agent is usually notified when customers do not pay in time, since agents' commissions are not paid until the premiums have been collected. Normally, the lapsed policy premium notices are sent 10 to 30 days after the premium due date, and uncollected premiums are then removed from the accounting records. The actual cancellation process may be held open for an extended period to accommodate policy renewals. However, this represents an internal administrative process that is unrelated to the actual reinstatement process required by insurance companies.

Agents' Balances

In addition to the direct billing basis, many companies also use an agency billing basis. This differs from the direct billing basis in that the insurance premiums are billed to the agent rather than to the insured. The agent in turn rebills the insured and is responsible for premium collections. Companies that write business through independent insurance agents will often utilize both the agency billing basis and the direct billing basis.

Independent insurance agents may prefer the agency billing basis because they are usually not required to remit the amounts due as they are collected. Rather, there is a specified due date for remitting the entire balance appearing on the agency statements prepared by the insurance company; the delayed collection period may extend for up to 45 days. The statement must be carefully prepared since there may be intervening transactions that create additional charges or credits in the agents' accounts prior to the original due date. For that reason, many insurance companies require that the accounts be paid from the agency statements of the insurance company. When this is not required, it will be necessary to reconcile the accounts periodically and account for the intervening transactions.

Where agency billing is used, the insurance policy will remain in force until the agent orders it canceled. Consequently, if the agent does not collect and remit the premiums in a timely fashion, the policy nevertheless remains in force, and the insurance company must look solely to the agent for payments.

Premiums and Agents' Balances Not Yet Due

Some companies may provide for a distinction between (1) uncollected premiums that are due but not yet paid and (2) uncollected premiums that are recorded but deferred because they are not yet due. The distinction between these two accounts is that the premiums are not recognized on amounts billed which are not yet due. On the other hand, the premiums of agents' balances in course of collection are recognized in premium income to the extent that such amounts have been earned pro rata from the due date.

However, many insurance companies include both types of premiums under the single caption of premiums and agents' balances in course of collection.

When these amounts are combined, the effect on operations is the same since the total amount of unearned premiums, including the amounts not yet due, are included in the liability for unearned premiums.

Allowances for Uncollectible Premiums

The premiums and agents' balances in the course of collection are analyzed to determine the amounts that should be written off or provided for in an allowance account. Bad accounts should be written off as soon as their status is determined.

For statutory reporting, a mandatory adjustment is made to the total outstanding balance if the accounts are not collected on a timely basis. The statutory provision requires that amounts outstanding for more than 90 days be treated as nonadmitted assets. This treatment causes the agents' balances or uncollected premiums to be stated net of these allowances in the balance sheet. However, the offset to these allowances is made by charging the nonadmitted assets directly to surplus. If the accounts are subsequently collected, surplus is credited.

For income tax reporting, no amounts are recognized as uncollectible until all reasonable efforts have been made to collect the accounts and the balances are deemed to be worthless.

Reinsurance Premiums Receivable

The amounts due from ceding insurance companies for reinsurance premiums are included in the uncollected premium account. The detail for these amounts is contained in a reinsurance listing (often called a "bordereau") prepared by the ceding company. Since the assuming company has no contact with the policyholders, the uncollected reinsurance premiums can be collected only from the ceding reinsurer. If any of these balances are due from companies that are not authorized to conduct business in the domicile state of the assuming insurance company, the entire amount must be offset by an unearned premium liability for reinsurance in unauthorized companies.

Audit Premiums Receivable

Premiums based on the amount of an insured payroll are initially set by estimating the payroll. The estimated premiums are recorded in the same manner as other premiums due from policyowners or agents. However, the final premium cannot be calculated until total payroll costs have been determined for the term of the policy. When the final determination is made for the payroll, the premiums are recomputed and adjusted for that period. This usually results in additional premiums that must be paid by the insured.

At any report date, the final payroll audits may not have been completed, and therefore the actual premiums are not known. It is necessary that an estimate be made of these additional amounts and recorded as uncollected premiums. The adjustments for these unrecorded amounts will result in an increase in premium income unless the original estimate of payroll costs was in excess of the actual incurred costs. In either case, the premium and uncollected premium accounts are adjusted. For statutory reporting, some companies do not adjust the uncollected premium account until the payroll audits have been completed. The latter method is not acceptable for income tax reporting unless an estimate of the amounts cannot be determined.

UNCOLLECTED PREMIUMS: LIFE INSURANCE AND ACCIDENT AND HEALTH INSURANCE

The uncollected premiums of these companies are combined with deferred life insurance and annuity premiums. For purposes of this material, only uncollected premiums are included; deferred premiums are discussed in connection with reserves for life and annuity contracts. Following statutory reporting practices, the uncollected life insurance and annuity premiums are separated from the accident and health premiums due and unpaid.

Uncollected life insurance premiums represent the amounts due for policies that have been extended by the grace period. The *grace period* is a policy feature that continues the policy in force beyond the premium payment date, usually for 30 days. That is, if the premiums are paid within 30 days after the premium due date, there is no interruption in protection. If the premiums are not paid within that period, the policies lapse and can be reinstated only if the reinstatement provisions are met. This may require proof of insurability to be furnished by the policyholder. While the grace period is usually 30 days, many companies do not process terminations until the end of the month following the date on which the policy would normally lapse. While a policyholder may not rely upon this further extension, the insurance company avoids the reinstatement process for policies that pay the premiums within that period. Losses that occur within the unofficial extension period likely will not be paid unless the late premium has been received prior to the loss date.

Uncollected life insurance premiums are adjusted to their net insurance basis. That is, the gross premium is reduced by a factor referred to as "loading," which represents the amount of the gross premium that is used to pay agents' commissions, operating expenses, and a margin for contingencies or profit. The loading factor is greater for the first-year premium than for renewal premiums. This is consistent with the actual occurrence of these costs for a policy's first year; the commissions and operating expenses are significantly larger in the year the policy is put on the books. In subsequent years, the commissions and cost of maintaining the policy are substantially reduced. In recording uncollected premiums, the net premiums are treated as an accounts receivable, the loading is treated as an expense, and the gross premium is included in premium income. These amounts are theoretically determined by listing each of the policies with premiums that are due but unpaid. Often, though, the calculations are made by the computer, and the total of the net premiums is determined without a detailed listing. Uncollected annuity premiums are determined in a manner consistent with the method followed for life insurance policies.

Uncollected premiums on accident and health policies are determined in a manner similar to that for property and liability insurance policies. The policies terminate if the premiums are not paid, although there is usually a grace period to accommodate late premium payments. Unlike property and liability insurance policies, however, which remain in force until a cancellation notice is given, many accident and health insurance policies terminate immediately upon nonpayment of premiums.

Some accident and health policies are written on a group basis that requires the group policyholder to pay all losses, expenses, and handling charges in connection with the insurance coverage. Under these circumstances, it is possible for amounts to be outstanding and unpaid for excess losses, expenses, and administrative charges over the premiums that have been collected. In this situation, the excess of losses and expense over the premiums-paid amount is carried as an uncollected premium and the related loss and expense items are recorded as a liability.

Regardless of the type of policy involved, there is no significant difference in the treatment of uncollected premiums for generally accepted accounting principles, statutory accounting practices, and income tax reporting.

BILLS RECEIVABLE TAKEN FOR PREMIUMS

Property and liability insurance companies are permitted to accept installment notes for premiums due. These notes arise in connection with the financing of policies requiring large premiums. In situations of this type, the insurance company provides installment credit in much the same manner as a loan company does. However, the security for these receivables consists of the unearned premiums on the policies that have been issued.

Generally, an initial payment is required to cover the cost of the policy during the first 2 or 3 months. Thereafter, the installments due include both principal and interest. The interest rate and payment dates are specified in the financing agreement. If the installment payment is not made when due, the policy will lapse and the premiums that are unearned will be reversed. The balances due on these installment receivables qualify as admitted assets to the extent that the unearned premiums on the policy are equal to or exceed the receivable balance. Any excess of the receivable over the unearned premium is classified as a nonadmitted asset.

Many property and liability insurance companies offer an installment payment basis for premiums. Because most of these arrangements are not considered to be financing arrangements, the installment payments represent a ratable part of the total premium plus a service charge for each installment that is made. The service charge is generally calculated to cover the cost of handling the additional premium payments and does not provide for financing charges in the nature of interest. These installment payments are included with uncollected premiums.

COLLATERAL LOANS

For insurance companies, these loans represent a limited investment opportunity. (They are more prevalent in the banking and investment brokerage business.) The basis of the loan is that it is fully collaterized by investments that are freely traded or easily exchanged. To carry such loans as admitted assets, it is necessary that the market value of the collateral always equal or exceed the current balance of the loan outstanding. The collateral is held by the insurance company under trust and a collateral assignment. The collateral note specifies the securities pledged and the interest rate and due date of the loan. Some state regulations prescribe that the fair market value of the securities must be greater than the amount of the note unless the securities pledged as collateral would qualify as investments for the insurance company, in which instance the fair market value must be at least equal to the loan amount. When the loan amount exceeds the fair market value of the collateral, then for statutory reporting the excess is treated as a nonadmitted asset. For income tax reporting, no write-off is permitted unless the loan becomes partially or entirely worthless. The details of outstanding collateral loans are reported in Schedule C of the annual statement blank.

AMOUNTS DUE FROM REINSURERS

These balances arise in connection with ceded reinsurance and assumed reinsurance. Some insurance companies have ceded reinsurance recoverable amounts only, while other companies have both ceded and assumed reinsurance amounts. In addition, there is some distinction between (1) life insurance and accident and health insurance companies and (2) property and liability insurance companies. The following explanations distinguish between the two:

Reinsurance Recoverable on Loss Payments: Property and Liability Insurance

These amounts are due from the assuming company for losses that have been ceded to them. They may arise from the excess of the loss payment on an individual policy over the maximum loss retained. They may also arise from excess loss provisions of reinsurance treaties, pro rata insured losses under quota share agreements, surplus protection treaties, and the like. Since the losses have been paid, these amounts are recoverable after loss payment reports have been filed. A reserve is not required so long as the amounts are due from solvent insurance companies. For statutory reporting, the amounts due from unauthorized reinsurance are included in this balance, even though some or all of the balance may have to be included separately as a liability. This latter liability balance may be reduced by the funds held for these companies. In addition, if amounts of reinsurance recoverable are outstanding for more than 90 days, they must be classified as a nonadmitted asset. The details of recoverable amounts are included in Schedule F, Part 1A, Section 1.

It should be noted that these receivable amounts are from actual loss payments only. Amounts estimated to be recoverable on unpaid losses are offset against the liability for unpaid losses.

Funds Held by or Deposited with Reinsured Companies: Property and Liability Insurance

These amounts are assets of the reinsurers and generally arise under two circumstances. First, since reinsurance settlements are made on a periodic basis, the ceding company may incur significant losses between reporting dates. The reinsurer will often make advances to the ceding company for such losses. The advances are for actual losses; however, since the detailed reports have not been compiled, the individual loss amounts cannot be identified. Advanced funds are treated by the reinsurer as an asset until the losses are actually reported and the amounts cleared.

The second circumstance occurs when the reinsurer permits the ceding company to withhold reinsurance premiums to the extent of the unearned premiums and unpaid losses covered in the reinsurance contract. This latter transaction occurs when the reinsurer is not authorized to conduct business in the domicile state of the ceding company or when the reinsurer is financing some of the reinsurance.

In either instance, some agreements provide for the payment of interest on the amounts that are withheld. The interest payments are accounted for in a manner similar to that for any other interest-bearing obligation.

A reserve against these outstanding balances is not required unless some of the amounts are deemed to be uncollectible from the ceding company. The amount of such reserves is determined in a manner similar to that for reserves for any other asset held by the insurance company. For statutory reporting, if the amounts held by or deposited with reinsured companies exceed the sum of the unearned premiums and outstanding losses on the reinsured policies, then the excess must be treated as a nonadmitted asset. For income tax reporting, the assets are not reduced until the balances are deemed to be partially or entirely worthless.

Reinsurance Ceded: Life Insurance and Accident and Health Insurance

In many respects, the asset balances arising from reinsurance transactions for life insurance and accident and health insurance companies are similar to those described for property and liability insurance companies. However, because of the long-term nature of life insurance and of some accident and health insurance, there are some distinctions. While these reinsurance transactions can take many forms, for the most part they will be reflected in the balances described below.

Amounts Recoverable from Reinsurers

These amounts represent the claims receivable from the reinsurer for losses that have been paid. As in every reinsurance arrangement, the writing company is responsible for the payment of all losses. Where these losses are covered by reinsurance, a claim is filed and the writing company is reimbursed for the losses previously paid. These recoverable amounts may arise from either life insurance coverages or accident and health insurance coverages. The amounts may be recoverable on either an excess loss or a pro rata loss basis. Such amounts represent either individual or group experience and are usually paid by the reinsurer as soon as the claim is filed.

An allowance for doubtful collections is usually not necessary for any of these accounts; however, for statutory reporting, amounts due from unauthorized companies in excess of funds deposited by or withheld from these reinsurers are treated as a liability. For income tax reporting, amounts from unauthorized companies are reported on a gross basis unless they become wholly or partially worthless. The details of all recoverable amounts are reported in the annual statement blank in Schedule S, Part 1.

Amounts recoverable from reinsurers for claims that have been reserved for but not paid are not recorded as an asset; but rather, these amounts are a deduction against the liability for policy claims outstanding.

Commission and Expense Allowances Due. The ceding company, under pro rata and related types of agreements, is reimbursed for agents' commissions and for other expenses incurred in writing the coverage. In recording the gross amount of the reinsurance transaction, the insurance company takes a credit on the income statement to reflect the reimbursement of these expenses. To the extent that premiums for this reinsurance have not been paid to the reinsurer, there is an offsetting asset amount that reflects the unrecovered commission and expense allowance. The collection of these amounts is assured since they will likely be paid at the time the premiums are remitted to the reinsurer.

Experience Rating and Other Refunds Due. Many reinsurance arrangements are settled on a tentative basis; that is, the net cost of the reinsurance is estimated and paid currently. The final determination of profit sharing is deferred until all the premiums have been received and all the losses and costs have been paid. The resulting income is then shared between the ceding company and the reinsurer.

This profit sharing arises because the estimated losses on these policies are usually greater than the actual loss experience. Under these conditions, there is an excess of revenue over the related costs and expenses, and a portion of this amount is returned to the ceding company. This amount must often be estimated, in which case it is subject to adjustment in subsequent periods. However, if careful estimates are made, then the assets may be stated on a gross basis and an allowance for uncollectible balances will not be necessary. These balances will be the same for generally accepted accounting principles, statutory accounting practices, and income tax reporting.

INVESTMENT INCOME DUE AND ACCRUED

This account includes amounts due from real estate income, interest-bearing investments, and equity investments paying cash dividends.

Real estate income includes all amounts received under rental arrangements with third parties; the rental arrangements can be for real or personal property.

Excluded from these amounts are lease payments from a sales-type or direct financing lease. The exclusion of these amounts is required for both generally accepted accounting principles and statutory accounting practices. When the due date of the rental amounts does not coincide with the year-end, any rents not received should be accrued and included in rental income. For statutory reporting, amounts due for rental income that are delinquent for over 30 days may be treated as nonadmitted assets.

Accrued amounts in this category can also arise from bonds, mortgage loans, policy loans, premium financing, and the like. When the interest payment dates do not coincide with the year-end, interest should be accrued to the financial reporting date. In addition, these interest amounts should include an adjustment made in order to accrue discounts and amortize premiums. Amounts deemed to be uncollectible should not be accrued. For statutory reporting, amounts past due 30 days or more may be classified as nonadmitted assets.

Dividends should be accrued for common stock and certain classes of preferred stock, based on the record date of the dividend declaration. Since traded stocks are reported at market value, dividends should not be accrued in the event that the market price has not been adjusted for the dividends.

ELECTRONIC DATA PROCESSING EQUIPMENT

The cost of equipment for processing policy information and providing accounting data is often substantial. The accounting treatment for these cash outlays is essentially the same for generally accepted accounting principles, statutory accounting practices, and income tax reporting. The amounts expended are amortized over the expected useful life of the equipment. Software costs are not included in the balance, except for programs required to make the equipment operational; the costs incurred in acquiring or developing any other software programs should be capitalized and the costs amortized over their expected useful life.

The reporting of electronic data processing equipment for statutory accounting practices is determined by state regulations. Some states provide that the cost will be capitalized and amortized over its useful life. In other states, companies must obtain permission from the insurance department before the cost can be carried as an admitted asset. Often, the regulations may provide for a minimum cost to be capitalized and for a maximum capitalizable cost, this representing a specified percentage of the insurance company's admitted assets or surplus. The period over which the costs are amortized seldom exceeds 5 years.

FEDERAL INCOME TAX RECOVERABLE

An insurance company may have income taxes which are payable for the current and prior years as well as income taxes which are recoverable from prior years. These payable and receivable amounts are often combined so that only the net amount payable or receivable is recorded. This method is appropriate when prior year's losses are offset against the current year's income. However, in some instances the combination of amounts receivable and payable may not be appropriate. For example, when current-year losses are carried back against prior years in which taxes were paid, the amount represents a refund of prior income taxes. In such instances, the refund amount is recorded as an asset and is not offset against a liability still due for any other year.

There may be other instances in which prior-year tax liabilities have not been settled and these amounts outstanding are recorded as liabilities. Generally, these amounts are not netted unless the claim for a refund arises in the same year for which there is an income tax liability.

For all reporting purposes, the amount of federal income taxes recoverable should reflect the best estimate of taxes and interest. The recognition of federal income taxes recoverable is the same whether the insurance company is filing a separate return or one consolidated with other companies. For consolidated returns, it is necessary to reflect the recoverable amount based on the federal income tax allocation method adopted by the consolidated group.

REAL ESTATE JOINT VENTURES

Real estate joint ventures offer the insurance company an opportunity to participate in the equity appreciation of real estate. Generally, the cash outlay required is less than for most other investments since the real estate joint venture funds a significant part of its activity with development loans. These joint-venture activities include office buildings, shopping centers, and condominium housing projects. The potential appreciation on these projects offers the insurance company the opportunity to achieve a maximum return on its investment. The insurance company furnishes the capital and joins with a developer who supplies the construction skills necessary for the successful completion of such a project. While an insurance company may function as a developer, it seldom does so.

An insurance company's contribution may be in two forms. First, the company may make an equity investment to cover the original development and land acquisition costs. Second, it may also provide the permanent debt financing for the project. These two types of investment are accounted for separately. Funds provided for capital are accounted for on the equity method; that is, the investment is carried at cost adjusted for the insurance company's share of undistributed joint-venture profits or losses. The investment in permanent debt financing is accounted for as a mortgage loan.

In the early stages of a real estate joint venture, there are usually losses since the project does not produce income until it is completed and occupied. The insurance company's share of these losses reduces the equity investment until it is extinguished. Thereafter, no further losses are recognized until the project develops income and all prior unrecorded losses are extinguished.

For statutory accounting practices, investments in real estate joint ventures are accounted for on the equity method. However, unlike generally accepted accounting principles (according to which all income and losses of the joint venture are taken directly to the income statement), only the amount of dividends received or declared is included in the income statement of an insurance company. Joint-venture losses, as well as income not distributed as dividends, are credited or charged directly to surplus. In addition, for a life insurance or accident and health insurance company, if the investment is in a subsidiary, the unrealized capital gain or loss may have to be included in the common stock reserve component of the mandatory securities valuation reserve. The effect of this latter adjustment is to eliminate unrealized gains or losses on real estate joint ventures from surplus. Any cash returned from the joint venture which does not represent earnings is applied to reduce the carrying value of the investment. The details of the investment are set out in Schedule BA.

FOREIGN CURRENCY EXCHANGE

An insurance company's operations may include financial transactions arising in foreign countries as a result of collecting premiums from, paying the losses of, or investing in securities of non-U.S. companies or as a result of owning another company that conducts its activities in a foreign country.

As a general rule, the business conducted in foreign countries is recorded in U.S. dollars until the transaction is closed. If the closed transaction results in a foreign currency gain or loss, this amount is included in the determination of current income. However, if the transaction is carried over to a new fiscal period, an allowance is made as of the end of the period to reflect the translation of outstanding amounts to U.S. dollars. Such differences are included as components of capital and surplus.

Statutory accounting practices require that the assets and liabilities pertaining to foreign operations be compared at the end of the year and that an adjustment be made on the net balance to reflect the conversion of this amount to U.S. dollars. Gains on foreign currency transactions are recorded as assets, and losses are recorded as liabilities. For property and liability insurance companies, the offset to this adjustment is made directly in the surplus account. For life insurance and accident and health insurance companies, the offsetting amount is included in Exhibit 4 and combined with the capital gains and losses on investments that are charged or credited directly to surplus.

AMOUNTS DUE FROM AFFILIATES

For statutory reporting, there is an exception to the usual rule that unsecured accounts receivable are required to be nonadmitted. The amounts due from affiliated companies that represent current accounts receivable for unsettled premiums, expenses, and the like are recognized as an admitted asset so long as the affiliate has the resources to repay the balance and maintains its account on a current basis. Amounts that have been invested in affiliates are not included in this balance.

OTHER ADMITTED ASSETS

The statutory annual statement blank contains some unlabeled lines that permit the insurance company to write in those other assets it owns which are permitted to be included in admitted assets. Examples of these are the cash value of life insurance policies owned by the company, unexpended deposits in statutory solvency pools or associations, capitalized lease equipment, trust funds, mineral rights, and refundable deposits.

NONADMITTED ASSETS

The annual statutory report filed by an insurance company provides for the exclusion of some assets in the determination of the company's financial condition. Even though these assets may be ultimately realized, they cannot be included with other admitted assets. Therefore, these assets are classified as nonadmitted. Examples of nonadmitted assets are:

- Advances made to life insurance agents
- Agents' balances which have been due for more than 90 days from property and liability insurance agents
- Equipment, furniture, and supplies
- Advances to officers and employees
- Loans on personal security which do not qualify as collateral loans
- Excess of amortized values of investments over the NAIC market value
- Interest due and accrued beyond 1 year
- Investments in excess of statutory limits
- Computer software
- Automobiles and trucks
- Prepaid expenses
- All unsecured receivables

Merely because an item is classified as nonadmitted does not alter the basic accounting requirement that it should be recorded in the accounting records. For example, furniture and equipment carried as an asset is subject to allowances for depreciation. Likewise, other receivables which are doubtful as to their collection should either be provided for in an allowance for doubtful accounts or be written off. In other words, assets which are deemed to be unrealizable in the normal course of operations should be written off and not accounted for as nonadmitted assets.

UNLISTED ASSETS: SCHEDULE X

This schedule is included in the statutory annual statement blank for the purpose of recording assets which are owned but which have no determinable value. The assets listed in this schedule are not included in the financial statement of the insurance company. Typical unlisted assets are investment securities which are deemed to be of no value even though the issuing company is still in business. Also, the schedule may include royalty and mineral rights which have been retained on properties previously sold. If any amounts are realized on these unlisted assets, they are included in current income. The assets are removed from this schedule when all claims or rights have been exhausted.

9

GOODWILL AND OTHER INTANGIBLES

Intangible assets *are capitalized expenditures which are expected to produce future benefits but which, unlike tangible assets, do not derive their value from a physical, material existence. The benefits produced by intangible assets may include legal rights, technical knowledge, customer acceptance, or future income. Examples of such assets are franchises, goodwill, patents, trademarks, stocks, organization costs, policy acquisition costs, and customer lists. Stocks and bonds, although intangible, are covered separately in Chapter 5, Investments in Securities. Deferred policy acquisition costs are covered in Chapter 10. Most of the remaining intangibles will be covered in this chapter. In connection with goodwill, Chapter 22, Mergers and Acquisitions, will provide additional useful information.*

Intangible assets may be developed internally or purchased from others. Intangibles may be specific, *meaning that they can be bought and sold by themselves, or they may be* nonspecific, *meaning that they cannot be transferred separately but are inseparably connected to a group of other assets or to the company itself. Patents and trademarks, for instance, are specific since they can be sold separately. Goodwill, on the other hand, is nonspecific since it cannot be sold by itself but must stay with the company. An outside party can acquire the goodwill of the company only by acquiring the company itself.*

ACCOUNTING FOR INTANGIBLES

Accounting for intangibles involves identifying them, classifying them, assigning an initial cost, and amortizing or otherwise handling that cost in future years. The accounting treatment will vary for statutory, GAAP, and tax purposes. The statutory treatment emphasizes a conservative balance sheet valuation, with the result that many intangibles must be treated as nonadmitted assets or expensed outright. Under generally accepted accounting principles (GAAP), intangibles are given much greater recognition, but still must be amortized over their useful life. In no event can the amortization period exceed 40 years, even if the intangible has an unlimited life; also, any unamortized balance must be expensed if the asset is determined to be worthless at some point. For tax purposes, an inconsistent approach is followed. In some cases the conservative statutory treatment is used; in other cases, intangibles are assigned a large value with an unlimited life.

In all situations, though, whether for statutory, GAAP, or tax purposes, intangibles are governed by the cost concept. Such assets can never be carried on the books for more than what was paid for them in cash or property. Complications may arise where the intangibles are acquired in exchange for noncash consideration, or where they are acquired as part of an asset package, but these complications are usually not important for statutory purposes, since most intangibles are given no value anyway.

For GAAP purposes, where a company is acquired in a pooling transaction (discussed in Chapter 22, Mergers and Acquisitions, under "GAAP Treatment,") the accounting for intangibles is also relatively easy since the intangible amounts recorded on the acquired company's books are merely carried over to the acquiring company. No new intangibles are created, and no intangible values change as a result of the transaction. Nothing occurs other than a combining of already existing amounts.

In any transaction other than pooling, though, an intangible may be recorded which previously had a different value or which was not recognized at all. The new cost of the intangible is the amount of cash paid or the fair market value of other property given up. However, if the fair market value of the intangible can be determined more readily than can the value of the other property given up, then the value of the intangible is used as the cost figure. Where the intangibles are acquired as part of a package, then all the *specific* intangibles, together with the tangibles acquired, are each assigned a cost equal to their individual fair market values. If the total purchase price exceeds the sum of these individual valuations, the difference is considered to be goodwill. If the total purchase price is less, the deficiency is allocated proportionately to noncurrent assets (other than marketable securities) to reduce their market values. If these noncurrent assets are reduced to zero, any remaining deficiency is considered to be a deferred credit and shall be amortized over the period estimated to be benefited, but not less than 40 years.

For tax purposes, intangibles acquired in a tax-free transaction (such as a merger, reorganization, or transfer to a controlled corporation) are treated in a manner similar to pooling for GAAP purposes. In other words, the values recorded on the books of the transferor are carried over to the books of the acquiror. No new intangibles are created and previous values do not change. Intangibles acquired in a taxable transaction are generally recorded in the same manner as for a GAAP nonpooling transaction; the cost is the cash or value of other property given up, unless the value of the intangible can be determined more readily than can the value of the other property. Where an asset package is acquired, though, the tax rules are slightly different from the GAAP rules. For tax purposes, the total purchase price is allocated among all assets, both tangible and intangible (other than cash and cash equivalents), in proportion to their individual fair market values. However, receivables are not allocated a basis in excess of face value.

This concept may be illustrated by the following example. Suppose that assets A, B, and C are acquired for $100. An appraiser later determines the individual value of A to be $30, B to be $30, and C to be $30. For GAAP purposes, each of the items would be recorded at $30, and the remaining $10 would be considered goodwill. For tax purposes, though, each item would be recorded at $33.33, which is each item's proportionate share of the total purchase price. This assumes that A, B, and C are assets other than cash, cash equivalents, or receivables.

For tax accounting purposes, if goodwill is known to be present in an acquisition, it theoretically should be given an individual value by appraisal, and thus it would receive its proportionate share of the purchase price as any other asset would. However, where goodwill is difficult to appraise, the GAAP method is sometimes used, and goodwill is merely given a value equal to the excess of the total purchase price over the sum of the individual values for the other assets. However, if the sum of the individual values exceeds the total price, then the market values of all assets (other than cash and its equivalent) are reduced proportionately to eliminate the deficiency. There is no "deferred credit."

GOODWILL

The above paragraphs have discussed goodwill in general terms, but the subject is much more complex. The accounting treatment is also extremely important since goodwill is often the largest intangible recorded when a company is acquired. As indicated previously, goodwill is recognized only when all or part of a business is purchased. It is not recorded under any other circumstances.

For statutory purposes, goodwill is not defined, but this is not significant since it is usually treated as a nonadmitted asset anyway. For GAAP purposes, *goodwill* is defined in a computational sense as the excess of the total purchase price of a business over the sum of the individual values of its other assets.

For tax purposes, there are many differing definitions of goodwill found in various court cases and revenue rulings. No single definition has received general acceptance. There is no point in quoting the many definitions. Suffice it to say that most definitions fall into one of the following categories:

1. The GAAP definition.
2. The ability of a business to earn more income than merely a fair rate of return on its tangible assets and investments.
3. The marketing appeal which makes customers continue to do business with a company.
4. The intangible value of trained employees, tested products, a distribution system, and other attributes which a new business starting out from scratch would not have even if it had the same tangible assets (buildings, computers, investments, etc.). These attributes are sometimes called "going concern value," and if goodwill is viewed according to one of the other definitions, goodwill and going concern value may even be treated as separate assets and given separate values.

For tax purposes, goodwill is generally valued either by the GAAP (also called the "residual") method or by a formula. Occasionally, a subjective lump-sum assignment of a round number (such as $5 million) is also used. The choice of the method is usually governed by the desire to minimize taxes. However, an unreasonable valuation would always be subject to IRS challenge.

The classic formula approach was originated by the IRS in Appeals and Review Memorandum (ARM) 34 and restated in Revenue Ruling 68-609. The IRS states that this method is a last resort which is to be used only if no other method is suitable. Despite this published disclaimer, however, both taxpayers and the IRS frequently use this method whenever it is to their advantage.

The formula consists of the following steps:

1. Determine the average net income of the entity over the last 5 years, excluding those years which had an abnormally high or low income because of extraordinary factors.
2. Determine the average amount of tangible assets and investments (less liabilities) over the last 5 years. Multiply this by the average industry rate of return on tangible assets. (This rate can be found in various publications, such as Dun & Bradstreet or Robert Morris Associates.)
3. Subtract step 1 from step 2 and capitalize the remainder at an appropriate rate which reflects average interest rates over the last 5 years, plus several additional percentage points as a risk premium since retaining goodwill is more difficult than collecting on a financial instrument. Generally, this rate will be higher than the rate of return used in step 2. The resulting capitalized figure is the goodwill.

Obviously, this computation reflects the second definition used above, namely, the ability of a business to earn more income than merely a fair rate of return on its tangible assets and investments. Various refinements to the formula are possible. More prior years may be introduced into the formula instead of just 5. A moving average may be used, which gives more weight to income earned in the latest years. Or historical income figures may be dispensed with completely and the formula based, instead, on projected future income in excess of a fair return on projected tangible assets, which excess would then be discounted back to the present at an appropriate rate.

Note that the IRS may attempt to place a value on goodwill by the formula method even where the appraised market values of the other assets exceed the total purchase price. (Of course, in this situation there would be no goodwill for GAAP purposes.) The total price would then be allocated to the individually appraised values, including that of goodwill. By introducing a separate value for goodwill in this situation, the IRS succeeds in allocating less of the total price to tangible assets, with the result that depreciation deductions are reduced.

Once the value of goodwill is determined, the next step is to determine whether it will be amortized. As mentioned previously, goodwill is a nonadmitted asset for statutory purposes, and therefore no amortization would be charged against operations since no continuing asset is recognized.

For GAAP purposes, goodwill is to be amortized over its expected useful life, but not more than 40 years. As a practical matter, most companies simply use the maximum of 40 years (rather than a shorter period) and expense the remaining balance if it is determined to become worthless in the meantime. The straight-line method of amortization is to be used, unless another method is clearly more appropriate due to special circumstances. If in future years a reduced life or value for goodwill becomes evident, then the reduced life or value should be used from that point forward. However, a reduction or total write-off of goodwill is not automatically required because of a few loss years.

For tax purposes, goodwill may not be amortized under any circumstances, but must be left on the books as an asset having an unlimited life. The IRS generally does not allow any write-off of goodwill until the acquired business is sold or liquidated in a taxable transaction. Where there is a partial sale of the business or other circumstances clearly indicating a loss in value, the IRS frowns on allowing any reduction of goodwill, but the courts may be somewhat more favorable to the taxpayer.

GOING CONCERN VALUE

As mentioned in the preceding section, *going concern value* is the intangible benefit of possessing trained employees, tested products, a distribution system, and similar attributes which a brand new business would not have, even though it had the same tangible assets and investments. As with goodwill, going concern value is recognized only when a business is purchased.

To put this discussion into its proper perspective, going concern value, if recognized at all, would only be a nonadmitted asset for statutory purposes. For GAAP purposes, going concern value is not recognized as a separate asset, but is included in the value of goodwill as the excess of the total purchase price over the sum of the individually appraised values for the other assets. If there is no goodwill, no amount is recognized for going concern value either.

Only for tax purposes does going concern value have any significance, and even here the concept does not have uniform acceptance. Many cases assume, either implicitly or explicitly, that going concern value is included in the goodwill value. In other situations, where a court has found that there is no goodwill due to a lack of earnings, a value is then placed on going concern value to reflect the advantage of an operating business over a new business, even though it is losing money. However, seldom if ever have the courts arrived at two separate values, one for goodwill and the other for going concern value.

Some appraisers, though, do calculate two separate values. The reason for this is to protect against having the IRS apply the residual (or GAAP) method of valuing goodwill and unidentified intangibles. If the residual method is applied, then depreciable assets receive a basis not exceeding market value. However, if *all* assets—including goodwill and going concern value—have separately appraised values, then the residual method is inappropriate. The total purchase price is then allocated proportionately among all assets, with the result that depreciable assets may receive a basis in excess of market value, thereby increasing depreciation deductions.

If separate amounts were not assigned to goodwill and going concern value, the IRS conceivably could argue that all intangibles were not individually appraised; consequently, the residual method should be used.

There is no single, generally accepted formula for arriving at going concern value. However, one approach that may be used is to measure the start-up costs of a new business which are avoided by purchasing an existing business. This may be done by the following process:

1. Estimate the start-up period, that is, the number of years required to transform a new business into a smoothly operating one in the same industry as the purchased business. Usually, this is 5 to 10 years.
2. Estimate the equity which would be invested in the business during the start-up period; then estimate what a fair return on this investment would be, based on bond yields. In effect, this is the "opportunity cost" of investing in a new business, since the investors are giving up the opportunity to earn this amount of income which they could have obtained by purchasing bonds or certificates of deposit.
3. Estimate the net income, if any, that the hypothetical new business would earn during the start-up period. Subtract this from the annual opportunity costs in step 2, and then discount the remaining opportunity costs back to the present at an appropriate discount rate. This rate would be based on current financial yields, plus several additional percentage points to reflect the risk that the new business might fail completely. The discounted amount represents the going concern value.

Where recognized for tax purposes, going concern value cannot be amortized, but (as with goodwill) must be left on the books until the acquired business is disposed of.

ORGANIZATION COSTS

These are the actual legal and similar costs required to start a new business. Unlike goodwill and going concern value, which are recorded only when one business is purchased by another business, every business records its own organization costs at the time of inception. The concept of organization cost is specifically addressed only in the tax law; accordingly, the rules that follow originate from tax sources.

At a minimum, organization costs include the legal fees for the articles of incorporation and the bylaws, together with the filing fees paid to the state for the same. Also included would be the legal costs and filing fees for the initial insurance license. Usually, there are also expenses for meetings and planning sessions prior to beginning operations, including the "organizational meeting."

Not included in organization costs are the expenses of underwriting the initial capitalization, preparing lease agreements, or any expenses of an "operating" nature, such as salaries, supplies, rent, or interest. The category of organization costs is really quite restrictive, and the lion's share of the items therein will consist only of attorneys' fees, accountants' fees, and filing fees paid to a government agency. Furthermore, the expenses must be incurred before the end of the taxable year in which the corporation begins business.

Organization costs must be capitalized, and an election may be made to amortize them on the straight-line basis over a period of 60 months or more, beginning with the month in which the corporation begins business. In the absence of a proper election, amortization is not allowed, and the capitalized costs cannot be written off until the corporation is liquidated. Several items should be noted in connection with the amortization:

1. Almost always, the minimum period of 60 months is used, rather than a longer period.
2. The month in which the corporation "begins business" occurs when the entity actually commences operations or acquires assets which will be used in operations. By itself, the mere obtaining of a corporate charter or the issuance of stock certificates does not constitute the beginning of business.
3. An election to amortize must be filed with the corporation's tax return for the year in which it begins business. The requirements of the election statement are contained in Income Tax Regulation 1.248-1(c). Failure to make a timely, proper election will result in the loss of the right to amortize the costs.
4. The expenses must be paid by the new corporation; if paid by another party, must be charged to the new corporation before the end of the year in which it begins business. Too often, a founder or an affiliated corporation will pay these expenses and forget to charge the new corporation, with the result that neither party gets to amortize them.
5. If the new corporation is dissolved before the end of the amortization period, any unamortized balance would be written off.

As mentioned previously, the above rules are taken from the tax law. Neither statutory nor GAAP pronouncements mention organization costs. However, any organization costs on the books would be nonadmitted assets for statutory purposes if the expenditures were not written off when incurred. For GAAP statements, most companies account for organization costs in the same manner as for tax purposes. This is the simplest approach to use for GAAP, considering the relative insignificance of organization costs to the total balance sheet and income statement.

START-UP COSTS

A new business, in addition to incurring organization costs, also incurs a variety of other expenses incident to the beginning of operations. Such expenses can fall into the following categories:

1. Preorganization Expenses

These are expenses incurred by the parent or founders prior to the formation of the entity. The most common examples are planning and investigative costs. For statutory purposes, these items are expensed by the parent or founder (if an insurance company). For GAAP purposes, such expenses are usually capitalized by the parent or founder and amortized over a period not to exceed 40 years (and expensed if the new entity is abandoned). For tax purposes, such expenses are capitalized and not amortized, but they may be expensed if and when the entity is abandoned.

2. Cost of Acquiring Funds

These costs are incurred to issue bonds or stock and include expenditures for underwriting and securities registration. They are expensed for statutory purposes and capitalized for GAAP and tax purposes. In the case of bonds or callable preferred stock, the capitalized costs would be amortized over the life of the security. In the case of noncancelable stock, GAAP amortization would be allowed and there would be no amortization for tax purposes. Stock issue costs are usually treated as a reduction of amounts paid in.

3. Preoperating Expenses

These are salaries, rent, and other expenses incurred by the entity after it is formed but before it begins operations. They are expensed for statutory and GAAP purposes. For tax purposes, they are often expensed as a practical matter, but the IRS may attempt to capitalize them if they are significant in amount and there is an extended period prior to operations.

4. Construction Period Interest and Taxes

These are incurred while an asset (usually a building) is being constructed and before the time it is placed in service or sold. Real estate taxes and interest on undeveloped land are in this category once construction activities begin, but not before. Construction activities are generally deemed not to begin until the land is actually altered, as opposed to the mere preparation of architect's plans.

Construction period interest and taxes are expensed for statutory purposes. For GAAP purposes, taxes are expensed and the interest is capitalized as a part of the asset cost and depreciated over the life of the asset. If there are no specific borrowings associated with the construction, a weighted average of the company's borrowing rates is used to impute the interest cost, which cannot exceed the total interest expense actually paid by the entity. For purposes of these computations, interest income is not offset against interest expense.

For tax purposes, real estate taxes as well as interest are capitalized. One-tenth of the capitalized amount is deducted in the year of disbursement, and the remaining 90 percent is amortized pro rata over 9 years, beginning with the year the asset is ready to be placed in service or sold.

5. Early Operating Expenses

The operating costs of the new company after it begins actively to conduct business are treated as expenses, exactly like the operating costs of a mature company. This is true even though the level of expenses and loss is higher for the new company. The expense requirement is the same for statutory, GAAP, and tax purposes. However, there may be special disclosures required for GAAP if the company is in a "development stage," meaning that significant revenue has not yet been received from operations. See Financial Accounting Standards Board (FASB) Statement 7.

RESEARCH AND DEVELOPMENT EXPENSES

The term "research and development" (R&D) has two different meanings. The first concerns technological or scientific research; the second covers marketing research and insurance product development. Another distinction is made between internally generated R&D and research results purchased from the outside.

For statutory purposes, all R&D expenditures are treated as expenses or as nonadmitted assets.

For GAAP purposes, R&D costs are also treated as expenses. However, the legal costs of applying for a patent would be capitalized and amortized over the patent's useful life of 17 years or less. The cost of acquiring or developing computer software is discussed in Chapter 8, Other Assets.

For tax purposes, the rules are a little more complex. Legal *and* research costs associated with purchasing or developing a patent would be amortized over the patent's remaining life of 17 years or less. Other internally incurred research costs of a technological or scientific nature may be expensed, or an election may be made to amortize them over a period of 60 months or more. In addition, there is a tax credit equal to 25 percent of the increase of such research expenditures over those of the previous year. Although the question is not completely settled, the internal cost of developing special software could be considered "technological research" and be treated under this category.

Internally incurred costs for marketing research and for insurance product development would generally be expensed as a practical matter, although conceivably the IRS could try to capitalize them and force them to be amortized over the product's expected useful life. No tax credit is available for increases in these expenditures.

The results of purchased research are usually expensed as a practical matter; however, if the amounts are large and a continuing life is evident, capitalization may be required. No tax credit is available.

TRADEMARKS AND TRADE NAMES

Insurance companies often have a variety of registered trademarks and trade names, both for the company and for individual products. For statutory purposes, all costs associated with a name or mark would be expensed or shown as a nonadmitted asset.

For GAAP purposes, the costs of developing or purchasing a name or mark would be capitalized and amortized over a period not to exceed 40 years. Any unamortized balance would be expensed if the name or mark were subsequently abandoned.

For tax purposes, the costs of development or purchase would also be capitalized, but they could not be amortized since the legal rights to the name or mark are generally renewable indefinitely. However, the costs could be expensed upon abandonment.

10

DEFERRED POLICY ACQUISITION COSTS

Policy acquisition costs are accounted for in some ways like prepaid expenses and in other ways like inventories. They are accounted for like prepaid expenses because these amounts benefit future periods. They are accounted for like inventories because policies must be in force and have continuing premiums to match with the unamortized expenses. For statutory reporting, policy acquisition costs cannot be deferred and become a period expense when they are paid. However, for statutory life insurance reporting, companies may be permitted to reduce the required reserves to a level that effectively defers the first-year acquisition costs to the second or third year. Such a method is not available for companies other than life insurance companies. Income tax reporting follows statutory reporting even though unearned premiums are recorded.

For generally accepted accounting principles, policy acquisition costs are deferred and amortized over future periods in order the more properly *to match them with future policy premiums. Since the accounting records of an insurance company are not maintained on the basis of generally accepted accounting principles, it is necessary to adjust the financial statements by the amount of unamortized acquisition costs.*

"Acquisition costs" has a meaning that is peculiar to financial reports prepared for insurance companies other than mutual life insurance and assessment companies and fraternal benefit societies. The term is not used in connection with statutory or income tax reports. These costs are defined as those related to the acquisition of new insurance contracts which require the payment of renewal premiums to continue them in force or as those having refundable unearned premiums. Costs which qualify as being deferrable are those which can reasonably be associated with the production of new business. The relationship of these costs to new business must be other than casual and should be easily identifiable as direct or allocated costs of production. For example, it could be asserted that the costs of developing new insurance products are incurred for the purpose of developing new business. However, until the new business is actually created and the premiums are received, those costs cannot be considered acquisition costs, although they may be deferrable as development or start-up costs.

In determining the adequacy of premiums, insurance companies must consider all expenses and generally make little distinction between acquisition or continuing expenses. For premium-determination purposes, the manner in which expenses are classified is much less important than assuring that all expenses are recoverable from policy premiums. Expenses are usually considered by separate "blocks" of business which must yield sufficient premiums to cover all expenses and yield a profit margin. By combining all business in a "block," a company can ignore special promotional products having losses because of inadequate premiums. Not all expenses included in a premium calculation will qualify as deferred policy acquisition costs.

Expenses reported on a statutory basis are classified as commissions and allowances, general expenses, and taxes, licenses, and fees for life and accident and health insurance companies—and as loss adjustment, other underwriting, and investment expenses for property and liability insurance companies. For that reason, it is necessary to understand the statutory expense classification in order more clearly to identify the costs that are subject to deferral and amortization.

Because of the differences in policy provisions between life insurance and accident and health insurance companies and property and liability insurance companies, deferred policy acquisition costs for each will be covered separately.

LIFE INSURANCE POLICIES

Most policies providing life insurance coverage are issued on a long-term basis and usually require the payment of periodic premiums for a fixed period or life. Deferred policy acquisition costs arise in the early years of a life insurance policy, with the bulk of the costs occurring in the first year. Because immediate recognition of these costs would distort the matching process with the related periodic premiums, such costs are accumulated at the beginning of the policy period and amortized in a reasonable manner over the future premium-paying periods. This process is the opposite of life insurance reserves, which are accrued ratably over the term of the policy to pay benefits when the policy matures.

In essence, the deferred policy acquisition costs provide a balancing account that prevents overstatement of future periodic income statements when acquisition costs are not incurred even though premiums continue to be paid. Although these amounts are not a component of life insurance reserves, they are often included as a factor in the formula for determining life reserves. This method ensures that the policy reserves and the related deferred acquisition costs are accrued and amortized using a single set of assumptions.

The factor method is preferable to the accountants' worksheet method, which determines the amortized portion of these costs in a manner similar to that used for determining depreciation for capital assets. The *accountants' worksheet method* is a simple matrix for allocating expenses ratably over a fixed number of years. The *factor method* is a mathematical method that directly relates both variable and fixed expenses to each policy in force. Since the factor method is an integral part of the life reserves calculation method, it will be determined on the same basis as for life reserves, i.e., seriatim basis, group basis, or other bases.

Expense Classifications

For purposes of determining gross premiums, expenses are usually classified as agents' compensation, other acquisition expenses, continuing maintenance expenses, termination expenses, and overhead expenses. These classifications include all statutory expenses and are allocated to each policy form for the purpose of determining gross premiums. For gross premium determination, the following allocations are made:

- Agents' compensation is usually allocated on a percentage-of-premium basis for each policy year.
- Other acquisition expenses are allocated on the basis of percentage of premium or on a dollar per policy or per unit of insurance for the first policy year.
- Maintenance expenses are allocated on the basis of dollars per policy for each policy year or a percentage of premiums for each policy year.
- Termination expenses are allocated on the basis of dollars per anticipated claims or dollars per units of insurance in force. Expenses related to voluntary terminations are usually allocated on the basis of dollars per each withdrawal.
- Overhead expenses are usually distributed to the preceding classification and allocated as previously described or separately allocated on the basis of dollars per policy for each policy year or a percentage of premium for each policy year.

The method used for allocating expenses for the gross premium calculation may be appropriate for determining deferred policy acquisition costs; however, the classification of specific expenses may be different. For purposes of determining those expenses qualifying for deferral as policy acquisition costs, the following analysis of statutory expense classifications will be helpful. Expense items appear in various exhibits and will be covered separately.

Commissions and Expense Allowances

Costs incurred in paying commissions on new and renewal business and reinsured policies are included in Exhibit 1, Part 2. Agents and brokers are paid a commission allowance on first-year and renewal premiums for the business they produce. The aggregate amount paid to agents and brokers for new business may be paid under a combination of compensation plans. These plans contemplate an incentive program for agents and brokers to offer and sell the policies underwritten by the company, to retain policies in force on previously written business, and to ensure quality control of the business by sharing profits on their production. Commission arrangements can be classified as follows:

Commissions on Premiums. Most commission arrangements are based on a percentage of premiums collected. Usually, the commissions are heaped into the first year, with smaller amounts paid for renewal premiums. Historically, this pattern of compensation has permitted the agent or broker to realize substantial commissions when the policies are written, while at the same time permitting a pattern of renewal commissions to provide long-term compensation benefits. The first-year commission rate is a competitive rate contemplated to encourage production of new business, but a maximum rate may be imposed by statute. The unregulated rate often ranges between 50 and 100 percent of the first-year premiums, although the amounts paid for selected policies may be lesser or greater than those amounts. The actual commissions paid are easily determined since they usually represent a percentage of premiums collected. These amounts qualify as deferred policy acquisition costs.

Contingent Commissions. Some companies have special arrangements with agents and brokers that permit the sharing of company profits for the business they produce. Often, the contingent amounts cannot be earned until the policies have been in force for more than 1 year and a specified minimum claim experience is met. Because contingent commissions depend upon future events, the amount of such commissions accrued either for statutory reporting or for inclusion in deferred policy acquisition costs should be based on the company's prior experience. For statutory and income tax reporting, the accrual of contingent commission results in a current period cost. For public reporting, these amounts qualify as deferred policy acquisition costs.

Bonuses, Trips, and Awards. To encourage the production of new business, special programs have been developed to provide agents and brokers with additional compensation in the form of bonuses, trips, and awards. These compensation programs are usually based on the attainment of production goals and are expressed in terms of new applications, new premiums, face amount of insurance, or a similar measurement basis. If at any reporting date these amounts are not fully earned, accruals must be provided based on production to date. For statutory and income tax reporting, the amounts so estimated are included as a period cost either as commissions or general expense. For public reporting, such amounts qualify as deferred policy acquisition costs.

Agents' Expense Reimbursement. Some agency agreements provide that the company will reimburse some or all of the expenses incurred in operating an agency office. The expenses may include rent and utilities, secretarial services, premium-collection costs, office equipment and supplies, and other related agency expenses. These programs usually have mutual benefits to the agent and the company and normally are not included in commission expenses. For statutory reporting, such amounts are often reported as agency expense allowances. However, to the extent that such expenses are more in the nature of branch office operations, they are included with the related other general expenses, and for public reporting, these amounts may qualify as deferred policy acquisition costs.

Other Commission Considerations. For statutory reporting, gross deferred premiums are offset by net premiums, which are recorded as an asset, and by an increase in loading on deferred premiums, which is recorded as a period cost. The commissions included in the increase in loading qualify as deferred policy acquisition costs to the extent that related gross deferred premiums are included in income. Often these amounts are reversed since reserves are restated to a midterminal basis, which eliminates the deferred premiums.

For statutory reporting, agents' commissions are allocated to ordinary, credit, industrial, and group life insurance. Deferred policy acquisition costs are determined by reallocating commissions to the various individual or group plans. For example, ordinary life insurance includes all life insurance policies issued other than industrial, credit, and group. The commissions applicable to individual life insurance contracts usually vary by the type of policy issued, and it is necessary to determine a commission factor for each policy or group of policies. For short-term contracts such as term insurance, commissions are generally expressed as a fixed percentage of the premiums. For ordinary life and endowment–type contracts, the commission factor includes some or all of the previously discussed compensation arrangements. The amount of commissions and other agents' compensation included in deferred policy acquisition costs should not vary significantly from the commission costs assumed in determining the premiums.

Agents or brokers are often paid a commission based on annual premiums even though the policyholder has elected to pay the premium semiannually, quarterly, or monthly. These excess amounts are often recorded as Agents' Balances, an asset. If for statutory reporting the excess amounts are included as a period cost, they should be reclassified when determining deferred policy acquisition costs. Agents' balances charged off may qualify as deferred policy acquisition costs if renewal premiums continue to be paid on the original policies. For statutory reporting, such amounts should not be written off if they can be recovered from terminated agents' nonvested future renewal commissions applicable to policies that created the excess commission payments.

Some agents' commission contracts provide for the commutation of renewal commissions. For statutory reporting, these amounts are accrued as a liability and charged as a period cost. For public reporting, such amounts should be deferred and amortized over the remaining period that premiums are collected.

For statutory reporting, if the sum of commissions, bonuses, awards, and special compensation arrangements exceeds the amount of commissions included in the loading factor for gross premiums, such excess amounts are recorded as a liability Cost of Collection on Premiums in Excess of Total Loading Thereon. This account has little if any bearing upon the determination of deferred policy acquisition costs; consequently, it should be eliminated.

For convenience of closing, companies often cease processing transactions a few days before the end of the year. This allows the company a little leeway in preparing year-end closing schedules. However, if premiums have been processed and included in income without providing for agents' compensation, an entry is required to record a liability for Commissions to Agents Due or Accrued, with an offsetting commission charged to period costs. Such commissions qualify for deferral and amortization.

For statutory reporting, a liability is recorded for Agents' Credit Balances even though the amounts due from agents are classified as nonadmitted assets. For public reporting, all agents' balances are combined to determine their effect on deferred policy acquisition costs.

Premiums collected before the end of the year but not processed are recorded in the statutory report as Remittances and Items Not Allocated. To the extent that these represent material amounts, they should be reclassified and recorded as premium income, with allowances made for agents' commissions. These commissions should be included in deferred policy acquisition costs.

Commissions and Expense Allowances on Reinsurance Assumed. These amounts are incurred in connection with business assumed from other producing companies. Often, the amounts are not separated between the amounts reimbursed to the ceding company for commissions and for other expenses. Consequently, for statutory reporting, the total commissions and expense allowances are recorded as a single item and separated by lines of business for industrial life, ordinary and group life, ordinary and group annuities, credit life, and accident and health coverage for group, credit, and other lines. These amounts are separately identified for amounts attributable to first-year business, renewal business, and single premium business.

For public reporting, the commissions and other expense allowances should be identified and, if possible, classified by product lines in a manner similar to that for costs identified for direct business. Reinsurance commissions and expense allowances incurred for assuming yearly renewable term products are not usually included in the deferred policy acquisition if it expires at the end of a calendar year. When policies expire at other dates, however, then for both interim reporting and annual reporting these amounts should be recorded as deferred policy acquisition costs to the extent that the business in force has an unearned premium balance.

For policies that are assumed and continue to be in force, such as with coinsurance agreements, the commission and expense allowances are treated the same as for direct business. However, to the extent that the amounts cannot be separated between commission and expense allowances, the total amount may be amortized as a single sum, using the factor approach.

Commissions and Expense Allowances on Reinsurance Ceded. For statutory reporting, these amounts are recorded as an income item even though they represent reimbursements for commissions and other expenses in producing such business. These amounts are reported separately by line of business in the annual statement for industrial, ordinary and group life, ordinary and group annuities, credit life, and accident and health group, credit, and other.

For public reporting, these amounts should be separately accounted for as commission, other expenses, and reinsurance profits. Ceding commissions and other expenses should be deducted from the direct expenses incurred in producing the business. Renewal commissions and expenses that are level and in proportion to premiums received should be charged as period costs. To the extent that allowances for coinsurance include a profit allowance, it should be amortized over the expected premium-paying period. Coinsurance allowances for single premium policies should be included as an offset to period costs.

Commission and expense allowances received in connection with the sale of a block of business should be recognized in full in the year of sale.

Commissions and expense allowances on ceded yearly renewable term business are treated as a current-period item unless there is an unearned premium balance on the policies ceded.

General Insurance Expenses

For statutory reporting, these expenses are included in Exhibit 5 and are separated between life insurance, accident and health insurance, and investment expenses. Investment expenses should reflect the direct and indirect costs of operating the investment department and should not enter into the determination of deferred policy acquisition costs. While commission expenses can be directly or reasonably related to the production of new business, other expenses are not so easily identified. Costs related to certain departments (such as underwriting and issue) should be included in deferred policy acquisition costs; however, such amounts cannot be derived from the statutory annual statement and must be determined by a separate costs analysis. Underwriting or selection costs include the salaries of supervisors and underwriters, clerical support salaries, inspection reports and medical examination fees, printing and forms, telephone, and other related costs. The costs of issuing the policies include the basic policy forms, the cost of calculating premiums and setting up records, and the cost of delivering the policies. Overhead costs—including executive management, electronic data processing costs, rent, and similar items—can be included if they are appropriately allocated to the basic deferred costs.

Following is an analysis of general expenses as they are classified in Exhibit 5 of the annual statement. To the extent that they are incurred to issue new premium-paying life insurance policies, these expenses qualify as deferred policy acquisition costs.

Rent. These expenses may be considered in two categories. Self-rent, the first category, is the amount charged for the company's occupancy of its own buildings. It is computed as a fair rental charge covering business use of their own property and is offset by a credit to real estate investment income. For public reporting, such rent does not affect deferred policy acquisition costs since the entries are eliminated.

The second category of rent includes amounts paid to third parties for home or branch office rent and amounts paid for utilities, taxes, building maintenance, and related services. Rent from sublease space is deducted. Rent expense incurred to support sales agencies, mail-order solicitations, underwriting, and issue functions should be included in deferred policy acquisition costs to the extent that they are directly or reasonably associated with the production of new business.

Salaries and Wages. In addition to basic payroll costs, this account includes directors' fees, amounts paid to agents in excess of commissions, and fees of consultants. Special studies must be done to determine amounts that qualify as deferred policy acquisition costs.

Salary costs which are paid to agents and to branch office and field managers and which are directly related to new production should be classified as deferred policy acquisition costs. Salary costs incurred to train new agents, develop new agencies, service existing business, and provide overall agency management should be excluded. Salary costs incurred in underwriting and issuing policies, whether or not the policies are taken, qualify as deferred policy acquisition costs. Salaries paid for home office agency administration and supervision and for clerical and office support usually do not qualify. Salary costs for executive supervision, maintaining records including electronic data processing salaries, personnel, printing, and other support services are in the nature of operating expenses and normally do not qualify as deferred policy acquisition costs.

For companies engaged in direct response business, a significantly larger portion of salaries and wages can be attributable to the production of new business. For example, advertising, electronic data processing, printing, mail processing, clerical typing, and supervisory and executive salaries may qualify as deferred policy acquisition costs, since they are more directly traceable to the production of new business than to similar expenses incurred by companies writing through agents and brokers.

Contributions for Benefit Plans for Employees. These costs include contributions for pension plans to cover current costs and a pro rata portion of prior service costs. They also include benefits for disability income protection, life insurance, health and accident insurance, and similar costs. For statutory reporting, some companies include the current pension contributions in this account and charge prior service costs directly to surplus. These costs are included in deferred policy acquisition costs to the extent that they relate to salaries and wages that are deferrable.

Contributions for Benefit Plans for Agents. These amounts are similar to those incurred for employee benefit plans. To the extent that these costs are incurred because of new business production, they should be included in deferred policy acquisition costs.

Other Employee Welfare. Expenses incurred for employees' meals, organizations' dues, extra military service pay, company-sponsored physical examination programs, recreational facilities, and similar benefits are included in this account. Because these benefits are not clearly associated with duties that are directly related to the production of new business, they are not included in deferred policy acquisition costs.

Legal Fees and Expenses. Costs incurred in administrative and court appearances, legislative hearings, and similar activities are included in this category. However, salaries paid to the company legal staff and outside costs incurred in connection with claims or real estate transactions are included under salaries and wages, claim costs, and real estate costs, respectively. These costs should not be deferred.

Medical Examination Fees. All fees incurred for medical examinations in connection with new business applications should be included in deferred policy acquisition costs. Fees incurred for reinstatement, policy changes, claims and employment should be excluded.

Inspection Report Fees. Inspection reports are an important part of underwriting new business, and such costs should be included as deferred policy acquisition costs. Any reporting fees related to reinstatements, policy changes, claims and employment should be excluded.

Fees of Public Accountants and Consulting Actuaries. These costs include fees for periodic examinations, income tax services, and consulting services for systems and policy design. These and similar fees are incurred on an ongoing basis and should not be deferred.

Expense of Investigation and Settlement of Policy Claims. Fees related to the investigation, litigation and settlement of policy claims are ongoing costs and should not be deferred.

Traveling Expenses. All travel costs of employees, directors, and agents are included in this category, as are the costs of maintaining and operating company-owned automobiles, of transferring employees, and of company entertainment. Little if any of these expenses qualifies as deferred policy acquisition costs.

Advertising. This account includes sales brochures, periodical advertising, specialty products such as calendars and pens, and similar expenses. Also, advertising agency fees, paper stock, and other supplies required for printing brochures and pamphlets are included. Direct response companies should include a significant amount of these expenses in deferred policy acquisition costs. Companies operating through agents and brokers should treat these costs as institutional advertising unless they can be reasonably associated with some units of production.

Postage, Express, and Telegraph and Telephone. For the most part, these items represent nonsalary period costs incurred for mailroom operations, telephone systems, freight, and similar costs. Companies having direct response marketing programs should defer an appropriate part of the postage and telephone costs. For most other companies, little if any of these costs should be deferred. However, costs incurred in purchasing mail-order equipment and telephone systems may qualify as costs that are otherwise amortizable.

Printing and Stationery. Costs included in this category include policy forms, rate books, in-house publications, financial reporting, office supplies and stationery, and related types of expenses. For statutory reporting, all purchases for supplies are charged to this account even though many may not be consumed during the current period. For public reporting, prepaid amounts may be amortized over the period benefited.

Cost or Depreciation of Furniture and Equipment. For statutory reporting, the cost of all furniture and equipment except home office building, mailroom, and telephone equipment may be reported in this account. Alternatively, the amounts may be capitalized and only the depreciation charge recorded here. In the latter instance, the undepreciated cost of such equipment is reported as a nonadmitted asset. For all other reporting purposes, the equipment should be capitalized and depreciated over its useful life. Depreciation expense qualifies for deferred policy acquisition costs to the extent that it relates to commissions or salary expenses that are deferred.

Rental of Equipment. All rental charges for office equipment, except for telephone rental equipment, is charged to this account and should not be deferred.

Books and Periodicals. The costs of current publications and books are charged to this account and do not qualify for deferral.

Bureau and Association Dues. These costs include dues and assessments related to business and professional organizations, except for amounts reported as employee and agents' welfare, and should not be included in deferred policy acquisition costs.

Insurance, Except on Real Estate. The costs of insurance for company property—other than on real estate, employee work-related injuries, fidelity and surety bonds, and related coverages—have only an incidental relationship to the production of new business and normally should not be included in deferred policy acquisition costs. However, to the extent that insurance premiums are prepaid, they may be deferred and amortized over the period benefited.

Miscellaneous Losses. Work-related losses not reimbursed by insurance represent period charges and should not be deferred.

Collection and Bank Service Charges. These costs are period charges and should not be deferred.

Sundry General Expenses. Most expenses that cannot be included in other expense categories are reported as sundry general expenses. However, if a single type of expense represents a significant portion of this category, it should be set out separately. Charitable contributions, company meetings and functions, costs of fees and services not includable in other expense categories, miscellaneous supplies, and similar items are typical sundry general expenses. These expenses usually represent period costs and should not be deferred.

Group Service and Administration Fees. Fees, allowances, and expense reimbursements incurred in connection with the sale and administration of group business should be included in this expense category. The portion of such costs that is related to the production of new business should be included in deferred policy acquisition costs. The portion of such costs incurred to provide continuous service for these policies is included under period costs and should not be deferred.

Agency Expense Allowances. Amounts included in this expense category include the costs of agency offices paid by the company, training expense allowances, and similar types of expenditures. Amounts paid to agents representing compensation for new business should be excluded from this account. Agency and branch office expenses incurred in connection with new business production should be included with other deferred policy acquisition costs. Other amounts represent period costs and should not be deferred.

Agents' Balances Charged Off. Advances made to agents which are not recoverable from them or from renewal commissions for business remaining in force are period costs and should not be deferred.

Agency Conferences Other than Local Meetings. All costs, including travel costs, incurred in connection with agency conferences should be included in this expense category. None of these costs should be deferred unless they are directly related to new business production.

Real Estate Expenses. All expenses directly related to real estate operations, whether home office, branch office, or investment properties, should be charged to this account. They include the salaries of home office and branch office employees exclusively involved in real estate operations, building maintenance and repair costs, property insurance, fees paid for real estate management, and related costs. These are operating costs and should not be included in deferred policy acquisition costs or separately deferred.

Investment Expenses Not Included Elsewhere. These costs include investment advisors, trustees, and custodian fees, fees and assessments to perfect rights as bond or stock owners, and similar nonrecurring costs. None of these costs should be deferred.

Depreciation on Real Estate. This cost is reported separately in Exhibit 2 and should not be included in deferred policy acquisition costs except to the extent that it may be directly related to other costs incurred in new business production.

Taxes, Licenses, and Fees (Excluding Federal Income Taxes)

For statutory reporting, these are classified in Exhibit 6 as real estate taxes, state insurance department license fees, state taxes on premiums, other state taxes (including amounts for employee benefits), social security taxes, and all other taxes. Amounts paid for insurance licenses and examination fees and for premiums represent period costs and should not be deferred. Real estate and social security taxes, to the extent that they relate to space used for or salaries paid for functions directly related to the production of new business should be allocated to those amounts. All other amounts represent operating costs and should not be deferred.

ANNUITY POLICIES

The elements of deferrable acquisition costs for annuities are the same as those described for life insurance policies. Whether any such costs should be deferred depends upon the premium-paying basis of the annuities. The following is a description of methods available for paying annuity premiums:

Annual Premium Deferred Annuities

These policies are written on a basis similar to that for ordinary life insurance policies. Periodic premium payments are required in order to receive the promised benefits in the future. During the premium-paying period, interest is added to the accumulation so that at the annuity starting date there will be sufficient funds, along with interest on the unpaid amounts, to pay the promised periodic benefits. The policy can be surrendered and funds withdrawn during the deferred period. A death benefit equal to the accumulated funds or to all prior premium payments will be paid prior to the annuity starting date. A policyholder who ceases paying premiums may request a paid-up annuity for a reduced amount. The policyholder may usually request an earlier or later annuity starting date, and appropriate adjustments will be made to the benefit amount.

Since these contracts require periodic premium payments, deferred policy acquisition costs are amortized in a manner similar to that for ordinary life insurance policies. The aggregate amount of deferred policy acquisition costs will vary, depending upon the assumptions made for interest, mortality, and withdrawal rates. Withdrawal estimates should reflect company or industry experience with such policies.

Single Premium Deferred Annuities

A future annuity paid for with a single lump sum will not produce deferred policy acquisition costs since there are no future premium payments required. Consequently, all costs incurred in selling and issuing the annuity become period costs when the deferred annuity is issued.

Single Premium Immediate Annuities

These annuities become payable to the policyholder immediately, as provided in the annuity contract. Consequently, no future premiums will be received and all costs incurred in selling and issuing the annuity should be expensed currently.

Flexible Premium Deferred Annuities

These policies are similar to annual premium deferred annuities except that fixed annual premium payments are not required. If the policies require premium contributions from time to time, some deferral of policy acquisition costs is appropriate. If, however, no future premium payments are required, then payments received should be considered single premium deferred annuity payments, and policy acquisition costs should not be deferred.

Annual Premium Deferred Variable Annuities

These annuity premiums are invested in a separate account of the insurance company. The value of each annuity is dependent upon the investment experience in that account. Deferred policy acquisition costs are recoverable from the initial premium sales charge and management fees paid by the separate account. If annual premiums are required, deferred policy acquisition costs may be matched with these amounts. First-year policy origination fees charged to the policyholder should be netted against the related first-year acquisition costs. Separate accounts are covered in more detail in Chapter 21, Variable Annuities and Life Insurance.

ACCIDENT AND HEALTH POLICIES

These policies provide reimbursement for costs of hospital and surgical expenses, major medical expenses arising from a single illness or accident, accident only policies, dental care policies, disability income protection policies, and specialized coverages for health and accident claims. The costs to be deferred on these policies are similar to the costs described under life insurance policies. The premium payment method and guarantees for continuing the policy in force are important considerations in determining the costs to be deferred. For purposes of determining deferred policy acquisition costs, these policies may be grouped in the following categories:

Cancelable Policies

Unlike life insurance and annuity policies, some accident and health insurance policies are cancelable at the option of the insurance company. Acquisition costs incurred to issue these policies normally expire annually. Therefore, these costs are amortized on a pro rata basis in proportion to earned premiums. The unexpired portion of deferred policy acquisition costs on these policies is usually determined by its ratio to unearned premiums. However, to the extent that a company's experience will support an assumption that cancelable policies will remain in force over an extended period of time, policy acquisition costs can be deferred similar to noncancelable policies.

Guaranteed Renewable Policies

Because these policies can be renewed by paying current premiums, it can usually be demonstrated that such policies will remain in force even though the premiums for all policyholders may be increased. The costs incurred in selling and issuing these policies, including nonlevel commission and other costs paid on renewal premiums, should be deferred and accounted for in a manner similar to that for life insurance policies.

Noncancelable Policies

These policies have provisions much like those for life insurance, since the premiums cannot be increased and the policies cannot be canceled as long as the scheduled premiums are paid. Deferred policy acquisition costs include commission, issue, and general expenses, much as is provided for life insurance policies. Nonlevel costs incurred in the first and renewal years should be aggregated and amortized, using appropriate estimates for withdrawals, morbidity, and interest. As with life insurance policies, these factors are usually included with the formula used in reserve computations.

Group Policies

These policies are usually cancelable, and the policy acquisition costs deferred are amortized over the period that the premiums are earned. Unless it can be demonstrated that such policies will continue in force for an extended period, the deferred costs expire at each annual premium-paying date.

CREDIT LIFE AND HEALTH POLICIES

Because these policies usually provide short-term protection, gross premiums are recognized in proportion to the amount of insurance in force. Deferred policy acquisition costs should be recognized ratably with earned premiums. If the reserves for these policies are calculated on the same basis as that for long-term contracts, the deferred policy acquisition costs should be amortized as part of the reserve calculation.

LOCKED-IN ASSUMPTIONS AND LOSS RECOGNITION

These two elements are considered together because they are interdependent in accounting for life insurance company operations. The concept that probable losses must be recognized currently and that reserve assumptions, whether liabilities or assets, once made should continue through future accounting periods, is based on a number of long-standing accounting rules. Some of the more significant accounting rules are the following:

- Revenues should not be anticipated.
- Cost of production should be matched against periodic revenue.
- A proper distribution of costs should be made between assets and expenses.
- Revenues should not be misused to shift income or losses arbitrarily from one period to another.
- Nonrecurring gains or losses should be recognized in the period in which they occur.
- All known liabilities should be recorded.
- Unexpired costs are those which are applicable to the production of future revenues.
- Accounting principles should be consistently applied between periods.

Locked-in Assumptions

Original assumptions should not be increased even though actual experience may indicate that the use of these assumptions may result in some mismatching of costs with future periodic revenue. The "penalty rule" that precludes these changes is that revenues should not be anticipated. The locked-in assumption rule is also necessary in order to ensure the consistent application of accounting principles between periods. Consequently, if subsequent experience demonstrates that there has been a favorable change in mortality, interest, or withdrawal assumptions, then the improvement is recognized in each period in which it occurs and is measured against the locked-in assumptions.

An opposite conclusion is reached if subsequent experience produces unfavorable experience that is expected to continue in the future. This is because of the rule that all known liabilities should be recorded currently. To do otherwise would be to defer losses into the future, whereas such losses should instead be recognized in the period in which they occur.

Loss Recognition

Losses on long-term policies occur because the assumptions used in determining premiums or in anticipating losses fail to materialize. Future policy premiums and benefits can be affected by unfavorable experience with mortality, investment earnings, withdrawals and terminations, and maintenance expenses. These losses can be summarized as a deficiency that arises when the sum of the expected future gross premiums and the current liability for future policy benefits is less than the sum of the expected future benefits, maintenance costs, and unamortized acquisition costs. If the deficiency becomes material in total, revised assumptions will be required in order to determine policy reserves. The effect of using restated reserves is that future profits will not emerge except to the extent that favorable experience develops. However, in determining revised assumptions, it is inappropriate to create current losses with the expectation that income in future periods will be realized.

Loss recognition may be determined on a policy-by-policy basis; however, it is more likely determined on a line-of-business basis. Even though a line of business develops profits, a loss on some policies should be recognized if failure to do so would result in line-of-business losses in future periods.

POLICIES WITH HIGH PREMIUMS AND BENEFITS

If these policies require a fixed annual premium, then deferred policy acquisition costs are accumulated and deferred in a manner similar to that for ordinary life insurance policies. If, on the other hand, the policyholder is permitted flexibility in making premium payments, then other factors must be considered in the accumulation and amortization of deferred policy acquisition costs. If future premiums cannot be reasonably determined, then each premium received should be considered a single premium, in which case deferred acquisition costs do not arise.

Because of diverse policy provisions, no single factor is controlling in the determination of expected future premiums. The following is a summary of significant factors that enter into the determination of expected future premiums:

Product Design

Some policies look very much like whole life insurance, with an emphasis on cash accumulation and investment return; some other policies require only an initial premium but permit payment of additional premiums to increase the cash value and insurance coverage; and other policies may require small annual premiums but permit payment of larger amounts. Even though policies do not require annual premiums, they are designed to provide greater benefits if annual premiums are paid. A review of policy provisions and of the underlying assumptions used in profit studies is necessary in order to determine the achievability of future premium projections.

Cost of Insurance Protection

Policies of this type normally use deductions from cash accumulation to cover the cost of pure insurance protection. The premium charge for this 1-year term coverage may exceed the net additions to the cash accumulation and cause the policy to terminate if future premiums are not received. The annual cost of the term insurance protection may affect the rate at which withdrawals occur.

Interest Guarantees

Guaranteed interest rates may be level for a number of years, short-term, or tied to outside investment sources. The amount of interest added to the cash accumulation may provide support for the achievability of annual premium projections.

Expense Charges

Some policies permit the deduction of an assumed cost for commission and other acquisition expenses from the initial and renewal premiums before cash accumulation accounts are increased. Other policies permit the inclusion of the entire premium in cash accumulation and impose a decreasing surrender charge over a period of years. Most policies include an annual maintenance expense charge; this charge, combined with other charges to the cash accumulation, may affect the manner in which renewal premiums are received.

Marketing

Policies may be sold by the company's ordinary individual agency sales force, by an insurance broker, or through salary savings plans. The extent to which policyholders are contacted about renewal premiums and the convenience with which premiums may be paid will affect the continuity of renewal premium payments.

Agents' Compensation

Sales commissions on these products may provide high first-year rates for initial premiums and low rates for renewal premiums. Some agency agreements provide a level commission rate based on a flat dollar amount per policy, a percentage of the premiums paid, and a level dollar amount per $1000 face amounts of the policy. The compensation program may determine agents' attitudes about the manner in which policyholders pay renewal premiums.

Replacement Pricing

Generally, there are no special pricing arrangements when existing policies of other companies are converted to policies with high premiums and benefits. However, if the replacement is internal (that is, if the company's current policies are replaced by its own newer high-premium and high-benefit policies), then the pricing of new products, the allowances made on policy surrenders, and the special agents' compensation arrangements will affect the gain or loss on the old policies and the continuity with which renewal premiums are paid.

The assumptions made about future premiums will determine the level of and the amortization period for the deferred policy acquisition costs for these policies. Because of the short-term experience which the insurance industry has had with these policies, the provision for adverse deviation is an important consideration for assumptions made about expected renewal premiums.

Replacement Costs

The accounting for replacement costs was usually ignored as being immaterial when only traditional life insurance products were offered. This was because there was little opportunity to convert accumulated cash values to a new policy that provided significantly lower term premiums and higher interest earnings. Newer policies, however, are often sold by making these cost and benefit comparisons and by creating a link between the replacement of old policies with the newer versions.

In order to avoid deferring replacement costs that result in future losses or to avoid charging current earnings with costs and losses that should be matched against future premiums, the following items should be considered in determining deferred policy acquisition costs:

External Policy Replacement. Initial premiums arising from the surrender benefits of policies sold by other companies do not create deferred policy replacement costs in the new companies. The unamortized deferred acquisition costs on surrendered policies are a current loss for the company paying the surrender benefits. The deferrable costs arising from external policy replacement are the same as those which qualify for deferral for other new business; they include commission and selling costs, underwriting and issue costs, and applicable portions of general overhead costs.

Internal Replacement Policies. All new qualifying acquisition costs incurred in issuing replacement policies should be deferred. In addition, the following items should be considered in determining those replacement costs which qualify for deferral:

- The unamortized balance of deferred policy acquisition costs on the old policy, to the extent that new costs do not exceed maximum deferral costs, should be considered for deferral.
- Nonrecoverable losses such as surrender costs, policy accounting costs, and similar items incurred in connection with the surrender of the old policy should be charged to current operations.
- Current operations should not be charged with the unamortized deferred acquisition costs of the replaced policy if this charge will result in creating income in future periods.
- The gains or losses on old policies arising from the difference between surrender proceeds and life insurance reserves released should be included in the determination of deferred policy acquisition costs.
- Investment gains or losses incurred to provide surrender benefits on old policies should be recognized in current operations.

□ The recoverability of deferred policy acquisition costs should be considered separately for replacement policies; it will likely require new assumptions about withdrawals, mortality, and interest.

Deferred policy acquisition costs on replacement policies are subject to the loss recognition tests required for all other life insurance policies.

PROPERTY AND LIABILITY INSURANCE POLICIES

Most property and liability insurance policies are issued on a short-term basis with premiums paid in advance. Although some policies may be issued for a term extending 1 to 5 years in the future or for periods of less than 6 months, most policies are issued for periods of 6 months to 1 year. These policies are usually renewable at the option of the issuing company, and the premiums may be adjusted at each renewal date. Consequently, new deferred policy acquisition costs arise each time a policy is renewed. Except for a few coverages requiring a single premium payment or providing guaranteed renewable options, all premiums are collected and earned over a short-term period.

Unlike most life insurance coverages, which pay a specified benefit, property and liability insurance provides indemnity against loss for all covered claims. Unless there are deductible provisions, all insured losses are indemnified up to the maximum policy limits. As the claims experience changes over time, premium adjustments are made in recognition of the change in claim cost. Because deferred policy acquisition costs are related to premiums earned, a change in premium rates can affect the total acquisition costs that may be deferred.

Statutory accounting rules require that all acquisition costs be expensed in the period in which they are incurred. Public reporting, on the other hand, requires that these costs be accrued and amortized over the period the premiums are earned. To achieve a matching of premiums and expenses, it is necessary to compare the acquisition costs incurred with the premiums written.

Premiums written are the sum of gross policy premiums, less return premiums, on all new and renewal business for the year. These amounts are summarized by line of business in Part 2C in the statutory annual statement and could be reproduced by adding gross premiums, less return premiums, on individual policies having new or renewal anniversary dates during the year. The premiums written constitute the denominator, which is compared to the incurred acquisition costs (the numerator). Applying this fraction to unearned premiums will provide an estimate of the unamortized balance of deferred acquisition costs. Companies writing many lines of business and using more advanced cost accounting methods will determine the unamortized balance for each line of business. Before the introduction of generally accepted accounting principles, companies would often use rule-of-thumb fractions to estimate these amounts—as a means of determining an amount described as "equity in unearned premiums."

Because of different policy terms, commission rates, and underwriting and inspection costs, advanced cost accounting methods should be used in determining unamortized acquisition costs for all except small companies or those having limited lines of business. In the latter instance, the aggregate method will likely be sufficient to demonstrate the reasonableness of unamortized acquisition costs.

Qualifying acquisition costs will vary depending upon how products are sold and issued. The nature of some costs incurred, such as agents' commissions and premium taxes, are generally recognized as qualifying for deferral, while other costs must be reviewed to determine whether they qualify. The following is a summary of costs incurred in operating a property and liability company:

Claims Adjustment Services

This category includes fees and expenses incurred in connection with the investigation and payment of policy claims. It includes the cost of independent adjusters and legal defense costs—including lawyers, bond premiums, court reporters, filing fees, medical and expert testimony, witness fees, medical examinations, processing fees, cost of credit report, and other related court costs and fees. Employee compensation costs incurred in an investigation, settlement, or defending claims are excluded from this category and reported as employee compensation and related expenses. All reinsured claim adjustment expenses, whether assumed or ceded, should be included.

The cost of claim adjustment services should not be included in deferred policy acquisition costs.

Commission and Brokerage

All payments to agents, managers, brokers, or others that are determined on the basis of a percentage of premiums for production are included in this account. Amounts of commission and brokerage paid to management, supervisors, or employees for commissions and brokerage not related to their duties as employees are also included. Commissions and other amounts paid for reinsurance assumed, except amounts that are paid for underwriting and claim expenses incurred under quota share or pooling arrangements, are also included in this account. Commissions and other allowances received on reinsurance ceded, except actual expense reimbursements for underwriting and claims in a quota share or pooling arrangement, are credited to this account. Contingent commissions paid on assumed business or received on ceded business and policy and membership fees are recorded separately.

This account does not include: any salary costs; allowances to managers, agents, or employees not computed as a percentage of premiums; payments for special services; or any other amounts paid that are not directly related to new or renewal business and not paid as a percentage of premiums or production.

All amounts included in commission and brokerage should qualify as deferred policy acquisition costs.

Allowances to Managers and Agents

All allowances paid to agents, brokers, managers, and other producers of new and renewal business, other than amounts classified as commission and brokerage, should be included in this account. The cost of travel expenses and costs related to conventions and meetings should also be included.

Amounts paid as reimbursement for incurred expenses, such as taxes, license fees, advertising and related expenses, should be excluded from this account and classified with other company expenses. Fees paid to agents and brokers for claim adjustment services, underwriting reports, audit of assureds' records, and similar items should also be excluded and reported in other expense classifications. Salaries paid for services other than production of new business should be included with other salary costs.

Most of the costs included in allowances to managers and agents should qualify as deferred policy acquisition costs.

Advertising

The cost of fees for advertising agents, public relations representatives, and other outside services should be included in this account. Other includable costs are television and radio spots, billboards, advertising space in newspapers and periodicals, artwork and printing for pamphlets, directory listings, advertising materials (such as calendars and signs made avaliable for agents' use or distribution), and similar expenses.

Employee salary costs, loss-prevention literature, recruiting advertisements, employee publications, and similar costs are excluded from advertising expenses and reported elsewhere.

The costs of advertising to promote company products and services should qualify for deferred policy acquisition costs. Costs incurred for institutional-type advertising generally do not qualify for deferral.

Boards, Bureaus, and Associations

Dues, fees, and assessments paid to rating organizations, statistical agencies, underwriting boards, and inspection bureaus qualify as deferred acquisition costs to the extent that they are associated with underwriting and issuing policies. Fees paid for rating plans and manuals qualify for deferral to the extent that changes in prices and coverages provide support for new and renewal business.

Amounts paid to other associations and advisory organizations usually constitute institutional costs, which do not qualify for deferral. The cost of services provided by engineering, loss prevention, and claim organizations usually do not qualify for deferral. Payments to state industrial commissions, security funds, and other agencies, as well as allowances made under reinsurance contracts for these expenses, are excluded from this account and classified separately elsewhere.

Surveys and Underwriting Reports

The cost of property surveys, credit checks, appraisals, commercial reporting services, fire records, medical examiners' fees, and similar items usually qualify for deferral as underwriting costs. All costs related to employees' salaries, credit reports for new employees, fees for physical examinations, and similar costs are excluded from this classification and included elsewhere.

Audit of Assureds' Records

Fees paid for auditing payrolls, as well as other premium-based costs, are included in this account and qualify for partial deferral to the extent that additional premium income is developed. If these costs are for routine checks to ascertain policyholders' compliance with payroll and other premium-based reporting, they should not be deferred.

Salaries

All salaries, overtime allowances, bonus and other contingent compensation payments, termination allowances, training allowances, and any other form of employee compensation are included in this classification. Since all employee salaries and other compensation are included except those related to company-owned real estate, it is necessary to review operating departments to ascertain the deferrable portion of these costs.

Generally, all costs incurred in agency operation (except for recruiting and training), in underwriting and issue, and in product advertising qualify for deferral. Allocable portions of executive and supervisory salaries may qualify for deferral to the extent that they are incurred in the production of new and renewal business. Salary costs incurred in electronic data processing functions that are directly related to underwriting and issue functions also qualify for deferral. Other salary costs incurred to provide policy maintenance and support services usually do not qualify for deferral, except to the extent that they are included in other overhead costs, which are allocable to the production of new business.

Employee Relations and Welfare

The cost of funding employee retirement programs, group life insurance, accident and health insurance, workers' compensation, and other similar employee benefit programs qualify for deferral to the extent that they are allocable to qualifying salaries. Other costs such as employee physical examinations, training programs, background checks, credit reports, recruiting costs, entertainment programs, and similar costs do not qualify for deferral. Costs incurred in providing employee meals are overhead costs that may be allocable to qualifying salary costs.

Insurance

Costs incurred for premiums to protect against losses arising from public liability, fidelity or surety, personal property, automobile, and similar claims do not qualify for deferral except to the extent that these amounts can be allocated as items of overhead.

Directors' Fees

Fees paid to directors and related costs for attending meetings usually do not qualify for deferral.

Travel and Travel Items

The costs of transportation, lodging, and meals and related expenses incurred by employees while traveling are included in this account. Also included are the costs of operating or renting automobiles; expenses incurred for transfer of employees; the dues and fees of social and civic clubs; membership dues and subscriptions for legal, accounting, actuarial, and other professional associations; and similar costs. Most of these costs are not incurred for the direct production of new and renewal business; however, some of these costs qualify as overhead that is allocable to deferred policy acquisition costs.

Rent and Rent Items

All rental costs for home and branch offices and all utilities, interest and taxes, repair and maintenance, and similar costs are included in this category. Rent charged for space occupied in company-owned buildings is also included in this account, but rental costs for furniture and equipment are included elsewhere. Portions of rental costs, excluding self-charged rent, are directly allocable to operations involved in selling, underwriting, and issuing new policies and should be included in deferred policy acquisition costs. Other costs do not qualify for deferral except to the extent that such amounts can be allocated to overhead items.

Equipment

The cost of renting or maintaining office equipment and furniture, as well as the depreciation on furniture and equipment, is included in this account. The cost of furniture and equipment charged to this account should be reclassified to a fixed asset account. Costs in this account are deferrable to the extent that they can be allocated to selling, underwriting, issue, and overhead costs.

Printing and Stationery

The costs of printing or purchasing policy forms qualify as deferred policy acquisition costs. Other costs incurred for printing or for purchasing office supplies, stationery, photocopies, newspapers and periodicals, and similar items do not qualify for deferred policy acquisition costs except to the extent that such costs can be allocated as overhead. Excess supplies intended for use in future periods may qualify for deferral as prepaid items.

Postage, Telephone and Telegraph, Exchange and Express

The cost of telephone service and postage, to the extent that it can be allocated to selling, underwriting, issue, or overhead, qualifies for deferral. Other costs incurred for freight, express charges, bank charges, and similar items generally do not qualify for deferral.

Legal and Auditing

These costs include fees paid for investment advice, legal costs (excluding claim costs), auditing fees, tax services, and custodian and transfer services. These and related costs generally do not qualify as deferred policy acquisition costs.

Taxes, Licenses, and Fees

The largest expenses in this category are the premium taxes paid to state and local governments. These taxes are incurred because of new and renewal premiums and qualify as deferred policy acquisition costs. Payroll taxes allocable to selling, underwriting, issue, and overhead also qualify for deferral.

Most other taxes and fees—including assessments for fire protection, state industrial commissions, state security funds, insurance department fees for agents' licenses, annual permit fees, and examinations—are institutional costs and usually do not qualify for deferral. Likewise, other taxes and fees paid on personal property, capital stock, corporation licenses, publication fees, and similar items are institutional costs and generally do not qualify for deferral.

Real Estate Expenses

This is the only expense category—other than salaries—in which the compensation of employees is included. The salaries and wages paid for all services related to the care and maintenance of real estate are included in this account. Other expenses include direct costs incurred for insurance, operating supplies, and similar costs. Real estate costs, to the extent that they can be allocated to selling, underwriting, issue, and overhead, qualify for deferral.

Real Estate Taxes

All taxes, licenses, and fees incurred as a result of owning real estate are included in this account. These costs should be combined with real estate expenses in determining the allocated portion that is deferrable.

Miscellaneous

Costs not includable in other expense categories are classified as miscellaneous. Such costs include charitable contributions, outside data processing services, and similar items and generally do not qualify for deferral.

LOSS RECOGNITION

The *concept* of loss recognition is the same for property and liability insurance companies and for life insurance companies. The long-standing accounting rules described early in this chapter under "Life Insurance Policies"—rules relating to the nonanticipation of revenues, to matching periodic costs with revenues, to recognizing as assets costs paid in advance, to recording all known liabilities, and to applying accounting principles on a consistent basis between periods—are equally applicable to short-duration property and liability contracts.

The difference in the *application* of the principles arises because short-term policies usually have premiums paid in advance which are recognized as deferred revenue that is earned ratably over the term of the policy. The related short-term deferred policy acquisition costs must bear the same relationship to deferred revenue that similar costs do in the case of life insurance contracts. For short-term policies, the deferral of acquisition costs is limited to the amount of actual costs incurred or to the balance of unearned premiums not required for future losses and maintenance expenses. If, upon testing, the unearned premiums are determined to be inadequate to cover anticipated losses, maintenance expenses, and the unamortized balance of deferred acquisition costs, then the latter amount must be reduced to the extent of the deficiency. If the deficiency is in excess of the balance of unamortized acquisition costs, a liability must be recorded for the excess.

TITLE INSURANCE COMPANIES

Because all premiums are paid at the inception of the policy, title insurance does not develop deferred policy acquisition costs. The costs incurred for title searches and for updating the title plant are period costs and are expensed as incurred. Other costs incurred in the purchase or construction of a title plant should be capitalized as a nonamortizable asset. This is because the title plant has an indefinite life, and the cost basis is not adjusted unless there is a change in statutes affecting titles or unless the plant becomes obsolete because of changes in circumstances or improper maintenance. When a write-down from the cost basis is indicated, it should be recognized currently.

JOINT EXPENSES

Expenses incurred for a group of affiliated companies are subject to rules of joint expense allocation for statutory reporting and to similar cost accounting rules for public and income tax reporting. In addition, joint expense allocation should be agreed to among the several companies. The agreement is not as much for the purpose of describing how expenses will be allocated as for the purpose of establishing that such allocations are representative of actual services performed and received by the companies. Joint expense allocations can be thought of as a sharing of expenses on an "arm's-length" basis. However, for statutory reporting, joint expense allocations are made on the basis of actual costs—whereas on an arm's-length basis, additional margins may be included for services and profits. In determining deferred policy acquisition costs, only actual expenses incurred by the joint parties should be shared. To do otherwise may result in an overstatement or understatement of the aggregate incurred policy acquisition costs.

Joint expense allocations should provide, wherever possible, that direct allocations be made. For salaries, direct allocation is often possible if employees work exclusively for one of the joint companies. If the employees' services cover more than one company, then time studies, units of production, or other bases may be used to allocate salary costs. For statutory reporting purposes, the companies may develop and use their own basis of allocation. If they do not, the following general guidelines for allocation must be used:

- *Direct allocation method*
  - Claim adjustment services
  - Commission and brokerage
  - Allowances to managers and agents
  - Directors' fees
  - State and local insurance taxes
  - Insurance department license and fees
  - Real estate taxes
  - Real estate expenses
- *Ratio-of-total-salaries method*
  - Employee relations and welfare
  - Insurance
  - Directors' fees (unless charged on a direct basis)
  - Rent and rent items
  - Equipment
  - Printing and stationery
  - Postage, telephone and telegraph, exchange and express
  - Payroll taxes
- *Ratio-of-premiums method*
  - Advertising
- *Special studies method*
  - Boards, bureaus, and associations
  - Surveys and underwriting reports
  - Audits of assureds' records
  - Travel and travel items
  - Legal and auditing
  - Miscellaneous
  - State and local insurance taxes (unless allocated directly)
  - Insurance department license and fees (unless allocated directly)
  - Real estate expenses (unless allocated directly)

The recommended allocation methods should always stand the test of appropriateness and applicability for the expenses being allocated. In some instances, it may be necessary to classify individual expenses separately and to apply to each category a different allocation method, one which bears a reasonable relationship to the purpose for which the expenses were incurred. The allocation method should be periodically updated so that they are current and applicable to present circumstances. Where joint expenses are included in reinsurance agreements, the results of such allocations should not vary significantly from the detailed allocations covered above.

11

UNEARNED PREMIUMS

The terms "unearned premium liability" and "unearned premium reserve" are used interchangeably to describe the unexpired portion of the gross insurance premium. For most insurance policies written by property and liability insurance companies, it represents the pro rata unexpired portion of the gross premium that would be returned to the policyholder if the policy were canceled by the issuer. For accident and health insurance policies, the unearned premium is an element in the total reserve held for those policies.

Unearned premiums should be thought of as deferred income. Since insurance premiums are collected in advance, it is necessary to prorate the premium over the policy term. In this respect, the unearned premiums represent neither a liability nor a reserve; rather, they represent the portion of the gross premium that has not yet expired. Premiums are earned based on the passage of time. Until the total period of time spec-

ified in the policy has elapsed, there remains an unfulfilled obligation to provide insurance coverage for the balance of the policy term.

An unearned premium, as the name implies, represents the amount of gross premium that should be excluded from the income statement. If, for accounting purposes, it were considered to be a reserve, it would be necessary to reduce the amount by the expected cancellations by policyholders and the company. If it were assumed that some policyholders will cancel, the unearned premium would be calculated by using a short-rate cancellation. This amount is specified in the policy and provides for a smaller return premium in the earlier months that the policy is in force, to allow the insurance company to recoup policy acquisition costs. If it were assumed that the policies will be canceled by the company, the unearned premium would be reduced by an estimate of the policies that would be canceled.

For statutory reporting, companies are required to provide a reserve for unearned premiums based on a method specified by statutes or regulations. The required reserve may be based on a formula for individual policies or may be a fixed percentage of all policies in force.

The determination of unearned premiums is affected by the following items:

POLICY COVERAGES AND TERMS

To make a precise computation of unearned premiums, the policies in force must be grouped by line of business and policy term. Insurance protection is available for losses suffered in connection with the ownership of property, the operation of a business, the risk of nonperformance of contracts, the risk of injury or illness, and the risk associated with the operation of automobiles, aircraft, and boats. This insurance protection is for the owners of property as well as for third parties who may suffer losses. Some insurance also offers protection for illness, work-related injuries, professional malpractice, violation of fiduciary duties, and a multitude of other potential losses.

The better to understand insurance terms and line of businesses, in this chapter the major insurance coverages included in unearned premium calculations are separated between property, personal and business, multiple-peril, and third-party insurance. The line-of-business reporting requirements for annual statutory statements can be classified within these groups.

Property Insurance

This insurance provides protection for property owners, both individual and business, from losses arising from insured perils. Some of the major peril coverages are described below.

Fire and Allied Lines. A fire insurance policy provides insurance protection against direct losses from fire and lightning. The protected property may be a business building or a dwelling, together with its attached structures, with materials and supplies used in construction or repair, and with building or dwelling equipment located on the premises.

Allied lines, or extended coverage in the case of dwellings, insure against perils such as windstorm, hail, explosion, riot, smoke, vandalism, and earthquake. Fire and additional coverages provide insurance protection for direct losses from these perils. Insurance for indirect losses, such as loss of income while damage is being repaired and extra expenses involved in getting a business back in operation, is purchased separately.

Building contents are usually covered in a single fire and allied lines insurance policy. This feature provides protection against fire and lightning for personal property but usually excludes automobiles, trucks, aircraft, and, in the case of manufacturing, certain other properties. It also may include protection for property held on consignment or in trust.

These policies are usually written for a term of 1 year.

Boiler and Machinery Insurance. Losses arising from the operation of steam boilers are usually excluded from fire and allied lines insurance contracts; therefore, this insurance protection must be purchased separately. The basic coverages offered are for damage to property of the insured or of a third party, bodily injury liability, legal expenses of settling claims, and extra expenses in expediting repairs. This insurance is for direct losses and usually excludes consequential damages to property. Losses arising as a consequence of lack of power, heat, refrigeration, and the like are not direct losses and are not covered unless the basic policy includes endorsement for such losses.

Boiler accidents may also cause business interruption and prevent a company from conducting its usual business, or at least cause it to operate on a reduced basis. This protection is also excluded from the boiler and machinery insurance unless separately endorsed or included in a separate contract.

Extensive inspection services and safety engineering reviews are required for boiler and machinery insurance. These services represent an important part of the total cost of insurance. Loss-prevention service and preventive maintenance reduce the hazard of boiler explosion and consequential business interruption and other losses. The cost of these services included in the premium probably exceeds the amount of direct losses.

Boiler and machinery insurance is usually written for a term of 1 year.

Glass Insurance. This insurance provides reimbursement for all glass breakage except for losses from fire and associated perils. The glass policy specifically insures against damage to plate glass and lettering and other ornaments described in the policy. This protection provides for the repair or replacement of the glass and encasement framings and for the installation of temporary covers. Glass insurance is seldom written individually for dwellings; rather, it is included as a part of regular property insurance protection. Damage to glass other than for breakage is usually not covered.

These policies are usually written for a term of 1 year.

Ocean and Inland Marine Insurance. Ocean marine insurance is a well-defined coverage and is offered by a limited number of insurance companies. Inland marine insurance, on the other hand, includes many coverages for loss to merchandise in transit, floating property, installment sales and deferred payment losses, and the like. It also includes protection for pleasure boats operated on inland waterways. These policies can be thought of as business or personal property insurance that is not otherwise provided for in any of the previously described coverages.

Transportation insurance, an inland marine coverage, provides protection for domestically shipped goods. It protects against the perils of fire, windstorm, collision, upset, and similar losses. The policies can be endorsed to include earthquake, landslide, and breakage. Theft of an entire shipment may also be insured; however, theft of a part of the total contents is usually not covered. Excluded are perils such as riot, strike, discoloring, rusting, rotting, and other perils arising from leakage or breakage unless they are specifically insured.

Property floater insurance, another inland marine coverage, provides protection to businesses and individuals for personal property that is not covered under one of the preceding forms. For businesses it may cover losses from the destruction of accounts receivable records, valuable papers and documents, fine art objects, advertising signs, and numerous other coverages. For individuals it covers stamp and coin collections, musical instruments, silverware, jewelry, personal property in automobiles, and many similar coverages.

Ocean and inland marine policies are usually written for a term of 1 year; however, they may cover a single trip or a specific period of time.

Automobile Property Damage Insurance. This insurance covers two types of physical damage: collision losses and comprehensive losses. They may be written in the same policy or may be purchased separately.

Collision insurance provides protection for collision with other vehicles and objects and for vehicle upset. It provides reimbursement for losses irrespective of fault or controversy with other parties. If the collision coverage is subject to a deductible amount, the insurance reimbursement excludes the deductible amount. Unlike some other types of insurance, the insured value is the actual cash value unless the vehicle has a stated value. Usually, stated value coverage is elected for antique or classic vehicles. Actual cash value is determined by the market price for comparable vehicles.

Comprehensive insurance offers protection against many perils. Normally, it provides reimbursement for losses other than collision and upset. These losses include those arising from fire, theft, explosion, windstorm, hail, vandalism, glass breakage, and flying objects. The insurance reimbursement for losses is based on replacement values. This is somewhat different than the reimbursement offered under collision protection, which uses the market value rule.

Automobile property damage insurance is written to cover an annual, a 6-month, or a 3-month term. The premiums may be payable on a monthly basis, but the term is seldom less than a 3-month period.

Aircraft Insurance. This insurance is written by a group of companies that have formed pools to insure these risks. This is because of the large potential losses that can result from hull damage. The property damage insurance is written for a fixed amount and may provide for more limited protection when the aircraft is not in flight. Only a limited number of insurance companies will provide aircraft insurance. The policies are written for a term of 1 year.

Personal and Business Insurance

In addition to being provided for under property insurance, a number of hazards are written as personal and business insurance. This insurance protects the personal and business assets of the insured from liability for negligence, malpractice, and losses arising from working conditions. In addition, it provides reimbursement for losses from accidents and health hazards, crime, and uninsured motorists. These insurance coverages may be purchased individually or in connection with other insurance coverages. Some of the more common forms of personal and business insurance are covered below.

Automobile Liability Insurance. This insurance protection covers losses for bodily injury and property damage that result from ownership or use of an automobile. The insurance will pay third parties for damages attributable to operation of a motor vehicle by a covered person up to the policy limit. It will also pay the cost to settle or defend claims.

The insurance extends to other "covered persons." These include family members and persons who use an automobile with the permission of the insured. Also included are other persons or organizations for losses caused them by the insured.

The use of nonowned automobiles is also covered if the automobile is operated with the permission of its owner. This insurance is an option that can be purchased to protect against claims arising from the negligent operation of automobiles by employees while performing services for the employer.

Bodily injury liability coverage is stated in thousands of dollars per occurrence, with an amount specified for each person and each accident. Property damage insurance is stated in thousands of dollars for each occurrence and covers damage to real and personal property. Liability insurance includes supplementary payments for the cost of bail bonds, premiums on appeal bonds, interest accruing after a judgment is entered in a lawsuit, a stipulated amount for loss of earnings, and other reasonable expenses that are incurred at the request of the insurance company.

Two other forms of indemnity payments may be covered in an automobile liability policy. The first coverage is for bodily injury arising from accidents where the other party is uninsured. The insured pays an additional premium to receive protection for these injuries that would be covered if the other party were insured. The bodily injury coverage is stated in thousands of dollars per each person and each accident. The second coverage is for medical payments. The insurance company pays reasonable expenses incurred for medical and funeral services arising from an accident of a covered person. The payment is limited to the amounts stated in the policy.

Liability Insurance Other than Automobile. The legal liability for negligence is imposed on individuals and businesses where there is a protected right and a duty is owed to one possessing that right. Negligence occurs when the required standard of care falls below that required by law and results in consequences that justify the payment of damages. A common example of negligence is the failure to maintain walkways in a reasonably safe condition, thus causing injuries to occur; this liability arises because property owners fail to make repairs and thereby endanger others using the walkway. The same standard of care applies when dangerous materials are stored in areas used by the public and injuries occur. In other words, negligence can occur because due care was not exercised in maintaining business properties or because business owners failed to use due care in protecting the public from dangerous materials.

The liability for these negligent acts may be partially or totally offset where the injured party has agreed to limitations or conditions of using property that exempts owners from liability or where the injured parties fail to exercise due care for their own safety. Liability for injuries also arises where the business owner acts wrongfully. An example of this liability is where untrue statements are published and result in damage to another's reputation or public image.

Losses may be claimed for special or general damages. Special damages consist of medical expenses, loss of earnings because of injury, repair or replacement of property, and the like. General damages represent intangible losses, such as pain and suffering. Punitive damages are in excess of special and general damages and are in the nature of punishment for intentional or malicious action.

The amount of protection offered is specified in the policy. The insurance protection covers the liability awards mentioned above as well as attorney fees, court costs, witness fees, and other out-of-pocket expenses incurred in defending against claims of liability.

Liability insurance is written in several forms, such as comprehensive general liability coverage; owners', landlords', and tenants' liability; garage liability; storekeepers' liability; contractors' coverage; manufacturers' coverage; and other special risks. Each liability coverage may be purchased separately or as blanket coverage in a comprehensive liability insurance policy. The latter type of policy provides broad coverages for some or all of the liability exposure. An example of a comprehensive-type policy is discussed below in this chapter under "Multi-Peril Insurance."

Crime, Burglary, and Theft Insurance. The risk of loss from criminal activity varies between types of property and location. Also, crimes may occur more frequently where there is poor building security or poor accounting controls. These insurance risks can be classified as property losses and cash losses. Property losses are reimbursable based on their fair value. Money losses are usually limited to a specified amount.

Crime insurance for a business includes loss protection from burglary, theft, extortion, robbery, forgery, loss from stolen credit cards, embezzlement, and the like. Personal crime insurance covers theft, burglary, vandalism, arson, mysterious disappearance, and related losses.

Many crime policies cover specific occurrences, such as inside and outside holdups, mercantile safe burglary, loss from safe-deposit boxes, and innkeepers' liability. Fidelity bonds provide coverage for employee losses. These bonds may be for specific positions or a blanket bond covering all employees.

Crime insurance may be purchased separately on an "all-risk" basis or may be included in a combination policy. These coverages are usually written on an annual basis.

Professional Liability Insurance. This is a specialty type of insurance coverage applicable to professional licensees. The "professional" group includes lawyers, physicians, accountants, architects, engineers, surveyors, druggists, consultants, and actuaries. Other licensees—such as insurance agents, brokers, and real estate salespeople—are insured under an errors and omission policy. Professional liability insurance and error and omission insurance provide protection in connection with losses from services rendered or services which should have been rendered but were not.

Professional liability claims are usually infrequent, but large. These claims may not be settled for many years following the event from which the claims arose. Such insurance is written on an "occurrence basis" or a "claims-made" basis. In the former instance, insurance protection is provided for occurrences during the policy year even though the claim may not be made until a subsequent year. In the latter instance, the insurance protection is for all the claims made against the insured during the policy year. Expected losses are easier to measure using the claims-made basis; consequently, such policies require a lower premium. Ultimate losses on an occurrence basis are more difficult to determine, and "cushions" result in a higher premium. In the long run, however, claim's cost will be the same for either basis.

These policies are usually written for a term of 1 year.

Accident and Health Insurance. This is a personal type of insurance protection. However, to the extent that employers fund an accident and sickness program for their employees, it can also be considered business insurance. The insurance can be written on an individual or a group basis. It can also be written to cover specific circumstances, such as accident and health insurance issued in connection with personal credit arrangements.

Accident and health insurance protection is not limited to payments by the insured for actual losses sustained. The benefits specified in the policy will be paid to the insured irrespective of other payments received. Most accident and health insurance policies can be classified into the following categories:

Loss of Income Protection. These policies contain a stated sum that is paid on a periodic basis if the insured becomes disabled because of sickness or injury. Separate policies may be written for disabilities arising from either sickness or accident; however, it is more common to find policies covering both perils. Disability income protection provides a fixed weekly or monthly payment for a specified period of disability. The period of disability payments may be for 2 years, 5 years, or life. Partial disability payments, if included in the protection, provide reduced payments during the partial disability period.

If the income protection pays benefits beyond 2 years, it is referred to as "long-term" disability insurance. Long-term disability insurance is often written to cover individuals engaged in highly skilled occupations, including business owners.

Most disability insurance includes an elimination or waiting period. Benefits under the policies do not become payable until the waiting period has expired. This provision eliminates claims arising from short periods of disability. It has the same effect as the self-insured deductible amount for medical expense coverages.

Medical Care Insurance. These insurance policies provide for payments to individuals or to the providers of medical care services. The insurance protection covers hospital costs, nursing care, physician and surgeon's charges, and other medical expenses. The policies may also provide for nursing home care, dental care, prescription drugs, psychiatric treatment, and the like.

The amount payable for medical care may be specified by a schedule of services in the policy or it may be in blanket form. The scheduled benefits specify the maximum amounts payable for daily hospital benefits, physician's care, surgeries, hospital supplies, nursing fees, and other charges. The blanket type of coverage specifies the maximum amount payable for all necessary medical expenses. Either form may specify a maximum amount for certain hospital care, such as maternity care or routine surgeries.

Major medical insurance is usually purchased separately and provides protection beyond the basic medical care insurance. These policies have a maximum benefit for each medical disability. Major medical insurance requires an initial deductible amount to be paid by the policyholder or another policy before the benefits begin. Amounts payable under the policy are usually reduced by participation provisions that require the insured to pay a specified percentage of the total benefits. The benefits payable usually include all reasonable charges incurred for necessary medical or surgical treatment.

Accident and health insurance policies, whether for disability or medical care insurance, are continued in force subject to the following options:

Noncancelable Insurance. These policies cannot be canceled by the insurance company so long as the premiums are paid. The premiums and the benefits are guaranteed at the inception of the policy and continue in force to a maximum specified age, usually age 65. Since the benefits are guaranteed irrespective of subsequent loss experience, the premiums are higher and the underwriting standards are stricter. Noncancelable insurance is more prevalent with disability income than with medical care.

Guaranteed Renewable. Policies issued under this form are similar to noncancelable policies, with one significant exception: The premium amount is not guaranteed. However, no premium adjustments can be made unless all policies for a class or age group are included. The initial premiums are usually less than for noncancelable policies and usually include both disability income and medical care.

Limited Renewable. These policies may be optionally renewable by the company or conditionally renewable. The former (optionally renewable) is applicable to each policy, and the insurer may increase the premium, add a benefit restriction, or decline to renew a policy. In the latter instance (conditionally renewable), the renewable provision applies to all policies of the same class, and individual policies will not be denied unless all policies of that class are not renewed.

Cancelable Policies. These are policies that can be canceled before the expiration of the policy period. Policy provisions specify the conditions under which such policies may be canceled. The cancelable feature may apply to individual policies or to a group or class of policies.

Term Policies. Some policies are written for a specified term and contain no renewal or termination provisions. These policies usually cover a specified period of time or specific trips.

Credit Accident and Health Insurance. This insurance is similar to disability income insurance except that the benefits are payable to an insured creditor. The payments continue until the total debt has been repaid or until the insured recovers.

Group Accident and Health Insurance. This insurance protection usually covers 25 or more individuals under a common policy. It can include disability income, medical care, or both. Additionally, it often includes dental care, prescription drugs, and outpatient treatments. Generally, the coverage must be offered to all qualified employees and none can be canceled individually. Group contracts usually have specified cancellation provisions.

Individual accident and health insurance is usually written for a term of 1 year, except for credit and trip insurance, which have a shorter and indeterminate term.

Multiple-Peril Insurance

Multiple-peril insurance represents an efficient way for insurance companies to provide protection, and it avoids gaps that might occur if individual peril policies were purchased by the insured. Most hazards can be insured under multiple-peril contracts, except for certain special risks. By using multiple-peril insurance contracts, the insurer is able to reduce the premium that would be charged if separate policies were issued. Because the insured pays only one insurance premium and the underwriting process is combined, there is a significant savings in administrative costs. The broad range of protection provided in such policies eliminates many of the concerns about types of insurance coverage needed to protect a business or an individual against unexpected loss.

Multiple-peril policies can be classified as commercial, homeowners', or farmowners'. Each classification is covered below.

Commercial Multiple-Peril Insurance. These policies are written in several forms and cover similar risks. The most common commercial multiple-peril policies are written for commercial, industrial, manufacturers', storeowners', public, and institutional property. Service businesses are usually written as special multiple peril. Certain businesses such as jewelry stores, musical instrument dealers, camera stores, fur dealers, businesses selling plants and animals, farm produce dealers, pawn brokers, secondhand stores, motels and hotels, theaters, bars, and restaurants are written under separate policies specifically designed for those businesses. All other businesses can be classified under one of the other multiple-peril policy forms.

Multiple-peril policies cover "all risks" except for losses arising from such hazards as war, mechanical breakdown, insects, fraud, neglect, leakage, and glass breakage. Losses to books, records, and securities are also not covered. Special multiple-peril policies may include liability, crime, and glass breakage coverage.

Commercial multiple peril policies may be written on two bases:

Named Perils. These policies specify the hazards that are insured. For example, the policy may cover fire, hail, windstorm, vandalism, and glass breakage. Insurance protection is provided for losses occurring from the named perils. Losses occurring from perils not named in the policy are not insured. The policy is a multiple-peril policy because it combines many coverages in a single policy.

All-Risk Policies. All perils are covered under this policy except those which are specifically excluded. The perils excluded often include such hazards as earthquakes, floods, crime, business interruption, and glass breakage. Any of these coverages may nevertheless be endorsed on and included in the policy.

There are two other features to commercial multiple-peril policies. First, most policies offer deductible arrangements which permit the insured to accept responsibility for smaller losses. The deductible provisions enable the insurer to reduce the premium by avoiding nuisance claims, which require a disproportionate administrative expense charge. The second feature is that most of these policies provide for inflation adjustments on an automatic basis. Under this provision, the insured values are increased automatically to reflect current inflation rates.

Commercial multiple-peril policies are generally written for a term of 1 year.

Homeowners' Insurance. This insurance is available to homeowners for an individual dwelling. Generally, it is not available for rented dwellings, apartment houses, and boarding houses. However, special limited form policies are available for condominium-unit owners.

Homeowners' insurance provides broad protection for loss to a dwelling, to personal property, or from a liability claim. The policies specify a dollar amount for dwelling losses, a percentage of the dwelling amount for appurtenant private structures and unscheduled personal property, and a fixed amount for additional living expenses. The comprehensive personal liability offers protection for losses of third parties for which the homeowner is liable, including medical payments for accidental injury and physical damage to third-party property. Some homeowners' policies may cover only named perils. However, most homeowners' policies are all-risk policies and cover all losses except those specifically excluded. Excluded coverage, which may be purchased separately, includes losses from earthquakes, floods, and the like.

There are several standard provisions included in a homeowners' policy. Dwelling losses are paid on the basis of actual cash value or replacement cost. Losses paid for unscheduled personal property are on the basis of actual cash value. Certain special risks are subject to a fixed limitation. These limited risks include losses of money, securities, stamp collections, furs, jewelry, manuscripts, boats, and the like. Losses arising from flood, earthquake, heating and power failure, steam boiler explosion, and similar losses often require special endorsements on policies.

Homeowners' insurance policies are generally written for a term of 1 year.

Farmowners' Insurance. These policies are written for farmowners and ranchowners and contain many of the insurance concepts included in a homeowners' policy. In addition, the policy provides protection against losses arising from the special needs of those engaged in the business of farming and ranching. The policies can be written on the basis of named perils or all risks. Typically, the perils insured against include losses from fire, lightning, windstorm, hail, explosion, vandalism, theft, collision, and related perils. The exclusions on these policies include losses from flood, earthquake and mudflow, power failure, and the like.

Losses on grain, hay, machinery, poultry, livestock, portable buildings, and similar items are subject to maximum limits. For example, livestock is usually limited to the actual cash value of the animal, a fixed dollar amount, or a calculated percentage of the total insurance on all livestock. Likewise damages to machinery are usually limited to a dollar maximum for each article.

Personal property can be insured on a blanket basis to an aggregate dollar value. The property may also be scheduled so that each individual item has a stated insurance value. In the former instance, where several personal property losses occur, the aggregate insurance protection is prorated to each scheduled loss. Excluded perils may be purchased separately and endorsed on the policy. Most farmowners' and ranchowners' policies include a loss deductible clause similar to the homeowners' policy.

These insurance policies are generally written for a term of 1 year.

Third-Party Insurance

In contrast to the protection provided to property owners for personal and business assets, third-party insurance provides protection to those dealing with individuals and businesses. Third-party insurance cannot always be distinguished from other insurance protection since it may also provide benefits to the insured. For the most part, however, it benefits another party and often may be required by statute or as a condition to a contract.

The major third-party insurance coverages are discussed below.

Workers' Compensation Insurance. All states require that employers provide compensation to workers for job-related injuries or diseases. The amount of insurance is specified in statutes or regulations. Some states require the insurance to be purchased from state "workers' compensation funds." Other states permit employers to maintain self-insurance funds to pay losses. However, the majority of employers purchase workers' compensation insurance from private insurers.

Most states specify a minimum and maximum benefit for temporary disabilities. These benefits as well as medical expense benefits are covered in workers' compensation policies. Generally, there is no policy limit for medical expense benefits. If a worker dies as a result of accident or disease related to employment, the dependents or estate are entitled to funeral expenses and a statutory compensation benefit.

Premiums charged for workers' compensation insurance are based on the employers' payroll cost. Consequently, premiums are estimated at the inception of the policy and are finally determined when all payroll costs have been incurred for the year.

Workers' compensation insurance is written for a 1-year term.

Fidelity and Surety Insurance. Fidelity insurance was discussed previously in connection with employee dishonesty or fraud. Fidelity insurance may also be required in connection with obtaining licenses and permits from regulatory bodies. In this circumstance, fidelity insurance is third-party insurance since the beneficiary is the agency issuing the license or the permit. Fidelity insurance is underwritten like other property and liability insurance protection.

Surety bonds, on the other hand, are often considered not to be insurance. Surety bonds cover specific performance and require the insurer to make good on any loss for nonperformance. To protect the issuer of the surety bonds, the insured is required to post collateral equal to the bond amount. The premium charged for surety protection is in the nature of a fee.

The two most common types of surety coverage are contractors' bonds and judicial bonds. Contractors' bonds are required in connection with contract bidding and construction to ensure that construction will be completed for the bid amount. If the contractor fails to perform, the surety will pay the cost of completing the construction even though the ultimate cost may exceed the original bid price.

Judicial bonds can be required in connection with indictments and lawsuits. For indictable crime, the bond is a guarantee that the plaintiff will appear at the appointed time for trial. For civil cases, the bond is a guarantee that the winning party to litigation will be protected where initial awards are appealed. Very few insurance companies write judicial bonds covering criminal indictments. Litigation bonds, on the other hand, are not significantly different than the contractors' bonds described above.

Fidelity bonds are usually written for a term of 1 year. Contractors' bonds remain in force until the construction is completed and accepted. Judicial bonds remain in force until discharged by the courts.

Mortgage Guarantee Insurance. This insurance provides protection to the lender if the borrower does not complete the payment of specified installments. The insurance provides protection for the total amount of the principal, interest, taxes, insurance, and other expenses. The policy benefits are automatically reduced as the mortgage payments are made. These policies are often required by financial institutions engaged in the business of providing residential mortgage financing. Since this is a specialized form of insurance, only a limited number of insurers issue it.

These insurance policies may be written for the full term of a mortgage loan or for a specified period. The expected average term for these policies is approximately 7 years.

Title Insurance. This insurance is similar to errors and omission insurance since it protects against defects that may arise in connection with the passing of title to real property. The mortgage lender requires the purchase of this insurance even though the title may appear to be without defects. The insurance protects a mortgage lender and the purchaser against losses that may occur because of a technical omission relating to inheritance or transfer of title. These defects may involve incomplete title transfers, missing signatures, forgeries, unpaid liens, and errors.

This insurance is written by a limited number of companies who possess extensive records on all properties in their operating area. The title records are necessary to establish continuity in ownership, which forms the basis on which title insurance is issued.

These policies are written for an indeterminate term and remain in force while property is owned by the purchasers of the insurance or their heirs.

OTHER TYPES OF INSURANCE

The preceding material covers the usual insurance policies included in the calculation of unearned premiums. There are several other types of insurance which have little effect on the unearned premium calculation. For example, crop and hail insurance is written to cover a growing season and very little of this coverage remains in force at the end of the year. Livestock insurance is written to reimburse for losses of livestock under limited conditions, such as while in transit or in holding pens; this insurance has little effect on the calculation of unearned premiums unless written in connection with farmowners' and ranchowners' policies. Other insurance protection such as rain insurance and pet insurance is written by a few companies and has no significant effect on the calculation of unearned premiums.

FACTORS AFFECTING POLICY COVERAGE AND TERM

There are many modifications that can be made to the policy coverage or term. Each of these changes must be considered in connection with calculating unearned premiums. The most significant coverage and term modifications are covered below.

Advanced Premiums

Property and liability insurance companies often bill premiums in advance of the due date. These amounts are included in premium income even though the insurance is not effective until a future date. None of these premiums has been earned and the entire advance premium should be included in unearned premiums. At the effective date of the policy, advance premiums are amortized with other premiums in force.

Additional Premiums

As a result of changes made to policy coverages or term, additional premiums may be charged to policyholders. These amounts should be included in unearned premiums in order to amortize the additional premium over the remaining term of the policy.

Returned Premiums

Returned premiums occur when policies are canceled or there is a change in coverage that reduces the insurance in force. The amount of premium returned to policyholders may not be the same as the remaining unamortized premium because of the use of short-rate cancellation factors. The amount subtracted from unearned premiums should be the unamortized amount of the original gross premium.

Audit Premiums

Some business insurance policies, such as workers' compensation, are determined on the basis of payroll costs. Since the payroll costs cannot be determined at the inception of the policy, an estimated premium (deposit premium) is charged to the policyholder. When the final annual payroll cost is determined, an adjustment is required for the difference between the estimated premium and the audited premium. The deposited premium as well as an estimate of the audited premium should be included in the unearned premium calculation. If the audited premiums are deemed to be immaterial, they may be included in premium income when they become due.

Changes in Coverage

Increases or decreases in policy limits, as well as additions or deletions of property insured, often require some modification to the original premium. These changes may affect the calculation of unearned premiums for both policy coverage and term. Changes that affect policy coverages are classified with the underlying premiums. Changes that affect the policy term result in additional premiums and return premiums, which are accounted for as described above.

Retrospective Premiums

Some policies provide for the redetermination of premiums based on the insured's loss experience, which may result in additional or return premiums. However, since the term of the coverage has expired, these amounts do not affect the calculation of unearned premiums except that an estimate of retrospective premiums may be included at year end. In the latter instance, such estimates are accounted for as additional premiums and return premiums, as described above.

Reinsurance Premiums

These premiums are payable to or recoverable from reinsurance companies for amounts that have been ceded to them. Reinsurance premiums, which include a part of or all of a risk, are determined in a manner similar to that for written premiums. The ceding company removes these amounts from unearned premiums and the assuming company includes the same amounts in its unearned premiums.

UNEARNED PREMIUM CALCULATION

Unearned premiums are determined from premium-in-force records and take into account advanced premiums, additional and return premiums, changes in coverage and terms, audit and retrospective premiums, and reinsurance. This is true whether unearned premiums are determined from each policy in force or are determined under the summary method—which combines like coverages and terms and applies an unearned premium factor. The grouping of premiums in like terms is important to the mathematical determination of unearned premiums. The grouping of policies by coverage is required in order to comply with statutory reporting requirements and to determine profitability by line of business.

Premiums in force include both collected and uncollected premiums. Some premiums are paid in installments and the actual collection of premiums has little bearing on the determination of unearned premiums. Premiums in force should include unpaid premiums when the policy is in a grace period; however, premiums deemed to be uncollectible should be eliminated immediately.

Unearned premiums which are calculated directly from policy master files may take into account an exact premium. That is, the calculation accounts for unearned premiums on a daily basis and this amount represents the actual premiums required to be returned if the company terminates the policy. The direct calculation may be made by summarizing premiums in force by policy term and applying unearned premium factors to each of the summarized totals. Advanced premiums will be included in the totals since none of these has yet been earned.

Unearned premiums may also be determined in another manner by summarizing total premiums in force adjusted for any modifications made to policy coverage or term. If all the premiums in force represent annual term premiums, the calculation can be made by applying a proration factor against each monthly total of premiums in force, using a ½-month convention (i.e., 1/24 for the first and last period). This method produces an approximate unearned premium which takes into account the monthly expirations of premiums in force. These amounts must be adjusted for reinsurance premiums ceded or assumed.

Any reasonable approximation that takes into account the policy coverage and term should be acceptable, except that for some statutory reporting purposes a minimum percentage factor must be assigned to the premiums in force (i.e., 40 percent for fire insurance).

Separate unearned premium determinations may be required for mortgage loan guarantee insurance, title insurance, and surety bond insurance. Unearned premiums for these coverages should be determined by the expected term, using the company's own experience. Where company experience is not available or deemed not to be useful, a fixed amortization period (such as 7 years for mortgage guarantee insurance) can be used that reflects a reasonable estimate of current unearned premiums.

12

LIFE INSURANCE COMPANY RESERVES

The provision for life insurance reserves is based upon predictable mortality, which is determined from the actual experience of large groups. This predictability permits a life insurance company to estimate required reserves that are significantly less than the face amount of the life insurance benefits. This same factor permits them to charge smaller premiums for life insurance benefits.

In addition to predicting mortality, a life insurance company must also estimate the level of investment earnings, the expenses of continuing the policies in force, and the probability of lapse or surrender (withdrawals) of policies over the expected premium-collection period. Similar estimates must be made to determine reserves for policies covering accident and health risks and annuity payments.

and remained in force at the end of the year, it could be assumed that a terminal reserve could be appropriate for a year-end valuation date; however, since policies are written throughout the year, it is not appropriate to assume that all premiums, investment earnings, and benefits applicable to these policies have been earned or incurred. Consequently, terminal reserves are not appropriate except for inconsequential policy riders and benefits.

Mean Reserves. The use of a mean reserve overcomes the deficiency of terminal reserves since it assumes that all policies are written at the middle of the year. The mean reserve method uses a simple average of the beginning and ending terminal reserves and the annual net valuation premium. This method assumes that policies have been issued proportionately throughout the year. It also assumes that all policy premiums have been paid to the policy anniversary date. Since many policy premiums are payable monthly, quarterly, and semiannually, the mean reserve is overstated by the amount of assumed premiums which have not been received. Consequently, an asset is recorded to recognize the net valuation premium that is due and unpaid or deferred from the valuation date to the policy anniversary date. Statutory reporting requires that this asset be recorded separately, rather than being deducted from the life insurance reserves.

Midterminal Reserves. Midterminal reserves are derived by using an average of the beginning and ending terminal reserves at each policy anniversary. Since the terminal reserve assumes that all premiums have been received, that all investment income has been earned, and that all policy benefits have been paid, the midyear estimate of life insurance reserves assumes that, on the average, the premiums have been paid through the middle of the year. Consequently, no provision needs to be made for premiums that are due or deferred to the next policy anniversary date. For statutory reporting, however, an additional reserve for unearned premiums is required in order to recognize the liability for that portion of the valuation premium which has been paid or which is due from the current valuation date to the next premium-paying date. Premiums paid beyond the next premium-paying date are accounted for separately.

Nonlevel Premium Reserves. Because the usual reserve valuations based on level premiums ignore the heavy expenses incurred in the early policy years, a series of other methods permitted to be used for statutory reporting has been developed. Sometimes referred to as "modified reserves," these methods assume that expenses are incurred on a level basis throughout the policy term. Modified reserves permit the deferral of first-year acquisition costs by requiring a smaller valuation premium in the earlier years and a larger valuation premium in later years. The most common modified reserves are as follows:

Full Preliminary Term Reserves. This method assumes that the first-year net valuation premium is the same as a 1-year term premium. It permits first-year premiums to be used for paying 1 year's mortality and first-year costs and expenses. This method does not distinguish between the costs incurred for a 1-

summary contains the amount of insurance in force, a single reserve factor can be applied to all policies in the group having a common issue year and attained age. The amount of insurance in force and the total policy count can be conveniently reconciled to other accounting files, which adds to the reliability of the grouping method.

Seriatim Calculation. This method involves applying a reserve factor to each policy in force in a manner similar to the way in which factors are applied to the PYA summaries. The reserve factors are stored with other policy information or are maintained in a separate file that is used during the valuation process. The seriatim and group calculation should produce substantially identical results.

Approximation Calculation. Approximation techniques are used to estimate reserves on an interim basis where more precise amounts are not required. Also, such methods may be used to determine reserves for nonstandard policies and supplemental policy benefits. The estimate may be made by applying factors to gross premiums or total insurance in force, or by applying an extra percentage to standard life insurance reserves to reflect additional risks, such as substandard risks. The approximation method should not be used as a substitute for one of the other more accurate reserve calculations.

Reserve Tables

To ease the burden of determining statutory life insurance reserves, actuarial tables have been developed that take into account the assumptions and calculations necessary to meet required reserves. The use of these tables eliminates much of the detailed reserve calculations. Besides being more efficient in determining reserves, the tables also provide the greater reliability of error-free calculations. Many companies prepare separate reserve files for computer applications, which enables them to produce life insurance reserves on an annual basis with a minimum of effort. This is especially true where companies modify the tables to take into account certain selection and underwriting practices. For example, if more demanding selection and underwriting practices are required in order to issue a policy, the tables can be modified to reduce the life insurance requirements during a select period after the policy is issued. Additionally, some companies may choose to determine life insurance reserves by working directly from the actuarial formulas that are stored in computer memory. A review of how the tables work will assist in understanding life insurance reserving practices.

For purposes of explaining the use of reserve tables, the 1958 CSO tables using 3 percent interest asumptions are covered below.

Commissioners' 1958 Standard Ordinary Mortality Table. This table was developed from the mortality experience of several large companies for the years 1950 through 1954. Its reliability was assumed, since it covered a very large cross section of typical policyowners who were subject to reasonable underwriting and selection standards. In adopting this table, state regulators assumed that it was

Curtate Reserves. The traditional method for determining reserves is based on the assumption that premiums are paid annually at the beginning of the policy and that death claims are paid at the end of the policy year. This method permits (1) the accrual of earnings on the premiums for the entire year and (2) the accrual of earnings through the incurred date to the end of the year on the amounts required to pay death claims. Consequently, reserve requirements are reduced by the interest factor on these assumptions.

Continuous Reserves. Most companies permit payment of premiums on a monthly, quarterly, or semiannual basis, rather than requiring payments on an annual basis; in addition, they usually pay claims on the incurred date of death; furthermore, they often promptly refund those paid premiums which cover periods from the date of death to the next annual premium-paying date. All three of these factors can result in a partial loss of interest. Consequently, reserves computed from the continuous functions will be greater than those computed from the curtate functions. These differences are illustrated in Table 12-1.

Net Level Premium Reserves

Net Level and Modified Reserve Tables. The differences that occur by using a range of assumptions and computation methods can be illustrated by comparing the results in reserves (Table 12-2). While the differences are not constant for each attained age, this illustration of a single policy and attained age will point out the degree of difference occurring between the methods.

The Commissioners' 1958 Standard Ordinary Mortality Table is widely used in the industry. Several other older tables are still used, to value reserves on carryover business written in prior years. The American Experience Table was developed before the turn of the century and was generally used until the Commissioners' 1941 Standard Ordinary Mortality Table was published. Currently, statutory reserves for new policies are based on the Commissioners' 1980 Standard Ordinary Mortality Table, which reflects more current mortality experience. In addition, the assumed interest rate has been raised to more realistic levels.

Table 12-1
Commissioners' 1958 Standard Ordinary 3% Mortality Table

$1000 Ordinary Life, Male, Age 35, Policy Duration 5 Years

	Curtate	Continuous
Net valuation premium	$16.29	$16.92
Terminal reserves	74.72	76.48

Table 12-3
Net Level-Premium Reserves, 3%
Interest (Curtate)

$1000 Ordinary Life Policy, Male, Age 30

	Mean Reserves	
Policy Duration	**1941 CSO**	**1958 CSO**
5 years	$ 68	$ 62
10 years	141	132
20 years	302	291
30 years	475	462
40 years	640	625
69 years	957	957

life insurance reserves provide the aggregate cushion against the probability that death benefits will be paid in a current period, it is important that mortality rates for each age be determined. For example, if the rate of mortality increases significantly for some periods, then the reserves must also increase significantly, and this increase may result in the periodic reporting of financial losses even though the expected ultimate mortality rate may prove to be accurate. Likewise, unusually low mortality rates for given periods may result in inflated financial reporting results. For short-term policies, premium rates can be increased to cover unanticipated losses. Long-term level-premium policies reflect the mortality rate variation only in the aggregate. Table 12-3 illustrates the year-to-year effect of mortality variance by comparing the results of tables which are similar but which use different mortality factors.

New life insurance companies or companies not having substantial policies in force find it difficult to establish their own experience and thus use the experience of other companies to determine reserves. Companies having reinsurance contracts with large companies may find the reinsurers' mortality tables to be representative. Others may use published mortality tables that are based on large-group experience. Since underwriting practice can significantly affect estimates of expected mortality, care must be exercised to ensure that the company's own experience has a reasonable relationship to the mortality tables it uses.

Interest Assumptions. In the determination of life insurance reserves, "interest" describes an estimate of investment earnings. These earnings may accrue from interest-bearing investments, dividends on common stocks, real estate investments, net gains from the sale of capital assets, and other earnings arising from investment activities. Investment earnings are compared with invested assets to arrive at an earnings rate, which is then expressed as "interest."

The interest assumptions used in determining life insurance reserves represent anticipated investment earnings that will accrue to the company and become available to pay policyholder benefits. The interest assumptions used should

Table 12-4
Commissioners' 1958 Standard Ordinary Table, CRVM, Curtate Function

$1000 Ordinary Life, Male, Age 30, Policy Duration 10 Years

	2½%	3%
Terminal reserves	$132.53	$121.87
Mean reserves	132.29	121.48
Net annual premium	15.32	13.95

be paid. The mortality assumptions served to reduce the present value of expected future premiums, thereby increasing the premiums payable by all surviving policyowners. Lapse (failure to pay policy premiums) and withdrawals (surrendering the policy for its then present benefits) affect the present value both of expected future premiums and benefits.

In determining a valuation premium of life insurance reserves, the incidence of lapse and withdrawals (sometimes referred to as "surrenders") has a significant effect on aggregate reserves. For example, if these items are overestimated, the reserve valuation premium will be understated. Conversely, if the items are underestimated, the valuation premium will be overstated. Since valuation premiums are compared to the amount of insurance in force, the understatement or overstatement of valuation premiums tends to be self-correcting. However, on certain policy forms, such as those containing high cash values, significant distortions in the amount of reserves can occur. In other words, high-benefit policies are more subject to reserving errors where withdrawal assumptions vary greatly from actual experience.

Withdrawal tables are often used in connection with the determination of policy premiums. Such withdrawal considerations tend to be averaged over the expected policy period since premiums are viewed in the aggregate before they are spread over the expected policy term. Life insurance reserves, on the other hand, are expressed as an amount to cover all current benefits for policies in force. For this reason, withdrawal tables often do not represent the company's own experience for each insurance plan, age and issue, policy duration, or method of premium payment. Where withdrawal tables are used, they should be representative of the company's expected experience with lapse and surrenders.

Some companies do not have adequate experience with voluntary terminations and consequently cannot rely on their own past experience to develop withdrawal rates. This is true for newer companies and for companies offering new types of life insurance coverage. For example, companies who have traditionally offered whole life–type policies may find their withdrawal experience to be inappropriate for a new line of jumbo term policies. In such instances, the company should look to its reinsurer or to industry experience in establishing withdrawal rates.

Cash Surrender Values. Minimum cash values are specified by statute. They usually represent an amount equal to the present value of future policy benefits minus an adjusted net premium that provides for the amortization of excess first-year expenses over the premium-paying period of the policy. Many companies modify this computation by reducing the excess first-year expenses or by amortizing the expenses over a period shorter than the premium-paying period. These adjustments usually provide larger cash values than the minimum cash value.

The cash value options must begin in the third policy year; however, most companies modify the option so that cash values will begin after the second or even the first policy year. The cash values in earlier years for traditional policies are usually less than the statutory reserve amount. With newer policies, which require significant annual cash premiums, the cash values will likely exceed statutory reserves and the higher value must be used for statutory reporting. Nontraditional cash value policies are discussed below in this chapter under "Reserves for Policies with High Premiums and Benefits."

The amount of cash value is determined from such factors as premium rates, acquisition and maintenance expenses, dividends, investment policies, and similar considerations. All of the cash value is available if the policy is surrendered.

In addition, most policies contain loan provisions which permit the policyholder to borrow up to 90 or 95 percent of the cash value. The policy loan has been a significant nonforfeiture benefit during periods of rising interest rates. Some current policies contain much higher borrowing rates and some of them are tied to current indexes, which diminishes some of the benefits of policy borrowing.

Extended Term Insurance. In lieu of surrendering a policy, the policyholder has the option to accept extended term insurance for the face amount of the policy, using cash value as a single premium payment. The face amount of the policy less policy loans outstanding is the extended term insurance benefit. The term of the benefit is determined by using the net cash surrender value (cash surrender value minus policy loans). All other policy benefits and riders terminate when this option is elected. The policy can be reinstated if the policyholder resumes paying premiums during the extended term period and usually requires the insured to show evidence of insurability before reinstatement.

If the cash value exceeds the amount required to pay the single term insurance premium, the excess cash value is usually applied to purchase a pure endowment benefit payable at the policy maturity date.

Paid-Up Insurance. Unlike extended term insurance, which continues the face amount of the policy (minus policy loans in force) for an extended period of time, the paid-up insurance option applies the cash surrender value to purchase fully paid insurance to maturity of the original policy. Cash value is used as a single premium to purchase a reduced face amount policy that remains in force to the original policy maturity date. If the original policy was a whole life policy, the paid-up amount will also be a whole life policy; if the original policy was an endowment-type policy, the reduced paid-up amount will be an endowment policy.

The reduced paid-up insurance option usually must be elected by the policy-

quently, only currently declared dividends are recorded as a liability and no dividend provision is included in life insurance reserves. The participating policyholders' share of surplus is held exclusively to support those policies and to pay future policy dividends. In all other respects, the life insurance reserves for participating policies are treated the same as nonparticipating policy reserves.

For statutory reporting, the provision for policy dividends consists of dividends due and unpaid and the estimated amount of dividends payable in the following calendar year. Dividends left with the company to accumulate at interest are accounted for separately.

Conversion Privileges

This benefit provides an option to upgrade policy benefits. The typical conversion option applies to term insurance. This permits a policyholder to convert a term policy to a permanent policy during a specified period.

The conversion privileges usually result in some adverse selection, since policyholders who are unable to purchase permanent insurance may elect to convert their term policies. All conversion privileges are accomplished with minimum costs and require the payment of premiums according to the new policy provisions and attained age; therefore, the implicit benefit cost to the company is measured by the risks that those electing the option will create an element of adverse selection. The anticipated cost of this adverse selection should be provided for either separately or as an implicit part of aggregate life insurance reserves.

For statutory reporting, the conservative mortality and interest assumptions required to provide aggregate reserves usually eliminate the need for a separate reserve covering conversion privileges.

Waiver of Premium Payments

The waiver of premium benefit is similar to the concept of disability benefits provided under accident and health insurance policies. The benefit is limited to the period that the insured becomes totally disabled. The benefit usually continues as long as the policyholder meets the disability requirements, except that it terminates at a specified age close to normal retirement.

The risk accepted by the life insurance company is limited to the loss of premiums during the disability period since the basic policy benefits were provided for by using the mortality, interest, and withdrawal assumptions covered in the preceding paragraphs. The waiver of premium benefit is an "add-on" to the basic policy premium and therefore must be separately reserved for. Since the amounts of premiums and risk of loss are relatively small, the accounting provisions for all reporting purposes are similar. As a practical matter, the statutory loss provision will likely represent a reasonable reserve for all reporting purposes.

Guaranteed Insurability Options

This benefit provides an option to purchase additional insurance at various dates in the future without evidence of insurability. The option matures at fixed

uct to a policyholder is that higher interest credits increase the cash benefit, which may be used to pay the insurance costs of the policy.

The following policy attributes are usually included in the high-premium–high-benefit policy:

Cash Accumulation

These policies provide for significant cash accumulation during the early term of the policy. The initial premiums are usually higher than for most other policies and are necessary to make the policy equation work effectively. This is more true where the initial expense charges are assessed at the beginning of the policy term. It is the cash accumulation benefit that provides a basis for all other policy benefits.

Flexibility of Premium Payments

Some policies require only an initial premium to keep the policy in force for a long period of time. Other policies require periodic premium payments at a minimum level to fund the other policy benefits. Most policies permit the policyowners to make larger or smaller premium payments or, in some instances, they may even skip policy premium payments. This flexible premium payment program provides an option that is not available in most traditional types of policies.

Excess Interest on Accumulations

An important feature of these policies is that interest is promised or projected to be at a much higher rate than the guaranteed interest contained in the policy form. This interest-crediting factor is usually determined monthly, quarterly, semiannually, or annually, or it may be promised at a rate that is tied to certain indexed investments. This feature provides the continuing basis for many of the other policy benefits.

Policy Face Amount Adjustments

Because the cost of insurance is tied to term insurance rates, policyholders usually have an option to increase or decrease the face amount of the policy within minimum and maximum limits. However, increases in the face amount may require evidence of insurability at the time the option is elected.

Partial Cash Withdrawals

Instead of borrowing against the policy or surrendering the policy, some of these policies permit a partial withdrawal of cash values. These withdrawals are usually subject to a minimum and maximum limit and may be made only at specified intervals during the year. A cash withdrawal does not affect the accrual of most other policy benefits—unless the withdrawal exceeds a specified amount, which may effectively cause the policy to be surrendered.

total reserve that is 130 percent of a standard risk. However determined, the additional reserve for the substandard risk, if material, must be provided for.

Payor Benefits Reserves

To ensure that a life insurance policy remains in force when the premiums are paid by other than the insured, a supplemental benefit is provided to cover the waiver of premiums in the event of the payor's disability or death. These reserves reflect the experience of the company or that of a major reinsurer with respect to waivers previously granted. This benefit is similar to the waiver of premium benefits offered to the insurer. The reserve estimated for reporting in the annual statement blank should be a reasonable estimate for such reserves for all other reporting purposes.

Nondeduction of Deferred Fractional Premiums

These amounts represent the mean reserve for the unpaid portion of an annual premium at the time of death. For statutory reporting, the amount is determined and reported separately in the annual statement blank. For income tax reporting, the reserve is recognized if it is calculated in connection with the life insurance reserve.

Supplementary Contract Reserves

These benefits do not arise until a life insurance policy matures. This option is usually available to the policyholder or surviving beneficiary and provides for paying the policy accumulation or face amount over a fixed period or for life.

reserves to protect against catastrophic occurrences within the group. Additional reserves are usually computed on the basis of a percentage of required credit life reserves.

ANNUITY RESERVES

The reserve amounts for annuities depend upon the type of annuity and the funding method chosen by the policyholder. In some circumstances annuities are more like a savings and investment fund, and in others more like a retirement fund. In a few instances, the annuity may provide for the payment of a death benefit. Annuity reserves are affected by the following factors:

Annuity Premiums

Unlike life insurance benefits, which pool policyholder premiums to accumulate promised benefits, annuities are funded by each policyholder from premium and interest accumulations. Premiums are accumulated in the following ways:

Annual Premium Deferred Annuities.. Future policy benefits are promised if all annual premium payments are made in accordance with the policy terms. The annual premiums are the discounted level payments that, when accumulated at interest, will provide sufficient funds to pay the annuity benefits when due.

Single Premium Deferred Annuities. Instead of making periodic annuity payments, the policyholder may pay as a single premium the discounted amount that, along with interest earnings, will pay the future promised benefits.

Flexible Premium Deferred Annuities. Annuity policies which do not require an annual or a fixed single premium and which do not promise specified annuity payments are flexible premium annuities. The promised benefits are determined based upon the premiums and interest earnings that are in the fund at the beginning of the benefit period.

Amounts withdrawn from the annuity accumulation prior to the benefit period are accounted for as surrenders. Consequently, annuity reserves prior to the benefit period or death are computed on the basis of net premium accumulation at interest. However, if these policies provide for refund guarantees or maximum annuity guarantees, additional reserves for these benefits must be provided for. For statutory reporting, where excess interest guarantees are made over an extended period, the amount of the guarantees in excess of policy interest will require an additional reserve.

Annuity benefits are usually available under several options. As the option becomes available and is elected by the policyholder, the annuity becomes imme-

mined at the beginning of the annuity will not be reduced when one of the joint annuitants dies. If the joint benefits are modified so that the survivor receives a reduced benefit, the joint benefit will be larger. The reserves for joint and survivor benefits are determined by using mortality assumptions applicable to the company's own experience, interest rates guaranteed in the policy, and expected excess interest payments. For statutory and income tax reporting, the reserves are usually determined by using prescribed mortality and interest tables. For statutory reporting, promised excess interest must be discounted at the policy-guaranteed rate.

Group Annuities

Annuities issued on a group basis are usually for the purpose of providing for retirement benefits during employees' active working years. The benefits can be accumulated under specific contracts or can be aggregated with the total benefits in a pool. Some contracts are accounted for on a liability method and others are accounted for as a regular annuity contract. The following summarizes the nature of group annuity contracts:

Group Deferred Annuities. The funds in this contract are allocated to each individual participant. The deposited funds are equal to the pension benefit earned during the year and are applied as a single premium to purchase a fully paid-up annuity for each employee. At retirement, the total paid-up annuity represents the pension fund for each individual participant. Under this arrangement, each participant is treated in a manner similar to that for individual annuity holders. The amount of each year's premium is determined based upon a defined future benefit, and premiums may change from year to year depending upon the current level of promised benefits. The accumulated funds during the deferred period (that is, up to the withdrawal or retirement date) are accounted for in a manner similar to that for annual premium deferred annuities. At maturity date, the annuity is then accounted for as an option for a straight-life annuity, a life annuity with a period certain, or a joint and survivor annuity.

Deposit Administration Contracts. These contracts use the funding mechanism of employer deposits to provide for promised pension benefits. The deposits are not allocated to individual employees; rather, they are accumulated by means of an actuarial formula in order to fund pension benefits over a long period of time. Individuals entitled to benefits under the contract are not separately accounted for during the deferred period. At retirement, amounts sufficient to fund a single premium annuity are removed from the deposit administration fund and used to purchase an annuity for the retiree. The unallocated deposit administration funds are accounted for in a manner similar to that for annual premium deferred annuities. Amounts withdrawn for single premium annuities are accounted for in a manner similar to that for straight-life annuities, joint and survivor annuities, and similar annuity options.

Immediate Participation Guarantee Contract. This is a modification of the deposit administration contract; it requires the employer to assume responsibil-

continue beyond the expiration date of the policy are usually valued at an estimate of settlement cost based on available claims history.

Accident and health reserves can be determined on a policy-by-policy basis or can be grouped in a manner similar to the method used for life insurance reserves. For statutory reporting, companies are required to use specific reserve tables. Certain accident and health policies may require additional reserves for contingencies.

Reserves are determined on the basis of the type of protection offered by the policy. The major policy forms are described below.

Disability Income Protection

This insurance provides benefits for loss of income from disability resulting from sickness or accident. Since the benefits are paid in fixed cash amounts, the term of the disability payments determines the total claim value.

The benefits offered under disability insurance are subject to numerous policy provisions that affect claim payments. These provisions and payment terms are summarized below.

Short-Term Disability Insurance. The benefits from this policy begin after a short waiting period, often 7 days, and continue for 1 or 2 years. Short-term disability benefits are often selected by employees who are not adequately covered under sick leave policies. The duration of the benefits is limited; therefore, the provision for loss reserves is predicated upon incurred claims and unearned premiums. Contingent benefits, such as maternity claims, require additional reserves. The provision for reserves required for statutory reporting will usually be a satisfactory estimate for all other reporting purposes.

Long-Term Disability Insurance. These benefits are delayed for several weeks or months after the disability has been incurred. However, the benefits are payable over a long period of time, often until the policyholder reaches age 65. The reserves for these policies are more difficult to determine since the rehabilitation periods are difficult to determine, and the occupation or employment opportunities may be limited.

The reserves for long-term disability benefits are determined in a manner similar to that for life insurance reserves. For companies that maintain extensive claim cost records, the reserves should be determined based upon their historical experience adjusted for current economic conditions. These reserves are determined by using (1) the mean or midterminal formula, (2) a reasonable discount rate based upon the company's historical and expected investment earnings, and (3) past history with lapsed and surrendered policies. Policies that provide for a return of premiums based upon claims experience require additional reserves. The risk for adverse deviation from reserve estimates can be included as an implicit part of the estimates or separately provided for. For statutory reporting, companies may be required to use specific morbidity tables and interest rates.

group coverage, the underwriting and selection process may be limited. For individual coverages, it is possible to underwrite each individual policy; consequently, some potential risks can be eliminated or separately charged for.

In the case of group policies, a significant policy feature allows coverage for all individuals in the group. Like the individual policy, the group policy usually excludes preexisting health conditions. For group insurance there is an element of antiselection, and a separate provision for that condition must be provided for. Group policies may be subject to experience rating adjustments which increase or decrease the net cost of insurance, and these contingencies must be included in the reserves.

REINSURANCE DEDUCTIONS

Reinsurance-ceded amounts should be deducted from the related reserves. The reinsured amounts affect reserves, claims that are unpaid, claims that are resisted, and incurred but not reported claims. The reinsurance-ceded amounts are calculated in a manner similar to that used in establishing primary reserves. If reserves are determined on a seriatim basis, then reinsurance is also calculated on that basis. Likewise, if a group calculation is used for the primary reserves, it is also used for the reinsurance-ceded calculation. Where liabilities are established for due and unpaid claims, the reserves for those policies and the reinsurance-ceded amounts should be removed.

Where companies have "bulk reinsurance" agreements, the reinsurance ceded will be equal to the primary reserves. Bulk reinsurance agreements are often used when the primary insurer continues to issue policies similar to those included in the bulk reinsurance contract. It is also used where assumption certificates are

Table 12-5
Commissioners' 1958 Standard Ordinary Mortality Table (Abbreviated)

Age	Number Living	Number Dying	Death Rate Per 1000	Life Expectancy Years
0	10,000,000	70,800	7.08	68.30
1	9,929,200	17,475	1.76	67.78
2	9,911,725	15,066	1.52	66.90
3	9,896,659	14,449	1.46	66.00
4	9,882,210	13,835	1.40	65.10
5	9,868,375	13,322	1.35	64.19
10	9,805,870	11,865	1.21	59.58
20	9,664,994	17,300	1.79	50.37
30	9,480,358	20,193	2.13	41.25
35	9,373,807	23,528	2.51	36.69
40	9,241,359	32,622	3.53	32.18
50	8,762,306	72,902	8.32	23.63
65	6,800,531	215,917	31.75	12.90
75	4,129,906	303,011	73.73	7.81
85	1,311,348	211,311	161.14	4.32
95	97,165	34,128	351.24	1.80
99	6,415	6,415	1000.00	0.50

ognized by first extinguishing unamortized acquisition costs and then making additions to reserves and liabilities. For statutory reporting, only the loss applicable to the current year is charged to operations; the balance is reported as a surplus adjustment.

Some reserve adjustments and increases in claim liabilities should be recog

Loss recognition is further described in Chapter 10, Deferred Policy Acquisition Costs, under "Locked-in Assumptions and Loss Recognition."

COMMISSIONERS' 1958 STANDARD ORDINARY MORTALITY TABLE (ABBREVIATED)

This table was developed from the mortality experience of several large companies for the years 1950 through 1954. It is presented here in abbreviated form (Table 12-5) to illustrate the mortality consideration included in a typical life insurance reserve calculation. Several other newer and older tables are used with or without modifications to approximate mortality experience.

13

PROPERTY AND LIABILITY LOSS RESERVES

Unlike life insurance reserves, which are based on rather reliable studies of prior mortality experience for large age groups, property and lia-

bility loss reserves must take into account expected loss experience, using everchanging risk circumstances. Prior experience with these risks is a significant factor in determining estimates of future claims payments; however, changes in policy conditions, laws, judicial determinations, inflation, and other factors may affect ultimate payments on outstanding losses. Consequently, no single formula will adequately measure property and liability risks as do the mortality tables for life insurance. Additionally, insurance protection offered for property and liability risks is broader in form and subject to deductible and coinsurance provisions not required for life insurance.

The following summary covers significant components of property and liability loss reserves:

REPORTED LOSSES

Losses are classified as reported as soon as the company or its agents receives and records a loss reported by an insured or a third party. Reported losses may be reserved separately under the following circumstances:

Filed but Not Investigated

These reported losses place the company on notice that claims have been made for benefits covered by their policies. Reserves for these losses are affected by the current status of claims files as follows:

Filed with Re[illegible] Proof [illegible]

Adjusted and Liability Determined

Often, where liability has been acknowledged by the company, the benefit amounts are fixed by the policy limits. Claim payment may be delayed because of required judicial approval, unresolved status of claimant's trustee, business disputes, or attorney's contingent fees. These losses include claims for bodily injury, professional liability, some workers' compensation, other liability, and fidelity and surety coverages. Other claims in this category include payments subject to changes in circumstances, such as claims for workers' compensation and disability income where changing health conditions could extend or terminate policy benefits. This category also includes surety policies where the cost of completing an insured project cannot be reasonably ascertained.

The reserves for long-term claims are often projected to their ultimate cost and discounted to present value to reflect the time value of money.

Adjusted and Liability Not Determined

These claims have been investigated and the review process completed, but the liability amount has not been determined because it is in dispute. Losses arising from bodily injury, workers' compensation, and professional liability are often difficult to determine since they may involve perceived as well as actual losses. When these claim investigations are completed and liability has been established, the company may propose an amount in settlement of the losses. If proposed settlement amounts are rejected, the determination of actual and perceived losses is subject to a negotiated settlement.

The reserve for these losses should take into account offers and counteroffers and litigation costs. For certain losses, such as claims for long-term disability, punitive damage claims must also be considered.

Claims in Litigation

Generally, these claims involve losses from fire and allied causes, bodily injury, professional and other liability, and boiler and machinery losses, except for small court claims and limited liability claims. These loss reserves are difficult to estimate since historical experience is limited and may not reflect the factual issues in the current suits. Amounts claimed may exceed the company's estimate of the liability and often exceed the entire policy face amount. At times, such claims are filed on a frivolous basis or may assert newly discovered judicial interpretations of contract liabilities.

Reserves for these losses are usually based on the company's best estimate of amounts at risk and legal counsel's estimate of the outcome of litigation.

Catastrophic Losses

These losses can occur for nearly all insured risks but most likely occur in connection with fire, windstorms, hailstorms, earthquakes, epidemics, and boiler explosions and other conflagrations. These losses become catastrophic when a single incident causes numerous, high-dollar-value claims. The incidents may occur regularly but are difficult to predict for either geographic location or severeness. Windstorms, hailstorms, and epidemics usually occur in a manner that permits an early determination of ultimate losses. Other catastrophic losses may involve claims against several parties, and the insurer's ultimate liability is often difficult to ascertain.

Loss reserves for claims that can be readily ascertained should be based on historical experience for similar claims, adjusted for current trends and factors. Losses on conflagrations where liability is difficult to ascertain should be considered in a manner similar to that for litigation losses.

UNREPORTED LOSSES

These losses, identified as IBNR (incurred but not reported), should be included in the current accounting period even though the company has no loss reports.

The delay in receiving notice of losses may have arisen because the losses were recently incurred, they were reported to the agent and not to the company, the policyholders were unaware that the losses were insured, there was a delay in postal delivery or mail processing, or the damage or injury has not yet been detected by policyholders or claimants. Also, some companies have early closing, resulting in 1 or 2 or more days of unprocessed losses. For workers' compensation, professional liability, and fidelity insurance, the losses may not be detected for a considerable period after being incurred.

For most unreported losses, a pattern of predictability emerges after several years of experience. Because incidents of unreported claims may vary by type of coverage, it is usually necessary to analyze subsequent loss experience by coverages to determine expected losses. Most of these losses are reported within a relatively short time after the end of an accounting period, exce compensation, professional liability, and fidelity insurance. Histor with the subsequent development of unreported losses, if modif trends and other factors, provides a reasonable basis for estimati these losses.

ADJUSTMENTS TO LOSS RESERVES

Pure loss reserves represent the aggregate estimated cost o paying all outstanding losses, including reported and unreporte unpaid loss adjustment expenses. The determination of these an on a best-estimate basis without regard to credits for reinsurar and for salvage or subrogation amounts. In order to report the o and expense reserves correctly, the following adjustments must b loss reserves:

Reinsurance Recoverable

Property and liability insurance companies purchase reinsurance from other insurers for excess losses. Reinsurance benefits and allowances permit a company to spread its adverse loss experience over an extended period of time. Reinsurance recoverable amounts arise from premiums paid for benefits designed to limit the following loss exposures:

Single Loss Occurrences. A common form of reinsurance provides loss protection for excess amounts over losses retained by the company, up to a specified limit. A *retained loss* is the agreed amount that the primary insurer must pay before claiming a benefit from the reinsurer. The retained amount may be as low as $10,000 to $25,000 for small companies, but up to a $1 million or more for larger companies. The recoverable excess amount is a direct offset against each single loss reserve. The single net loss reserve consists of the retained amount plus the excess, if any, of the loss over the reinsured amount. The allowance for reinsurance is determined for each single loss reserve. If loss reserves for long-term disability, workers' compensation, and other long-term benefits have been discounted, then reinsurance allowances should also be discounted to their present value.

Aggregate Loss Reserves. In addition to reinsuring single loss reserves, most companies purchase reinsurance to protect against surplus drains arising from adverse aggregate loss experience. Examples of these reinsurance agreements are covered in Chapter 16, Reinsurance Ceded and Assumed, under "Categories of Business." To determine its allowances for this reinsurance, a company classifies its losses by coverage and year incurred, including outstanding amounts, and thereby ascertains the amounts by which its incurred losses exceed its aggregate retained amounts. The aggregate loss reserves for each line of business are reduced for these recoverable amounts.

and Subrogation Recoverable

tory financial reporting, companies are not permitted to recognize until they are received in cash. For public reporting, these d be estimated, net of expenses, and used to reduce pure loss may affect the amount of reinsurance recoverable.

:s in connection with the payment of property losses when the ı has paid them retains the right to dispose of salvageable residue :s. These amounts often arise in connection with fire, windstorm, :rical, and vehicular damage.

arises because the insured losses have been paid and the rights of ıd recovery from third parties have passed to the company. These arise in connection with property or liability losses involving neg- : parties or employee wrongdoing for fidelity claims.

:coverable amounts are usually determined for single losses but ın historical experience adjusted for current trends and factors.

LOSS RESERVE CALCULATIONS

Although loss reserves are insurance liabilities, the assets available to pay such reserves when due represent a principal source of investable funds for a property liability insurance company. In that respect, reserves can be thought of as representing assets. In terms of financial reporting, however, the reserves represent the liability for losses incurred but not yet paid.

In determining loss reserves, a property liability company therefore gives little consideration to its investable assets. This is in recognition that its primary function is to pay policy benefits as soon as they are ascertained. Consequently, loss reserves are calculated, for the most part, on a pure loss basis. This reserving concept differs from life insurance in that most property and liability benefits are payable over a short period of time, whereas life insurance benefits are usually payable many years in the future and are discounted to their present value.

Since property and liability loss reserves are subject to changing circumstances by factors such as inflation, supervision practices, loss file procedures and controls, legislative changes, and current court attitudes, reserves may be determined by using one or more of the following methods:

Individual Case Estimates

These reserves are determined from the factual circumstances reported in the claim file and represent an estimate of the ultimate settlement cost. An initial review of claim files usually results in eliminating small cases for which the cost of settlement is obvious or for which the facts indicate that an arbitrary amount can be assigned. These small cases are usually segregated, and settlements are routinely approved when all loss documents are received. Other claim files are reviewed by examiners experienced in estimating losses for one or more lines of business. The accuracy with which claims are estimated depends upon the skills and the experience of the claim examiner. The level of skills and experience varies by the type of loss.

Property Losses. Most property losses occur in connection with policies covering fire and allied lines, multiple perils, ocean and inland marine, automobile physical damage, and specialized coverages such as earthquakes, aircraft, glass breakage, burglary and theft, and boiler and machinery risks.

Losses from fire, windstorm, hail, explosion, and similar accidents usually involve loss estimates based on cost recovery or on cost to replace: (1) Cost recovery represents the insured amount less estimated normal wear and tear or depreciation. Determining this value usually requires an inspection of the property and an estimate of the percent of destruction in relation to the total insured amount. When the insured amount less normal wear and tear or depreciation is multiplied by the estimated destruction percentage, the result is an estimate of the ultimate loss. The estimating process is the same for factory or business buildings, home or farm buildings, machinery and equipment, office and home furnishings, and similar insured property. (2) When the loss is measured by the replacement value, historical cost is replaced by current cost for the addition(s) required to replace the property. Replacement costs are more difficult to determine than cost recovery values are because they take several factors into account: the quality of construction; the availability of similar construction materials; the acceptability of like-kind replacements for machinery, equipment, furnishings, and supplies; and inflation.

Determining the losses for inventoriable items is often difficult because the accounting records may be incomplete, partially destroyed, or totally lost. Other valuation methods, including consultants and appraisal reports, may be required in order to estimate the loss amount. Production records, sales journals, shipping ledgers, and other primary source documents may provide a reasonable basis for estimating losses related to manufactured inventory, outstanding accounts receivable, and work in process. Estimates of property losses should be offset by reinsurance recoverable and salvage and subrogation, except that for statutory reporting, salvage and subrogation is ignored.

Liability Losses. Determining liability loss reserves is more difficult than determining property losses because as many claims include intangible amounts. Liability losses may be incurred in connection with circumstances which were not contemplated when the insurance policy was issued but which developed because of dynamic changes in statutes and court decisions. For example, the principle of third-party negligence may have been defined beforehand by legislators but later interpreted by the judiciary in a fashion which results in unexpected liability payments. Liability losses vary by the type of policy coverage.

The following are some of the significant classes of liability insurance:

Automobile Liability. The operators of motor vehicles are responsible for injuries to others caused by their negligent actions. States having comparative negligence laws permit each party to claim damages based on even minor negligence on the part of one party. In some jurisdictions, guests riding with the operator are not covered except to the extent of incurred medical expenses. To eliminate contention about medical expenses, loss of wages, and other injuries for small claims, many states have no-fault laws under which each driver must look to his or her own insurance carrier for recoveries.

Automobile liability claims are often settled on a negotiated basis. First, after a thorough review, the claim examiner determines whether liability exists and estimates the total loss. These estimates represent individual case estimates and should in each case reflect the ultimate settlement cost, including a margin for possible adverse deviations from the estimate. Actual settlements of the loss amounts are then negotiated with the injured parties or their legal representative.

Some claims are settled in litigation instituted by the injured party. These claims may be exaggerated because of perceived losses that cannot be verified. Claims in litigation are established on the same basis as nonlitigated claims—except that the additional issues raised by the claimant, as well as the cost of litigation and adjustment services, must be considered. Often, new facts are discovered as these claims develop; in this event, adjustments are made to the individual case estimates to reflect additional liabilities. In the event that claim examiners have determined that no liability exists, it may still be necessary to provide for the costs incurred in order to dispose of such claims.

Besides arising from personal injuries, automobile liability claims arise from wrongful death, lost wages, loss of services of a spouse, and compensatory damages. These liability claims may also arise in connection with the negligence of an operator permitted to use the owner's vehicle.

Personal and Business Liabilities. Ownership of property, whether it is used as a personal residence or for a business activity, gives rise to claims resulting from hazardous conditions—such as broken sidewalks and steps; defective doors; falling objects; unprotected machinery, pipes, and radiators; animal bites; negligent action of employees; improper use of recreational vehicles; and uncleared ice and snow. Some states require the injured parties to bear a proportionate share of the liability for their lack of due care and attention. Claim examiners evaluate these claims on the basis of reported facts and establish an estimated liability for each open case. If the claims are not settled through negotiation and proceed to litigation, the liabilities are estimated on the same basis as are litigated automobile liabilities.

Some risks may be separately regulated, especially when the liabilities arise from specific nonperformance, such as for dramshops, pension plan management, and fiduciary and trust arrangements. Special skills may be required in order to estimate these case liabilities since they are subject to separate statutes governing the actions of individuals and businesses in these risk categories. In several states, there are also special laws governing farm-related accidents.

Workers' Compensation Liabilities. This is required work-related liability insurance that protects both employee and employer. It protects the employee because the benefits are guaranteed for medical expenses and loss of time for injuries determined to be job-related. It protects the employer's assets because these work-related benefits are defined and are required to be covered by insurance. Unlike other liability claims, which may be subject to considerable negotiations, workers' compensation benefits are payable in a fixed and determinable amount when the facts and circumstances develop that a work-related injury has occurred. The litigation of workers' claims usually involves a determination that a valid claim exists rather than a determination about the exact amount of damages.

Workers' compensation benefits include (1) payment of all medical-related expenses incurred as a result of injury and (2) subsequent loss-of-wage benefits during periods of unemployment or underemployment. Estimating the losses for these claims requires a determination of the potential medical benefits to be paid and of the period of unemployment. Medical expenses incurred to treat and heal the injuries to full recovery are easier to estimate than are those related to injuries requiring long-term recovery periods or long-term benefits for unemployment or underemployment.

Unlike most other property and liability claims, workers' compensation benefits payable over a long period are discounted to their present value. This discounting is permitted when following statutory accounting because these benefits are not required to be paid in a lump sum. Where benefits appear certain to be paid for an extended period or for life, they may be negotiated with the claimant and paid in a single lump sum.

Product Liabilities. This is a special class of losses arising from an implied warranty that products are not defective. Losses arising from defective products do not require proof of negligence but only proof that the products are unsalable or unfit for a particular use. These implied warranties may be disclaimed if the product is properly labeled to disclose the purpose for which it should be used. Product claims often involve circumstances in which the user asserts that the producer has failed to exercise care and caution in producing or labeling the product and that this has resulted in losses.

When determining loss reserves, claim examiners must ascertain that implied warranties were violated or that due care and caution in construction was not observed. Estimated actual damages are often difficult to ascertain since losses may involve actual and perceived injuries and punitive damages may be asserted.

Professional Liabilities. Claims against physicians, attorneys, accountants, actuaries, and other skilled tradespeople is an insurance loss area requiring special skills.

These claims arise because of an alleged breach of contract or because of negligence. Breach-of-contract claims involve a failure to perform the services as agreed. Negligence claims involve a failure to exercise the required standard of care. The standard of care required is usually specified in the statutes or in the canons and ethics of the profession. Failures to follow the appropriate standard, resulting in losses, are the basis of claims for negligence. While some of these claims are litigated, for the most part they are subject to negotiated settlements. Some claims may not emerge for a number of years following the alleged negligence; consequently, the estimate of incurred but not reported claims becomes a significant factor in determining loss reserves for professional liability.

Many professional liability policies are now written on a claims-made basis. Under this type of policy, only the claims that are reported during the policy period are covered. Claims made after the policy period, even though the loss is alleged to have occurred during the period, are excluded, thus avoiding long-term exposure. Incurred but not reported claims usually arise only because of a failure in the company's reporting network.

Accident and Health Insurance. Claims from these policy coverages include medical expense reimbursement and short- and long-term disability. Medical expense reimbursement usually arises from guaranteed policy benefits paying a fixed indemnity; most policy benefits are paid during a short duration, such as 1 or 2 years. Travel accident policies usually limit benefits to claims arising during a specified travel period. Disability income protection policies providing benefits from loss of wages for periods of 1 or 2 years are classified as short-term disability policies; benefits payable over longer period or for life are classified as long-term disability policies.

Reserves for medical expense reimbursement and short-term disability income protection are based on the facts and circumstances of each file, as are other liability benefits. Long-term disability benefits are more difficult to determine since facts and circumstances can change with time and ultimate benefits are adjusted for these expected changes.

Credit accident and health policies are issued on a group basis and the benefits are more limited, usually providing protection for the purpose of insuring payment of debts. These policies are usually reserved on a group basis unless circumstances indicate that a file should be reserved separately.

Fidelity and Surety. Fidelity claims arise because an insured individual deliberately or inadvertently caused the disappearance of money or property. Whether the fidelity insurance covers an individual or a position, loss reserves are determined by estimating provable amounts up to the policy limits. In some instances, such losses may be partly or wholly recoverable from the individual causing the loss.

Claims for surety benefits occur by failure of the insured party to perform as agreed. Since the surety agrees to perform if the insured does not, the actual loss incurred may be only to replace old management or may require total funding to complete a project. If there is a series of projects, the surety may undertake to complete all of them in order to minimize its losses. The insured's collateral on deposit is used to reduce amounts paid by the surety. Reserves for these losses should be based on the facts and circumstances, including the cost of performing all outstanding insured contracts.

Formula Estimates

Reserves determined by formula may be the primary estimate for some lines of unpaid losses, for a reasonableness check on aggregate loss reserves, or for temporary estimates for specific losses before individual case estimates are determined.

All formula reserves are based on the prior years' experience either of a company or of the industry. Small dollar volumes or small policyholder counts for a line of business will not provide a reliable basis for estimating future reserves. In order to achieve reliable estimates, the experience data base used must be large enough to avoid those distortions from unusual losses which may occur when using only limited historical experience. Industry experience is useful for determining formula reserves only if it parallels the company's underwriting practices, the geographic location of its risks, and its claim-settling practices. Since formula reserves are based on prior experience, the computational factors must be modified for current trends in claim settlements and policy benefits, for underwriting changes, and for inflation, and must include reasonable margins for errors in estimates.

The reliability of formula reserves depends upon the accuracy with which loss data is recorded. Errors in coding for type of coverage, partial payments, loss expenses, salvage and subrogation, and reinsurance, if significant in total, will distort the results of formula computations. Incorrectly tabulating the claim counts, failing to reopen claim files for additional payments, and combining multiple losses in a single coverage will distort the average claim costs computations.

Formula estimates should be based on net paid losses, except that reinsurance not related to specific claim files should be determined separately. Formula reserves are seldom applied to large losses since they are usually subject to a separate review and may involve nonroutine settlement conditions, which are not easy to codify in a formula estimate. Catastrophic losses usually involve the participation of reinsurers and are estimated separately. The statistical data used in determining loss reserves should include experience for at least 3 to 5 prior years to ensure that trends in claim settlements are adequately considered.

Ideally, each reported claim and each incurred but not reported claim would be held open until all loss payments were made and the file closed. This would provide an exact claim history on which formula reserves could be developed. Accumulating this data is usually impractical, however; instead, formulas are developed by using loss experience based on payments accounted for by accident year or calendar year. Paid losses must be identified by coverage or line of business since aggregate loss experience is not meaningful when determining formula estimates. Where losses are reported by accident year, the formula reserve factors include incurred but not reported losses which must be separated for financial reporting. Where claim payments are classified by calendar or reported year, the incurred but not reported losses are not included and must be reserved separately.

Of the numerous formulas used to estimate loss reserves, most can be included in the following two categories:

Extrapolation Estimates. Extrapolation often involves the determination of an interim value when both the beginning and ending values surrounding the interim period are known. It may also involve determining an ultimate value when the interim value is known. The latter computation is used to extrapolate estimated ultimate claim costs. It should not be confused with computational methods which use discounting to determine the present value of future costs. The ultimate costs for property and liability insurance, other than for workers' compensation and disability insurance, are the gross expected payments made to settle a policy claim.

The extrapolation estimate is based on the relationship of prior paid losses to ultimate paid amounts. Losses already paid are extrapolated to ultimate estimated losses by using a ratio of paid losses to ultimate losses at each stage of development. The sum of ultimate estimated losses is reduced by currently paid losses to determine current unpaid amounts. Prior years' paid claims are classified by accident year, developed through successive periods, and expressed as a percentage of ultimate development. Since the losses are developed by accident year, they include a provision for incurred but not reported claims, which for statutory reporting are separated and reported as a separate item.

This method of estimating ultimate costs is often referred to as the "payment development method." To work effectively, the method must be based on a consistent loss-reporting system. It also assumes that developed prior-year loss levels will be relatively consistent in the future; if claims are not incurred in a relatively stable and proportional manner, the extrapolation method should be modified to reflect changes in the frequency and the severity of reported losses. Unlike other formula methods, extrapolation estimates do not require the use of claim counts. After the development of prior years' paid loss percentages, the computation of ultimate estimated losses is easily accomplished by a series of arithmetic computations.

Average Cost Estimates. Average claim costs are based on claim counts and dollar amounts paid. The average claim valuation method is especially useful for smaller recurring claims because it is an efficient method that avoids the necessity of individual valuation of each claim. The average cost method requires the accumulation of claim counts and dollar values by coverage or by line of business. To develop reliable data, a large volume of claim activities must be included in the computation to avoid significant and infrequent variations from the claim payment pattern. This formula method likely will not be used to estimate ultimate losses for catastrophic risks, professional liability, long-term disability, fidelity and surety, and other specialized risks.

The average claim valuation method requires accurate data about the frequency and severity of losses incurred. It is not a simple arithmetic average, but takes into account the various types of claims as well as projected trends in loss payments. Using detailed claim counts and loss payments by coverages, a formula can be developed to determine the average historical paid losses.

Estimated ultimate losses are derived by using unpaid loss counts and the average values of paid losses adjusted for current trends in loss payments and inflation. Ultimate losses are reduced by payments already made to determine current unpaid losses. Where ultimate estimated claim counts are used, reserves include an estimate for incurred but not reported losses, which for statutory reporting must be segregated and separately reported. If a current unpaid loss count is used, a separate estimate must be made of incurred but not reported losses.

Average cost estimates require continual updating for changes made in policy forms, legislative and judicial decrees, and inflation. Larger claim payments and unusual losses should be excluded from the computation. Reinsurance recoveries and salvage and subrogation should be included in the average cost, except that for statutory reporting, expected salvage and subrogation recovery should be ignored.

OTHER LOSS RESERVE CONSIDERATIONS

Several factors affect the ultimate reserves. Some arise from statutory rules, some from special treatment of particular products, and others because of their own common occurrences.

The following are some of the significant other considerations affecting the determination of loss reserves:

Statutory Reserves

These reserves arise from four principal sources:

Unearned Premiums. For certain lines of business, such as credit life insurance and credit accident and health insurance, companies are required to hold specified amounts of unearned premiums as a special loss reserve (Schedule K reserves). Other special reserves include deferred maturity benefits, return premiums on retrospective rating plans, and noncancelable accident and health benefits. To the extent that unearned premium reserves represent an excess over actual unearned premiums, they are statutory reserves which are not included in public reporting financial statements.

Unauthorized Reinsurance. Reinsurance companies not licensed in states in which they accept reinsurance risks are classified as unauthorized companies. Amounts due from such companies on paid and unpaid losses are subject to a separate statutory reserve requirement. Where such amounts exceed funds held or retained by the company for the account of unauthorized companies, the excess must be held as a special reserve. To the extent that these excess amounts are deemed to be recoverable, the statutory reserve is eliminated for public reporting financial statements.

Schedule P Reserves. For automobile liability, other liability, medical malpractice, and workers' compensation, a special reserve calculation is made, and to the extent that it exceeds the experience ratio, these amounts are classified as Schedule P statutory reserves. The lowest loss ratio in the 5 preceding years is compared to premiums earned for the years in determining the adequacy of these reserves. For automobile and other liabilities, if the lowest loss ratio is less than 60 percent, then a 60 percent factor must be computed and the excess over previously determined amounts is included as a statutory reserve. For workers' compensation liability, the minimum statutory loss ratio is 65 percent and the maximum is 75 percent. For credit insurance, the minimum loss ratio is 50 percent. Schedule P reserves are not required for public reporting financial statements.

Voluntary Reserves. Companies writing protection for catastrophic events may include voluntary reserves in anticipation of losses that may have occurred or will be incurred in the future and for which other reserves have not been provided. The concept of statutory voluntary reserves reflects a conservative attitude about future loss events. These amounts cannot be arbitrarily determined but must be based on reasonable assumptions about their loss experience. For public reporting, such reserves are not permitted.

Other Reserve Considerations

However determined, loss reserves represent an inventory of incurred losses for which reserve estimates must be provided. Consequently, an accurate cutoff at the end of an accounting period is important in order to preclude incurred losses from being deferred to a subsequent accounting period.

Conservative accounting practices may result in providing for losses in excess of the ultimate cost. Redundancies in reserves may result in mismatching current revenue against cost and expenses as well as in overstating the loss experience used to calculate current policy premiums.

STRUCTURED SETTLEMENTS

In recent years, many companies have begun to arrange settlements with claimants involving liability losses by using the "structured payment settlement." The use of this payment method permits a company to offer long-term installment payments on a discounted basis. Except for workers' compensation and long-term disability payments, most insurers are required to provide the gross liability for long-term periodic payments. This results in a surplus strain that can be avoided by utilizing the "structured payment method."

The method is designed to provide additional benefits to a claimant and permits the closing of the insurer's claim file with a discounted lump-sum payment. The actual payment is negotiated between the insurer and the claimant and is funded by a single annuity payment made by the insurer. For example, if the claim has a value of $100,000, a structured settlement payment may be arranged to provide the claimant with periodic payments over a long-term aggregating amounts in excess of $100,000 and which may be funded by the insurer for amounts less than $100,000. This arrangement requires the insurer to purchase an annuity contract from an authorized life insurance company and provides for payments to be made directly to the claimant on behalf of the insurer, permitting the claimant to receive all the periodic payments on a tax-free basis. If, on the other hand, an annuity contract is purchased by the claimant, future interest earnings on the annuity will be taxable. The insurer, although usually contingently liable for such payments, may nevertheless close the claim file as being fully paid.

If insurers were permitted to discount these liabilities for their current and expected earnings rate, an annuity contract would not be required.

TITLE INSURANCE

Losses incurred by title insurance companies are more in the nature of errors and omission losses. If the title search fails to detect mistakes in public records, forgeries and impersonations, incomplete probate of wills, and undisclosed or unlocated heirs, a loss may be incurred to correct the title flaws or to reimburse the purchasers for their losses in attempting to acquire the property. Often, these errors and omissions can be corrected by affidavits received in consideration of payments made to former or undisclosed heirs. If the property was transferred by forgeries, falsification of records, or impersonation, the real owner may reclaim the property or accept consideration for properly transferring title. Where defects cannot be corrected, the purchasers are reimbursed, up to the policy limits, for the total cost and expenses incurred by them. Liability seldom involves intangible claims, but tangible losses in relinquishing defective titles may be considered.

To match revenue from title insurance policies properly, ultimate estimated claim costs should be recognized concurrently with the premium revenue. For statutory reporting, title insurance companies are often required to maintain an unearned premium reserve based on a fixed percentage of title insurance revenue. To the extent that these reserves approximate estimated ultimate costs, they may be used by public reporting companies as loss reserves; otherwise, unearned premium reserves required by statutory accounting should be eliminated. To the extent that the initial estimated ultimate claim costs are deficient, incurred losses, including incurred but not reported losses, are recorded when they are reported. Amounts recovered from errors and omission policies owned by title insurance companies should be applied to reduce losses.

MORTGAGE GUARANTEE INSURANCE

Mortgage guaranteed losses are more in the nature of bad debt losses incurred by the primary lender. That is, the losses are not the result of a casualty, except to the extent that the borrower's earning power is interrupted because of a casualty loss. Losses occur because the borrower's personal financial situation renders the borrower unable or unwilling to meet mortgage obligations or because of adverse local or national economic conditions. Although the mortgage guaranty company has a right to underwrite each risk separately, generally the lenders' policies on mortgage loans are approved and the insurers' losses should parallel expected bad debt losses on all lenders' mortgages. Losses tend to be higher during the earlier periods, when borrowers have smaller equities. As their equities increase, the risk of loss should correspondingly decrease.

Mortgage insurance losses are recognized as liabilities when incurred. Consequently, loss reserves must include a provision for reported and incurred but not reported losses. Loss reserves are based on the company or industry historical experience adjusted for local and national economic trends.

Generally, foreclosure on mortgaged real estate is better handled by the lender. However, there may be circumstances that require the mortgage insurance company to pay the insured loss and accept conveyance of the unsold property. Real estate acquired in foreclosure is excluded from investments and separately reported, except that for statutory reporting it is combined with other real estate owned by the company. Such real estate is reported at fair value, and costs in excess of that amount are expensed currently. Realized gains and losses on the sale of foreclosed real estate should be recognized in the period of sale as an adjustment to claim costs.

Some companies are required by statute to maintain a contingency reserve against possible losses from adverse economic cycles. The contribution to these reserves may represent a portion of earned premiums or a percentage of loan amounts outstanding. These reserve amounts are required to be maintained for a 10-year period and are released on a first-in–first-out basis. Contingency reserves can be released on a current basis if actual losses exceed the required additions. To the extent that contingency reserves are deemed redundant, they should be excluded for public reporting. If contingency reserves are included, they should be adjusted for tax deductions permitted to the extent that the company invests in special U.S. Mortgage Guarantee Tax and Loss Bonds.

14

LOSS ADJUSTMENT EXPENSES

Loss adjustment expenses are incurred in connection with all policy claims even though the claims may be denied. The reserves for loss adjustment expenses represent the estimated future expenses to settle all claims in process. These expenses should be accrued at the same time that the liability for a loss is recognized. For some property and medical claims, only a minor amount of claims expense is incurred and the reserves are usually smaller. For liability claims, adjustment expenses are significant and result in a larger reserve. For title insurance, claims adjustment expenses are usually not reserved but are recognized as incurred since losses are easily ascertained and settled.

Since loss adjustment expenses are not incurred uniformly, it is necessary to identify loss expenses by coverage and line of business. Preferably, these expenses should be determined by specific claims; this results in a more accurate estimate of ultimate unpaid loss adjustment expenses. For larger losses, allocated claims adjustment expenses can be estimated on an individual case basis, as are loss reserves. However, because many loss adjustment expenses cannot be allocated, especially those incurred internally, it is usually necessary to estimate these reserves on a formula basis.

Loss adjustment expenses are divided into the following categories:

ALLOCATED LOSS ADJUSTMENT EXPENSES

These expenses can usually be identified as costs related to an individual claim file. The cost of services for outside adjusting services, attorneys' fees, service and court costs, police reports, expert witness fees, appraisal costs, and private investigators are some of the more common allocated loss adjustment expenses.

The amount of allocated loss expenses varies by companies and is affected by the level of claim activity, catastrophic events, geographic areas served without internal claim adjusters, litigation activities, and available independent adjusting services. Many companies have adequate internal staff to adjust their own claims and seldom use outside services. Others have less internal staff and serve a wide geographic area, which requires the use of more external claims adjusting services. Consequently, industry experience with allocated loss expenses is less useful as a guide for the adequacy of such reserves than is comparable experience with actual losses.

Allocated loss adjustment expenses are often determined by accident reporting year and exclude incurred but not reported losses, which must be provided for separately.

UNALLOCATED LOSS ADJUSTMENT EXPENSES

These expenses are those incurred in settling claims which cannot be identified by claim files. They include expenses incurred in audits of assureds' records, claims department salaries and employee relations and benefits, portions of expenses for insurance, travel rental items, equipment repair and maintenance, printing and stationery, and postage and telephone. Costs such as real estate expenses and taxes, commissions and allowances, advertising, boards and associations, and underwriting reports are excluded because they do not apply or, in the case of real estate expenses, are separately charged as rental items.

Unallocated expenses incurred during the period are separated between underwriting, investment, and loss adjustment expenses. Certain expenses, such as salaries, employee benefits, and travel, are by their nature relatively easy to identify and to separate between cost centers. Other expenses are subject to less objective measurements. However determined, the separation of paid expenses between underwriting, investment, and loss adjustment permits reporting these amounts separately in the statement of operations. Unpaid amounts for underwriting and investment expenses are similarly relatively easy to determine. Unpaid loss adjustment expenses, on the other hand, cannot be accrued except by the use of a cost accounting system. *Cost allocation* and *cost accounting* differ in that the latter provides a basis for determining future costs, whereas the former provides only a current basis for identifying costs related to current operations.

COST ACCOUNTING FOR LOSS ADJUSTMENT EXPENSES

Cost accounting provides the basis for preferable expense allocation through a series of operations: the recording, classification, and summarization of operating costs. A cost accounting system consists of a design of systems and procedures for operations that permit the determination of costs by functions, activities, products, periods, and departments and territories. It enables the user to forecast future costs by the use of standard or other cost measurements. A cost accounting system is based on historical costs modified for anticipated changes in operations, selections of alternative costs, and inflation.

The goal in using cost accounting systems is to provide accurate data on current operations as well as to forecast future operations. As with any cost system, variations from estimated standard costs are recognized in the period they occur, resulting in current operations being charged with actual incurred costs. By the use of a standard cost system, deviations from standards can be recognized in future estimates, providing a more accurate determination of future costs.

Cost accounting for loss adjustment expenses may involve the use of cost allocation methods and standard costs.

Cost Allocation

All property and liability insurance companies must devise a system for distributing direct and indirect costs to underwriting, investment, and loss adjustment expenses. Most cost allocations are accomplished by using a direct basis for identifiable costs and an estimated basis for indirect costs.

The cost system should take into account the actual time spent for services of employees for each related cost center. Salary costs incurred by claims department personnel on an exclusive basis should be allocated 100 percent to loss adjustment expenses. This distribution formula includes services at all levels of the claims department, from manager through entry-level employees. However, care must be exercised to ensure that employees participating in other company programs are identified and separately charged to that function; this method represents the direct cost exception method, whereby minor functions are allocated on an exception basis. Such allocations should be made by comparing total time incurred to time spent on other functions. Costs should be determined on the basis that provides for the sharing of total employee costs, including those paid for nonworking hours, so that costs are shared equitably between functions.

Employee costs for functions which cannot be identified with a specific cost center should be allocated on the basis of the relative contribution made to each operating unit. Cost may be measured on a direct time basis or measured by comparing the volume of units or services furnished to the total cost incurred. Ideally, a cost system should provide for a double allocation to account for non-working or nonproductive time. However, the details required to make these determinations often cannot be identified and the total cost is allocated on a single formula basis.

Nonservice costs such as equipment, printing and stationery, postage, and utilities should be allocated on the usage basis for each function or service area. Periodic testing of the allocation of such costs should ensure that the costs are spread between functions in a manner based on current usage.

Statutory Methods

Where cost allocation programs are not used, a statutory allocation method is imposed. This allocation follows the Underwriting and Investment Exhibit, Part 4, and is described below.

Expense Allocation

Basis of Allocation	*Expenses*
□ Direct charges	Claims adjustment services; commission and brokerage; advertising; boards, bureaus, and associations; surveys and underwriting reports; and audits of insureds' records
□ Studies of employees' activities	Salaries
□ Pro rata on salary ratios	Employee relations and welfare, insurance, directors' fees, rent and rent items, equipment, printing and stationery, and postage and telephone and telegraph.
□ Special studies	Travel and travel items, legal and auditing, taxes, license and fees (except payroll taxes), and miscellaneous
□ Investment expenses	Real estate expenses and real estate taxes

In addition to the allocation method for expenses incurred by the company, a specific formula is prescribed for apportionment of the joint expenses of a group of companies sharing personnel and facilities. Shared expenses are reported as an increase or decrease to each expense item among the several companies, and management charges are usually not permitted except for items incurred with a noninsurance holding company.

Where other apportionment bases are not established, companies are required to share expenses on the basis of a joint expenses allocation.

Joint Expenses Allocation

Apportionment Basis	*Expenses*
□ Percentage of premiums	Advertising
□ Special studies	Boards, bureaus, associations, surveys and underwriting reports, audits of insured's records, travel and travel items, legal and auditing, and miscellaneous
□ Salary basis	Employee relations and welfare, insurance, rent and rent items, equipment, printing and stationery, postage and telephone, and payroll taxes

Federal income taxes do not enter into the allocation of loss adjustment expenses but are usually shared among a group of companies filing a consolidated return on the basis of income tax expense incurred as if a separate return were filed.

ESTIMATING LOSS ADJUSTMENT EXPENSES

Loss adjustment expenses vary significantly by line of business and are not consistent between companies. The line of business variance is caused by the type of loss incurred. The amount of time spent by a claim adjuster to determine the loss amount of a business fire will likely be greater than the time spent by claim adjusters to determine an automobile collision loss. Oftentimes, even losses within a line will develop significantly different amounts of claims adjustment expenses. An automobile liability claim for which the losses are readily determinable and agreed to by the claimant requires a minimum of claim adjustment effort; on the other hand, where multiple injuries occur in an automobile accident, claim adjustment services may be required over an extended period of time.

Another factor affecting loss adjustment expenses is the amount of time elapsing between the incurred date and the settlement date. Generally, the older the claim, the greater the increase in loss adjustment expenses. Loss adjustment expenses should be reviewed several times during the year to take into account changes in policy forms, legislative changes, and judicial interpretations. The accumulation of historical data about loss adjustment expenses is the most significant element in arriving at an accurate estimate of such future costs.

Case Basis

The preferable way to determine loss adjustment expense reserves is by specific claims. This results in a more accurate estimate of ultimate unpaid loss adjustment expenses which have been reduced for the amount of cost paid to date. Few companies maintain cost records with sufficient detail to permit them to use this method; however, to the extent that it can be used, the data developed about loss adjustment expense reserves can be the more reliable.

Paid-to-Paid Basis

One of the most universally applied techniques for estimating loss adjustment expense reserves is the ratio of paid loss adjustment expenses to paid losses. If this method is used without modification, it will probably miss the actual experience by a considerable amount. If all losses are paid within a short period of time, the paid-to-paid ratios will likely reflect a reasonable average experience for estimating these reserves. However, most losses are not paid on a current basis, and this results in a mismatching of loss adjustment expenses and losses. If the paid-to-paid ratios are modified in a manner that changes the weight given to currently paid loss adjustment expenses, the method may be more appropriately used. For example, some companies may use a 3-year weighted average of paid loss adjustment expenses to paid losses where the current year's average weighting is equal to 100 percent, the first preceding year's 66⅔ percent, and the second preceding year's 33⅓ percent. This weighting method emphasizes the current year's experience without ignoring the effects of prior years' paid-to-paid experience.

Generally, the use of paid-to-paid ratios results in understating loss adjustment expense reserves because these costs tend to increase as losses remain unpaid. A bulk factor may be added to the paid-to-paid ratio, raising the loss adjustment expense reserves to a more realistic level.

Incurred-to-Incurred Basis

Incurred losses and expenses are derived by accounting for these items on an accident year basis. Allocated loss adjustment expenses can be accumulated with losses by accident year. Unallocated loss expenses are not so easy to identify; consequently, they are usually distributed on the basis of an arbitrary formula. The formula is based on a best estimate, and it usually results in assigning one-half of the unallocated loss adjustment expense when the loss is incurred and assigning the balance over all open claims years based on loss payments for each year in relationship to total loss payments. For companies which have developed a comprehensive statistical base, it may be possible to assign unallocated loss expenses based on claim counts for line of business and coverage.

The incurred-to-incurred basis should provide a more realistic formula for estimating unpaid loss adjustment expenses. This is partly true since, as previously mentioned, paid loss adjustment expenses tend to continue after loss payments are made.

Combination Basis

The most accurate method of estimating loss adjustment expenses usually involves a combination of case basis and formula basis. Case-basis expenses are developed to their ultimate cost and reduced by expenses incurred to date. The formula basis for unallocated loss expenses may likewise be calculated on a case basis, using claim counts by line and coverage and determining average unallocated costs for each type of loss. Where the unallocated losses cannot be determined on a case basis, they may be estimated by using a bulk amount determined on the basis of the ratio of unallocated to allocated expenses.

Just as in the determination of loss reserves, considerable judgment must be applied to any formula basis—taking into account infrequent costs, catastrophic events, changes in policy forms, legislative mandates, judicial interpretations, and inflation.

CALCULATING LOSS ADJUSTMENT EXPENSE RESERVES

However the estimates are determined, they must be applied to unpaid claims files. The factor amount applied to each claim file must be reduced for loss adjustment expenses already incurred. As previously indicated for unallocated expenses, it is often determined that 50 percent of the costs are incurred when the loss is reported. However, this percentage tends to be rather arbitrary and to ensure that loss adjustment expense reserves are adequate, some companies, either by testing historical results or by using extra margins, will estimate incurred expenses to be less than 50 percent.

For statutory reporting in Schedules O and P, the unallocated loss expenses paid during the calendar year must be distributed on the basis of assigning 45 percent to the most recent year, 5 percent to the next most recent year, and the balance to all years (including the most recent year) in proportion to the amount of loss payments paid for each year during the most recent calendar year. If that formula produces an amount for any year in excess of 10 percent of earned premiums, the excess should be redistributed to all years.

Since loss adjustment expense reserves are directly related to loss reserves, any understatement or overstatement of loss reserves will likely affect the loss adjustment expense reserves.

OTHER RESERVE CONSIDERATIONS

Although the liability for a loss adjustment expense is not separated between allocated and unallocated items for public reporting, such balances should be developed, using historical data in order to determine more accurately the total outstanding liability. The total of these expenses represents the estimate of future payments to close a claim file; totals will vary by line of business, coverage, and company. The reliability of the statistical records is extremely important to the accurate determination of these reserves.

Allocated expenses should be accounted for by accident date to provide the basis for the incurred-to-incurred ratio method of estimating loss adjustment expense reserves.

The ratio applied to unpaid losses is based on an estimate of ultimate losses minus loss expenses paid to date. In applying the ratio to incurred but not reported losses, it should be assumed that no loss adjustment expenses have been paid to date.

Historical data, once determined, should be regularly updated. And to the extent that actual results vary significantly from estimated results, the prior years' experience should be restated to reflect actual subsequent development.

For certain lines, such as title insurance, loss adjustment expense reserves are not required for public reporting (but may be for statutory reporting) since it may be assumed that such costs are incurred evenly—given that they are usually incurred by internal staff as part of their routine functions.

Where "examiners' formula methods" (see pages 248 and 249) are used, they should be challenged to ensure that they reflect current costs. This can be accomplished by comparing loss adjustment expenses incurred to losses incurred and comparing loss adjustment expense reserves to loss reserves.

Where loss adjustment expense reserves are strengthened, the reserve addition should be charged to current operations—except that for statutory reporting, amounts attributable to prior years' strengthening may qualify as an adjustment to surplus.

15

CAPITAL AND SURPLUS

Capital and surplus constitute the equity of the company. Together, they are the difference between total assets and liabilities. They also equal the capital contributions by shareholders (or policyholders) plus net income and minus capital distributions and net losses since inception.

Within this general framework, however, capital and surplus have different meanings for GAAP (generally accepted accounting principles), statutory, and tax purposes. The definitions also vary with the type of company (stock, mutual, or reciprocal) and the type of insurance (life, property, etc.). Before getting into a detailed discussion, a brief overview of the various kinds of capital and surplus will be presented in the following paragraphs.

Companies fall into three different categories based on their capitalization: stock, mutual, and reciprocal. Stock insurance companies obtain their initial capitalization in the same manner as does a regular business entity. In other words, shares of stock are sold for cash (or occasionally property), and the shareholders own the equity of the company and elect the board of directors which governs company operations. The ultimate goal of such a company is to make a profit for the shareholders. Initial funds may also be obtained through borrowing, but such funds are generally not included in capital and surplus.

Mutual companies are common in the insurance business but unusual in many other industries. They are similar to a cooperative in that there is no stock and that the equity of the company is owned by its customers—the policyholders. The board of directors is elected by the policyholders, and the goal of the company is to operate efficiently in order to provide policyholders with the lowest possible insurance cost. The company's initial funds can be contributed by the original policyholders, but because of the large initial capital requirement, this is seldom done. More commonly, a group of investors will provide the needed funds in exchange for bonds or guarantee certificates. These amounts are included in legal capital and surplus because repayment is not allowed until the surplus accumulated from operations reaches a sufficient level. Some states also restrict the payment of interest on these instruments if surplus is below a minimum amount. As a practical matter, the motivation of such an investor is not the interest income, but the opportunity to have a management position or some other profitable business arrangement with the company.

A reciprocal insurance company is now rare, and in fact is really not a company at all but rather an unincorporated loss-sharing arrangement. In other words, the insureds pool their funds and agree to pay claims out of the pool. From an economic standpoint, a reciprocal is similar to a mutual, but legally there is a difference since a reciprocal does not involve a corporation or other separate entity which owns the pooled funds. A reciprocal is managed by an agent called an "attorney-in-fact"; this agent, however, is not the owner but merely a hired manager appointed by the insureds. As with a mutual, the initial capital and surplus requirements could be provided by the insureds, but more commonly the attorney-in-fact provides the needed funds in exchange for bonds or certificates of contribution. These amounts are included in surplus because repayment of principal (and sometimes interest) is restricted until sufficient surplus levels are achieved from operations. The incentive for the attorney-in-fact to provide the funds is the opportunity to charge a management fee for operating the reciprocal; often, the fee is a percentage of premiums.

For GAAP, the terms commonly used for capital and surplus are "capital" and "retained earnings," which together constitute "stockholders' equity" (or "policyholders' surplus" in the case of mutual companies). These amounts are not intended to represent the strength or value of the company (although some individuals may erroneously interpret them as such), but are instead a historical repository of the capital contributions, capital distributions, and cumulative GAAP net income or loss since inception.

For statutory accounting, capital and surplus, together known as "policyholders' surplus," are intended to measure the strength of the company for regulatory purposes. They equal the difference between admitted assets and liabilities. Because of conservative statutory accounting practices, including the exclusion of nonadmitted assets, the policyholders' surplus does provide an estimate of the minimum financial strength of the company available for protection of the policyholders. However, the policyholders' surplus is not intended to reflect the value of the company or its maximum potential strength.

For tax purposes, the role of capital and surplus is more vague and less important. In fact, the primary tax effect is really not on the company but on the shareholders of a stock company (a mutual company would not be affected). The concept of surplus is roughly reflected in the term "earnings and profits," which is basically the cumulative taxable income and loss since inception, with several special adjustments. Earnings and profits (E&P) have significance since shareholders are taxed on company dividends to the extent of the company's E&P.

GAAP ACCOUNTING

There are really no special insurance rules for GAAP capital and surplus. Rather, the accounting principles applicable to all types of businesses are applied. The only exception would be in the special terminology used for mutual or reciprocal companies. In the case of a stock company, *stockholder's equity* usually consists of Capital Stock, Paid-in Capital, and Retained Earnings accounts. There may also be accounts for Capital Stock Subscribed, Preferred Stock, or Treasury Stock.

Capital Stock

This account consists of the number of common shares issued, times the par value per share (or stated value per share in the case of no par stock). The total amount in the Capital Stock account (plus the par value of any preferred shares) is sometimes called the "stated capital."

A few companies have more than one class of common stock. Where there are two classes, usually the main difference is that one is voting and the other nonvoting. Such companies may maintain two separate capital stock accounts, one for each class. On the balance sheet, both accounts may be combined, but disclosure of the characteristics of the two classes must be made, either parenthetically or in footnotes to the financial statements.

Note that only the par value of *issued* shares is taken into account. The number of *authorized* shares has no significance for accounting purposes. "Authorized shares" simply refer to the maximum number of shares that the company is permitted to issue under its articles of incorporation. This number can be increased at any time simply by amending the articles. Only after the corporation has decided to issue the shares, though, do they take on any economic significance.

The concept of par value for common stock is a historical relic that has virtually no significance today. Technically, if the original shareholders did not pay at least par value for their shares, they could be liable to the company's creditors for the difference between the par value and what they paid. However, issuing shares for less than par would never be allowed by the state insurance departments, and this hardly occurs even in the case of noninsurance businesses since a typical par value is $1 per share (it could even be 1 cent per share—whatever is set forth in the articles of incorporation). Par value is also used by some states for determining the annual corporation fee, but this fee is usually less than $1,000 per year in any case. Thus, par value has little real significance, but the separate account of Capital Stock is traditionally maintained for the total par value of all issued shares.

All states provide for the issuance of no par stock. The board of directors will then determine a "stated value" for the shares, which is treated for accounting and legal purposes the same as par value. The distinction between par and no par stock is merely a semantic difference rather than a significant one, except that in a few states there could be a difference in the corporate annual fee.

Stock is usually issued for cash, but it may also be issued for property (whether tangible or intangible) or for services actually performed. The property or services would be recorded at fair value, and in the absence of fraud the determination of the board of directors as to value would be binding. However, stock may not be issued for a promissory note of the buyer or for future services. Where the buyer gives a promissory note, the transaction is treated as a subscription for shares, which are not actually issued until the note is fully paid (see "Stock Subscriptions," below in this chapter).

Capital stock increases whenever additional stock is issued, or if the articles of incorporation are amended to increase the par value (an unusual occurrence). Capital stock decreases whenever shares are canceled or redeemed, or if the articles of incorporation are amended to reduce the par value. Capital stock does not decrease if the company repurchases shares without canceling them (see the discussion on "Treasury Stock," below in this chapter). Likewise, capital stock does not change where there is a stock split in which a corresponding adjustment is made to the par value per share. Thus, where $1 par value shares are split 2 for 1, if the par value of the split shares is reduced to $0.50, there is no change in the total dollar amount of capital stock. In the event of a stock dividend, though (or a stock split without a corresponding adjustment to par value), the capital stock will increase (see "Retained Earnings," below in this chapter).

Paid-in Capital

Paid-in capital (sometimes called "paid-in surplus") consists of the amount paid for newly issued stock in excess of par value. Thus, if $1 par value stock is issued for $50, the Capital Stock account would be credited for $1 and Paid-in Capital would be credited for $49. Together, the two accounts reflect the total amount paid into the company for issued stock. It is important to note that only amounts *paid into the company* for stock are reflected; neither Capital Stock nor Paid-in Capital is affected by subsequent sales by shareholders after the stock is issued.

Changes in Paid-in Capital often correspond to changes in Capital Stock. The account increases when additional shares are issued for more than par value, or when the par value of existing shares is reduced (the entry would be to debit Capital Stock and credit Paid-in Capital). An increase would also occur when existing shareholders contribute capital without receiving additional shares in exchange. (Such transactions are generally encountered only in closely held corporations.) The Paid-in Capital account decreases when shares are canceled or the par value of existing shares is increased.

When a company repurchases its own shares for cancellation, Capital Stock is debited for the par value of the shares and Cash is credited for the repurchase price. If the repurchase price is less than the original issue price of the shares, Paid-in Capital is debited for the difference between the par value and the repurchase price. If the repurchase price exceeds the original issue price, the difference between the par value and the repurchase price is debited to Paid-in Capital to the extent that the account has a credit balance attributable to the same class of shares. Any remaining difference is debited to Retained Earnings.

Stock Subscriptions

These represent shares which have not yet been issued, but which the corporation has agreed to issue once they are paid for in full. Stock subscription agreements may be used where the shares are being paid for in installments or where a prospective shareholder intends to purchase stock from the corporation at a future date. Such agreements are now relatively uncommon and generally would only be encountered in the case of a new, closely held company.

Where there is doubt about whether the prospective shareholder will actually pay for the shares, the company probably should not make any accounting entries until cash is received, although the existence of the subscription contract would, of course, be disclosed in footnotes to the financial statements. In other cases the following entry would be made at the time the subscription agreement is entered into:

Subscriptions Receivable	xx	
Capital Stock Subscribed		xx
Paid-in Capital		xx

The debit would be for the subscription price, and the credit to Capital Stock Subscribed would be for the total par value of the subscribed shares. Paid-in Capital would be debited for any difference. As cash is received, the receivable would be reduced, and when the final payment is made, the Capital Stock Subscribed account would be debited for its balance, with a corresponding credit to Capital Stock.

On the balance sheet, Capital Stock Subscribed may be shown as a separate item in the equity section, or it may be combined with the Capital Stock account with either a parenthetical or a footnote disclosure. Subscriptions Receivable may be shown as an asset, or as a separate negative item in the equity section. For statements filed with the Securities and Exchange Commission, the latter presentation is required. Subscriptions Receivable, as with any receivable, would be subject to the requirement of an allowance for doubtful collectibility where appropriate.

Special procedures must be followed where a prospective shareholder defaults on a stock subscription. In most states, if less than 50 percent of the subscription price has been paid in, the stock is not issued and any monies paid are forfeited to the corporation. Thus, the following entry would be made:

Capital Stock Subscribed	Full $ balance	
Paid-in Capital	Plug	
Subscriptions Receivable		Remaining $ balance

If at least 50 percent of the subscription price has been paid in, then most states require the subscribed shares to be offered for sale for at least the unpaid balance plus expenses of sale. If someone buys the shares, any excess proceeds over this minimum sales price are returned to the defaulting subscriber, to the extent that he or she paid the corporation under the subscription contract. This would result in the following entry (assuming no expenses of sale):

Cash	Sales proceeds	
Capital Stock Subscribed	Full $ balance	
Capital Stock		Total par value
Subscriptions Receivable		Remaining $ balance
Payable to Defaulter		Plug

In the event that the sales proceeds exceeded the total original subscription price (plus expenses of sale), any excess would be credited to Paid-in Capital.

Preferred Stock

Most insurance companies do not issue preferred stock. These are shares which, in comparison to common stock, have priority treatment with respect to liquidation and dividends. In other words, if the company is liquidated, the holders of preferred stock will receive the par value of their shares before the common stockholders receive anything. (Of course, though, creditors would have a higher priority in liquidation than either preferred or common stockholders.) Likewise, the preferred stock shareholders are entitled to receive their stipulated amount of dividends before any dividend can be paid on the common stock for that year.

However, the payment of dividends is not mandatory and must be approved by the board of directors. The only right of preferred shareholders is that *if* dividends are paid, the preferred shareholders will receive theirs before the common shareholders receive any.

Unlike that of common stock, the par value of preferred stock is significant since this is the amount that will be paid for the shares in the event of liquidation, if assets after the payment of creditors are sufficient. The most frequent par value is $100 per share. Also, the stipulated dividend amount may be expressed as a percentage of par value, or as a specific dollar amount per share.

In addition to its two basic characteristics (priority with respect to liquidation and dividends), preferred stock can take on many optional variations, such as being redeemable, callable, convertible, cumulative, noncumulative, participating, voting, and nonvoting.

- Redeemable shares may be cashed in for their par value at the option of the shareholder; usually, this can occur only after a specific date.
- Callable shares must be cashed in if the company so requests; usually, the company can do this only after a specific date.
- Convertible shares may be exchanged for a predetermined number of common shares at the option of the shareholder.
- Cumulative shares entitle the preferred shareholder to be paid all dividends "in arrears" for both the current and all prior years before the common shareholders receive anything. *Dividends in arrears* are any stipulated preferred dividends which remain unpaid as of the current date. Thus, if $10 is the stipulated dividend per share and such amounts are not paid in 19x0 and 19x1, the preferred shareholders must be paid $30 per share befor any common stock dividends could be paid in 19x2.
- Noncumulative shares do not have the right to receive unpaid "catch-up" dividends for prior years. In the preceding example, if the shares were noncumulative, only $10 per share would need to be paid on the preferred stock in 19x2 prior to any common dividends. The preferred right pertains only to the current year, and dividends in arrears for prior years are disregarded.
- Participating shares are those which are eligible to receive dividends in excess of the basic stipulated amount. The basic stipulated amount is paid before the common shares receive anything, as with regular preferred stock, but on top of this, the participating preferred stock can share in additional dividends along with the common stockholders according to a predetermined formula.
- Preferred shares may be either voting or nonvoting, although shares with regular voting rights are relatively uncommon and are usually encountered only in closely held corporations. Most preferred shares, however, do have the right to vote on any amendments to the articles of incorporation which affect their rights, and many shares have contingent voting rights which come into effect if a certain number of dividend payments are missed.

The accounting for preferred stock is relatively simple. When issued, Preferred Stock is credited for the par value, with any excess proceeds credited to Paid-in Capital. A separate Paid-in Capital (or Stock Premium) account may be maintained for preferred shares. If the preferred shares are issued for less than par, then the discount is shown as a deduction from the par value in the Preferred Stock account. Unpaid dividends in arrears would not be shown as a liability, but would be disclosed in the footnotes to the financial statements. The characteristics and rights of the preferred shares would also be disclosed (i.e., dividend rate, voting arrangements, cumulative rights, convertibility).

If preferred stock is converted into common, the par value of the preferred is debited, the par value of the common is credited, and any difference is recorded in Paid-in Capital. If separate Paid-in Capital accounts were maintained for the two classes, there would be a transfer between them, of course. If preferred shares are called or redeemed, Preferred Stock is debited for the par value, and any difference between that and the payment for the shares would generally be recorded in Paid-in Capital.

Treasury Stock

Corporations sometimes repurchase their own shares without canceling them. Such repurchased but still existing shares are shown as "treasury stock." They are still considered to be *issued* shares, but they are not *outstanding*. Dividends are generally not paid on treasury shares.

The primary reason for not canceling the shares is to leave open the possibility that the shares may be resold at a later date. Of course, the company could cancel the shares and later issue new ones to obtain the same economic result, but this would require more paperwork and might involve a different accounting treatment in the interim. Also, treasury shares, unlike newly issued shares, may be resold by the company for less than par value without a potential liability attaching to the buyer.

The most common method of accounting for treasury stock is the cost method. When shares are repurchased by the company, the Treasury Stock account is debited and Cash is credited, both for the amount of the repurchase price. Treasury Stock is shown as a negative item in the equity section of the balance sheet, usually beneath Retained Earnings.

If the treasury shares are later resold, Cash is debited for the proceeds and Treasury Stock is credited for its existing balance attributable to those shares. If the sales proceeds exceed what the company paid to repurchase the shares, Paid-in Capital is credited for the excess. (Although the company did have a "gain" on the transaction, the income statement is not affected. The gain, as indicated, goes to Paid-in Capital.) If the sales proceeds are less than what the company paid to repurchase the shares, the deficiency is debited to Paid-in Capital to the extent that Paid-in Capital contains a credit balance attributable to that class of shares. Any deficiency in excess of this would be debited to Retained Earnings. Again, although the company had a "loss" on the transaction, the income statement is not affected—the loss is debited instead to Paid-in Capital and then to Retained Earnings if Paid-in Capital has an insufficient balance for that class.

If the treasury shares are later canceled without being resold, the par value of the shares is debited to Capital Stock, and Treasury Stock is credited for its balance (the repurchase price). The difference between the repurchase price and the par value is debited to Paid-in Capital to the extent that this account has a credit balance arising from shares of the same class. Any remaining difference would be debited to Retained Earnings.

Instead of using the cost method, treasury shares may also be accounted for as if they had been actually canceled, although this accounting practice is less frequent. In such a situation, no Treasury Stock account is established. Instead, the par value is debited to Capital Stock and Cash is credited for the repurchase price. Any difference is debited to Paid-in Capital to the extent that this account has a credit balance for the same class of shares. Any further debit would be to Retained Earnings. If the shares are later resold, they would be accounted for in the same manner as a new issue.

Retained Earnings

Unlike capital stock and paid-in capital, retained earnings are not obtained by contributions from outside the corporation, but rather by earnings generated from within. In fact, the term "retained earnings" describes the usual composition of the account quite well: cumulative corporate earnings that have been retained rather than distributed to shareholders as dividends.

The primary item which increases the Retained Earnings account is net income after taxes. Retained Earnings is reduced by net losses, dividends to shareholders, and certain other adjustments. Where dividends are paid in property, Retained Earnings is reduced by the fair market value of the property, and a gain or loss on the property would be recognized.

If dividends are paid in shares of the company's stock, the treatment differs depending on whether the stock dividend is large or small. A small dividend is one which is less than approximately 20 or 25 percent of the previously outstanding shares. In such a situation, Retained Earnings is debited for the fair market value of the shares, Capital Stock is credited for the par value of the stock dividend, and Paid-in Capital is credited for the difference. A large stock dividend is accounted for at par value rather than market value; Retained Earnings is debited and Capital Stock is credited, both for the par value of the shares. The assumption underlying this rule is that a large stock dividend will cause the market value per share to decrease, whereas a small stock dividend is presumed not to affect the market price per share significantly. If a stock dividend is near the 20 to 25 percent range, the accountant would use his or her best judgment to determine whether the dividend is large or small based on the effect on the market price.

Retained Earnings may also be decreased where stock is redeemed for more than the original issue price and Paid-in Capital is exhausted for that class of shares.

On a few occasions, Retained Earnings may be adjusted for amounts arising in prior periods which do not flow through the income statement. Such prior-period adjustments which bypass the income statement are not allowed except to correct an error or to reflect the benefit from preacquisition tax loss carryforwards of a subsidiary. An "error" is defined somewhat narrowly; it does not include revisions of estimates from the benefit of hindsight; nor does it include retroactive changes from one acceptable accounting method to another. However, a change from an unacceptable accounting method to an acceptable one would constitute the correction of an error.

Finally, a deficit in Retained Earnings may be eliminated by means of a quasi reorganization. This is strictly an accounting procedure which does not require the company to declare bankruptcy or go through other court proceedings; however, shareholder approval must be obtained. A quasi reorganization allows a company to cleanse its GAAP records of prior losses and start over with a zero balance in Retained Earnings. This is done by the following procedure:

1. Assets are written down to their fair market value. Upward adjustments are not permitted except to offset write-downs within the same asset category. The net write-down is debited to Retained Earnings.
2. Retained Earnings is then credited to eliminate its debit balance. Paid-in Capital is debited by the same amount if there is a sufficient credit balance. If the Paid-in Capital account is not sufficient, the par value of the shares must be reduced by the amount needed to absorb the credit to Retained Earnings. If the par value is insufficient, then a quasi reorganization is not permitted.
3. The Retained Earnings portion of the financial statement should show the date of the quasi reorganization for an extended period, generally the next 10 years.

Normally, a credit balance in Retained Earnings is available for the payment of dividends, absent some legal or contractual restriction beyond the scope of GAAP, such as state insurance department requirements. However, the board of directors may choose to segregate part or all of the Retained Earnings balance into a special category to show that it is unavailable for dividends. This category is known as "Appropriated Retained Earnings." Retained Earnings may be appropriated for any purpose the board desires, such as company expansion or a contingency loss reserve. The remaining balance in Retained Earnings is called "Unappropriated" and is available for dividends, although there is no requirement or inference that any dividends will in fact be paid. The board is free to appropriate Retained Earnings or to return amounts from the appropriated category back to the unappropriated category. The classification is made primarily to inform stockholders and financial statement readers of the board's intentions; it has little legal effect, since the board can change its mind at any time.

STATUTORY ACCOUNTING

Statutory accounting follows many basic GAAP accounting principles. Certain differences exist for the purpose of presenting a more conservative measurement of capital for the protection of policyholders. Another difference is that statutory accounting does not use the term "retained earnings." Instead, the capital accounts used are Paid-up Capital, Gross Paid-in and Contributed Surplus, Special Surplus Funds, and Unassigned Surplus.

State regulatory requirements govern the minimum amount of capital and surplus that a company must have to begin and to continue operations. The purpose of these rules is to ensure that the company will have an adequate amount of funds to meet possible claims. In this respect an insurance company is treated differently from a regular business, since most noninsurance businesses (other than banks and similar entities) are not subject to minimum capital requirements.

Capital and surplus requirements typically range from $1 million to $3 million but may vary depending on the state, the type of company (stock, mutual, or reciprocal), and the type of insurance (life, property and casualty, etc.). Mutual companies may also be required to have a minimum number of policyholders.

Paid-up Capital

This account is generally the same as Capital Stock for GAAP purposes. It consists of the total number of shares issued, times the par value per share (or stated value in the case of no par stock). Statutory accounting for changes in the account would be the same as that for GAAP. The par value of any preferred stock would be included in this account as well.

Gross Paid-in and Contributed Surplus

This corresponds to the Paid-in Capital account for GAAP since it consists of the proceeds from the issuance of stock in excess of par value. Together with Paid-up Capital, these two accounts constitute the amount contributed to the company in exchange for its stock. Changes in the Gross Paid-in and Contributed Surplus account would occur in the same manner as for the GAAP Paid-in Capital account.

Special Surplus Funds

This category is similar to GAAP Appropriated Retained Earnings, but is not exactly the same. Special Surplus Funds is not a single account, but rather a group of accounts, each of which contains an amount of surplus earmarked for a specific purpose. The nature and balance of each fund account is determined by the board of directors, and such amounts are not available for the payment of dividends unless the board transfers the amounts back to Unassigned Surplus (discussed below). An exception to this restriction on dividends occurs in connection with the Reserve for Undeclared Policyholder Dividends.

Special Surplus Funds are generally established by the board on a voluntary basis, and in many states it is theoretically possible that a company could have no Special Surplus Funds if it so desired. Some states, though, require a Guarantee or Insolvency Fund to be established in the Special Surplus Funds category. However, most reserves or funds *required* by state regulation are shown as liabilities rather than as a Special Surplus Fund.

Special Surplus Funds may be established for a variety of reasons. The main reasons are to allocate funds for possible excessive claims or investment losses over and above the amount of required reserves. An allocation for eventual reserve strengthening is another reason. While amounts may be placed in Special

Surplus Funds for any purpose, most companies do not use this category for noninsurance items such as reserves for building expansion or asset acquisitions, even though GAAP Retained Earnings is sometimes appropriated for these purposes.

Some of the more common Special Surplus Funds are described below (the exact terminology will vary among companies).

Reserve for Undeclared Policyholder Dividends. This account would contain any anticipated policyholder dividends which have not been recorded as a liability. Of course, dividends which have been declared or which otherwise meet the criteria for liabilities would not be recorded as a Special Surplus Fund but rather as a liability (see Chapter 17, Policyholder Dividends).

Reserve for Taxes on Unrealized Capital Gains. This reflects the taxes that will be incurred when appreciated assets are disposed of in the future. Currently unrealized losses in other investments should be considered in setting this amount, if they would be disposed of to offset the capital gain. Note that unrealized capital gains for which a deferred tax liability is provided would not be included in Special Surplus Funds since liabilities rather than surplus are affected by such amounts (see Chapter 19, Federal Income Taxes).

Investment Fluctuation Reserve. Chapter 3, Relationship of Generally Accepted Accounting Principles and Statutory Accounting Practices, discusses the mandatory securities valuation reserve (MSVR). This reserve is a liability and not a surplus fund. However, the company may wish to establish an additional voluntary reserve in addition to the MSVR. This voluntary reserve would be included in Special Surplus Funds. The reserve could include a general buffer against unforeseen fluctuations and/or a specific amount based on actual decreases in value after the year end but before the issuance of the statement blank. (Since the MSVR is based on year-end values, such declines in value after the year-end would not be reflected in the MSVR.)

Guarantee or Insolvency Fund. This is a reserve required by some states to provide a pool for compensating the policyholders of an insolvent company. The insurance companies would not have to make an actual payment until an insolvency occurs, but in the meantime they are required to have this amount set aside within the company and unavailable for dividends. This set-aside amount, usually a fractional percentage of premiums, is not treated as a liability or as an expense but as a Special Surplus Fund. Of course, an actual payment out of the Fund would be treated as an expense. This Fund, since it is mandatory, is an exception to the general rule that Special Surplus Funds are voluntary. It should be noted that some states, while they require insurers to pick up the tab if another insurance company in the state becomes insolvent, do not require a Guarantee or Insolvency Fund to be established to provide a reserve.

Mortality Fluctuation Reserve. This is a reserve, over and above the statutory reserve, for potential excess losses which could be caused by an epidemic or other special circumstances. This is especially applicable to group life insurance when there is a concentration of risks. New York State requires such a surplus reserve to be established for group insurance.

Annuity Contingency Reserve. This is similar to the Mortality Fluctuation Reserve, except that it guards against the "problem" of too many people living for too long.

Contingency Reserve for Large Risks. Where a company writes policies with very high coverages (life insurance, aviation insurance, etc.) and does not reinsure them, it may wish to establish a supplementary reserve to protect against the occurrence of several losses or perhaps even of one single loss which would exceed the actuarially established reserves.

Unassigned Surplus

This is somewhat similar to the GAAP Unappropriated Retained Earnings account, since it is whatever is left of Capital and Surplus accounts after Paid-up Capital, Gross Paid-in and Contributed Capital, and Special Surplus Funds are subtracted. Unassigned Surplus is generally free from any restrictions and is available for the payment of dividends. It is the only account out of which normal dividends can be paid.

Unassigned Surplus is increased by company income and by transfers from a Special Surplus Fund. Unassigned Surplus is decreased by losses, dividends, and transfers to a Special Surplus Fund. Unassigned Surplus is also affected by a number of adjustments peculiar to the insurance industry. These adjustments are made directly to surplus rather than passing through the results of operations. The most common of these adjustments are as follows:

Changes in Nonadmitted Assets. An increase in nonadmitted assets—such as furniture, automobiles, and premiums more than 90 days overdue—reduces surplus. A decrease in nonadmitted assets would increase surplus. (See Chapter 8, Other Assets.)

Changes in the Liability for Unauthorized Reinsurance. Where the company reinsures with another company which is not authorized to do business in the first company's state of domicile, a liability for the reinsured reserves or unearned premiums must be established and subtracted from surplus, except to the extent that the first company holds funds of the reinsurer. (See Chapter 16, Reinsurance Ceded and Assumed.)

Capital Gains and Losses: Life Insurance. For a life insurance company, both realized and unrealized capital gains and losses (net of federal income taxes) are charged directly to surplus except to the extent charged to the mandatory securities valuation reserve (MSVR). Capital gains are added to the MSVR until the MSVR reaches its maximum limit, and then to surplus. Capital losses are deducted from the MSVR until it reaches zero and are then deducted from surplus. When making the entry to surplus, capital gains and losses are netted against each other.

Capital Gains and Losses: Property and Liability. For a property and liability insurance company, realized capital gains and losses are income statement items and not direct adjustments to surplus. Unrealized capital gains and losses, though, are a direct adjustment to surplus, in the same manner as for a life insurance company.

Changes in the MSVR. Any change in the MSVR is charged directly to surplus and not to operations.

Changes in Foreign Exchange Adjustment. Assets and liabilities valued in foreign currencies must be adjusted at the end of each year for current exchange rates. The difference between beginning and year-end exchange balances is charged directly to surplus.

Change in Reserve Valuation Basis. This is usually encountered only in connection with life and health insurance. Where the reserve valuation method is changed, the cumulative effect of the change which is attributable to *prior* years is charged to surplus and not to current operations. Of course, the portion of the change attributable to the current year would be charged to operations. Examples of valuation method changes include different interest rate assumptions, or a change from the net level method to the preliminary term method. (See Chapter 12, Life Insurance Company Reserves.)

Change in Excess of Statutory Reserves over Statement Reserves. This is usually encountered only in connection with property and liability insurance, and is reflected in Schedules K and P of the statutory statement. (See Chapter 13, Property and Liability Loss Reserves.)

Stock Issue Expenses. Legal, underwriting, commission, and other expenses of stock issuance are charged directly to surplus rather than to operations or paid-in capital.

Changes from Insurance Department Examinations. Where the insurance department requires changes with respect to items arising in prior years, states generally allow the prior-period adjustment to be charged to surplus rather than to current operations.

Changes in Surplus of Separate Accounts. Where separate accounts are maintained, the change in surplus for each separate account is recorded in the company's surplus section.

Unassigned Surplus is the only capital and surplus account which can have a negative balance. Paid-up Capital, Gross Paid-in and Contributed Capital, and Special Surplus Funds can never have a balance of less than zero. Losses, though, are debited to Unassigned Surplus, and continued losses would increase the negative balance until the company became insolvent. A negative balance could not be caused by dividends (other than liquidating dividends), however, since they can be paid only out of a positive balance in Unassigned Surplus.

It is common for a young company to have a negative balance in Unassigned Surplus as a result of policy acquisition and other start-up costs. However, if the negative balance is large enough to cause total capital and surplus to fall below the required level, a capital impairment occurs, and if additional capital and surplus is not obtained, the state insurance department may close down the company or take over its management.

Treasury Stock. Treasury stock is handled in much the same manner for statutory purposes as for GAAP. However, the cost method rather than the par value method would be used until the stock is canceled (meaning that the stock is accounted for at its repurchase price). If the stock is canceled, the par value is removed from Paid-up Capital, and the remainder of the repurchase price is debited to Gross Paid-in and Contributed Capital, but not to exceed the amount of Gross Paid-in and Contributed Capital attributable to those particular shares. Any excess of the repurchase price over these amounts is debited to Unassigned Surplus. Unlike GAAP, Gross Paid-in and Contributed Capital is not debited for more than the amount attributable to those particular shares (for GAAP, the limiting factor is the total Paid-in Capital attributable to that entire class of stock).

Treasury Stock is shown as a separate item which reduces surplus. State regulations restrict the amount of treasury stock that a company may acquire, and in some states permission from the insurance department is needed to make the purchase.

Stock Dividends. All stock dividends for statutory purposes are treated in the same manner as a "large" stock dividend under GAAP. In other words, Paid-up Capital is credited for the par value of the shares, and Unassigned Surplus is debited for the same amount. The fair market value of the dividend shares is not a factor, regardless of the number of shares involved.

Subordinated Surplus Debentures. Unlike a regular business, an insurance company can include a special type of debt in capital and surplus, rather than accounting for it as a liability. The terminology may vary, but "Special Surplus Debenture" is the term most commonly applied to these debt instruments.

To be included in surplus, the debentures must meet state requirements. These requirements typically provide that the instruments must be subordinated to other debt and that payments on the debentures are allowed only if total surplus is adequate. Surplus debentures are usually issued in connection with mutual or reciprocal insurance, but stock companies have the right to issue them as well (although some states require shareholder approval for their issuance).

TAX ACCOUNTING

Capital and surplus have less significance for tax purposes than for GAAP and statutory purposes. A "tax" balance sheet is not presented to the public, and the IRS has no interest in whether surplus levels are adequate for the policyholders. Since the regular corporate tax computation is based on income, the capital and surplus generally have no tax impact as far as the corporation is concerned. The special insurance company tax returns (Forms 1120L and 1120M) do not even have space for a balance sheet, although a copy of the statutory statement blank must be attached.

Where capital and surplus do have a tax impact is on the shareholders of a stock company. This is because any distributions to shareholders (with certain exceptions) is taxable to them as a dividend to the extent of either current or accumulated earnings and profits (E&P). Accumulated E&P is somewhat comparable to GAAP Retained Earnings.

Usually, the existence of sufficient E&P is not an issue since state insurance regulations limit dividends to statutory Unassigned Surplus. While Unassigned Surplus, Retained Earnings, and E&P are not identical to each other, in a broad sense they all consist of the cumulative profits and losses of the company, less taxes and dividends. Thus, if sufficient Unassigned Surplus exists to permit a shareholder distribution, it is likely that sufficient E&P exists to make the distribution taxable to shareholders as a dividend—as ordinary income, in other words.

However, there are special circumstances under which the amount of E&P is significant. For this reason, the E&P computation rules will be discussed briefly below.

Also, capital transactions may affect the tax treatment of shareholders in several other ways. First, where a dividend is paid in shares of the company's stock, special rules govern whether the stock dividend will be taxable or not. Second, where stock is redeemed by the company, certain tests are applied to determine how the redeeming shareholder will be taxed. These rules will also be summarized.

E&P Computation Rules

As the starting point in calculating accumulated earnings and profits, the company's taxable income less taxable losses is summed for each year since inception, but not before March 1, 1913. However, the taxable income or loss must be adjusted to reflect only straight-line depreciation for 1973 and later years, even if accelerated depreciation was used on the tax return. Furthermore, for assets acquired after 1980 which qualify for the accelerated cost recovery system (ACRS), special extended useful lives must be utilized in the revised depreciation deductions for E&P purposes (5 years for 3-year property, 12 years for 5-year property, and 40 years for 15-year real property.) Also, construction period interest and taxes are not amortized over the regular 10-year schedule but are added to the basis of the asset and depreciated over its full life.

For property acquired after 1982, the depreciable basis for E&P purposes is not reduced by one-half of the investment credit, even if such a reduction is made for tax return purposes. Also, if the $5000 expense election for fixed assets is used, the deduction must be spread over 5 years in the E&P calculation. There are other E&P adjustments as well, but most of them generally do not affect insurance companies.

In determining accumulated E&P, reductions are made for any federal income taxes paid and for shareholder dividends. Where dividends are paid in property, only the adjusted basis of the property reduces E&P. For dividends paid in shares of company stock, a reduction of E&P is made only if the stock dividend is taxable, in which case the reduction is equal to the fair market value of the stock.

Accumulated E&P is also reduced when the company redeems its own shares. The reduction is usually equal to the redemption price, less the par value and additional paid-in capital attributable to the shares, but the reduction cannot exceed the percentage of E&P which is equal to the percentage of stock redeemed. Other special adjustments will sometimes be necessary as well.

Capital Transaction Rules

As mentioned earlier, distributions to shareholders are treated as dividends if paid out of either *current* or *accumulated* earnings and profits. Current E&P is simply the increase in accumulated E&P for the present year (taxable income plus the special depreciation adjustments, less federal income taxes). Thus, even if the company had a large negative accumulated E&P at the beginning of the year, distributions would still be treated as dividends to the extent of current E&P, even if the current E&P were not sufficient to eliminate the deficit in accumulated E&P. Current E&P for the entire year is used in the dividend calculation, regardless of when during the year the dividend was paid. On the other hand, if the company had a taxable loss for the current year (negative current E&P), distributions would still be treated as dividends to the extent of any positive balance in accumulated E&P.

Dividend distributions to shareholders are taxable as ordinary income. However, individuals may apply a $100 exclusion against total dividends. Corporations may generally use an 85 percent dividend exclusion, which is increased to 100 percent in the case of an affiliated group (see Chapter 23, Subsidiary Companies). In the case of property dividends, individuals are taxable on the fair market value, while corporations are taxable on the lesser of fair market value or adjusted basis. If the distribution exceeds E&P, the excess is treated as a tax-free return of capital to the extent of the shareholder's basis in the stock, and any remaining part of the distribution is treated as a capital gain.

Where a dividend is paid in shares of company stock, a complex set of rules determines whether it is taxable, assuming that E&P is sufficient. Basically, such a stock dividend is taxable if any one of the following applies:

- The shareholder had the option (whether or not exercised) to take cash or property instead of stock.
- The stock dividend changes the ownership percentage of the shareholder.
- The stock dividend is paid to preferred shareholders.

In the case of a nontaxable stock dividend, a proportionate part of the basis of the underlying stock must be allocated to the dividend shares, based on their fair market value. This allocation is not mandatory where the value of the stock dividend is less than 15 percent of the value of the underlying stock. Even if a stock dividend is nontaxable, though, if it is other than common stock paid on common stock, then any gain on a subsequent sale of the stock may be ordinary income under the Internal Revenue Code, Section 306.

Where a corporation repurchases its stock (or purchases stock in a related corporation), the proceeds from the stock sale may be treated as a dividend (assuming sufficient E&P) unless one of the following exceptions applies (they are presented in summary form only):

- Neither the shareholder nor any related party was other than strictly a preferred shareholder.
- The total voting percentage and the total common stock ownership percentage of the shareholder and any related parties are reduced to less than 80 percent of what these percentages were before the redemption, and the shareholder (together with any related party) has less than 50 percent of the total voting power after the redemption.
- All the stock of the shareholder is redeemed. If there are related shareholders who are not fully redeemed, then additional requirements must be met in order to come under this exception from dividend treatment.
- In the case of an individual shareholder, the distribution consists of an autonomous business segment (or proceeds from the sale thereof) which was operated by the corporation for at least 5 years.

16

REINSURANCE CEDED AND ASSUMED

Insurance companies issue policies to individuals and businesses to provide indemnity against unexpected losses. The premium charged for such protection is based on past loss experience for a large number of policyholders. To protect themselves against the possibility that future loss experience may exceed the anticipated levels, insurance companies may contract with other insurance companies for reinsurance.

Reinsurance agreements involve an insurer, sometimes referred to as the primary writing or "ceding" company, who pays or shares premiums with a reinsurer (the "assuming" company) in return for its agreement to indemnify or share in losses incurred by policyholders. This transaction is sometimes referred to as "insurance for the insurance company." Premiums and losses ceded to a reinsurance company are included as a part of its operations. (The accounting for reinsurance premiums and losses is discussed in this chapter under "Accounting for Reinsurance.")

Reinsurance transactions occur in nearly all life, accident and health, and property and liability insurance companies. The details of reinsurance transactions vary between companies and coverages, but the underlying need for reinsurance protection is essentially the same. It permits the primary writing company to issue policies for larger amounts and to protect its surplus from loss due to large unexpected claims. Without the benefits of reinsurance, the primary writing company would place limits on the policies offered and would risk insolvency when unexpected losses occur.

Reinsurance agreements can only be made between insurance companies. Individuals and businesses receive all their policy benefits from the primary writing company and are usually unaware of reinsurance arrangements. The detailed contract provisions are agreed to by the ceding and the assuming insurance companies and, in some instances, may require advance approval from state insurance regulators. Except where there are state solvency funds, the ceding company depends upon the financial strength of the assuming company for loss indemnity payments. If the assuming company fails, the ceding company must honor all the benefits promised in the policies it issued.

CATEGORIES OF REINSURANCE

All reinsurance agreements can be classified into broad categories of risk sharing. The terms used to describe these categories are conceptual; the reinsuring agreements contain the details of their reinsurance arrangements. The broad categories of reinsurance are described below.

Facultative Reinsurance

This plan allows each risk to be reinsured separately. The primary writing company determines the amount of risk it will retain and offers the excess to a reinsurer. The reinsurer underwrites each risk offered to it and accepts or declines each insured. Primary insurers with limited underwriting facilities may prefer a facultative reinsurance arrangement since it permits them to rely on the reinsurer's opinion about the risk before the policy is issued.

To avoid the time lag in accepting new risks, facultative reinsurance may be written on an automatic basis. Under this arrangement, the primary writer and the reinsurer agree upon underwriting standards, and risks are reinsured—up to a retention limit—without any further action by the reinsurer. The automatic plan requires the primary writing company to cede and the reinsuring company to accept all policies issued up to the maximum agreed amount.

Facultative reinsurance may also be written on a treaty basis for a class of insureds, with an option that permits either party to include or exclude individual risks.

Treaty Reinsurance

Treaty reinsurance is automatic and covers one or more classes of risk. The reinsurance arrangement specifies the types and amounts of coverage included; unlike the arrangement for facultative reinsurance, individual policies are not negotiated. Treaty reinsurance assumes that the primary writing company will accept risks on the basis of its established underwriting practices, and the reinsurer binds itself to accept all such risks up to the maximum specified amount of reinsurance.

Pro Rata Reinsurance

This reinsurance arrangement, sometimes referred to as "proportional" reinsurance, provides for sharing the premiums and losses between the primary writing company and the reinsurer. Under this arrangement, each of the companies participates in its share of the underwriting gains or losses for the risks covered. Pro rata reinsurance can be written on two bases:

Quota Share. Quota share agreements provide that each company will share in every policy based on a fixed percentage of premiums and losses. The primary writing company cedes a fixed percentage of the premiums and the reinsurer agrees to pay its share of each policy loss. The reinsurer also agrees to pay a ceding commission to cover the acquisition costs of business assumed.

Surplus Share. The pro rata sharing of premiums and losses for this category of reinsurance is separately determined for each policy. The agreement specifies the amount of each policy risk that will be retained by the primary writing company, and the reinsurer accepts the balance of the risk up to a maximum amount. The reinsurer's share of premiums and losses is determined by the ratio of the amount it assumes over the total policy amount. The reinsurer has no share of the policy if the primary writing company's retention is equal to or greater than the total policy amount.

Excess Loss Reinsurance

Excess loss reinsurance protects the primary writing company for losses in excess of a certain dollar amount. This reinsurance is written on two bases:

Excess Loss per Risk. Excess loss reinsurance protects the primary writing company for losses in excess of the amount retained for each risk, up to a maximum limit. The premium charged by the reinsurer is based on its estimate of the excess losses to be paid. This differs from pro rata surplus share reinsurance since all losses in excess of the retention, up to the maximum, are paid by the reinsurer.

Aggregate Excess of Loss. This is often referred to as "stop loss" reinsurance. It differs from excess loss per risk reinsurance since all losses in a class of risks are combined to determine the losses paid by the reinsurer. The reimbursable losses are determined by the ratio of losses to net premium income. When the ceding company's loss percentage exceeds that specified in the reinsurance policy, the reinsurer will pay all of the excess losses up to a fixed dollar amount.

Catastrophic Reinsurance

This protects the ceding company against excess losses arising from a single catastrophe (a windstorm, earthquake, or other calamity). The reinsurer is responsible for the excess of losses over the amount of losses retained by the primary writing company, up to a maximum limit. This reinsurance differs from aggregate excess loss reinsurance since it applies to losses arising from a single event or a series of events rather than to losses incurred over a specified period of time.

Since there are significant differences between reinsurance transactions for life, accident and health, and property and liability insurance, they are covered separately below.

LIFE REINSURANCE

There are two implicit factors in the business of issuing life insurance policies that create a demand for reinsurance arrangements. First, the face amount of a life insurance policy is much larger than the periodic premium charged to the policyholder, and this results in a significant risk to the company if losses occur in excess of those predicted when the policy was issued. Second, the cost of issuing a life insurance policy may be greater than the initial premium received from the policyholder, resulting in a drain on the company's surplus. The reinsurance agreements described below have been developed to meet these needs.

Yearly Renewable Term (YRT)

This reinsurance agreement, sometimes described as "annual renewable term (ART)," is designed to protect the primary writing company from large unexpected losses. The reinsurer charges the ceding company a 1-year term premium to insure the net amount at risk; the *net amount at risk* is the face amount of the policy less the terminal reserve. Since this is term insurance protection, it does not cover other policy benefits, such as cash values and dividends. This reinsurance is renewable annually and the net amount at risk decreases with each terminal reserve increase. These reinsurance agreements normally expire at the end of the year and are immediately reissued at the beginning of the next year.

Coinsurance

Under the terms of this agreement, the reinsurer shares in the policy premiums and all the policy benefits. This is pro rata insurance, requiring the ceding company to pay a proportional part of the original premium to the reinsurer. The premium paid to the reinsurer is a pro rata share of the original premium, as opposed to the separate risk premium charged for yearly renewable term reinsurance. The reinsurer agrees to reimburse the ceding company for its share of policy claims and benefits as well as for agents' commissions and other expenses incurred in writing the policy.

Since the agreement does not terminate at the end of the year, the reinsurer must provide for its share of policy reserves. Also, because commissions and other costs incurred when the policy is issued may exceed the first-year premium, coinsurance removes some of the surplus drain for newly issued policies and permits the ceding company to reduce its exposure for unexpected losses.

Modified Coinsurance

This differs from coinsurance in that it requires the ceding company to maintain all the life insurance reserves. At year-end, the reinsurer owes the ceding company an amount equal to the increase in the mean reserve on reinsured policies—and since the ceding company has held the reserve funds, it owes the reinsurer interest on the prior year's mean reserve at the rate specified in the agreement. The result is a net transfer of funds from the reinsurer (that is, a transfer of the difference between these amounts); this is referred to as the "modified coinsurance reserve adjustment." In all other respects, the agreement is the same as other coinsurance and provides similar benefits to the ceding company.

PROPERTY AND LIABILITY REINSURANCE

Most property and liability insurance coverages are written for a term of 1 year or less, with the expectation that such policies will continue in force over a long period of time. The risk of adverse claims experience in relation to the expected claims is greater than for most life insurance coverages; this is because the property and liability policies are issued for a much shorter term, and accident statistics consequently provide a less reliable measure of future losses than do statistics covering mortality experience. Therefore, the purpose of property and liability reinsurance is to serve as a buffer against adverse claim experience occurring in the short term. Since the premiums for these policies can be adjusted at each renewal period, any short-term adverse claim experience can of course be absorbed over the long term through future premium increases; however, property and liability insurance companies need reinsurance to be able to share their adverse loss experience over the short term.

These companies may also require some relief from the surplus drains that occur with the issuance and renewal of policies. A surplus drain occurs because the cost of marketing and writing a policy is expensed when incurred, whereas the policy's premiums are earned over its term.

Property and liability reinsurance can be classified into the following categories:

Surplus Lines Reinsurance

This reinsurance protects the insurer from the risk of large losses. The primary writing company determines the amount of risk it can retain on individual coverages and cedes the balance of the coverage to reinsurers. The reinsurance may be issued in layers so that a number of reinsurers are participating in a single risk. For example, if the total risk is $500,000 and the primary writing company retains $100,000, separate reinsurance agreements may cover the excess of $400,000. If the first reinsurer accepts an excess of $100,000, that contract is referred to as "first surplus" reinsurance. Additional layers accepted by other reinsurers are referred to as "second surplus," "third surplus," etc.

Surplus lines reinsurance permits the primary writing company to issue coverage beyond the amount it wishes to retain. If reinsurers are not found for each required layer of reinsurance, the primary writer must accept that portion of the risk.

Each reinsurer receives a proportionate part of the premium for the risk. In the above example, each reinsurer would receive the portion of the premium that was charged for the layer it reinsured.

Excess Loss Reinsurance

In this reinsurance, the reinsurer agrees to pay all losses in excess of the amount retained by the primary company, up to a maximum limit. Excess loss reinsurance is often used by insurance companies that are able to retain a large portion of the initial risk. Consequently, fewer losses pass through to the reinsurance company, resulting in a smaller administrative cost and a smaller risk premium. By reinsuring only the larger losses, the primary writing company purchases reinsurance only for the losses that would cause unusual fluctuations in its loss experience.

Catastrophic Reinsurance

Because large losses arise from a single occurrence, such as fire, windstorm, or hail, the primary writing company often needs reinsurance in order to avoid the surplus drains that result from such events. Under catastrophic reinsurance, all the losses attributable to a single occurrence are aggregated and the losses in excess of a specified amount are paid by the reinsurer, up to a maximim limit. For example, the reinsurance company may be responsible for all or for a fixed percentage (i.e., 90 percent) of the aggregate losses in excess of the specified amount arising from a single catastrophe. The reinsurer will reimburse these excess losses (up to a fixed maximum amount), which occur during a calendar year. Alternatively, the reinsuring agreement may provide for a maximum loss ratio (i.e., 65 percent) to be borne by the ceding company, after which the reinsurer will pay all or a fixed percentage of the excess losses up to a maximum amount.

The premium paid for catastrophic reinsurance covers the expected excess losses plus administrative costs and profit. The marketing and underwriting costs of the primary writing company are retained by it and not assumed by the reinsurer.

Quota Share Reinsurance

This reinsurance agreement requires the primary writing company to cede a part of each risk it insures within the class of policies covered in the agreement. For example, a 50/50 quota share agreement requires the ceding company to retain 50 percent of the premiums and to remit 50 percent of the premiums to the reinsurer. Likewise, the ceding company retains 50 percent of the losses and cedes 50 percent of the losses to the reinsurer. The reinsurer pays a ceding commission to the primary writing company to reimburse it for marketing and underwriting expenses and to afford it a profit margin. The ceding commission may be subject to adjustment, depending on subsequent claims experience.

Quota share reinsurance is easy to administer, since premiums and losses are accounted for in the aggregate. It is commonly used by smaller insurers with limited surplus and by insurance companies that need to strengthen their surplus immediately by reducing unearned premiums.

Quota share reinsurance does not apply to amounts previously reinsured under surplus or excess reinsurance agreements. While quota share reinsurance is useful in specific circumstances, such as those described above, it does require the ceding company to share its profitable policies with the reinsurer.

Facultative Reinsurance

This reinsurance is used by property and liability companies to enable them to write large cases. For example, a primary writing company writing fire insurance may retain $100,000 of each risk. If a very large case is written for $10 million, the capacity of existing reinsurance agreements may be exceeded; therefore, the primary writing company may offer to share the individual risk with reinsurers in order to reduce its share of the risk to a permitted level. If in the above instance the total capacity of the primary writing company (including reinsurance) is $5 million, then facultative reinsurers must be found to accept the excess $5 million. These policies are underwritten separately by each reinsurer.

Portfolio Reinsurance

A primary writing company may wish to discontinue writing a single line of business or to withdraw its writings from a geographic area. Portfolio reinsurance (sometimes described as "bulk reinsurance") permits it to cede an entire block of insurance in force. This reinsurance is similar to quota share, except that 100 percent of the risk is transferred to the reinsurer. The primary writing company may continue to service the business in force for a fee.

Portfolio reinsurance may require the reinsurer to issue assumption certificates to the policyholders. If it does, the primary writing company is relieved of all responsibility for future losses. But in any event, the reinsurer pays the primary writing company a ceding commission for marketing expenses, underwriting costs, and profit margin. Many states require advance approval of these reinsurance agreements.

ACCIDENT AND HEALTH REINSURANCE

To a great extent, reinsurance for accident and health risks is similar to property and liability reinsurance. This is because (except for noncancelable and guaranteed renewable coverages) accident and health risks are written for a short period of time and are subject to nonrenewal and cancellation. Similarly, too, the losses on these coverages are more difficult to estimate than are life insurance risks which are determined from reliable mortality experience. The losses are also subject to the risk of cost escalation from adverse selection; that is, those who have claims are likely to continue the insurance in force for as long as possible. Insureds who incur fewer claims are more likely not to renew their policies when premiums are increased to recover past adverse loss experience.

Accident and health insurance is written by life, accident and health, and property and liability insurance companies. However, only life insurance companies are permitted to issue noncancelable and guaranteed renewable policies. The reinsurance agreements generally follow the provisions in the policies issued by the ceding company. For example, coinsurance and modified coinsurance are the types of reinsurance agreements used when accident and health insurance is written by a life insurance company. Quota share and excess loss reinsurance agreements are generally used when accident and health insurance is written by a property and liability company.

There is a distinctive feature to reinsurance agreements covering loss of income. For long-term disability claims, the reinsurer may agree to take a larger share of the losses after an extended elimination period. For example, the reinsurer may pay no losses until after 2 years' benefits have been paid by the primary writing company and thereafter may assume a much larger share of losses than would be typical for excess loss reinsurance. This type of reinsurance permits the primary writing company to accept the costs of losses and administration for short-term claims and to rely on the reinsurer to cover long-term disability claims.

REINSURANCE POOLS

A group of insurers may join together and jointly underwrite reinsurance. Some reinsurance pools will reinsure member companies only, while others may issue a specific type of reinsurance for all insurers. Others may be specifically authorized by state governments.

Often, reinsurance pools are organized and managed by a reinsurance intermediary. The intermediary is a broker who arranges the placement of reinsurance and provides administration for the collection and payment of premiums and losses. Reinsurance pools created by an intermediary assume the income and losses from a number of primary writing companies and redistribute the premiums and losses on an agreed-upon basis to participants of the pool. This arrangement permits companies to participate in larger insurance risks than they otherwise might have been able to. The reinsurance pool is the vehicle that permits insurers to smooth out their loss experience. Pools participated in by related companies are operated similarly.

Many of the government-sponsored pools are called "joint underwriting associations." Their purpose is to provide insurance coverage for those not reasonably able to obtain it in the voluntary market. A joint underwriting association works much like a voluntary reinsurance pool does, except that the participation of each insured is often required. Consequently, each reinsured guarantees its share of the solvency of the joint underwriting association. The association collects the premiums, pays the losses and administrative costs, and passes a proportionate share of the costs to each member. If the losses and expenses exceed the premiums, the reinsureds may be subject to an assessment by the joint underwriting association to make up the difference. The insured may receive a policy from an individual company, but in reality the policy is underwritten by all members of the association.

The reinsurance pools may purchase reinsurance themselves in much the same manner that an individual company may choose to reinsure a portion of its risks.

ACCOUNTING FOR REINSURANCE

The primary writing company is usually responsible for providing the accounting data necessary to record reinsurance transactions. The assuming company is responsible for determining that the data supplied to it properly reflects its share of the reinsurance transaction. Often, the reinsurer does not inspect the original records, but it does have a right to do so, for if erroneous data is furnished by the primary writing company, the reinsurer cannot properly report its own financial condition. The arrangement for furnishing data and inspecting records is covered in the reinsurance agreement.

In terms of cash flow, reinsurance transactions are netted so that only small cash payments are required in order to settle the accounts (this applies to all but bulk reinsurance or quota share reinsurance transactions involving a significant amount of unearned premiums). However, for accounting purposes, reinsurance transactions should be reported in gross amounts by the primary writing company and the reinsurer.

The following material covers reinsurance accounting for life, property and liability, and accident and health insurance.

Life Reinsurance

There are fewer accounting entries necessary for recording yearly renewable term reinsurance than there are for coinsurance; however, the accounting for both types of transactions is similar. These transactions are summarized below.

Reinsurance Premiums. All original premiums ceded, whether collected or uncollected, should be reported by the primary writing company as reinsurance premiums ceded. This amount is subtracted from the total premiums (Exhibit 1, annual statement) in determining the net premium income for the year. To the extent that reinsurance premiums have not been paid to the assuming company, they are included as a liability. Due and uncollected premiums on reinsurance ceded should be subtracted from the asset representing due and uncollected premiums. The assuming company includes the reinsurance premiums assumed in premium income (Exhibit 1, annual statement) and the due and uncollected premiums, whether due from the policyholder or the ceding company, with other due and uncollected premiums.

Reinsurance Losses. For yearly renewable term reinsurance, the ceding company is reimbursed for incurred claims on reinsured policies. The amounts recovered from the reinsurer are applied to reduce the amount of death benefits paid by the primary writing company. Claims incurred which have not been paid by the reinsurer are reported as an asset for amounts due from the reinsurer for losses paid. The assuming company reports the losses paid with other death benefits and reports as a liability those amounts incurred which have not been paid.

Losses incurred under coinsurance arrangements are reported the same as yearly renewable term losses are. However, coinsurance covers other benefits, such as surrender values and policyholder dividends. These amounts are reported in the same manner as death benefits, except that the reinsured amounts are included in surrender benefits and policyholder dividends by both the ceding and assuming companies.

All reinsurance annuity benefits, including death benefits and supplementary contracts, are applied by the ceding company to reduce annuity benefits or supplementary benefits with and without life contingencies. The assuming company includes all benefits that it pays in annuity benefits or in supplementary contract benefits with and without life contingencies.

Reinsurance Expenses. Yearly renewable term reinsurance does not cover commissions, taxes, and other acquisition expenses incurred by the primary writing company; consequently, it has no effect on the expenses of either the ceding or the assuming company.

Coinsurance, on the other hand, requires the assuming company to pay a proportionate share of the acquisition expenses. These include agents' commissions, premium taxes, and other acquisition expenses included in the contract. However, unlike policy benefits, the actual reimbursement received from the reinsurer cannot always be identified by specific expenses and includes a share of expected profits. To the extent that reimbursed expenses are identifiable, they should be reported as a reduction from similar expenses incurred by the primary writing company. For statutory reporting, the total amount is reported as commissions on reinsurance ceded—an income item.

The reinsurer, to the extent that the expenses can be identified, reports these amounts as additional expenses incurred for commissions, premium taxes, and other expense items. For statutory reporting, the total amount is reported as commissions on reinsurance assumed—an expense item.

Experience Refund. In consideration of reinsuring policies on a yearly renewable term basis, the assuming company includes an element of profit in the premium charge to the primary writing company. The realization of this profit is contingent on an estimate of the losses the reinsurer expects to pay. These contracts often provide for a return of part of the premium if the actual loss experience is better than the expected loss experience which was used to calculate the premium. The method for determining the experience refund is specified in the policy and is usually payable annually.

The amount received by the primary writing company should be reported as premium income. For statutory reporting, the amounts are set out separately as "experience refunds"—an income item. Amounts due but uncollected, including an estimate of contingent refunds, should be included as an asset by the primary writing company. For statutory reporting, contingent amounts are often reported as nonadmitted assets.

The reinsurer reports experience refunds as a reduction of its premium income and records unpaid amounts, including contingent amounts, as a liability.

Coinsurance contracts may also include a provision for experience refunds and may include investment earnings. The experience ratings for these contracts are reported as described above (under "Life Insurance") for yearly renewable term reinsurance.

Reinsurance Reserves. Policy reserves are adjusted for all reinsurance arrangements of yearly renewable term and coinsurance. The reserve adjustment for modified coinsurance is treated differently. Reinsurance reserve adjustments for each of the contracts are covered below.

Yearly Renewable Term. These policy reserves may be calculated on two bases: The reserve may be the unearned portion of reinsurance premiums paid to the assuming company, or it may be determined by the mean reserve of 1-year term coverage for the reinsurance ceded, utilizing the mortality and interest assumptions used to value the policy, before reinsurance. The ceding company reduces both the policy reserves and the increase in reserves by the amount of reinsured reserves. The assuming company increases its policy reserves and the increase in reserves by the amount it computes for the net amount at risk. For statutory reporting, the credit taken by the ceding company on reinsured policies is limited to the lesser of (1) the reserves recorded by the assuming company or (2) the ceding company's reserve for those policies.

Coinsurance. Policy reserves under a coinsurance arrangement are transferred pro rata to the reinsurers. That is, the reserves are determined by the ceding company and a pro rata portion is ceded to the reinsurer. The ceding company reduces its policy reserves and its increase in reserves by the amount of policy reserves ceded to the reinsurer. The assuming company increases its policy reserves and its increase in life reserves for the amount of life reserves assumed.

For statutory reporting, the maximum deduction for reinsurance reserves is limited to the pro rata amount determined by the ceding company for those policies before the reinsurance transaction, even though the assuming company may use a different policy reserve method.

Modified Coinsurance. Most modified coinsurance agreements provide that the assuming company will transfer to the ceding company the annual increase in mean reserves on policies reinsured. The reserves may be transferred at the end of the year or on a monthly pro rata basis. In either instance, the ceding company increases its policy reserves by the amount of funds received from the reinsurer for such reserves, and the assuming company treats such a transfer as a return of reinsurance premiums.

For statutory reporting, it is assumed that the ceding company has established the reserves (as though there was no reinsurance) by having increased both its policy reserves and the increase in aggregate reserves for life policies. The amounts received from the reinsurer are recorded as other income—reserve adjustments on reinsurance ceded.

Modified Coinsurance Interest Adjustment. Under modified coinsurance, an interest adjustment is made for the reinsured policy reserves held by the ceding company. The interest rate specified in the agreement applies to funds held by the ceding company to support the reinsured reserves. This adjustment is usually made at the end of the year and applies to all reinsured mean reserves at the beginning of the year. The modified coinsurance interest adjustment is reported as a reduction of reinsurance premiums ceded by the ceding company and as a reduction of reinsurance premiums assumed by the assuming company.

Property and Liability Reinsurance

The accounting entries necessary to record transactions involving reinsurance are similar for all categories of property and liability reinsurance. These transactions are summarized below.

Reinsurance Premiums. All reinsurance premiums paid for surplus lines, excess loss, catastrophic, quota share, facultative, and portfolio reinsurance are reported as a reduction to premiums written by the ceding company and as an addition to premiums written by the assuming company. Unpaid reinsurance premiums are reported as reinsurance amounts payable by the ceding company and as uncollected premiums by the assuming company.

Unearned premiums with respect to reinsurance premiums are deducted from unearned premiums by the ceding company and added to unearned premiums by the assuming company.

For statutory reporting, all reinsurance premiums are reported by line of business written.

Reinsurance Losses. All recoveries on losses ceded should reduce the loss payments reported by the ceding company and increase the loss payments reported by the reinsurer. Reinsurance recoverable on loss payments is reported as an asset by the ceding company and is included in unpaid losses by the assuming company.

Reinsurance recoverable on losses in the process of adjustment is used to reduce the loss reserve and losses incurred of the ceding company and to increase the loss reserves and losses incurred of the assuming company.

If loss adjustment expenses are included in the reinsurance agreement, the ceding company reports such amounts as a reduction in loss adjustment expense reserves and loss expense incurred, and the assuming company reports them as additions to loss adjustment expense reserves and loss expense incurred.

For statutory reporting, reinsurance losses are reported separately by line of business for both the ceding and assuming companies. Since these reinsured losses decrease the losses incurred by the ceding company, they will cause an increase in the excess of statutory reserves over statement reserves if the reported loss experience for liability insurance is less than the minimum required to be reported. For the assuming company, the increase in its incurred losses will reduce the excess of statutory reserves over statement reserves when its loss experience is less than the statutory minimum.

Reinsurance Expenses. There are usually no expense reimbursements to the ceding company on excess loss and catastrophic reinsurance. Rather, the premiums include amounts necessary to cover expected losses, expenses, and profit. Therefore, reinsurance premiums for excess loss and catastrophic reinsurance have no effect on the acquisition expenses incurred by the primary writing company.

On the other hand, reinsurance premiums for surplus lines, quota share, facultative, and portfolio reinsurance are offset by a commission which permits the primary writing company to be reimbursed for its policy acquisition costs and afforded a margin of profit. The amount of these expenses is aggregated in a single account—Reinsurance Commissions (a reimbursed expense for the ceding company and an expense for the reinsurer).

Reinsurance commissions reimburse the primary writing company for agents' commissions, premium taxes, other underwriting expenses, and a pro rata portion of the profit assumed in the original premiums. However, these amounts are not set out separately and usually cannot be identified by their individual components. Reinsurance commissions are applied by the ceding company to reduce the underwriting expenses and by the assuming company to increase the underwriting expenses—except that where reinsurance profits can be identified, such amounts should be reported as an adjustment to premium income.

Reinsurance commissions are usually expressed as a percentage of the reinsurance premiums. Often, the commission is provisional and may be increased or decreased depending upon the loss experience of the reinsured policies. At the close of an accounting period, the contingent adjustment should be estimated and reported as an adjustment to commissions on reinsurance assumed or ceded. Additional commissions owed to the primary writing company should be recorded as a liability by the reinsurer and as an asset by the ceding company; for statutory reporting, however, the asset amount may be classified as nonadmitted in some state jurisdictions. For statutory reporting, all commissions on reinsurance ceded, including any profits, must be applied to increase or decrease the underwriting expenses.

Accident and Health Reinsurance

Since these policies may be written by life insurance or property and liability insurance companies (except that guaranteed renewable and noncancelable policies may only be written by life insurance companies), the accounting entries are based on the type of company. The accounting for accident and health reinsurance is summarized below.

Life Insurance Companies. Accident and health insurance policies are often reinsured by using coinsurance. The ceding company reduces its premium income, losses, expenses and reserves as explained above in this chapter under "Life Reinsurance." No distinction is made in the reinsurance credit between the amounts applicable to unearned premiums and the other reserve credits applicable to guaranteed renewable and noncancelable policies. The assuming company increases its premiums, losses, expenses, and reserves for its proportionate share of the coinsurance.

If accident and health reinsurance is reinsured as yearly renewable term insurance, the premiums, losses, and reserves are adjusted as explained above under "Life Reinsurance." Expenses are not adjusted since they are not considered in the reinsurance premium.

Accident and health policies reinsured on a facultative or similar basis are reported in the same manner as for coinsurance.

Property and Liability Insurance Companies. Reinsurance premiums are reported as an adjustment to premium income and are deducted by the ceding company and added by the assuming company. Reserve credits consist of a pro rata portion of unearned premiums and are deducted by the ceding company and added by the assuming company. Unpaid reinsurance premiums are reported as reinsurance amounts payable by the ceding company and as uncollected premiums by the assuming company. For statutory reporting, these amounts are reported as a separate line of business.

Reinsurance losses are reported as a decrease in paid losses by the ceding company and as an increase in paid losses by the assuming company. Losses unpaid at the closing date are reported by the ceding company as reinsurance recoverable on losses paid and by the assuming company as unpaid losses. For statutory reporting, these losses are reported by line of business.

Reinsurance expenses consist of agents' commissions, taxes, other underwriting expenses, and profits; these expenses are reported as a reduction of underwriting expenses by the ceding company and as an addition to underwriting expenses by the assuming company. As explained in regard to the reinsurance profits of life insurance companies, if these amounts can be identified, they should be reported as an adjustment to premium income.

Unauthorized Reinsurance

For statutory reporting, reinsurance companies which are not authorized to do business in the domicile state of the ceding company may cause the ceding company to classify certain reinsurance balances as nonadmitted. Whether a reinsurer is an authorized company must be determined on a state-by-state basis. If the reinsurer is considered to be unauthorized, amounts recoverable and reinsurance credits due from it may not be admitted for statutory reporting. The exception to this rule is that these balances may be admitted to the extent that the ceding company holds funds deposited by the reinsurer, including any amounts held that are due the reinsurer for reinsurance premiums.

The ceding company must report all funds held under reinsurance contracts as a liability, and the assuming company must report such funds held by or deposited with ceding companies as an asset. Neither of these amounts is adjusted by the liability for unauthorized reinsurance.

17

POLICYHOLDER DIVIDENDS

Insurance companies which issue participating policies generally pay dividends to the policyholders. The idea is that the policyholder is charged a premium larger than "necessary" by using conservative estimates for mortality and investment earnings and that some or all of the "excess" premium is returned to the policyholder after the end of the year. This excess is determined based on the actual mortality experience, investment return, and overall profitability of the company. The company need not repay all of the excess but may retain part of it for a general contingency fund. A true policyholder dividend, as distinguished from an experience refund, is never determined based on the actual experience of an individual policyholder (such as an employer) but is instead based on the experience of the whole insurance company or of a class of policies; nevertheless, experience refunds are sometimes called "dividends."

Another important point is that there is no legal or contractual obligation to declare policy dividends; the board of directors holds the final authority in the matter. In practice, however, dividends in some amount are declared on participating policies virtually without fail. Once declared, dividends constitute a legal liability.

Participating policies are most commonly identified with life insurance—and mutual life insurance companies in particular, since the pur-

pose of such companies is to return profits to the policyholders. However, not all policies issued by mutual life insurance companies are participating; occasionally, nonparticipating ones are issued as well. Both whole life and term policies may be participating, and stock life insurance companies can and do issue participating policies, although these are in the minority. Property and liability insurance may also be issued on a participating basis. While this chapter will primarily discuss life insurance dividends, the principles also apply to property and liability dividends; important distinctions between the two types of dividends will be noted where necessary.

Dividends are generally paid annually, usually sometime after the date of the policy anniversary. To compensate for the initial acquisition costs, some policies do not include a dividend for the first or second year, or they make the dividends for these years conditional upon payment of the next premium. In other respects, annual payments are now the general rule. Deferred dividend policies, for which payments are not made for a number of years, are rare if they are issued at all. A few policies provide for "extra" dividends after a certain number of years in addition to the regular annual dividends.

Policyholder dividends are not all paid at the same time. In the case of a dividend paid on stock, of course, all of the shareholders receive their payments simultaneously. But for policy dividends, while there is a single declaration date (usually in December or January), the actual payments are not made until after a particular policyholder's anniversary date. Thus, if the dividend is declared on December 31, the dividend payments could be spread over the next 365 days according to all the different anniversary dates.

DIVIDEND CALCULATIONS

The level of dividends on participating policies is determined not only by the company's internal experience but by competitive conditions in the marketplace. The intensity of the competition between companies determines in part how close a company will come to paying the maximum dividend possible without endangering the security of the policyholders. Also, there is a tendency for companies to loosely follow a dividend "scale" from year to year in order to minimize uncertainty and instability; the level of dividends would therefore be "smoothed" to some extent. Thus, in a poor year the company might invade its general contingency fund in order to keep up the historical level of dividends, and in a good year it might pay less than the maximum possible in order to avoid erratic annual fluctuations.

But while competitive conditions and historical patterns do influence the dividend calculation, generally the most important factor is the company's own experience for the year. The first step is for the board of directors to determine that year's *divisible surplus*; this is the total amount available to pay dividends to all policyholders. Obviously, the divisible surplus is simply the portion of total earnings that the company decides not to retain, in view of internal needs and market conditions.

The next step is to allocate the divisible surplus among the various policyholder categories. A *category* is defined in terms of the type of the policy, the duration of the policy, and the age of the policyholder. The portion of divisible surplus—the dividend—that each category receives is based on the estimated contribution of that category to the total divisible surplus. Although there are a number of ways to make this estimate, probably the most common is the *contribution method,* which analyzes three factors—excess interest, mortality savings, and loading savings—to determine the amount of dividend that each category receives.

- *Excess interest* is the amount of investment income earned by the company over and above the assumed reserve rate. This excess is then allocated among policy categories based on asset shares (see Chapter 12, Life Insurance Company Reserves, under "Reserves for Policies with High Premiums and Benefits"). There are different practices as to (1) whether capital gains are treated as investment income; (2) whether the base in the asset share calculation is limited to interest-bearing liabilities and surplus; (3) whether the initial reserve, the mean reserve, or the initial reserve less one-half of the annual insurance cost is used for actuarial values; and (4) how expenses and income taxes are allocated to investment income.
- The mortality factor is based on the actual experience of the company with policyholders of a particular category as compared to the assumed mortality used in computing reserves.
- The loading factor reflects the level of the company's other expenses. These expenses are often allocated to policies based on a percentage of the premium plus a constant dollar amount per $1000 of insurance coverage.

In theory, the sum of the individual dividends paid should exactly equal the divisible surplus; however, there is usually a slight discrepancy. As noted earlier, the divisible surplus and the allocation formula are determined by board declaration on a single date, and then the individual payments are spread over the next 365 days based on anniversary dates. Thus, if a policy is canceled after the declaration date but before the anniversary date, the individual dividend computed on this policy will not have to be paid, which would make the sum of the dividends paid less than the divisible surplus. Also, if a policy which had lapsed before the declaration date is reinstated before the anniversary date, a dividend will be paid even though this was not included in the allocation made at the declaration date; this would tend to make the sum of the individual dividends more than the divisible surplus.

DIVIDEND OPTIONS

Policyholder dividends are generally available in the form of cash, but policyholders may choose from among a variety of alternatives to cash. The most common options in addition to cash are accumulation at interest, paid-up insurance, and 1-year term insurance.

The cash option can consist either of receiving a check for cash or of using the dividend to reduce the next year's premium; both have basically the same effect on the policyholder. In passing, we should note that policy dividends, unlike dividends paid on shares of stock, are not taxable income to the policyholders but are treated as premium refunds. Of course, if the policyholder is taking a business deduction for the premium payment, the dividend would reduce the deduction when received.

Closely related to the cash option is the accumulation option, in which the dividends are simply left with the insurance company to accumulate at interest until withdrawn by the policyholder. Depending on the insurance contract, the rate of interest may either be fixed in the policy or left to the discretion of the company. Usually, the accumulated dividends may be withdrawn at will, but sometimes the policyholder must wait until an anniversary date. At the time of death, any accumulated dividends and interest would of course be paid to the beneficiaries. The interest would be taxable income to policyholders when made available for their withdrawal, regardless of whether they actually withdraw it.

The amount of the dividend may also be used to purchase paid-up additions to the policy. The additional coverage is equal to what may be purchased by using the dividend as a single premium, generally at net rates. This is attractive to many policyholders, not only because of the net rates but also because there is generally no need to demonstrate insurability and there are no tax consequences to the policyholder.

Another common option is to use the dividend to purchase 1-year term insurance. Again, the amount of the coverage is calculated by using the dividend as a single premium. The advantages to policyholders are generally the same as those for paid-up additions. The difference is that significantly more coverage is purchased, but it expires after 1 year.

A less frequent option is to accumulate the dividends toward a paid-up or endowment contract. The policy may be considered a paid-up contract when the surrender value plus the accumulated dividends (and interest thereon) equals the net single premium. The policy may be considered an endowment when the surrender value plus dividends and interest equals the maturity value.

GAAP ACCOUNTING

When dividends are incurred, the debit is to Dividends Expense. The credit side of the entry is determined by the particular dividend option chosen. If paid in cash, the credit is to Cash. If applied to reduce premiums, the credit is to Premium Income. If accumulated at interest, the credit is to Dividend Deposits, a liability account. If used to purchase additional insurance, the credit is to Premium Income for the particular type of additional insurance.

Under generally accepted accounting principles (GAAP), however, the company cannot wait until the transaction has been consummated before recording the dividend. Where a cash dividend will be paid, the liability must be booked prior to the cash payment. Although from a legal standpoint, a dividend is not a binding obligation until declared by the board of directors, under GAAP an estimate of undeclared dividends must be accrued when there is a reasonable expectation that they will be paid. This is in keeping with the overall GAAP principle that *contingent* liabilities must be booked whenever they are susceptible to estimation and payment appears likely.

In the case of virtually all companies which issue participating policies, there is a consistent historical pattern of paying dividends. Thus, barring some extraordinary change in circumstances, the accountant may assume that a dividend will be paid with respect to the current year. The key is to make an estimate of what the amount will be. Since companies generally tend to use the same computation formula from year to year, the historical formula may be applied to current-year information to generate the estimate. Of course, the company is under no obligation to continue using the same formula, so if the accountant has reason to believe that there will be a change in the dividend practice, an appropriate adjustment to the estimate should be made. Prior formulas cannot be applied blindly—but must be used with common sense, based on current knowledge.

In addition to determining the estimated amount of the dividend, it is also important to allocate the liability to the proper period. The objective is to match the dividend liability against the premium giving rise to the dividend, since the dividend is really just a refund of part of that premium. Thus, the estimated dividends incurred on premiums earned during the year would be booked as expenses and as liabilities for the same year. Care must be taken to see that dividends paid currently with respect to prior years' premiums are debited to the liability account and not to the expense account. Of course, the estimate of dividends will usually vary slightly from the actual payments, and this difference may be run through the income statement for the following year. (Life insurance dividends are discussed more fully in Chapter 12, Life Insurance Company Reserves.)

STATUTORY ACCOUNTING

The statutory treatment of life insurance dividends does not vary significantly from the GAAP treatment. Dividends are recorded as an expense in the year that the underlying premiums are earned. If they are undeclared at the time the statutory statement blank is prepared, an estimate must be made in the same manner as for GAAP purposes. Total dividends are described in Exhibit 7 of the life statement.

Since dividends are generally not paid by year end, a liability for the unpaid amounts must be established. Statutory accounting recognizes four different liability accounts:

1. *Dividends Due and Unpaid*: dividends which should have been paid during the year but were not. This category is rather narrow. It does not include dividends which are to be paid in the following year with respect to current-year premiums; instead, it only includes such items as the following:
   - The dividend is conditional upon receiving the next premium payment, which was due but not received by year end.
   - The dividend is to be credited to the next premium, but the next premium

has not been paid and the full amount has been recorded as due and uncollected.

- The dividend was due to be paid, but the check was not mailed out because of the lack of an address, or other unusual circumstances.

2. *Dividends Apportioned for Payment in the Following Calendar Year*: dividends which have been declared with respect to premiums earned in the current year and for which payment is to be made in the next year. Most declared dividends fall into this category. A liability should be recorded even if the dividend is contingent upon payment of a renewal premium.
3. *Dividends Not Yet Apportioned for Payment in the Following Calendar Year*: basically the same as the previous category, except that the formality of declaration has not been performed at the end of the year. An estimate of the undeclared dividends to be paid with respect to premiums earned in the current year is made in a manner similar to that for GAAP. Of course, if the declaration is made after the end of the year but before the statutory statement blank is prepared, this "actual" figure could be used as the end-of-year "estimate."
4. *Dividend Accumulations*: simply dividends which the policyholder has elected to leave on deposit with the company. This account also includes any interest accrued on the deposits, whether or not the interest has been posted or credited to the policyholder's account. Thus, a special end-of-year accrual calculation must be made for statement purposes if the company does not already do this. The Dividend Accumulations account is shown in Exhibit 10 of the life statement.

A few policies include coupons which mature on the policy anniversary and are used to guarantee an annual rate of return on the policy. The coupon is essentially an annual pure endowment. Matured coupons which have not yet been presented for payment should be treated as a dividend accumulation and should accrue interest. The liability for an unmatured coupon should be treated as a policy reserve or as a separate policy liability.

Nonparticipating group insurance or pension contracts often include a provision for experience rating refunds. These are treated as premium refunds and are similar to a policy dividend except that the calculation is made based on the experience of the group rather than on the experience of the entire company or on a class of policies. The accounting entries are basically the same as for policy dividends. To determine the estimated liability at the end of the year, the experience of the group as of that date should be obtained and a calculation made from this data.

Dividends on property and liability insurance are accounted for in a manner similar to that for life insurance. One difference would be the absence of dividend options for additional insurance. Also, the liability is generally not recorded until the dividends have been declared.

TAX ACCOUNTING

Under tax accounting, dividends are treated as an expense (subject to a limitation described below) and unpaid dividends are treated as a liability. For tax purposes, a *dividend* is defined as an amount which is paid to a policyholder and which is not fixed in the policy but instead depends on the experience of the company or the discretion of management. This definition is somewhat broader than that used for GAAP and statutory purposes. It, of course, includes payments to participating policyholders out of divisible surplus. It also includes experience refunds—whether paid on participating or nonparticipating policies—where the experience of the company is a factor. Although these experience refunds or rate credits may be considered as return premiums for other purposes, they are dividends for tax purposes. The definition of *return premiums* is quite narrow; it includes only those amounts fixed in the contract, such as refunds resulting from policy cancellations or from erroneous premium calculations.

For tax purposes, as for other purposes, dividends do not include interest payments, such as interest payments on dividend accumulations. Dividends also do not include payments by one life insurance company to another with respect to reinsurance ceded, even if these amounts are not fixed in the contract but depend on experience or on the discretion of management.

While the tax definition of a dividend is broader than that under GAAP and statutory accounting, the tax rules are more strict as to when an unpaid dividend may be booked as an accrued expense. For GAAP and statutory purposes, the objective is to match the dividend against the underlying premium as it is earned; this in turn creates the necessity for estimates in the event that the dividends are undeclared. For tax accounting, however, the use of estimates is much more restricted, since the main objective is not matching, but allowing a deduction only after it becomes a certainty.

For an unpaid dividend to be accrued, it must be declared by the board of directors (or otherwise caused to become a legal obligation) by the 15th day of the third month after the year's end. This would be March 15 for most companies. The dollar amount must either be stated in the board resolution or the resolution must prescribe a fixed formula for computing the dividend. Thus, in the case of a formula resolution, the dollar amount can be calculated later, but the formula itself cannot be changed after the declaration date. The 2½-month period after the year's end would normally give the company enough time to determine the dividend or the dividend formula. However, failure to meet the 2½-month deadline would cause the accrual of unpaid dividends to be lost for tax purposes.

Where the dividends cannot be accrued for tax purposes, the regulations are structured to allow a deduction for these amounts when they are actually paid. This is because the tax deduction for any given year is equal to the dividends paid during the year, plus those properly accrued at the end of the year (by declaration within 2½ months after year end), less those properly accrued at the beginning of the year. Thus, were the deadline to be missed, the unpaid dividends would not be properly accrued at the beginning of the next year and would therefore be deductible when paid.

For life insurance companies, there is still another restriction on dividends. Dividends are deductible only against gain from operations, not from taxable investment income. Furthermore, the deduction for dividends—together with the special percentage deductions on nonparticipating, group life, and accident and health policies—cannot exceed $250,000 plus any excess of gain from operations (before these deductions) over taxable investment income. (This formula limitation and its current treatment are discussed more fully in Chapter 19, Federal Income Taxes.) This limitation constitutes a significant difference between tax accounting on the one hand and GAAP and statutory accounting on the other. For GAAP and statutory purposes, the entire amount of dividends is treated as an expense without any limitation. For tax purposes, any dividends which exceed the $250,000 formula limitation are lost forever—they cannot be carried forward.

For property and liability companies, however, policyholder dividends are generally deductible in full, provided that they meet the definition of "dividend" and are properly accrued. The one exception would be for a small mutual company other than life or marine ("small" means gross receipts over $150,000 but less than $500,000). Such a company is generally taxed on taxable investment income only, and dividends are not deductible against this, but only against underwriting income.

For years beginning in 1984, the Tax Reform Act provides that dividends are deductible in full. (See Chapter 19, Federal Income Taxes.)

18

PREMIUM AND OTHER TAXES

In addition to the federal income tax, the most costly tax imposed on the insurance industry, insurance companies pay a number of other taxes. Some, such as the state premium tax, are unique to the insurance industry, while others, such as payroll or property taxes, are common to all forms of businesses. These other taxes may be paid to federal, state, or local governments.

PREMIUM TAXES

The second largest tax paid by the insurance industry consists of premium taxes levied by state governments. Unlike the complex federal income tax, the premium tax structure is relatively simple, consisting basically of a flat percentage applied to gross premiums received for risks within the state—similar to a sales tax.

However, in one respect premium taxes are more complicated—for whereas there is only a single federal income tax system, there are 50 different state premium tax systems, and none is exactly the same. Each state has its own rules governing the rate of tax and the definition of the tax base. Because of the many different rules, this chapter can only present a general overview of premium taxes.

Tax Rates

Rates of tax range from 1.5 to 4 percent, but the most common are 2 to 2.5 percent. A state may charge different rates depending on the type of company (life, property, etc.), the type of premium written (life, annuity, fire, windstorm, etc.), and the domicile of the company—whether it is foreign or domestic. Certain companies, such as fraternal insurers or nonprofit entities like Blue Cross and Blue Shield, are often exempt from the tax altogether. Likewise, certain types of premiums, such as annuity or pension premiums, are exempt from tax in many states.

Some states charge foreign (i.e., out-of-state) insurers a higher rate than they do domestic companies (those based within the state). This discriminatory practice has led to most states adopting "retaliatory" tax provisions, based on the principle of "do unto others as they do unto you." For example, state X may generally charge a rate of 2 percent. However, if state Y charges 3 percent to insurers domiciled in X, then state X will also charge 3 percent, instead of 2 percent, to insurers domiciled in Y. These retaliatory provisions, while occasionally working an injustice to individual companies, have produced the beneficial effect of generally stabilizing tax rates. A state contemplating a rate increase would have to be cautious, since its own insurance companies could be injured by retaliation.

Tax Base

The tax is generally imposed on direct premiums written on risks within the state. Reinsurance premiums received are generally excluded from direct premiums and are thus not subject to tax. Return premiums are also subtracted from direct premiums.

Some states stop right here and apply the tax rate to these gross direct premiums. Other states allow for deductions against gross premiums before applying the tax rate. There is no uniformity among the states as to the nature of these deductions. Some of the deductions allowed are for policyholder dividends, reinsurance premiums paid, property taxes, insurance department fees, and certain investments within the state.

In computing the premium tax, it is helpful to begin with Schedule T in the annual statement; it shows the premium income by state. The property and liability annual statement also has a separate Exhibit of Premiums and Losses for each state, immediately following Exhibit 3.

Payment of Tax

After the tax is computed, it may be reduced by credits in certain states for state income or franchise taxes. Many states also require the estimated premium tax to be prepaid on a quarterly or semiannual basis. The tax due for a year is shown in the annual statement as follows:

- Life: Exhibit 6, Line 3
- Property: Underwriting and Investment Exhibit, Part 4, Line 18(a)

EXCISE TAX ON FOREIGN INSURERS

There are no federal premium taxes. However, there is a federal excise tax on premiums for U.S. risks which are paid to foreign insurers or reinsurers. The tax is based on gross premiums, but unlike a state premium tax, the excise tax is paid by the premium payor, not by the recipient. Also unlike state premium taxes, reinsurance premiums are subject to the excise tax.

The tax rate on direct property and casualty premiums is 4 percent. The rate on life and reinsurance premiums is 1 percent. The tax is paid quarterly on Form 720. Life insurance companies which pay this tax would report it in Exhibit 6, Line 6. Property and liability companies would report it in the Underwriting and Investment Exhibit, Part 4, Line 18(d).

PAYROLL TAXES

Insurance companies pay a variety of payroll taxes to federal and state governments. Some of these taxes are withheld from the wages of employees; others are imposed directly on the employer itself.

Payroll taxes are imposed only on wages paid to *employees*. The definition of an employee, as opposed to an independent contractor, has given rise to many controversies. The general rule is that where a company is able to control the manner and means of a person's work, and not just the results, an employment relationship exists. This rule is often hard to apply, so the following factors may be helpful in making a determination:

- Who sets the person's hours?
- Is the person free to work for other companies?
- Does the person provide his or her own equipment and work area?

The above factors are only items to consider, for the determination of an employment relationship depends on the facts and circumstances of each situation. However, payroll taxes will not be imposed where the company had reasonable grounds for treating the person as an independent contractor, filed all required reports on that basis, and treated all persons performing similar jobs as independent contractors since 1977. (Full-time life insurance salespeople, though, may be statutory employees—as discussed just below in regard to FICA taxes.)

Federal payroll taxes consist of income tax withholding, social security taxes, and unemployment taxes.

Income taxes are withheld from the wages of employees according to IRS tables based on the wage amount, the pay period, the employee's marital status, and the number of exemptions claimed.

Social security (FICA) taxes are imposed on both the employer and the employee. For 1985, the employer pays a 7.05 percent rate and the employee has 7.05 percent withheld from wages. Wages in excess of $39,600 per person are not subject to this tax. A full-time life insurance sales agent, even if not meeting the regular definition of an employee, may still be considered a *statutory employee* subject to FICA taxes. This occurs if the agent performs duties on a continuing basis, does not have a substantial personal investment in equipment (other than a car), and cannot substitute another person to do his or her work. The compensation of such an agent is subject to FICA taxes, but not to income tax withholding or unemployment taxes unless the agent also meets the regular definition of an employee.

Federal unemployment (FUTA) taxes are imposed on the first $7,000 of wages paid to each person. The gross rate is 3.5 percent, but a credit may be taken for some or all of the state unemployment taxes paid, with the result that in most cases the effective FUTA rate is 0.8 percent.

State payroll taxes consist of state income tax withholding (in states having an income tax) and state unemployment taxes. Rates are set by each state, and the unemployment tax rates are generally based on the employer's historical experience of unemployment claims filed by former employees.

Federal income tax withholding and FICA taxes are reported on Form 941, which is filed on a quarterly basis. However, advance deposits are required if the cumulative unpaid taxes equal or exceed $500. In such a situation the taxes must be deposited by the 15th day of the following month. However, if the cumulative total equals or exceeds $3000 at any time, deposits are required more frequently.

Federal unemployment taxes are reported on Form 940, which is filed annually. If the cumulative unpaid FUTA taxes exceed $100, a deposit must be made by the last day of the next month.

Each state provides its own forms and deposit requirements.

In addition to the above returns, the wages and withholding for each employee must also be reported on Form W-2, which is submitted annually to the IRS with Form W-3.

Payments to independent contractors (as opposed to employees) are not reported on any of the above returns. However, if the payments to any person equal or exceed $600 during a calendar year, the total paid must be reported on Form 1099-MISC. Withholding is generally not required, but if the person fails to provide an identifying number or the IRS notifies the company that such number is inaccurate, the 20 percent "backup" withholding is required, which is reported on Form 941 and deposited along with employee withholding and FICA taxes.

For accounting purposes, amounts withheld from wages (income tax withholding and the employee's share of FICA tax) are reported as part of gross salaries, and not as a tax. (Likewise, any backup withholding on independent contractor payments would be shown as part of the contract payment and not as a tax.) The reason for this, of course, is that employees, rather than the company itself, are paying these items. Other payroll taxes (unemployment taxes and the employer's share of FICA tax) are reported as taxes on the following lines of the annual statement:

- Life: Exhibit 6, Line 4 (state unemployment), Line 5 (FICA), and Line 6 (FUTA)
- Property: Underwriting and Investment Exhibit, Part 4, Line 18(c)

REAL ESTATE TAXES

Insurance companies pay real estate taxes to state and local governments based on the assessed value of the real property. Except for the development phase of a project, such taxes are charged against income for GAAP, statutory, and income tax purposes. The following lines of the annual statement are used:

- Life: Exhibit 6, Line 1
- Property: Underwriting and Investment Exhibit, Part 4, Line 20.

Property taxes may be accrued in several different ways: by prorating the tax over the year to which the tax relates (as determined under state law), by considering the entire tax to accrue on the date the tax becomes a lien, or by accruing the tax on the date that the tax must be paid. In many states the payment date for such taxes is 12 or more months after the year to which the tax relates, and sometimes the exact rate of tax is not known until after the end of this earlier year. Also, some states use a fiscal period for assessing the tax which does not coincide with the insurance company's calendar year. For these reasons, it is usually acceptable to account for property taxes by any of the three methods—or by any other rational basis which produces a similar result. (A pure cash basis would not be acceptable if there was a material omission or bunching of tax payments.) Consistency in accounting is the most important consideration.

Often, the accounting treatment will be determined when the real estate is acquired, since the purchase contract specifies the allocation of tax liability between buyer and seller.

For federal income tax purposes, real estate taxes are deductible on the date that they become a lien or a personal liability of the company, unless an election is made to accrue them ratably over the year to which the tax relates. This election must be made for the first year that the company becomes subject to real estate taxes. When real estate is bought or sold, the property tax liability for that year must be prorated between buyer and seller based on the sale date, regardless of how the purchase agreement prorates the taxes.

As a practical matter, IRS agents usually allow a deduction for the amount of real estate taxes shown in the annual statement rather than force the company to follow the income tax deduction guidelines strictly, since any difference is generally immaterial and would only be a shifting of deductions between years. Legally speaking, though, the IRS always has the right to require compliance with the income tax rules.

For a discussion of how property taxes during the development stage of a project are accounted for, see Chapter 9, Goodwill and Other Intangibles, under "Construction Period Interest and Taxes."

PERSONAL PROPERTY TAXES

Insurance companies generally incur few if any personal property taxes. Inventory, equipment, and furniture are some of the items that may be subject to such taxes. The accounting and income tax rules for accruing any personal property taxes are the same as for real estate taxes. However, if the amount of tax is immaterial, it is usually acceptable to use the cash basis for convenience purposes. The amount of tax would be reported as "Other taxes" in the annual statement as follows:

- Life: Exhibit 6, Line 6
- Property: Underwriting and Investment Exhibit, Part 4, Line 18(d)

STATE FRANCHISE OR INCOME TAXES

Although most states impose an income or franchise tax on regular businesses, insurance companies are subject to these taxes less frequently because states rely on the premium tax to raise funds from the insurance industry. Furthermore, in most situations where an income or franchise tax is encountered, the state allows its premium tax to be reduced by the amount of income or franchise tax. Thus, the income or franchise tax often has no net effect on the company.

Where imposed, a state income tax will usually be patterned after the federal income tax. A franchise tax, on the other hand, is supposedly a "fee" for the privilege of doing business in the state. The fee may be computed in a variety of ways, but is often a percentage of net income, total assets, or total equity. A franchise tax is "in lieu" of an income tax, and therefore a company would not be subject to both income and franchise taxes in the same state.

State income and franchise taxes are accounted for on the accrual basis and are reported on the following lines of the annual statement:

- Life: Exhibit 6, Line 4
- Property: Underwriting and Investment Exhibit, Part 4, Line 18(a)

MISCELLANEOUS STATE TAXES

Insurance companies pay several other state taxes and fees in addition to those previously discussed. Annual license fees are charged by every state for the authority to do business. Such fees may be a flat amount (usually several hundred dollars) or may be a fractional percentage of assets, stock, or equity. Insurance departments also charge companies for the cost of performing an NAIC audit every 3 years.

Almost all states impose a tax on surplus lines (insurance on risks which cannot be provided by licensed companies). Usually, though, the tax is paid by the broker or agent, and not by the insurance company.

A fire department or fire marshal tax may be imposed as a percentage of fire premiums. This generally reduces the premium tax.

A tax may be charged on workers' compensation premiums (or claims paid) to support the Workers' Compensation Commission, rehabilitation programs, and second-injury funds.

Another tax may be charged to support a state guarantee fund, which reimburses the policyholders of insolvent insurance companies.

Some states also charge a tax to administer motor vehicle financial responsibility laws and to pay unsatisfied judgments of uninsured drivers.

These and other miscellaneous state taxes are accounted for on the accrual basis, or the cash basis can be used if the amounts are immaterial (which they often are). The following lines of the annual statement are used:

- Life: Exhibit 6, Line 2 (insurance department licenses and fees), and Line 6 (other)
- Property: Underwriting and Investment Exhibit, Part 4, Line 18(b) (insurance department licenses and fees), and Line 18(d) (other)

19

FEDERAL INCOME TAXES

The material on insurance company taxation is included for two reasons. First, the accountant may be called upon to prepare the tax return or to answer basic tax questions. Second, the calculation of deferred taxes is extremely important for an insurance company, and a general understanding of the tax rules is necessary in order to make this calculation.

Since this is primarily an accounting handbook, the discussion of taxes is restricted to the basic knowledge needed to perform the above functions. No attempt is made to cover complex tax planning or to discuss the many intricacies found in the regulations, rulings, and cases applicable to insurance companies.

TYPES OF INSURANCE COMPANIES FOR TAX PURPOSES

The first task is to determine whether the company qualifies as an *insurance company* for tax purposes. As a general rule, a company qualifies if over half of its business is insurance. Usually, this is not a problem. However, the mere fact that a company has an insurance license and calls itself an "insurance company" has little or no bearing. The nature of the actual business conducted determines the tax qualification. Thus, if two-thirds of a so-called insurance company's income comes from the lending business, the company will not be treated as an insurance company for tax purposes, but merely as a regular corporation.

Once the company qualifies for tax purposes, the next step is to determine the type of category under which it will be taxed. All such insurance companies will fall into one of the following four categories:

1. *Tax-exempt organizations:* primarily fraternal or local benevolent life associations. Since there are no special insurance tax rules for these entities, they will not be covered.
2. *Life insurance companies:* those with over 50 percent of their reserves attributable to life or noncancelable health or accident insurance.
3. *Mutual companies other than life or marine:* for simplicity, called "mutual casualty companies," but mutual property and liability insurance companies also fall into this category.
4. *All other insurance companies:* including stock property and liability companies, title companies, mutual marine companies, and life companies which do not meet the 50 percent reserve test.

The tax treatment of each category is different and is covered in a separate section of this chapter. An insurance company can be in only one category for any particular year, but it can be in different categories for different years. In different years, it can even switch back and forth from insurance company to non-insurance company status. However, there are special rules governing the use of loss carryovers and carrybacks when a company changes its category or status. A loss from a non-insurance company year may not be used in an insurance company year, and vice versa. A loss arising in an insurance company year may be used in another insurance company year even if the company is a different type of insurance company for that year. But the loss is limited to what it would be if the company had been the same type of insurance company in all years as it is in the year the loss is carried to. Thus, a loss may be carried from a mutual casualty year to a stock casualty year, but it is limited to what the loss would be if the company had been stock all along.

Subject to the above rules, losses may be carried back 3 years and forward 15 years. The time period continues to elapse even if a loss cannot be used in a particular year—for instance, if the company temporarily goes into a noninsurance status.

Two other points about insurance companies in general should be mentioned. First, all insurance companies must be on the calendar year, except to the extent required by the consolidated return regulations. Second, the primary source of tax data is the statutory statement. Unless there is a specific tax rule to the contrary, most items of taxable income and expense are taken directly off the statutory statement.

Life Insurance Companies—Pre-1982

The tax scheme for life insurance companies is far more complex than for other types of insurance companies. To be subject to this tax, the company must be an insurance company in which the life reserves plus unearned premiums on noncancelable (or guaranteed renewable) accident and health policies exceed more than 50 percent of the total insurance reserves. Note that being an "insurance company" is required in addition to the 50 percent reserve test; otherwise, a manufacturing or other noninsurance business could use the favorable life insurance tax rules simply by issuing a single life policy but no nonlife policies. On the other hand, an insurance company which issued some life policies but failed the 50 percent test would be taxed as an "other insurance company."

If a company qualifies for the life insurance tax rules, its taxable income is the smaller of its taxable investment income or its gain from operations, plus 50 percent of any excess of gain from operations over taxable investment income. In addition, any amounts removed from its Policyholders' Surplus Account are also included in taxable income. The taxes are paid at regular corporate rates but reported on a special return, Form 1120L.

Definition of Reserves. To be a *life insurance reserve* for purposes of the 50 percent test and other tax computations, the reserve must be (1) computed by using recognized mortality or morbidity tables together with an assumed rate of interest, (2) set aside to meet future unaccrued claims, and (3) required by law or insurance department regulations. Three other items should be noted:

- Life insurance reserves do not include so-called deficiency reserves, which are the excess of discounted future claims over discounted future premiums on a policy.
- The amount of reserves for any year is the average of the beginning and ending reserve balances.
- The average amount of policy loans outstanding is subtracted in computing life insurance reserves.

Total insurance reserves for purposes of the 50 percent test include life insurance reserves, unearned premiums on noncancelable accident or health policies, and all other insurance reserves required by law, except for deficiency reserves. Total reserves are computed on an average basis, reduced by the average amount of any policy loans.

Taxable Investment Income. Conceptually, the object in computing taxable investment income is to separate the investment income necessary to build up life insurance or pension reserves from that earned on funds used for other purposes. Only the latter amount is included in taxable investment income.

First, *gross investment income* must be computed. This consists of interest, dividends, rents, royalties, short-term capital gains in excess of long-term losses, and income from any trade or business other than the insurance business. Note that tax-exempt interest is included. Premiums on all bonds must be amortized, as must all original issue discounts and all discounts on tax-exempt bonds. At the election of the taxpayer, market discounts on taxable bonds need not be amortized.

Second, the following expenses are subtracted from gross investment income to arrive at the *investment yield:*

- □ Real estate expenses and depreciation on investment property. No deduction is allowed for the expenses of real estate used by the company, except the investment department.
- □ Depletion.
- □ Expenses connected with a noninsurance trade or business, other than losses on the sale of capital or fixed assets.
- □ Investment expenses. If any general or overhead expenses are allocated here, then the total investment expenses (not just the allocation) are subject to a limit. The limit is 0.0025 of the mean assets, plus mortgage service fees, plus the greater of (1) ¼ of the excess of investment yield (without deduction for investment expenses) over 3¾ percent of the mean assets, minus mortgage service fees; or (2) 0.0025 of the mean of mortgages that are without service fees. *Mean assets* are the average of all company assets, except real estate and fixed assets used for insurance offices. Real estate and stocks are valued at fair market value, while other assets are valued at their adjusted basis.

The investment yield is then divided by the mean assets (as defined above) to produce the *current earnings rate.* The lower of the current earnings rate or the average earnings rate over the last 5 years is called the "adjusted reserve rate."

Next, the adjusted reserve rate is multiplied by the *adjusted life insurance reserves.* These are the average reserves (described earlier) multiplied by a percentage—which is 100 percent, plus 10 times the average interest rate assumed in calculating the reserves, minus 10 times the adjusted reserve rate.

To this result is added the product of the mean pension reserves times the current earnings rate. These two numbers (adjusted life reserves and pension reserves, times their respective rates), plus interest paid by the company, constitute the *policy and other contract liability requirement,* which essentially is the amount of investment income excluded from taxation as being necessary to build up reserves.

However, we are not yet finished computing taxable investment income.

Next, the policyholder and other contract requirement is divided by the investment yield. The difference between this percentage and 100 percent is called the "company's share." The company's share percentage is then multiplied by each of the individual categories of income and expense making up the investment yield. The sum of these individual products—less the company's share of tax-exempt interest, less the 85 percent dividend-received deduction on the company's share of dividends, less a special deduction of $25,000 (or 10 percent of investment yield, if smaller), and plus 100 percent of any long-term capital gains in excess of short-term losses—is the taxable investment income.

For purposes of calculating the dividend-received deduction here, the deduction is limited to 85 percent of taxable investment income before the deduction. However, this limit does not apply if deducting the full 85 percent of dividends received would produce a taxable investment loss.

Gain from Operations. After calculating taxable investment income, the next step is to calculate the gain from operations. This takes into account all aspects of company income, both investments and premiums. There are basically three elements:

- The company's share of investment yield
- The gain from premium income
- The net long-term capital gain in excess of short-term loss

The total investment yield used in this calculation is the same as that for taxable investment income. However, the company's share is computed differently: To obtain this, the required interest is divided by the investment yield to determine the policyholders' share. Here, the *required interest* is the interest rate assumed in calculating reserves (as opposed to an actual earnings rate), multiplied by the mean reserves computed at that rate. (See the section, "Special Reserve Calculations," just below.) The company's share percentage is the difference between that for the policyholders' share and 100 percent. This percentage is then multiplied by each individual item of investment yield to determine the taxable portion.

Next, the gain from premium income must be determined. This consists of premiums, decreases in reserves (see "Special Reserve Calculations," below), and all other income other than investment income and capital gains. In the case of deferred and uncollected premiums, only the net valuation portion (not the loading) is included in premium income, as well as in assets and reserves. Subtracted from these income items are the following deduction items:

1. Return premiums and reinsurance premiums. Amounts returned (other than in connection with reinsurance) which depend on the experience of the company or the discretion of management are treated not as returned premiums but as policyholder dividends (item 10 below).
2. Claims accrued during the year.
3. Increases in reserves (see "Special Reserve Calculations," below).
4. The company's share of tax-exempt income.
5. The 85 percent dividend-received deduction on the company's share of dividends, limited to 85 percent of the gain from operations before this deduction and before the special policyholder deductions in items 10, 11, and 12, below.
6. Business or investment deductions not allowed in computing investment yield.

7. A special deduction of $25,000 (but not to exceed 10 percent of the investment yield).
8. Charitable contributions (limited to 10 percent of gain from operations before the deductions for contributions and for items 10, 11, and 12, with a 5-year carryforward of any excess).
9. Bad debts computed on the direct write-off method. The reserve method is not allowed.
10. Policyholder dividends. (See special limits, below).
11. Ten percent of the increase in reserves on nonparticipating policies or, if greater, 3 percent of the premiums on nonparticipating policies which are guaranteed renewable for 5 years or more. Group policies are not counted here. (See special limits, below.)
12. Two percent of accident and health premiums and group life premiums. The accumulated deduction for the current year plus all prior years cannot exceed 50 percent of such premiums in the current year. (See special limits, below).

The total deductions under items 10, 11, and 12 cannot exceed $250,000 plus any excess of gain from operations (before the deductions) over taxable investment income.

After these deductions have been subtracted from the gain from premium income, what remains is the second element of life insurance taxation—the gain from operations.

Special Reserve Calculations. A number of special rules govern how reserves are computed for tax purposes. One provision is that only life insurance reserves are considered in computing the policyholder's share of taxable investment income, while additional reserves are considered in computing gain from operations. These additional reserves are:

- Unearned premiums and unpaid losses on any kind of insurance.
- Annuity certain reserves.
- Dividend accumulations or amounts held at interest.
- Advanced premiums and premium deposit funds.
- Special contingency reserves on group plans for retired lives or premium stabilization.
- Deficiency reserves, however, are still excluded.

This larger group of reserves is used to figure the policyholder's share of investment yield in computing the gain from operations. This group of reserves is also used to calculate the income or deduction element in gain from operations for reserve decreases or increases, respectively.

In computing this income or deduction item for changes in the reserve balance, the required interest (or investment yield, if smaller) is subtracted from the ending reserve balance. (The *required interest* is the assumed rate times the reserve.) This adjustment is necessary in order to prevent a double tax benefit, since the required interest is reflected both in the reserve buildup and also as the excluded portion of investment yield.

In the event that there is a change during the year in the method of computing reserves, the old method is used for both the beginning and ending reserve balances. The adjustment in reserves due to the change (the difference between the ending reserve on the old method and the ending reserve on the new method) is taken into the tax return at the rate of 10 percent a year for 10 years. If the change in method causes the reserves to increase, the 10 percent each year is a deduction from the gain from operations. If the change causes the reserves to decrease, the 10 percent is an income item in the gain from operations. Note that if the company ceases to be a life insurance company (because its life reserves fell below 50 percent), any unamortized amount from the method change is taken into the tax return for the previous year.

All life insurance companies are eligible to increase their reserves by what is known as the "preliminary term election." For statutory accounting purposes, companies may be allowed to set up only a special term reserve for newer whole life policies. For tax purposes, such companies may elect to revalue the reserves on these policies to a level-premium basis. Such an election, once made, may not be revoked without IRS consent. If the election is initially made in the current year, both the beginning and ending reserves must be revalued on the level-premium basis. Unlike other adjustments to reserve balances, this election is not considered a change in method and there is no 10-year spread of the adjustment. The initial adjustment to the beginning reserve balance will never enter into the tax return.

Companies making the election must revalue all reserves—they cannot pick and choose. Either the *exact* or the *approximate* revaluation method may be used, so long as the same one is applied consistently. The sole exception to this is that, even while the approximate method can still be used for all other policies, the exact method *must* be used on noncancelable accident and health (A&H) policies. Under the approximate method, all preliminary term reserves are increased by the sum of:

1. $21 per $1000 of the insurance in force under such contracts (other than term), less 2.1 percent of the reserves under such contracts; and
2. $5 per $1000 of the term insurance in force under such contracts which at the time of issuance cover more than 15 years, less 0.5 percent of the reserves under such contracts

Note that the revalued reserves are used for all tax computations, other than for the 50 percent reserve test used for purposes of determining life insurance company qualification.

Subtractions from Policyholders' Surplus Account. The third element of life insurance taxation consists of subtractions from the Policyholders' Surplus Account. To determine this element, the Shareholders' Surplus and Policyholders' Surplus accounts must first be defined.

The Shareholders' Surplus Account begins with a zero balance on January 1, 1958, to which is added life insurance company taxable income since that date (other than subtractions from the Policyholders' Surplus Account), together with tax-exempt income and the dividend-received deduction (both the company's and the policyholders' shares), the special $25,000 deduction, and the nontaxable part of capital gains attributable to the pre-1959 appreciation. The account is also increased by any subtractions from the Policyholders' Surplus Account that are not actually distributed, and decreased by any federal income taxes on the taxable investment income or the gain from operations.

The Policyholders' Surplus Account begins with a zero balance on January 1, 1959, to which is added the untaxed portion (50 percent) of the gain from operations in excess of the taxable investment income. Also added are the special 10 percent deduction for nonparticipating contracts and the 2 percent deduction for A&H policies.

After the two accounts are adjusted for the above items at the end of the current year, the next four subtractions are made in the following order from the Policyholders' Surplus Account and included in taxable income:

1. Distributions to stockholders in excess of the balance in the Shareholders' Surplus Account.
2. Amounts removed from the account at the election of the company. Any amount may be removed, but this is generally done only to use up an expiring loss carryover or to take advantage of the lower rates on the first $100,000 of taxable income.
3. Any balance in the account in excess of the greater of:
   a. Fifteen percent of life reserves at the end of the year
   b. Twenty-five percent of the excess of ending life reserves over life reserves on December 31, 1958
   c. Fifty percent of net premiums and other considerations received with respect to insurance contracts
4. Any balance in the account if the company ceases to be an insurance company for 1 year or a life insurance company for 2 consecutive years.

Mutual Property and Liability Insurance Companies

Although insurance taxation reaches its maximum complexity in the case of life insurance companies, property and liability insurance companies are also subject to special rules. However, while both stock and mutual life insurance companies are basically taxed the same—with a few exceptions—mutual property and liability companies are taxed much differently than stock property and liability insurance companies. A stock company is taxed as an "other" insurance company, which is like a regular corporation in many respects (see "Other Insurance Companies," below in this chapter). Mutual companies, though, have a scheme of taxation all their own.

Any mutual company other than life or marine is subject to these rules. A mutual company, of course, is one controlled by the policyholders. Surplus is distributed in the form of policy dividends. The identification of a mutual company is usually not difficult, although in a few rare instances there could be some doubt.

For income tax purposes, mutual property and liability companies are divided into three categories:

- Regular mutuals (those receiving more than $500,000 in gross receipts annually)

- Small mutuals (those with annual gross receipts of between $150,000 and $500,000 annually)
- Exempt mutuals (those with $150,000 or less in gross receipts annually)

For the purpose of determining these classifications, gross receipts do not include capital gains.

Regular Mutuals. The taxable income of a regular mutual is the sum of its taxable investment income, statutory underwriting income, and subtractions from the protection against loss account.

Taxable Investment Income. This consists of interest, dividends, rents, royalties, capital gains, and gross income from any noninsurance business, less the following items:

- Tax-exempt interest.
- Depreciation and other expenses connected with real estate investments. No deduction is allowed for expenses attributable to real estate occupied by the company, except for its investment department.
- Depletion.
- Expenses connected with a noninsurance business.
- Interest expense.
- The 85 percent dividend-received deduction, limited to 85 percent of taxable investment income before the deduction (unless taking the full 85 percent of dividends received would produce a net investment loss, in which case there is no limit).
- Capital losses. As with regular corporations, capital losses are normally limited to the amount of capital gains (with a 3-year carryback and a 5-year carryforward of any excess). However, mutuals are allowed an additional deduction for capital losses incurred to raise funds to pay claims or policyholder dividends. This additional capital loss deduction is limited to the excess of (1) gross receipts from the sale of capital assets—plus interest, dividends, rents, royalties, and net premiums—over (2) losses paid, expenses paid, and policyholder dividends. *Net premiums* mean gross premiums minus returned premiums and reinsurance premiums. Those amounts returned which depend on the experience of the company or the discretion of management are considered policyholder dividends and not return premiums.
- Investment expenses. These are expenses of the investment department. General and overhead expenses may be allocated to the investment department, but if such an allocation is made, the total investment expenses (not just the allocation) become subject to a limit. The limit is 0.0025 of the average book value of the investment assets, plus ¼ of the excess of the taxable investment income (without reduction for investment expenses) over the sum of the tax-exempt interest, the dividend-received deduction, and 3¾ percent of the average book value of invested assets. Note that in calculating the taxable investment income, the bond discount (whether original issue or market) does not need to be amortized.

Statutory Underwriting Income. After computing the taxable investment income, the statutory underwriting income must be determined. This is the total company income less the sum of the total company expenses, the taxable investment income, the special $6000 deduction, and the protection against loss deduction. (A taxable investment loss would be added back.)

The total company income and total company expenses are calculated as for a regular corporation, with the following modifications peculiar to the insurance business:

- An adjustment is made for unearned premiums.
- Bad debts must be accounted for by the direct write-off method rather than by the reserve method.
- Capital losses are calculated in the same way as for taxable investment income.
- Policyholder dividends are deductible.
- Unlike the computation for taxable investment income, investment expenses are deductible in full and the 85 percent dividend-received deduction is limited to 85 percent of total taxable income, not just to 85 percent of taxable investment income.

The special $6000 deduction is equal to $6000 less 1 percent of the gross receipts (other than capital gains) over $500,000. Because of the 1 percent cutback, this deduction disappears when the gross receipts equal or exceed $1,100,000. Also, this deduction cannot reduce statutory underwriting income below zero.

Protection Against Loss (PAL) Account. This account is the most complex part of mutual company taxation. Additions to the account are treated as deductions from underwriting income, whereas subtractions from the account are the third element of mutual company taxable income (the other elements being the investment income and underwriting income).

The annual addition to the PAL account is the sum of the following items:

- One percent of losses incurred during the year, reduced by salvage and reinsurance recoverable.
- Twenty-five percent of statutory underwriting income before the PAL deduction.
- A special amount for concentrated risk companies. If over 40 percent of a company's premiums come from insurance for natural disasters (windstorm, hail, flood, earthquake, etc.) within either one state or a 200-mile radius, then this deduction is available. The deduction is equal to the statutory underwriting income (before the PAL deduction) times the percentage that these concentrated risk premiums exceed 40 percent.

As mentioned before, subtractions from the PAL account are a separate element of taxable income. Five specific items are subtracted from the PAL account:

1. Any statutory underwriting loss for the current year (but not to exceed the current PAL addition).
2. Any loss found by combining the taxable investment income (or loss) with the

statutory underwriting income (or loss). Before subtracting this loss from the PAL account, the loss is reduced by any amount in item 1 above.
3. Any loss carryovers to the current year.
4. Any PAL account addition from the fifth preceding taxable year, except for 12½ percent of that earlier year's statutory underwriting income before the PAL deduction. In making this calculation, the current year's amounts from items 1, 2, and 3 are first subtracted from the earlier PAL additions, beginning with the fifth prior year.
5. Any balance in the PAL account in excess of the greater of (a) 10 percent of the premiums earned minus policyholder dividends, or (b) the balance in the PAL account at the end of the previous year. To determine the PAL account balance for this purpose, current-year additions and subtractions (except for item 5) are made. However, amounts in the PAL account for concentrated risk premiums in any year are excluded from the balance in this computation.

If a company ceases to be taxed as a regular mutual property and liability insurance company, the entire balance in the PAL account is triggered into taxable income. Likewise, a company may elect to have the entire balance in its PAL account taxed. This election normally would be made only where there is an expiring loss carryover or where the company wishes to be taxed as a small mutual.

A regular mutual pays tax at the same rates as a normal corporation, with one exception. If the taxable income is less than $12,000, the tax is only 30 percent of the taxable income in excess of $6000. Form 1120M is used to report the tax.

The loss carryover rules for a regular mutual are the same as for all insurance companies, with three exceptions:

- The general rule is that if an insurance company is taxed under different categories for the loss year and the use year, the loss is limited to what the amount would have been if the company had been taxed as the same type of insurance company for all years as the loss year. For regular mutuals, this limitation also applies if the company was taxed as other than a regular mutual for any year *between* the loss year and the use year.
- If a regular mutual company converts to a stock company, the loss carryovers are reduced by 25 percent of the policyholders' dividends in each loss year.
- A loss may not be carried to, or from, any year that the company is taxed as a small mutual.

Small and Exempt Mutuals. A mutual property and liability insurance company with gross receipts (other than capital gains) not exceeding $150,000 is exempt from tax.

A mutual with gross receipts (other than capital gains) over $150,000 but less than $500,000 is taxed on taxable investment income only (computed in the same manner as for a regular mutual), provided that no consolidated return is filed and that there is no balance in the PAL account. Such a company is called a "small" mutual. In this situation, any underwriting income would be tax-free. Furthermore, if the applicable gross receipts are over $150,000 but less than $250,000, the tax is reduced by the percentage that the difference between the receipts and $250,000 bears to $100,000. This phase-in provision prevents an abrupt tax if a company crosses the $150,000 line from exempt to taxable status.

A small mutual uses the normal corporate tax rates, except that if its taxable income is less than $6000, the tax is only 30 percent of the excess over $3000. As with a regular mutual, Form 1120M is used to report this tax. Losses may not be carried from, or to, any year that the company is taxed as a small mutual.

A small mutual may elect to be taxed as a regular mutual, meaning that the statutory underwriting gain and PAL account will enter into the tax calculation, in addition to investment income. There would be no phase-in of tax where the gross receipts are between $150,000 and $250,000. Such an election is irrevocable not only for the current year but for all future years, unless the IRS consents to a change. Obviously, an election would normally be made only where significant tax benefits are anticipated from underwriting losses or additions to a PAL account. Instead of making an election, a small mutual that has a subsidiary which it has held for 5 years may file a consolidated return. This will make the company taxable as a regular mutual, but the company could revert to a small mutual status merely by liquidating the subsidiary in order to eliminate the consolidated return.

Other Insurance Companies

This is a catchall category for an insurance company other than a tax-exempt one, a qualifying life company, or a mutual property and liability company. Commonly included in this category are stock property and liability companies, title companies, mutual marine companies, and life companies failing the 50 percent reserve test. Also included are mutual fire and flood companies which exclusively issue perpetual policies, or whose primary business is issuing policies of varying length for an identical premium amount, if the unearned portion of the premium is returned to the policyholder at the end of the contract.

The tax rules for "other" insurance companies are much simpler than for life insurance or mutual property and liability insurance companies, being basically the normal corporate tax rules with a few modifications. Reporting is made on the normal corporate Form 1120, and the normal corporate tax rates apply. Consolidated returns may be filed with noninsurance companies under the regular consolidated return rules.

Taxable income and expense are computed in the same manner as for a normal corporation, with the following adjustments:

- Unearned premiums are not taxed. Furthermore, life insurance reserves are allowed on life or annuity policies even if the company does not qualify as a life insurance company for tax purposes.
- Losses are deductible when incurred, with adjustments for salvage and reinsurance recoverable.
- Bad debts are deducted on the direct write-off method instead of the reserve method.
- Dividends to policyholders are deductible.
- Capital losses are deductible in the same manner as for a mutual property and liability company. In other words, capital losses can offset not only capital gains, but also ordinary income if incurred to raise funds to pay claims or div-

idends. The ordinary deduction is limited to the excess of (1) gross receipts from the sale of capital assets—plus interest, dividends, rents, royalties, and net premiums—over (2) losses paid, expenses paid, and policyholder dividends.

- Mortgage or lease guarantee companies and municipal bond insurance companies are allowed a deduction for their legal reserve requirements for the current year and the past 8 years, to the extent that such previous reserves were not deducted. The current reserve addition cannot exceed 50 percent of the premiums earned for the year, and the entire reserve deduction cannot produce a taxable loss. To take advantage of this deduction, tax and loss bonds equal to the tax benefit must be purchased. Mortgage companies are required to take into income the reserve deduction for the tenth preceding year, and lease and municipal bond insurance companies the deduction for the twentieth preceding year. A reduction in state reserve requirements can also result in income, and a discontinuance of the business can cause a recapture of all deductions.
- A mutual fire company exclusively issuing perpetual policies is not taxed on its single deposit premiums.
- A mutual fire or flood company primarily selling policies of varying lengths with identical premiums is taxed on 2 percent of its premiums earned for the year (net of premiums returned).

Deferred Federal Income Taxes

The complexity of insurance taxation has a spin-off in the financial reporting process. As with any other commercial enterprise, insurance companies must provide for deferred income taxes when variations between the tax return and financial statement are caused by timing differences. However, the unique method of taxing insurance companies often makes deferred tax calculations much more difficult than for other commercial enterprises.

The income tax return and the financial statements for an insurance company will always be different. The tax return is largely based on the statutory statement, with numerous special modifications. The statutory statement emphasizes a conservative valuation of surplus for state regulatory purposes; for example, insurance companies are required to expense first-year acquisition costs and, in the case of life insurance, are required to use low interest rates for reserves. The special tax modifications to the statutory statement were designed to raise revenue, to distribute the tax burden fairly among different types of companies, or to give companies a tax cushion for catastrophic losses. On the other hand, financial statements prepared in accordance with generally accepted accounting principles (GAAP) attempt to measure enterprise income for the current period realistically, without regard to the public policy decisions underlying the statutory statement. For this reason, variations between GAAP income and tax income are inevitable.

The differences between GAAP income and tax income may be either of a permanent nature, such as the nondeductibility of penalties for tax purposes, or of a temporary nature in which the amounts are booked and taxed in different years, but in the long run are equal. For instance, first-year commissions may be expensed for tax purposes but amortized for financial statement purposes. The financial statement expense does not occur in the same year as the tax deduction, but eventually, at the end of the amortization period, the commission will have been fully charged off for both book and tax purposes.

Where the differences are permanent, no deferred taxes should be provided, since accounting for the item in a different manner for financial purposes will not cause tax effects in future periods. The tax liability (if any) shown on the current return for this item is all that will ever be owed. The tax return liability under these circumstances will be the liability for financial reporting purposes. On the other hand, a timing difference means that the tax return effect and the book accounting of the transaction will not occur in the same year. Deferred taxes are provided simply to carry out the matching requirement: That the tax effect of a transaction is shown on the financial statements in the same year that the transaction itself is shown.

Basic Computation Concepts. To calculate deferred taxes, the following procedure is followed. First, differences between the financial statement amounts and the tax return amounts must be classified between permanent differences and timing differences. Second, deferred taxes are recorded on timing differences by using the current tax rate (as opposed to using the rates expected in future years when the timing differences reverse). This calculation is made on a with-and-without basis. In other words, the deferred taxes are the difference between the liability shown on the tax return and what the liability would have been if the return had been prepared from the financial statements after excluding permanent differences. Or it is possible to get the same result by calculating the deferred taxes as the difference between the tax return liability and what the liability would have been if the return had been adjusted for timing differences.

The above procedure determines deferred taxes under the *net change* method; this means that both the new timing differences and the older differences which are now reversing are lumped together. Current tax rates determine the deferred taxes on the net amount. A more difficult, but acceptable, alternative is to use the *gross change* method; here, the deferred taxes on the new timing differences are calculated by using current rates, and the deferred taxes on the older, reversing differences are calculated by using the tax rates for the year in which the difference originated. Obviously, this method is more difficult because detailed records of prior timing differences and deferred taxes must be maintained. The net change method is easier if deferred taxes have been provided, or reconstructed, for all prior years. If deferred taxes have not been previously provided, such as when a company first converts to GAAP, a balance for deferred taxes at the beginning of the year must be reconstructed, or else the gross change method must be used.

APB Opinion 11 permits the tax effects of timing differences to be computed either on an individual item basis or by grouping similar items. Thus, the tax effect of depreciation differences could be determined either asset by asset or by combining the depreciation differences for all assets. Obviously, the grouping method is almost always used because of its simplicity. However, dissimilar differences may not be grouped together. For instance, depreciation differences would not be combined with life reserve differences. Instead, the tax effects of each group would be calculated separately, using the with-and-without computation. Both tax effects, of course, go into the deferred tax account.

It should be noted that despite this requirement of APB Opinion 11, many companies make only a single with-and-without computation anyway, in which all timing differences are grouped together. If this aggregate computation produces the same deferred taxes as separate computations, there is no harm. But in other situations, separate computations may provide different results.

The gross change and net change concepts may be illustrated by the following example (a 50 percent tax rate is assumed for the current year and a 40 percent rate for prior years):

	Gross Change Method	Net Change Method
Pretax accounting income	$500	$500
Depreciation timing differences:		
Originating	200	
Reversing	(50)	
Net change		150
Bad debt timing differences:		
Originating	100	
Reversing	(80)	
Net change		20
Permanent differences (i.e., municipal interest)	(30)	(30)
Taxable income	$640	$640
Tax return liability (50%)	$320	$320
TAX EFFECT OF DEPRECIATION TIMING DIFFERENCES		
Taxable income	$640	$640
Depreciation:		
Originating	200	
Net change		150
	$840	$790
Tax on above	$420	$395
Tax on reversing differences ($50 × 40%)	(20)	
Tax return liability	(320)	(320)
Tax effect of depreciation timing differences	$ 80	$ 75
TAX EFFECT OF BAD DEBT TIMING DIFFERENCES		
Taxable income	$640	$640
Bad debt timing differences:		
Originating	100	
Net change		20

	Gross Change Method	Net Change Method
Total	$740	$660
Tax on above	$370	$330
Tax effect of reversing differences ($80 × 40%)	(32)	
Tax return liability	(320)	(320)
Tax effect of bad debt timing differences	$ 18	$ 10
TAX PROVISION		
Current liability (per tax return)	$320	$320
Deferred liability:		
Depreciation	80	75
Bad debts	18	10
Total provision	$418	$405

Treatment of Losses. If there is a net operating loss or excess credit shown on the return, the tax benefit of any GAAP carryback may be shown in the current year. However, the tax benefit of loss or credit carryforwards generally may not be recognized until the future year in which it is actually realized. Current recognition of tax carryforwards is allowed only where the future realization is virtually certain, which is defined in APB Opinion 11 as where (1) the loss is due to an identifiable nonrecurring cause and the company has been consistently profitable in the past and (2) sufficient future taxable income appears to be assured.

The above paragraph deals with carrybacks rather than with deferred taxes. However, operating losses also have implications in the deferred tax area. Although generally, as mentioned above, future tax refunds may not be currently recognized, the future turnaround of existing timing differences is a certainty, assuming that the company remains in operation. Thus, the tax effect of GAAP loss carryforwards may be recognized currently in the deferred tax liability account to the extent that timing differences will reverse in the carryforward period (generally 15 years).

The following example should illustrate how the tax effects of losses are accounted for:

	1980	1981	1982	1983
Taxable income	$100	$150	$ 80	$(700)
Timing differences	20	30	20	40
GAAP taxable income	$120	$180	$100	$(660)
Tax return liability	$ 50	$ 75	$ 40	
Deferred taxes (50%)	10	15	10	
Tax expense	$ 60	$ 90	$ 50	

Additional Assumptions

- Net change method used
- Total deferred tax liability on December 31, 1979 = $90
- Total deferred tax liability on December 31, 1982 = $125 ($90 + $10 + $15 + $10)
- Total timing differences on December 31, 1983 = $290
- Total timing differences on December 31, 1983, which will reverse within the next 15 years = $250

To compute the 1983 tax provision, the following steps are necessary:

1. Compute the GAAP tax carryback, which is $400. Since the $660 GAAP taxable loss exceeds the GAAP taxable income ($120 + $180 + $100) for the past 3 years, the total tax expense for the prior 3 years of $60 + $90 + $50 is the GAAP "refund."
2. Compute the GAAP tax carryforward. This is $260, consisting of the 1983 GAAP loss of $660 less the $400 carryback.
3. Compute the tax effect of timing difference reversals within the carryforward period (15 years). Total timing differences = $290, of which $250 is assumed to reverse within 15 years. The deferred tax liability on December 31, 1983, is:

Balance on December 31, 1982	$125
Deduct 3 years' deferred liability eliminated by the carryback ($10 + $15 + $10)	(35)
Balance on December 31, 1983	$ 90

Now take the ratio fraction $^{250}/_{290}$ (the proportion of total timing differences which will reverse within 15 years) and multiply it by the deferred tax balance to get the tax effect of these reversals, which is $78 ($90 × $^{250}/_{290}$).
4. Take the lower of step 2 or 3, which is $78, and add it to the GAAP refund of $200 in step 1 for a total 1983 tax benefit of $278.
5. Divide this amount into the current portion of $165 (the actual tax return carryback refund of $50 + $75 + $40) and the deferred portion of $113 (what remains of the $278 after subtracting the current portion). In future years, the tax benefits of the loss carryforward are not recognized as income until they first restore the total deferred tax liability to what it would have been at the end of 1983 had there been no 1983 loss. At the end of 1983, the deferred taxes (but for the loss) would have been $145 (1982 balance of $125, plus 50% of the $40 timing difference in 1983). However, in actuality, the deferred taxes at the end of 1983 are only:

1982 balance	$125
Less deferred taxes absorbed by carryback ($10 + $15 + $10)	(35)
Less the benefit of future reversals recognized in 1983	(78)
Balance on December 31, 1983	$ 12

Thus, the first $123 ($135 − $12) of future GAAP tax benefits is credited not to income but to the deferred liability account. If future tax rates stay at 50 percent, this means that the first $246 of future GAAP taxable income will be so utilized. If future tax rates change in the carryforward years, the future rates (not the 1983 rates) are used to calculate the restoration to the deferred liability account in those years.

Once deferred taxes have been restored by carryforward benefits to the proper balance of $135, additional tax benefits from the carryforward would be booked as an extraordinary item of income when realized.

1982–1983 LIFE TAX PROVISIONS

The Tax Equity and Fiscal Responsibility Act of 1982 made several changes to the life insurance company tax laws. Some of the changes were made to stop tax abuses, while others were designed to correct the perceived imbalance in the comparative tax burdens borne by mutual versus stock companies that had developed over the years since the existing life insurance tax act was passed in 1959. Some of the many changes causing this imbalance were inflation, high interest rates, reduced mortality, and new insurance products.

Congress recognized that the changes were significant enough to justify a complete rewrite of the 1959 act; however, since a rewrite would require extensive study, it was decided to repair the existing 1959 "three-phase" tax system and retain it for a 2-year period, in anticipation of a complete rewrite being ready by 1984. Thus, the tax changes effective for 1982 and 1983 are known as the "stopgap" provisions.

Deduction for Policyholder Dividends

One major stopgap provision allows both a greater maximum limit for the deductibility of policyholder dividends and special deductions for nonparticipating and group contracts. (The special deductions are basically 10 percent of the increase in nonparticipating reserves and 2 percent of accident and health insurance and group life insurance premiums, with certain modifications.) Under the 1959 act, the total deduction for policyholder dividends and special deductions was limited to $250,000, plus any excess of gain from operations (before deducting these items) over taxable investment income.

The stopgap provision changes the $250,000 amount to $1 million. However, the $1 million is reduced by 25 cents for each dollar that the total dividends and special deductions exceed $4 million. Thus, when the total dividends and special deductions reach $8 million, the $1 million will have been reduced to zero, leaving a deductibility limit equal to just the excess (if any) of the gain from operations over taxable investment income.

However, the stopgap rules introduce an alternative formula for the limit on dividends and special deductions, and this formula may be elected if it produces a larger amount. First, the alternative formula allows a full deduction for policyholder dividends paid to a qualified pension plan. Next, it allows a deduction for the first $1 million of other (nonpension) dividends and special deductions, and 77.5 percent of any excess over $1 million for a mutual company (85 percent of any excess for a stock company). As with the first formula, the $1 million amount in the alternative formula is reduced by 25 cents for each dollar that the total dividends and special deductions exceed $4 million.

In both formulas, only a single $1 million amount is allowed for each controlled corporate group.

Menge Formula Revised

In computing taxable investment income, the policyholder's share of investment yield is determined by dividing the adjusted reserves rate by adjusted life reserves. Under the 1959 act, adjusted life reserves were equal to average reserves, multiplied by a percentage which is 100 percent plus 10 times the average interest rate assumed in calculating the reserves, minus 10 times the adjusted reserves rate. This is known as the "Menge formula."

Because of high interest rates, the "10 times" part of the Menge formula became distorted and has been replaced in the stopgap provisions by a geometric formula. For 1982–1983, the adjusted life reserves are equal to the average reserves times 0.9 raised to the power of n. The power of n is 100 times the average interest rate assumed in calculating the reserves, minus 100 times the adjusted reserves rate.

Approximate Method for Preliminary Term Revaluation

A company using the preliminary term method for state statutory purposes may revalue its reserves to the net level method for tax purposes, using either the exact or the approximate method. Under the 1959 act, the approximate method caused preliminary term reserves to be increased by the sum of $21 per $1000 of non-term insurance, minus 2.1 percent of such reserves, plus $5 per $1000 of term insurance, minus 0.5 percent of such reserves.

Under the stopgap provisions, the approximate revaluation for non-term insurance is changed to $19 for each $1000 of insurance, minus 1.9 percent of such reserves. Only reserves established after March 31, 1982, are affected. The revaluation formula for term insurance was not changed.

Reserve Deductions for Guaranteed Interest

Some policies contain a guaranteed rate of interest. Before 1982, the future guaranteed interest could be considered when establishing current reserves. After 1981, the stopgap provisions prohibit reserves from including interest guaranteed beyond the end of the current year for which the reserves are being computed. (Of course, reserves will still take into account the minimum assumed interest rate prescribed by state law.)

Changes to Treatment of Reinsurance

Modified coinsurance is an arrangement whereby the ceding company continues to hold the assets and reserves subject to the reinsurance agreement and periodically settles up with the reinsurer for any gain or loss on the reinsurance. A special tax election, however, treated the reinsurer as holding the assets and reserves. This provided a means of converting the investment income on the reinsured assets into underwriting income when paid to the reinsurer, with the result that both companies could sometimes reduce their taxes, depending on which phase of taxation they were in under the 1959 three-phase system.

Because of this potential tax abuse, the stopgap provisions repeal the modified coinsurance election after 1981. Because of the retroactive nature of the repeal on existing reinsurance agreements, the additional tax caused by the repeal may be paid in three annual interest-free installments.

Also, for purposes of computing taxable investment income, interest expense incurred by the ceding company to fund a conventional coinsurance contract is disallowed after 1981.

In another provision, a reinsurer is given a "dividends-reimbursed" deduction on the accrual basis for policyholder dividends which it must reimburse the ceding company for under a reinsurance agreement. Previously, a court decision had held that this deduction must be computed on the cash basis.

Finally, the IRS is given the authority to reallocate taxable income where reinsurance agreements are entered into between related parties.

Other Changes

In computing the policyholders' share of investment yield after 1981, the interest liability on group pension contracts is limited to the amount actually credited to the contracts during the year.

In computing the deduction for interest on a nonparticipating guaranteed annuity with life contingencies, the full amount of interest may be used if guaranteed beyond 12 months; it may be used either as a set rate or, where the company has no control over the factors, as determined by a formula. In the case of a participating guaranteed annuity with life contingencies, a full deduction is allowed for the permanently guaranteed interest and a 92.5 percent deduction is allowed for interest credited in excess of the guaranteed rate.

Life company consolidated returns are to be filed using the "bottom-line" approach in which the final taxable incomes of the separate companies are combined. The "phase-by-phase" method of arriving at consolidated income is not to be used.

POST-1983 LIFE TAX PROVISIONS

The Deficit Reduction Act of 1984 contained a complete rewrite of the life insurance tax laws. Although a few provisions from the 1959 law were carried over, the new act basically represents a clean break with the past. The overall approach of the new law is a more logical measurement of economic income. However, despite the more logical concept, the details of the new law are probably just as complex as those of the old law.

The old law contained a three-phase scheme in which a company could be taxed either on its share of investment income or on its total operating income. The new law abandons the three-phase concept and replaces it with a single phase applicable to all companies.

In computing taxable income under the single-phase scheme, the most significant changes occur in four areas:

1. Policyholder dividends are now deductible without limit, unlike prior law. However, mutual companies will have their dividend deduction reduced by an assumed return on equity.
2. Reserves are now computed under a new method which reflects current economic conditions rather than state statutory requirements.
3. Small companies receive a special deduction of 60 percent of their first $3 million of life insurance taxable income. This deduction is phased out as income increases over $3 million.
4. All companies receive a deduction of 20 percent of their taxable income (after being reduced by any small company special deduction).

Policyholder Dividends

Generally. As mentioned above, the old law contained a formula limitation on the deduction for policyholder dividends. There was no logical reason for this limit, other than to allocate the comparative tax burdens borne by the mutual and stock segments of the insurance industry.

The new law abolishes any limit on policyholder dividends after 1983. In addition, the definition of a policyholder dividend is expanded to include experience refunds, premium adjustments, and interest credited on policies in excess of the assumed rate.

The deduction is for dividends paid or accrued during the year. Accruals are determined by using the "all-events" test. Thus, there is no longer any deduction for a reserve for policyholder dividends after 1983.

Stock companies need read no further. The treatment of their policyholder dividends is completely covered in the above paragraphs.

Mutual Companies. Mutual companies, however, must compute a complicated "differential earnings amount" which reduces their deduction for policyholder dividends (and their deduction for reserves, if policyholder dividends are insufficient). The reason for this is that policyholder dividends include a return on each policyholder's ownership equity in the company. Congress decided that this return on equity should not be deductible, just as a stock company cannot deduct the return on the equity of its owners (the shareholders).

For 1984, and for purposes of 1985 estimated taxes, the differential earnings amount is equal to the average equity base times 7.8 percent (Schedule F of the tax return).

For 1985 and later years, the differential earnings amount is determined by the following formula:

$$(\text{Imputed stock earnings rate} - \text{average mutual earnings rate}) \times \text{average equity base}$$

The *imputed stock earnings rate* and the *average mutual earnings rate* are industry wide figures determined by the secretary of the treasury—individual companies do not have to compute these rates themselves. It should be noted that the average mutual earnings rate used in the formula is the rate for the second prior year.

Because of this time lag for the average mutual earnings rate, the effect of any difference between the rate used and that which is finally determined for the current year is taken as an adjustment to taxable income in the following year. However, if the company ceases to be a mutual company, any such adjustment is made to the final mutual year.

The *average equity base* must be computed by each mutual company. This is the average of the equity bases at the beginning and the end of the year. It consists of the following items:

1. Surplus and capital shown on the annual statement.
2. Nonadmitted *financial* assets, defined as stocks, bonds, real estate, mortgages on real estate, and other invested assets. On the other hand, furniture, agent's balances, and premiums receivable are examples of nonadmitted assets which are not financial and thus are not included in the equity base.
3. The excess of statutory reserves over tax reserves.
4. The mandatory securities valuation reserve.
5. Any deficiency reserve or voluntary reserve.
6. Fifty percent of any liability for policyholder dividends to be paid in a future year.

If a mutual company has a stock life insurance subsidiary, the stock subsidiary is treated as a mutual company and its equity base is combined with that of the parent. Subsidiaries other than life companies are valued at their NAIC values for purposes of the parent's equity base.

There are also a number of reductions in computing the equity base. The most common reduction is for *high-surplus* companies—those for which the average equity base in 1984 is more than 14.5 percent of average assets. The average equity base of such a company is reduced by the following formula:

$$A\% \times [\text{average equity base} - (\text{average assets} \times B\%)]$$

A% is equal to the following depending on the year:

1984	100%
1985	80
1986	60
1987	40
1988	20
1989 and later	0

B% is equal to the following, depending on the year:

1984	14.5%
1985–1986	14.0
1987–1988	13.5

Thus, the high-surplus exclusion reduces every year and is completely eliminated by 1989. The exclusion in each of the years 1985–1988 cannot exceed the exclusion, if any, for 1984.

The average equity base is also reduced by the following items:

1. Guaranteed interest in future years on insurance policies issued before 1985, pursuant to insurance plans in existence on July 1, 1983
2. The percentage of a company's total life insurance business which is attributable to western hemisphere countries other than the United States, Canada, or Mexico
3. In the case of a mutual company which became the successor to a fraternal benefit society in 1950 or March of 1961, the amount of the surplus assumed from the fraternal society, increased by 7 percent interest annually until 1984 and by the average mutual earnings rate for later years

Small Company Deduction

A deduction equal to 60 percent of the first $3 million of tentative life insurance company taxable income (LICTI) is allowed to qualifying small companies. The deduction is reduced by 15 percent of any tentative LICTI in excess of $3 million, with the result that the deduction is eliminated when tentative LICTI reaches $15 million (Schedule H).

A *small company* is defined as one with assets of less than $500 million at the end of the year. Total assets are measured by the adjusted basis, except that real estate and stock are measured by the fair market value. The adjusted basis in a partnership or trust interest is disregarded, and the company is deemed to hold its proportionate share of the underlying partnership or trust assets.

Furthermore, the assets of all companies (including nonlife companies) within a controlled group are combined for purposes of the $500 million test. A limited exception applies for 1984 only. Under this exception, only the assets of insurance companies and financial intermediaries (such as banks, finance companies, and securities brokers) within the controlled group are combined for the small company test. This exception is available only if (1) a life-nonlife consolidated return is not filed, (2) no life company is added to the group after September 27, 1983, and (3) any capital contributions received by the life companies do not exceed the shareholder dividends paid by the life companies during the year.

For purposes of calculating the small company deduction, tentative LICTI is determined by excluding the small company deduction, the special 20 percent life insurance deduction, and any item from a noninsurance business. However, operations loss deductions are taken into account. Also, all life insurance companies (but not other companies) within a controlled group are combined to determine the LICTI. The single small company deduction for the group would then be apportioned back to the individual life companies based on their own LICTIs.

In calculating the LICTI, income from an insurance business includes income from investment activities traditionally carried on by life insurance companies. This includes investments in stock, real estate, and oil and gas limited partnerships. However, except in the case of real estate, these functions must be passive investments, without active participation in the business by the life company.

Thus, a securities brokerage operation or participation in an oil and gas venture as a *general* partner or manager would be considered a noninsurance business since these activities are not merely passive investments for the life company.

A special rule also treats fees for administering pension, life insurance, or accident and health insurance plans as being derived from the insurance business.

The following example illustrates how the small company deduction is computed. Assume that the tentative LICTI is $8 million.

Maximum small company deduction ($3,000,000 × 60%)		$1,800,000
Less reduction:		
Tentative LICTI	$8,000,000	
Maximum base	− 3,000,000	
Excess	5,000,000	
	× 15%	
Reduction		−750,000
Net small company deduction		$1,050,000

On the other hand, if tentative LICTI had been only $2,000,000, then the small company deduction would simply be 60 percent of this, or $1,200,000.

Special 20 Percent Life Company Deduction

All life insurance companies, whether "small" or not, are allowed a special deduction equal to 20 percent of tentative life insurance company taxable income

(LICTI) after having reduced the LICTI by any 60 percent small company deduction allowed (Schedule J).

Thus, if a company has a tentative LICTI of $2,000,000, a 60 percent small company deduction of $1,200,000 would be allowed. The special 20 percent deduction would then be 20 percent × ($2,000,000 − $1,200,000) = $160,000. The final taxable income would therefore be $2,000,000 − $1,200,000 − $160,000 = $640,000.

On the other hand, if tentative LICTI was $20 million, no 60 percent small company deduction would be allowed (since this disappears when tentative LICTI exceeds $15 million), and the special 20 percent deduction would simply be 20 percent × $20,000,000 = $4,000,000.

In computing the special 20 percent deduction, all life insurance companies within a controlled group are combined, and the deduction is then apportioned back to each individual company based on its own tentative LICTI. Since there is no upper limit on the 20 percent deduction, the only effect of this controlled group provision is to cause companies with losses to be offset against companies with income, which reduces the overall 20 percent deduction.

However, when computing the 20 percent deduction, an election may be made to avoid having to offset one life company's loss against the income of other life companies within the controlled group, if the profitable companies do not file a consolidated return with the loss company. If this election is made, the use of the life company's loss for other purposes is restricted. Only 80 percent of the loss—to the extent that the loss would otherwise be offset against other companies' income in calculating the 20 percent deduction (but for the election)—may be used against nonlife income or carried back against pre-1984 life insurance company taxable income.

This may be illustrated by the following example. Assume that companies B and C file a consolidated return and that company A is a member of the same controlled group but does not join in the consolidated return. Also assume that there is no 60 percent small company deduction.

Life company A's tentative LICTI	$500	
Life company B's tentative LICTI	($700)	consolidated
Nonlife company C's taxable income	$1,000	consolidated

Without an election, there is no special 20 percent deduction since the loss from B totally eliminates the positive income of A. Thus, A's LICTI is not reduced below $500, and the consolidated return of B&C is $1000 − $700 = $300.

However, if an election is made, the loss of B is not offset against A's income and thus A receives a special 20 percent deduction of $100, giving it a taxable income of $500 − $100 = $400. On the other hand, since $500 of B's $700 loss was spared from being offset against A, only 80 percent of this $500 (which equals $400) can be used against the nonlife income of C in the consolidated return. The remaining $200 of B's $700 loss can be used in full against C's income. Thus, the B&C consolidated income is $1000 − $400 − $200 = $400.

To change the example slightly, assume that B's loss is only ($300) instead of ($700). Without an election, A would have a special deduction of 20 percent × ($500 − $300) = $40, giving it a taxable income of $500 − $40 = $460. The B&C consolidated income would be $1000 − $300 = $700.

If an election was made, A would receive a special 20 percent deduction of $100, giving it a taxable income of $400. However, since A's LICTI is spared from being reduced by the entire amount of B's $300 loss, only 80 percent of B's $300 loss (which equals $240) may be used against C's nonlife income, resulting in a B&C consolidated taxable income of $1000 − $240 = $760.

Note that in both examples (and most other situations) the combined taxable income of all the entities together will remain the same, whether an election is made or not. For instance, in the first example, the combined taxable income is $800 without an election (A = $500; B&C = $300), while if an election is made, the combined taxable income is still $800 (A = $400; B&C = $400). The election has the effect of reallocating income among members of the controlled group and would be made to take advantage of individual company circumstances, such as loss carryovers or tax credits.

New Reserve Rules

Generally. Under prior law, reserves were measured for tax purposes by the amount reported in the statutory statement, except that statutory preliminary term reserves could be revalued to the net level basis for tax purposes. Reserve assumptions varied from company to company and from state to state. An addition to reserves during the year decreased taxable income, while an increase in reserves was a deduction.

Under the new law, a decrease in reserves is still added to income, and an increase is still a deduction (Schedule B). However, the manner of computing reserves has completely changed. Reserves should generally be lower in the new calculations, and the amounts will be determined in a uniform manner for all companies, rather than allowing for a variation in assumptions among different companies and different states. The initial decrease in reserves caused by switching from the old law to the new law on January 1, 1984, will not affect taxable income. There will no longer be a revaluation election for preliminary term reserves.

After January 1, 1984, the tax reserve is the greater of the net surrender value or a tax-prescribed reserve calculation, but the tax reserve (whether the net surrender value or the tax-prescribed calculation) cannot exceed the statutory reserve. The comparison between the net surrender value and the tax-prescribed calculation may be made on an individual contract basis or by groups of similar policies.

The *net surrender value* is defined as the cash surrender value less any surrender penalty. Market value adjustments are not considered to be a surrender penalty.

In computing the tax reserve for pensions, the net surrender value is deemed to be the balance in the policyholder's fund, less any surrender penalty. Again, market value adjustments are not taken into account.

Tax-Prescribed Reserve Calculation. The tax-prescribed reserve calculation sets forth a uniform method, interest rate, and mortality table for each type of policy. As stated above, the tax reserve is the greater of this tax-prescribed calculation or the net surrender value, not to exceed the statutory reserve. In the tax-prescribed calculation, the following reserve methods are required:

- *Life insurance:* Commissioners' Reserve Valuation Method (CRVM)
- *Annuities:* Commissioners' Annuity Reserve Valuation Method (CARVM)
- *Noncancelable accident and health:* 2-year full preliminary term (except that the net level method can be elected if it has been used for both statutory and tax purposes since 1982)
- *Other contracts:* an NAIC-approved method

Note: Deficiency reserves are not allowed.

The interest rate to be used in computing reserves is the prevailing state-assumed rate at the beginning of the year in which the contract was issued. In the case of reinsurance agreements, the date the underlying contract was issued is used for this purpose, not the date of the reinsurance contract. Except for annuity contracts, an election may be made to use the prevailing rate at the beginning of the year preceding the year of issue. This election is made on a contract-by-contract basis.

The *prevailing* state-assumed rate is the highest assumed rate permitted by at least 26 states. The limitations on rates contained in nonforfeiture laws are ignored. If there is no prevailing assumed rate for noncancelable accident and health insurance, the prevailing rate for whole life insurance is used.

The *prescribed* mortality or morbidity table is that which was permitted by the laws of at least 26 states when the contract was issued. Unlike the rules for prevailing interest rates, there is a 3-year grace period when prevailing tables change. During this grace period, either the old or the new tables may be used. Thus, if Table A is prevailing (permitted by at least 26 states) in 19x1, but Table B becomes accepted by 26 states in 19x2, either Table A or Table B may be used in 19x2, 19x3, and 19x4. Beginning in 19x5, only Table B may be used (assuming that it is still permitted by at least 26 states).

Modifications to the tables may be made for substandard risks or other special factors not considered in the tables.

Supplemental Reserves. In addition to the reserve computed on the basic contract, under certain circumstances an additional reserve may be used for tax purposes, with the result that total reserves are higher, creating larger deductions. Additional reserves are allowed for certain supplemental benefits, substandard risks, and riders for term insurance or annuities.

A *supplemental* benefit is defined as one of the following: guaranteed insurability, accidental death and disability, convertibility, disability waiver, and any other benefit prescribed by regulations. If there is a separately identifiable charge for one of the above, and the net surrender value for other benefits cannot be used to fund this charge (other than by loan), the statutory reserve for such benefit is allowed for tax purposes, in addition to the tax reserve for the basic contract. If one of the listed supplemental benefits does not meet the requirement of a separate charge not funded by the net surrender value, then the statutory reserve for such benefit is added to the tax-prescribed reserve calculation for the basic reserve. In these circumstances, tax reserves would only increase if the tax-prescribed reserve calculation for the basic contract plus the statutory reserve for the supplemental exceeded the net surrender value of the basic.

For example, assume that for the basic contract the net surrender value is $1000 and the tax-prescribed calculation is $700. The statutory reserve for a listed supplemental benefit is $200. If the benefit has a separate charge and the net surrender value cannot fund it, then the total tax reserve is $1200 ($1000 net surrender value plus $200 benefit reserve). If the listed benefit does not meet the above requirements, then the tax reserve is the net surrender value of $1000, since this exceeds the sum of the tax-prescribed reserve ($700) plus the benefit reserve ($200). However, if the reserve for a listed benefit not meeting the requirements was $400, then the tax reserve would be $700 + $400 = $1100.

An additional reserve is allowed for riders providing term insurance or annuities if (1) the contracts are issued before 1989 pursuant to a plan of insurance in effect on January 1, 1984, and if (2) there is a separately identifiable charge for the rider and the net surrender value cannot be used to fund it (other than by loan). The additional reserve is determined by the tax rules rather than by statutory rules, except that the tax reserve cannot exceed the statutory reserve.

A separate tax reserve is allowed for substandard risks if the company has a separate charge, maintains a separate statutory reserve, does not adjust the net surrender value, and does not regularly use the net surrender value to pay the charge for the substandard risk. The computation of the tax reserve is made in accordance with the tax reserve rules, except that the reserve cannot exceed the premium charges for the risk, plus interest, less the mortality charges. The separate reserve for substandard risks cannot be used on more than 10 percent of the insurance in force (other than term insurance). If the substandard contracts exceed 10 percent, then the excess is not eligible for separate reserve treatment, but may be considered in setting the amount of the reserve for the basic contracts.

Certain Foreign Reserves. In the case of certain foreign reserves, the tax reserve will be the greater of the tax reserve computed under regular rules or the minimum reserve required by the foreign government. However, the tax reserve in either case cannot exceed the NAIC net level reserve.

This special treatment is allowed where the foreign country is other than Canada and Mexico, the policy is issued by a foreign branch office maintained in that country, and the country has required that branch office to be maintained in the country since the company began doing business there.

Interest Guaranteed Beyond End of Year. Interest guaranteed beyond the end of the year in excess of the prevailing state-assumed rate is not included in reserves. This is a modification of the 1982–1983 law which used the contract-assumed rate instead of the prevailing state-assumed rate.

Deferred and Uncollected Premiums. After 1983, no reserve will be allowed for deferred and uncollected premiums (and such items will be excluded from gross income). This reverses the *Standard Life* case.

Small Company Elections. A small company (defined as one with less than $100 million of assets) can elect to continue the use of statutory reserves after 1983 for tax purposes for contracts issued before 1984, with the condition that no tax reserve can be maintained for deferred and uncollected premiums.

A company making this election has the choice of making a further election, if it has less than $3 million of tentative LICTI for 1984. Under this second election, the company can continue to use statutory reserves for contracts issued from 1984 through 1988 for tax purposes. However, the statutory reserves must be modified by the geometric Menge formula (a concept introduced by the 1982–1983 law), except that the Menge formula under the new law uses the prevailing state-assumed rate instead of the adjusted reserves rate.

To illustrate, assume that the statutory reserves are $100,000, the prevailing state-assumed rate is 8 percent, and the average rate assumed by the company in computing the reserves is 5 percent. Under the Menge formula, the statutory reserves of $100,000 are multiplied by 0.9^3 (where the exponent of 3 comes from 8 percent minus 5 percent). This produces a tax reserve of $72,900.

Fresh Start Adjustment. In most cases the reserves on January 1, 1984, under the new law will be substantially lower than the tax reserves on December 31, 1983. However, a special transitional "fresh start" provision makes this one-time decrease in reserves tax-free, with a few exceptions.

1. Under the old law, a change in reserves due to reserve weakening or strengthening was amortized over 10 years for tax purposes. Under the new law, any unamortized balance for reserve weakening under the old law will not be added to income after 1983. However, if there is an unamortized balance for reserve strengthening under the old law, any excess of this unamortized balance over the fresh start adjustment will still be deductible after 1983. For instance, if a reserve strengthening of $100,000 took place in 1980, then by December 31, 1983, $30,000 of this would have been amortized, leaving an unamortized balance of $70,000. If the fresh start adjustment for these particular reserves was $50,000 (in other words, a decrease of $50,000 on January 1, 1984, due to the law change), the difference of $20,000 ($70,000 unamortized balance less $50,000 fresh start) may still be taken as a deduction for reserve strengthening after 1983. However, the law is unclear as to when this $20,000 is deducted.
2. Reserve strengthening or a reinsurance agreement entered into between September 27, 1983, and December 31, 1983, is deemed to have taken place on January 1, 1984 (thereby eliminating the fresh start benefit). The reserve strengthening would then be amortized over 10 years for tax purposes.
3. A section 818(c) preliminary term election made after September 27, 1983, will not be allowed. There is a narrow exception in which more than 95 per-

cent of the 818(c) reserves arise from contracts issued under a plan of insurance filed between March 1, 1982, and September 27, 1983.

4. When a recapture of policies under a conventional coinsurance contract occurs after 1983, the fresh start adjustment is allocated between the ceding and assuming companies and amortized over 10 years.

Definition of a Life Insurance Company. Despite the new definition of reserves for computing the taxable income, statutory reserves will generally still be used in the test for determining whether a company meets the definition of a life insurance company.

Policyholders' Share of Exempt Items

As in the past, tax-exempt income and the 85 percent dividends-received deduction must be allocated between the company's share and the policyholders' share. Only the company's share of these items produces a tax benefit. The new law, however, introduces an extremely complicated method of computing the company's share, and only the basic concept will be discussed here. The following steps would be performed:

1. Compute the policy interest, consisting of the required interest on reserves at the prevailing state-assumed rate. Add the deductible excess interest, amounts credited to pension funds, and amounts credited to deferred annuities (Schedule L).
2. Compute the investment portion of the policy dividends. First, take the policyholder dividends and subtract deductible excess interest, dividends on pension funds, dividends on deferred annuities, and premium and mortality charges on excess interest contracts. Multiply the remainder by the following ratio (Schedule K, Part I):

$$\frac{\text{Investment income} - \text{policy interest}}{\text{Gross income} + \text{tax exempt income} - \text{increase in reserves}}$$

3. Add the amounts obtained in steps 1 and 2. This is the policyholder's share amount (Schedule K, Part I).
4. Multiply the gross investment income by 90 percent. (The law in effect assumes a 10 percent expense ratio.) Subtract the policyholder share amount (step 3). This gives the company's share of net investment income (Schedule K, Part II).
5. Divide this by 90 percent of the gross investment income. The result is the company's share percentage. The difference between this percentage and 100 percent is the policyholders' share percentage (Schedule K, Part II).

Only the company's share percentage times the total 85 percent dividends-received deduction is allowed as a deduction for the life insurance company (Schedule G).

The policyholders' share percentage times any tax-exempt income is used to reduce the reserves at year end (Schedule B).

Note that the 100 percent dividends-received deduction (applicable to dividends from a subsidiary controlled by 80 percent or more) is not prorated between the company's and the policyholders' share. The entire amount is allowed as a deduction. However, if the subsidiary itself has tax-exempt income or the 85 percent dividends-received deduction and either of these is distributed up to the parent, then these amounts would be prorated between the company's share and the policyholders' share.

Pre-1984 Policyholders' Surplus Account

Under the old law, there was a "Phase III" addition to taxable income consisting of distributions out of the policyholders' surplus account. This occurred when dividends were paid after having exhausted the shareholders' surplus account, when the policyholders' surplus account exceeded a prescribed ceiling, or when the company ceased to be a life insurance company for 2 consecutive years or ceased to be an insurance company for any year.

The policyholders' surplus account consisted of the nontaxed one-half of the excess of gain from operations over taxable investment income, plus special deductions on nonparticipating contracts.

The shareholders' surplus account consisted of the cumulative taxable income of the company since 1958, less income taxes paid.

Under the new law, no further additions will be made to the policyholders' surplus account after 1983. Distributions out of the policyholders' surplus account after 1983 will continue to be taxable (Schedule N).

The new law allows continued additions to the shareholders' surplus account after 1983, consisting of taxable income (but not less than zero) plus the 20 percent special deduction, the 60 percent small company deduction, and tax-exempt income (Schedule M). Income taxes and dividends paid to shareholders continue to be deductions from the account.

Segregated Asset Accounts

Several modifications are made to the treatment of segregated asset accounts under the new law. Variable life insurance contracts may now be included in such accounts, in addition to the variable annuities and pension contracts included under the old law.

Capital gains in a segregated asset account are no longer taxed to the company (previously, only capital gains with respect to pension contracts were exempt). As before, ordinary income allocable to policyholders is not taxed to the company.

Regulations will be issued which require that investments in segregated asset accounts be diversified.

20

FINANCIAL STATEMENTS

Financial statements for insurance companies are prepared on the basis of statutory accounting practices specified for use in preparing the annual statement or on the basis of generally accepted accounting principles (GAAP) required for use in connection with public reporting companies. The financial statements discussed in this material are presumed to be those which are issued to polichyolders or stockholders and which contain the disclosures required following GAAP. Reports prepared for internal use may take any form deemed to be useful in managing company operations, and such reports are excluded from this material.

Financial reports following statutory accounting practices should contain: a balance sheet; statements of income or operations, capital and surplus, and changes in financial position; and notes to financial statements. These reports are prepared from data extracted from the annual statement filed with the commissioner of insurance. While there is no prohibition on publishing supplementary data, such as is included in the exhibits and schedules of the annual statements, such data is not required for a fair presentation of the financial conditions and results of operations of the company.

Financial statements prepared on the basis of GAAP must include the financial statements and disclosures required by professional literature and, for public reporting companies, must include the additional disclosures prescribed by the Securities and Exchange Commission. The financial statements discussed here presume that all such disclosures are required.

Financial statements of mutual life insurance companies and their wholly owned stock life insurance company subsidiaries prepared on the basis of statutory accounting practices are considered to be in accordance with GAAP for such companies. Financial statements for mutual property and liability insurance companies prepared on the basis of statutory accounting practices are not considered to be in accordance with GAAP.

Most state jurisdictions prescribe the permissible method for filing financial statements for policyholders or stockholders, and such reports are considered to be in the nature of special reports unless they include the disclosures required by GAAP.

FINANCIAL STATEMENTS: STATUTORY BASIS

These financial statements are prepared on the basis of the forms and instructions contained in the annual statement blank. The following describe the principal components of these statements:

Property and Liability Insurance Companies

Statement of Assets, Liabilities, Surplus, and Other Funds. The accountable assets include bonds, stocks, mortgage loans on real estate, real estate investments, collateral loans, cash, short-term investments, other invested assets, agents' balances and uncollected premiums, funds held by reinsurance companies, reinsurance recoverable on loss payments, accrued investment income, and similar types of assets.

The liabilities include unpaid losses and adjustment expenses; other accrued expenses; accrued taxes, licenses, and fees; accrued federal income taxes; unearned premiums; funds held under reinsurance treaties; reinsurance amounts payable; and similar accrued amounts.

The Capital and Surplus account includes common and preferred stock and either other contributed surplus (in the case of a stock company) or (for mutual companies) other surplus, including guarantee fund certificates.

Statement of Income. This statement includes all income, costs, and expenses except those specifically reported in the Capital and Surplus account. Included are premiums earned, net investment income, net realized capital gains and losses, finance and service charges, other income, losses and loss expenses incurred, other underwriting expenses, dividends to policyholders, and federal income taxes.

Capital and Surplus Account. In addition to capital changes, net income, dividends to stockholders, and extraordinary charges or credits, changes to this account include net unrealized capital gains or losses, nonadmitted assets, unauthorized reinsurance, foreign exchange adjustments, and statutory reserves.

Statement of Changes in Financial Position. The funds provided in this statement include underwriting and investment gains and other income, less dividends to policyholders and federal income taxes, adjusted for changes in liabilities for loss and adjusting expenses, unearned premiums, underwriting expenses, agents' balances, reinsurance receivable or payable, nonadmitted assets, and similar amounts. It also includes funds provided from the sale or maturity of investments, realized capital gains or losses, capital paid-in funds, borrowed money funds, and other similar funds. The funds applied include acquired investments, dividends to stockholders, changes in foreign exchange, and other amounts requiring funds. These accounts are reconciled to the cash on hand and on deposit at the beginning and end of the year.

Notes to Financial Statements. The following disclosures are required:

- Basis of presentation
- Basis of valuation of invested assets
- Federal income tax allocation
- Information concerning parent, subsidiaries, and affiliates
- Deferred compensation and retirement plans
- Capital and surplus and shareholders' dividend restrictions
- Borrowed money
- Contingent liabilities
- Leases
- Subsequent events

Included in the Appendix is a sample of the annual statement of a property and liability insurance company. This sample references the basic financial statements to the parts, exhibits, and schedules that provide detailed information about the amounts appearing in the financial statements.

Life Insurance and Accident and Health Insurance Companies

Statement of Assets, Liabilities, Surplus, and Other Funds. The assets included are bonds; stocks; mortgage loans on real estate; real estate investments; policy loans; collateral loans; cash; short-term investments; other invested assets; reinsurance recoverable for losses, expenses, and allowances; premiums deferred and uncollected; accrued investment income; and similar types of assets.

The liabilities include reserves for life and accident and health benefits; supplementary contracts; unpaid life and accident and health claims; policyholder dividend accumulations; provisions for policyholder dividends for the subsequent year; premiums received in advance; discounted premiums; commissions due agents and for reinsurance assumed; accrued general expenses; unpaid taxes, licenses, and fees; accrued federal income taxes; unearned investment income; mandatory securities valuation reserve; and similar liability amounts. Companies owning separate accounts have contra assets and liability amounts representing the total separate account values.

The Capital and Surplus account includes common and preferred stock and either other contributed surplus (in the case of a stock company) or (for mutual companies) other surplus, including guarantee fund certificates.

Summary of Operations. This statement includes all income (excluding capital gains and losses) and costs and expenses except those specifically reported in the Capital and Surplus account. Included are premium and annuity considerations, funds from deposits and supplementary contracts, net investment income, reinsurance commissions and allowances, reinsurance reserve adjustments, and similar income items. Costs and expenses include death, maturity, annuity, disability, and surrender benefits; interest on contract funds; payments on supplementary contracts; increases in all reserves; agents' commissions and expense allowances; general insurance expenses; taxes, licenses, and fees; loading on premiums; transfers to separate accounts; dividends to policyholders; and federal income taxes.

Capital and Surplus Account. In addition to capital changes, dividends to stockholders, and extraordinary charges and credits, changes to this account include net realized and unrealized capital gains, nonadmitted assets, unauthorized reinsurance, mandatory securities valuation reserve, and other surplus adjustments.

Statement of Changes in Financial Position. The funds provided in this statement include net gains from operations after policyholder dividends and federal income taxes, adjusted for depreciation on real estate and amortization of premiums and discounts on investments. It also includes funds provided from the sale or maturity of investments, capital paid-in funds, borrowed money funds, and similar funds. The funds applied include acquired investments, dividends to stockholders, increases in policy loans, and other amounts requiring funds. These accounts are reconciled to the cash on hand and on deposit at the beginning and end of the year.

Notes to Financial Statements. The following disclosures are required:

- Basis of presentation
- Basis of valuation of invested assets
- Investment income by category
- Federal income tax allocation
- Information concerning parent, subsidiary, and affiliates
- Deferred compensation and retirement plans
- Capital and surplus and shareholders' dividend restrictions
- Borrowed money
- Life and annuity actuarial reserves

- □ Premium and annuity considerations deferred and uncollected
- □ Contingent liabilities
- □ Leases
- □ Subsequent events

Included in the Appendix is a sample of the annual statement of a life insurance and accident and health insurance company. This sample references the basic financial statements to the exhibits and schedules that provide detailed information about the amounts appearing in the financial statements.

FINANCIAL STATEMENTS: PUBLIC REPORTING BASIS

The two primary sources for the accounting and disclosure rules for insurance companies are the Financial Accounting Standards Board and the Securities and Exchange Commission (SEC). Some of the rules have specific application to insurance companies, and others apply to all public reporting companies. Where specific accounting and disclosure rules are not found in documents prepared by either of these organizations, the reporting rules are governed by other authoritative sources. The general rules apply to all reporting companies unless there is a specific rule for insurance companies and if neither general nor specific rules apply, other authoritative sources must be used.

The accounting and reporting rules adopted by the SEC in Regulation S-X include considerable detail about the treatment of individual captions appearing in the financial statements. It can be presumed that companies following the form and content rules for financial statements contained in Regulation S-X will comply in all respects with the general financial reporting and disclosure requirements.

Financial Statement Requirements: Regulation S-X

Regulation S-X contains the form and content and the requirements for financial statements for insurance companies subject to the Securities Act of 1933 and the Securities and Exchange Act of 1934. These rules apply to all public reporting, whether in a registration statement, a proxy filing, or the annual report to the SEC on Form 10-K. If the annual report to shareholders complies with the form and content disclosures requirements, the reports can be incorporated by a reference in the annual report on Form 10-K and in many registration statements.

Article 7 of Regulation S-X applies specifically to financial statements of insurance companies, but the statements must also comply with Articles 1, 2, 3, 3A, and 4.

Article 1 covers the definition of terms used in Regulation S-X. Most of these definitions have a universal meaning; however, for purposes of reporting, some terms have a specific application. The following are examples of specific applications:

- *Development stage company.* This category includes (1) companies which are totally involved in establishing a new business and which have commenced no principal operations and (2) companies having no significant revenue from planned principal operations.
- *Insurance holding company.* A company which owns the securities of one or more insurance companies and has the ability to exercise control is classified as an insurance holding company.
- *Promoter.* A person who receives 10 percent or more of a class of securities or of the proceeds from the sale of securities for services or property, excluding underwriting commissions or amounts received solely in exchange for property, is deemed to be a promoter.
- *Related parties.* In addition to the registrant and its affiliates, management, and subsidiaries accounted for on the equity method, the principal owners of more than 10 percent of the voting interest of the reporting entity are considered to be related parties.
- *Significant subsidiaries.* A subsidiary is deemed to be significant when the investments in and advances to it exceed 10 percent of the consolidated assets of the parent, when the assets of the subsidiary are equal to or greater than 10 percent of the consolidated assets of the parent, or when the net income of the subsidiary exceeds 10 percent of the consolidated parent net income. In a pooling-of-interest transaction, the subsidiary is deemed to be significant if the numbers of common shares exchanged for it exceed 10 percent of the total common shares outstanding at the date of the combination. If either the parent or its tested subsidiary (but not both) incurred a loss, the equity in the income or loss of the tested subsidiary should be excluded from the consolidated net income for purposes of making the 10 percent computation. If the income of the parent is at least 10 percent lower than the average net income, excluding loss years, for the last 5 years, the average net income should be substituted in the computation.

Article 2 covers the qualifications and the report concerning the qualifications of accountants.

Article 3 specifies the statements to be filed, the timing of the filings, the years to be covered, the treatment of acquired companies, and other specialized reporting.

Article 3A covers the principles governing the filing of consolidated and combined financial statements.

Article 4 contains the rules of general application, including the following required notes to financial statements:

- Principles of consolidation or combination
- Assets subject to lien and assets collateralized
- Defaults in principal, in interest, and in sinking fund or redemption provision for securities or credit agreements
- Preferred shares and liquidation preferences
- Restrictions which limit the payment of stockholder dividends
- Significant changes in bonds, mortgages, and similar debts
- Summarization of financial information about the assets, liabilities, and net

income of significant unconsolidated subsidiaries and of 50 percent or less owned entities

- Income tax expenses, including the currently payable and deferred income tax expense, the timing differences for each deferred income tax component of 5 percent or more, and a reconciliation of current taxes to the applicable statutory rates, showing components of 5 percent or more separately
- Warrants or rights outstanding, including aggregate amounts and exercise dates
- Leased assets and leased commitments
- Interest cost expensed and capitalized
- Material, related party transactions which affect the financial statements

Article 4 also includes general rules covering special reporting items not usually applicable to insurance companies.

Article 7 is applicable to financial statements filed for all insurance companies except mutual life insurance companies and their wholly owned stock insurance subsidiaries. Summarized below are the financial statement requirements for (1) life insurance and accident and health insurance and (2) property and liability insurance companies. Where specific items apply to one category, they are so noted.

Balance Sheets

Assets. The following disclosures should be made for each caption:

- *Investments other than in related parties.*
  - Fixed maturities include bonds, notes, marketable certificates of deposits with maturities beyond 1 year, and redeemable preferred stock.
  - Equity securities include common stock and nonredeemable preferred stock.
  - Mortgage loans on real estate.
  - Investment real estate net of accumulated depreciation and amortization but excluding real estate acquired in settling title claims, mortgage guarantee claims, and similar insurance claims which are included in other assets.
  - Policy loans. (Life companies.)
  - Other long-term investments.
  - Short-term investments, including commercial paper and marketable certificates of deposits maturing within 1 year, savings accounts, time deposits, and interest-earning cash accounts.

The basis of determining the amounts of fixed maturities and equity securities and the alternative amount representing cost or aggregate value should be disclosed. Investments in a single person or its affiliates, excluding United States government securities, which exceed 10 percent of the stockholders' equity should be identified separately. Investments which have been non-income-producing for 12 months should be identified.

- *Cash not otherwise restricted.* Restricted cash should be shown separately and the restrictions described.

- *Securities and indebtedness of related parties–stated separately.*
- *Accrued investment income.*
- *Accounts and notes receivable.* This category includes amounts receivable from agents and insureds, and other receivables less allowances for doubtful accounts.
- *Reinsurance recoverable on paid losses.*
- *Deferred policy acquisition costs.*
- *Property and equipment, less depreciation and amortization.*
- *Title insurance plant.*
- *Other assets.*
- *Assets held in separate accounts.* (Life companies.)

Liabilities. The minimum required disclosures include the following:

- *Future policy benefits.* (Life companies.) The footnotes should include the basis of assumptions used in determining these benefits, including interest rates, mortality, and withdrawals.
- *Unpaid losses and loss expenses.* (Property and liability companies.)
- *Unearned premiums.* (Property and liability companies.)
- *Other policy claims and benefits payable.*
- *Other policyholders' funds.* (Life companies.) Included in this category are supplementary contracts without life contingencies, policyholders' dividend accumulations, undistributed earnings on participating business, dividends to policyholders, and similar items. Individual items in excess of 5 percent of the total liabilities should be shown separately.
- *Other liabilities.* Included are accrued payrolls, commissions, interest, taxes, and other individual items exceeding 5 percent of the liabilities which should be disclosed separately.
- *Federal income taxes.*
- *Notes payable, bonds, mortgages, and similar obligations, including capitalized leases.* Short-term debt and long-term debt, including capitalized leases, should be shown separately.
- *Indebtedness to related parties.*
- *Liabilities related to separate accounts.* (Life companies.) This is an offset to the assets held in separate accounts.
- *Commitments and contingent liabilities.*

The following additional footnote disclosures should be made about liabilities:

- Reinsurance transactions—including a description of significant reinsurance agreements, the nature and effect of material nonrecurring transactions, and contingent reinsurance liabilities—should be explained.
- The relative significance of participating life insurance should be expressed as a percentage of insurance in force and premium income, and the methods of determining allocable income and dividends should be explained.
- The amount of income taxes payable and of deferred income taxes should be disclosed, including deferred income taxes applicable to unrealized appreciation of equity securities.
- If the aggregate of short-term borrowings from banks, factors, and other finan-

cial institutions exceeds 5 percent of the total liabilities, the general character of each type of debt—including the interest rate, date of maturity, principal repayment plan, debt priority, and conversion privileges—should be disclosed.

Minority Interest. If the amount represented by preferred stock and the applicable dividend requirements are material in relation to the stockholders' equity, such amounts should be disclosed in the footnotes.

Redeemable Preferred Stocks. This includes preferred stocks with mandatory redemption requirements or with redemption privileges outside the control of the issuer. The number of shares authorized, issued, and outstanding and the redemption amount should be disclosed.

Stockholders' Equity

- *Nonredeemable preferred stocks.* The class of preferred shares, the number of shares issued or outstanding, and the dollar value should be described.
- *Common stocks.* Each class of common stock should be shown separately and described in terms of the number of shares issued and outstanding, the dollar amount, and convertible features, if any.
- *Other stockholders' equity.* Additional paid-in capital, other additional capital, and retained earnings (appropriated and unappropriated) should be shown separately. The amount of statutory stockholders' equity as of each balance sheet date should be described in the footnotes.

Statements of Income

Revenues. The following disclosures should be made for each caption:

- *Premiums.* This caption should include premiums from reinsurance assumed less reinsurance ceded.
- *Net investment income.* The details of investment income, applicable expenses, and income from each category of investment that exceeds 5 percent of total investment income should be disclosed in the footnotes.
- *Other income.* Amounts in excess of 5 percent of total revenue should be disclosed separately.

Benefits, Losses, and Expenses. The minimum required disclosures include the following:

- *Benefits, claims, losses, and settlement expenses.* For life insurance and accident and health insurance companies, this includes death, annuity, disability, and surrender benefits, matured endowments, payments of supplementary contracts and deposits, and increases in all reserves. For property and liability insurance companies, it includes losses and loss expenses.
- *Policyholders' share of earnings on participating policies, dividends, and similar items.* (Life companies.)
- *Underwriting, acquisition, and insurance expenses.* Amortized deferred pol-

icy acquisition costs and other significant operating expenses should be shown separately.

- *Income or loss before income tax expense, and other.*
- *Income tax expense.*
- *Minority interest in income of consolidated subsidiaries.*
- *Equity in earnings of unconsolidated subsidiaries and of 50 percent or less owned entities.* The amount of gain or loss on investments should be excluded from this caption and included with realized gains or losses. The amount of dividends received from these entities should be disclosed.
- *Income or loss before realized gains or losses on investments and extraordinary items.*
- *Realized gains or losses on investments other than investments in affiliates, less applicable tax.* Amounts applicable to equity and to 50 percent owned companies should be shown separately. The method of determining the cost of investment should be disclosed. The amount of realized and unrealized investment gains or losses should be shown separately for fixed maturities and equity securities.
- *Discontinued operations.*
- *Income or loss before extraordinary items and cumulative effect of change in accounting principles.*
- *Extraordinary items less applicable tax.*
- *Cumulative effects of changes in accounting principles.*
- *Net income or loss.*
- *Earnings-per-share data.*

Statements of Stockholders' Equity. An analysis of the changes in each caption of stockholders' equity is required as a separate statement or in footnotes. The analysis is a reconciliation of the accounts at the beginning and end of each period for which an income statement is required and describes all significant reconciling items.

The following are typical captions and disclosures:

- *Common stock.* Changes resulting from stock issued or repurchased for cash, from stock issued in acquisitions, as options, to effect stock splits, and from similar transactions should be disclosed separately.
- *Additional paid-in capital.* Changes resulting from the sale or repurchase of stock for cash and from acquisitions, contributions of capital, and similar transactions should be reported separately.
- *Unrealized appreciation or depreciation of equity securities.* The net change in the valuation of equity securities for the year, other adjustments resulting from acquisition or disposition of subsidiary companies, and similar items should be reported separately.
- *Retained earnings.* The net income for the year, the cash dividends paid (including the amount per share for each class of shares), the changes arising from acquisition or disposition of subsidiaries, and similar items should be reported separately.

Statements of Changes in Financial Position. This statement is required for all financial statements and should reflect the changes either in working capital or in cash. Since insurance companies generally report an unclassified balance sheet, this statement will usually reflect the increase (decrease) in cash. The statement should begin with the income or loss before extraordinary items, with adjustments for those amounts included in income or loss which did not use or provide cash during the period. Since items which did not provide cash are not sources or uses of cash, they should be described as items recognized in net income which did not require outlays of cash for the current period. The sum of these amounts is described as cash provided from (used in) operations for the period, exclusive of extraordinary items. Extraordinary items of income or loss should be shown separately. Other sources and use of funds should be described for each significant element which provided or used funds during the period.

Other specific disclosures include funds arising from the purchase or sale of each significant long-term asset, changes in common stock resulting from conversion features of long-term debt or preferred stock, changes in long-term debt, sale or repurchase of capital stock for cash, cash dividends to shareholders, and similar significant changes.

Some of the typical changes reported in these statements are described below:

- *Net income.* Extraordinary items, if any, should be reported separately.
- *Changes in items not affecting funds in the current period.* Typical items include changes in future policy benefits, losses and adjusting expenses, unearned premiums, other benefits payable, reinsurance amounts, deferred policy acquisition costs, accrued investment income, depreciation and amortization, agents' balances and uncollected premiums, deferred federal income taxes, and similar accrued or deferred items.
- *Sale, maturity, or repayment of investments.* Each significant category of investments for fixed and equity securities, mortgage loans, real estate, policy loans, and short-term investments should be shown separately.
- *Other sources of funds.* This caption includes all other items, such as borrowed funds, decreases in notes and other receivables, disposition of subsidiaries, and proceeds from the sale of capital or preferred stock.

Funds derived from operations and investment activities should disclose all significant transactions. Typical applications of funds include the following:

- *Acquisition of investments.* Individual categories for fixed and equity securities, mortgage loans, real estate, policy loans, short-term investments, and similar significant items should be reported separately.
- *Other applications of funds.* These include increases in premiums and other receivables, cash dividends, additions to property and equipment, deferred policy acquisition costs, reduction of debt, repurchase of common or preferred stock, acquisition of subsidiary companies, and similar transactions.

The net change in the sources and applications of funds represents the increase (decrease) in cash and should be used to reconcile the cash at the beginning and end of the year.

Included in the next section are examples of financial statements for public reporting property and liability insurance and life and accident and health insurance companies.

ILLUSTRATIVE FINANCIAL STATEMENTS

Table 20-1
Balance Sheets*

Property and Liability Insurance Company

	(000s Omitted) December 31	
	19XX	19XX
ASSETS		
Investments:		
Fixed maturities—at amortized cost—market: $176,393 and $162,840, respectively	$180,798	$168,474
Equity securities—at market—cost $17,202 and $16,870, respectively	17,670	17,000
Mortgage loans on real estate	100	110
Total investments	198,568	185,584
Cash	1,201	201
Accrued investment income	4,750	4,300
Receivables:		
Agents' balances and uncollected premiums	5,400	5,200
Due from reinsurers	410	490
Recoverable federal income taxes	100	100
	5,910	5,790
Deferred policy acquisition costs	9,940	9,090
Property and equipment—at cost less accumulated depreciation of $3,430 and $2,260, respectively	23,770	24,040
Other assets	418	318
Total assets	$244,557	$229,323
LIABILITIES AND STOCKHOLDERS' EQUITY		
Reserves and liabilities:		
Unpaid losses and loss expenses	$ 76,000	$ 72,200
Unearned premiums	45,185	43,285
Other liabilities	13,825	18,083
Federal income taxes:		
Current	1,100	1,000
Deferred	3,970	3,630
	5,070	4,630
Mortgage note on real estate	4,000	4,500
Total reserves and liabilities	144,080	142,698
Stockholders' equity:		
Common stock, $1 par value:		
Authorized 10,000 shares; issued 5000 shares	5,000	5,000
Additional paid-in capital	20,000	20,000
Unrealized appreciation of equity securities	468	130
Retained earnings	75,009	61,495
Total stockholders' equity	$100,477	86,625
Total liabilities and stockholders' equity	$244,557	$229,323

*See Notes to Financial Statements, pages 350–353.

Table 20-2
Statements of Income*

Property and Liability Insurance Company

	(000s Omitted) Year Ended December 31	
	19XX	19XX
Revenues:		
Premiums	$165,800	$157,600
Net investment income	11,150	9,914
Other income	170	150
Total revenues	177,120	167,664
Benefits, losses, and expenses:		
Losses	92,600	94,323
Loss expenses	14,400	15,200
Commissions	17,140	16,810
Other underwriting expenses	19,360	21,320
Amortization of deferred acquisition costs	13,050	12,640
Total benefits, losses, and expenses	156,550	160,293
Income before income taxes and net realized gains on investments	20,570	7,371
Federal income taxes:		
Current	6,650	2,561
Deferred (credit)	220	(370)
	6,870	2,191
Income before net realized gains on investments	13,700	5,180
Net realized gains on investment, less applicable income taxes	314	280
Net income	$ 14,014	$ 5,460
Earnings per share:		
Income before net realized gains on investments	$ 2.74	$ 1.03
Net realized gains on investments	.06	.06
Total	$ 2.80	$ 1.09

*See Notes to Financial Statements, pages 350–353.

Table 20-3
Statements of Stockholders' Equity*

Property and Liability Insurance Company

	(000s Omitted)				
	Common Stock	**Additional Paid-in Capital**	**Unrealized Appreciation of Equity Securities**	**Retained Earnings**	**Total**
Balance on January 1, 19XX	$5,000	$20,000	$ 30	$56,535	$ 81,565
Net income for 19XX				5,460	5,460
Unrealized appreciation of equity securities			100		100
Cash dividends on common stock ($0.10 per share)				(500)	(500)
Balance on December 31, 19XX	5,000	20,000	130	61,495	86,625
Net income for 19XX				14,014	14,014
Unrealized appreciation of equity securities			338		338
Cash dividends on common stock ($0.10 per share)				(500)	(500)
Balance on December 31, 19XX	$5,000	$20,000	$468	$75,009	$100,477

*See Notes to Financial Statements, pages 350–353.

Table 20-4
Statements of Changes in Financial Position*

Property and Liability Insurance Company

	(000s Omitted) Year Ended December 31	
	19XX	19XX
SOURCE OF FUNDS		
Net income	$14,014	$ 5,460
Increase (decrease) in items not affecting funds:		
Losses and adjusting expenses	3,800	2,900
Unearned premiums	1,900	1,700
Depreciation and amortization	1,270	1,230
Accrued investment income	(450)	(200)
Deferred policy acquisition costs, less amortization	(850)	(810)
Other assets	220	300
Current and deferred federal income taxes	440	260
Other liabilities	(4,258)	4,840
Funds from operations	16,086	15,680
Proceeds from sale, maturity, or repayment of investments, excluding realized gains	6,807	2,514
Total source of funds	$22,893	$18,194
APPLICATION OF FUNDS		
Acquisition of investments	$20,393	$16,844
Purchase of property and equipment	1,000	750
Dividends paid to stockholders	500	500
Increase in cash	1,000	100
Total application of funds	$22,893	$18,194

*See Notes to Financial Statements, pages 350–353.

Notes to Financial Statements

Note A: Significant Accounting Policies

The financial statements have been prepared in conformity with generally accepted accounting principles, which differ in some respects from the accounting practices followed in the preparation of financial statements submitted to state insurance departments. (See Note F.)

INVESTMENTS

Fixed maturities (bonds and redeemable preferred stock) are reported at amortized cost and adjusted for other than temporary market value declines. Equity securities (common and non-redeemable preferred stock) are reported at current market value, except that subsidiaries are reported at equity in underlying net asset value. All other investments are reported at cost. Unrealized appreciation and depreciation of equity securities, less applicable deferred income taxes, are reported separately in stockholders' equity. Realized gains and losses are determined on the specific identification basis.

DEFERRED POLICY ACQUISITION COSTS

The cost of acquiring new business (commissions and other costs which vary directly with and are primarily related to new business), to the extent recoverable, have been deferred and are amortized over the term of the related policies.

UNPAID LOSSES AND LOSS EXPENSES

The liability for unsettled claims, which are reported net of all reinsurance amounts, includes losses and adjustment expenses, all determined by using case-basis evaluations and statistical analyses. These amounts are necessarily subject to future changes in claim severity and other factors and are continuously reviewed. Adjustments (if any) to these estimates are reported in current operations.

PREMIUM REVENUES

Premiums, except for unearned amounts, are reported as income when due.

UNEARNED PREMIUMS

Premiums which are not earned are reported net of all reinsurance amounts and are calculated on a pro rata basis over the term of the policies remaining in force.

REINSURANCE

Policy premiums ceded to or assumed from other companies have been netted against premium income and unearned amounts. Loss amounts related to ceded or assumed premiums have been netted against losses and loss expenses incurred and against unpaid amounts. Commissions on ceded and assumed premiums are netted against underwriting expenses.

FEDERAL INCOME TAXES

Policy acquisition and certain other costs are reported for income tax in periods different from when such amounts are reported in the financial statements. Deferred income taxes arising from the different reporting dates are recorded in the financial statements. Investment tax credits are accounted for by the "flow-through" method. (See Note C.)

EARNINGS PER SHARE

Net income per share is based on the weighted average number of shares of common stock outstanding during the year.

Note B: Investment Operations

The major categories of investment income are summarized below.

	(000s Omitted) Year Ended December 31	
	19XX	19XX
Fixed maturities	$11,602	$10,197
Equity securities	858	834
Real estate	552	540
Other	1	1
	13,013	11,572
Less investment expenses	1,863	1,658
Total	$11,150	$ 9,914

Unrealized and realized gains (losses) are summarized below.

Unrealized:		
Equity securities	$ 468	$130
Income taxes*	-0-	-0-
Total	$ 468	$130
Realized:		
Fixed maturities	$ 85	
Equity securities	349	$ 360
	434	360
Income taxes	120	80
Total	$ 314	$ 280

*Offset by capital loss carryover.

Note C: Federal Income Taxes

A reconciliation of the difference between total income tax expense and amounts computed by applying the expected federal tax rate (46%) to income before income taxes and realized investment gains is presented below.

	(000s Omitted) Year Ended December 31	
	19XX	19XX
Computed income tax at 46% rate	$ 9,462	$ 3,901
Tax-exempt investment income	(2,202)	(1,504)
Other	(390)	(206)
Provision for federal income taxes	$ 6,870	$ 2,191

Deferred taxes resulting from the timing differences of reporting tax expenses for tax and financial reporting purposes are presented below.

Deferred policy acquisition costs	$340	$(450)
Other	(120)	80
Total	$220	$(370)

Note D: Mortgage Note Payable

The 9% mortgage payable, which is collateralized by the company home office building, is payable at $500,000 annually plus interest.

Note E: Retirement Plan

The company has a noncontributory self-insured defined benefit pension plan covering substantially all full-time employees. Past service costs are fully funded and annual contributions provide for normal current costs. Contributions charged to expense amount to $370,000 and $340,000 for 19XX and 19XX, respectively. The actuarial present value of accumulated plan benefits at July 31, 19XX, using an assumed rate of interest of 7%, total $1,780,000 (19XX $1,610,000), including $970,000 and $810,000 (19XX $830,000 and $780,000) of vested and nonvested benefits respectively. Net assets available for benefits total $1,360,000 (19XX $1,140,000).

Note F: Financial Reporting Basis

A reconciliation of the net income and stockholders' equity of the company—as reported in conformity with accounting practices required for use in reporting to regulatory authorities in contrast to that reported in the accompanying financial statements—is as follows:

	(000s Omitted)			
	Net Income Year Ended December 31		Stockholders' Equity December 31	
	19XX	19XX	19XX	19XX
As reported to regulatory authorities	$13,504	$5,200	$ 89,007	$76,783
Deferred policy acquisition costs	850	770	9,940	9,090
Additional regulatory reserves			3,000	2,900
Equipment, furniture, and other assets nonadmitted			2,500	2,100
Deferred income taxes	(340)	(510)	(3,970)	(3,630)
Unrealized appreciation of equity securities				(618)
As reported herein	$14,014	$5,460	$100,477	$86,625

The amount ($11,002 on December 31, 19XX) by which retained earnings reported in these statements exceed unassigned surplus reported to regulatory authorities is restricted and cannot be distributed as dividends to stockholders.

Note G: Reinsurance

The company reinsures risks with other companies and treats expected recoveries on unpaid losses as risks for which the company is not liable. To the extent that the reinsuring companies are unable to meet their obligations under these reinsurance agreements, the company is contingently liable for all such losses.

Note H: Property and Equipment

The major categories of property and equipment are as follows:

	(000s Omitted) December 31	
	19XX	19XX
Land	$ 3,000	$ 3,000
Buildings and improvements	17,000	16,500
Furniture, fixtures, and equipment	7,200	6,800
	27,200	26,300
Less accumulated depreciation	3,430	2,260
Total	$23,770	$24,040

Table 20-5
Balance Sheets*

Life Insurance Company

	(000s Omitted) December 31	
	19XX	19XX
ASSETS		
Investments:		
Fixed maturities—at amortized cost—market: $439,910 and $421,740, respectively	$483,290	$454,640
Equity securities—at market—cost $23,964 and $23,346, respectively	25,654	24,966
Mortgage loans on real estate	27,270	26,940
Policy loans	95,642	89,760
Short-term investments	25,273	4,064
Other invested assets	830	703
Total investments	657,959	601,073
Cash	370	1,765
Accrued investment income	6,982	6,746
Receivables:		
Agents' accounts	2,350	3,510
Amounts due from reinsurers	10,943	12,110
Other receivables	930	1,020
	14,223	16,640
Deferred policy acquisition costs	61,980	58,360
Property and equipment—at cost less accumulated depreciation of $5,090 and $3,930 respectively	12,862	12,272
Separate account assets	205,408	196,110
Total assets	$959,784	$892,966

*See Notes to Financial Statements, pages 358–363.

Table 20-5
Balance Sheets* (*Continued*)

Life Insurance Company

	(000s Omitted) December 31	
	19XX	19XX
LIABILITIES AND STOCKHOLDERS' EQUITY*		
Policy and Other Liabilities		
Policy liabilities and accruals:		
Future policy benefits:		
Life and annuity	$404,892	$378,259
Accident and health	10,603	8,699
Unearned premiums	8,040	7,910
Other policy claims and benefits	4,068	3,310
	427,603	398,178
Other policyholders' funds	67,763	66,760
Other liabilities:		
Accrued expenses	8,194	7,520
Premium and other taxes	894	718
Federal income taxes:		
Current	3,924	3,670
Deferred	1,790	1,670
Notes payable	2,960	3,067
	17,762	16,645
Total policy and other liabilities	513,128	481,583
Separate account liabilities	205,408	196,110
Total liabilities	718,536	677,693
Stockholders' Equity		
Common stock, $1 par value:		
Authorized 10,000 shares; issued 2,500 shares	2,500	2,500
Additional paid-in capital	22,500	22,500
Unrealized appreciation of equity securities	1,690	1,620
Retained earnings	214,558	188,653
	241,248	215,273
Total liabilities and stockholders' equity	$959,784	$892,966

*See Notes to Financial Statements, pages 358–363.

Table 20-6
Statements of Income*

Life Insurance Company

	(000s Omitted) Year Ended December 31	
	19XX	19XX
Revenues:		
Premiums:		
Life and annuity	$ 87,781	$ 83,410
Accident and health	7,999	7,280
Supplementary contracts and dividends left on deposit	4,768	4,490
Investment income—net of expenses (19XX $4,752; 19XX $4,632)	59,416	57,960
Other income	431	550
Total revenues	160,395	153,690
Benefits and Expenses:		
Death benefits	24,480	27,860
Annuity benefits	14,290	15,110
Accident and health benefits	2,770	3,280
Surrender benefits	13,274	21,930
Supplementary contracts and dividend accumulations payments	4,858	5,420
Other benefits	3,140	3,290
Increase in future policy benefits:		
Life and annuity	26,633	18,090
Accident and health	2,034	1,070
Other contracts	816	360
Dividends to policyholders	900	800
Underwriting, acquisition, and insurance expenses:		
Commissions	12,490	9.630
General expenses	12,835	10,720
Insurance taxes	2,736	2,665
Policy acquisition cost deferred	(12,456)	(11,285)
Amortization of deferred policy acquistion costs	8,836	8,175
Total benefits and expenses	117,636	117,115
Income before income taxes and net realized gains on investments	42,759	36,575
Federal income taxes:		
Current	15,432	11,710
Deferred	120	108
	15,552	11,818
Income before net realized gains on investments	27,207	24,757
Net realized gains on investments, less taxes of: 19XX $299; 19XX $436.	1,198	1,670
Net income	$ 28,405	$ 26,427
Earnings per share:		
Income before net realized gains on investments	$ 10.88	$ 9.90
Net realized gains on investments	.48	.67
Total	$ 11.36	$ 10.57

*See Notes to Financial Statements, pages 358–363.

Table 20-7
Statements of Stockholders' Equity*

Life Insurance Company

	000s Omitted				
	Common Stock	Additional Paid-in Capital	Unrealized Appreciation of Equity Securities	Retained Earnings	Total
Balance on January 1, 19XX	$2,500	$22,500	$1,580	$164,726	$191,306
Net income for 19XX				26,427	26,427
Unrealized appreciation of equity securities			40		40
Cash dividends on common stock ($1 per share)				(2,500)	(2,500)
Balance on December 31, 19XX	2,500	22,500	1,620	188,653	215,273
Net income for 19XX				28,405	28,405
Unrealized appreciation of equity securities			70		70
Cash dividends on common stock ($1 per share)				(2,500)	(2,500)
Balance on December 31, 19XX	$2,500	$22,500	$1,690	$214,558	$241,248

*See Notes to Financial Statements, pages 358–363.

Table 20-8
Statements of Changes in Financial Position*

Life Insurance Company

	(000s Omitted) Year Ended December 31	
	19XX	19XX
SOURCE OF FUNDS		
Net income	$28,405	$26,427
Increase (decrease) in items not affecting funds:		
Future policy benefits	29,425	19,520
Deferred policy acquisition costs, less amortization	(3,620)	(3,110)
Other policyholder funds	1,003	970
Federal income taxes	374	260
Accrued investment income	(236)	(241)
Amounts held by reinsurers	1,167	1,032
Depreciation	1,160	1,040
Accrued expenses	850	720
Funds from operations	58,528	46,618
Proceeds from sale, maturity, or repayment of investments, excluding realized gains	22,084	25,667
Decrease in receivables	1,250	920
Total source of funds	$81,862	$73,205
APPLICATION OF FUNDS		
Acquisition of investments	$73,018	$58,970
Increase in policy loans	5,882	7,734
Dividends paid to stockholders	2,500	2,500
Decrease in notes payable	107	1,105
Additions to property and equipment—net	1,750	3,206
Decrease in cash	(1,395)	(310)
Total application of funds	$81,862	$73,205

*See Notes to Financial Statements, pages 358–363.

Notes to Financial Statements

Note A: Significant Accounting Policies

The financial statements have been prepared in conformity with generally accepted accounting principles, which differ in some respects from the accounting practices followed in the preparation of financial statements submitted to state insurance departments. (Note F.)

INVESTMENTS

Fixed maturities (bonds and redeemable preferred stock) are reported at amortized cost and adjusted for other than temporary market value declines. Equity securities (common and nonredeemable preferred stock) are reported at current market value. Unrealized appreciation and depreciation of equity securities, less applicable deferred income taxes, are reported separately in stockholders' equity. Mortgage loans and policy loans are reported at unpaid principal amounts. Real estate is reported at the lower of cost or estimated net realizable value. All other investments are reported at cost.

DEFERRED POLICY ACQUISITION COSTS

The costs of acquiring new business (commissions and other costs which vary directly with and are primarily related to new business), to the extent recoverable from related renewal premiums, have been deferred. Such costs are being amortized over the premium-paying period of the related policies, using the same assumptions as to interest, mortality, and withdrawals as are used for computing liabilities for future policy benefits.

FUTURE POLICY BENEFITS

The liabilities for future policy benefits have been determined on a net level basis. Interest assumptions for all policies issued after 19XX are at an initial rate of 7½% graded to 4½% after 15 years. For policies issued before 19XX and after 19XX, the initial rate is 6½% graded to 4% after 20 years. For all policies issued before 19XX, interest rates remain at a substantially level rate of 4%. Annuity interest rates vary from 4% to 8% guaranteed rates. The current provision for annuity interest rates varies, depending upon money market rates, which, for the current year, vary from 9% to 13%. Mortality and withdrawal assumptions are based on the company's experience, except that those policies for which the company has insufficient experience are based on currently published mortality and withdrawal tables prepared by their primary reinsurer.

PREMIUM REVENUES AND RELATED COSTS

Premiums are recognized as earned when due. Benefits and expenses are associated with earned premiums so as to result in recognization of policy profits over the life of the contract. This is accomplished by means of the provisions for liabilities of future policy benefits and the amortization of deferred acquisition costs over the term of the policy period.

REINSURANCE

Premiums, expenses, and future policy benefits are stated net after the deduction of amounts related to reinsurance ceded to or assumed from other companies.

PROPERTY AND EQUIPMENT

Real estate and other property and equipment are reported at cost less accumulated depreciation. Depreciation expense is computed by using the straight-line method over the estimated useful lives of the assets.

FEDERAL INCOME TAXES

The provision for federal income taxes includes amounts currently payable and deferred income taxes arising from timing differences from reporting acquisition costs and future policy benefits in different periods for financial and income tax reporting. Investment tax credits are accounted for by the flow-through method. (See Note C.)

SEPARATE ACCOUNTS

The transactions in the separate accounts are charged or credited directly to them and are excluded from the statements of income

EARNINGS PER SHARE

Net income per share is based on the weighted average number of shares of common stock outstanding during the year.

Note B: Investment Operations

The major categories of investment income are summarized below.

	(000s Omitted) Year Ended December 31	
	19XX	19XX
Fixed maturities	$48,088	$47,714
Equity securities	1,530	1,564
Mortgage loans	2,180	2,116
Policy loans	6,910	6,326
Short-term investments	5,280	4,206
Other	180	670
	64,168	62,596
Less investment expenses	4,752	4,636
Total	$59,416	$57,960

Unrealized and realized gains (losses) are summarized below.

Unrealized:		
Equity securities	$ 1,690	$1,620
Income taxes*	-0-	-0-
Total	$ 1,690	$1,620
Realized:		
Fixed maturities	$ (23)	$636
Other investments	210	100
Equity securities	1,310	1,370
	1,497	2,106
Income taxes	299	436
Total	$1,198	$ 1,670

*Offset by capital loss carryover.

Note C: Federal Income Taxes

A reconciliation of the difference between total income tax expenses and amounts computed by applying the expected federal income tax rate (46%) to income before income taxes and realized investment gains is presented below.

	(000s Omitted) Year Ended December 31	
	19XX	**19XX**
Computed income tax at 46% rate	$18,858	$16,824
Tax-exempt investment income	(980)	(972)
Income not presently subject to tax	(1,801)	(2,521)
Special deductions	(229)	(586)
Other	(296)	(927)
Total	$15,552	$11,818

Deferred taxes resulting from the timing differences of reporting tax expenses for tax and financial reporting purposes are presented below.

Deferred policy acquisition costs	$ 80	$ 40
Future policy benefits	70	48
Other	(30)	20
Total	$ 120	$ 108

Note D: Notes Payable

The notes payable are subordinated to all policyholder claims, are due in annual installments of $175,000 plus 10% interest on the unpaid amounts, and are callable at face amount at the option of the company.

Note E: Retirement Plan

The company has a noncontributory self-insured defined benefit pension plan covering substantially all full-time employees. Past service costs are fully funded and annual contributions provide for normal current costs. Contributions charged to expense amount to $930,000 and $885,000 for 19XX and 19XX, respectively. The actuarial present value of accumulated plan benefits at July 31, 19XX, using an assumed rate of interest of 7%, total $4,674,000 (19XX $3,970,000) including $2,863,000 and $1,811,000 (19XX $2,547,000 and $1,423,000) of vested and nonvested benefits, respectively. Net assets available for benefits total $4,562,000 (19XX $3,880,000).

Note F: Financial Reporting Basis

A reconciliation of the net income and stockholders' equity of the company—as reported in conformity with accounting practices required for use in reporting to regulatory authorities in contrast to that reported in the accompanying financial statements—is as follows:

	(000s Omitted)			
	Net Income Year Ended December 31		Stockholders' Equity December 31	
	19XX	19XX	19XX	19XX
As reported to regulatory authorities	$21,980	$17,470	$111,805	$ 93,455
Deferred policy acquisition costs	3,620	4,610	61,980	58,360
Future policy benefits	4,655	4,910	59,830	55,175
Net investment gains	110	750		
Mandatory securities valuation reserve			8,493	7,833
Federal income taxes:				
Current	(782)	(460)		
Deferred	(120)	(108)	(1,790)	(1,670)
Nonadmitted assets	(1,230)	(960)	4,242	5,472
Due and deferred premiums	(66)	(67)	(6,150)	(6,084)
Other adjustments—net	238	282	2,838	2,732
As reported herein	$28,405	$26,427	$241,248	$215,273

The amount ($127,753 on December 31, 19XX) by which retained earnings reported in these statements exceed unassigned surplus reported to regulatory authorities is restricted and cannot be distributed as dividends to stockholders.

Note G: Reinsurance

The company reinsures risks with other companies and treats expected recoveries of direct losses as risks for which the company is not liable. To the extent that the reinsuring companies are unable to meet their obligations under these reinsurance agreements, the company is contingently liable for all such losses.

Note H: Property and Equipment

The major categories of property and equipment are as follows:

	(000s Omitted) December 31	
	19XX	19XX
Land	$ 2,000	$ 2,000
Buildings and improvements	10,780	10,402
Furniture, fixtures, and equipment	5,172	3,800
	17,952	16,202
Less accumulated depreciation	5,090	3,930
	$12,862	$12,272

21

VARIABLE ANNUITIES AND LIFE INSURANCE

BENEFITS FROM INVESTMENT EARNINGS

Variable annuities and variable life insurance were developed to offer policyholders an alternative to the traditional fixed benefits policies. Fixed benefits are determined either by quoting an absolute rate that continues during the period that the policy is in force or by guarantying a measurement standard that permits benefits to be determined on an annual basis at earning rates prevailing at the time the premiums are paid. The features of fixed benefits, investment year benefits, and variable benefits are summarized in this chapter in order to point out the available benefits from investment earnings that may lead a policyholder to consider purchasing a variable annuity or variable life insurance policy.

Fixed Benefits

Fixed-benefit policies provide living and death benefits based on a guaranteed earnings rate for premiums paid during an accumulation period. The actual amount of the guaranteed earnings benefit is usually not known by the policyholder since it is included as an implicit part of the premium calculation. When comparing policies with similar benefits, it is therefore necessary to compare the premiums and cash value accumulations in order to determine which policy has the most favorable fixed benefits.

These fixed benefits should not be confused with the statutory minimum guaranteed benefits used to provide life insurance and annuity reserves. Fixed-benefit policies are usually calculated on the earnings of an investment portfolio and these earnings fluctuate from year to year. Over a period of years, however, the level of earnings tends to average out as a percentage of the portfolio rate. Fixed-benefit policies have an advantage over other forms since benefits will not decrease even though the portfolio rate decreases. On the other hand, policies with nonparticipating fixed benefits cannot be enhanced even though current earnings may cause the portfolio rate to greatly exceed the fixed-benefit rate.

Investment Year Benefits

Some policies are issued with benefits determined by the earnings rate prevailing at the time that each premium is paid. The level of these benefits depends upon the ability of the company to achieve current investment earnings in excess of the promised minimum benefit. The investment year benefit is an operating concept that does not require codification in the financial statements. For financial reporting, investment earnings are accounted for in the aggregate and promised benefits are included in the reserves.

Investment year benefits are attractive to policyholders during periods of high interest rates and slow economic growth in equity securities. The concept does not rely solely on money-market returns, which can change rapidly, but usually relies on intermediate term investments, which provide a higher rate of return over several years. Investment year benefits are considered the more reliable the more closely they are tied to the most current investment securities. This investment concept differs from the traditional fixed-benefit program in which long-term securities are often purchased to fund the fixed benefits, in which instance the long-term nature of the investments is as important as their earnings rates.

Variable Benefits

Unlike either fixed or investment year benefits, variable benefits are tied directly to an investment portfolio. The change in cash or retirement benefits is directly affected by investment performance. During the deferred period, the amounts accumulating depend upon the new premiums paid and the aggregate performance of the investment portfolio. Policies having variable benefits shift the risk of changes in investment opportunities and economic growth from the company directly to the policyholder. This permits the policyholders to accrue all the investment growth and at the same time requires them to take the risk that benefits may decrease during periods when investment returns and economic growth decline.

The concept of variable benefits places the policyholders in a position to protect the purchasing power of their premiums and investment growth by matching the benefits to the current economic conditions. During the periods of accelerated growth, the benefits are contemplated to increase, and during periods of lesser growth, the benefits are contemplated to decline. Whether variable benefits perform in such a fashion depends upon many factors, including the overall performance of specific investment programs.

Some variable benefit policies permit policyholders to choose between programs that are tied to equity securities, long-term bond investments, money-market investments, and several other investment programs. These policies usually permit the transfer of accumulated funds between available investment programs at least once during an annual period.

Most benefits can be tied to one or more of the preceding programs. The concept of fixed benefits programs and of high-premium and high-benefit programs has been covered in Chapter 4, Revenue Recognition, under "Life Insurance Premiums." The remainder of this chapter covers the accounting and compliance aspects of programs offering variable benefits.

SEPARATE ACCOUNTS

Most state jurisdictions permit an insurance company to establish a separate investment account to provide variable benefits. It may be called a "separate" account, a "segregated asset" account, a "variable" account, or a similar designation, but each has the common purpose of providing a facility for determining benefits that depend upon investment performance. Separate account investment performance includes: amounts received or accrued for interest and dividends; gains, losses, sales, or other disposition of securities; and a market adjustment to recognize unrealized gains or losses on investments.

These separate accounts are creatures of law and exist solely to accommodate the variable benefit–type policy. For many years, the annuities have been the primary source of investable assets for such accounts. However, more and more companies are working on life insurance programs that are tied to the variable benefit features of separate accounts. The features of annuity and life insurance accounts are similar, although life insurance separate accounts are not as well established as are annuity accounts.

The following discussions cover typical, although not universal, ways in which separate accounts are permitted to function:

Trust Concept

The separate account is sometimes thought of as a "trust" account, but in fact it is not. Rather, it is a separate and distinct investment account that has for its purpose an investment program that may create benefits more in line with general economic growth.

A *trust* is a restrictive creature of law that imposes upon the trustee or manager a set of prescribed duties for the benefit of another. The statutory rules regulating trust activities and trust funds are generally set out in detail and do not permit the usual discretionary actions allowed to executive management. To the extent that the separate account restricts the type of investments that may be executed, it may be thought of as a trust; however, since the separate account is created by statute, the actions of executive management in regard to a separate account are not restricted by trust statutes.

Separateness Concept

The laws governing the creation of a separate account permit the allocation of amounts arising from settlement or dividend options to be segregated in a separate account to provide annuities or life insurance. Additionally, separate accounts are permitted to hold funds for pension plans and life insurance that are contributed by or designated for investment in a separate account. Investment accounts usually include all annuities whether or not they are made on behalf of a qualified pension plan.

The separateness concept usually includes some or all of the following provisions:

- All separate account assets are owned by the company and administered under the statutes governing these accounts. Since the company owns its separate accounts, it does not function in the capacity of a trustee.
- The assets are separate and distinct from the general assets held by the company and are not subject to claim by general creditors.
- Separate accounts are not subject to the investment limitation imposed upon general account assets.
- All assets are valued at market, except that the commissioner of insurance may approve another value when in his or her judgment the market value is not appropriate.
- All income from separate account investments, including realized and unrealized gains and losses, is credited or charged to the separate account and does not affect the surplus of the general account.
- Assets cannot be exchanged with the general account except with special permission by the commissioner of insurance, and then only at market value.
- Policy benefits can be payable in a fixed or variable amount but cannot be guaranteed without special approval of the commissioner of insurance.

- □ Participants in the separate account must be provided with a statement about how the account values and units are determined.
- □ Separate accounts must comply with all federal or state laws governing the issue of variable policies that are deemed to be securities.

Participant's Account

An important element of the separate account is the manner in which the value of the participant's account is determined. The basic equation for each account is based on the value of invested assets over the dollar amount of each single or periodic payment. Generally, the value is expressed as a unit which has a starting amount equal to the original dollars invested in the account. Thereafter, the unit value may increase or decrease based on the investment performance of all separate account assets, including adjustments to state assets at market value. The current unit value determines the number of units credited for new dollars paid into the account. This value functions in a manner similar to that for the per share value of a mutual fund. As new dollars are paid in on accounts already in force, the participant's account fluctuates with the investment results.

This investment program is intended to offer the advantage of "dollar averaging" for deferred accounts as well as for those in the payout period. The payout benefits can be in a fixed amount and will continue as long as there is a balance in the investment account. The payout units may also be made in variable amounts for a fixed number of units that are based on current investment results. In either instance the amounts of the benefits are not guaranteed, as are those of nonvariable policy benefits, unless an election is made at maturity to transfer the variable values to a fixed-benefit policy.

Investment Alternatives

The following are examples of the investment alternatives available to fund separate accounts offering policies with variable benefits. This listing is not exhaustive but does represent a group of typical investment programs.

Type of Program	*Objectives*
□ Bonds	Long-term interest guarantees
□ Growth stock	Long-term stock appreciation and reasonable dividend income
□ Income stock	Current dividend benefits with long-term opportunity for market appreciation
□ Money market	Maximum current money-market interest rates with short-term investment commitments
□ Real estate	Long-term property appreciation with reasonable rental earnings

□ Combination	Combined benefits of two or more other investment programs

Variable Life Insurance

The preceding discussions of separate accounts apply equally to annuity and life insurance products. However, the death benefit feature of life insurance causes variable life products to provide a guaranteed floor of life insurance; this feature requires some of the premiums paid into the variable account to be used to guarantee the minimum life benefit. While some annuity accounts guarantee the return of premiums, such amounts are fully funded, whereas life insurance death benefits are not. Cash value accumulation for variable life insurance is affected in the same manner as for all other variable policy benefits. Some variable life insurance provides for the payment of flexible premiums so long as there are sufficient accumulated funds to maintain a minimum amount of life insurance benefits. Although variable life insurance products have not yet been marketed on the same scale as other variable products have, the concept of life insurance benefits nevertheless applies to a separate account equally as well as does the concept of annuity benefits.

REGISTRATION AND REPORTING

Because benefits are based on investment performance, many separate accounts must not only comply with individual state registration requirements but are subject to registration with the Securities and Exchange Commission (SEC) as well. Most registrations are governed by the Investment Company Act of 1940, although some separate accounts may be registered solely under the Securities Act of 1933.

The registration is required because of the investment features that affect annuity benefits, death benefits, and cash values. The policyholder of a separate account assumes the investment risks underlying the benefits—whereas for fixed benefits, the company has that risk. Because the policyholder assumes the investment risk, the policy contract takes on the characteristics of a security and the benefits are determined in much the same fashion as are the investments in mutual funds.

Some separate accounts are exempt from registration if policyholder funds consist of stock bonus, pension, or profit-sharing plans properly qualified under specific sections of the Internal Revenue Code. These plans are exempt because the investments are designated by the managers of such plans as part of an overall investment program and the individual participants do not make investment decisions. Typically, such separate accounts may limit their investment to a single pension plan for their own or other employees and permit the transfer to the separate account.

All plans not specifically exempted are required to file registration statements with the SEC and to comply with applicable state securities laws.

The following discussion of registration and reporting covers the registration forms, periodic reports, and financial statements required for most variable annuities and life insurance policies funded through separate accounts.

Registration Forms

By regulation, the SEC has adopted forms to be used under the Securities Act of 1933 and the Investment Company Act of 1940. The information required in these forms and in a prospectus includes such items as condensed financial information; general information and history; investment objectives and policies; tax status; directors, officers, and advisory board members; brokerage allocation; custodian; transfer agent and dividend paying agent; investment advisory and other services; general information about the plans; yield quotations; financial statements; principal underwriters; management services; distribution expenses; and other similar information.

Separate accounts must also include the following information: description of the registrant and sponsor, deductions of expenses, general description of variable annuity and life insurance contracts, annuity periods and death benefits, purchases and redemptions, and locations of accounts and records. Each registration form has a specific list of requirements which are applicable to each type of separate account operation.

The following are the most commonly used registration forms:

Form	*Use*
□ Form N-1	This form was designed for use by open-end management companies prior to the adoption of Form N-1A and is prescribed for use by separate accounts selling scheduled premiums or flexible-premium variable life insurance. It was also prescribed for use by variable annuities funded through separate accounts and registered as management investment companies prior to the adoption of Form N-3.
□ Form N-8B-2	This form is used by unit investment trusts and by separate accounts which fund variable life insurance and which are registered as unit investment trusts. It was required for variable annuities funded by a separate account registered as unit investment trusts prior to the adoption of Form N-4.
□ Form N-3	This form is prescribed for use by all separate accounts which fund variable annuity contracts and which are reg-

istered as management investment companies. It is used for all registrations required by the Investment Company Act of 1940 or the Securities Act of 1933.

- □ Form N-4 — This form is prescribed for use by all separate accounts which fund variable annuity contracts registered as unit investment trusts. It is used for all required registrations under the Investment Company Act of 1940 and the Securities Act of 1933.
- □ Form S-1 — This form is prescribed for all registrations under the Securities Act of 1933 for which another form is not required. Separate accounts which fund variable annuity contracts and which are not registered under the Investment Company Act of 1940 are required to use this form. Separate accounts registered only under the Securities Act of 1933 are subject to all the reporting and disclosure requirements applicable to commercial companies.
- □ Form S-6 — This form is prescribed for use by unit investment trusts registered under the Securities Act of 1933 and for separate accounts which fund scheduled or flexible-premium variable life insurance policies and which are registered as unit investment trusts.

Most registration forms contain a prospectus which specifies the information required to be reported. The prospectus (along with additional information and statements) is enclosed separately in the registration statement.

Reporting Requirements

Separate accounts required to file registration statements must also furnish semiannual reports to the SEC and to policyholders.

Securities and Exchange Commission Reports. The semiannual report to the SEC is filed on Form N-SAR. This form replaces N-1R for all separate accounts funding variable annuities and life insurance except those registered as unit investment trusts which file on N-30A-2.

Form N-SAR contains specific sections to be completed by different types of companies, depending upon how they have registered. Unlike form N-1R reports, audited financial statements are not required in the semiannual reports since the annual reports to policyholders, which contain audited financial statements, must also be filed with the SEC. Nor does the required summary financial information need to be reviewed by independent accountants, as was required under previous forms; however, each annual report must include a letter from independent accountants indicating that internal controls are sufficient to provide reasonable assurance that any material inadequacy existing either at the date of the examination or during the year would be disclosed. In addition, Form N-SAR is designed to eliminate the need to repeat items from previous reports where no change has occurred. This form does not eliminate the need to file quarterly reports on Form N-IQ.

Semiannual Reports to Policyholders. All separate accounts registered as a management investment company must furnish semiannual reports to policyholders containing the following information:

- *Balance sheet.* The balance sheet must be accompanied by a statement of the aggregate value of investments on the date of such balance sheet.
- *Securities owned.* This is a list showing the amounts and values of securities owned on the date of the balance sheet.
- *Income statement.* The income statement must cover the period reported on, and individual income or expense items representing more than 5 percent of total income or expense must be itemized separately.
- *Surplus statement.* This statement must itemize each charge or credit to the account which represents more than 5 percent of the total charges or credits during the period.
- *Remuneration paid.* The amounts paid by the company during the period to all directors, advisory board members, and officers must be disclosed in statements.
- *Purchase and sale of securities.* The statements must disclose the aggregate dollar amount of purchases and sales of investment securities, other than government securities, made during the period covered by the report.

Separate accounts registered as unit investment trusts and investing substantially all the assets in securities issued by a management investment company must furnish financial statements of such companies for the same fiscal period.

Separate accounts funding variable annuities and life insurance and filing only under the Securities Act of 1933 are required to file Form 10-K annually with the Securities and Exchange Commission as well as to provide reports to policyholders.

Financial Statement Requirements: Regulation S-X

Regulation S-X contains the form and content and the requirements for financial statements of all companies subject to the Securities Act of 1933, the Securities and Exchange Act of 1934, the Investment Company Act of 1940, and other acts governing the offering and sale of securities.

Special reporting provisions for registered management investment companies and for companies required to be registered as management investment companies include the following financial statements:

- An audited balance sheet or statement of assets and liabilities at the end of the most recent fiscal year
- An audited statement of operations for the most recent fiscal year (including statements of income and expense, realized gains or losses on investments, and unrealized appreciation or depreciation of investments) which must conform to the appropriate company category requirements as specified in Article 6
- Audited statements of changes in net assets for the 2 most recent fiscal years conforming to the requirements specified in Article 6

All types of management investment companies are required to conform to the general rules of Articles 1, 2, 3, and 4 as well as to the rules in Article 6 applicable to each category of the management investment company. Article 1 covers the application of Regulation S-X and the definitions of terms used therein. Article 2 covers the qualifications and reports of accountants. Article 3 covers the general instructions for preparation of financial statements, and Rule 3-18 covers special provisions for companies required to be registered as management investment companies. Article 3A covers the consolidated and combined financial statements. Article 4 covers the rules of general application, including the form, order, and terminology; required general notes to the financial statements; and other rules of general application.

Rules 6-01 to 6-10 are applicable to financial statements for separate accounts registered as management investment companies. These rules describe the elements of the balance sheet, including the disclosures about capital shares and surplus, undistributed net income, accumulated net realized gain or loss on investments, and unrealized appreciation or depreciation of assets. The rules governing the statement of income and expense require a division between income items for cash dividends, interest, and other income and expenses, including the total of management and other service fees of unaffiliated and affiliated persons. All separate income and expense items exceeding 5 percent of the respective totals must be disclosed. Rules 6-05 and 6-06 require the disclosure of realized and unrealized gains and losses on securities as well as of the aggregate costs and proceeds from the sale of investments, showing affiliated and United States government obligations separately. Rule 6-08 requires the separate disclosure of net income, realized gains or losses on investments, increase or decrease of unrealized appreciation or depreciation of assets, securities issued and repurchased, distribution of capital for dividends (both from net income and realized capital gains), and the balance of net assets at the beginning and close of the period.

Separate accounts registering as unit investment trusts must comply with Rules 6-10a to 6-13. Rule 6-11 requires a statement of condition (balance sheet), which discloses the investments in securities and in other assets and liabilities and the title and number of outstanding units applicable to the aggregate policyholders' interest. Rule 6-12 requires a statement of income and distributable funds which includes investment and other income as well as details of expenses relating to management fees, legal and audit fees, and other expenses, with each significant amount stated separately. These amounts are reconciled between the beginning and end of the year for net income, realized gains and losses, and distributions to policyholders.

Rules 6-30 through 6-34 are applicable to employee stock purchases, savings, and similar plans. These rules may also be applicable to separate accounts of those companies preparing reports which are subject to filings made under the Securities Act of 1933.

Additional financial information prepared on the basis of an accumulation unit outstanding throughout the period must disclose the following:

- Investment income
- Expenses
- Net investment income
- Net realized and unrealized gains (losses) on securities
- Net increase (decrease) in accumulation unit value
- Accumulation unit value at the beginning and end of the period
- Expenses and net investment income to average net assets
- Portfolio turnover rate
- Number of accumulation units outstanding at the end of the period

This information must be shown for the current and four preceding periods for reports to policyholders (10 years for registration statements).

Other Registration and Reporting

Life insurance companies are the sponsors of separate accounts and are usually the investment advisors and principal underwriters of these policies.

To qualify as an investment advisor, the company or its designated subsidiary must comply with the reporting and disclosure requirements imposed by the SEC, including furnishing an audited balance sheet in connection with shareholder or participant proxy notification.

If the company or its designated subsidiary is also the principal underwriter of the separate account, its agents must be qualified and licensed as Registered Representatives. In addition, the principal underwriter must comply with the reporting requirements of the Securities and Exchange Act of 1934, including filing an annual report on Form X17A-5 and filing other reports required by such broker-dealers.

Most states have securities laws governing many aspects of the activities and business undertakings of broker-dealers and require periodic reports from them.

22

MERGERS AND ACQUISITIONS

This chapter covers the accounting that is necessary when one business acquires another business. Such acquisitions can be made in a number of ways, and the treatment for each type of acquisition varies for tax and accounting purposes.

GAAP TREATMENT

Under generally accepted accounting principles (GAAP), a business acquisition is accounted for either as a *pooling of interests* or as a *purchase*. If a group of detailed requirements is met, the pooling method must be used. If all the requirements are not met, then the purchase method must be used. The two methods are not alternatives which a company may choose from. One, and only one, method will be applicable to each acquisition. The purchase method is a catchall category which is used only where the pooling method does not apply.

Furthermore, a particular transaction cannot be treated as part pooling and part purchase. It must be all one or the other. However, the acquisition of a minority stock interest in a subsidiary in a later transaction is always accounted for as a purchase, even if the original acquisition of the majority interest was accounted for as a pooling.

On the other hand, transfers between a parent and its wholly owned subsidiary, or between two wholly owned subsidiaries of the same parent, are always accounted for by using the pooling concept.

The basic concept behind pooling is that the accounts of two companies are combined without modification. Prior book values of both entities are carried over to the combined entity. There is no "step-up" or other change in basis. Such treatment is justified where the shareholders of both entities become shareholders of the combined entity and where no shareholders are bought out. Thus, the transaction is more of a change in corporate form than a purchase of stock or assets.

In the case of a purchase, a significant percentage of the former shareholders of the acquired entity are bought out with assets and do not continue as shareholders of the combined entity. Thus, there is more than a mere change in corporate form—since assets have exited from the combined entity and there has been a change in the underlying ownership. In these circumstances, the acquired entity should be accounted for at the value paid for it rather than at the depreciated cost previously carried on the acquired entity's books.

Pooling Method

The pooling method must be used if three groups of requirements are met in full. The requirements pertain to (1) the characteristics of the combined entities, (2) the manner of the acquisition, and (3) the absence of certain planned transactions after the acquisition.

1. *Characteristics.* Prior to the acquisition, both of the entities must have been autonomous and also independent of each other. *Autonomous* means that neither entity was a subsidiary of any other corporation at any time within 2 years before the acquisition. Exceptions to this rule occur when one of the entities was a subsidiary within the 2-year period but was divested pursuant to a government order, or when a triangular merger takes place. A *triangular merger* occurs when one entity merges into a subsidiary of another entity. Such a transaction is not disqualified if the parent of the acquiring subsidiary was not itself the subsidiary of another corporation within the 2-year period.

   Furthermore, as mentioned above, the two combining entities must have been *independent* of each other. This means that on the date of acquisition, neither entity owned more than 10 percent of the outstanding voting common stock of the other entity.

   Exception: As indicated above, transfers not involving outsiders, such as parent-subsidiary or subsidiary-subsidiary transfers within a wholly owned corporate group, are accounted for by the pooling concept.
2. *Manner.* In the acquisition, one entity must exchange solely its own voting common stock for at least 90 percent of the voting common stock of the other entity. The other 10 percent of the acquired entity's stock can be acquired for something other than voting common stock (i.e., cash, property, preferred stock), or need not be acquired at all. Likewise, preferred stock, nonvoting common stock, or debt instruments of the acquired entity may be purchased with cash or property, or need not be acquired at all.

The key requirement, once again, is that voting common stock is exchanged for at least 90 percent of the voting common stock of the acquired entity. Cash or other property can be given up so long as it is not pro rata and so long as no more than 10 percent of the voting common stock is acquired in this manner.

If the acquired entity owns any voting common stock of the acquiring entity prior to the combination, the 90 percent computation becomes more complicated. (This refers to a prior ownership interest of not more than 10 percent; a larger interest would disqualify the transaction for pooling.) In such a situation, the following calculation must be made:

a. Take the number of shares the acquiree holds in the acquiror, and translate this number into an appropriate number of acquiree shares by means of the exchange ratio.
b. Reduce the number of acquiree shares exchanged for the acquiror's voting common stock by the translated number in step (a) above.
c. If the reduced number in step (b) is not at least 90 percent of the outstanding voting common stock of the acquiree, then the transaction does not qualify for pooling.

An example may help to clarify this somewhat confusing computation. Assume the following facts:

- Acquiree has 1000 voting common shares outstanding.
- Acquiree owns 50 shares of acquiror (assumed to be less than a 10 percent interest).
- Acquiror will exchange 1 of its shares for each 2 shares of acquiree. All 1000 acquiree shares will be acquired in this manner.

a. The acquiree's 50 shares in the acquiror are translated by the 2:1 acquiree's exchange ratio into 25 shares of the acquiree.
b. The 25 is subtracted from the 1000 outstanding shares of the acquiree that the acquiror obtained in the exchange.
c. Since the remainder of 975 exceeds 90 percent of the acquiree's 1,000 outstanding shares, the transaction is not disqualified for pooling. However, if the acquiror obtained only 920 shares of the acquiree in exchange for voting common stock, the 920 would be reduced by the 25 translated shares in step (a), giving a remainder of 895. Since this is less than 90 percent of the acquiree's 1000 outstanding shares, the transaction would be disqualified for pooling.

Intercompany holdings also cause computation problems for the acquiror. The number of voting common shares which the acquiror issues in the exchange is reduced by:

a. The number of acquiror shares which are held by the acquiree, and
b. The translated number of shares of the acquiree which are held by the acquiror. This calculation is made by taking the number of acquiree shares held by the acquiror and multiplying it by the ratio of total outstanding acquiree shares over the number of acquiror shares issued in the exchange.

At least 90 percent of the acquiree's voting common shares must be acquired by this reduced number of shares. To elaborate on the previous example, assume that the acquiror already owns 80 shares of the acquiree. Implicit in the facts given is that the acquiror will issue 500 shares in the exchange (1 share for every 2 of the acquiree's 1000 shares). The 500 issued shares would then be reduced by the following amounts:

a. The 50 acquiror shares held by the acquiree.
b. The translated number of acquiree shares held by the acquiror. This is 80 shares multiplied by 1000/500, or 160.

Thus, the reduced number of acquiror shares issued is 500 − 50 − 160, or 290. Since 290 acquiror shares would not obtain 90 percent of the acquiree shares in an exchange, the transaction does not qualify for pooling. However, if the acquiror did not own any acquiree shares (instead of 80), then the 500 shares would be reduced only by the 50 acquiror shares held by the acquiree. The remaining 450 shares would obtain exactly 90 percent of the acquiree shares in the exchange (according to the acquiror's 1:2 exchange ratio), and thus the transaction would barely qualify for pooling as far as the 90 percent rule is concerned.

A further requirement states that the acquisition must be completed within 1 year, unless there is a delay due to governmental action or litigation beyond the control of the combining entities. Acquiree stock obtained either before or after the 1-year period would not count towards the 90 percent requirement.

Finally, the terms of the plan of exchange cannot be altered once it is put into effect, unless earlier exchanges of stock under the plan are adjusted to meet the new terms. Thus, a change in the exchange ratio without a corresponding adjustment for prior exchanges under the plan would disqualify the transaction for pooling. However, no adjustment would be required for intercompany shares obtained before the plan was put into effect.

3. *Absence of certain planned transactions after the acquisition.* To qualify for pooling, requirements must be met which relate not only to the characteristics of the entities and the manner of the combination but also to the conduct of the parties after the acquisition. In particular, the following items must be complied with:
   a. There must be no agreement, direct or indirect, that the acquiror will buy back its shares issued to the acquiree's shareholders. However, the former acquiree shareholders may sell or transfer their acquiror shares to an outside party at any time. Following a pooling acquisition, there is no "continuity-of-interest" rule as there is in the tax law following a tax-free acquisition.
   b. There must be no financial arrangements that negate the nature of the equity interest received by the former acquiree shareholders. For instance, the acquiror cannot guarantee loans for the former acquiree shareholders that are secured by the acquiror stock issued in the exchange. As a practical matter, this would have the effect of transforming the issued shares into debt—and is therefore not permitted.
   c. The acquiror cannot plan to dispose of a significant part of the assets obtained from the acquiree within 2 years after the acquisition. Exceptions are for dispositions in the normal course of business (sale of inventory, rou-

tine retirement of obsolete equipment, etc.), dispositions of duplicate facilities or excess capacity, or dispositions under a government order.

d. Generally, there can be no contingent consideration involved in the acquisition. Thus, additional shares or other consideration cannot be given for postacquisition events such as attaining certain profit levels or reaching a certain security price. However, the number of shares issued may be adjusted where a contingency in existence at the time of the exchange is settled at an amount different from that recorded. The most common example occurs with litigation. If the litigation is concluded for more or less than was recorded at the time of the exchange, the number of shares issued may be revised accordingly. This would not only include litigation where one of the entities is a defendant, but also where one of the entities is a plaintiff.

e. There is no rule that the acquiree be dissolved, or not dissolved, after the exchange. Thus, the acquiree could merge into the acquiror and disappear as a separate entity, or it could continue a separate existence as a subsidiary of the acquiror—or both entities could disappear and be replaced by a new third entity. There is also no requirement as to which corporate entity survives (in the case of a merger) or which is the parent (if a subsidiary remains in existence). Thus, for tax or legal reasons, the smaller corporation could be used as the survivor or as the parent. These factors, by themselves, have no effect on the pooling requirements.

Once the acquisition is determined to qualify for pooling, the next step is to make the proper entries in the accounting records and on the financial statements. As indicated before, the basic principle behind pooling is that existing account balances are simply combined without further modification. Thus, accounting for pooling can be relatively easy. Net incomes of both entities for the whole year are combined, regardless of when the acquisition took place during the year. Thus, even though an acquisition took place on December 31 for two calendar-year entities, there would be only one income statement. This would be issued by the surviving corporation and would combine the income of both entities for the entire calendar year. Likewise, balance sheet accounts would simply be combined. The surviving corporation would issue one balance sheet, and it would reflect not only the "old" assets but also those that were recently acquired.

While in principle this sounds easy, being a mere exercise in arithmetic, in practice there can be complications. First, the acquired entity's books must be placed on the same accounting methods as those used by the acquiror. Thus, if the acquiror uses a last-in–first-out (LIFO) inventory method, the acquiree's books must be restated to reflect LIFO even if the acquiree had previously used a first-in–first-out (FIFO) or some other method. Not only must the combined income statement for the year reflect identical accounting methods, but all balance sheet accounts of the acquiree must also be restated to reflect what they would have been had the acquiree used the acquiror's accounting methods since the acquiree's inception. Also, in the audit report for the current year, if prior years' financial statements are presented for comparative purposes, these prior statements must reflect combined amounts for the acquiree and the acquiror, all restated in accordance with the accounting methods used by the acquiror.

The combined statements, in addition to being made uniform with respect to accounting methods, must also reflect identical accounting periods. This is not a problem where both the acquiror and the acquiree had been on the same fiscal year prior to the acquisition. (If one insurance company acquired another insurance company, then both would of course be on the calendar year.) However, adjustments are necessary if the same years were not previously used: for the year of acquisition, the income statement will show the combined results of both entities, based on the acquiror's year.

For example, suppose that the acquiror was on the calendar year while the acquiree was on a June 30 fiscal year. The acquisition takes place on May 31, 19x5. The calendar-year 19x5 statement for the acquiror reflects the acquiror's operations for 19x5, together with the acquiree's operations from 1/1/x5 to 12/31/x5. The acquiree's operations from 7/1/x4 to 12/31/x4 are disregarded for purposes of the 19x5 income statement. Likewise, the acquiree's operations for 1/1/x5 to 5/31/x5 are included in the acquiror's income statement, even though these months were prior to the acquisition. Where prior years' income statements are presented for comparative purposes, these must also be restated in a similar manner so as to reflect calendar-year reporting for the combined operations.

Whenever combined statements are presented, certain intercompany transactions between the acquiree and the acquiror should be eliminated (even though the transactions took place before the acquisition, when both companies were independent). Intercompany transactions affecting current assets, current liabilities, revenue, cost of sales, and retained earnings should be eliminated to the extent possible. Intercompany transactions involving long-term assets and liabilities may also be eliminated, but this is not required; if these transactions are not eliminated, their nature and their effect on earnings per share shall be disclosed.

Also, any costs of implementing the pooling acquisition must be expensed in the current year for GAAP purposes (but not for tax purposes). These expenses could include securities registration fees, legal expenses, and accounting costs.

In the financial statements for the year of acquisition, a number of items must be disclosed in footnotes. There must be:

- A description of the enterprises combined.
- A reference to the pooling-of-interests method of accounting for the acquisition.
- Details about the number and types of shares involved in the exchange.
- Details of the results of operations of the separate entities for the period from the beginning of the acquiror's year to the date of the acquisition. The details should include revenue, extraordinary items, net income, changes in stockholder's equity, and the amount and nature of intercompany transactions. The separate information may be as of the end of the interim reporting period nearest the date of the acquisition.
- A summary of the accounting practices of the combined entity, and a summary of the adjustments made to the acquiree's books in order to bring the accounting methods into uniformity.

- □ The effect on retained earnings from changing the fiscal year of the acquiree. The details of this should include revenue, expenses, extraordinary items, net income, and other changes in stockholder's equity for any part of the acquiree's last year which is excluded from the combined income statement for the year of acquisition. (This is not required where both entities were previously using the same fiscal year.)
- □ A reconciliation of revenues and earnings between the combined enterprise, and the acquiror on a separate basis, as if no acquisition had taken place.

Purchase Method

As previously mentioned, the purchase method is to be used in all business acquisitions to which the pooling method does not apply. Since the use of the purchase method is defined in this negative sense, there is no checklist of requirements that must be met in order to qualify for the purchase method. The purchase method is simply used whenever an acquisition does not meet *all* of the requirements for pooling.

Once the purchase method is determined to be applicable to an acquisition, the next step is to set up the proper accounting treatment. Unlike pooling, which conceptually consists of nothing more than a combining of previously existing amounts, the purchase method causes the previous account balances of the acquiree to disappear and to be replaced by completely new balances, which are based on an allocated amount of the total purchase price.

Thus, the first step is to determine the total purchase price. This consists of the sum of the following items:

1. The cash paid to the sellers.
2. The fair market value of stock, notes, or other property transferred to the sellers. The value of stock can be determined by appraisal, unless there is a quoted market price that is appropriate in light of the number of shares transferred and of any restrictions on the shares.

   The value of the debt obligations transferred to the seller is their face amount if the stated interest rate reflects currently prevailing interest rates for similar instruments. If the stated rate is different, then the scheduled payments must be discounted to the present at a fair rate in order to determine the value; in this situation, the cost of the company acquired is debited for the present value of the debt instrument, a liability account is credited for the face amount, and any difference is recorded as a premium or discount. (See Chapter 5, Investments in Securities, for a discussion of how the premium or discount is amortized in future years.)

   The fair value of other property transferred can be determined by appraisal. The use of book values would not be appropriate unless they approximated market values or unless the amounts were immaterial.
3. The present value of any liabilities assumed in the transaction. This may differ from the face amount of the liabilities where currently prevailing interest rates differ from the face rate for instruments of similar risk and duration. In such a situation, the payments due must be discounted back to the present at

the current fair rate. The cost of the company acquired is then debited for the present value of the liability, a liability account is credited for the face value, and the difference is recorded as Deferred Interest Receivable. The application of this requirement calls for judgment, and a present-value adjustment generally would not be made where it is immaterial. This could occur where the fair rate is relatively close to the face rate, or where the duration of the liability is short (i.e., trade payables). A 2 percent difference between the face rate and current rates on a $10,000 debt might not be significant, but even a 1 percent difference could be significant for a $10 million liability.

4. The direct expenses incurred in relation to the acquisition. These could include costs for legal, accounting, underwriting, and investigative services. (This is different from the pooling method, for which such expenditures are considered to be current expenses rather than a component of asset cost.) However, indirect or general expenses—those which would be incurred regardless of whether the acquisition took place—are treated as current expenses and are not included in the asset cost.

If for some reason it is more difficult to value the property surrendered than the property received, then the value of the property received may be used as the cost figure. This might occur where the acquiror transfers stock which is not publicly traded in exchange for stock that is publicly traded (and the transaction does not qualify for pooling). In most situations, though, it will be at least as easy to determine the value surrendered. and therefore that amount is used as the cost.

Contingent consideration may also affect the total cost. If the amount of contingent consideration is reasonably determinable at the balance sheet date, it shall be included in the cost at that time; otherwise, the contingent consideration shall be disclosed in footnotes to the financial statements for that year. Disclosure would continue in future years until the consideration were either paid or the obligation appeared to have lapsed.

Contingent consideration which is later paid, and which is based on earnings reaching a certain level, is recorded as an additional cost of acquisition. Generally, this additional cost is added to goodwill and amortized over the remaining life of the goodwill. However, if the previously recorded acquisition cost was less than the fair market value of the acquired assets, the additional cost would result in a proportionate restatement of all noncurrent asset values.

On the other hand, contingent consideration based on security prices does not change the total acquisition cost. When paid, such contingent consideration is recorded at its fair market value, but the consideration issued is written down by a corresponding amount.

Where contingent securities are held by an escrow agent, any dividends or interest amounts paid on those securities are not added to the acquisition cost until such time as the securities are transferred to the seller.

Tax effects may also affect the total acquisition cost. The tax savings from deducting imputed interest on contingent consideration reduce the total cost where the contingency is based on earnings. Where the contingency is based on security prices, capital is increased by the tax savings. (Note that contingent consideration paid more than 1 year after the exchange will almost always give rise to imputed interest for tax purposes under section 483; however, there would be no imputed interest for GAAP purposes).

If the acquired entity has tax loss or credit carryforwards, the tax benefits from these carryforwards are used to reduce goodwill when the benefits are realized. If the amount of goodwill is not sufficient to absorb these benefits, the values of all other noncurrent assets (other than marketable securities) would be reduced proportionately.

Once the total acquisition cost is determined, the next step is to allocate the total cost among the individual assets acquired. First, each of the tangible and specific intangible assets (those intangibles which can be bought and sold separately) is assigned an amount equal to its fair market value (which may differ from its prior book value). Any excess of the total price over the sum of the individual values is then assigned to goodwill, which is amortized over 40 years or less.

In some situations, however, the total acquisition cost will be less than the sum of the individual fair market values. In these circumstances, there is no goodwill, and the values of all noncurrent assets (other than marketable securities) are reduced proportionately until the sum of the individual amounts equals the total cost. If noncurrent assets other than marketable securities are reduced to zero and the total cost still exceeds the value of the remaining assets, the difference is recorded as a deferred credit and amortized over a period of 40 years or less.

For a complete discussion of accounting for goodwill and other intangibles obtained in an acquisition, see Chapter 9, Goodwill and Other Intangibles.

TAX TREATMENT

For tax purposes, mergers and acquisitions may be classified into two categories: taxable and nontaxable. In a broad sense, nontaxable transactions may be thought of as roughly comparable to GAAP pooling, and taxable acquisitions may be compared to the purchase method. However, multitudinous rules and variations often make the tax treatment much more complex and in many ways different than the GAAP treatment. Under some circumstances, a GAAP pooling transaction may be taxable, and a GAAP purchase transaction may be nontaxable. What follows is a general overview of the tax principles; a complete discussion would fill a whole volume.

Nontaxable Transactions

In the area of nontaxable corporate reorganizations, there are several subcategories: acquisitions, liquidations, separations, and section 351 transfers (transfers to a controlled corporation). Each in turn has several variations, as described in the following:

Acquisitions. There are basically five types of tax-free corporate acquisitions. All five are contained in section 368 of the Internal Revenue Code:

1. *Type A.* This is a merger or consolidation performed in accordance with state law. In the case of a merger, the acquiror transfers its own stock and possibly

other property to the acquiree's shareholders, who surrender all of their stock. The acquiree corporation then goes out of existence, and all of its assets and liabilities are now held by the acquiror. A consolidation is similar to a merger, except that both the acquiror and the acquiree go out of existence and are replaced by a new corporate entity which succeeds to all assets and liabilities of the former corporation.

To qualify for Type A tax-free treatment, at least 50 percent of the consideration going to the acquiree shareholders must consist of acquiror stock. The test is made on an aggregate basis, not on an individual shareholder basis; thus, some shareholders could receive only stock and others only cash, so long as at least 50 percent of the total is stock. The stock used need not be voting common stock alone; it could be preferred or nonvoting stock. However, the recipients of stock must plan to continue as acquiror shareholders and cannot immediately dispose of their stock after the acquisition; this is known as the *continuity-of-interest* requirement and differs from pooling, since for GAAP purposes the stock can be transferred immediately, so long as the transfer is to an outside party. Also, there must be a *business purpose* for the acquisition; this requirement is relatively easy to satisfy since any substantial nontax motive—such as financial, legal, marketing, or administrative—will usually suffice. Finally, there must be a *continuity of enterprise,* which means that the acquiror must either continue at least one of the acquiree's historical lines of business or use a significant amount of the acquiree's historical assets in a postacquisition business. One of the reasons for this requirement was to reduce the number of tax-motivated mergers of operating businesses into mutual funds which would then dispose of the business.

2. *Type B.* Here, the acquiror obtains at least 80 percent of each class of acquiree stock solely in exchange for acquiror voting stock (or stock of a corporation controlling the acquiror). After the acquisition, the acquiree continues to exist as a subsidiary of the acquiror. Note that no cash or other property can be used in acquiring the requisite 80 percent of the acquiree; only voting stock may be given. The other 20 percent can be obtained for cash or other property, but only if the transaction is separate and unrelated.

   As with a Type A acquisition, the continuity-of-interest, continuity-of-enterprise, and business purpose requirements apply. There can be no prearranged plan for the former acquiree shareholders to dispose of their new acquiror stock.

3. *Type C.* Here the acquiror obtains "substantially all" of the acquiree's assets in exchange for acquiror voting stock (or stock of a corporation controlling the acquiror). The corporate shell of the acquiree is not obtained —only its assets and liabilities. *Substantially all* of the assets is defined as 70 percent of the gross assets and 90 percent of the net assets (assets less liabilities). Note that in determining whether the exchange is for acquiror voting stock, the assumption of acquiree liabilities is permitted. Furthermore, a special rule permits cash or other property to be given to the acquiree shareholders. However, *if* any cash or other property is so given, then the cash or other property, *plus the assumed liabilities,* cannot exceed 20 percent of the total consideration given. But if no cash or other property is given, then the assumed liabilities

are not subject to the 20 percent limit. Again, the continuity-of-interest, continuity-of-enterprise, and business purpose requirements apply.

4. *Type (a)(2)(D)*. This is a "triangular" merger of the acquiree into a subsidiary of the acquiror. The subsidiary must obtain substantially all of the acquiree assets (as defined above), and the acquiree's shareholders receive acquiror stock and possibly other property. The acquiror stock need not be voting, but as with a Type A merger, the stock must constitute at least 50 percent of the total consideration. The continuity-of-interest, continuity-of-enterprise, and business purpose requirements also apply.
5. *Type (a)(2)(E)*. This is a "reverse triangular" merger in which the acquiree mergers into a subsidiary of the acquiror but in which the acquiree, rather than the first subsidiary, survives the merger to continue as a subsidiary of the acquiror. After the merger, the acquiree must hold substantially all of its former assets, together with the assets of the disappearing first subsidiary. The former shareholders of the acquiree must have exchanged at least 80 percent of each class of acquiree stock in exchange solely for voting stock of the acquiror's parent, as with the Type B acquisition. The continuity-of-interest, continuity-of-enterprise, and business purpose requirements also apply.

Liquidations. Under section 332 of the Internal Revenue Code, a subsidiary in which the parent owns at least 80 percent of each class of stock (other than nonvoting preferred) may be liquidated into the parent on a tax-free basis if several requirements are met: First, there must be a plan of liquidation; second, the liquidation must be complete; and third, the liquidation must be completed within 3 years from the close of the taxable year in which the first liquidating distribution is made (assuming that the complete liquidation is taking place in stages).

Transfers under Section 351. Transfers may be made on a tax-free basis to a corporation in which the transferors own at least 80 percent of each class of stock immediately after the transfer.

The most common example of this occurs when a new corporation is formed. The incorporators can generally avoid taxes on property transferred to the new corporation at its inception since they will own 100 percent of the corporation immediately afterwards.

Section 351 can also apply to transfers to existing corporations. For instance, a parent may transfer property to its wholly owned subsidiary. Note, however, that tax-free treatment does not apply to transfers to an investment company, to stock issued for services, or (under certain circumstances) to transfers of liabilities to the new corporation.

The continuity-of-interest requirement also applies to section 351. Thus, tax-free treatment may be unavailable if the shareholders have a prearranged plan to dispose of their stock after the transfer.

Separations. If certain requirements contained in section 355 are met, the assets of a single corporation can be divided among two or more corporations on a tax-free basis. The separation can take the form of a spin-off, a split-up, or a split-off.

A *spin-off* consists of transferring a line of business to a new corporation and then distributing the stock in that new corporation to the shareholders of the first corporation on a pro rata basis.

A *split-up* consists of dividing all the assets of a corporation between two new corporations, and then distributing the stock of the new corporations to the shareholders of the first corporation on a pro rata basis. The first corporation then goes out of existence.

A *split-off* consists of the transfer of a line of business to a new corporation, as with a spin-off, but the stock of the new corporation is not distributed pro rata. Instead, one group of shareholders surrenders its stock in the first corporation in exchange for all of the stock in the new corporation. Thus, the original shareholder group is separated into two groups: one owning all of the first corporation, and one owning all of the new corporation.

To qualify for a tax-free separation, each of the corporations in existence after the separation must own a complete, active line of business which was owned by the first corporation for at least 5 years prior to the separation (or which was acquired within 5 years in a tax-free transaction). The active-line-of-business requirement is somewhat nebulous, but generally the operation should include the functions of (1) purchasing or production, (2) sales, and (3) collection of receivables. Mere investment assets would not constitute an active line of business. Furthermore, the continuity-of-interest and business purpose requirements apply to corporate separations.

Basis Determination. In any type of tax-free corporate reorganization (acquisition, liquidation, separation, or section 351 transfer), the carryover of prior book values is similar to that for the GAAP pooling method. Thus, any assets involved in a tax-free reorganization retain the same tax basis after the reorganization as that which they had before the reorganization, even though a different corporation may hold the assets.

Taxable Transactions

Any corporate acquisition which does not qualify for some type of nontaxable category as described above is a *taxable transaction*. Again, the purchase/pooling analogy continues. There are no specific requirements that must be met in order to qualify for a taxable transaction. The specific requirements apply to nontaxable transactions—and if the requirements are not met, the transaction simply becomes taxable.

A taxable transaction can take the form of an asset acquisition or a stock acquisition. Where assets are acquired, the assets take on a new tax basis equal to the total cost of the acquisition, which consists of:

1. The cash paid.
2. The face amount of notes issued to the seller. However, if the interest rate on the notes is less than the minimum rate required by the IRS under section 483, then the note is discounted for imputed interest. Under current regulations, if at least 9 percent is not charged, a 10 percent rate will be imputed (rates are changed periodically). Imputed interest would reduce the amount of the notes for purposes of calculating the cost of the acquisition.

3. The face value of liabilities assumed. Unlike the GAAP purchase method, the face amounts of liabilities are not adjusted, regardless of interest rates.
4. The fair market value of stock or other property transferred, unless the other property is of a *like-kind* nature (property exchanged for other property of a similar type). In the latter situation, a basis carryover may apply instead of the fair market value.
5. Legal, accounting, underwriting, and similar expenses connected with the acquisition.
6. Contingent consideration issued in the form of cash, notes, or other property. If the contingent consideration is payable more than 1 year after the acquisition, then the amount is discounted for imputed interest under section 483 as previously discussed.

Once the total cost of the acquisition is determined, it must then be allocated to the individual assets acquired in proportion to their fair market values. However, cash and cash equivalents receive a face amount basis, while receivables are never allocated a basis in excess of face value (although less than face could be allocated). This allocation thus differs from that under the GAAP purchase method, in which the assets receive a basis *equal* to fair market value, with any excess going to goodwill. For tax purposes, though, the allocation is made *in proportion* to fair market values. Goodwill can be separately appraised instead of simply receiving the excess of the purchase price over the values of the other assets. The result is that where the total price exceeds the sum of individual market values, the individual assets will receive a basis in excess of market value. Of course, if the total price is less than the sum of the individual market values, then all assets other than cash and equivalents will receive a basis of less than market value. (Unlike as for the GAAP purchase method, all assets other than cash and equivalents would be reduced, not just the noncurrent assets.) For a complete discussion of how goodwill and other intangibles would be valued in an acquisition, see Chapter 9, Goodwill and Other Intangibles.

Where the stock of a corporation is acquired instead of assets, the stock will normally take on a basis equal to the total cost of the acquisition, as defined above. The assets held by the acquired corporation would continue to retain their former tax basis without any change because of the acquisition. However, an election can be made under section 338 to change this outcome, and such an election is usually made where the purchase price exceeds the net book value of the acquired company's assets. The basic principle of such an election is that the assets of the acquired corporation receive a new tax basis equal to what the basis would be if assets were acquired instead of stock. In other words, the formality of acquiring stock is disregarded for this tax purpose and the transaction is treated as an asset acquisition. The total purchase price of the stock would then be allocated among the individual assets as was discussed in the preceding paragraph (except that a special adjustment is necessary if less than 100 percent of the acquiree stock was received). The reason that the election is usually made is to obtain a basis for depreciable assets which is higher than the book value carried by the acquired company.

To qualify for a section 338 election, the acquiror must obtain at least 80 percent of each class of acquiree stock (other than nonvoting preferred) by "purchase" within a 12-month period. *Purchase* basically means a taxable transaction with an unrelated party. An acquisition of a corporation from a related party would not generally qualify. In addition, the acquiror must file an election statement with the IRS within 75 days after the 80 percent threshold is reached. Acquisitions of the other 20 percent of the acquiree stock may take place outside of the 12-month period, but at least 80 percent must be obtained within any 12-month period (this 12-month period can overlap 2 taxable years).

Section 338 is the successor provision to the well-known section 334(b)(2) liquidation, which no longer applies. Under section 338, though, a liquidation of the acquiree is not required. But similar to section 334(b)(2), if a section 338 election is made, depreciation and investment credit recaptures will be incurred on the deemed sale of the assets.

23

SUBSIDIARY COMPANIES

The existence of a parent-subsidiary relationship creates some special accounting considerations. These include consolidated financial statements, intercompany transactions, carrying values, dividends, and the equity method of accounting for earnings. Each of these considerations is treated differently for generally accepted accounting principles (GAAP), tax, and statutory purposes.

GAAP PRINCIPLES

The GAAP rules governing parent-subsidiary relationships are usually triggered by a 20 percent ownership interest in another company, and sometimes by an even smaller percentage. An ownership interest ranging from 20 to 50 percent will generally cause the equity method to be used; an interest in excess of 50 percent will usually cause consolidated financial statements to be required.

Under the equity method, income statements are not combined, but the parent generally reports its percentage share of the subsidiary's earnings (whether distributed or not) as a single item of income or loss. Likewise, balance sheets are not combined, but the parent's ownership interest in the subsidiary is shown as an investment asset on the parent's balance sheet.

In contrast, under the consolidated method all the individual accounts of both entities are combined, with certain adjustments. The income statement is combined on an account-by-account basis rather than showing the subsidiary's net income or loss as a single lump-sum item. Similarly, the balance sheet is combined on an account-by-account basis rather than showing a single item for the investment in the subsidiary. When combining the subsidiary accounts with the parent's, the subsidiary is treated as if it were wholly owned. For example, 100 percent of the subsidiary's revenue is combined with the parent's revenue, even if the parent owns only 65 percent of the subsidiary.

To correct for this overbooking of subsidiary accounts, however, when the subsidiary is not wholly owned, an adjustment is made for the minority interest. On the income statement, the portion of the subsidiary's net income attributable to minority shareholders is shown as a single negative item just above the bottom-line consolidated net income. On the balance sheet, the portion of the subsidiary's equity attributable to the minority shareholders is shown as a separate item in the equity section or as a liability.

EQUITY METHOD

Requirements

The equity method must be used where the parent's investment in the voting stock of another corporation "gives it the ability to exercise significant influence over operating and financial policies" of the second corporation. This is really the only guideline, but there are various objective and subjective criteria to be used in interpreting the language of this rule. (In the following discussion, *parent* will denote the investor corporation and *subsidiary* the investee corporation, even if 50 percent control in the legal sense is lacking.)

The objective criterion is the rebuttable presumption that the parent has "significant influence" if it owns (directly or indirectly) 20 percent or more of a corporation's voting stock. For these purposes, only stock that has present voting rights is considered. Potential voting privileges which may be obtained through the exercise of options or the occurrence of a contingency are disregarded (even though they may be taken into account for earnings-per-share or other purposes). It does not matter whether the voting stock is common or preferred; thus, nonvoting common stock would be ignored just as would nonvoting preferred. There is no definition of exactly what an "indirect" interest would include for purposes of the 20 percent calculation. Stock held by a nominee for the benefit of the parent would seem to be included, and stock held by another subsidiary of the parent which is over 50 percent controlled probably also would be included. Other situations would be a gray area requiring the use of judgment.

As mentioned above, the 20 percent guideline is a rebuttable presumption of significant influence. While the presumption would usually be upheld, there are some situations in which an interest larger than 20 percent would still not constitute significant influence. Likewise, there could be situations in which an interest of less than 20 percent would nonetheless constitute significant influence.

To determine whether a departure from the 20 percent guideline is justified, subjective indications of influence should be considered. These include the extent of the parent's representation on the subsidiary's board of directors; the parent's participating in policymaking; large intercompany transactions; overlap of managers; and technological dependency on the parent. Also, the size of the parent's stock interest should be compared to that of other ownership blocks. Thus, even though the parent owns 25 percent, if an outside shareholder owns 60 percent of the subsidiary, there is a good chance that the parent does not have significant influence. However, the existence of other large blocks of stock, or even of a block exceeding 50 percent, does not automatically preclude the use of the equity method. An examination would have to be made as to whether the other shareholders in fact control the subsidiary without regard to the views of the parent.

Other circumstances which may indicate that a larger-than-20 percent interest is not significant influence include:

1. Opposition to the parent by the subsidiary through litigation, complaints to government agencies, or similar tactics
2. A shareholder agreement which limits the voting or corporate rights of the parent
3. The inability of the parent to obtain that financial information from the subsidiary which is needed to compute the equity method
4. Unsuccessful attempts by the parent to obtain representation on the subsidiary's board of directors

The above list is not all-inclusive, and there could be other subjective factors which may cause the 20 percent guideline to be disregarded. Of course, the mere existence of one or more of these factors does not automatically override the 20 percent guideline. Professional judgment must be used to weigh the importance of each item.

Income Statement

As indicated above, under the equity method the parent records its percentage share of the subsidiary's net income. This statement sounds simple, but many complexities can arise from its interpretation.

First, the net income of the subsidiary must be determined. Ideally, the determination is made as if the subsidiary was on the parent's fiscal year, even though the subsidiary may use a different year for its own accounting purposes. However, this is often burdensome, so Accounting Principles Board (APB) opinion

18 allows the parent to use the most recently available subsidiary financial statements so long as the lag in reporting is consistent from year to year. For instance, suppose that the parent is on the calendar year but that the subsidiary is on a May 31 fiscal year. For purposes of applying the equity method, the ideal solution would be to reconstruct the subsidiary's income statement as if it was on the calendar year as well and then to apply the parent's ownership percentage to this figure. Indeed, this may be possible where the subsidiary prepares accurate monthly financial statements, or where the subsidiary's quarter-end coincides with the parent's year-end. But in our example, it would be impractical to do this unless the subsidiary has reliable monthly statements. Furthermore, the quarterly statements prepared by the subsidiary would not match the calendar year since the subsidiary's quarters end on August 31, November 30, February 28, and May 31. In this situation, the parent would be allowed to use the subsidiary's net income for the 12 months ended November 30 in applying the equity method, so long as this pattern was followed every year. The parent could not switch the subsidiary's computation period back and forth between November 30 and another quarter-end.

In addition, the subsidiary's net income must be computed with the elimination of intercompany profits and losses. A full discussion of intercompany eliminations may be found in the discussion of GAAP consolidated financial statements. Also, all declared preferred stock dividends, together with undeclared dividends on cumulative preferred shares, are subtracted in computing the subsidiary's net income. (Of course, preferred dividends paid in the form of stock would be disregarded.) In all other respects, the subsidiary's net income would be that which is computed in conformity with normal GAAP rules.

The next step is to determine the parent's share of this net income. This is based on the parent's ownership of common stock divided by the total number of subsidiary common shares. Note that, unlike the 20 percent guideline calculation discussed above, *both voting and nonvoting* common shares are included in this computation. Excluded from the computation are preferred shares (whether voting, nonvoting, or convertible), stock options, stock warrants, and convertible debt.

If the parent's ownership percentage fluctuates during the year, the computation becomes more complicated. The parent cannot simply use its year-end percentage in such a situation. Instead, the parent's varying ownership throughout the year must be applied to the subsidiary's actual earnings for that portion of the year. Thus, if the parent's percentage went from 20 to 40 percent at the midpoint of the year, the parent would record 20 percent of the subsidiary's net income for the first 6 months and 40 percent of the subsidiary's earnings for the last 6 months. In most situations, of course, changes of ownership do not conveniently occur at the midpoint of the year. Where it is impractical to determine the subsidiary's actual earnings between ownership changes, the net income may be estimated in an appropriate manner, such as on a pro rata basis if the earnings are fairly level throughout the year.

Where the parent is using the equity method and then its ownership percentage drops below 20 percent (and subjective factors do not give the parent substantial influence even though it owns less than 20 percent), the parent must discontinue using the equity method unless or until its percentage again reaches 20 percent. The subsidiary's net income would be estimated up to the date that the parent's share dropped below 20 percent, and the parent would record its share of that amount. After that date, the parent would account for its investment by the cost method, using as a starting point the carrying value at the time the ownership interest went below 20 percent. The cost method would be applied only on a prospective basis, and the application of the equity method up to that point would not be disturbed. Future dividends would be recorded as income to the extent of the parent's share of the subsidiary earnings since the cost method was started. Dividends in excess of this would not be recorded as income but would be used to reduce the investment account. Losses or undistributed earnings of the subsidiary would not be recorded by the parent.

Where the parent is not using the equity method and goes over the 20 percent guideline, or subjective factors give it substantial influence, then the approach is different. A retroactive calculation is made. Basically, the account balances and financial statements are restated *as if* the equity method had been used since the first acquisition of common stock in the subsidiary, no matter how small. In other words, once substantial influence (generally 20 percent) is obtained, then the financial results for the time previous to this point are recomputed on the assumption that substantial influence existed all along, even when the parent had only a 1 percent interest or less in the subsidiary.

To illustrate this concept, suppose that the parent acquired 5 percent on 1/1/x1, an additional 10 percent on 1/1/x2, and 10 percent more on 1/1/x3. The subsidiary is on the calendar year, has a net income of $100,000 annually, and pays $40,000 in dividends each year. In its original financial statements for 19x1, the parent would show dividend income of $2000 (5 percent × $40,000) and would show $6000 of dividend income for 19x2 (15 percent × $40,000). Since the parent went over 20 percent on 1/1/x3, it would use the equity method and show income of $25,000 for that year (25 percent × $100,000). In addition, the accounts would be restated to reflect the use of the equity method for 19x1 and 19x2 as well. Thus, an additional $3000 of income would be picked up for 19x1 (5 percent × $100,000, less $2000 of dividends already reported) and an additional $9000 for 19x2 (15 percent × $100,000, less $6000 of dividends already reported). These corrected figures would be shown on any 19x1 or 19x2 income statements included for comparative purposes in reports for 19x3 or later years. Also, the investment account and retained earnings would be restated to reflect the use of the equity method since 19x1.

The parent's share of subsidiary earnings is ordinarily shown as a single line item on the income statement. However, the parent's share of subsidiary extraordinary items or prior-period adjustments is shown separately, unless immaterial to the parent.

The parent's share of subsidiary losses is usually reported in the same manner as is a share of positive income. However, the parent will ordinarily discontinue reporting losses after they exceed the carrying value of the subsidiary stock (common and preferred) plus net advances to the subsidiary. Exceptions to the nonreporting of excess losses occur where the parent has guaranteed debts for the subsidiary, where the parent is otherwise committed to provide additional funds to the subsidiary (perhaps by stock subscription agreements or lines of credit), or where an imminent return to profitable operations by the subsidiary seems certain (such as where the loss is due to a nonrecurring event). Where one of these exceptions does not apply and excess losses are not reported, future net income of the subsidiary is not reported, either, until the excess losses are first absorbed.

The parent's income statement can also be affected by a number of subsidiary items other than the share of net income. A permanent decline in the value of the subsidiary stock below its carrying value would be recorded as a loss. "A permanent decline in value" is a subjective concept and would depend on such factors as the parent's ability to recover the carrying value and the subsidiary's future earnings capacity. Dividends paid by the subsidiary are generally not taken into income, but instead reduce the carrying value of the investment. However, dividends are recorded as income in certain instances. These include preferred dividends received, undeclared dividends on cumulative preferred, and dividends in excess of the carrying value.

Balance Sheet

Handling the balance sheet under the equity method is easy once the income statement amounts are determined. The starting point is the adjusted cost of the subsidiary common stock at the time the equity method is adopted. The investment account is adjusted upward for the parent's share of subsidiary net income after that date, together with any further purchases of common stock or contributions to capital. The investment account is adjusted downward for the parent's share of subsidiary losses, common stock dividends, permanent declines in value, and sales or redemptions of common stock.

The common stock investment is generally shown as a single line item in long-term assets. Other types of investments in the subsidiary are accounted for separately—for instance, preferred stock, warrants, options, notes, or bonds.

Disclosures

A parent which uses the equity method must make a number of disclosures in its financial statements. The extent of disclosure depends in part on the materiality of the equity in the subsidiary compared to the parent. Where there is more than one subsidiary, disclosures on a combined basis may be considered. The following items should generally be disclosed:

1. The name of the subsidiary and the percentage of common stock held.
2. The name of any corporation in which the parent owns over 20 percent but does not use the equity (or consolidated) method, together with the name of any corporation in which the parent owns less than 20 percent but does use the equity method. The reasons for deviating from the 20 percent guideline should be given.
3. The manner of accounting for the investment in the subsidiaries described in items 1 or 2—i.e., the equity method, the consolidated method, or the cost method.

4. The difference between the carrying value of any subsidiary and the parent's percentage of the subsidiary's underlying equity, and how such difference is handled for accounting purposes.
5. The quoted market price, if available, of the subsidiary stock (other than one which is over 50 percent controlled).
6. If unconsolidated subsidiaries over 50 percent controlled are material on a combined basis, then summarized data on assets, liabilities and net income should be presented for such corporations.
7. The possible effect on the parent's reported share of subsidiary income or loss from the potential exercise of outstanding warrants, options, or convertible securities. Although this contingent effect is disclosed, as noted earlier, it is not recorded in the accounts.

CONSOLIDATED METHOD

As mentioned earlier, the consolidated method generally produces the same amount of subsidiary income or loss recognition as the equity method does. The differences between the two methods occur in the manner of presentation and in the amount of detail shown. Whereas the equity method reflects the ownership of the subsidiary in only a single line item on the parent's income statement and balance sheet, the consolidated method basically causes the parent and subsidiary amounts to be combined on an account-by-account basis, with certain adjustments. For instance, where the parent's balance sheet shows the Cash balance, under the equity method this is the parent's cash balance only, but under the consolidated method this is the balance of both parent and subsidiary put together. Likewise, where the parent's income statement shows Gross Revenues, under the equity method this is the parent's revenues only, but under the consolidated method this is the revenue for both companies.

Of course, a mere combining of accounts will cause distortions where the subsidiary is not wholly owned by the parent. If no further adjustment was made, the parent would in effect be claiming the benefit of *all* the subsidiary's assets and earnings, when in fact the parent owns only a percentage of these and outside shareholders own the remainder. Thus, a single line item on the income statement and the balance sheet contains the adjustment necessary to reflect the minority interest in the subsidiary's equity and earnings. Although the Cash balance shows *all* of the subsidiary's cash, the minority interest in cash and other assets (net of the minority interest in liabilities) would appear as a negative (debit) item above the equity section of the consolidated balance sheet. On the income statement, Gross Revenues would continue to show all of the subsidiary's revenues, but the minority interest in net earnings would appear as a negative (debit) item near the bottom of the income statement, just above Consolidated Net Income, which is the total net income less the minority interest.

Qualification

The basic requirement for consolidation is that the parent own, directly or indirectly, over 50 percent of the outstanding voting stock of the subsidiary. The definition of *voting stock* is the same as for the equity method: it does not matter whether the voting stock is common or preferred, and options, warrants, convertible securities, and nonvoting common shares are excluded.

There are certain circumstances in which consolidation is not appropriate even if over 50 percent of the voting stock is owned. However, consolidation is never appropriate where the parent does not own over 50 percent. (This is unlike the equity method, which may be used under certain circumstances even if the ownership is below 20 percent.)

The circumstances in which consolidation *might* not be appropriate even with over 50 percent ownership include:

1. Control by the parent is likely to be only temporary—for instance, where the subsidiary is about to be sold.
2. The parent does not have control because of a bankruptcy or similar proceeding.
3. The minority interest is so large, in relation to the consolidated equity, that separate statements would be more meaningful than a consolidated one. An example of this might be where the parent has a negative equity by itself and the subsidiary has a large positive equity. If both the parent's deficit and the minority interest were large enough, it is even conceivable that the value of the minority interest could constitute over half of the combined equities. Obviously, consolidation probably would not be meaningful in these circumstances.
4. One of the entities is a special type of enterprise that is incompatible with the other entities. For instance, it would not be particularly meaningful to consolidate a bank or an insurance company with a manufacturing enterprise. In fact, such consolidated statements could be positively misleading, and separate statements would be better. On the other hand, consolidating a bank or insurance company with another type of financial entity might be appropriate. Note that a captive leasing company (one whose primary customer is the parent) should always be consolidated with the parent.
5. The subsidiary is in a foreign country, and exchange controls, instability, or other serious problems make it prudent to exclude the subsidiary. For instance, it would be misleading to combine a parent's inadequate working capital with a subsidiary's excessive working capital if the latter could not be repatriated.

The above list is not all-inclusive, and there may be other factors which make consolidation inappropriate. On the other hand, the mere presence of one or more of these factors does not automatically make consolidation improper. Professional judgment must be applied to weigh and evaluate all of the circumstances. The primary objective in such an evaluation should be to make the financial statements as meaningful as possible. If consolidation is more informative, then it should be done, assuming that over 50 percent of the vote is controlled. If separate statements would be more informative, then this option should be chosen. The above-listed factors are merely items to consider and should not be applied in a mechanical or mindless manner.

Where there is a foreign subsidiary, the following four alternatives should be considered in addition to the ordinary consolidated treatment:

1. To consolidate domestic subsidiaries only, and to disclose in the financial statements summary information about foreign subsidiaries. The summary should include assets, liabilities, net income or loss, and the parent's equity in the subsidiary (and how this was determined). If prior foreign earnings are included in the consolidated retained earnings, this amount should be noted. Even though the foreign entity is not consolidated, intercompany eliminations shall still be made as if it were consolidated.
2. To consolidate both foreign and domestic subsidiaries, and also to furnish the summary information in alternative 1 above.
3. To present two sets of consolidated statements: one including both foreign and domestic subsidiaries, and one with domestic subsidiaries only.
4. To include foreign subsidiaries in the consolidation, and also to furnish parent company financial statements showing the investments in and income from foreign subsidiaries separate from domestic subsidiaries.

Procedure

The simplest and most common method of preparing consolidated statements is to use columnar paper. The left-hand side shows the account titles, and then there is a separate column for the trial balance amounts of each entity. Then there is an Eliminations column, and finally a Consolidated column. The Consolidated column consists of the sum of the separate entity columns, less amounts in the Eliminations column.

As with the equity method, it is easiest if all the entities have the same accounting year. However, the lack of a uniform year does not make consolidation inappropriate. Often, a trial balance for a subsidiary can be converted from a different year to the parent's year through the use of interim or monthly financial statements. If this is not practical, and the subsidiary's year-end is within 3 months of the parent's year-end, then the results for the subsidiary's regular year-end may be used. The treatment, however, must be consistent from year to year—it would not be acceptable to change back and forth between the subsidiary's year-end and subsidiary amounts converted to the parent's year-end. Also, where different years are used for the parent and subsidiary, any material intervening events should be disclosed in the financial statements.

Once the trial balances for each entity are recorded in the applicable columns of the consolidating worksheet, the next step is to complete the Eliminations column. The following elimination entries should be made:

Intercompany Transactions. All intercompany transactions should be eliminated. These include intercompany sales, rents, interest, loans, and dividends. Since the concept of consolidation is to present the results of many entities as if they were a single entity, intercompany transactions must be eliminated since the "single entity" could not make sales or loans to itself.

"Simple" Transactions. Intercompany transactions can be broken down into two categories. The "simple" category consists of those in which an intercompany gain does not become capitalized in an asset account. Examples are loans, rentals, interest, services, or dividends. These types of intercompany transactions can be eliminated simply by reversing the original entry. For instance, if the parent loaned $100,000 to the subsidiary, the following original entries would be made:

	DR	CR
PARENT		
Accounts Receivable	$100,000	
Cash		$100,000
SUBSIDIARY		
Cash	100,000	
Accounts Payable		100,000

To perform an elimination, both of the entries could simply be reversed. Thus, the eliminations column would show a debit to Cash and a credit to Accounts Receivable for $100,000, and a debit to Accounts Payable and a credit to Cash, also for $100,000. However, notice that in the reversing process, Cash has been both debited and credited for $100,000—so there is no net effect on consolidated cash. Therefore, a shortcut elimination entry would be simply to debit Accounts Payable and credit Accounts Receivable for $100,000. This single entry reaches the same result as the two previous reversals.

A similar procedure would be followed for other intercompany transactions in the simple category. The following list shows sample elimination entries for the common types of transactions within the category (assume that all of the transactions were for $100,000 paid in cash):

	DR	CR
INTERCOMPANY INTEREST PAYMENT		
Interest Income	$100,000	
Interest Expense		$100,000
INTERCOMPANY RENT PAYMENT		
Rent Income	100,000	
Rent Expense		100,000

INTERCOMPANY SERVICES (I.E., CONSULTING, DATA PROCESSING)

Services Income	100,000	
Services Expense		100,000

INTERCOMPANY DIVIDEND

Dividend Income	100,000	
Retained Earnings		100,000

If the above transactions were not paid in cash but were instead accrued, then the following additional elimination entry would have to be made in each instance to take care of the intercompany accrual:

Accounts Payable	$100,000	
Accounts Receivable		$100,000

"Complex" Transactions. The second, or "complex" category of intercompany transactions consists of those in which an intercompany gain becomes part of an asset account. (In the simple category, any intercompany income was offset by an equal amount of intercompany expense, or by a debit to retained earnings in the case of a dividend.) The two most common examples would be the intercompany sale of inventory or fixed assets. However, other transactions could be included as well, such as intercompany interest or services for which the payor capitalizes part of the payment (i.e., payment of construction period interest by one entity to another).

In such a situation the intercompany gain must be eliminated from the asset account in every year that the asset contains the gain. The elimination entry will contain more than two accounts, unlike the simple eliminations described above.

For intercompany sales of inventory, there are two objectives: to reduce retained earnings and beginning inventory for prior year's intercompany gains that are still in the beginning inventory, and to eliminate the effect of intercompany sales made during the year. To accomplish the first objective, a worksheet must be kept from year to year which identifies the intercompany inventory still on hand at the end of the year and the amount of intercompany gains contained in the cost thereof.

For instance, assume that at the beginning of the year the parent has on its books $100,000 of inventory which was purchased from the subsidiary in a prior year. The subsidiary's cost for this inventory was $80,000; thus, there is an intercompany gain of $20,000 contained in the $100,000 of inventory. If the elimination entry was being made at the *beginning* of the year, the entry would be to debit Retained Earnings and credit Inventory for $20,000. Of course, though, elimination entries are made at the *end* of the year, not at the beginning. Since beginning inventory is not shown on the year-end statements, the credit must be to the cost of sales, which has the same effect (the beginning inventory increases the cost of sales, so reducing the beginning inventory is the same as reducing the cost of sales).

Next, the effect of current-year intercompany sales must be eliminated. This is accomplished by debiting sales and crediting the cost of sales for the gross sales price, then debiting the cost of sales and crediting inventory for the intercompany profits remaining in the inventory at the end of the year. Assume that $200,000 of sales is made to the parent by the subsidiary during the year, at a profit of $50,000. At the end of the year, $30,000 of intercompany profits remains in inventory on hand.

The elimination entries for the year would be:

	DR	CR
PRIOR YEAR'S GAINS		
Retained Earnings	$ 20,000	
Cost of Sales		$ 20,000
CURRENT YEAR SALES		
Sales	200,000	
Cost of Sales		200,000
ENDING INVENTORY PROFITS		
Cost of Sales	30,000	
Inventory		30,000

The elimination entries are somewhat different where a fixed asset is sold within the consolidated group because of the effect of depreciation. First, though, let us look at the elimination entry for the sale of a nondepreciable asset within the group—such as raw land or marketable stock. To record the original transaction, the seller would have debited Cash, and credited the Asset account for its cost and Gain for the difference. The buyer would have debited Asset for the sales price and credited Cash. Observe that the Cash entries exactly offset, as do the Asset entries *to the extent of the original cost.* Thus, the only elimination necessary to reverse the effect of the transaction is to debit Gain and credit Asset for the same amount. For each future year that the asset is held, the same entry must continue to be made, except that the debit is to Retained Earnings instead of to the Gain account.

Depreciable Assets. Now suppose that the asset is depreciable. The existence of the intercompany gain means that a larger value for the asset will be depreciated, which creates an excessive depreciation deduction. The excess depreciation in the current year (the part of the gain that is depreciated this year) must be eliminated, as must the excess depreciation taken in prior years.

To illustrate this concept, suppose that the subsidiary sold a machine to the parent for $100,000. The subsidiary's gain on the sale was $20,000. The parent is taking straight-line-depreciation over 10 years, with a full year's depreciation being taken in year 1. The following elimination entries would be made in the first year:

	DR	CR
TO ELIMINATE THE GAIN ON THE SALE		
Gain on Sale	$20,000	
Machine		$20,000
TO ELIMINATE EXCESS DEPRECIATION		
Accumulated Depreciation	2,000	
Depreciation Expense		2,000
($20,000 gain/10 years)		

Now let us look at the elimination entries for year 2:

TO ELIMINATE GAIN IN THE ASSET ACCOUNT		
Retained Earnings	$20,000	
Machine		$20,000
TO ELIMINATE CURRENT EXCESS DEPRECIATION		
Accumulated Depreciation	2,000	
Depreciation Expense		2,000
TO ELIMINATE PRIOR EXCESS DEPRECIATION		
Accumulated Depreciation	2,000	
Retained Earnings		2,000

In years 3 through 10, the elimination entries would remain the same as for year 2, except that the amounts in the third entry—to eliminate prior excess depreciation—would increase by $2,000 each year.

After year 10, of course, no further depreciation would be taken and entry 2 would be inapplicable. In entries 1 and 3, Retained Earnings would be both debited and credited for $20,000, so Retained Earnings could be ignored in elimination. The elimination entry would simply be a debit to Accumulated Depreciation and a credit to Machine for $20,000.

If at some point the machine is sold to an outside party, the intercompany transaction can be closed out. The above elimination entries need not be made, except to eliminate any excess depreciation for the current year, if such was taken (entry 2). The only other elimination entry needed would be to debit Retained Earnings and credit Gain (or Loss) for the difference between the intercompany gain and the excess accumulated depreciation. Thus, if the above asset was sold on the first day of year 3, the following elimination entry would be the only one made (assuming no depreciation in year 3):

Retained Earnings	$16,000	
Gain (Loss) on Sale		$16,000

The $16,000 is the difference between the $20,000 intercompany gain and the $4,000 of excess accumulated depreciation ($2,000 for each year). The rationale for this entry is that if there had been no intercompany sale at all and the subsidiary had made the sale to the outside party, its cost would be $20,000 lower than the parent's, but it would have had $4,000 less of accumulated depreciation than was recorded by the parent. The result is that the subsidiary would show a gain $16,000 larger than what the parent showed.

If income taxes have been paid on intercompany gains, which could occur where the entities do not file a consolidated tax return (which many insurance companies do not), then deferred taxes should be provided (as discussed in Chapter 19, Federal Income Taxes).

Note that there is one situation in which intercompany gains are not required to be eliminated: in a regulated industry where one of the entities in the consolidated group manufactures or constructs assets for another entity in the group, to the extent that the intercompany profit "is substantially equivalent to a reasonable return on investment ordinarily capitalized in accordance with the established practice of the industry" (*Accounting Research Bulletin* 51).

Investment Account and Minority Interest. In addition to eliminating intercompany transactions, it is also necessary to eliminate the investment of the parent in the subsidiary; otherwise, there would be a duplication of values: The subsidiary's net assets would be reflected once in the combination of accounts and once in the price paid by the parent for those assets (the Investment account).

The elimination entry is really quite simple. In the case of a wholly owned subsidiary, the Investment in Subsidiary account is credited for its entire balance, and the subsidiary's equity accounts (Common stock, Paid-in Capital, and Retained Earnings) are debited for their entire balance. If the subsidiary was acquired in a pooling transaction (see Chapter 22, Mergers and Acquisitions), then this entry will automatically be in balance. If the subsidiary was acquired in a purchase transaction (anything other than a pooling), any difference between the debits and credits is recorded as Goodwill.

Where Goodwill is recorded, it is also necessary to amortize the Goodwill as described in Chapter 9, Goodwill and Other Intangibles. Generally, the amortization is over a 40-year period, and it is recorded in the Eliminations column.

To illustrate the eliminations for a wholly owned subsidiary, assume that it was acquired by purchase and that the parent's investment account is $100,000. The Capital Stock account of the subsidiary is $1,000, the Paid-in Capital account is $9,000, and the Retained Earnings account is $70,000. The following entries would be made:

	DR	CR
ELIMINATE THE INVESTMENT		
Capital Stock	$ 1,000	
Paid-in Capital	9,000	
Retained Earnings	70,000	
Goodwill	20,000	
Investment in Subsidiary		$100,000
AMORTIZE GOODWILL		
Amortization Expense	500	
Accumulated Amortization—goodwill ($20,000/40 years)		500

Of course, in many instances the subsidiary will not be wholly owned. In such a situation, a provision must be made to reflect the equity in the subsidiary which is owned by outsiders—such equity is not an intercompany holding and therefore should not be eliminated.

Eliminating the minority interest is relatively easy. Where the subsidiary has no preferred stock, simply compute the minority interest percentage (minority common shares divided by total outstanding shares), and do not eliminate that percentage of the subsidiary's equity accounts (Common Stock, Paid-in Capital, and Retained Earnings). For instance, in the previous example, suppose that the subsidiary was only 90 percent owned. In that situation, the investment elimination entry would be:

Capital Stock	$ 900	
Paid-in Capital	8,100	
Retained Earnings	63,000	
Goodwill	28,000	
Investment in Subsidiary		$100,000

In other words, the elimination entry is the same as before, except that only 90 percent of the subsidiary equity accounts is eliminated. The 10 percent attributable to minority interests is left on the books. Goodwill continues to be a *plug* amount (the difference between the equity eliminations and the investment eliminations) which is amortized over a period not to exceed 40 years.

Actually, there are a number of ways to present the minority interest on the balance sheet, although this is probably the easiest to comprehend. The other methods involve only differences in presentation or style; they do not involve different dollar results in a substantive sense. For instance, all of the subsidiary equity accounts could be eliminated, with the minority interest being reflected by a single line item equal to the minority percentage times the total subsidiary equity. Such an entry would appear as follows:

Capital Stock	$ 1,000	
Paid-in Capital	9,000	
Retained Earnings	70,000	
Goodwill	28,000	
Investment in Subsidiary		$100,000
Minority Interest		8,000

The $8,000 Minority Interest is equal to 10 percent of the subsidiary equity of $1,000 + $9,000 + $70,000. Note that the elimination for Investment in Subsidiary does not change, and that Goodwill, the plug, continues to be $28,000.

This Minority Interest of $8,000 can be shown as a separate line item in consolidated equity. However, some companies show it as a separate line item in the liability section instead of the equity section; sometimes it is also shown as a separate item between the liability and equity sections.

Where the subsidiary has preferred stock outstanding and there is a minority interest, an extra wrinkle is thrown into the elimination entry. (Of course, where the parent owns all of both the preferred and common stock, then all of the subsidiary equity is simply eliminated without any further "wrinkles.") In such a situation, a preferred stock elimination entry must be made prior to the common equity elimination entry. In the preferred stock elimination entry, the par value of the parent's interest in preferred is eliminated from equity, together with the investment in preferred stock on the asset side. Then a common equity elimination entry is made, just like the ones we have been using in examples, except that the total subsidiary equity is reduced by the par value of *all* preferred stock for purposes of this computation (which leaves only the "common" equity).

To illustrate, suppose that the subsidiary has $100,000 of preferred stock outstanding, $10,000 of par value common stock, $90,000 of common paid in capital, and $300,000 of retained earnings. The parent owns all of the preferred stock and 90 percent of the common stock. The parent has an investment (cost) of the preferred equal to $100,000, and an investment account for the common stock equal to $420,000. The following entries would be made:

	DR	CR
ELIMINATION OF PREFERRED STOCK		
Preferred Stock (equity account)	$100,000	
Investment in Preferred Stock		$100,000
ELIMINATION OF COMMON EQUITY		
Capital Stock	9,000	
Paid-in Capital	81,000	
Retained Earnings	270,000	
Goodwill	60,000	
Investment in Subsidiary		420,000
AMORTIZATION OF GOODWILL		
Amortization Expense	1,500	
Accumulated Amortization ($60,000/40 years)		1,500

Now assume the same facts, except that the parent owns only 60 percent of the preferred stock:

ELIMINATION OF PREFERRED STOCK		
Preferred Stock (equity account)	$ 60,000	
Investment in Preferred Stock		$ 60,000
ELIMINATION OF COMMON EQUITY		
Capital Stock	$ 9,000	
Paid-in Capital	81,000	
Retained Earnings	270,000	
Goodwill	60,000	
Investment in Subsidiary		$420,000
AMORTIZATION OF GOODWILL		
Amortization Expense	1,500	
Accumulated Amortization		1,500

You undoubtedly noted that entries 2 and 3 were exactly the same, regardless of the percentage of preferred stock held by the parent. In fact, if the parent held all of the $100,000 in preferred stock, or none of it, entries 2 and 3 would still remain the same. Only entry 1 changes. The end result is that, after eliminations, the consolidated balance sheet shows only that part of the subsidiary equity (whether preferred or common) which is not held by the parent.

On the income statement, a minority interest adjustment must also be made, although this is much simpler than the balance sheet adjustment. At the bottom of the income statement, the minority interest percentage of total subsidiary net income is simply shown as a deduction in arriving at consolidated net income, which is the parent's net income plus the parent's share of subsidiary net income (after elimination of intercompany transactions).

To illustrate, assume the following two separate income statements. There are no intercompany transactions.

	Parent	Subsidiary
Gross revenue	$100,000	$40,000
Expenses	(70,000)	(25,000)
Net income	$ 30,000	$15,000

If the parent owned 90 percent of the subsidiary's common stock, the consolidated income statement would appear as follows:

Revenue	$140,000
Expenses	(95,000)
Minority share of net income	(1,500)
Net income	$ 43,500

(Note that the Minority Share of $1500 is 10 percent of the separate subsidiary income of $15,000. If there were intercompany transactions, it would be 10 percent of the subsidiary's separate income after elimination of intercompany items.)

Even when a minority interest exists, it is still necessary to eliminate the entire amount of all intercompany transactions—the elimination is not limited to the parent's percentage share only. You are permitted to allocate the total elimination between the majority and minority interests, but this is merely a difference in presentation and would not change the consolidated net income. From the standpoint of simplicity, it is preferable to make a total elimination without the allocation.

One other point should be made concerning minority interests and the income statement. The minority interest will share in losses as well as income, of course, but if the cumulative minority losses exceed the minority interest in the subsidiary's equity, further losses attributable to the minority interest shall be charged against the majority interest. If the subsidiary then earns profits, the majority interest would absorb all profits until the majority interest has been "repaid" for the excess minority losses charged to it.

Changes in Control

The preceding section has illustrated the elimination entries that are needed to convert the mere combination of separate financial statements into consolidated statements. However, they were simplified since they assumed that the parent owned a constant percentage of the subsidiary. In reality, the parent's percentage frequently fluctuates up and down. Consolidated accounting in this situation requires more adjustments.

Let us first consider the year in which the parent initially obtains control and begins to account for the subsidiary under the consolidated method. In this case, the parent's income for prior years must be restated to reflect the use of the consolidated method for all years that the parent owned common stock in the subsidiary, even if its interest was only 1 percent or less. (This restatement of income, of course, would affect retained earnings at the beginning of the year in which control was obtained.) However, no restatement is necessary if the subsidiary was previously accounted for under the equity method, since the parent would already have reported its share of the subsidiary's income for prior years.

Suppose that the parent has no ownership in the subsidiary in 19x0, obtains 1 percent in 19x1, 10 percent more in 19x2, and 40 percent more in 19x3. For purposes of simplicity, assume that all transactions take place on January 1. In the original income statements prior to 19x3, the parent would account for its interest in the subsidiary under the cost method, meaning that the investment account would be carried at the purchase price (less any permanent declines in value). Dividends would have been reported as income and generally would not affect the investment carrying value. The equity method would not have been used since the parent did not have a 20 percent interest prior to 19x3.

Beginning in 19x3, the parent must use consolidated reporting since its interest now exceeds 50 percent (assuming that none of the special circumstances of noncontrol apply). Thus, in 19x3 51 percent of the subsidiary's income would be included in consolidated income, after elimination of the 49 percent minority interest. However, the parent's income for 19x1 and 19x2 must also be restated. The revised parent's income for 19x1 would include 1 percent of the subsidiary's 19x1 income just as if it had been consolidated for that year (thus, intercompany transactions would be eliminated). The parent's revised income for 19x2 would include 11 percent of the subsidiary's income. Years prior to 19x1 would be unaffected since the parent had no interest.

The effect of the restatement would appear only on financial statements for 19x1 or 19x2 which appear as comparative statements in reports for 19x3 and thereafter. The original financial statements issued for 19x1 and 19x2 would not have to be recalled. Also, the parent's retained earnings on January 1, 19x3, would be restated to reflect the revised income for 19x1 and 19x2.

Now let us change the previous example by assuming that the parent did not acquire an additional 40 percent in 19x3, but only 20 percent (giving it a total interest of 31 percent for the year). In 19x4, the parent acquired still another 20 percent, giving it 51 percent. Of course, in this situation the parent would not begin consolidated accounting until 19x4. However, it would begin using the equity method in 19x3 since it went over 20 percent in that year. Pursuant to the equity method rules, in 19x3 the parent would still restate its 19x1 and 19x2 income to account for its 1 and 11 percent interests in the subsidiary, respectively (see the discussion above in this chapter under "Equity Method"). The parent's January 1, 19x3, retained earnings would be correspondingly restated. Therefore, when consolidated accounting is begun in 19x4, no further restatement of prior income is necessary since it had already been restated under the equity method. (Recall that the equity and consolidated methods have the same effect on net income and that the differences between the two relate only to the manner in which the individual components of net income are presented.)

In the above example, we assumed that the acquisitions took place on the first day of the year. If an acquisition occurs on any other day, then the year must be divided into two parts. Suppose that the parent acquired its initial 1 percent on July 31, 19x1, instead of January 1, 19x1. When restating its 19x1 income, the parent would pick up none of the subsidiary's income prior to July 31, and would pick up 1 percent of the subsidiary's income for the last 5 months of the year. The subsidiary's 19x1 income can be prorated for this purpose if it produces a reasonable approximation.

If the parent goes over the 50 percent mark on any day other than the first of the year, then the same type of concept applies. Suppose that a parent which had no prior stock ownership acquired 51 percent of the subsidiary on June 30. Both entities are on the calendar year; thus, none of the subsidiary's net income for the first 6 months would be included in consolidated net income, and 51 percent of the subsidiary's income for the last 6 months would be included. However, there are two different methods of presenting this result. One method which can be used is to consolidate the total income of both entities for the entire year and then to deduct the subsidiary's preacquisition net income, together with the postacquisition minority interest, at the bottom of the income statement. It is also acceptable, though, to consolidate only the subsidiary's postacquisition operations with those of the parent.

Where the parent's interest is reduced during the year but it still retains over 50 percent, the subsidiary's income is apportioned between the minority and majority interests according to their varying percentages during the year. Thus, if the parent had 80 percent for the first 6 months and 60 percent for the last 6 months, the subsidiary's total operations would be consolidated, but the minority interest in net income would consist of 20 percent of the income for the first 6 months and 40 percent for the last 6 months.

If the parent loses control during the year, generally none of the subsidiary's operations are consolidated for the year. If the parent continued to own at least 20 percent, it would simply use the equity method from the first of the year forward. Thus, if the parent had 60 percent for the first 6 months and 40 percent for the last 6 months, consolidated statements would not be prepared, but the parent would report 60 percent of the subsidiary's income for the first 6 months and 40 percent for the last 6 months, using the equity method of presentation.

If the parent also went below 20 percent during the year, the equity method would be used from the first of the year up until the point that the parent's interest fell below 20 percent, and the cost method would be used thereafter. Suppose that the parent had 60 percent for the first 6 months and 10 percent for the last 6 months. Consolidated statements would not be prepared, but the parent would use the equity method to report 60 percent of the subsidiary's net income for the first 6 months. The parent would report none of the subsidiary's net income for the last 6 months and thereafter, since it owns less than 20 percent. The carrying value of the Investment in Subsidiary account at the end of the first 6 months would become the "cost" for purposes of applying the cost method beginning with the last 6 months.

Reciprocal and Multiple Stockholdings

Thus far we have dealt with the simple situation in which the parent owns a percentage of the subsidiary and there are no other interrelated holdings. However, it is possible that the subsidiary may own some of the parent stock as well, or that the parent may own stock in other entities which in turn own stock in the subsidiary. The first situation will be referred to as a "reciprocal" holding, and the second as a "multiple" holding.

In the case of a reciprocal holding, the subsidiary would report income from the parent under the cost method if the subsidiary owns less than 20 percent of the parent. For the rare situation in which the subsidiary owns 20 percent or more of the parent, it is possible that the subsidiary might use the equity method to report income from the parent. However, your authors would discourage the use of the equity method in this situation for three reasons: (1) the equity method is based on the concept of substantial influence, and it seems somewhat illogical to say that a subsidiary has substantial influence over the parent when in fact the parent controls the subsidiary; (2) the dual use of the equity method would require a complicated algebraic computation; and (3) the effect of the subsidiary's use of the equity method would be eliminated in the consolidation anyway.

Where, as is usually the case, the subsidiary uses the cost method to account for its investment in and income from the parent, two eliminating adjustments must be made. First, the subsidiary's Investment in Parent account must be eliminated. This is accomplished by crediting the Investment in Parent account for its entire balance and debiting Treasury Stock (a negative equity account) for the same amount. Next, any parent dividends received by the subsidiary must be eliminated, which is accomplished by debiting Dividend Income and crediting Retained Earnings. These adjustments simply reflect the concept that all intercompany holdings and transactions should be eliminated in consolidation.

Multiple holdings occur where the parent owns stock in A and B, and A also owns stock in B. Multiple holdings may in turn be broken down into a number of different situations, depending on the level of each shareholding.

Where the parent directly owns over 50 percent of both A and B, it is obvious that consolidated statements will include all three entities. The first step is to eliminate the interest of A in B, as well as any A-B intercompany transactions. This is done regardless of whether A reports its income from B under the cost method or the equity method. Suppose that A owns 10 percent of B, and that its interest was acquired for $50,000. The total Capital Stock of B is $100,000, and the total Retained Earnings account is $300,000. Also, B paid $4,000 in dividends to A. The following elimination entries would be made (assuming no other intercompany transactions):

	DR	CR
ELIMINATE INTERCOMPANY INVESTMENT		
Capital Stock (10%)	$10,000	
Retained Earnings (10%)	30,000	
Goodwill (plug)	10,000	
Investment in B		$50,000
ELIMINATE INTERCOMPANY DIVIDEND		
Dividend Income	$4,000	
Retained Earnings		$4,000

If A had a 25 percent interest and used the equity method, the same concept would be followed, but the entries would look somewhat different. Take the facts in the previous example, except that the carrying value of the Investment in B account is $150,000 and the net income of B is $50,000:

ELIMINATE INTERCOMPANY INCOME		
Equity in Income from B (25% × $50,000)	$12,500	
Investment in B (plug)		$8,500
Retained Earnings (for amount of the dividend)		4,000
ELIMINATE INTERCOMPANY INVESTMENT		
Capital Stock (25%)	25,000	
Retained Earnings (25%)	75,000	
Goodwill (plug)	41,500	
Investment in B (remaining balance of $150,000 − $8,500)		141,500

Next, the parent's interest in B would be eliminated. This would be done in the normal manner already described for elimination entries, just as if A had owned nothing in B. The end result would be that after the parent and A have both made their eliminations in B, the Investment in B accounts of both would be zero. Also, the only equity and net income of B *not eliminated* would be that belonging to the minority interest—defined as shareholders other than the parent or A. (Thus, in short, A is not treated as a minority shareholder even though it owns only 25 percent.)

Finally, the parent's interest in A is eliminated. Again, this is made in the normal manner and nothing "tricky" should be involved. After all the eliminations are made, all intercompany investments, dividends, and bookings of income under the equity method will be gone. All operations will be combined, and there will be minority interests in A and B (and remember, A is not a minority shareholder in B). However, these minority interests will be in equity and income after the elimination of intercompany equity method accruals, not before the elimination of these accruals.

There will also be circumstances in which the parent does not have direct control of both A and B. The parent may own 60 percent of A but only 30 percent of B. However, A may own 25 percent of B. Obviously, the parent may consolidate with A, but may B be included? The answer is yes. Although the parent does not directly have over 50 percent of B, it can determine how A votes its 25 percent interest by virtue of its controlling interest in A. Thus, the parent's direct interest of 30 percent plus the indirect interest of 25 percent give it control of B and allow all three entities to be consolidated. The eliminations would be made in the same manner as described for the situation in which the parent directly controls A and B.

Unconsolidated Subsidiaries

Where consolidated statements are prepared, the parent may also own stock in entities which are not included in the consolidation. The unconsolidated entities could be omitted because of an interest of 50 percent or less or because of special circumstances which negate control even with a greater-than-50 percent interest.

Where the parent has a greater-than-50 percent interest in the unconsolidated entity, the cost method rather than the equity method would generally be used to account for the entity, since the special circumstances negating the consolidated method would also negate the equity method. In such a situation, a number of disclosures shall be made:

1. The cost of the stock in the unconsolidated entity
2. The consolidated group's share of the equity and earnings of the subsidiary
3. The dividends received from the subsidiary
4. Any material effect on depreciation and amortization that would occur if the entity had been acquired for more than book value and then was consolidated
5. If the unconsolidated entities are material in the aggregate, summary information regarding their assets, liabilities, and operating results

The above disclosures may either be made for each unconsolidated subsidiary or be given in total for all such subsidiaries. Also, intercompany transactions with such subsidiaries generally should be eliminated, but it is not required to eliminate intercompany gains where the gains do not exceed the consolidated group's unrecorded equity in undistributed earnings in the subsidiary. However, such uneliminated gains should be disclosed if they are material.

If the unconsolidated entity is accounted for by the equity method or if there is a 20 percent or greater interest (even where the equity method is not used), then another set of disclosures must be made. These disclosures are described above in this chapter under "Equity Method."

Combined Statements

Consolidated statements are applicable in a parent-subsidiary context. Sometimes, though, two or more entities may be commonly controlled in a brother-sister configuration rather than a parent-subsidiary one. This would seldom if ever occur where a publicly held company is involved, but is quite common in closely held situations. The simplest example would be where one individual owns all the stock of two separate corporations. Often, though, a shareholder group such as a family owns a controlling but not an entire interest in each of the entities.

The mere fact that a small shareholder group controls two or more corporations does not automatically make combined statements suitable. In fact, strictly speaking, there are no circumstances in which combined statements are actually *required*. However, there are circumstances in which combined statements may be a more meaningful alternative than separate statements. No hard-and-fast rules exist to decide this. Professional judgment, as opposed to mechanical tests, must be used.

The two main factors in determining the suitability of combined statements are control and relatedness. The tighter the controlling shareholder group and the greater the amount of its control, the more likely that combined statements would be appropriate. The controlling shareholder group sometimes can be large but still remain "tight" and act in a unified manner, such as when children, grandchildren, and trusts own shares of stock.

The second criterion is relatedness. If the entities are similar or complement each other in an integrated operation, then combined statements might be more meaningful than separate statements. A finance company and a credit life company would be an ideal example. However, if the entities are significantly different—for instance, an insurance company and a manufacturing company—then it is less likely that combined statements would be suitable.

In addition to the above factors, combined statements may also be appropriate for a group of unconsolidated subsidiaries or for entities under common management (as opposed to shareholder control).

Combined statements are prepared in basically the same manner as consolidated statements are. The main difference is that normally there is no elimination of investment in subsidiary accounts and subsidiary equity accounts, since these are not applicable in a brother-sister context in which neither entity owns stock in the other. However, if one entity does own some stock in the other, then such an elimination would be necessary. As with consolidated statements, there should be an elimination of intercompany transactions.

Parent Company Statements

Although there are circumstances in which a parent company is required to prepare consolidated statements, there is no prohibition against making additional disclosures of separate company financial information within the same consolidated report. For instance, separate parent company statements may be included along with the consolidated statements in the same report, although the parent company statements generally would not be issued in an audited report all by themselves. The disclosure of parent data within the consolidated report could be useful to creditors or preferred shareholders of the parent. Likewise, financial statements for specific subsidiaries or a group of subsidiaries could be included in the consolidated report. This is simply in keeping with the objective of making the complete GAAP financial report as meaningful as possible to readers.

STATUTORY ACCOUNTING

The statutory accounting treatment for subsidiaries is generally easier than the GAAP treatment. This is because statutory statements are not consolidated; rather, a separate statement blank is prepared for each individual insurance company. On occasion, the separate company statements may be supplemented by an additional statutory statement blank which combines the operations of several affiliated insurance companies.

No specific definition of a subsidiary is provided for statutory purposes. The following discussion applies to stock of a company which the "insurer is either the parent of, or under direct or indirect common control, or affiliated" with the insurer.

Balance Sheet Treatment

Although statutory statements are not consolidated, subsidiaries will affect the parent's balance sheet as an investment item. On the asset exhibit, the investment in subsidiary will be included in the general category of Stocks. On Schedule D, the summary of stocks and bonds, there is a separate line for subsidiary and related investments. The stock in each subsidiary would be listed individually on Schedule D, Part 2.

The carrying value for the investment in subsidiary is the most important aspect of the balance sheet treatment. There are six possible methods of determining the carrying value, as discussed below. The first four may be used for either insurance or noninsurance company subsidiaries; the last two are restricted to one or the other. A company may use different methods for different subsidiaries—it is even conceivable that a parent might use all six methods if it had six or more subsidiaries. (Of course, as a practical matter, it is unlikely that a parent would choose to use that many different methods.) However, once a method is chosen for a particular subsidiary, that valuation method must continue to be used for that particular subsidiary, unless written permission to change is obtained from the NAIC Subcommittee on Valuation of Securities.

Valuation Methods Available for Both Insurance and Noninsurance Subsidiaries

1. The stock in the subsidiary may be valued as if the subsidiary's assets were owned directly by the parent. (This method must be used if the subsidiary is a foreign insurer.) In other words, the subsidiary's separate existence is ignored, and the subsidiary's net assets would be accounted for by using statutory principles, whether or not the subsidiary was an insurance company.

Nonadmitted assets would be left out, and subsidiary liabilities would reduce the gross asset amount. Note that although the individual subsidiary assets are valued as if owned directly by the parent, the aggregate of these individual subsidiary asset values is listed under Stocks as an investment in subsidiaries, rather than being spread throughout the parent's balance sheet. Thus, the statutory value of real estate owned by a subsidiary appears under Stocks in the parent's balance sheet rather than under Real Estate.

2. A concept similar to the GAAP equity method may also be used for both insurance and noninsurance subsidiaries. The starting point is the cost of the subsidiary's stock. The cost is then adjusted for the parent's share of the results of subsequent subsidiary operations, and reduced by any dividends received from the subsidiary. In the case of insurance subsidiaries, statutory accounting is used to measure the subsidiary's operations. For noninsurance companies, GAAP is used. However, if the noninsurance subsidiary in turn has its own insurance subsidiary, the carrying value of the noninsurance subsidiary must be adjusted to reflect the statutory net assets of its second-tier insurance subsidiary. Thus, suppose that parent A owns a noninsurance company B which in turn owns an insurance company C. Suppose further that under the GAAP equity method B is valued at $1 million, which includes a value for C of $400,000, also under the GAAP equity method. However, the net assets of C under statutory principles are only $300,000. Therefore, A carries B on its balance sheet at $900,000. Under the equity method, there is also a limit on the amount that can be assigned to goodwill and other intangibles; this is discussed below under "Modifications."
3. The subsidiary stock may also be carried at market value if the shares are listed on a national securities exchange or on the over-the-counter NASDAQ system.
4. Finally, any other reasonable method may be used to value the stock if approved by the NAIC subcommittee.

Valuation Method for Insurance Subsidiaries Only

5. Insurance subsidiaries can be carried at *statutory book value,* defined as the capital and surplus on the last annual statement or subsequent examination report (less reserves required by statute, policyholders' surplus, and the par value—or redemption value, if greater—of preferred stock), divided by the number of common shares issued and outstanding, multiplied by the number of shares owned by the parent.

Valuation Method for Noninsurance Subsidiaries Only

6. If the noninsurance company is audited by an independent CPA, that subsidiary's GAAP net worth for its most recent fiscal year-end may be used. If the audit is not completed at the time for filing the parent's statutory statement, as estimate may be used, with any variation between the estimate and the final audited figures being reported to the subcommittee at a later date. As under method 2 above (the equity method), if the noninsurance subsidiary has its own second-tier insurance subsidiary, the GAAP value must be

adjusted to reflect the statutory net assets of the second-tier subsidiary. Also, the limitation on goodwill and intangibles applies here, as discussed below under "Modifications."

Modifications

1. Unless the subsidiary is carried at a listed market value (method 3 above), the carrying value must be reduced by any subsidiary assets which would be nonadmitted in the parent's hands if the assets were leased to or used by the parent, or if they were acquired from the parent or for its benefit under circumstances indicating an intent to circumvent the nonadmitted asset rules.
2. Preferred stock of a wholly owned subsidiary is accounted for in the same manner as is the subsidiary's common stock. Preferred stock of a subsidiary not wholly owned would be accounted for under the regular rules for valuing preferred stock (see Chapter 5, Investments in Securities).
3. Where a subsidiary is valued under the equity method (method 2) or the GAAP method (method 6), the value must be adjusted to reflect the statutory net assets of a second-tier insurance subsidiary. See method 2 above for a more complete discussion of this adjustment.
4. Where a subsidiary is valued under the equity method (method 2) or the GAAP method (method 6), the amounts attributable to goodwill and other intangibles of all subsidiaries together shall not exceed 10 percent of the capital and surplus of the parent, as reported in its last annual statement. This applies both to the acquisition year and to all years thereafter. The amount of goodwill and other intangibles falling within this limitation shall be written off over a period not exceeding 10 years. Amounts in excess of the limitation shall be written off immediately against surplus. *Goodwill* means the difference between the cost of a purchased subsidiary and the value of the net assets on the predecessor company's books (using statutory accounting if the subsidiary is an insurance company). The 10 percent limitation does not apply to subsidiaries acquired before June 15, 1972. The goodwill of such subsidiaries must be written off over 20 years or less and may be charged to the common stock component of the mandatory securities valuation reserve, if any.
5. Foreign insurance subsidiaries may be valued only by method 1 above.

Filing and Approval. The basis of valuing subsidiaries must be filed with the subcommittee by April 1 of each year, and within 30 days after the acquisition of a subsidiary.

The subcommittee retains the right to require accounting treatment different from that discussed above in unusual circumstances.

Income Statement Treatment

The statutory income statement treatment for subsidiary accounting is also relatively simple. Since consolidated statements are not filed, income from the subsidiary is reported either as dividends or as a change in the carrying value.

Dividends from affiliates are reported on the applicable lines of Exhibit 3 for a life company, and Part 1 of the Underwriting and Investment Exhibit for a property and liability company.

The change in carrying value (or book value) for a subsidiary is reported as an unrealized capital gain or loss. For a property and liability company, this is shown in Part 1A of the Underwriting and Investment Exhibit and constitutes a direct charge to surplus. For a life company, this is shown in Exhibit 4 and constitutes a direct charge to surplus and an adjustment to the mandatory securities valuation reserve in current or subsequent years.

APPENDIX

*ANNUAL STATEMENTS**

*Printed Annual Statement Forms reprinted courtesy of John S. Swift Co., Inc., St. Louis, Missouri.

Note: In the case of reciprocal exchanges and other types of insurers using special terminology, the printed items and references in this blank, if not appropriately changed, shall be construed to apply to such insurers in respect to corresponding data and information as the context may require.

ANNUAL STATEMENT

For the Year Ended December 31, 19

OF THE CONDITION AND AFFAIRS OF THE

PROPERTY-LIABILITY INSURANCE Co.

NAIC Group Code: NAIC Company Code: Employer's ID Number:

Organized under the Laws of the State of ______________________, made to the

INSURANCE DEPARTMENT OF THE STATE OF

PURSUANT TO THE LAWS THEREOF

Incorporated ______________ Commenced Business ______________

Home Office ______________ (Street and Number), ______________ (City or Town, State and Zip Code)

Mail Address ______________ (Street and Number), ______________ (City or Town, State and Zip Code)

Main Administrative Office ______________ (Area Code) (Telephone Number)

Contact Person and Phone Number ______________

OFFICERS

President ______________

Secretary ______________

Treasurer ______________

Vice-Presidents ______________

DIRECTORS OR TRUSTEES

State of ______________
County of ______________ } ss

______________ President, ______________ Secretary, ______________ Treasurer

of the ______________ being duly sworn, each for himself deposes and says that they are the above described officers of the said insurer, and that on the thirty-first day of December last, all of the herein described assets were the absolute property of the said insurer, free and clear from any liens or claims thereon, except as herein stated, and that this annual statement, together with related exhibits, schedules and explanations therein contained, annexed or referred to are a full and true statement of all the assets and liabilities and of the condition and affairs of the said insurer as of the thirty-first day of December last, and of its income and deductions therefrom for the year ended on that date, according to the best of their information, knowledge and belief, respectively.

Subscribed and sworn to before me this

______________ day of ______________, 19 ______________ President

______________ ______________ Secretary

______________ Treasurer

Note: The pages identified by the symbol (®) in this annual statement were reproduced by the John S. Swift Company from master forms copyright 19 by the John S. Swift Company, Incorporated.

Name

ASSETS	(1) Current Year	(2) Previous Year
	~~(000 omitted)~~	
1. Bonds (Schedule D-Part I)	180,798	168,474
2. Stocks:		
2.1 Preferred stocks (Schedule D-Part 2-Section 1)	8,870	8,400
2.2 Common stocks (Schedule D-Part 2-Section 2)	8,800	8,600
3. Mortgage loans on real estate (Schedule-B)	100	110
4. Real estate:		
4.1 Properties occupied by the company (less $ 4,000 encumbrances) (Schedule A-Part I)	14,470	14,740
4.2 Other properties (less $ encumbrances)		
5. Collateral loans (Schedule C-Part I)		
6.1 Cash on hand and on deposit (Schedule N)	1,201	201
6.2 Short-term investments (Schedule DA)		
7. Other invested assets (Schedule BA)		
7a. Subtotals, cash and invested assets (Items 1 to 7)	214,239	200,525
8. Agents' balances or uncollected premiums:		
8.1 Premiums and agents' balances in course of collection	5,400	5,200
8.2 Premiums, agents' balances and installments booked but deferred and not yet due		
9. Funds held by or deposited with reinsured companies	220	200
10. Bills receivable, taken for premiums		
11. Reinsurance recoverable on loss payments (Schedule F-Part IA-Section 1)	190	290
12. Federal income tax recoverable	100	100
13. Electronic data processing equipment	3,200	3,000
14. Interest, dividends and real estate income due and accrued (Part I-Col. 6)	4,750	4,300
15. Receivable from affiliates		
16. Equities and deposits in pools and associations	18	18
17.		
18.		
19.		
20.		
21.		
22. TOTALS (Items 7a through 21)	228,117	213,633

Note: The items on this page to agree with Exhibit 1, Col. 4.

The Notes to Financial Statements are an integral part of this statement.

LIABILITIES, SURPLUS AND OTHER FUNDS	(1) Current Year	(2) Previous Year
	(000 OMITTED)	
1. Losses (Part 3A, Column 5, Item 31)	65,300	61,800
2. Loss adjustment expenses (Part 3A, Column 6, Item 31)	10,700	10,400
3. Contingent commissions and other similar charges	300	300
4. Other expenses (excluding taxes, licenses and fees) (PART 4)	1,400	1,500
5. Taxes, licenses and fees (excluding federal and foreign income taxes) (PART 4)	3,700	3,800
6. Federal and foreign income taxes (excluding deferred taxes)	1,100	1,000
7.		
8. Borrowed money		
9. Interest, including $.......... on borrowed money		
10. Unearned premiums (Part 2B, Column 7, Item 31)	45,185	43,285
11. Dividends declared and unpaid:		
(a) Stockholders		
(b) Policyholders	170	170
12. Funds held by company under reinsurance treaties		
13. Amounts withheld or retained by company for account of others	2,640	2,400
14a. Unearned premiums on reinsurance in unauthorized companies $..........		
14b. Reinsurance on paid losses $.......... and on unpaid reported losses $.......... and on incurred but not reported losses $.......... recoverable from unauthorized companies $..........		
14c. Paid and unpaid allocated loss adjustment expenses recoverable from unauthorized companies $..........		
14d. Total $..........		
15. Less funds held or retained by company for account of such unauthorized companies as per Schedule F, Part 2, Column 6 $..........		
16. Excess of statutory reserves over statement reserves (Schedule P, Parts 1A, 1B, 1C, 1D and Schedule K)	3,000	2,900
17. Net adjustments in assets and liabilities due to foreign exchange rates		
18. CEDED REINSURANCE BALANCES PAYABLE	1,000	1,000
19. Drafts outstanding	200	200
20. Payable to affiliates		
21. Payable for securities	1,300	1,000
22. OTHER LIABILITIES	3,115	7,095
23. Total liabilities (Items 1 through 22)	139,110	136,850
24. Special surplus funds:		
(a)		
(b)		
(c)		
25A. Capital paid up	5,000	5,000
25B.		
26A. Gross paid in and contributed surplus	20,000	20,000
26B. Unassigned funds (surplus)	64,007	51,783
26C. Less treasury stock, at cost:		
(1) .... shares common (value included in Item 25A $..........)		
(2) .... shares preferred (value included in Item 25A $..........)		
27. Surplus as regards policyholders (Items 24 to 26B, less 26C) (Page 4, Item 40)	89,007	76,783
28. TOTALS (Page 2, Item 22)	228,117	213,633

Name

UNDERWRITING AND INVESTMENT EXHIBIT
STATEMENT OF INCOME

	(1) Current Year	(2) Previous Year
	~~(000 OMITTED)~~	
UNDERWRITING INCOME		
1. Premiums earned (Part 2, Column 4, Item 31)	165,800	157,600
DEDUCTIONS		
2. Losses incurred (Part Column 7, Item 31)	92,600	94,323
3. Loss expenses incurred (Part 4, Column 1, Item 22)	14,700	15,200
4. Other underwriting expenses incurred (Part 4, Column 2, Item 22)	51,200	51,540
5.		
6. Total underwriting deductions (Items 2 through 5)	158,500	161,063
7. Net underwriting gain or loss (—) (Item 1 minus 6)	7,300	(3,463)
INVESTMENT INCOME		
8. Net investment income earned (Part 1, Item 16)	12,450	10,914
9. Net realized capital gains or losses (—) (Part 1A, Item 11)	434	360
9A. Net investment gain or loss (—) (Items 8+9)	12,884	11,274
OTHER INCOME		
10. Net gain or loss (—) from agents' or premium balances charged off (amount recovered $ 210 amount charged off $ 40)	170	150
11. Finance and service charges not included in premiums (Schedule T, Column 8 total)		
12.		
13.		
14.		
15.		
16.		
17. Total other income (Items 10 through 16)	170	150
18. Net income before dividends to policyholders and before federal and foreign income taxes (Items 7+9A+17)	20,354	7,961
18A. Dividends to policyholders (Exhibit 3, Item 16 plus Page 3, Item 11b, Column 1 minus 2)	200	200
18B. Net income, after dividends to policyholders but before federal and foreign income taxes (Item 18 minus 18A)	20,154	7,761
19. Federal and foreign income taxes incurred	6,650	2,561
20. Net income (Item 18B minus 19) (to Item 22)	13,504	5,200
CAPITAL AND SURPLUS ACCOUNT		
21. Surplus as regards policyholders, December 31 previous year (Page 4, Column 2, Item 40)	51,783	47,283
GAINS (+) AND LOSSES (—) IN SURPLUS		
22. Net income (from Item 20)	13,504	5,200
23. Net unrealized capital gains or losses (Part 1A, Item 12)	(280)	(200)
24. Change in non-admitted assets (Exhibit 2, Item 32, Col. 3)	(400)	(100)
25. Change in liability for unauthorized reinsurance (Page 3, Item 15, Column 1 minus 2)		
26. Change in foreign exchange adjustment		
27. Change in excess of statutory reserves over statement reserves (Page 3, Item 16, Column 1 minus 2)	(100)	100
28. Capital changes:		
(a) Paid in (Exhibit 3, Item 6)		
(b) Transferred from surplus (Stock Divd.)		
(c) Transferred to surplus		
29. Surplus adjustments:		
(a) Paid in (Exhibit 3, Item 7)		
(b) Transferred to capital (Stock Divd.)		
(c) Transferred from capital		
30. Net remittances from or to Home Office (Exhibit 3, Items 4b minus 12b)		
31. Dividends to stockholders (cash)	(500)	(500)
32. Change in treasury stock (Page 3, Item 26C (1) and (2), Column 1 minus 2)		
33. Extraordinary amounts of taxes for prior years		
34.		
35.		
36.		
37.		
38.		
39. Change in surplus as regards policyholders for the year (Items 22 through 38)	12,224	4,500
40. Surplus as regards policyholders, December 31 current year (Items 21 plus 39) (Page 3, Item 27)	64,007	51,783

STATEMENT OF CHANGES IN FINANCIAL POSITION

	(1) Current Year	(2) Previous Year
	(000 OMITTED)	
FUNDS PROVIDED		
FROM OPERATIONS:		
1. Underwriting gain (Page 4, Item 7)	7,300	(3,463)
Charges (+) credits (—) to underwriting gain not affecting funds:		
2. Change in liability for losses and adjusting expenses	3,800	2,900
3. Change in liability for unearned premiums	1,900	1,900
4. Change in liability for other underwriting expenses	(200)	200
5. Change in agents' balances	(200)	(100)
6. Change in net reinsurance receivable or payable	80	200
7. Change in non-admitted assets (Page 4, Item 24)	400	100
8. Change in amounts withheld for account of others	240	170
9. Change in other items:		
9.1 Balances with affiliates		
9.2 Electronic data processing equipment	(200)	(200)
9.3 Other assets		(100)
9.4 Other liabilities	(3,680)	4,993
0. Funds provided from underwriting (Items 1 to 9.4)	9,440	6,400
1. Investment gain (Page 4, Item 9A)	12,884	11,274
Charges (+) credits (—) to investment gain not affecting funds:		
2. Change in liability for investment expenses		
3. Change in interest, dividends and real estate income accrued	(450)	(200)
4. Depreciation and amortization	405	300
5. Other items:		
15.1		
15.2		
Funds provided from investments (Items 11 to 15.2)	12,839	11,374
Other income (Page 4, Item 17)	170	150
Dividends paid to policyholders	(200)	(200)
Federal income taxes paid	(6,550)	(2,400)
Funds provided from operations (Items 10, 16, 17, 18 and 19)	15,699	15,324
FROM INVESTMENTS SOLD, MATURED OR REPAID:		
Bonds	5,750	2,000
Stocks	1,000	500
Mortgage loans	10	10
Real estate		
Collateral loans		
Other invested assets		
Net change in investments acquired and disposed of during year		
Realized capital gains (—) losses (+) (Page 4, Item 9)	434	360
Funds provided from disposition of investments (Items 21 to 28)	7,194	2,870
Other funds provided:		
30.1 Capital and surplus paid in		
30.2 Borrowed money $ 200 less repaid $ 200		
30.3 Other sources		
Total other funds provided (Items 30.1 to 30.3)		
Total funds provided (Items 20, 29 and 31)	22,893	18,194
FUNDS APPLIED		
COST OF INVESTMENTS ACQUIRED:		
Bonds	19,523	16,504
Net increase (+), decrease (—) short-term investments		
Stocks	1,670	790
Mortgage loans		
Real estate	200	300
Collateral loans		
Other invested assets		
Total cost of investments acquired (Items 33 to 38)	21,393	17,594
Other funds applied:		
40.1 Dividends to stockholders	500	500
40.2 Change in foreign exchange		
40.3		
Total other funds applied (Items 40.1 to 40.3)	500	500
Total funds applied (Items 39 and 41)	21,893	18,094
Increase in cash (Items 32 minus 42)	1,000	100
CASH ON HAND AND ON DEPOSIT:		
Beginning of year	201	101
End of year	1,201	201

UNDERWRITING AND INVESTMENT EXHIBIT

PART 1 – INTEREST, DIVIDENDS AND REAL ESTATE INCOME

(000 OMITTED)

(1)	(2) Schedule	(3) Collected During Year Less Paid For Accrued On Purchases	Paid in Advance (4) Current Year	(5) Previous Year	Due and Accrued‡ (6) Current Year	(7) Previous Year	(8) Earned During Year (3) + (5) + (6) − (4) − (7)
1. U. S. government bonds	D*	645			22	21	646
1.1 Bonds exempt from U. S. tax	D*	1,474			424	435	1,463
1.2 Other bonds (unaffiliated)	D*	9,146			3,717	3,370	9,493
1.3 Bonds of affiliates	D*						
2.1 Preferred stocks (unaffiliated)	D	730			260	165	825
2.11 Preferred stocks of affiliates	D						
2.2 Common stocks (unaffiliated)	D	32			16	15	33
2.21 Common stocks of affiliates	D						
3. Mortgage loans	B†	1					1
4. Real estate	A§	1,835			311	294	1,852
5. Collateral loans	C						
6.1 Cash on hand and on deposit	N						
6.2 Short-term investments	DA**						
7. Other invested assets	BA						
8. Financial options and futures	DB						
9.							
10. Totals		13,863			4,750	4,300	14,313

	Deductions	
11. Total investment expenses incurred (Part 4, Col. 3, Item 22)	1,393	
12. Depreciation on real estate (for companies which depreciate annually on a formula basis)	470	
13.		
14.		
15. Total deductions (Items 11 to 14)		1,863
16. Net Investment Income Earned (Item 10 minus Item 15—to Page 4, Item 8)		12,450

* Includes $ 128 accrual of discount less $ 63 amortization of premium.
† Includes $........ accrual of discount less $........ amortization of premium.
§ Includes $ 1,300 for company's occupancy of its own buildings.
** Includes $........ accrual of discount less $........ amortization of premium.
‡ Admitted items only. State basis of exclusions........

PART 1A – CAPITAL GAINS AND LOSSES ON INVESTMENTS

(000 OMITTED)

(1)	Schedule	(2) Profit on Sales or Maturity	(3) Loss on Sales or Maturity	(4) Increases by Adjustment in Book Value	(5) Decreases by Adjustment in Book Value	(6) Net Gain (+) or Loss (−) from Change in Difference Between Book and Admitted Values	(7) Total (Net of Cols. (2) to (6) incl.) (2) − (3) + (4) − (5) + (6)
1. U. S. government bonds	D						
1.1 Bonds exempt from U. S. tax							
1.2 Other bonds (unaffiliated)		90	5			(10)	75
1.3 Bonds of affiliates							
2.1 Preferred stocks (unaffiliated)							
2.11 Preferred stocks of affiliates							
2.2 Common stocks (unaffiliated)		410	61			(270)	79
2.21 Common stocks of affiliates							
3. Mortgage loans	B						
4. Real estate	A				‡		
5. Collateral loans	C						
6.1 Cash on hand and on deposit	N						
6.2 Short-term investments	DA						
7. Other invested assets	BA						
8. Financial options and futures	DB						
9.							
10. Totals		500	66			(280)	154

(Distribution of Item 10, Col. 7)

11. Net realized capital gains or losses* (Page 4, Item 9) (Col. 2−3, Item 10)	434
12. Net unrealized capital gains or losses* (Page 4, Item 23) (Col. 4 − 5 + 6, Item 10)	(280)

* Attach statement or memorandum explaining basis of division.
‡ Excluding $........ depreciation on real estate included in Part 1, Item 12.

UNDERWRITING AND INVESTMENT EXHIBIT

PART 2—PREMIUMS EARNED (000 OMITTED)

LINE OF BUSINESS	(1) Net Premiums Written per Column 4, Part 2C	(2) Unearned Premiums Dec. 31 Previous Year—per Col. 3, Last Year's Part 2	(3) Unearned Premiums Dec. 31 Current Year—per Col. 7, Part 2B	(4) Premiums Earned During Year Cols. (1) + (2) — (3)	
1. Fire	5,600	1,840	2,240	5,200	1
2. Allied lines	3,500	960	760	3,700	2
3. Farmowners multiple peril	750	210	260	700	3
4. Homeowners multiple peril	21,600	6,800	6,700	21,500	4
5. Commercial multiple peril	29,400	8,200	7,500	30,100	5
8. Ocean marine					8
9. Inland marine	550	180	230	500	9
10.					10
11. Medical malpractice					11
12. Earthquake					12
13. Group accident and health					13
14. Credit accident and health (group and individual)					14
15. Other accident and health					15
16. Workers' compensation	7,400	2,100	2,300	7,200	16
17. Other liability	1,300	460	560	1,200	17
19. Auto liability	63,600	14,270	15,070	62,800	19
21. Auto phys. damage	31,700	7,600	8,900	30,600	21
22. Aircraft (all perils)					22
23. Fidelity					23
24. Surety					24
25. Glass	30	10	20	20	25
26. Burglary and theft	90	30	20	100	26
27. Boiler and machinery	190	65	75	180	27
28. Credit	1,200	420	420	1,200	28
29. International					29
30. Reinsurance	790	140	130	800	30
31. TOTALS	167,700	43,285	45,185	165,800	31

PART 2A—PREMIUMS IN FORCE

(1) In Force Dec. 31 Last Year Without Deducting Reinsurance	(2) Premiums Written or Renewed During Year per Cols. 1 and 2, Part 2C	(3) Excess of Original Premiums over Amount Received for Additional Premiums and Reinsurance	(4) Deduct Expirations and Excess of Original Premiums over Return Premiums on Cancellations	(5) In Force At End of Year (1) + (2) + (3) — (4)	(6) Deduct Reinsurance In Force (Schedule F) Authorized and Unauthorized Companies	(7) Net Premiums In Force (5) — (6)	
							1
							2
							3
							4
							5
							8
							9
							10
							11
							12
							13
							14
							15
							16
							17
							19
							21
							22
							23
							24
							25
							26
							27
							28
							29
							30
							31

SUPPLEMENTARY INFORMATION

UNDERWRITING AND INVESTMENT EXHIBIT

PART 2B—RECAPITULATION OF ALL PREMIUMS

†Gross premiums (less reinsurance) and unearned premiums on all unexpired risks and reserve for return premiums under rate credit or retrospective rating plans based upon experience, viz.: (000 OMITTED)

PART 2C—PREMIUMS WRITTEN (000 OMITTED)

DETAILS OMITTED

LINE OF BUSINESS	Running One Year or Less From Date of Policy		Running More Than One Year from Date of Policy		(5) Advance Premiums (100%)	(6) Reserve for Rate Credits and Retrospective Returns Based on Experience	(7) Total Reserve for Unearned Premiums (2)+(4)+(5)+(6)		Gross Premiums (Less Return Premiums), Including Policy and Membership Fees, Written and Renewed During Year				
	(1) Premiums In Force	(2) Amount Unearned*	(3) Premiums In Force	(4) Amount Unearned*					(1) Direct Business	(2) Reinsurance Assumed	(3) Reinsurance Ceded	(4) Net Premiums Written (1) + (2) − (3)	
1. Fire			(c)					1	5,750	70	220	5,600	1
2. Allied lines								2	3,580	60	140	3,500	2
3. Farmowners multiple peril								3		750		750	3
4. Homeowners multiple peril								4	22,470	200	1,070	21,600	4
5. Commercial multiple peril								5	30,190	660	1,450	29,400	5
8. Ocean marine								8					8
9. Inland marine								9	550			550	9
10.								10					10
11. Medical malpractice								11					11
12. Earthquake								12					12
13. Group accident and health						(b)		13					13
14. Credit accident and health (group and individual)**								14					14
15. Other accident and health						(b)		15					15
16. Workers' compensation								16	7,150	370	120	7,400	16
17. Other liability								17	1,245	120	65	1,300	17
19. Auto liability								19	64,380	160	940	63,600	19
21. Auto phys. damage								21	31,590	230	120	31,700	21
22. Aircraft (all perils)								22					22
23. Fidelity								23					23
24. Surety								24					24
25. Glass								25	30			30	25
26. Burglary and theft								26	90			90	26
27. Boiler and machinery								27	206		16	190	27
28. Credit								28		1,200		1,200	28
29. International								29					29
30. Reinsurance								30		1,400	610	790	30
31. TOTALS	95,110	43,185			2,000		45,185	31	167,231	5,220	4,751	167,700	31

*By gross premiums is meant the aggregate of all the premiums written in the policies or renewals in force.

(b) Including $ .... reserved for deferred maternity and other similar benefits.

(c) Including $ .... premium deposits on perpetual fire insurance risks.

UNDERWRITING AND INVESTMENT EXHIBIT

PART 3 – LOSSES PAID AND INCURRED
(000 OMITTED)

LINE OF BUSINESS	LOSSES PAID LESS SALVAGE				(5) Net Losses Unpaid Current Year (Part 3A, Col. 5)	(6) Net Losses Unpaid Previous Year	(7) Losses Incurred Current Year (4) + (5) — (6)	(8) Ratio Losses Incurred (Col. 7, Part 3) to Premiums Earned (Col. 4, Part 2)	
	(1) Direct Business	(2) Reinsurance Assumed	(3) Reinsurance Recovered	(4) Net Payments (1) + (2) — (3)					
1. Fire	1,120	60		1,180	840	620	1,400		1
2. Allied lines	1,840	120		1,960	560	420	2,100		2
3. Farmowners multiple peril		730		730	130	160	700		3
4. Homeowners multiple peril	12,000	240	40	12,200	3,600	3,200	12,600		4
5. Commercial multiple peril	15,697	763	360	16,100	9,800	8,700	17,200		5
8. Ocean marine								SUPPLEMENTARY INFORMATION	8
9. Inland marine	123			123	27	30	120		9
10.									10
11. Medical malpractice									11
12. Earthquake									12
13. Group accident and health									13
14. Credit accident and health (group and individual)*									14
15. Other accident and health									15
16. Workers' compensation	2,630	120		2,750	1,100	2,650	1,200		16
17. Other liability	610	60		670	390	450	610		17
19. Auto liability	34,390	110	500	34,000	42,100	40,300	35,800		19
21. Auto phys. damage	17,340	60		17,400	4,700	3,800	18,300		21
22. Aircraft (all perils)									22
23. Fidelity									23
24. Surety									24
25. Glass									25
26. Burglary and theft	20			20	10	10	20		26
27. Boiler and machinery	30			30	30	20	40		27
28. Credit		450		450	350	100	700		28
29. International									29
30. Reinsurance		1,487		1,487	1,663	1,340	1,810		30
31. TOTALS	85,800	4,200	900	89,100	65,300	61,800	92,600		31

*Business not exceeding 120 months duration.

UNDERWRITING AND INVESTMENT EXHIBIT

PART 3A — UNPAID LOSSES AND LOSS ADJUSTMENT EXPENSES

(000 OMITTED)

LINE OF BUSINESS	ADJUSTED OR IN PROCESS OF ADJUSTMENT		(2)	(3)	INCURRED BUT NOT REPORTED		(5)	(6)	
	(1a) Direct	(1b) Reinsurance Assumed per Schedule F, Part 1A, Sec. 2, Col. 2	Deduct Reinsurance Recoverable from Authorized and Unauthorized Companies per Schedule F, Part 1A, Sec. 1, Col. 2	Net Losses Excl. Incurred But Not Reported (1a + 1b—2)	(4a) Direct	(4b) Reinsurance Assumed Less Ceded	Net Losses Unpaid Excluding Loss Adjustment Expenses 3+4a+4b	Unpaid Loss Adjustment Expenses	
1. Fire	826	20	90	756	60	24	840	67	1
2. Allied lines	513		20	493	30	37	560	28	2
3. Farmowners multiple peril	130		10	120	10		130	14	3
4. Homeowners multiple peril	3,122	310	220	3,212	380	8	3,600	290	4
5. Commercial multiple peril	9,260	420	960	8,720	920	160	9,800	1,270	5
8. Ocean marine									8
9. Inland marine	27			27			27	3	9
10.									10
11. Medical malpractice									11
12. Earthquake									12
13. Group accident and health							(a)		13
14. Credit accident and health (group and individual)*									14
15. Other accident and health							(a)		15
16. Workers' compensation	493	320		813	240	47	1,100	220	16
17. Other liability	390			390			390	83	17
19. Auto liability	37,093	1,277	1,400	36,970	3,900	1,230	42,100	8,100	19
21. Auto phys. damage	2,826		120	2,706	1,900	94	4,700	360	21
22. Aircraft (all perils)									22
23. Fidelity									23
24. Surety									24
25. Glass									25
26. Burglary and theft	10			10			10		26
27. Boiler and machinery	30			30			30		27
28. Credit	380		30	350			350	50	28
29. International									29
30. Reinsurance		1,303		1,303	360		1,663	215	30
31. TOTALS	55,100	3,650	2,850	55,900	7,800	1,600	65,300	10,700	31

(a) Including $ .... for present value of life indemnity claims and $ .... reserved for deferred maternity and other similar benefits.

*Business not exceeding 120 months duration.

UNDERWRITING AND INVESTMENT EXHIBIT

PART 4 — EXPENSES

(000 OMITTED)

	(1) LOSS ADJUSTMENT EXPENSES	(2) OTHER UNDERWRITING EXPENSES	(3) INVESTMENT EXPENSES	(4) TOTAL
1. Claim adjustment services:				
(a) Direct	4,250			4,250
(b) Reinsurance assumed	200			200
(c) Reinsurance ceded	50			50
(d) Net claim adjustment services (a+b–c)	4,500			4,500
2. Commission and brokerage:				
(a) Direct		16.400		16.400
(b) Reinsurance assumed		1,200		1,200
(c) Reinsurance ceded		460		460
(d) Contingent—net				
(e) Policy and membership fees				
(f) Net commission and brokerage (a+b–c+d+e)		17.140		17.140
3. Allowances to managers and agents		1,100		1,100
4. Advertising		800		800
5. Boards, bureaus and associations		900		900
6. Surveys and underwriting reports		700		700
7. Audit of assureds' records	49	100	1	150
8. Salaries	5,500	15,100	185	20,785
Employee relations and welfare	400	900	20	1,320
Insurance	29	70	1	100
Directors' fees		30		30
Travel and travel items	1,004	1.400	10	2.414
Rent and rent items	809	1,600	1	2.410
Equipment	500	2.400	14	2.914
Printing and stationery	400	1.300	30	1.730
Postage, telephone and telegraph, exchange and express	1,100	2.200	20	3,320
Legal and auditing		260		260
Totals (Items 3 to 17)	9.791	28.860	282	38.933
Taxes, licenses and fees:				
(a) State and local insurance taxes		4.000		4,000
(b) Insurance department licenses and fees		160		160
(c) Payroll taxes	400	1,000	10	1,410
(d) All other (excluding federal and foreign income and real estate)	9	40	1	50
(e) Total taxes, licenses and fees (a+b+c+d)	409	5,200	11	5,620
Real estate expenses			800	800
Real estate taxes			300	300
Miscellaneous (itemize):				
(a)				
(b)				
(c)				
Total expenses incurred	14.700	51,200	1,393	67,293
Less unpaid expenses—current year	16,700	5,000	100	15,800
Add unpaid expenses—previous year	10,400	5,200	100	15.700
Total expenses paid (Items 22—23+24)	14,400	51.400	1,393	67,193

EXHIBIT 1 — ANALYSIS OF ASSETS (000 OMITTED)

	(1) Ledger Assets	(2) Non-Ledger Including Excess of Market (or Amortized) Over Book Values	(3) Assets Not Admitted Including Excess of Book Over Market (or Amortized) Values	(4) Net Admitted Assets (Cols. 1 + 2 − 3)
1. Bonds (Schedule D)	180,820		22	180,798
2. Stocks (Schedule D):				
2.1 Preferred stocks	9,742		872	8,870
2.2 Common stocks	7,460	1,340		8,800
3. Mortgage loans on real estate (Schedule B):				
(a) First liens	100			100
(b) Other than first liens				
4. Real estate, less encumbrances (Schedule A)	14,470			14,470
5. Collateral loans (Schedule C)				
6.1 Cash on hand and on deposit:				
(a) Cash in company's office	1			1
(b) Cash on deposit (Schedule N)	1,200			1,200
6.2 Short-term investments (Schedule DA)				
7. Other invested assets (Schedule BA)				
8. Agents' balances or uncollected premiums (net as to commissions and dividends):				
8.1 Premiums and agents' balances in course of collection (after deducting ceded reinsurance balances payable of $ 200)	5,400			5,400
8.2 Premiums, agents' balances and installments booked but deferred and not yet due (after deducting ceded reinsurance balances payable of $..........)				
9. Funds held by or deposited with reinsured companies	220			220
10. Bills receivable, taken for premiums				
11. Reinsurance recoverable on loss payments (Schedule F, Part 1A, Col. 1)	190			190
12. Federal income tax recoverable	100			100
13. Electronic data processing equipment	3,200			3,200
14. Interest, dividends and real estate income due and accrued		4,750		4,750
15. Receivable from affiliates				
16. Equities and deposits in pools and associations	18			18
17. Other assets (give items and amounts):				
17.1 Equipment, furniture and supplies	2,100		2,100	XXX
17.2 Bills receivable, not taken for premiums				XXX
17.3 Loans on personal security, endorsed or not				XXX
17.4 OTHER	400		400	
18.				
19.				
20.				
21.				
22. Totals	225,421	6,090	3,394	228,117

EXHIBIT 2—ANALYSIS OF NON-ADMITTED ASSETS

Excluding Excess of Book over Market (or Amortized) Values and Item 14, Col. (3), Exhibit 1

(000 OMITTED)

	(1) End of Previous Year	(2) End of Current Year	(3) Change for Year Increase (−) or Decrease (+) (Col. 1 − 2)
23. Loans on company's stock			
24. Deposits in suspended depositories, less estimated amount recoverable			
25. Agents' balances or uncollected premiums over three months due:			
25.1 Premiums and agents' balances in course of collection			
25.2 Premiums, agents' balances and installments booked but deferred and not yet due			
26. Bills receivable, past due, taken for premiums			
27. Excess of bills receivable, not past due, taken for risks over the unearned premiums thereon			
28. Equipment, furniture and supplies	1,800	2,100	(300)
29. Bills receivable, not taken for premiums			
30. Loans on personal security, endorsed or not			
31. Other assets not admitted (itemize):			
(a) OTHER	300	400	(100)
(b)			
(c)			
(d)			
(e)			
(f)			
(g)			
(h)			
(i)			
(j)			
32. Total change (Col. 3) (Carry to Item 24, Page 4)	XXXXX	XXXXX	(400)

EXHIBIT 3—RECONCILIATION OF LEDGER ASSETS

INCREASE IN LEDGER ASSETS

1. Net premiums written (Part 2, Col. 1, Item 31)
2. Interest, dividends and real estate income received (Part 1, Item 10, Col. 3)
3. From sale or maturity of ledger assets (Part 1A, Col. 2, Item 10)
4. Other income items or increases, viz.:
   - (a) Agents' balances previously charged off
   - (b) Remittances from home office to U.S. branch (gross)
   - (c) Funds held under reinsurance treaties (net)
   - (d) Borrowed money (gross)
   - (e) Amounts withheld or retained for account of others (net)
   - (f)
   - (g)
   - (h)
   - (i) SUPPLEMENTARY INFORMATION
   - (j)
   - (k)
   - (l)
5. Adjustment in book value of ledger assets (Part 1A, Item 10, Col. 4)
6. Capital paid in (Page 4, Item 28a)
7. Surplus paid in (Page 4, Item 29a)
8. Total (Items 1 to 7)

DECREASE IN LEDGER ASSETS

9. Net losses paid (Part 3, Col. 4, Item 31)
10. Expenses paid (Part 4, Item 25, Col. 4)
11. From sale or maturity of ledger assets (Part 1A, Col. 3, Item 10)
12. Other disbursement items or decreases, viz.:
    - (a) Agents' balances charged off
    - (b) Remittances to home office from U. S. branch (gross)
    - (c) Funds held under reinsurance treaties (net)
    - (d) Borrowed money (gross)
    - (e) Amounts withheld or retained for account of others (net)
    - (f)
    - (g)
    - (h)
    - (i)
    - (j)
    - (k)
    - (l)

. Adjustment in book value of ledger assets (Part 1A, Item 10, Col. 5) and depreciation (Item 12, Part 1)

. Federal and foreign income taxes paid

Dividends paid stockholders

Dividends to policyholders on direct business, less $.................. dividends on reinsurance assumed or ceded (net)

Total (Items 9 to 18)

RECONCILIATION BETWEEN YEARS

Amount of ledger assets as per balance December 31 of previous year

Increase (+) or decrease (−) in ledger assets during the year (Item 8 minus Item 19)

Balance = ledger assets December 31 of current year

NAIC GROUP CODE:

EXHIBIT OF PREMIUMS AND LOSSES

NAIC COMPANY CODE:

BUSINESS IN THE STATE OF DURING THE YEAR

(1) LINE OF BUSINESS	Gross Premiums, Including Policy and Membership Fees, Less Return Premiums and Premiums on Policies Not Taken (2) Direct Premiums Written	(3) Direct Premiums Earned*	(4) Dividends Paid or Credited to Policyholders on Direct Business	(5) Direct Losses Paid (deducting salvage)	(6) Direct Losses Incurred	(7) Direct Losses Unpaid
1. Fire						
2. Allied lines						
3. Farmowners multiple peril						
4. Homeowners multiple peril						
5. Commercial multiple peril						
8. Ocean marine						
9. Inland marine						
10.						
11. Medical malpractice						
12. Earthquake						
13. Group accident and health						
14. Credit A & H (Group and Individual)						
15.1 Collectively renewable A & H			*Supplementary Information*			
15.2 Non-cancellable A & H						
15.3 Guaranteed renewable A & H						
15.4 Non-renewable for stated reasons only						
15.5 Other accident only						
15.6 All other A & H						
16. Workers' compensation						
17. Other liability						
19.1 Private passenger auto no-fault (personal injury protection)						
19.2 Other private passenger auto liability						
19.3 Commercial auto no-fault (personal injury protection)						
19.4 Other commercial auto liability						
21.1 Private passenger auto physical damage						
21.2 Commercial auto physical damage						
22. Aircraft (all perils)						
23. Fidelity						
24. Surety						
25. Glass						
26. Burglary and theft						
27. Boiler and machinery						
28. Credit						
31. TOTALS						

Finance and service charges not included in Lines 1 to 31: $

*Direct premiums earned may be estimated by formula on the basis of country-wide ratios for the respective lines of business except where adjustments are required to recognize special situations.

CREDIT ACCIDENT AND HEALTH INSURANCE
(Included in the Above Exhibit)

To be submitted not later than April 1.

(1)	(2) Direct Premiums (Excluding Reinsurance Accepted and without Deduction of Reinsurance Ceded)	(3) Direct Premiums Earned (prior to Dividends and Retrospective Rate Credits Paid or Credited)	(4) Dividends Paid or Credited on Direct Business	(5) Direct Losses Paid	(6) Direct Losses Incurred	(7) Direct Losses Unpaid
32.1 Group A & H Policies — Loans of 60 or LESS months' duration						
32.2 Group A & H Policies — Loans of GREATER THAN 60 MONTHS' DURATION BUT NOT GREATER THAN 120 MONTHS						
33. Other A & H Policies						
34. Totals (Items 32.1 + 32.2 + 33)						

GENERAL INTERROGATORIES

1. Have there been included in this statement proper reserves to cover liabilities which may have been actually incurred on or before December 31 but of which no notice was received at the home office until subsequently? ANSWER:
2. Does the company issue both participating and non-participating policies? ANSWER: .... If so, state the amount of net premiums in force on both participating and non-participating policies. ANSWER:
3. (Mutual Companies and Reciprocal Exchanges only):
   (a) Does company issue assessable policies? ANSWER: .... (b) Does company issue non-assessable policies? ANSWER:
   (c) If assessable policies are issued, what is the extent of the contingent liability of the policyholders? ANSWER:
   (d) Total amount of assessments laid or ordered to be laid during the year on deposit notes or contingent premiums $
4. (Reciprocal Exchanges only):
   (a) Does the Exchange appoint local agents? ANSWER: .... If so, is the commission paid out of Attorney-in-Facts' compensation or as a direct expense of the Exchange? ANSWER:
   (b) What expenses of the Exchange are not paid out of the compensation of the Attorney-in-Fact? ANSWER:
   (c) Has any Attorney-in-Fact compensation, contingent on fulfillment of certain conditions, been deferred? ANSWER: .... If so, give full information
5. CAPITAL STOCK OF THIS COMPANY

CLASS	NUMBER SHARES AUTHORIZED	NUMBER SHARES OUTSTANDING	PAR VALUE PER SHARE	REDEMPTION PRICE IF CALLABLE	IS DIVIDEND RATE LIMITED?	ARE DIVIDENDS CUMULATIVE?
Preferred						
Common				X X X X	X X X X	X X X X

6. Does the company own any securities of a real estate holding company or otherwise hold real estate indirectly? ANSWER: .... If so, explain
   Name of real estate holding company .... Number of parcels involved .... Total book value $
7a. Is the company a member of an insurance Holding Company System consisting of two or more affiliated persons, one or more of which is an insurer? ANSWER:
7b. If the answer to General Interrogatory 7a is yes, did the company register and file with its domiciliary State Insurance Commissioner, Director or Superintendent, or with such regulatory official of the State of domicile of the principal insurer in the Holding Company System, a registration statement providing disclosure substantially similar to the standards adopted by the National Association of Insurance Commissioners in its Model Insurance Holding Company System Regulatory Act and model regulations pertaining thereto, or is the company subject to standards and disclosure requirements substantially similar to those required by such Act and regulations? ANSWER: .... State regulating
8. Total amount loaned during the year to directors or other officers, $ .... ; to stockholders not officers, $ .... Total amount of loans outstanding at end of year to directors or other officers, $ .... ; to stockholders not officers, $
9. Did any person while an officer, director or trustee of the company receive directly or indirectly, during the period covered by this statement, any commission on the business transactions of the company? ANSWER:
9a. Did any person while an officer, director, trustee or employee receive directly or indirectly, during the period covered by this statement, any compensation in addition to his regular compensation on account of the reinsurance transactions of the company? ANSWER:
9b. Has the company an established procedure for disclosure to its board of directors or trustees of any material interest or affiliation on the part of any of its officers, directors, trustees, or responsible employees which is in or is likely to conflict with the official duties of such person? ANSWER:
9c. Except for retirement plans generally applicable to its staff employees and agents and contracts with its agents for the payment of commissions, has the company any agreement with a person whereby it agrees that for any service rendered or to be rendered, he shall receive directly or indirectly any salary, compensation or emolument that will extend beyond a period of 12 months from the date of the agreement? ANSWER:
10. What amount of installment notes is owned and now held by the company? ANSWER:
11. Have any of these notes been hypothecated, sold or used in any manner as security for money loaned within the past year? .... If so, what amount? ANSWER:
12. Largest not aggregate amount insured in any one risk (excluding workers' compensation). ANSWER:
13. What provision has this company made to protect itself from an excessive loss in the event of a catastrophe under a workers' compensation contract issued without limit of loss? ANSWER:
14. Has this company guaranteed any financed premium accounts? ANSWER: .... If so, give full information
15. Has this company reinsured any risk with any other company and agreed to release such company from liability, in whole or in part, from any loss that may occur on the risk, or portion thereof, reinsured? ANSWER: .... If so, give full information
16. If the company has assumed risks from another company, there should be charged on account of such reinsurances a reserve equal to that which the original company would have been required to charge had it retained the risks. Has this been done? ANSWER:
17. Has this company guaranteed policies issued by any other company and now in force? ANSWER: .... If so, give full information
18. Were all the stocks, bonds and other securities owned December 31 of current year, in the actual possession of the company on said date, except as shown by the schedules of special and other deposits? ANSWER: .... If not, give full and complete information relating thereto:
18a. Does the company own any investments in letter stock or other restricted securities? ANSWER: .... If yes, are they identified by appropriate symbol or otherwise in Schedule D? ANSWER:
18b. Have all private placement investments which were the subject of renegotiation or modification of their terms during the year been disclosed to the Valuation of Securities Office of the NAIC, with full details as to the provisions renegotiated or modified? ANSWER:
18c. Have filings been made with the Valuation of Securites Office of the NAIC in connection with acquisition and disposition of securities as required by Section 8 of the Valuation Procedures and Instructions for Bonds and Stocks? ANSWER:
19. Were any of the stocks, bonds or other assets of the company loaned, placed under option agreement, or otherwise made available for use by another person during the year covered by this statement? ANSWER: .... If yes, give full and complete information relating thereto
    Show all information if any securities were involved under a reverse repurchase agreement
20. State as of what date the latest financial examination of the company was made or is being made, and by what department or departments. ANSWER:
21. Has any change been made during the year of this statement in the charter, by-laws, articles of incorporation, or deed of settlement of the company? ANSWER: .... If so, when? .... If not previously filed, furnish herewith a certified copy of the instrument as amended.
22. Has any direct new business been solicited or written in any state where the company was not licensed? ANSWER: Yes .... No .... If answer is "yes," explain
23. Is the purchase or sale of all investments of the company passed upon either by the board of directors or a subordinate committee thereof? ANSWER:
24. Does the company keep a complete permanent record of the proceedings of its board of directors and all subordinate committees thereof? ANSWER:
25. Have the instructions for completing the blank required by this Department been followed in every detail? ANSWER:
    (Only United States branches of foreign companies need answer interrogatories 26 and 27):
26. What changes have been made during the year in the United States manager or the United States trustees of the company? ANSWER:
27. Does this statement contain all business transacted for the company through its United States branch, on risks wherever located? ANSWER:
28. Are any of the liabilities for unpaid losses and unpaid loss adjustment expenses discounted to present value at a rate of interest greater than zero? ANSWER: .... If so, state maximum rate of interest used: .... % and the aggregate amount of discount: $
29. During the period covered by this Statement, did (a) any agent, general agent, broker, sales represenative, non-affiliated sales/service organization, or any combination thereof under common control (other than salaried employees of the company),(b) any sales/service organization owned in whole or in part by the company or an affiliate, receive credit or commissions for or control a substantial part (more than 20 percent of any major line of business measured on direct premiums) of (i) sales of new business? (ii) renewals? ANSWER: (a)(i) .... (ii) .... (b)(i) .... (ii)
30. If the company underwrites commercial insurance risks, such as workers' compensation, are premium or promissory notes accepted from its insureds covering unpaid premiums and/or unpaid losses? .... If so, what was the range of interest rates charged under such notes during the period covered by this statement? .... % to .... %

    Are letters of credit or collateral and other funds received from insureds being utilized by the company to secure premium or promissory notes taken by the company, or to secure any of the company's reported direct unpaid loss reserves, including unpaid losses under loss deductible features of commercial policies? .... If so, state the amount thereof at December 31 of the current year. Letters of Credit $ .... Collateral and other funds $
31. What interest, direct or indirect, has this company in the capital stock of any other insurance company? ANSWER:

GENERAL INTERROGATORIES

32. Ceded Reinsurance Report

SECTION 1. Annual Report of Reinsurance Transactions (including facultative and pooling transactions)

1. What is the maximum amount of return commission which would have been due reinsurers if they or you had cancelled all of your company's reinsurance or if you or a receiver had cancelled all of your company's direct business and reinsurance assumed as of the end of the period covered by this Annual Statement, with the return of the unearned premium reserve? Intercompany pooling agreement:............, All other reinsurance:............, Total:............
2. What would be the amount of the reduction in surplus as shown on this Annual Statement if adjustments were made to reflect the full amount described in Question 1? Intercompany pooling agreement:............, All other reinsurance:............, Total:............
3. On the basis of loss experience to date, have you accrued earned additional premiums which would be payable or return reinsurance commissions which would be refundable in the future if the reinsurer or you cancelled all of your company's reinsurance as of the end of the period covered by this Annual Statement? Answer:............ If you have not so accrued, what would be the amount of such additional premium or return commission? Intercompany pooling agreement:............, All other reinsurance:............, Total:............
4. What would be the amount of the reduction in surplus as of the end of the period covered by this Annual Statement if adjustments were made to reflect the full amount described in Question 3? Intercompany pooling agreement:............, All other reinsurance:............, Total:............
5. What would be the percentage reduction in surplus as of the end of the period covered by this Annual Statement from the combined effects of the amounts described in Questions 2 and 4? Intercompany pooling agreement:............, All other reinsurance:............, Total:............
6. What is the amount of additional reinsurance premiums, computed at the maximum level provided by the reinsurance contracts, in excess of amounts previously paid and presently accrued (including as accrued the amount shown in response to Question 3) on retrospective adjustment periods covering the most recent three years? Intercompany pooling agreement:............, All other reinsurance:............, Total:............
7. What is the amount of return reinsurance commission, computed at the minimum level provided by the reinsurance contracts, in excess of amounts previously paid and presently accrued (including as accrued the amount shown in response to Question 3) on retrospective adjustment periods covering the most recent three years? Intercompany pooling agreement:............, All other reinsurance:............, Total:............
8. What would be the percentage reduction in surplus as of the end of the period covered by this Annual Statement from the combined effects of the amounts described in Questions 6 and 7? Intercompany pooling agreement:............, All other reinsurance:............, Total:............
9. What would be the percentage reduction in surplus as of the end of the period covered by this Annual Statement from the combined effects of the amounts described in Questions 2, 4, 6 and 7? Intercompany pooling agreement:............, All other reinsurance:............, Total:............

SECTION 2. Supplementary Report of Reinsurance Transactions

Whenever the company enters into a new reinsurance contract or alters the terms of any existing ceded reinsurance contract, during the year following the date of this Annual Statement, it shall answer the questions set forth in Section 1 as of the date of such new or altered contracts. If the answer to Question 5 shows a reduction in the then current surplus of 30% or more, it shall report such fact within 15 days after the date of such new contract or alteration to each Regulatory Authority with which this Annual Statement was filed.

SECTION 3. Requirements for Reinsurance Credit

Whenever the answer to Question 5 shows a reduction in surplus of 30% or more, or whenever the answer to Question 8 shows a reduction in surplus of 50% or more, or whenever the answer to Question 9 shows a reduction in surplus of 60% or more the company shall not take credit for its ceded reinsurance unless:

A. The company shall file in respect of each reinsurer separately as of the end of each calendar quarter, a statement of balances which shall include cash balances, unearned premium reserves, loss reserves and accruals for retrospective adjustments. Such statement shall be certified by the reinsurer and filed by the company within 45 days after the end of each calendar quarter with each Regulatory Authority with which the Annual Statement is filed; and,

B. Its reinsurance contract provides that in the event of termination the reinsurer shall continue to be obligated, with respect to business in force, for 90 days or until the earliest date thereafter as of which such original business may be terminated, but in no event more than 12 months; and,

C. In the event of insolvency of the company, the reinsurer shall be entitled to recoup unearned ceding commission only to the extent that original commissions and taxes are recouped by the company; and,

D. The company submits all reinsurance contracts in force and thereafter negotiated to each Regulatory Authority with which the Annual Statement is filed; and,

E. The reinsurance agreements for which credit is claimed by the company contain provisions protecting the company from an element of risk from ultimate underwriting loss; or,

F. The reduction is attributable to a reinsurance pooling agreement between affiliated companies which has been approved by the insurance regulatory authority in the company's domiciliary state.

Consistent with the purpose of this report, the Regulatory Authority (ies) in appropriate cases may waive one or more of these instructions.

Instructions for Completing Ceded Reinsurance Report

Question 1. This amount should be computed by applying the fixed or provisional commission rates for each treaty to the unearned premium reserve for each such treaty. For this calculation, it shall be assumed that all reinsurance is entirely cancelled, with return of unearned premium and commission.

Question 2. The amount determined in response to Question 1 should be reduced to reflect applicable income taxes and unearned premium reserves ceded to unauthorized companies, if any.

Question 3. The amount determined in response to this question should be based on loss experience to date reflecting amounts claimed as reinsurance recoverable on paid and unpaid losses as set forth in Schedule F, Part 1A, Section 1.

Question 4. The amount determined in response to Question 3 should be adjusted to reflect applicable income taxes.

Question 5. Divide the sum of the answers to Questions 2 and 4 by Surplus As Regards Policyholders as shown on Page 3, Item 27 of this Annual Statement.

Questions 6 and 7. These instructions apply to retrospective rated contracts and sliding scale commission contracts.

The amounts below should be computed separately for each retrospective adjustment period which is currently in force or which was in force during the most recent three years:

(a) In regard to retrospective adjustment periods which commenced within the most recent three years and ended during this period, the amount should be computed at the maximum level provided by the reinsurance contracts less amounts previously paid to reinsurers and less amounts presently accrued (including as accrued the amount shown in response to Question 3).

(b) In regard to retrospective adjustment periods which commenced prior to the most recent three years and which ended during this period, the amount should be determined as in (a) above, but should be pro rata reduced for the period of time of the retrospective adjustment period which is prior to the most recent three-year period.

(c) In regard to retrospective adjustment periods which commenced within the most recent three years but will end after this period, the amount should be computed at the maximum level provided by the reinsurance contracts on the basis of inception to statement date premium data. Otherwise, with this exception the instructions in (a) above should be followed.

(d) In regard to retrospective adjustment periods which commenced prior to the most recent three years and which will end after this period, the amount should be determined at the maximum level provided by the reinsurance contracts on the basis of inception to statement date premium data. This amount should be pro rata reduced for the period of time of the retrospective adjustment period which is prior to the most recent three-year period. Otherwise, with these exceptions the instructions in (a) above should be followed.

Question 8. Divide the sum of the amounts determined as answers to Questions 6 and 7, less applicable income taxes by Surplus As Regards Policyholders as shown on Page 3, Item 27 of this Annual Statement.

Question 9. Divide the sum of the answers to Questions 2, 4, 6 and 7 (adjusted by applicable income taxes) by Surplus As Regards Policyholders as shown on Page 3, Item 27 of this Annual Statement.

NOTES TO FINANCIAL STATEMENTS

asis of Presentation.

The accompanying financial have been prepared in conformity with ccounting practices prescribed or permitted by the National Assoc-ation of Insurance Commissioners and the State of ______________.

asis of Valuation of Assets.

Assets are generally stated as follows: Bonds at amortized cost; referred stocks at cost; common stocks at market; unconsolidated ıbsidiaries on the equity basis; property and equipment at depreciated ost, less encumbrances. Depreciation is calculated on a straight ine basis over the estimated useful life of each asset. Subsidiary mpanies are valued in accordance with Section 4(B)(IV) of the ecurities Valuation Handbook.

deral Income Tax Allocation.

The Company does not file consolidated income tax returns with its bsidiary companies. Federal income taxes incurred and available for coupment in the event of future net losses are; current year ,550,000; first preceeding year $2,400,000; second preceeding year ,400,000. The Company has capital loss carryover of $32,000 which pires in 19XX.

formation Concerning Subsidiaries.

All the outstanding shares of ABC Financial Services, Inc. and bsidiaries are owned by the Company.

tirement Plan.

The Company has a noncontributory pension plan covering substantially employees. As a matter of policy, pension costs are funded as they rue and vested benefits are fully funded.

ital and Surplus and Shareholder Dividend Restrictions.

The maximum amount of dividends which can be paid by the Company shareholders without prior approval of the Insurance Commissioner approximately $13,000,000. Dividends are paid quarterly as de-mined by the Board of Directors. Dividends paid during the current r were $500,000. The Company has no preferred stock outstanding.

rowed Money.

The Company has outstanding a real estate mortgage loan on its e office property which requires annual payments of $500,000 s interest.

tingent Liabilities.

The Company has no unrecorded contingent liabilities.

Company does not have any material lease obligations at this time.

Note.—In case the following schedules do not afford sufficient space, companies may furnish them on separate forms, provided the same are upon paper of like size and arrangements and contain the information asked for herein and have the name of the company printed or stamped at the top thereof.

SPECIAL DEPOSIT SCHEDULE

Showing all deposits or investments NOT held for the protection of ALL the policyholders of the Company

(1) WHERE DEPOSITED	(2) DESCRIPTION AND PURPOSE OF DEPOSIT (Indicating literal form of registration of Securities)	(3) PAR VALUE	(4) STATEMENT VALUE	(5) MARKET VALUE
	DETAILS OMITTED			
	Totals			

SCHEDULE OF ALL OTHER DEPOSITS

Showing all deposits made with any Government, Province, State, District, County, Municipality, Corporation, firm or individual, except those shown in Schedule N, and those shown in "Special Deposit Schedule" above

(1) WHERE DEPOSITED	(2) DESCRIPTION AND PURPOSE OF DEPOSIT (Indicating literal form of registration of Securities)	(3) PAR VALUE	(4) STATEMENT VALUE	(5) MARKET VA
	Totals			

SCHEDULE OF EXAMINATION FEES AND EXPENSES

(1) TYPE OF EXAM (a)	(2) STATE INITIATING EXAM (b)	(3) STATES PARTICIPATING (b)	(4) DATE BEGUN	(5) DATE COMPLETED	(6) DATE REPORT PUBLISHED	FEES AND EXPENSES INCURRED IN CURRENT YEAR (7) AMOUNT (c)	(8) STATE (b)	(9) OFFSETTING CREDITS, IF ANY
			DETAILS OMITTED					
					Total			

(a) "M" for marketing conduct, "F" for financial condition, describe others
(b) Use 2 digit post office abbreviation
(c) Show amount paid to each state (or representatives thereof) separately. The total amount plus $ .... for other state insurance department licenses and fees should agree with Page 11, Column 4, Item 18(b).

FIVE-YEAR HISTORICAL DATA

All Figures Taken From or Developed From Annual Statements of Corresponding Years

Show amounts in whole dollars only, no cents; show ratios and percentages to one decimal place, i.e. 17.6.

	(1) 19	(2) 19	(3) 19	(4) 19	(5) 19
Gross Premiums Written (Page 8, Part 2C, Cols. 1 & 2)					
1. Liability Lines (Items 11, 16, 17 & 19)					
2. Property Lines (Items 1, 2, 9, 12, 21, 25 & 26)		DETAILS	OMITTED		
3. Property and Liability Combined Lines (Items 3, 4, 5, 8, 22 & 27)					
4. All Other Lines (Items 10, 13, 14, 15, 23, 24, 28, 29 & 30)					
5. Total (Item 31)					
Net Premiums Written (Page 8, Part 2C, Col. 4)					
6. Liability Lines (Items 11, 16, 17 & 19)					
7. Property Lines (Items 1, 2, 9, 12, 21, 25 & 26)					
8. Property and Liability Combined Lines (Items 3, 4, 5, 8, 22 & 27)					
9. All Other Lines (Items 10, 13, 14, 15, 23, 24, 28, 29 & 30)					
10. Total (Item 31)					
Statement of Income (Page 4)					
11. Net Underwriting Gain or Loss (Item 7)					
12. Net Investment Gain or Loss (Item 9A)					
13. Total Other Income (Item 17)					
14. Dividends to Policyholders (Item 18A)					
15. Federal and Foreign Income Taxes Incurred (Item 19)					
16. Net Income (Item 20)					
Balance Sheet Items (Pages 2 and 3)					
17. Total Admitted Assets (Page 2, Item 22)					
18. Agents' Balances or Uncollected Premiums (Page 2)					
18.1 In Course of Collection (Item 8.1)					
18.2 Deferred and Not Yet Due (Item 8.2)					
19. Total Liabilities (Page 3, Item 23)					
20. Losses (Page 3, Item 1)					
21. Loss Adjustment Expenses (Page 3, Item 2)					
22. Unearned Premiums (Page 3, Item 10)					
23. Capital Paid Up (Page 3, Item 25A)					
24. Surplus as Regards Policyholders (Page 3, Item 27)					
Percentage Distribution of Cash and Invested Assets (Page 2) (Item divided by Page 2, Item 7a) x 100.0					
25. Bonds (Item 1)					
26. Stocks (Items 2.1 and 2.2)					
27. Mortgage Loans on Real Estate (Item 3)					
28. Real Estate (Items 4.1 and 4.2)					
29. Collateral Loans (Item 5)					
30. Cash and Short-term Investments (Item 6.1 and 6.2) (1981 and prior, Item 6)					
31. Other Invested Assets (Item 7)					
32. Cash and Invested Assets (Item 7a)	100.0	100.0	100.0	100.0	100.0
Investments in Parent, Subsidiaries and Affiliates					
33. Bonds (Page 29, Item 29, Col. 6)					
34. Preferred Stocks (Page 29, Item 47, Col. 3)					
35. Common Stocks (Page 29, Item 65, Col. 3)					
36. Short-term Investments (Schedule DA, Part 1, Col. 10)					
37. Total of above Items 33, 34, 35 & 36					
38. Percentage of Investments in Parents, Subsidiaries and Affiliates to Surplus as Regards Policyholders (Item 37 above divided by Page 3, Col. 1, Item 27 × 100.0)					

FIVE-YEAR HISTORICAL DATA
(Continued)

	(1) 19	(2) 19	(3) 19	(4) 19	(5) 19
Capital and Surplus Accounts (Page 4)					
Net Unrealized Capital Gains or Losses (Item 23)					
Dividends to Stockholders (Cash) (Item 31)		DETAILS OMITTED			
Change in Surplus as Regards Policyholders for the Year (Item 39)					
Gross Losses Paid (Page 9, Part 3, Cols. 1 & 2)					
Liability Lines (Items 11, 16, 17 & 19)					
Property Lines (Items 1, 2, 9, 12, 21, 25 & 26)					
Property and Liability Combined Lines (Items 3, 4, 5, 8, 22 & 27)					
All Other Lines (Items 10, 13, 14, 15, 23, 24, 28, 29 & 30)					
Total (Item 31)					
Net Losses Paid (Page 9, Part 3, Col. 4)					
Liability Lines (Items 11, 16, 17 & 19)					
Property Lines (Items 1, 2, 9, 12, 21, 25 & 26)					
Property and Liability Combined Lines (Items 3, 4, 5, 8, 22 & 27)					
All Other Lines (Items 10, 13, 14, 15, 23, 24, 28, 29 & 30)					
Total (Item 31)					
Operating Ratios (Page 4) (Item divided by Page 4, Item 1) x 100.0					
Premiums Earned (Item 1)	100.0	100.0	100.0	100.0	100.0
Losses Incurred (Item 2)					
Loss Expenses Incurred (Item 3)					
Other Underwriting Expenses Incurred (Item 4)					
Net Underwriting Gain or (Loss) (Item 7)					
ther Ratios					
ther Underwriting Expenses to Net Premiums Written Page 4, Items 4 + 5—17 divided by Page 8, Part 2C, ol. 4, Item 31 x 100.0)					
osses and Loss Expenses Incurred to Premiums Earned Page 4, Items 2 + 3 divided by Page 4, Item 1 x 100.0)					
et Premiums Written to Policyholders' Surplus (Page 8, art 2C, Col. 4, Item 31, divided by Page 3, Item 27, ol. 1 x 100.0)					
ne Year Loss Development (000 omitted) chedule "O", Page 54					
evelopment in estimated liability on unpaid losses curred prior to current year (Part 1, Item 31, Col. 18)					
evelopment in estimated liability for loss expenses losses incurred prior to current year Part 2, Item 31, Col. 18)					
chedule "P", Page 59					
evelopment in estimated losses and loss expenses curred prior to current year (Part 2, Item 11, l. 7 less Col. 6)					
tal of above Items 60, 61 & 62					
atio of development of loss and loss expenses incurred policyholders' surplus of previous year end (Item 63 ove divided by Page 4, Item 21, Col 1 x 100.0)					
wo Year Loss Development (000 omitted) hedule "O", Page 54					
velopment in estimated liability on unpaid sses incurred 2 years before the current year d prior (Part 1, Item 31, Col. 19)					
evelopment in estimated liability for loss penses on losses incurred 2 years before the rrent year and prior (Part 2, Item 31, Col. 19)					
hedule "P", Page 59					
velopment in estimated losses and loss expenses urred 2 years before the current year and prior art 2, Item 9, Col. 7 less Col. 5)					
tal of above Items 65, 66 & 67					
tio of development of loss and loss expenses incurred reported policyholders' surplus of second previous ar end (Item 68 above divided by Page 4, Item 21, . 2 x 100.0)					

ANNUAL STATEMENT FOR THE YEAR 19 OF THE PROPERTY-LIABILITY INSURANCE Co.

Name

SCHEDULE A—Part 1

Showing All Real Estate OWNED December 31 of Current Year, the Cost, Book and Market Value thereof, the Nature and Amount of all Liens and Encumbrances thereon, including Interest Due and Accrued, etc.

(000 OMITTED)

NO.	(1) QUANTITY, DIMENSIONS AND LOCATION OF LANDS; SIZE AND DESCRIPTION OF BUILDINGS (Nature of encumbrances, if any, including interest due and accrued)	(2) DATE ACQUIRED	(3) NAME OF VENDOR	(4) AMOUNT OF ENCUMBRANCES	(5) *ACTUAL COST	(6) BOOK VALUE LESS ENCUMBRANCES	(7) †MARKET VALUE LESS ENCUMBRANCES	(8) INCREASE BY ADJUSTMENT IN BOOK VALUE DURING YEAR	(9) DECREASE BY ADJUSTMENT IN BOOK VALUE DURING YEAR	(10) GROSS INCOME LESS INTEREST ON ENCUMBRANCES	(11) EXPENDED FOR TAXES, REPAIRS AND EXPENSES	(12) NET INCOME	RENTAL VALUE OF SPACE OCCUPIED BY (13) Company	(14) Parents, Subsidiaries and Affiliates	(15) YEAR OF LAST APPRAISAL
	LOT 100 - COUNTY PLAZA	19XX	BUSINESS BUILDERS	4,000	19,500	14,000	14,000		450	1,775	1,490	310	1,250	560	
	LOTS 3 & 4 ANYPLACE	19XX	COMMERCIAL BUILDERS		500	470	470		20	60	10	50	50		
			Totals	4,000	20,000	14,470	14,470		470	1,835	1,500	360	1,300	560	

*Including cost of acquiring title, and, if the property was acquired by foreclosure, such cost shall include the amounts expended for taxes, repairs and improvements prior to the date on which the company acquired title. †State basis on which market value was determined

CLASSIFICATION

Showing the total amount of Real Estate owned in each State and Foreign Country

STATE	MARKET VALUE	STATE	MARKET VALUE	STATE	MARKET VALUE	STATE	MARKET VALUE	FOREIGN COUNTRY	MARKET VALUE
				DETAILS OMITTED					
								Total	

ANNUAL STATEMENT FOR THE YEAR 19 OF THE Property-Liability Insurance Co.
Name

SCHEDULE A—Part 2

Showing All Real Estate ACQUIRED During the Year and Showing also Amounts Expended for Additions and Permanent Improvements Made During said Year to ALL Real Estate

NO.	(1) QUANTITY, DIMENSIONS AND LOCATION OF LANDS; SIZE AND DESCRIPTION OF BUILDINGS (OR) NATURE OF ADDITIONS AND PERMANENT IMPROVEMENTS MADE DURING THE YEAR (Nature of encumbrances, if any)	(2) DATE ACQUIRED	(3) HOW ACQUIRED	(4) NAME OF VENDOR	(5) COST TO COMPANY DURING THE YEAR	(6) AMOUNT EXPENDED FOR ADDITIONS AND PERMANENT IMPROVEMENTS DURING THE YEAR	(7) BOOK VALUE DECEMBER 31 OF CURRENT YEAR LESS ENCUMBRANCES
		Details Omitted					
				Totals			

SCHEDULE A—Part 3

Showing All Real Estate SOLD or Otherwise Disposed of During the Year Including Payments During the Year on "Sales under Contract"

NO.	(1) QUANTITY, DIMENSIONS AND LOCATION OF LANDS; SIZE AND DESCRIPTION OF BUILDINGS (Nature of encumbrances, if any)	(2) DATE SOLD	(3) NAME OF PURCHASER	(4) †COST TO COMPANY	(5) INCREASE BY ADJUSTMENT IN BOOK VALUE DURING YEAR	(6) DECREASE BY ADJUSTMENT IN BOOK VALUE DURING YEAR	(7) ††BOOK VALUE AT DATE OF SALE LESS ENCUMBRANCES	(8) ‡AMOUNT RECEIVED INCLUDING PAYMENTS ON SALES UNDER CONTRACT	(9) PROFIT ON SALE	(10) LOSS ON SALE	(11) GROSS INCOME DURING YEAR LESS INTEREST ON ENCUMBRANCES	(12) EXPENDED FOR TAXES, REPAIRS AND EXPENSES DURING YEAR
				Details Omitted								
			Totals									

†Including cost of acquiring title, and, if the property was acquired by foreclosure, such cost shall include the amounts expended for taxes, repairs and improvements prior to the date on which the company acquired title. In reporting sales under contract, include payments received during the current year only.
‡Indicate payments on "Sales under Contracts" in Part 3 by inserting the letter "P" after the number of the parcel.
††In case of sales under contract, include payments received during current year only, until book value per Part 1 is exhausted.

SCHEDULE A—Verification Between Years

1. Book value, December 31, previous year (Item 4, Col. 1, Exhibit 1, prior year statement) . . . ______
2. Increase by adjustment:
   - (a) Totals, Part 1, Col. 8 . . . ______
   - (b) Totals, Part 3, Col. 5 . . . ______
3. Cost of acquired, Part 2, Col. 5 . . . ______
4. Cost of additions and permanent improvements, Part 2, Col. 6 . . . ______
5. Profit on sales, Part 3, Col. 9 . . . ______
6. Total . . . ______
7. Decrease by adjustment:
   - (a) Totals, Part 1, Col. 9 . . . ______
   - (b) Totals, Part 3, Col. 6 . . . ______
8. Received on sales, Part 3, Col. 8 . . . ______
9. Loss on sales, Part 3, Col. 10 . . . ______
10. Book value, December 31, current year (Item 4, Col. 1, Exhibit 1) . . . ______

Form 2

ANNUAL STATEMENT FOR THE YEAR 19 OF THE Property-Liability Insurance Co.

Name

SCHEDULE B

Showing all Long-term MORTGAGES OWNED December 31 of Current Year, and all Mortgage Loans Made, Increased, Discharged, Reduced or Disposed of During the Year

Indicate by symbols FHA and VA if loans are so insured. All such FHA and VA insured loans not in process of foreclosure may be summarized by year and state of issue and combined values may be shown for land and buildings.

(000 OMITTED)

(1)	DATE		RECORD OF MORTGAGE				PRINCIPAL						INTEREST				(18)	(19)	(20)	(21)
NUMBER	(2) Year Given	(3) Year Due	(4) State	(5) County	(6) Book	(7) Page	(8) Amount Unpaid Dec. 31 of Previous Year	(9) Amount Loaned During Year (A)	(10) Amount Paid on Account or in Full During Year (B)	(11) Amount Unpaid Dec. 31 of Current Year (8) + (9)—(10)	(12) Date Due	(13) Rate of	(14) Amount Past Due Dec. 31 of Current Year	(15) Am't Accrued Dec. 31 of Current Year	(16) Gross Am't Rec'd During Year	(17) Paid for Accrued Interest on Mortgages Acquired During Year	VALUE OF LANDS MORTGAGED	VALUE OF BUILDINGS	AMOUNT OF FIRE INSURANCE HELD BY COMPANY ON THE BUILDINGS	LOCATION AND DESCRIPTION (State if this mortgage is being foreclosed, or if there are any prior liens. State name of mortgagor if mortgagor is a parent, subsidiary, affiliate, officer or director.)
	XX	XX	IL	Page			110		10	100	XX				1		20	140	200	Page County, IL
				Totals			110		10	100	XX	XX			1		XXX	XXX	XXX	

(A) Including all mortgages "purchased" or otherwise acquired during the year and all increases during the year on loans outstanding December 31 of previous year

(B) Including mortgages under which Company has secured title and possession by foreclosure

CLASSIFICATION

Showing the Total Amount of Long-term Mortgage Loans on Real Estate in Each State and Foreign Country

STATE	AMOUNT	STATE	AMOUNT	STATE	AMOUNT	STATE	AMOUNT	FOREIGN COUNTRY	AMOUNT
								Total	

...lume derived from non-cancellable accident and health policies, may report on Schedule B forms of the Life Blank in lieu of this schedule.

Form 2

ANNUAL STATEMENT FOR THE YEAR 19 OF THE Property-Liability Insurance Co.

Name

SCHEDULE B A—PART 1

Showing Other Long-term Invested Assets OWNED December 31, Current Year

(1) NUMBER OF UNITS AND DESCRIPTION*	(2) YEAR ACQUIRED	(3) LESSEE OR LOCATION	(4) AMOUNT OF ENCUMBRANCES	(5) COST TO COMPANY	(6) BOOK VALUE AT DECEMBER 31, LESS ENCUMBRANCES	(7) STATEMENT VALUE AT DECEMBER 31	(8) MARKET OR INVESTMENT VALUE AT DECEMBER 31, LESS ENCUMBRANCES	(9) ADDITIONS TO (+) OR REDUCTIONS IN (—) INVESTMENT†	(10) DECREASE (—) OR INCREASE (+) BY ADJUSTMENT IN BOOK VALUE DURING YEAR‡	(11) GROSS INCOME RECEIVED DURING YEAR	(12) NET INCOME RECEIVED DURING YEAR §	(13) AMOUNTS ACCRUED AT DECEMBER 31 §§	(14) AMOUNTS PAST DUE AT DECEMBER 31 §§
					NONE								
Grand Totals													

*Give detailed description of investment and of underlying security (Footnotes may be used to describe leases for each class in the aggregate). Indicate statutory category of investment, i.e. real estate, mortgage, security, or other. Include in this Schedule, showing subtotals by class and grand total for all classes: (1) All loans on or investments in oil and gas production payments except those listed in Schedule D, Part 1 or Schedule DA. (2) All Transportation Equipment. (3) Timber Deeds. (4) Mineral Rights carried as admitted assets. (5) Motor Vehicle Trust Certificates. (6) Any other class of admitted investment not clearly includable in other statement schedules.

†Include additional investments made, or portion of investment repaid.
‡Include depreciation on real estate and transportation equipment, etc., amortization of preimum and accrual of discount if applicable.
§After appropriate reduction for interest paid to manufacturer during year and depletion and amortization of mineral rights.
§§After appropriate reduction for due and accrued interest payable to manufacturers.

SCHEDULE B A—VERIFICATION BETWEEN YEARS

1. Book value of other invested assets (Exhibit 1, Item 7, prior year annual statement) . . . ______
2. Cost of acquisitions during year:
   - (a) Column 5, Part 2 . . . ______
   - (b) Column 9, Part 1 . . . ______
   - (c) Column 7, Part 3 . . . ______ ______
3. Increase by adjustment during year:
   - (a) Column 10, Part 1 . . . ______
   - (b) Column 8, Part 3 . . . ______ ______
4. Profit on disposition, Column 9, Part 3 . . . ______
5. Total . . . ______
6. Deduct consideration on disposition, Column 5, Part 3 . . . ______
7. Reductions in investment during year:°
   - (a) Column 9, Part 1 . . . ______
   - (b) Column 7, Part 3 . . . ______ ______
8. Decrease by adjustment during year:
   - (a) Column 10, Part 1 . . . ______
   - (b) Column 8, Part 3 . . . ______ ______
9. Loss on disposition, Column 10, Part 3 . . . ______
10. Book value of other invested assets, Exhibit 1, Item 7, current year . . . ______

°Cash payments on account of capital, e.g., depletion and amortization of mineral rights.

ANNUAL STATEMENT FOR THE YEAR 19 OF THE Property-Liability Insurance Co.
Name

SCHEDULE B A – PART 2

Showing Other Long-term Invested Assets ACQUIRED During Current Year

(1) NUMBER OF UNITS AND DESCRIPTION*	(2) DATE ACQUIRED	(3) LESSEE OR LOCATION	(4) COST TO COMPANY	(5) CONSIDERATION PAID DURING CURRENT YEAR	(6) NAME OF VENDOR
		None			
Grand Totals					

SCHEDULE B A – PART 3

Showing Other Long-term Invested Assets DISPOSED OF During Current Year

(1) NUMBER OF UNITS AND DESCRIPTION*	(2) DATE DISPOSED OF	(3) LESSEE OR LOCATION	(4) NAME OF PURCHASER OR NATURE OF DISPOSITION	(5) CONSIDERATION	(6) BOOK VALUE AT DATE OF SALE	(7) ADDITIONS TO (+) OR REDUCTIONS IN (—) INVESTMENT	(8) DECREASE (—) OR INCREASE (+) BY ADJUSTMENT IN BOOK VALUE DURING YEAR	(9) PROFIT ON SALE	(10) LOSS ON SALE	(11) NET INCOME
			None							
Grand Totals										

* Include in this Schedule, showing subtotals by class and grand total for all classes. (1) All loans on or investments in oil and gas production payments except those listed in Schedule D Part 1 or Schedule DA. (2) All Transportation Equipment. (3) Timber Deeds. (4) Mineral Rights carried as admitted assets. (5) Motor Vehicle Trust Certificates. (6) Any other class of admitted investment not clearly includable in other statement schedules.

ANNUAL STATEMENT FOR THE YEAR 19 OF THE PROPERTY-LIABILITY INSURANCE Co.
Name

SCHEDULE C — Part 1

Showing All Long-term Collateral Loans IN FORCE December 31 of Current Year

(1) NO.	(2) DESCRIPTION OF SECURITIES HELD AS COLLATERAL DECEMBER 31 OF CURRENT YEAR (Give in this column the number of shares of each block of stock and rate of interest and year of maturity of each bond held as collateral)	(3) PAR VALUE	(4) RATE USED TO OBTAIN MARKET VALUE	(5) MARKET VALUE DEC. 31 OF CURRENT YEAR	(6) AMOUNT LOANED THEREON	(7) DATE OF LOAN	(8) MATURITY OF LOAN	INTEREST (9) Rate on Loan	INTEREST (10) Amount Past Due Dec. 31 of Current Year	INTEREST (11) Amount Accrued Dec. 31 of Current Year	INTEREST (12) Amount Received During Year	(13) NAME OF ACTUAL BORROWER (State if the borrower is a parent, subsidiary, affiliate, officer or director)
					NONE							
	Totals		XXX			XXX	XXX	XXX				

SCHEDULE C — Part 2

Showing All Long-term Collateral Loans MADE During the Year

(1) NO	(2) DESCRIPTION OF SECURITY ACCEPTED AS COLLATERAL WHEN LOAN WAS MADE	(3) PAR VALUE	(4) RATE USED TO OBTAIN MARKET VALUE	(5) MARKET VALUE AT DATE OF LOAN	(6) AMOUNT LOANED THEREON	(7) DATE OF LOAN	(8) MATURITY OF LOAN	(9) RATE OF INTEREST ON LOAN	(10) NAME OF ACTUAL BORROWER (State if the borrower is a parent, subsidiary, affiliate, officer or director)
			NONE						
	Totals		XXX			XXX	XXX	XXX	

ANNUAL STATEMENT FOR THE YEAR 19 OF THE PROPERTY-LIABILITY INSURANCE Co.
Name

SCHEDULE C — Part 3

Showing All Long-term Collateral Loans DISCHARGED in Whole or in Part During the Year

(1) NO. Indicate partial payments by the letter "P"	(2) DESCRIPTION OF COLLATERAL RELEASED WHEN LOAN WAS DISCHARGED (In case of partial payments enter collateral released only)	(3) PAR VALUE	(4) RATE USED TO OBTAIN MARKET VALUE	(5) MARKET VALUE AT DATE OF DISCHARGE	(6) AMOUNT OF LOAN REPAID	(7) DATE OF LOAN	(8) DATE OF REPAYMENT	INTEREST (9) Rate on Loan	INTEREST (10) Amount Received During Year	(11) NAME OF ACTUAL BORROWER (State if the borrower is a parent, subsidiary, affiliate, officer or director)
					NONE					
	Totals		XXX			XXX	XXX	XXX		

SCHEDULE C — Part 4

Showing All Substitutions of Collateral During the Year

(1) NO. (To Correspond with No. Shown in Parts 1, 2 and 3)	(2) AMOUNT OF LOAN Col. (6) of Parts 1, 2 or 3	COLLATERAL SUBSTITUTED (3) Description	COLLATERAL SUBSTITUTED (4) Date	COLLATERAL SUBSTITUTED (5) Par Value	COLLATERAL SUBSTITUTED (6) Market Value	COLLATERAL RELEASED (7) Description	COLLATERAL RELEASED (8) Date	COLLATERAL RELEASED (9) Par Value	COLLATERAL RELEASED (10) Market Value
					NONE				
Totals		XXX	XXX			XXX	XXX		

SCHEDULE D—SUMMARY BY COUNTRY

Long-term Bonds and Stocks OWNED December 31 of Current Year

(000 OMITTED)

(1) DESCRIPTION		(2) BOOK VALUE	(3) †MARKET VALUE (Excluding accrued interest)	(4) ACTUAL COST (Excluding accrued interest)	(5) PAR VALUE OF BONDS	(6) *AMORTIZED OR INVESTMENT VALUE
BONDS Governments (Including all obligations guaranteed by governments)	1. United States	9,129	9,070	9,131	9,115	9,127
	2. Canada					
	3. Other Countries					
	4. Totals	9,129	9,070	9,131	9,115	9,127
States, Territories and Possessions (Direct and guaranteed)	5. United States					
	6. Canada					
	7. Other Countries					
	8. Totals					
Political Subdivisions of States, Territories and Possessions (Direct and guaranteed)	9. United States	27,820	27,820	27,642	27,940	27,820
	10. Canada					
	11. Other Countries					
	12. Totals	27,820	27,820	27,642	27,940	27,820
Special revenue and special assessment obligations and all non-guaranteed obligations of agencies and authorities of governments and their political subdivisions	13. United States	125,690	122,767	125,740	127,210	125,703
	14. Canada					
	15. Other Countries					
	16. Totals	125,690	122,767	125,740	127,210	125,703
Railroads (unaffiliated)	17. United States					
	18. Canada					
	19. Other Countries					
	20. Totals					
Public Utilities (unaffiliated)	21. United States	4,340	3,556	3,893	4,720	4,386
	22. Canada					
	23. Other Countries					
	24. Totals	4,340	3,556	3,893	4,720	4,386
Industrial and Miscellaneous (unaffiliated)	25. United States	13,841	13,180	13,638	13,973	13,762
	26. Canada					
	27. Other Countries					
	28. Totals	13,841	13,180	13,638	13,973	13,762
Parent, Subsidiaries and Affiliates	29. Totals					
	30. **Total Bonds**	180,820	176,393	180,044	182,958	180,798
PREFERRED STOCKS Railroads (unaffiliated)	31. United States					
	32. Canada					
	33. Other Countries					
	34. Totals					
Public Utilities (unaffiliated)	35. United States	8,342	7,570	8,342		
	36. Canada					
	37. Other Countries					
	38. Totals	8,342	7,570	8,342		
Banks, Trust and Insurance Companies (unaffiliated)	39. United States					
	40. Canada					
	41. Other Countries					
	42. Totals					
Industrial and Miscellaneous (unaffiliated)	43. United States	1,400	1,300	1,400		
	44. Canada					
	45. Other Countries					
	46. Totals	1,400	1,300	1,400		
Parent, Subsidiaries and Affiliates	47. Totals					
	48. **Total Preferred Stocks**	9,742	8,870	9,742		
COMMON STOCKS Railroads (unaffiliated)	49. United States					
	50. Canada					
	51. Other Countries					
	52. Totals					
Public Utilities (unaffiliated)	53. United States					
	54. Canada					
	55. Other Countries					
	56. Totals					
Banks, Trust and Insurance Companies (unaffiliated)	57. United States					
	58. Canada					
	59. Other Countries					
	60. Totals					
Industrial and Miscellaneous (unaffiliated)	61. United States	5,760	6,610	5,760		
	62. Canada					
	63. Other Countries					
	64. Totals	5,760	6,610	5,760		
Parent, Subsidiaries and Affiliates	66. Totals	1,700	2,190	1,700		
	66. **Total Common Stocks**	7,460	8,800	7,460		
	67. **Total Stocks**	17,202	17,670	17,202		
	68. **Total Bonds and Stocks**	198,022	194,063	197,246		

†Statement value for Preferred Stocks. For certain bonds, values other than actual market may appear in this column (See Schedule D Part 1 for details). *Companies, societies, and associations which do not amortize their bonds should leave this column blank.

The aggregate value of bonds which are valued at other than actual market is $

SCHEDULE D—Verification Between Years

DETAILS OMITTED

Book value of bonds and stocks, per Items 1 and 2, Col. 1, Exhibit 1, previous year . . . . ______

Cost of bonds and stocks acquired, Col. 5, Part 3 . . . ______

Increase by adjustment in book value:

(a) Col. 10, Part 1 . . . . ______

(b) Col. 9, Part 2, Sec. 1 . ______

(c) Col. 8, Part 2, Sec. 2 . ______

(d) Col. 9, Part 4 . . . . ______ ______

Profit on disposal of bonds and stocks, Col. 11, Part 4 ______

Total . . . . ______

6. Deduct consideration for bonds and stocks disposed of, Col. 5, Part 4 . . . . ______

7. Decrease by adjustment in book value:

(a) Col. 11, Part 1 . . . . ______

(b) Col. 10, Part 2, Sec. 1 . ______

(c) Col. 9, Part 2, Sec. 2 . ______

(d) Col. 10, Part 4 . . . . ______ ______

8. Loss on disposal of bonds and stocks, Col. 12, Part 4 . . . . ______

9. Book value of bonds and stocks, per Items 1 and 2, Col. 1, Exhibit 1, current year . . . . ______

SCHEDULE D — PART 1A

Maturity Distribution of Long-term Bonds Owned December 31, Current Year at Statement Values

(1) MATURITY	(2) GOVERNMENTS SCHEDULE D (Group 1)	(3) POLITICAL SUBDIVISIONS, GOVERNMENTAL AGENCIES AND AUTHORITIES (Groups 2, 3 & 4)	(4) OTHER (Unaffiliated) (Groups 5, 6 & 7)	(5) PARENT SUBSIDIARIES AND AFFILIATES (Group 8)	(6) TOTAL BONDS
1. 1 year or less					
2. Over 1 year through 3 years					
3. Over 3 years through 5 years			DETAILS OMITTED		
4. Over 5 years through 10 years					
5. Over 10 years through 15 years					
6. Over 15 years through 20 years					
7. Over 20 years					
8. Totals					

3. Political Subdivisions of States, Territories and Possessions (direct and guaranteed).
4. Special revenue and special assessment obligations and all non-guaranteed obligations of agencies and authorities of governments and their political subdivisions.
5. Railroads. (unaffiliated)
6. Public Utilities. (unaffiliated)
7. Industrial and Miscellaneous. (unaffiliated)
8. Parent, Subsidiaries and Affiliates.

ANNUAL STATEMENT FOR THE YEAR 19 OF THE PROPERTY-LIABILITY INSURANCE CO.

Name

SCHEDULE D — Part 1

Showing all Long-term BONDS Owned December 31 of Current Year (000 OMITTED)

Supplemental columns for data concerning Amortization. SEE NOTE

(1) **DESCRIPTION		(2) INTEREST		(3) DATE OF				(4)	(5)	(6)	(7)	(8)	INTEREST		(10)	(11)	(12)	(13)	(14)	(15)	(16)	(17)	(18)
CUSIP Identification ***	Give complete and accurate description of all bonds owned, including the location of all street railway and miscellaneous companies. If bonds are "serial" issues give amount maturing each year.	Rate of	*How Paid	Maturity Year	Maturity Month	††Option Year	††Option Call Price	BOOK VALUE	PAR VALUE	Rate Used to Obtain Market Value	‡‡MARKET VALUE (excluding accrued interest)	ACTUAL COST (excluding accrued interest)	(9.1) Amount Due and Accrued Dec. 31 of Current Year on bonds not in default	(9.2) Gross Am't Received During Year	Increase by Adjustment in Book Value During Year	Decrease by Adjustment in Book Value During Year	Amount of Interest due and accrued Dec. 31, current year, on bonds in default as to principal or interest	§NAIC Designation	Year Acquired	Effective Rate of Interest at Which Purchase Was Made	†Amortized or Investment Value Dec. 31 of Current Year	‡Increase in Amortized Value During Year	‡Decrease in Amortized Value During Year
GOVERNMENT																							
009121809	U S TREASURY BOND	6.5	JJ	XX	JAN			99	100	98	98	99	3	7				YES	XX	6.5	100		
	SUB-TOTAL GOVERNMENT							9,129	9,115		9,070	9,131	22	644	3	2	—				9,127		
POLITICAL SUBDIVISIONS																							
187661CUB	MAINE MUNICIPAL BOND	5.0	JJ	XX	JAN	XX	PAR	459	500	AMOR	459	499	14	27				YES	XX	5.1	459		
	SUB-TOTAL POLITICAL SUBDIVISIONS							27,820	27,940		27,820	27,642	424	1,440	41	7					27,820		
REVENUE																							
516820DG7	TUSON WATER WORKS	6.2	JJ	XX	JUL	XX	PAR	532	500	AMOR	532	535	16	31		1		YES	XX	6.1	532		
	SUB-TOTAL REVENUE							125,690	127,210		122,767	125,740	3,600	7,931	67	42					125,703		
PUBLIC UTILITIES																							
109980AOAE	CITIES GAS COMPANY	4.8	MN	XX	NOV			49	49		49	49	1	2				YES	XX	4.8	49		
	SUB-TOTAL PUBLIC UTILITIES							4,340	4,720	AMOR	3,556	3,893	50	394							4,386		
INDUSTRIAL + MISCELLANEOUS																							
224399AF2	CRANE CO.	10	JD	XX	DEC	XX	PAR	146	150	AMOR	146	146	9	15	1			YES	XX	10.4	146		
	SUB-TOTAL INDUSTRIAL + MISC.							13,841	13,973		13,180	13,638	67	791	16	11		YES	XX		13,762		
	TOTAL							180,820	182,958		176,393	180,044	4,163	11,200	127	62					180,798		

‡‡Where amortized value or any value other than the market value published in the NAIC Valuation of Securities Manual is entered in Column 7, insert a symbol alongside of the amount reported.

*Insert initial letters of months in which interest is payable.

**Where a bond is payable in a foreign currency the par value and purchase price in that currency should be included as a part of the description.

***From entry in the previous year's Annual Statement if owned at that time; from the purchase confirmation (or certificate) if purchased subsequently. Leave blank for private placements.

†Perpetual bonds, bonds in default as to principal or interest and bonds not amply secured, are to be entered in this column at market value.

‡Companies which use "Amortized Values" as "Book Values" may omit entering figures in these columns, and provide the following footnote:
"The increases and decreases in amortized values are the same as those shown in columns for 'Increase and Decrease by Adjustment in Book Value,' excepting as otherwise indicated."

§Insert the NAIC designation for such security printed in the NAIC Valuation of Securities Manual.

NOTE — This supplemental information, required of all Companies which amortize their bonds, is not to be used as a substitute for the information required in the preceding columns but in addition thereto.

††Show year and call price pertaining to option, if any, on which amortization is based. On bonds purchased at a premium, the maturity date or call feature producing lowest amortized value should be used.

Form 29

Stocks to be grouped in following order and each group arranged alphabetically:
Railroads. (unaffiliated)
Public Utilities. (unaffiliated)
Banks, Trust and Insurance Companies. (unaffiliated)
Industrial and Miscellaneous. (unaffiliated)
Parent, Subsidiaries and Affiliates.

ANNUAL STATEMENT FOR THE YEAR 19 OF THE PROPERTY-LIABILITY INSURANCE CO.

Name

SCHEDULE D – Part 2 – Section 1

Show sub-totals for each group. *Showing all* PREFERRED STOCKS *Owned December 31 of Current Year*

(000 OMITTED)

(1) DESCRIPTION: CUSIP Identification ***	(1) DESCRIPTION: Give complete and accurate description of all preferred stocks owned, including redeemable options, if any, and location of all street railway, bank, trust and miscellaneous companies.	(2) NO. OF SHARES	(3) PAR VALUE PER SHARE	(4) BOOK VALUE	(5) *RATE PER SHARE	(6) STATEMENT VALUE	(6a) RATE PER SHARE USED TO OBTAIN MARKET VALUE	(6b) MARKET VALUE	(7) ACTUAL COST	DIVIDENDS (8 1) DECLARED BUT UNPAID	DIVIDENDS (8 2) AMOUNT RECEIVED DURING YEAR	(9) INCREASE BY ADJUSTMENT IN BOOK VALUE DURING YEAR	(10) DECREASE BY ADJUSTMENT IN BOOK VALUE DURING YEAR	(11) §NAIC DESIG-NATION	(12) YEAR ACQUIRED
PUBLIC UTILITIES															
341081 20C	FLORDIA PW. & LT. INC.	10	100	821	46.75	468	46.75	468	827		45			US	19XX
	TOTAL PUBLIC UTILITIES			8,342		7,570		7,570	8,342	189	634				
INDUSTRIAL AND MISCELLANEOUS															
371028903	GENERAL TEL. & TEL.	5	50	275	100	275	100	275	275	5	19			AS	VARIOUS
	TOTAL INDUSTRIAL AND MISC.			1,400		1,300		1,300	1,400	71	96				
	TOTAL PREFERRED STOCK			9,742		8,870		8,870	9,742	260	730				

*Insert the word "cost" for preferred stocks eligible for stabilization under Section 3 (D) (d) of the NAIC Valuation Procedures. Insert the market value rate for preferred stocks not eligible for stabilization.

***From entry in the previous year's Annual Statement if owned at that time; from the purchase confirmation (or certificate) if purchased subsequently. Leave blank for private placements.

NOTES: Complete information must be furnished in connection with any holding of preferred or common stock on the statement date which is optioned or restricted in any way as to its sale by the insurer. Identify all such securities by the symbol "R" to be inserted beside the figure shown as the rate per share to obtain market value. Transferable shares only, of Savings and Loan or Building and Loan Associations to be reported herein.
§Insert the NAIC designation for such security printed in the NAIC Valuation of Securities Manual.

Stocks to be grouped in following order and each group arranged alphabetically:
Railroads (unaffiliated)
Public Utilities (unaffiliated)
Banks, Trust and Insurance Companies (unaffiliated)
Industrial and Miscellaneous (unaffiliated)
Parent, Subsidiaries and Affiliates

Show sub-totals for each group.

ANNUAL STATEMENT FOR THE YEAR 19 OF THE PROPERTY-LIABILITY INSURANCE CO.

Name

SCHEDULE D—Part 2—Section 2

Showing all COMMON STOCKS *Owned December 31 of Current Year*

(000 OMITTED)

CUSIP Identification ***	(1) DESCRIPTION Give complete and accurate description of all common stocks owned, including redeemable options, if any, and addresses (City and State) of all street railway, banks, trust and insurance companies, savings and loan or building and loan associations and miscellaneous companies.	(2) NO. OF SHARES	(3) BOOK VALUE	(4) RATE PER SHARE USED TO OBTAIN MARKET VALUE	(5) MARKET VALUE	(6) ACTUAL COST	DIVIDENDS (7.1) DECLARED BUT UNPAID	DIVIDENDS (7.2) AMOUNT RECEIVED DURING YEAR	(8) INCREASE BY ADJUSTMENT IN BOOK VALUE DURING YEAR	(9) DECREASE BY ADJUSTMENT IN BOOK VALUE DURING YEAR	(10) §NAIC DESIG-NATION	(11) YEAR ACQUIRED
	INDUSTRIAL AND MISCELLANEOUS											
30229012	OIL CORP	10	237	33.00	330	237		12				VARIOUS
	TOTAL INDUSTRIAL AND MISC.		5,760		6,610	5,760	16	31				
	PARENT, SUBSIDIARIES, AND AFFILIATED											
	ABC SUBSIDIARY	1	700		900	700						
	TOTAL PARENT, SUBSIDIARIES & AFF.		1,700		2,190	1,700						
	TOTAL COMMON STOCK		7,460		8,800	7,460	16	31				

NOTES: Complete information must be furnished in connection with any holding of preferred or common stock on the statement date which is optioned or restricted in any way as to its sale by the insurer.
Identify all such securities by the symbol "R" to be inserted beside the figure shown as the rate per share to obtain market value.
Transferable shares only, of Savings and Loan or Building and Loan Associations to be reported herein.

***From entry in the previous year's Annual Statement if owned at that time; from the purchase confirmation (or certificate) if purchased subsequently. Leave blank for private placements.
§Insert the NAIC designation for such security printed in the NAIC Valuation of Securities Manual.

ANNUAL STATEMENT FOR THE YEAR 19 OF THE PROPERTY-LIABILITY INSURANCE CO.

Name

Bonds, preferred stocks and common stocks to be grouped separately showing sub-totals for each group.

SCHEDULE D — Part 3

Showing all Long-term Bonds and Stocks ACQUIRED During the Current Year (000 OMITTED)

(1) DESCRIPTION§ CUSIP Identification ***	Give complete and accurate description of each bond and stock, including location of all street railway, bank, trust and miscellaneous companies.††	(2) DATE ACQUIRED*	(3) NAME OF VENDOR*	(4) NO. OF SHARES OF STOCK	(5) ACTUAL COST (Excluding Accrued Interest and Dividends)	(6) PAR VALUE OF BONDS	(7) PAID FOR ACCRUED INTEREST AND DIVIDENDS
	DETAILS OMITTED	XX	XXXX	XXX	XXX	XXX	

*The items with reference to each issue of bonds and stocks acquired at public offerings may be totaled in one line and the word "Various" inserted in Columns 2 and 3. [illegible] the totals of Columns 6, 7 and 15 of Part 5. All bonds and stocks acquired and fully disposed of during the year are not to be itemized in this Part.

***From entry in the previous year's Annual Statement if owned at that time; from the purchase confirmation (or certificate) if purchased subsequently. Leave blank for private placements.

††If bonds are serial issues give amounts maturing each year. Securities acquired under a reverse repurchase agreement must be identified.

Form 1249

Bonds, preferred stocks and common stocks to be grouped separately showing sub-totals for each group.

ANNUAL STATEMENT FOR THE YEAR 19 OF THE PROPERTY-LIABILITY INSURANCE Co.

Name

SCHEDULE D—Part 4

Showing all Long-term Bonds and Stocks SOLD, REDEEMED or Otherwise DISPOSED OF During the Current Year

(000 OMITTED)

CUSIP Identification ***	(1) DESCRIPTION‡ Give complete and accurate description of each bond and stock, including location of all street railway, bank, trust and miscellaneous companies.††	(2) DISPOSAL DATE**	(3) NAME OF PURCHASER (If matured or called under redemption option, so state and give price at which called.)	(4) NO. OF SHARES OF STOCK	(5) CONSIDERATION (Excluding Accrued Interest and Dividends)	(6) PAR VALUE OF BONDS	(7) ACTUAL COST (Excluding Accrued Interest and Dividends)	(8) BOOK VALUE AT DISPOSAL DATE	(9) INCREASE BY ADJUSTMENT IN BOOK VALUE DURING YEAR	(10) DECREASE BY ADJUSTMENT IN BOOK VALUE DURING YEAR	(11) PROFIT ON DISPOSAL	(12) LOSS ON DISPOSAL	(13) INTEREST ON BONDS RECEIVED DURING YEAR†	(14) DIVIDENDS ON STOCKS RECEIVED DURING YEAR†
	OTHER BONDS (DETAILS OMITTED)	XX	XXXX		XXX	XXX	XXX	XXX	1	1	90	5	1	
	COMMON STOCKS (DETAILS OMITTED)	XX	XXXX	X	XXX		XXX	XXX			410	61		

‡Enter as a summary item the totals of Columns 6 to 14 of Part 5. All bonds and stocks acquired and fully disposed of during the year are not to be itemized in this Part.
**Companies may at their option summarize all bonds of the same issue called, matured or redeemed during the year and omit disposal dates.
***From entry in the previous year's Annual Statement if owned at that time; from the purchase confirmation (or certificate) if purchased subsequently. Leave blank for private placements.

†Including accrued interest and dividends on bonds and stocks disposed of.
††If bonds are serial issues give amounts maturing each year.
Securities sold under a reverse repurchase agreement must be identified.

ANNUAL STATEMENT FOR THE YEAR 19 OF THE PROPERTY-LIABILITY INSURANCE Co.

Name

Bonds, preferred stocks and common stocks to be grouped separately showing sub-totals for each group.

SCHEDULE D – Part 5

Showing all Long-term Bonds and Stocks ACQUIRED During the Current Year and Fully DISPOSED OF During the Current Year

(1) DESCRIPTION		(2)	(3)	(4)	(5)	(6)	(7)	(8)	(9)	(10)	(11)	(12)	(13)	(14)	(15)
CUSIP identification ***	Give complete and accurate description of each bond and stock, including location of all street railway, bank, trust and miscellaneous companies.††	DATE ACQUIRED*	NAME OF VENDOR*	DISPOSAL DATE**	NAME OF PURCHASER (If matured or called under redemption option, so state and give price at which called.)	PAR VALUE (BONDS) OR NUMBER OF SHARES (STOCKS)	COST TO COMPANY (Excluding Accrued Interest and Dividends)	CONSIDERATION (Excluding Accrued Interest and Dividends)	BOOK VALUE AT DISPOSAL DATE	INCREASE BY ADJUSTMENT IN BOOK VALUE DURING YEAR	DECREASE BY ADJUSTMENT IN BOOK VALUE DURING YEAR	PROFIT ON DISPOSAL	LOSS ON DISPOSAL	INTEREST AND DIVIDENDS RECEIVED DURING YEAR†	PAID FOR ACCRUED INTEREST AND DIVIDENDS
					NONE										

*The items with reference to each issue of bonds and stocks acquired at public offerings may be totaled in one line and the word "Various" inserted in Columns 2 and 3.
**Companies may at their option summarize all bonds of the same issue called, matured or redeemed during the year and omit disposal dates.
***From entry in the previous year's Annual Statement if owned at that time; from the purchase confirmation (or certificate) if purchased subsequently. Leave blank for private placements.

†Including accrued interest and dividends on bonds and stocks disposed of.
††If bonds are serial issues give amounts maturing each year.
Securities acquired or disposed of under a reverse repurchase agreement must be identified

SCHEDULE D – PART 6 – Section 1

Questionnaire Relating to the Valuation of Shares of Certain Subsidiary, Controlled or Affiliated Companies

(1) Name of Subsidiary, Controlled or Affiliated Company	(2) Do Insurer's Admitted Assets Include Intangible Assets Connected with Holding of Such Company's Stock?	(3) If Yes, Amount of Such Intangible Assets	Common Stock of Such Company Owned by Insurer on Statement Date	
			(4) No. of Shares	(5) % of Outstanding
Details Omitted				
	Total		X X X X	X X X X

Amount of Insurer's Capital and Surplus (Page 3, Item 27 of previous year's statement filed by the insurer with its domiciliary insurance department): $

SCHEDULE D – PART 6 – Section 2

(1) Name of Lower-tier Company	(2) Name of Company Listed in Section 1 which controls Lower-tier Company	(3) Amount of Intangible Assets Included in Amount Shown in Column (3), Section 1	Common Stock of Lower-tier Company Owned Indirectly by Insurer on Statement Date	
			(4) No. of Shares	(5) % of Outstanding
Details Omitted				
	Total		X X X X	X X X X

ANNUAL STATEMENT FOR THE YEAR 19 OF THE Property-Liability Insurance Co.
Name

SCHEDULE DA – PART 1

Showing All SHORT-TERM INVESTMENTS† *Owned December 31 of Current Year*

(1) DESCRIPTION**		(2)	(3)	(4) §INTEREST		(5) §DATE OF MATURITY		(6)	(7)	(8)	(9)	(10)	(11)	(12) INTEREST		(13)	(14)	(15)
CUSIP Identification ***	Give complete and accurate description of all investments owned, including identifying the kind of investment vehicle if other than short-term bond.	§DATE ACQUIRED	§NAME OF VENDOR	Rate Of	*How Paid	Year	Month	BOOK VALUE	INCREASE (+) OR DECREASE (−) BY ADJUSTMENT IN BOOK VALUE DURING YEAR	PAR VALUE	RATE USED TO OBTAIN STATEMENT VALUE	STATEMENT VALUE (Excluding Accrued Interest)	ACTUAL COST (Excluding Accrued Interest)	Amount Due and Accrued Dec. 31 of Current Year on Bonds not in default	Gross Amount Received	PAID FOR ACCRUED INTEREST	NAIC DESIG-NATION ††	EFFECTIVE RATE OF INTEREST AT WHICH PURCHASE WAS MADE §
			NONE															
									†††									

* Insert initial letters of months in which interest is payable.
** Where an investment is payable in a foreign currency, the par value and the purchase price in that currency should be included as a part of the description.
*** From the purchase confirmation (or certificate). Leave blank for private placements.
† ... at time of acquisition were one year or less. Identify "Repos"

†† Insert the NAIC designation for such security printed in the NAIC Valuation of Securities Manual.
††† Includes $ .... other than accrual of discount and amortization of premium.
§ Purchases of various issues of the same issuer of short-term investments may be totalled on one line and the word "various" inserted in the columns.

ANNUAL STATEMENT FOR THE YEAR 19 OF THE Property– Liability Insurance Co.
Name

SCHEDULE DA—PART 2

Verification of SHORT-TERM INVESTMENTS between Years

	(1) TOTAL*	(2) BONDS	(3) COLLATERAL LOANS	(4) MORTGAGE LOANS	(5) OTHER SHORT TERM INVESTMENT ASSETS**	(6) INVESTMENTS IN PARENT SUBSIDIARIES AND AFFILIATES
1. Book value, previous year						
2. Cost of short-term investments acquired		None				
3. Increase by adjustment in book value						
4. Profit on disposal of short-term investments						
5. Subtotals (Total of Items 2 to 4)						
6. Consideration received on disposal of short-term investments						
7. Decrease by adjustment in book value						
8. Loss on disposal of short-term investments						
9. Subtotals (Total of Items 6 to 8)						
10. Book value, current year						

*Column (1) amounts equal the sum of Columns (2) through (6). Column (1), Line 10 equals Part 1, Column (6), total

**Indicate the category of such assets, for example, joint ventures, transportation equipment

Form 1349

ANNUAL STATEMENT FOR THE YEAR 19 OF THE PROPERTY-LIABILITY INSURANCE CO.

Name

40

Separate financial options into 2 groups, put options and call options; within each group, show separately fixed income, equity and other financial options. Show subtotals for each group and category.

SCHEDULE DB – PART A – Section 1

Showing All Financial Options Owned December 31 of Current Year

(1) DESCRIPTION OF ALL FINANCIAL OPTIONS OWNED, INCLUDING DESCRIPTION OF UNDERLYING SECURITY(S) OR CONTRACT(S)	(2) EXPIRATION DATE	(3) EXERCISE PRICE	(4) INDICATION OF EXISTENCE OF HEDGE*	(5) DATE ACQUIRED	(6) ACTUAL COST	(7) INCREASE/DECREASE BY ADJUSTMENT IN BOOK VALUE	(8) BOOK VALUE	(9) MARKET VALUE	(10) STATEMENT VALUE	(11) GAIN/(LOSS) (a) Recognized	(11) GAIN/(LOSS) (b) Deferred
					NONE						
Grand Totals	XXX	XXX	XXX	XXX							

SCHEDULE DB – PART A – Section 2

Showing All Financial Options Acquired During Current Year

(1) DESCRIPTION OF ALL FINANCIAL OPTIONS ACQUIRED, INCLUDING DESCRIPTION OF UNDERLYING SECURITY(S) OR CONTRACT(S)	(2) EXPIRATION DATE	(3) EXERCISE PRICE	(4) INDICATION OF EXISTENCE OF HEDGE*	(5) NAME OF VENDOR	(6) DATE ACQUIRED	(7) ACTUAL COST
		NONE				
Grand Total	XXX	XXX	XXX	XXX	XXX	

* ... description of the hedge program been made available to the domiciliary state? ....

Form 1249

ANNUAL STATEMENT FOR THE YEAR 19 OF THE PROPERTY-LIABILITY INSURANCE Co.

Name

Separate financial options into 2 groups, put options and call options; within each group, show separately fixed income, equity and other financial options. Show subtotals for each group and category.

SCHEDULE DB – PART A – Section 3

Showing All Financial Options Terminated During Current Year

(1) DESCRIPTION OF FINANCIAL OPTIONS TERMINATED INCLUDING DESCRIPTION OF UNDERLYING SECURITY(S) OR CONTRACT(S)	(2) EXPIRATION DATE	(3) EXERCISE PRICE	(4) INDICATE EXERCISE EXPIRATION OR SALE	(5) DATE ACQUIRED	(6) DATE TERMINATED	(7) ACTUAL COST	(8) INCREASE/DECREASE BY ADJUSTMENT IN BOOK VALUE DURING YEAR	(9) BOOK VALUE AT TERMINATION DATE	(10) CONSIDERATION RECEIVED ON TERMINATION	(11) PREMIUMS ALLOCATED TO PURCHASE COST OR SALE PROCEEDS ON EXERCISE	(12) GAIN/(LOSS) ON TERMINATION		
											(a) Deferred	(b) Recognized	(c) Used to adjust basis of hedge
						NONE							
Grand Totals	X X X	X X X	X X X	X X X	X X X								

SCHEDULE DB – PART A – Section 4

Verification Between Years of Book Value of Financial Options Owned

1. Book value of options owned, December 31, previous year (Sec. 4, Line 7, previous year) . . . . ________
2. Cost of options acquired (Sec. 2, Col. 7) . . . . ________
3. Increase/(decrease) by adjustment in book value of options (Sum of Sec. 1, Col. 7 and Sec. 3, Col. 8) . . . . ________
4. Deduct (gain)/loss on termination of options:
   - (a) deferred (Sec. 3, Col. 12a) . . . . ________
   - (b) recognized (Sec. 3, Col. 12b) . . . . ________
   - (c) used to adjust basis of hedge (Sec. 3, Col. 12c) . . . . ________ ________
5. Deduct consideration received on termination of options (Sec. 3, Col. 10) . . . . ________
6. Deduct premiums allocated to purchase cost or sale proceeds on exercise (Sec. 3, Col. 11) . . . . ________
7. Book value of options owned, December 31, current year (Sec. 1, Col. 8, current year) . . . . ________

Form 1249

ANNUAL STATEMENT FOR THE YEAR 19 OF THE PROPERTY-LIABILITY INSURANCE CO.
Name

Separate financial options into 2 groups, put options and call options; within each group, show separately fixed income, equity and other financial options. Show subtotals for each group and category.

SCHEDULE DB – PART B – Section 1

Showing All Financial Options Written and in Force December 31 of Current Year

(1) DESCRIPTION OF FINANCIAL OPTIONS WRITTEN AND IN FORCE INCLUDING DESCRIPTION OF UNDERLYING SECURITY(S) OR CONTRACT(S)	(2) XX	(3) EXPIRATION DATE	(4) EXERCISE PRICE	(5) INDICATION OF EXISTENCE OF HEDGE*	(6) DATE ISSUED	(7) CONSIDERATION RECEIVED	(8) MARKET VALUE	(9) STATEMENT VALUE	(10) GAIN/(LOSS) (a) Recognized	(10) GAIN/(LOSS) (b) Deferred
						NONE				
Grand Totals	XXX	XXX	XXX	XXX	XXX					

SCHEDULE DB – PART B – Section 2

Showing All Financial Options Written During Current Year

(1) DESCRIPTION OF ALL FINANCIAL OPTIONS ISSUED, INCLUDING DESCRIPTION OF UNDERLYING SECURITY(S) OR CONTRACT(S)	(2) XX	(3) EXPIRATION DATE	(4) EXERCISE PRICE	(5) INDICATION OF EXISTENCE OF HEDGE*	(6) DATE ISSUED	(7) CONSIDERATION RECEIVED
			NONE			
Grand Total	XXX	XXX	XXX	XXX	XXX	

*Has a comprehensive description of the hedge program been made available to the domiciliary state? .... If not, attach a description with this statement.

XX If a call option, indicate "no" if the underlying investment was not owned at the time option was written; otherwise leave blank.

Form 1249

ANNUAL STATEMENT FOR THE YEAR 19 OF THE PROPERTY-LIABILITY INSURANCE CO.

Name

Separate financial options into 2 groups, put options and call options; within each group, show separately fixed income, equity and other financial options. Show subtotals for each group and category

SCHEDULE DB – PART B – Section 3

Showing All Financial Options Written That Were Terminated During Current Year

(1) Description of All Financial Options Terminated Including Description of Underlying Security(s) or Contract(s)	(2) Expiration Date	(3) Exercise Price	(4) Date Issued	(5) Date Terminated	(6) Indication of Exercise Expiration or Closing Purchase Transaction	(7) Consideration Received	(8) Cost of Termination	(9) Premiums Allocated to Purchase Cost or Sale Proceeds on Exercise	(10) Gain/(Loss) on Termination		
									(a) Deferred	(b) Recognized	(c) Used to adjust basis of hedge
						NONE					
Grand Totals $	X X X	X X X	X X X	X X X	X X X						

SCHEDULE DB – PART B – Section 4

Verification Between Years of Consideration Received for Financial Options Written

1. Consideration received for financial options written and outstanding, previous year (Sec. 4, Line 6, previous year) . . . . . ______
2. Consideration received for options written during year (Sec. 2, Col. 7) . . . . . ______
3. Deduct cost of terminating options by closing purchase transaction during year (Sec. 3, Col. 8) . . . . . ______
4. Deduct gain/(loss) on termination:
   - (a) deferred (Sec. 3, Col. 10a) . . . . . ______
   - (b) recognized (Sec. 3, Col. 10b) . . . . . ______
   - (c) used to adjust basis of hedge (Sec. 3, Col. 10c) . . . . . ______ ______
5. Deduct premiums allocated to purchase cost or sale proceeds on exercise (Sec. 3, Col. 9) . . . . . ______
6. Consideration received for financial options written and outstanding, current year (Sec. 1, Col. 7, current year) . . . . . ______

Form 1249

Separate financial futures contracts into 2 groups, long positions and short positions; within each group, show separately interest rate futures and other financial futures contracts. Show subtotals for each group and category.

ANNUAL STATEMENT FOR THE YEAR 19 OF THE PROPERTY-LIABILITY INSURANCE CO.

Name

SCHEDULE DB – PART C – Section 1

Showing All Financial Futures Contracts Open December 31 of Current Year

(1)	(2)	(3)	(4)	(5)	(6) FUTURES CONTRACTS			(7) MARGIN INFORMATION		
DESCRIPTION OF ALL FINANCIAL FUTURES CONTRACTS OPEN	NUMBER OF CONTRACTS	DATE OF MATURITY	INDICATION OF EXISTENCE OF HEDGE*	XX	(a) Original Price	(b) Current Price	(c) Difference	(a) Initial Deposit Requirement	VARIANCE MARGIN (b) Deferred Gain/(Loss)	VARIANCE MARGIN (c) Recognized Gain/(Loss)
					NONE					
Grand Totals	XXX	XXX	XXX	XXX						

SCHEDULE DB – PART C – Section 2

Showing All Financial Futures Contracts Opened During Current Year

(1) DESCRIPTION OF EACH FINANCIAL FUTURES CONTRACT EXECUTED	(2) NUMBER OF CONTRACTS	(3) NAME OF VENDOR	(4) DATE OF OPENING POSITION	(5) DATE OF MATURITY	(6) XX	(7) INDICATION OF EXISTENCE OF HEDGE*	(8) ORIGINAL PRICE OF FUTURES CONTRACTS	(9) INITIAL MARGIN DEPOSIT REQUIREMENT
		NONE						
Grand Totals	XXX	XXX	XXX	XXX	XXX	XXX		

*Has a comprehensive description of the hedge program been made available to the domiciliary state? ...... If not, attach a description with this statement

XX If contract requires the company to deliver securities at the contract maturity date, indicate "no" if the underlying instruments were not owned at the time the futures contract was opened, otherwise leave blank

Form 1249

Separate financial futures contracts into 2 groups, long positions and short positions, within each group, show separately interest rate futures and other financial futures contracts. Show subtotals for each group and category.

ANNUAL STATEMENT FOR THE YEAR 19 OF THE PROPERTY-LIABILITY INSURANCE Co.

Name

SCHEDULE DB – PART C – Section 3

Showing All Financial Futures Contracts That Were Terminated During Current Year

(1) DESCRIPTION OF EACH FINANCIAL FUTURES CONTRACT TERMINATED	(2) NUMBER OF CONTRACTS	(3) DATE OF TERMINATION	(4) INDICATION OF EXISTENCE OF HEDGE*	(5) FUTURES CONTRACTS			(6) MARGIN INFORMATION		
				(a) Original Price	(b) Closing Transaction Price	(c) Gain/(Loss) on Termination	(a) Gain/(Loss) Utilized to Adjust Basis of Hedge	(b) Gain/(Loss) Recognized in Current Year	(c) Gain/(Loss) Deferred Over Year End
				NONE					
Grand Totals	X X X	X X X	X X X						

*Has a comprehensive description of the hedge program been made available to the domiciliary state? ....
If not, attach a description with this statement.

SCHEDULE DB – PART C – Section 4

Verification Between Years of Deferred Gain/(Loss) on Financial Futures Contracts

1. Deferred gain/(loss), December 31, previous year (Sec. 4, Line 6, previous year) . . . . ________
2. Change in deferred gain/(loss) on open contracts (Difference between years – Sec. 1, Col. 7b) . . . . ________
3. a. Gain/(loss) on contracts terminated during the year (Sec. 3, Col. 5c) . . . . ________
   b. Less:
      (i) Gain/(loss) used to adjust basis of hedge (Sec. 3, Col. 6a) . . . . ________
      (ii) Gain/(loss) recognized in current year (Sec. 3, Col. 6b) . . . . ________
      (iii) Subtotal (Line 3b(i) plus 3b(ii)) . . . . ________
   c. Subtotal (Line 3a minus Line 3b(iii)) . . . . ________
4. Subtotal (Line 1 + Line 2 + Line 3c) . . . . ________
5. Less:
   Disposition of gain/(loss) on contracts terminated in prior years:
   (a) recognized . . . . ________
   (b) used to adjust basis of hedge . . . . ________ ________
6. Deferred gain/(loss), December 31, current year (Line 4 minus Line 5) . . . . ________

SCHEDULE F – Part 1A – Section 1

Ceded Reinsurance as of December 31, Current Year

(000 OMITTED)

NAME OF REINSURER*	NAIC COMPANY CODE	LOCATION**	(1) REINSURANCE RECOVERABLE ON PAID LOSSES	(2) REINSURANCE RECOVERABLE ON UNPAID LOSSES	(3) PREMIUMS IN FORCE	(4) UNEARN PREMIUM (Estimate
Affiliates:						
DETAILS OMITTED						
		Grand Totals	190	2,850		

*All companies should be listed in straight alphabetical order

**Show the precise location of the reinsurance company

SCHEDULE F – Part 1A – Section 2

Assumed Reinsurance as of December 31, Current Year
(To be filed not later than April 1)
(000 omitted)

NAME OF REINSURED*	NAIC COMPANY CODE	LOCATION**	(1) REINSURANCE PAYABLE ON PAID LOSSES	(2) REINSURANCE PAYABLE ON UNPAID LOSSES	(3) UNEARNED PREMIUMS (Estimated)
...tes:					
DETAILS OMITTED					
		Totals—Affiliates			
...iliates:					
		Totals—Non-affiliates			
		Grand Totals		3,650	

*All companies should be listed in straight alphabetical order.

**Show the precise location of the reinsurance company.

SCHEDULE F – Part 1B

Portfolio Reinsurance Effected or Cancelled (-) during Current Year

NAME OF COMPANY	NAIC COMPANY CODE	(1) DATE OF CONTRACT	(2) AMOUNT OF ORIGINAL PREMIUMS	(3) AMOUNT OF REINSURANCE PREMIUMS
(a) Reinsurance Ceded				
NONE				
Total Reinsurance Ceded by Portfolio	XXX	XXX		
(b) Reinsurance Assumed				
NONE				
Total Reinsurance Assumed by Portfolio	XXX	XXX		

ANNUAL STATEMENT FOR THE YEAR 19 OF THE PROPERTY-LIABILITY INSURANCE Co.

Name

SCHEDULE F – Part 2

Funds Withheld on Account of Reinsurance in Unauthorized Companies as of December 31, Current Year

NAME OF REINSURER	NAIC COMPANY CODE	(1) UNEARNED PREMIUMS (Debit)	(2) (a) PAID AND UNPAID LOSSES RECOVERABLE (Total of Amounts in Cols. (1) + (2) of Schedule F Part 1A Section 1 for unauthorized companies) (Debit)	(2) (b) INCURRED BUT NOT REPORTED LOSSES RECOVERABLE (Estimates of amounts recoverable from unauthorized companies) (Debit)	(2) (c) PAID AND UNPAID ALLOCATED LOSS ADJUSTMENT EXPENSES RECOVERABLE (Debit)	(3) TOTAL (1) + (2a) + (2b) + (2c)	(4) DEPOSITS BY AND FUNDS WITHHELD FROM REINSURERS (Credit)	(5) MISCELLANEOUS BALANCES (Credit)	(6) SUM OF (4) + (5) BUT NOT IN EXCESS OF (3)
				NONE					
Totals	XXX								

NOTES Total of Column (6) to agree with deduction taken in Item 15, Page 3
Securities held on deposit shall be valued in accordance with N.A.I.C. valuations

Letters of credit are to be included in Column (4) and indicated by an asterisk (*). Letters of credit are not to be included in assets or liabilities on Pages 2 or 3 or supporting pages or exhibits

SCHEDULE G

Showing Net Losses Paid on Fidelity and Surety claims that were undisposed of December 31st of the following years, as compared with Estimated Liability per Annual Statement of the respective years and at end of Current Year.

(1) NET LOSSES UNPAID DECEMBER 31ST PER ANNUAL STATEMENT FOR EACH OF THE FOLLOWING YEARS (INCLUDING RESERVES FOR CLAIMS INCURRED BUT NOT REPORTED) VIZ	(2)	(3) TOTAL AMOUNT PAID TO DATE SINCE DECEMBER 31 OF YEAR IN COLUMN (1)	(4) ESTIMATED LIABILITY DECEMBER 31ST CURRENT YEAR	(5) TOTAL (3) + (4)	(6) INCREASE OR (—) DECREASE ESTIMATED LIABILITY (5) — (2)
FIDELITY					
SURETY					
FIDELITY					
SURETY			NONE		
FIDELITY					
SURETY					
FIDELITY					
SURETY					
FIDELITY					
SURETY					
FIDELITY					
SURETY					
FIDELITY					
SURETY					

SCHEDULE K

Computation of Excess of Statutory Reserve over Statement Reserves — Credit

1. Net unpaid losses on policies expired prior to October 1, current year		
2. Reserve for losses on policies expired in October, November and December, current year:		
(a) Net premiums written on such policies		
(b) 50% of (a)		
(c) Net losses paid under such policies		
(d) Difference (b) — (c)		NONE
(e) Net losses unpaid under such policies		
(f) Difference (d) — (e), show zero if negative		
3. Reserve for accrued losses on policies in force December 31, current year:		
(a) Net premiums earned under such policies		
(b) 50% of (a)		
(c) Net losses paid under such policies		
(d) Difference (b) — (c)		
(e) Net losses unpaid under such policies		
(f) Difference (d) — (e), show zero if negative		
4. Excess of Statutory Reserve over Statement Reserves 2(f) + 3(f)		

Note Sum of 1 + 2(e) + 3(e) should equal Page 10, Column 5, Item 28.

Form 12

ANNUAL STATEMENT FOR THE YEAR 19 OF THE Property-Liability Insurance Co.
Name

SCHEDULE H—ACCIDENT AND HEALTH EXHIBIT

	(1) TOTAL		(2) GROUP ACCIDENT AND HEALTH		(3) CREDIT* (Group and Individual)		(4) COLLECTIVELY RENEWABLE		OTHER INDIVIDUAL POLICIES									
									(5) NON-CANCELLABLE		(6) GUARANTEED RENEWABLE		(7) NON-RENEWABLE FOR STATED REASONS ONLY		(8) OTHER ACCIDENT ONLY		(9) ALL OTHER	
	Amount	%†	Amount	%†	Amount	%†	Amount	%†	Amount	%†	Amount	%†	Amount	%†	Amount	%†	Amount	%†
PART 1. ANALYSIS OF UNDERWRITING OPERATIONS																		
1. Premiums written																		
2. Premiums earned (see note b)																		
3. Incurred claims																		
4. Increase in policy reserves																		
5. Commissions*																		
6. General insurance expenses																		
7. Taxes, licenses and fees																		
8. Total expenses incurred																		
9. Gain from underwriting before dividends to policyholders																		
10. Dividends to policyholders																		
11. Gain from underwriting after dividends to policyholders																		
PART 2. RESERVES AND LIABILITIES																		
A. PREMIUM RESERVES:																		
1. Unearned premiums																		
2. Advance premiums																		
3. Reserve for rate credits																		
4. Total premium reserves, current year							None											
5. Total premium reserves, previous year																		
6. Increase in total premium reserves																		
B. POLICY RESERVES:																		
1. Additional reserves																		
2. Reserve for future contingent benefits (deferred maternity and other similar benefits)**																		
3. Total policy reserves, current year																		
4. Total policy reserves, previous year																		
5. Increase in policy reserves																		
C. CLAIM RESERVES AND LIABILITIES:																		
1. Total current year																		
2. Total previous year																		
3. Increase																		
PART 3. TEST OF PREVIOUS YEAR'S CLAIM RESERVES AND LIABILITIES																		
1. CLAIMS PAID DURING THE YEAR:																		
a. On claims incurred prior to current year																		
b. On claims incurred during current year																		
2. CLAIM RESERVES AND LIABILITIES, DEC. 31, CURRENT YEAR:																		
a. On claims incurred prior to current year																		
b. On claims incurred during current year																		
3. TEST:																		
a. Line 1a and 2a																		
b. Claim reserves and liabilities, Dec. 31, previous year																		
c. Line a minus Line b																		
PART 4. REINSURANCE																		
A. REINSURANCE ASSUMED:																		
1. Premiums written																		
2. Premiums earned (see note b)																		
3. Incurred claims																		
4. Commissions																		
B. REINSURANCE CEDED:																		
1. Premiums written																		
2. Premiums earned (see note b)																		
3. Incurred claims																		
4. Commissions																		

*Business not exceeding 120 months duration.
†In each column of Part 1, show the percentages of Line 2 for Lines 3 through 11 inclusive.

*Includes $............ reported as "Policy, membership and other fees retained by agents."
**If not included in claim reserves.
(b) Premiums earned are before adjustment for the increase in policy reserves which has been treated as a separate deduction.

SCHEDULE M – PART 1

Showing all direct or indirect payments of more than $100 (exclusive of expenses paid in connection with settlement of losses, claims and salvage under policy contracts) in connection with any matter, measure or proceeding before legislative bodies, officers or departments of government during the year, excluding company's share of such expenditures made by organizations listed in Part 4 below.

(1) PAYEE		(2) AMOUNT PAID	(3) MATTER, MEASURE OR PROCEEDING
NAME	ADDRESS		
	Details Omitted		

SCHEDULE M – PART 2

Showing all payments (other than salary, compensation, emoluments and dividends) to or on behalf of any officer, director or employee which exceeded $1,000 or amounted in the aggregate to more than $10,000 during the year. (Excluding reimbursement of expenditures for transportation, board and lodging of Company Auditors, Inspectors, Claims Investigators and Adjusters, and Special Agents, and excluding payments listed in Part 1.)

(1) NAME OF PAYEE AND TITLE OF POSITION	(2) AMOUNT PAID	(3) OCCASION OF EXPENSE
Details Omitted		
	$	

SCHEDULE M – PART 3

Showing all payments for legal expenses which exceeded $500 or aggregated more than $5,000 during the year, exclusive of payments in connection with settlement of losses, claims and salvage under policy contracts. (Excluding payments listed in Part 1.)

(1) PAYEE		(2) AMOUNT PAID	(3) OCCASION OF EXPENSE
NAME	ADDRESS		
	DETAILS OMITTED		

SCHEDULE M – PART 4

Showing all payments in excess of $1,000 to each Trade Association, Service Organization, Statistical, Actuarial or Rating Bureau during the year. (A service organization is defined as every person, partnership, association or corporation who or which formulates rules, establishes standards, or assists in the making of rates, rules, or standards for the information or benefit of insurers or rating organizations.)

(1) PAYEE		(2) AMOUNT PAID	(3) OCCASION OF EXPENSE
NAME	ADDRESS		
DETAILS OMITTED			

SCHEDULE N

Showing all Banks, Trust Companies, Savings and Loan and Building and Loan Associations in which deposits were maintained by the company at any time during the year and the balances, if any (according to Company's records) on December 31, of the current year. Exclude balances represented by a negotiable instrument.

(000 Omitted)

(1) DEPOSITORY* (Give Full Name and Location. State if depository is a parent, subsidiary or affiliate.) Show rate of interest and maturity date in the case of certificates of deposit or time deposits maturing more than one year from statement date.	(2) AMOUNT OF INTEREST RECEIVED DURING YEAR	(3) AMOUNT OF INTEREST ACCRUED DECEMBER 31 OF CURRENT YEAR	(4) BALANCE
OPEN DEPOSITORIES			
Details Omitted			
Totals—Open Depositories			
SUSPENDED DEPOSITORIES			
Totals—Suspended Depositories			
Grand Totals—All Depositories			1,201

TOTALS OF DEPOSITORY BALANCES ON THE LAST DAY OF EACH MONTH DURING THE CURRENT YEAR

		APRIL		JULY		OCTOBER	
		MAY		AUGUST		NOVEMBER	
		JUNE		SEPTEMBER		DECEMBER	

*In each case where the depository is not incorporated and subject to governmental supervision, the word "PRIVATE" in capitals and in parentheses, thus—(PRIVATE), should be inserted to the left of the name of the depository. Any deposit in a suspended depository which is taken credit for should have a star placed opposite the amount in the schedule.

Deposits in federally insured depositories not exceeding $40,000 may be combined and reported in opposite the caption "Deposits in (insert number) depositories which do not exceed the $40,000 amount in any one depository."

Short-term certificates of deposit to be reported in Schedule DA. Long-term negotiable certificates of deposit to be reported in Schedule D.

SCHEDULE O – PART 1 – LOSS DEVELOPMENT
(000 omitted)

(1)	(2) Losses paid during the year less reinsurance received during the year (a)	(3)	(4)	(5) Salvage and subrogation received in the current year	(6)	(7)	(8)	(9)	(10) Losses unpaid December 31 of current year	(11)	(12)	(13)	(14) Development	(15)	(16) Estimated liability on unpaid losses	(17)	(18) Change in such estimated liability	(19)
	On losses incurred during 19	On losses incurred during 19	On losses incurred prior to 19	On losses incurred during 19	On losses incurred during 19	On losses incurred prior to 19	Total (Col. 2 + 3 + 4 − 5 − 6 − 7) net disbursements per Col. 4 Part 3	Losses paid during 19 on losses incurred prior to 19 (Col. 3 + 4, Sch. O, 19)	On losses incurred during 19	On losses incurred during 19	On losses incurred prior to 19	Total per Col. 5 Part 3A (Col. 10 + 11 + 12) (b)	On losses incurred prior to 19 (Col. 3 + 4 + 11 + 12)	On losses incurred prior to 19 (Col 4 + 9 + 12)	Dec. 31, 19 per Col. 5, Part 3A, 19 (b)	Dec. 31, 19 per Col. 5, Part 3A, 19 (b)	Dec. 31, 19 (Col 14 less Col. 16)	Dec. 31, 19 (Col. 15 less Col. 17)
1. Fire																		
2. Allied lines																		
9. Inland marine																		
10.																		
12. Earthquake																		
13. Group accident and health																		
14. Credit accident and health (group and individual)**																		
15. Other accident and health																		
21. Auto phys. damage																		
23. Fidelity									*			*			*	*		
24. Surety									*			*			*	*		
25. Glass																		
26. Burglary and theft																		
28. Credit																		
29. International																		
30. Reinsurance																		
31. TOTALS																		

SUPPLEMENTARY INFORMATION

*Exclude reserves for Fidelity and Surety losses incurred but not reported.
(a) Reinsurance as used in Columns 2, 3 and 4 include (1) received in cash, and (2) recoverable (charged during year of statement) if carried as a ledger asset.
(b) Fidelity and Surety reserves obtained from Column 3 Lines 23 and 24, Part 3A
**Business not exceeding 120 months duration.

SCHEDULE O – PART 2 – LOSS EXPENSE DEVELOPMENT
(000 omitted)

(1)	(2) Allocated loss expense payments during the year	(3)	(4)	(5) Unallocated loss expense payments during the year (a)	(6)	(7)	(8)	(9)	(10) Unpaid loss adjustment expenses December 31 of current year	(11)	(12)	(13)	(14) Development	(15)	(16) Estimated liability on unpaid loss adjustment expenses	(17)	(18) Change in such estimated liability	(19)
	On losses incurred during 19	On losses incurred during 19	On losses incurred prior to 19	On losses incurred during 19	On losses incurred during 19	On losses incurred prior to 19	Total (Col. 2 + 3 + 4 + 5 + 6 + 7) net disbursements	Loss expenses paid during 19 on losses incurred prior to 19 (Col. 3 + 4 + 6 + 7, Schedule O, Part 2, 19)	On losses incurred during 19	On losses incurred during 19	On losses incurred prior to 19	Total per Col. 6 Part 3A (Col. 10 + 11 + 12)	On losses incurred prior to 19 (Col. 3 + 4 + 6 + 7 + 11 + 12)	On losses incurred prior to 19 (Col. 4 + 7 + 9 + 12)	Dec. 31, 19 per Col. 6, Part 3A 19	Dec. 31, 19 per Col. 6, Part 3A, 19	Dec. 31, 19 (Col 14 less Col. 16)	Dec. 31, 19 (Col 15 less Col. 17)
1. Fire																		
2. Allied lines																		
9. Inland marine																		
10.																		
12. Earthquake																		
13. Group accident and health																		
14. Credit accident and health (group and individual)**																		
15. Other accident and health																		
21. Auto phys. damage																		
23. Fidelity																		
24. Surety																		
25. Glass																		
26. Burglary and theft																		
28. Credit																		
29. International																		
30. Reinsurance																		
31. TOTALS																		

SUPPLEMENTARY INFORMATION

(a) See Schedule P—Part 1F footnote (g) for method of distribution.
**Business not exceeding 120 months duration.

ANNUAL STATEMENT FOR THE YEAR 19 OF THE PROPERTY-LIABILITY INSURANCE Co
Name

SCHEDULE O – PART 3 – SUMMARY – LOSS AND LOSS EXPENSE
(000 omitted)

(1)	(2)	(3)	(3a)	(d) LOSS EXPENSE PAYMENTS				(6)	(7)	(8)	(9)	(10)	(11)	(12)
Years in Which Premiums Were Earned and Losses Were Incurred	Premiums Earned	Loss Payments (b)	Salvage Received (c)	(4) Allocated	(4a) Ratio 4 ÷ 3 %	(5) (g) Unallocated	(5a) Ratio 5 ÷ 3 %	Loss and Loss Expense Payments (3 + 4 + 5)	Ratio 6 ÷ 2 %		Losses Unpaid	(d) Loss Expense Unpaid	Total Losses and Loss Expense Incurred (6 + 9 + 10)	Ratio 11 ÷ 2 %
1 Prior to 19										X X X				
2 19										X X X				
3 19				SUPPLEMENTARY INFORMATION						X X X				
4 19										X X X				
5 19										X X X				
6 19										X X X				
7 19										X X X				
8 19										X X X				
9 19										X X X				
10 19										X X X				
11 TOTALS										X X X				X X X

(b) Include amounts reportable in Columns 2, 3 and 4 of Schedule O—Part 1. (For lines other than current year, amounts reported herein should include loss payments made in prior years as well as loss payments made in current year.)

(c) Include amounts reportable in Columns 5, 6 and 7 of Schedule O—Part 1. (For lines other than current year, amounts reported herein should include salvage received in prior years as well as salvage received in current year.)

(g) The unallocated loss expense payments paid during the most recent calendar year should be distributed to the various years in which losses were incurred as follows: (1) 45% to the most recent year, (2) 5% to the next most recent year, and (3) the balance to all years, including the most recent, in proportion to the amount of loss payments paid for each year during the most recent calendar year. If the distribution in (1) or (2) produces an accumulated distribution to such year in excess of 10% of the premiums earned for such year, disregarding all distributions made under (3), such accumulated distribution should be limited to 10% of premiums earned and the balance distributed in accordance with (3). Are they so reported in this statement? ANSWER: ....

(d) The term "loss expense" includes all payments for legal expenses, including attorney's and witness fees and court costs, salaries and expenses of investigators, adjustors and field men, rents, stationery, telegraph and telephone charges, postage, salaries and expenses of office employees, home office expenses and all other payments under or on account of such losses, whether the payments are allocated to specific claims or are unallocated. Are they so reported in this statement? ANSWER: ....

SCHEDULE P—PART 1—SUMMARY

(000 OMITTED)

(1) Years in Which Premiums Were Earned and Losses Were Incurred	(2) Premiums Earned	(3) Loss Payments	(d) LOSS EXPENSE PAYMENTS				(6) Loss and Loss Expense Payments (3 + 4 + 5)	(7) Ratio 6 ÷ 2 %	(8) Number of Claims Outstanding	(9) Losses Unpaid	(10) (d) Loss Expense Unpaid	(11) Total Losses and Loss Expense Incurred (6 + 9 + 10)	(12) Ratio 11 ÷ 2 %
			(4) Allocated	(4a) Ratio 4 ÷ 3 %	(5) (g) Unallocated	(5a) Ratio 5 ÷ 3 %							
1 Prior to 19													
2 19													
3 19													
4 19													
5 19													
6 19													
7 19													
8 19													
9 19													
10 19													
11 TOTALS													X X X

DETAILS OMITTED

SCHEDULE P—PART 1A—AUTO LIABILITY†

(1)	(2)	(3)	(4)	(4a)	(5)	(5a)	(6)	(7)	(8)	(9)	(10)	(11)	(12)
1 Prior to 19													
2 19													
3 19													
4 19													
5 19													
6 19													
7 19													
8 19													
9 19													
10 19													
11 TOTALS													

DETAILS OMITTED

COMPUTATION OF EXCESS OF STATUTORY RESERVE OVER STATEMENT RESERVES—AUTO LIABILITY

19 $ .... 19 $ .... 19 $ 3,000 Total $ .... Calculation Method— 61 % of Column 2, less Column 11, if negative enter zero. See Note a.

SCHEDULE P—PART 1B—OTHER LIABILITY†

(1)	(2)	(3)	(4)	(4a)	(5)	(5a)	(6)	(7)	(8)	(9)	(10)	(11)	(12)
1 Prior to 19													
2 19													
3 19													
4 19													
5 19													
6 19													
7 19													
8 19													
9 19													
10 19													
11 TOTALS													

DETAILS OMITTED

COMPUTATION OF EXCESS OF STATUTORY RESERVE OVER STATEMENT RESERVES—OTHER LIABILITY

19 $ .... 19 $ .... 19 $ .... Total $ .... Calculation Method— .... % of Column 2, less Column 11, if negative enter zero. See Note a.

See Schedule P—Part 1F for footnotes.

ANNUAL STATEMENT FOR THE YEAR 19 OF THE Property-Liability Insurance Co.
Name

SCHEDULE P–PART 1C–MEDICAL MALPRACTICE

(1) Years in Which Premiums Were Earned and Losses Were Incurred	(2) Premiums Earned	(3) Loss Payments	(d) LOSS EXPENSE PAYMENTS (4) Allocated	(4a) Ratio 4÷3 %	(5) (g) Unallocated	(5a) Ratio 5÷3 %	(6) Loss and Loss Expense Payments (3+4+5)	(7) Ratio 6÷2 %	(8) Number of Claims Outstanding	(9) (f) Losses Unpaid	(10) (d) Loss Expense Unpaid	(11) Total Losses and Loss Expense Incurred (6+9+10)	(12) Ratio 11÷2 %
1 Prior to 19													
2 19													
3 19													
4 19					Details Omitted								
5 19													
6 19													
7 19													
8 19													
9 19													
10 19													
11 Totals													X X X

COMPUTATION OF EXCESS OF STATUTORY RESERVE OVER STATEMENT RESERVES–MEDICAL MALPRACTICE
19 $ 19 $ 19 $ Total $ Calculation Method— % of Column 2, less Column 11, if negative enter zero. See Note a.

SCHEDULE P—PART 1D—WORKERS' COMPENSATION

(1)	(2)	(3)	(4)	(4a)	(5)	(5a)	(6)	(7)	(8)	(9)	(10)	(11)	(12)
1 Prior to 19													
2 19													
3 19													
4 19													
5 19					Details Omitted								
6 19													
7 19													
8 19													
9 19													
10 19													
11 Totals													

COMPUTATION OF EXCESS OF STATUTORY RESERVE OVER STATEMENT RESERVES–WORKERS' COMPENSATION
19 $ 19 $ 19 $ Total $ Calculation Method— % of Column 2, less Column 11, if negative enter zero. See Note a.

SCHEDULE P–PART 1E–FARMOWNERS MULTIPLE PERIL, HOMEOWNERS MULTIPLE PERIL, COMMERCIAL MULTIPLE PERIL, OCEAN MARINE, AIRCRAFT (ALL PERILS) AND BOILER AND MACHINERY

(1)	(2)	(3)	(4)	(4a)	(5)	(5a)	(6)	(7)	(8)	(9)	(10)	(11)	(12)
1 Prior to 19													
2 19													
3 19													
4 19													
5 19					Details Omitted								
6 19													
7 19													
8 19													
9 19													
10 19													
11 Totals													X X X

ⓐ See Schedule P–Part 1F for footnotes.

SCHEDULE P – PART 1F – INCURRED BUT NOT REPORTED LOSSES

(1) Years in Which Losses Were Incurred	(h) INCURRED BUT NOT REPORTED LOSSES UNPAID INCLUDED IN COLUMN 9 OF:					(i) ONE YEAR DEVELOPMENT OF IBNR LOSSES INCLUDED IN COLUMNS 3 AND 9 OF:				
	(2) Part 1A	(3) Part 1B	(4) Part 1C	(5) Part 1D	(6) Part 1E	(7) Part 1A	(8) Part 1B	(9) Part 1C	(10) Part 1D	(11) Part 1E
1 Prior to 19										
2 19										
3 19										
4 19										
5 19				DETAILS OMITTED						
6 19										
7 19										
8 19										
9 19										
10 19						X X X X	X X X X	X X X X	X X X X	X X X X
11 TOTALS										

Footnotes:

(a) The percentage to be used is based on the company's actual loss ratios in the five years immediately prior to the most recent three, provided that at least three of the five years have at least $1 million in Column 2. Use the lowest ratio in Column 12 for these years using only years which have at least $1 million in Column 2. If the lowest qualifying ratio is less than 60%, then use 60% (65% for Workers' Compensation). If the lowest qualifying ratio is more than 75%, then use 75%. If at least three of the five years do not have at least $1 million in Column 2, use 60% (65% for Workers' Compensation). Round percentage to nearest tenth of one per cent. Indicate percentage used.

(d) The term "loss expense" includes all payments for legal expenses, including attorney's and witness fees and court costs, salaries and expenses of investigators, adjustors and field men, rents, stationery, telegraph and telephone charges, postage, salaries and expenses of office employees, home office expenses and all other payments under or on account of such injuries, whether the payments are allocated to specific claims or are unallocated. Are they so reported in this statement? ANSWER: ....

(f) State maximum rate of interest used in determining present values of future workers' compensation payments .... %.

(g) The unallocated loss expense payments paid during the most recent calendar year should be distributed to the various years in which losses were incurred as follows: (1) 45% to the most recent year, (2) 5% to the next most recent year, and (3) the balance to all years, including the most recent, in proportion to the amount of loss payments paid for each year during the most recent calendar year. If the distribution in (1) or (2) produces an accumulated distribution to such year in excess of 10% of the premiums earned for such year, disregarding all distributions made under (3), such accumulated distribution should be limited to 10% of premiums earned and the balance distributed in accordance with (3). Are they so reported in this statement?
ANSWER: ....

(h) Totals on Line 11 to agree with the reserve shown on Page 10, Columns 4a + 4b of this statement. The IBNR reserve estimates in Columns 2 through 6 should be sufficient to cover claims which may be reopened in future periods.

(i) Include payments and reserves in respect to losses incurred more than one year prior to the date of this statement and reported during the current year.

[1]Includes only Bodily Injury Liability prior to 1971

SCHEDULE P – PART 2 – SUMMARY

(1)	INCURRED LOSSES AND LOSS EXPENSE REPORTED AT END OF YEAR (000 OMITTED)						INCURRED LOSS AND LOSS EXPENSE RATIO REPORTED					
Years in Which Losses Were Incurred	(2) 19	(3) 19	(4) 19	(5) 19	(6) 19	(7) 19	(8) 19	(9) 19	(10) 19	(11) 19	(12) 19	(13) 19
Prior to 19			Details Omitted				X X X	X X X	X X X	X X X	X X X	X X X
19												
Cumulative Total							X X X	X X X	X X X	X X X	X X X	X X X
19	X X X						X X X					
Cumulative Total	X X X						X X X	X X X	X X X	X X X	X X X	X X X
19	X X X	X X X					X X X	X X X				
Cumulative Total	X X X	X X X					X X X	X X X	X X X	X X X	X X X	X X X
19	X X X	X X X	X X X				X X X	X X X	X X X			
Cumulative Total	X X X	X X X	X X X				X X X	X X X	X X X	X X X	X X X	X X X
19	X X X	X X X	X X X	X X X			X X X	X X X	X X X	X X X		
Cumulative Total	X X X	X X X	X X X	X X X			X X X	X X X	X X X	X X X	X X X	X X X
19	X X X	X X X	X X X	X X X	X X X		X X X	X X X	X X X	X X X	X X X	

SCHEDULE P – PART 2A – AUTO LIABILITY

Prior to 19			Details Omitted				X X X	X X X	X X X	X X X	X X X	X X X
19												
Cumulative Total							X X X	X X X	X X X	X X X	X X X	X X X
19	X X X						X X X					
Cumulative Total	X X X						X X X	X X X	X X X	X X X	X X X	X X X
19	X X X	X X X					X X X	X X X				
Cumulative Total	X X X	X X X					X X X	X X X	X X X	X X X	X X X	X X X
19	X X X	X X X	X X X				X X X	X X X	X X X			
Cumulative Total	X X X	X X X	X X X				X X X	X X X	X X X	X X X	X X X	X X X
19	X X X	X X X	X X X	X X X			X X X	X X X	X X X	X X X		
Cumulative Total	X X X	X X X	X X X	X X X			X X X	X X X	X X X	X X X	X X X	X X X
19	X X X	X X X	X X X	X X X	X X X		X X X	X X X	X X X	X X X	X X X	

SCHEDULE P – PART 2B – OTHER LIABILITY

Prior to 19			Details Omitted				X X X	X X X	X X X	X X X	X X X	X X X
19												
Cumulative Total							X X X	X X X	X X X	X X X	X X X	X X X
19	X X X						X X X					
Cumulative Total	X X X						X X X	X X X	X X X	X X X	X X X	X X X
19	X X X	X X X					X X X	X X X				
Cumulative Total	X X X	X X X					X X X	X X X	X X X	X X X	X X X	X X X
19	X X X	X X X	X X X				X X X	X X X	X X X			
Cumulative Total	X X X	X X X	X X X				X X X	X X X	X X X	X X X	X X X	X X X
19	X X X	X X X	X X X	X X X			X X X	X X X	X X X	X X X		
Cumulative Total	X X X	X X X	X X X	X X X			X X X	X X X	X X X	X X X	X X X	X X X
19	X X X	X X X	X X X	X X X	X X X		X X X	X X X	X X X	X X X	X X X	

SCHEDULE P – PART 2C – MEDICAL MALPRACTICE

Prior to 19			Details Omitted				X X X	X X X	X X X	X X X	X X X	X X X
19												
Cumulative Total							X X X	X X X	X X X	X X X	X X X	X X X
19	X X X						X X X					
Cumulative Total	X X X						X X X	X X X	X X X	X X X	X X X	X X X
19	X X X	X X X					X X X	X X X				
Cumulative Total	X X X	X X X					X X X	X X X	X X X	X X X	X X X	X X X
19	X X X	X X X	X X X				X X X	X X X	X X X			
Cumulative Total	X X X	X X X	X X X				X X X	X X X	X X X	X X X	X X X	X X X
19	X X X	X X X	X X X	X X X			X X X	X X X	X X X	X X X		
Cumulative Total	X X X	X X X	X X X	X X X			X X X	X X X	X X X	X X X	X X X	X X X
19	X X X	X X X	X X X	X X X	X X X		X X X	X X X	X X X	X X X	X X X	

SCHEDULE P – PART 2D – WORKERS' COMPENSATION

	(1) Years in Which Losses Were Incurred	Incurred Losses and Loss Expense Reported at End of Year (000 Omitted)						Incurred Loss and Loss Expense Ratio Reported					
		(2) 19	(3) 19	(4) 19	(5) 19	(6) 19	(7) 19	(8) 19	(9) 19	(10) 19	(11) 19	(12) 19	(13) 19
1	Prior to 19			Details Omitted				X X X	X X X	X X X	X X X	X X X	X X
2	19												
3	Cumulative Total							X X X	X X X	X X X	X X X	X X X	X X
4	19	X X X						X X X					
5	Cumulative Total	X X X						X X X	X X X	X X X	X X X	X X X	X X
6	19	X X X	X X X					X X X	X X X				
7	Cumulative Total	X X X	X X X					X X X	X X X	X X X	X X X	X X X	X X
8	19	X X X	X X X	X X X				X X X	X X X	X X X			
9	Cumulative Total	X X X	X X X	X X X				X X X	X X X	X X X	X X X	X X X	X X
10	19	X X X	X X X	X X X	X X X			X X X	X X X	X X X	X X X		
11	Cumulative Total	X X X	X X X	X X X	X X X			X X X	X X X	X X X	X X X	X X X	X
12	19	X X X	X X X	X X X	X X X	X X X		X X X	X X X	X X X	X X X	X X X	

SCHEDULE P – PART 2E – FARMOWNERS MULTIPLE PERIL, HOMEOWNERS MULTIPLE PERIL, COMMERCIAL MULTIPLE PERIL, OCEAN MARINE, AIRCRAFT (ALL PERILS) AND BOILER AND MACHINERY

		(2)	(3)	(4)	(5)	(6)	(7)	(8)	(9)	(10)	(11)	(12)	(13)
1	Prior to 19		Details Omitted					X X X	X X X	X X X	X X X	X X X	X
2	19												
3	Cumulative Total							X X X	X X X	X X X	X X X	X X X	X
4	19	X X X						X X X					
5	Cumulative Total	X X X						X X X	X X X	X X X	X X X	X X X	X
6	19	X X X	X X X					X X X	X X X				
7	Cumulative Total	X X X	X X X					X X X	X X X	X X X	X X X	X X X	X
8	19	X X X	X X X	X X X				X X X	X X X	X X X			
9	Cumulative Total	X X X	X X X	X X X				X X X	X X X	X X X	X X X	X X X	X
10	19	X X X	X X X	X X X	X X X			X X X	X X X	X X X	X X X		
11	Cumulative Total	X X X	X X X	X X X	X X X			X X X	X X X	X X X	X X X	X X X	X
12	19	X X X	X X X	X X X	X X X	X X X		X X X	X X X	X X X	X X X	X X X	

SCHEDULE P—PART 3—SUMMARY

Calendar Year Premiums Earned, Accident Year Loss and Loss Expense Incurred

	DOLLARS (000 omitted)							PERCENTAGES						
	(1) 19	(2) 19	(3) 19	(4) 19	(5) 19	(6) 19	(7) 19	(8) 19	(9) 19	(10) 19	(11) 19	(12) 19	(13) 19	(14) 19
	Summary Data from Schedule P—Part 1—Summary													
...ums Earned Loss Exp. Inc'd.		DETAILS OMITTED						100.0	100.0	100.0	100.0	100.0	100.0	100.0
	Loss & Loss Expense through 1 year													
...e (2)—(3)														
	Loss & Loss Expense through 2 years													
...e (2)—(5)							XX XX							XX XX
	Loss & Loss Expense through 3 years													
...e (2)—(7)						XX XX	XX XX						XX XX	XX XX
	Loss & Loss Expense through 4 years													
...e (2)—(9)					XX XX	XX XX	XX XX					XX XX	XX XX	XX XX
	Loss & Loss Expense through 5 years													
...e (2)—(11)				XX XX	XX XX	XX XX	XX XX				XX XX	XX XX	XX XX	XX XX

SCHEDULE P—PART 3A—AUTO LIABILITY

Calendar Year Premiums Earned, Accident Year Loss and Loss Expense Incurred

	DOLLARS (000 omitted)							PERCENTAGES						
	(1) 19	(2) 19	(3) 19	(4) 19	(5) 19	(6) 19	(7) 19	(8) 19	(9) 19	(10) 19	(11) 19	(12) 19	(13) 19	(14) 19
	Summary Data from Schedule P—Part 1A													
...ns Earned ...oss Exp. Inc'd.		DETAILS OMITTED						100.0	100.0	100.0	100.0	100.0	100.0	100.0
	Loss & Loss Expense through 1 year													
(2)—(3)														
	Loss & Loss Expense through 2 years													
(2)—(5)							XX XX							XX XX
	Loss & Loss Expense through 3 years													
(2)—(7)						XX XX	XX XX						XX XX	XX XX
	Loss & Loss Expense through 4 years													
(2)—(9)					XX XX	XX XX	XX XX					XX XX	XX XX	XX XX
	Loss & Loss Expense through 5 years													
(2)—(11)				XX XX	XX XX	XX XX	XX XX				XX XX	XX XX	XX XX	XX XX

SCHEDULE P—PART 3B—OTHER LIABILITY

Calendar Year Premiums Earned, Accident Year Loss and Loss Expense Incurred

	DOLLARS (000 omitted)							PERCENTAGES						
	(1) 19	(2) 19	(3) 19	(4) 19	(5) 19	(6) 19	(7) 19	(8) 19	(9) 19	(10) 19	(11) 19	(12) 19	(13) 19	(14) 19
	Summary Data from Schedule P—Part 1B													
...s Earned ...s Exp. Inc'd.		DETAILS OMITTED						100.0	100.0	100.0	100.0	100.0	100.0	100.0
	Loss & Loss Expense through 1 year													
(2)—(3)														
	Loss & Loss Expense through 2 years													
(2)—(5)							XX XX							XX XX
	Loss & Loss Expense through 3 years													
(2)—(7)						XX XX	XX XX						XX XX	XX XX
	Loss & Loss Expense through 4 years													
(2)—(9)					XX XX	XX XX	XX XX					XX XX	XX XX	XX XX
	Loss & Loss Expense through 5 years													
(2)—(11)				XX XX	XX XX	XX XX	XX XX				XX XX	XX XX	XX XX	XX XX

SCHEDULE P – PART 3C – MEDICAL MALPRACTICE

Calendar Year Premiums Earned, Accident Year Loss and Loss Expense Incurred

	DOLLARS (000 omitted)							PERCENTAGES					
	(1) 19	(2) 19	(3) 19	(4) 19	(5) 19	(6) 19	(7) 19	(8) 19	(9) 19	(10) 19	(11) 19	(12) 19	(13) 19
	Summary Data from Schedule P—Part 1C												
1 Premiums Earned								100.0	100.0	100.0	100.0	100.0	100.0
2 Loss & Loss Exp. Inc'd.		DETAILS OMITTED											
	Loss & Loss Expense through 1 year												
3 Paid													
4 Reserve (2)—(3)													
	Loss & Loss Expense through 2 years												
5 Paid							X X						
6 Reserve (2)—(5)							X X						
	Loss & Loss Expense through 3 years												
7 Paid						X X	X X						X X
8 Reserve (2)—(7)						X X	X X						X X
	Loss & Loss Expense through 4 years												
9 Paid					X X	X X	X X					X X	X X
10 Reserve (2)—(9)					X X	X X	X X					X X	X X
	Loss & Loss Expense through 5 years												
11 Paid				X X	X X	X X	X X				X X	X X	X X
12 Reserve (2)—(11)				X X	X X	X X	X X				X X	X X	X X

SCHEDULE P — PART 3D — WORKERS' COMPENSATION

Calendar Year Premiums Earned, Accident Year Loss and Loss Expense Incurred

	DOLLARS (000 omitted)							PERCENTAGES					
	(1) 19	(2) 19	(3) 19	(4) 19	(5) 19	(6) 19	(7) 19	(8) 19	(9) 19	(10) 19	(11) 19	(12) 19	(13) 19
	Summary Data from Schedule P—Part 1D												
1 Premiums Earned								100.0	100.0	100.0	100.0	100.0	100.
2 Loss & Loss Exp. Inc'd.		DETAILS OMITTED											
	Loss & Loss Expense through 1 year												
3 Paid													
4 Reserve (2)—(3)													
	Loss & Loss Expense through 2 years												
5 Paid							X X						
6 Reserve (2)—(5)							X X						
	Loss & Loss Expense through 3 years												
7 Paid						X X	X X						X
8 Reserve (2)—(7)						X X	X X						X
	Loss & Loss Expense through 4 years												
9 Paid					X X	X X	X X					X X	X
10 Reserve (2)—(9)					X X	X X	X X					X X	X
	Loss & Loss Expense through 5 years												
11 Paid				X X	X X	X X	X X				X X	X X	X
12 Reserve (2)—(11)				X X	X X	X X	X X				X X	X X	X

SCHEDULE P – PART 3E – FARMOWNERS MULTIPLE PERIL, HOMEOWNERS MULTIPLE PERIL, COMMERCIAL MULTIPLE PERIL, OCEAN MARINE, AIRCRAFT (ALL PERILS) AND BOILER AND MACHINERY

Calendar Year Premiums Earned, Accident Year Loss and Loss Expense Incurred

	DOLLARS (000 omitted)							PERCENTAGES					
	(1) 19	(2) 19	(3) 19	(4) 19	(5) 19	(6) 19	(7) 19	(8) 19	(9) 19	(10) 19	(11) 19	(12) 19	(13) 19
	Summary Data from Schedule P—Part 1E												
1 Premiums Earned								100.0	100.0	100.0	100.0	100.0	100
2 Loss & Loss Exp. Inc'd.		DETAILS OMITTED											
	Loss & Loss Expense through 1 year												
3 Paid													
4 Reserve (2)—(3)													
	Loss & Loss Expense through 2 years												
5 Paid							X X						
6 Reserve (2)—(5)							X X						
	Loss & Loss Expense through 3 years												
7 Paid						X X	X X						X
8 Reserve (2)—(7)						X X	X X						X
	Loss & Loss Expense through 4 years												
9 Paid					X X	X X	X X					X X	X
10 Reserve (2)—(9)					X X	X X	X X					X X	X
	Loss & Loss Expense through 5 years												
11 Paid				X X	X X	X X	X X				X X	X X	
12 Reserve (2)—(11)				X X	X X	X X	X X				X X	X X	

SCHEDULE X – PART 1 – UNLISTED ASSETS

**Showing all property owned by or in which the Company had any interest, on December 31 of current year, which is not entered on any other schedule and which is not included in the financial statement for the current year*

(1) DESCRIPTION	(2) FROM WHOM ACQUIRED	(3) DATE WHEN ACQUIRED	(4) DATE WHEN CHARGED OFF FROM STATEMENT	(5) PAR VALUE	(6) ACTUAL COST	(7) BOOK VALUE WHEN CHARGED OFF	(8) MARKET VALUE DECEMBER 31 OF CURRENT YEAR	(9) GROSS INCOME THEREFROM DURING YEAR	(10) OUTLAYS MADE DURING YEAR	(11) REASONS FOR NOT CARRYING PROPERTY ON BOOKS
					NONE					
			Totals							XXXX

SCHEDULE X – PART 2

Showing all property acquired or transferred to Schedule X, Part 1, during the year except that shown in invested asset schedules and except furniture, fixtures and supplies

(1) DESCRIPTION	(2) DATE OF ACQUISITION	(3) FROM WHOM ACQUIRED	(4) PAR VALUE	(5) ACTUAL COST
	NONE			
		Totals		

SCHEDULE X – PART 3

Showing all property sold or transferred from Schedule X, Part 1, during the year except that shown in invested asset schedules

(1) DESCRIPTION	(2) DATE OF ACQUISITION	(3) FROM WHOM ACQUIRED	(4) PAR VALUE	(5) ACTUAL COST	(6) DATE OF SALE	(7) TO WHOM SOLD	(8) CONSIDERATION	(9) GROSS INCOME THEREFROM DURING YEAR	(10) OUTLAY THEREON DURING YEAR OTHER THAN COST
				NONE					
		Totals			XXX	XXX XXX XXX XXX XXX			

*Companies should limit entries in this schedule to items transferred from asset accounts.

SCHEDULE Y — ORGANIZATIONAL CHART

Attach a chart or listing presenting the identities of and interrelationships among all affiliated insurers and all other affiliates, identifying all insurers as such. No non-insurer affiliate need be shown if its total assets are less than ½ of 1% of the total assets of the largest affiliated insurer.

DETAILS OMITTED

NOTE: All members of a Holding Company Group shall prepare a common Schedule for inclusion in each of the individual annual statements and the consolidated Fire and Casualty Annual Statement of the Group.

SCHEDULE T—EXHIBIT OF PREMIUMS WRITTEN

Allocated by States and Territories

(1) STATES, ETC.	(1a) IS INSURER LICENSED? (Yes or No)	GROSS PREMIUMS, INCLUDING POLICY AND MEMBERSHIP FEES, LESS RETURN PREMIUMS AND PREMIUMS ON POLICIES NOT TAKEN		(4) DIVIDENDS PAID OR CREDITED TO POLICYHOLDERS ON DIRECT BUSINESS	(5) DIRECT LOSSES PAID (Deducting Salvage)	(6) DIRECT LOSSES INCURRED	(7) DIRECT LOSSES UNPAID	(8) FINANCE AND SERVICE CHARGES NOT INCLUDED IN PREMIUMS
		(2) DIRECT PREMIUMS WRITTEN	(3) DIRECT PREMIUMS EARNED					
ama AL								
a AK								
na AZ								
nsas AR								
ornia CA								
ado CO								
ecticut CT								
ware DE								
Columbia DC								
la FL								
gia GA								
i HI								
ID								
s IL								
a IN								
IA								
s KS								
cky KY								
ana LA								
ME								
and MD								
chusetts MA								
gan MI								
sota MN								
sippi MS								
uri MO								
na MT								
ska NE								
NV								
Hampshire NH								
ersey NJ								
Mexico NM								
ork NY								
arolina NC								
akota ND								
OH								
ma OK								
OR								
lvania PA								
Island RI								
rolina SC								
kota SD								
see TN								
TX								
UT								
t VT								
VA								
gton WA								
ginia WV								
sin WI								
g WY								
n Samoa AS								
GU								
Rico PR								
gin Is. VI								
CN								
en (Aggregate) **OT								
	††							

DETAILS OMITTED

Explanation of Basis of Allocation of Premiums by States, etc.

*Total for Column 2 to agree with the total of Column 1 in Part 2C, Page 8. Total for Column 5 to agree with the total of Column 1 in Part 3, Page 9. Total for Column 6 to agree with the sum of totals for Columns 5 and 7 less the total for Column 7 in the previous annual statement.
Total for Column 7 to equal Part 3A, Page 10, totals for Columns 1a and 4a. Total for Column 8 to agree with Item 11, Page 4.
**All U. S. business must be allocated by state regardless of license status.
††Insert the number of yes responses except for Canada and Other Alien.

SUPPLEMENTAL EXHIBITS AND SCHEDULES
INTERROGATORIES

DETAILS OMITTED

The following supplemental reports are required to be filed as part of your annual statement filing. However, in the event that your company does not transact the type of business for which the special report must be filed, your response to the specific interrogatory will be accepted in lieu of filing a "NONE" report.

1. Will Supplement A to Schedule T (Medical Malpractice Supplement) be filed with this Department by March 1? Answer (yes or no):.......... If answer is "no," please explain:..........

2. Will Schedule SIS (Stockholder Information Supplement) be filed with this Department by March 1? Answer (yes or no):.......... If answer is "no," please explain:..........

3. Will the Credit Accident and Health Insurance section on page 14 of the annual statement be filed with this Department by April 1? Answer (yes or no):.......... If answer is "no," please explain:..........

4. Will the Insurance Expense Exhibit be filed with this Department by April 1? Answer (yes or no):.......... If answer is "no," please explain:..........

5. Will Schedule H be filed with this Department by April 1? Answer (yes or no):.......... If answer is "no," please explain:..........

6. Will Schedule F, Part 1A, Section 2 be filed with this Department by April 1? Answer (yes or no):.......... If answer is "no," please explain:..........

7. Will the Statement of Opinion relating to loss and loss adjustment expense reserves be filed with this Department by April 1? Answer (yes or no):.......... If answer is "no," please explain:..........

8. Will the Credit Life and Accident and Health Exhibit be filed with this Department by May 1? Answer (yes or no):.......... If answer is "no," please explain:..........

9. Will the Products Liability Supplement be filed with this Department by May 1? Answer (yes or no):.......... If answer is "no," please explain:..........

10. Will the Accident and Health Policy Experience Exhibit be filed with this Department by June 30? Answer (yes or no):.......... If answer is "no," please explain:..........

SUPPLEMENT "A" TO SCHEDULE T
EXHIBIT OF MEDICAL MALPRACTICE PREMIUMS WRITTEN
Allocated by States and Territories

†DESIGNATE THE TYPE OF HEALTH CARE PROVIDERS REPORTED ON THIS PAGE:

(1) STATES, ETC.		(2) NUMBER OF EXPOSURES	(3) DIRECT PREMIUMS WRITTEN*	(4) DIRECT PREMIUMS EARNED*	DIRECT LOSSES PAID (5) AMOUNT	DIRECT LOSSES PAID (6) NO. OF CLAIMS‡	(7) DIRECT LOSSES INCURRED	DIRECT LOSSES UNPAID (8) AMOUNT REPORTED	DIRECT LOSSES UNPAID (9) NO. OF CLAIMS‡	(10) DIRECT LOSSES INCURRED BUT NOT REPORTED
abama	AL									
aska	AK									
izona	AZ				None					
kansas	AR									
lifornia	CA									
lorado	CO									
nnecticut	CT									
laware	DE									
st. Columbia	DC									
rida	FL									
orgia	GA									
waii	HI									
ho	ID									
nois	IL									
iana	IN									
a	IA									
nsas	KS									
tucky	KY									
isiana	LA									
ne	ME									
yland	MD									
sachusetts	MA									
higan	MI									
nesota	MN									
sissippi	MS									
souri	MO									
tana	MT									
raska	NE									
ada	NV									
Hampshire	NH									
Jersey	NJ									
Mexico	NM									
York	NY									
Carolina	NC									
Dakota	ND									
	OH									
homa	OK									
on	OR									
sylvania	PA									
e Island	RI									
arolina	SC									
akota	SD									
essee	TN									
	TX									
	UT									
ont	VT									
ia	VA									
ngton	WA									
Virginia	WV									
nsin	WI									
ing	WY									
can Samoa	AS									
	GU									
Rico	PR									
Virgin Is.	VI									
a	CN									
alien (itemize)	**OT									
(a)										

*Gross premiums, including policy and membership fees, less return premiums on policies not taken. Include in this Exhibit the medical malpractice portion of any policy for which the premiums for medical malpractice are separately stated. Include all indivisible premium policies for which at least one-half of the premium is for medical malpractice coverage.

†A separate Supplement "A" must be used for each designated type of health care provider, which are (1) Physicians - including surgeons and osteopaths, (2) Hospitals; (3) Other health care professionals, including dentists; (4) Other health care facilities; and (5) Medical malpractice policies effective prior to January 1, 1976.

‡If a claim count is included in losses paid, it must not be included in losses unpaid, or vice versa.

**All U. S. business must be allocated by state regardless of license status.

NOTE. See additional instructions on reverse side.

NOTES

ANNUAL STATEMENT

For the Year Ended December 31, 19

OF THE CONDITION AND AFFAIRS OF THE

LIFE INSURANCE COMPANY

NAIC Group Code: NAIC Company Code: Employer's ID Number:

Organized under the Laws of the State of ____________________, made to the

INSURANCE DEPARTMENT OF THE STATE OF

PURSUANT TO THE LAWS THEREOF

Incorporated ________________ Commenced Business ________________

Home Office ________________ (Street and Number), ________________ (City or Town, State and Zip Code)

Mail Address ________________ (Street and Number), ________________ (City or Town, State and Zip Code)

Main Administrative Office ________________ (Area Code) (Telephone Number)

Contact Person and Phone Number ________________

OFFICERS

President ________________

Secretary ________________

Treasurer ________________

Actuary ________________

Vice-Presidents

DIRECTORS OR TRUSTEES

State of
County of } ss

, President, , Secretary, , Treasurer,

the , being duly sworn, each for himself poses and says that they are the above described officers of the said insurer, and that on the thirty-first day of December last, all of the herein described assets were the absolute prop-y of the said insurer free and clear from any liens or claims thereon, except as herein stated, and that this annual statement, together with related exhibits, schedules and explanations erein contained, annexed or referred to are a full and true statement of all the assets and liabilities and of the condition and affairs of the said insurer as of the thirty-first day of Decem- last, and of its income and deductions therefrom for the year ended on that date, according to the best of their information, knowledge and belief, respectively.

President Secretary Treasurer

Actuary

Subscribed and sworn to before me this

day of , 19

Note: The pages identified by the symbol (S) in this annual statement were reproduced by the John S. Swift Company from master forms copyright 19 by the John S. Swift Company, Incorporated.

ASSETS	(1) Current Year	(2) Previous Year
	(000 OMITTED)	
1. Bonds (SCHEDULE D - PART 1)	480,430	451,8
2. Stocks:		
2.1 Preferred stocks (SCHEDULE D - PART 2 - SECTION 1)	2,860	2,
2.2 Common stocks (SCHEDULE D - PART 2 - SECTION 2)	25,654	24,
3. Mortgage loans on real estate (SCHEDULE B - PART 1 - SECTION 1)	27,270	26,
4. Real estate:		
4.1 Properties occupied by the company (less $ encumbrances) (SCHEDULE A - PART 1)	8,690	8,
4.2 Properties acquired in satisfaction of debt (less $ encumbrances)		
4.3 Investment real estate (less $ encumbrances)		
5. Policy loans	95,642	89,
6. Premium notes, including $ for first year premiums		
7. Collateral loans (SCHEDULE C - PART 1)		
8.1 Cash on hand and on deposit (SCHEDULE E)	370	1,
8.2 Short-term investments (SCHEDULE DA)	25,273	4,
9.		
10. Other invested assets	830	
10A. Subtotals, cash and invested assets (Items 1 to 10)	667,019	611,
11. Reinsurance ceded:		
11.1 Amounts recoverable from reinsurers	8,002	9,
11.2 Commissions and expense allowances due	210	
11.3 Experience rating and other refunds due	2,731	2,
11.4		
12.		
13. Electronic data processing equipment	3,210	3,
14. Federal income tax recoverable		
15.		
16.		
17. Life insurance premiums and annuity considerations deferred and uncollected	6,045	5
18. Accident and health premiums due and unpaid	105	
19. Investment income due and accrued (EXHIBIT 3 - COLUMNS 3 + 4)	6,982	6
20. Net adjustment in assets and liabilities due to foreign exchange rates		
21.		
22.		
23.		
24.		
25.		
26. Subtotals (Items 10A to 25)	694,304	63
27A. From Separate Accounts Statement	205,408	19
27B. From Variable Life Insurance Separate Accounts Statement		
28. TOTALS (Items 26 to 27B)	899,712	83

NOTE: The items on this page to agree with Exhibit 13, Col. 4.

The Notes to Financial Statements are an integral par

LIABILITIES, SURPLUS AND OTHER FUNDS	(1) Current Year (000 OMITTED)	(2) Previous Year
;gregate reserve for life policies and contracts $ (Exh. 8, Line H) less $ included in Item 7.3	465,393	434,781
;gregate reserve for accident and health policies (Exhibit 9, Line C, Col. 1)	17,972	15,262
pplementary contracts without life contingencies (Exhibit 10, Line 7, Col. 5)	3,721	3,522
icy and contract claims:		
Life (Exhibit 11, Part 1, Line 4d, Column 1 less sum of Columns 9, 10 and 11)	2,175	1,890
Accident and health (Exhibit 11, Part 1, Line 4d, sum of Columns 9, 10 and 11)	1,893	1,420
icyholders' dividend and coupon* accumulations (Exhibit 10, Line 7, Col. 6 plus Col. 7)	59,107	58,490
licyholders' dividends $ and coupons $ due and unpaid (Exhibit 7, Line 10)	58	52
ovision for policyholders' dividends and coupons payable in following calendar year—estimated amounts:		
Dividends apportioned for payment to , 19	910	770
Dividends not yet apportioned		
Coupons and similar benefits		
ount provisionally held for deferred dividend policies not included in Item 7		
miums and annuity considerations received in advance less $ discount;		
uding $ 107 accident and health premiums (Exhibit 1, Part 1, Col. 1, sum of Lines 4 and 14)	1,623	1,704
bility for premium and other deposit funds	4,884	4,692
cy and contract liabilities not included elsewhere:		
Surrender values on cancelled policies		
Provision for experience rating refunds		
Other amounts payable on reinsurance assumed		
Amounts Payable for Reinsurance Ceded	3,705	3,320
missions to agents due or accrued-life and annuity $ 1,132 accident and health $ 110	1,242	1,370
missions and expense allowances payable on reinsurance assumed		
eral expenses due or accrued (Exhibit 5, Line 12, Col. 4)	866	764
sfers to Separate Accounts due or accrued, excluding Variable Life Insurance (net)		
sfers to Variable Life Insurance Separate Accounts due or accrued (net)		
s, licenses and fees due or accrued, excluding federal income taxes (Exhibit 6, Line 9, Col. 4)	872	690
ral income taxes due or accrued, including $ 782 on capital gains (excluding deferred taxes)	3,924	3,670
t of collection" on premiums and annuity considerations deferred and uncollected in excess of total loading thereon		
rned investment income (Exhibit 3, Line 10, Col. 2)	261	150
ınts withheld or retained by company as agent or trustee	174	190
ınts held for agents' account, including $ 96 agents' credit balances	96	96
ttances and items not allocated	2,170	1,920
adjustment in assets and liabilities due to foreign exchange rates		
ity for benefits for employees and agents if not included above		
owed money $ 2,810 and interest thereon $ 150	2,960	3,067
ends to stockholders declared and unpaid		
llaneous liabilities (give items and amounts):		
Mandatory securities valuation reserve (Page 29A, final Item)	8,493	7,833
Reinsurance in unauthorized companies		
Funds held under reinsurance treaties with unauthorized reinsurers		
Unreimbursed expenditures by a parent, affiliate or subsidiary company		
Drafts outstanding		
Separate Accounts Statement	205,408	196,110
Variable Life Insurance Separate Accounts Statement		
Total Liabilities (Items 1 to 25B)	787,907	741,763
paid up	25,000	25,000
paid in and contributed surplus (Page 3, Item 28, Col. 2 plus Page 4, Item 46a, Col. 1)	-	-
surplus funds:		
gned funds (surplus)	86,805	68,455
easury stock, at cost:		
shares common (value included in Item 27A $)		
shares preferred (value included in Item 27A $)		
(total Items 27B + 28 + 29A + 29B − 29C)	86,805	68,455
f Items 27A and 29D (Page 4, Item 50)	111,805	93,455
Totals of Items 26 and 30 (Page 2, Item 28)	899,712	835,218

a, guaranteed annual pure endowments and similar benefits.

SUMMARY OF OPERATIONS
(Excluding Capital Gains and Losses)

	(1) Current Year	(2) Previous Y
	(000 OMITTED)	
1. Premiums and annuity considerations (Exhibit 1, Part 1, Line 20d, Col. 1)	95,780	89.
1A. Annuity and other fund deposits		
2. Considerations for supplementary contracts with life contingencies (Exhibit 12, Line 3)	660	
3. Considerations for supplementary contracts without life contingencies and dividend accumulations (Exhibit 12, Lines 4 and 5)	4,108	3,
3A. Coupons left to accumulate at interest (Exhibit 12, Line 5A)		
4. Net investment income (Exhibit 2, Line 7)	61,251	58.
5. Commissions and expense allowances on reinsurance ceded (Exhibit 1, Part 2, Line 26a, Col. 1)	310	
5A. Reserve adjustments on reinsurance ceded (Exhibit 12, Line 10A)		
6. OTHER INCOME	121	
7. TOTALS (Items 1 to 6)	162,230	153,4
8. Death benefits	24,480	27,8
9. Matured endowments (excluding guaranteed annual pure endowments)	3,140	3,2
10. Annuity benefits (Exhibit 11, Part 2, Line 6d, Cols. 4 + 8)	14,290	15,1
11. Disability benefits and benefits under accident and health policies	2,770	3,2
11A. Coupons, guaranteed annual pure endowments and similar benefits (Exhibit 7, Line 15, Cols. 3 + 4)		
12. Surrender benefits	13,274	21,9
13. Group conversions		
14. Interest on policy or contract funds	1,240	1,1
15. Payments on supplementary contracts with life contingencies (Exhibit 12, Line 22.1)	3,098	3,7
16. Payments on supplementary contracts without life contingencies and of dividend accumulations (Exhibit 12, Lines 22.2 + 23)	520	4.
16A. Accumulated coupon payments (Exhibit 12, Line 23A)		
17. Increase in aggregate reserves for life and accident and health policies and contracts	33,322	21,1
18. Increase in reserve for supplementary contracts without life contingencies and for dividend and coupon accumulations	816	3
19.		
20. TOTALS (Items 8 to 19)	96,950	98,4
21. Commissions on premiums and annuity considerations (direct business only) (Exhibit 1, Part 2, Line 30, Col. 1)	11,330	9,6
21A. Commissions and expense allowances on reinsurance assumed (Exhibit 1, Part 2, Line 26b, Col. 1)		
22. General insurance expenses (Exhibit 5, Line 10, Cols. 1 + 2)	12,470	11,
23. Insurance taxes, licenses and fees, excluding federal income taxes (Exhibit 6, Line 7, Cols. 1 and 2)	2,730	2,6
24. Increase in loading on and cost of collection in excess of loading on deferred and uncollected premiums	1,150	
24A. Net transfers to (+) or from (—) Separate Accounts (excluding Variable Life Insurance)		
24B. Net transfers to (+) or from (—) Variable Life Insurance Separate Accounts		
25.		
26. TOTALS (Items 20 to 25)	124,630	123,
27. Net gain from operations before dividends to policyholders and federal income taxes (Item 7 minus Item 26)	37,600	30,
28. Dividends to policyholders (Exhibit 7, Line 15, Cols. 1 and 2)	970	
29. Net gain from operations after dividends to policyholders and before federal income taxes (Item 27 minus Item 28)	36,630	29,
30. Federal income taxes incurred (excluding tax on capital gains)	14,650	11,
31. NET GAIN FROM OPERATIONS AFTER DIVIDENDS TO POLICYHOLDERS AND FEDERAL INCOME TAXES (excluding tax on capital gains) (Item 29 minus Item 30)	21,980	17,

CAPITAL AND SURPLUS ACCOUNT

	(1) Current Year	(2) Previous Y
32. Capital and surplus, December 31, previous year (Page 3, Item 30, Col. 2)	93,455	78.
33. Net gain (Item 31)	21,980	17,
34. Net capital gains (Exhibit 4, Line 10.2)	770	1,
35. Change in non-admitted assets and related items (Exhibit 14, Line 13, Col. 3)	(1,240)	(
36. Change in liability for reinsurance in unauthorized companies, increase (–) or decrease (+) (Page 3, Item 25.2, Col. 1 minus 2)		
37. Change in reserve on account of change in valuation basis, increase (–) or decrease (+) (Exh. 8A, Line 7, Col. 4)		
38. Change in mandatory securities valuation reserve, increase (–) or decrease (+) (Page 3, Item 25.1, Col. 1 minus 2)	(660)	(
39.		
40.		
41. Change in treasury stock, increase (–) or decrease (+) (Page 3, Items 29C (1) & (2), Col. 1 minus 2)		
42.		
43. Change in surplus in Separate Accounts Statement		
44. Change in surplus in Variable Life Insurance Separate Accounts Statement		
45. Capital changes:		
(a) Paid in		
(b) Transferred from surplus (Stock Dividend)		
(c) Transferred to surplus (Exhibit 12, Line 29)		
46. Surplus adjustments:		
(a) Paid in		
(b) Transferred to capital (Stock Dividend) (Exhibit 12, Line 30, inside amount for stock $)		
(c) Transferred from capital (Exhibit 12, Line 29)		
47. Dividends to stockholders	(2,500)	(2,
48.		
49. Net change in capital and surplus for the year (Items 33 through 48)	18,350	14,
50. Capital and surplus, December 31, current year (Items 32 + 49) (Page 3, Item 30)	111,805	93.

NOTE: Items 1 to 31 to agree with Page 5, Col. 1, Items 1 to 31.

STATEMENT OF CHANGES IN FINANCIAL POSITION

	(1) Current Year	(2) Previous Year
	(000 OMITTED)	
FUNDS PROVIDED		
PERATIONS:		
et gain from operations after dividends to policyholders and federal income taxes xcluding tax on capital gains) (+)	21,980	17,470
arges (+) credits (—) not affecting funds:		
crease (+) in policy reserves	33,322	21,170
crease (+) in policy and contract claims	758	960
crease (+) in other policy or contract liabilities	1,161	1,030
crease in net reinsurance payables (+) receivables (—)	1,552	2,190
crease (+) in liability for policyholder dividends, coupons and experience rating refunds	146	80
crease (+) in commissions, expenses and taxes (other than federal income taxes) due or accured	156	110
crease (+) in federal income taxes due or accrued, excluding tax on capital gains	254	230
crease (—) in premiums receivable	66	70
crease in net investment income receivable (—)	(125)	(120)
preciation on real estate and other invested assets (+)	987	840
nortization of premium (+)	59	53
crual of discount (—)	(1,790)	(1,660)
al funds provided from operations (Items 1 to 16)	58,526	42,443
VESTMENTS SOLD, MATURED OR REPAID:		
nds	12,863	15,007
cks	5,924	6,110
rtgage loans	2,977	3,760
l estate		
er invested assets	320	790
Gains (+) or Losses (—) on investments acquired and disposed of during year		
on capital gains (—)	(782)	(410)
al investments sold, matured or repaid (Items 18 to 24)	21,302	25,257
HER FUNDS PROVIDED:		
ital and surplus paid in (+)		
rowed money $ 2,493 less amounts repaid $ 2,600	107	
l other funds provided (Items 26 to 28)	107	
l funds provided (Items 17, 25 and 29)	79,935	67,700
FUNDS APPLIED		
ESTMENTS ACQUIRED:		
ls	40,996	33,860
increase (+) decrease (-) in short-term investments	21,209	3,920
ks	6,702	11,210
gage loans	3,307	4,760
estate	1,377	2,700
r invested assets	447	960
investments acquired (Items 31 to 37)	74,038	57,410
ER FUNDS APPLIED:		
lends to stockholders	2,500	2,500
Increase (+) decrease (—) in policy loans	5,882	7,920
r items (net)	(1,090)	(920)
other funds applied (Items 39 to 43)	7,292	9,500
funds applied (Items 38 and 44)	81,330	69,910
ase (+) Decrease (—) in Cash (Item 30 minus Item 45)	(1,395)	790
I ON HAND AND ON DEPOSIT:		
nning of year (Item 48, Column 2)	1,765	975
of year (Items 46 + 47)	370	1,765

Form 1.

ANNUAL STATEMENT FOR THE YEAR 19 OF THE *Life Insurance Company*

Name

ANALYSIS OF OPERATIONS BY LINES OF BUSINESS
(Gain and Loss Exhibit) (Excluding Capital Gains and Losses)

	(1)	(2)	Ordinary			(6)	Group		Accident and Health		
	Total**	Industrial Life	(3) Life Insurance	(4) Individual Annuities	(5) Supplementary Contracts	Credit Life* (Group and Individual)	(7) Life Insurance†	(8) Annuities	(9) Group	(10) Credit* (Group and Individual)	(11) Other
1. Premiums and annuity considerations					X X X						
1A. Annuity and other fund deposits					X X X						
2. Considerations for supplementary contracts with life contingencies			X X X	X X X					X X X	X X X	X X X
3. Considerations for supplementary contracts without life contingencies and dividend accumulations											
3A. Coupons* left to accumulate at interest											
4. Net investment income											
5. Commissions and expense allowances on reinsurance ceded											
5A. Reserve adjustments on reinsurance ceded											
6.											
7. Totals (Items 1 to 6)											
8. Death benefits				X X X				X X X	X X X	X X X	X X X
9. Matured endowments (excluding guaranteed annual pure endowments)				X X X				X X X	X X X	X X X	X X X
10. Annuity benefits			X X X			X X X	X X X		X X X	X X X	X X X
11. Disability benefits and benefits under accident and health policies											
11A. Coupons, guaranteed annual pure endowments and similar benefits											
12. Surrender benefits				X X X				X X X	X X X	X X X	X X X
13. Group conversions				X X X				X X X			
13A. Transfers on account of group package policies and contracts	X X X	X X X	X X X	X X X	X X X						X X X
14. Interest on policy or contract funds											
15. Payments on supplementary contracts with life contingencies			X X X	X X X					X X X	X X X	X X X
16. Payments on supplementary contracts without life contingencies and of dividend accumulations											
16A. Accumulated coupon* payments											
17. Increase in aggregate reserves for life and accident and health policies and contracts											
18. Increase in reserve for supplementary contracts without life contingencies and for dividend and coupon* accumulations											
19.											
20. Totals (Items 8 to 19)											
21. Commissions on premiums and annuity considerations (direct business only)											
21A. Commissions and expense allowances on reinsurance assumed											
22. General insurance expenses											
23. Insurance taxes, licenses and fees, excluding federal income taxes											
24. Increase in loading on and cost of collection in excess of loading on deferred and uncollected premiums											
24A. Net transfers to (+) or from (—) Separate Accounts (excluding Variable Life Insurance)											
24B. Net transfers to (+) or from (—) Variable Life Insurance Separate Accounts											
25.											
26. Totals (Items 20 to 25)											
27. Net gain from operations before dividends to policyholders and federal income taxes (Item 7 minus Item 26)											
28. Dividends to policyholders											
29. Net gain from operations after dividends to policyholders and before federal income taxes (Item 27 minus Item 28)											
30. Federal income taxes incurred (excluding tax on capital gains)											
31. Net gain from operations after dividends to policyholders and federal income taxes (excluding tax on capital gains) (Item 29 minus Item 30)											

SUPPLEMENTARY INFORMATION

† [illegible] 120 months duration. *Includes coupons, guaranteed annual pure endowments and similar benefits. **The items in this column to agree with Page 4, Column 1.

Form 1

ANNUAL STATEMENT FOR THE YEAR 19 OF THE Life Insurance Company
Name

ANALYSIS OF INCREASE IN RESERVES DURING THE YEAR
(Gain and Loss Exhibit)

	(1) TOTAL	(2) INDUSTRIAL LIFE	ORDINARY			(6) CREDIT LIFE[a] (GROUP AND INDIVIDUAL)	GROUP	
			(3) LIFE INSURANCE	(4) INDIVIDUAL ANNUITIES	(5) SUPPLEMENTARY CONTRACTS		(7) LIFE INSURANCE	(8) ANNUITIES
1. Reserve Dec. 31 of previous year								
2. Tabular net premiums or considerations								
3. Considerations for supplementary contracts without life contingencies and dividend accumulations								
4. Present value of disability claims incurred					X X X			
5. Tabular interest								
6. Tabular less actual reserve released		X X X						
7. Increase in reserve on account of change in valuation basis								
8. Other increases (net)								
9. TOTALS (Items 1 to 8)								
10. Tabular cost					X X X			
11. Reserves released by death				X X X	X X X			X X X
12. Reserves released by other terminations (net)								
13. Annuity, supplementary contract, disability and accumulated dividend payments								
13A. Net transfers to (+) or from (—) Separate Accounts (excluding Variable Life Insurance)								
13B. Net transfers to (+) or from (—) Variable Life Insurance Separate Accounts								
14. TOTAL DEDUCTIONS (Items 10 to 13B)								
15. Reserve Dec. 31 of current year								

SUPPLEMENTARY INFORMATION

[a] Business not exceeding 120 months duration.

Form 1

ANNUAL STATEMENT FOR THE YEAR 19 OF THE LIFE INSURANCE COMPANY
Name

7

EXHIBIT 1 — PART 1 — PREMIUMS AND ANNUITY CONSIDERATIONS
(000 omitted)

DETAILS OMITTED

	(1) Total	(2) Industrial Life	Ordinary: (3) Life Insurance	Ordinary: (4) Individual Annuities	(5) Credit Life* (Group and Individual)	Group: (6) Life Insurance	Group: (7) Annuities	Accident and Health: (8) Group	Accident and Health: (9) Credit* (Group and Individual)	Accident and Health: (10) Other	
FIRST YEAR (other than single)											
CURRENT YEAR 1. Uncollected											1.
2. Deferred											2.
3. Deferred & uncollected:											3.
a. Direct											a.
b. Reinsurance assumed											b.
c. Reinsurance ceded											c.
d. Net (Line 1 + Line 2)											d.
4. Advance											4.
5. Line 3d − Line 4											5.
6. Collected during year:											6.
a. Direct											a.
b. Reinsurance assumed											b.
c. Reinsurance ceded											c.
d. Net											d.
7. Line 5 + Line 6d											7.
8. Previous year (uncollected + deferred − advance)											8.
9. First year premiums and considerations:											9.
a. Direct											a.
b. Reinsurance assumed											b.
c. Reinsurance ceded											c.
d. Net (Line 7 − Line 8)	26,190		12,700	7,200		2,760	1,430	1,460		640	d.
SINGLE											
10. Single premiums and considerations:											10.
a. Direct											a.
b. Reinsurance assumed											b.
c. Reinsurance ceded											c.
d. Net	7,870		2,720	5,150							d.
RENEWAL											
CURRENT YEAR 11. Uncollected											11.
12. Deferred											12.
13. Deferred & uncollected:											13.
a. Direct											a.
b. Reinsurance assumed											b.
c. Reinsurance ceded											c.
d. Net (Line 11 + Line 12)											d.
14. Advance											14.
15. Line 13d − Line 14											15.
16. Collected during year:											16.
a. Direct											a.
b. Reinsurance assumed											b.
c. Reinsurance ceded											c.
d. Net											d.
17. Line 15 + Line 16d											17.
18. Previous year (uncollected + deferred − advance)											18.
19. Renewal premiums and considerations:											19.
a. Direct											a.
b. Reinsurance assumed											b.
c. Reinsurance ceded											c.
d. Net (Line 17 − Line 18)	61,720		29,400	18,200		4,940	3,280	4,700		1,200	d.
TOTAL											
20. Total premiums and annuity considerations:											20.
a. Direct	96,650		45,590	30,550		7,800	4,710	6,160		1,840	a.
b. Reinsurance assumed	420		420								b.
c. Reinsurance ceded	(1,290)		(1,190)			(100)					c.
d. Net (Lines 9d + 10d + 19d)	95,780		44,820	30,550		7,700	4,710	6,160		1,840	d.

*Business not exceeding 120 months duration.

Form 1

ANNUAL STATEMENT FOR THE YEAR 19 OF THE LIFE INSURANCE COMPANY
Name

EXHIBIT 1 — PART 2 — DIVIDENDS AND COUPONS* APPLIED, REINSURANCE COMMISSIONS AND EXPENSE ALLOWANCES AND COMMISSIONS INCURRED (direct business only)

(000 OMITTED)

	(1) TOTAL	(2) INDUSTRIAL LIFE	ORDINARY (3) LIFE INSURANCE	ORDINARY (4) INDIVIDUAL ANNUITIES	(5) CREDIT LIFE* (Group and Individual)	GROUP (6) LIFE INSURANCE	GROUP (7) ANNUITIES	ACCIDENT AND HEALTH (8) GROUP	ACCIDENT AND HEALTH (9) CREDIT* (Group and Individual)	ACCIDENT AND HEALTH (10) OTHER	
DIVIDENDS AND COUPONS* APPLIED (included in Part 1)											
21. To pay renewal premiums (Exhibit 7, Line 1)											21.
22. All other (Exhibit 7, Lines 2, 3 & 4)				DETAILS OMITTED							22.
REINSURANCE COMMISSIONS AND EXPENSE ALLOWANCES INCURRED											
23. First year (other than single):											23.
a. Reinsurance ceded											a.
b. Reinsurance assumed											b.
c. Net ceded less assumed											c.
24. Single:											24.
a. Reinsurance ceded											a.
b. Reinsurance assumed											b.
c. Net ceded less assumed											c.
25. Renewal:											25.
a. Reinsurance ceded	310										a.
b. Reinsurance assumed											b.
c. Net ceded less assumed	310										c.
26. Totals:											26.
a. Reinsurance ceded (Page 5, Item 5)											a.
b. Reinsurance assumed (Page 5, Item 21A)											b.
c. Net ceded less assumed											c.
COMMISSIONS INCURRED (direct business only)											
27. First year (other than single)											27.
28. Single											28.
29. Renewal											29.
30. Totals (to agree with Page 5, Item 21)	11,330										30.

*Business not exceeding 120 months duration.
*Includes coupons, guaranteed annual pure endowments and similar benefits.

(000 OMITTE

EXHIBIT 2 — NET INVESTMENT INCOME

1. Gross investment income (Exhibit 3, Line 10, Col. 7)	66,01
2. Investment expenses (Exhibit 5, Line 10, Col. 3)	3,16
3. Investment taxes, licenses and fees, excluding federal income taxes (Exhibit 6, Line 7, Col. 3)	62
4. Depreciation on real estate and other invested assets	98
5.	
6. Total (Lines 2 through 5)	4,76
7. Net Investment Income—Line 1 less Line 6 (to Page 4, Item 4)	61,25
8. Ratio of net investment income to mean assets (see instructions)	

†Includes $............ investment expenses and $............ investment taxes, licenses and fees, excluding federal income taxes, attributable to Separate Accounts.

EXHIBIT 3 — GROSS INVESTMENT INCOME

(000 OMITTED)

Schedule		(1) Collected During Year	Current Year (2) Unearned	(3) Due	(4) Accrued	(5) Non-Admitted	(6) Previous Year (3) + (4) — (2) — (5)	(7) Earned Duri[ng] (1) — (2) + (4) — (5)
1. U.S. government bonds	D	* 2,100			690		630	2,
1.1 Bonds exempt from U.S. tax	D	* 940			280		240	
1.2 Other bonds (unaffiliated)	D	* 43,334		538	4,514	170	3,488	44,
1.3 Bonds of affiliates	D	*						
2.1 Preferred stocks (unaffiliated)	D	‡ 240			20		20	
2.11 Preferred stocks of affiliates	D	‡						
2.2 Common stocks (unaffiliated)	D	1,540					10	
2.21 Common stocks of affiliates	D							
3. Mortgage loans	B	** 2,160	50	20	240		190	
4. Real estate	A	§ 1,870					20	
5. Premium notes, policy loans and liens		6,890	200		390		170	
6. Collateral loans								
7.1 Cash on hand and on deposit	DA	100						
7.2 Short-term investments	BA	† 5,260			310		290	
8. Other invested assets	D	80	11				(11)	
9.								
9.1 Financial options and futures								
10. Totals		64,514	261	558	6,424	170	5,047	66

*Includes $ 1,790 accrual of discount less $ 59 amortization of premium and less $............ paid for accrued interest on purchases.
‡Excludes $............ paid for accrued dividends on purchases.
**Includes $............ accrual of discount less $............ amortization of premium and less $............ paid for accrued interest on purchases.
§Includes $............ for company's occupancy of its own buildings; and exclude $............ interest on encumbrances.
†Includes $ 1,835 accrual of discount less $............ amortizatio[n] of premium and less $............ paid for accrued interest on purchases.

*EXHIBIT 4 — CAPITAL GAINS AND LOSSES ON INVESTMENTS

(000 OMITTED)

Schedule		(1) Increase in Book Value	(2) Profit on Sale or Maturity	(3) Decrease in Book Value	(4) Loss on Sale or Maturity	(5) Net Gain (+) or Loss (—) from Change in Difference Between Book and Admitted Values	(6) Net Gain[s] or Losse[s] (1) + (2) — (4) +
1. U.S. government bonds	D		40				
1.1 Bonds exempt from U.S. tax	D						
1.2 Other bonds (unaffiliated)	D		1,120		350	(1,140)	(3
1.3 Bonds of affiliates	D						
2.1 Preferred stocks (unaffiliated)	D		320		40	160	
2.11 Preferred stocks of affiliates	D						
2.2 Common stocks (unaffiliated)	D		1,920		260	(388)	1,
2.21 Common stocks of affiliates	D						
3. Mortgage loans	B		210				
4. Real estate	A			**			
5. Premium notes, policy loans and liens							
6. Collateral loans							
7.1 Cash on hand and on deposit							
7.2 Short-term investments	DA						
8. Other invested assets	BA			**		(40)	
9. Foreign exchange		X X X	X X X	X X X	X X X		
9.1 Financial options and futures	DB						
9.2							
10. Totals			3,610		650	(1,408)	1

10.1 Less federal income taxes incurred on capital gains	
10.2 Balance to Surplus Account, Page 4, Item 34	
Distribution of Line 10.2, Col. 6. (Attach statement or memorandum explaining basis of division.)	
11. Net realized capital gains (+) or losses (−) on assets disposed of during the year $............ less $............ reflected in previous years' statements and less $ 782 federal income tax incurred on capital gains	2
12. Net unrealized capital gains (+) or losses (−) of the year	(

*Adjustments due to amortization to be reported in Exhibit 3.
**Excluding $............ depreciation on real estate and $............ depreciation on other invested assets included in Exhibit 2, Line 4.

EXHIBIT 5 — GENERAL EXPENSES

(000 OMITTED)

	INSURANCE (1) LIFE	INSURANCE (2) ACCIDENT AND HEALTH	(3) INVESTMENT	(4) TOTAL
Rent	1,588	67	185	1,840
Salaries and wages	4,090	270	1,135	5,495
11 *Contributions for benefit plans for employees	760	40	130	930
12 *Contributions for benefit plans for agents	377	35		412
21 Payments to employees under non-funded benefit programs				
22 Payments to agents under non-funded benefit programs				
31 Other employee welfare	235	15	130	380
32 Other agent welfare	350	45		395
Legal fees and expenses	22	15	3	40
Medical examination fees	265	55		320
Inspection report fees	110	40		150
Fees of public accountants and consulting actuaries	80	30	30	140
Expense of investigation and settlement of policy claims	15	20		35
Traveling expenses	280	35	25	340
Advertising	230	50	30	310
Postage, express, telegraph and telephone	245	20	25	290
Printing and stationery	350	50	30	430
Cost or depreciation of furniture and equipment	140	35	25	200
Rental of equipment	130	20	20	170
Books and periodicals	20	10	5	35
Bureau and association dues	50	15	20	85
Insurance, except on real estate	25	15	10	50
Miscellaneous losses	25	5		30
Collection and bank service charges			10	10
Sundry general expenses	448	5	85	538
Group service and administration fees				
Agency expense allowance	570	60		630
Agents' balances charged off (less $ 10 recovered)	8	15		23
Agency conferences other than local meetings	60	30		90
Real estate expenses			1,262	1,262
Investment expenses not included elsewhere				
GENERAL EXPENSES INCURRED	10,473	997	3,160	14,630
Reconciliation with Exhibit 12	(To Page 4, Item 22)		(To Exhibit 2, Line 2)	
General expenses unpaid December 31, previous year	614	110	40	764
General expenses unpaid December 31, current year	691	125	50	866
General expenses paid during year (10+11−12)	10,396	982	3,150	14,528
	X X X	X X X	X X X	(To Exhibit 12, Line 27)

ORDINARY LIFE INSURANCE AND INDIVIDUAL ANNUITY BUSINESS ONLY

Compensation to agents on a plan other than commissions, included in Col. (1): First year $.........., Renewal $..........

Agency supervision, except home office, included in Col. (1): Line 2 $.........., Line 5.1 $.........., Line ..... $..........

Branch office expenses other than those in A and B included in Col. (1): Line 1 $.........., Line 2 $.........., All other lines $..........

*These items include $.......... on account of prior service.

EXHIBIT 6 — TAXES, LICENSES AND FEES (EXCLUDING FEDERAL INCOME TAXES)

(000 OMITTED)

	INSURANCE (1) LIFE	INSURANCE (2) ACCIDENT AND HEALTH	(3) INVESTMENT	(4) TOTAL
Real estate taxes			535	535
State insurance department licenses and fees	60	10	20	90
State taxes on premiums	1,790	160		1,950
Other state taxes, incl. $.......... for employee benefits				
U.S. Social Security taxes	455	30	55	540
All other taxes	205	20	10	235
TAXES, LICENSES AND FEES INCURRED	2,510	220	620	3,350
Reconciliation with Exhibit 12	(To Page 4, Item 23)		(To Exhibit 2, Line 3)	
Taxes, licenses and fees unpaid December 31, previous year	560	40	90	690
Taxes, licenses and fees unpaid December 31, current year	712	50	110	872
Taxes, licenses and fees paid during year (7+8—9)	2,358	210	600	3,168
	X X X	X X X	X X X	(To Exhibit 12, Line 28.1)

NOTE: Canadian and other foreign taxes are included appropriately in Lines 1, 2, 3, 4 and 6.

EXHIBIT 7 — DIVIDENDS AND COUPONS* TO POLICYHOLDERS

(000 OMITTED)

	DIVIDENDS (1) LIFE	DIVIDENDS (2) ACCIDENT AND HEALTH	COUPONS* (3) LIFE	COUPONS* (4) ACCIDENT AND HEALTH
Applied to pay renewal premiums	200			
Applied to shorten the endowment or premium-paying period				
Applied to provide paid-up additions	44			
Applied to provide paid-up annuities				
TOTAL LINES 1-4	244			
Paid in cash	270			
Left on deposit with the company	310			
TOTAL LINES 5-8	824			
Amount due and unpaid (Item 6, Page 3)	58			
Provision for annual dividend and coupon* policies (Item 7, Page 3, in part)	910			
Terminal dividends (Item 7, Page 3, in part)				
Provision for deferred dividend policies (Item 7, Page 3, in part)				
Amount provisionally held for deferred dividend policies not included in line 12 (Item 8, Page 3)				
TOTAL LINES 10-12A	968			
Line 13 of previous year	822			
TOTAL DIVIDENDS AND COUPONS* TO POLICYHOLDERS (LINES 9+13 - 14)	970			
	(To Page 4, Item 28)		(To Page 4, Item 11A)	

*Includes coupons, guaranteed annual pure endowments and similar benefits

Name

Form

EXHIBIT 8—AGGREGATE RESERVE FOR LIFE POLICIES AND CONTRACTS

(000 OMITTED)

(1) VALUATION STANDARD	(2) TOTAL	(3) INDUSTRIAL	(4) ORDINARY	(5) CREDIT* (Group and Individual)	(6) GROUP
A. LIFE INSURANCE:					
1. 1958 CSO 4% NLP	27,840		24,620		3,2
2.					
3.					
4.					
5.					
6.					
7.					
8.					
9.					
10.					
11.					
12.					
13.					
14. DETAILS OMITTED					
15.					
16.					
17.					
18.					
19.					
20.					
21.					
22.					
23.					
24.					
25.					
26.					
27.					
28.					
29.					
30.					
31.					
32. TOTALS (Gross)	327,933		300,843		27,0
33. Reinsurance ceded	4,840		4,840		
34. TOTALS (Net)	323,093		296,003		27,
B. ANNUITIES (excluding supplementary contracts with life contingencies):					
1. 1971 IAM 4½% - DEFERRED	17,640	X X X	16,130	X X X	1
2.		X X X		X X X	
3.		X X X		X X X	
4.		X X X		X X X	
5.		X X X		X X X	
6. DETAILS OMITTED		X X X		X X X	
7.		X X X		X X X	
8.		X X X		X X X	
9.		X X X		X X X	
10.		X X X		X X X	
11.		X X X		X X X	
12.		X X X		X X X	
13.		X X X		X X X	
14.		X X X		X X X	
15.		X X X		X X X	
16.		X X X		X X X	
17.		X X X		X X X	
18. TOTALS (Gross)		X X X		X X X	
19. Reinsurance ceded		X X X		X X X	
20. TOTALS (Net)	139,600	X X X	122,850	X X X	16,
C. SUPPLEMENTARY CONTRACTS WITH LIFE CONTINGENCIES:					
1. 1955 AMERICAN ANNUITY 3.5%	400		400		
2.					
3.					
4.					
5. TOTALS (Gross)					
6. Reinsurance ceded					
7. TOTALS (Net)	400		400		
D. ACCIDENTAL DEATH BENEFITS:					
1. 1959 ADB 3%	620		620		
2.					
3.					
4.					
5. TOTALS (Gross)	620		620		
6. Reinsurance ceded	20		20		
7. TOTALS (Net)	600		600		
E. DISABILITY—ACTIVE LIVES:					
1. 1952 DISABILITY 3%	940		940		
2.					
3.					
4.					
5.					
6.					
7. TOTALS (Gross)	940		940		
8. Reinsurance ceded	40		40		
9. TOTALS (Net)	900		900		
F. DISABILITY—DISABLED LIVES:					
1. 1952 DISABILITY 3%	825		825		
2.					
3.					
4.					
5.					
6.					
7. TOTALS (Gross)	825		825		
8. Reinsurance ceded	25		25		
9. TOTALS (Net)	800		800		

*Business not exceeding 120 months duration.

EXHIBIT 8 – AGGREGATE RESERVE FOR LIFE POLICIES AND CONTRACTS (Continued)

(000 OMITTED)

VALUATION STANDARD (1)	TOTAL (2)	INDUSTRIAL (3)	ORDINARY (4)	CREDIT* (Group and Individual) (5)	GROUP (6)
scellaneous Reserves:					
For excess of valuation net premiums over corresponding gross premiums on respective policies, computed according to the standard of valuation required by this state	INCLUDED IN OTHER RESERVES				
For non-deduction of deferred fractional premiums or return of premiums at the death of the insured					
For surrender values in excess of reserves otherwise required and carried in this schedule					
Totals (Gross)					
Reinsurance ceded					
Totals (Net)					
Grand Totals (Net)—(Item 1, Page 3)	465,393		421,553		43,840

EXHIBIT 8A – CHANGES IN BASES OF VALUATION DURING THE YEAR

(Including supplementary contracts set up on a basis other than that used to determine benefits)

DESCRIPTION OF VALUATION CLASS (1)	VALUATION BASES: CHANGED FROM (2)	VALUATION BASES: CHANGED TO (3)	INCREASE IN ACTUARIAL RESERVE DUE TO CHANGE (4)
NONE			
Total (Item 7, Page 6)			

GENERAL INTERROGATORIES

the company ever issued both participating on-participating policies? Answer: YES

the company at present issue both cipating and non-participating policies? er: YES

, state which kind is issued. er: ....

the company any assessment or stipulated ium policies in force? Answer: NO

state:

unt of insurance $..........

unt of reserve $..........

of reserve: ....

Basis of regular assessments: ....

Basis of special assessments: ....

Assessments collected during year $..........

4. If the policy loan interest rate guaranteed in any one or more of its currently issued policies is less than 5%, not in advance, state the policy loan rate guarantees on any such policies. Answer: ....

5. Does the company hold reserves for any annuity contracts which are less than the reserves that would be held on a standard basis? Answer: NO

If so, state the amount of reserve on such policies (a) on the basis actually held: $..........; (b) which would have been held (on an exact or approximate basis) using the actual ages of the annuitants; the interest rate(s) used in (a); and the same mortality basis used by the company for the valuation of comparable annuity benefits issued to standard lives. If the company has no comparable annuity benefits for standard lives to be valued, the mortality basis shall be the table most recently approved by the state of domicile for valuing individual annuity benefits: $..........; and (c) attach statement of methods employed in their valuation.

EXHIBIT 9 – AGGREGATE RESERVE FOR ACCIDENT AND HEALTH POLICIES

(000 OMITTED)

	TOTAL (1)	GROUP ACCIDENT AND HEALTH (2)	CREDIT* (GROUP AND INDIVIDUAL) (3)	COLLECTIVELY RENEWABLE (4)	OTHER INDIVIDUAL POLICIES: NON CANCELLABLE (5)	GUARANTEED RENEWABLE (6)	NON-RENEWABLE FOR STATED REASONS ONLY (7)	OTHER ACCIDENT ONLY (8)	ALL OTHER (9)
A. Active Life Reserve									
ed premium reserve .	8,040	6,110			1,930				
nal reserves*	230	175			55				
for future contingent (deferred maternity her similar benefits) .									
for rate credits . .									
ls (Gross)	8,290	6,285			1,985				
surance ceded	40	30			10				
ls (Net)	8,230	6,255			1,975				
B. Claim Reserve									
value of amounts not on claims**	9,922	7,540			2,382				
for future contingent (deferred maternity er similar benefits) .									
s (Gross)	9,922	7,540			2,382				
urance ceded	180	136			44				
s (Net)	9,742	7,404			2,338				
nd Totals (Net) 2, Page 3)	17,972	13,659			4,313				
ar interest on policy		DETAILS OMITTED							

ach statement as to valuation standard used in calculating this reserve, specifying reserve bases, interest rates and methods.

cludes reserves for unaccrued benefits on incurred but unreported claims. Accrued benefits should be reported in Exhibit 11, Part 1, Lines 2.2 and 3.

*Business not exceeding 120 months duration.

BIT 10—SUPPLEMENTARY CONTRACTS WITHOUT LIFE CONTINGENCIES, DIVIDEND ACCUMULATIONS, AND COUPON* ACCUMULATIONS

VALUATION RATE (1)	CONTRACT RATE OR RATES ‡ (2)	SUPPLEMENTARY CONTRACTS WITHOUT LIFE CONTINGENCIES: PRESENT VALUE OF AMOUNTS NOT YET DUE (3)	AMOUNTS LEFT ON DEPOSIT (4)	TOTALS (5)	DIVIDEND ACCUMULATIONS (6)	COUPON* ACCUMULATIONS (7)
3½%	3½%				59,107	
4	4	3,721		3,721		
ls (Items 3 and 5, Page 3). . . .		3,721		3,721	59,107	

ontract rate or rates corresponding to each valuation rate.

*Includes coupons, guaranteed annual pure endowments and similar benefits.

Form 1

Name

EXHIBIT 11 – POLICY AND CONTRACT CLAIMS

PART 1 – Liability End of Current Year (000 omitted)

DETAILS OMITTED

	(1) TOTAL	(2) INDUSTRIAL LIFE	ORDINARY (3) LIFE INSURANCE	(4) INDIVIDUAL ANNUITIES	(5) SUPPLEMENTARY CONTRACTS	(6) CREDIT LIFE* (Group and Individual)	GROUP (7) LIFE INSURANCE	(8) ANNUITIES	ACCIDENT AND HEALTH (9) GROUP	(10) CREDIT* (Group and Individual)	(11) OTHER
1. Due and unpaid:											
a. Direct											
b. Reinsurance assumed											
c. Reinsurance ceded											
d. Net											
2. In course of settlement:											
2.1 Resisted: a. Direct									X X X	X X X	X X X
b. Reinsurance assumed									X X X	X X X	X X X
c. Reinsurance ceded									X X X	X X X	X X X
d. Net			†	†		†	†		X X X	X X X	X X X
2.2 Other: a. Direct											
b. Reinsurance assumed											
c. Reinsurance ceded											
d. Net			†	†		†	†		†	†	†
3. Incurred but unreported — net as to reinsurance			†	†		†	†		†	†	†
4. Totals:											
a. Direct											
b. Reinsurance assumed											
c. Reinsurance ceded											
d. Net	4,068	*	* 1,493	420	100		* 22	140	1,273		620

*Including matured endowments (but not guaranteed annual pure endowments) unpaid amounting to $ ______ in Column 2, $ ______ in Column 3 and $ ______ in Column 7.

†Include only portion of disability and accident and health claim liabilities applicable to assumed "accrued" benefits. Reserves (including reinsurance assumed and net of reinsurance ceded) for unaccrued benefits for Ordinary Life Insurance $ ______, Individual Annuities $ ______, Credit Life (Group and Individual) $ ______ and Group Life $ ______ are included in Page 3, Item 1 (See Exhibit 8, Section F); and for Group Accident and Health $ ______, Credit (Group and Individual) Accident and Health $ ______ and Other Accident and Health $ ______ are included in Page 3, Item 2 (See Exhibit 9, Section B).

* Business not exceeding 120 months duration.

Form 1

ANNUAL STATEMENT FOR THE YEAR 19 OF THE LIFE INSURANCE COMPANY

Name

EXHIBIT 11 – POLICY AND CONTRACT CLAIMS

PART 2 – Incurred During the Year (000 OMITTED)

	(1) TOTAL	(2) INDUSTRIAL LIFE*	ORDINARY (3) LIFE INSURANCE**	ORDINARY (4) INDIVIDUAL ANNUITIES	ORDINARY (5) SUPPLEMENTARY CONTRACTS	(6) CREDIT LIFE* (Group and Individual)	GROUP (7) LIFE INSURANCE***	GROUP (8) ANNUITIES	ACCIDENT AND HEALTH (9) GROUP	ACCIDENT AND HEALTH (10) CREDIT* (Group and Individual)	ACCIDENT AND HEALTH (11) OTHER
1. Settlements during the year:											
a. Direct											
b. Reinsurance assumed											
c. Reinsurance ceded											
d. Net	†										
2. Liability December 31, current year from Part 1:	DETAILS OMITTED										
a. Direct											
b. Reinsurance assumed											
c. Reinsurance ceded											
d. Net											
3. Amounts recoverable from reinsurers December 31, current year (Schedule S, Part 1, Col. 3)											
4. Liability December 31, previous year:											
a. Direct											
b. Reinsurance assumed											
c. Reinsurance ceded											
d. Net											
5. Amounts recoverable from reinsurers December 31 previous year											
6. Incurred Benefits:											
a. Direct											
b. Reinsurance assumed											
c. Reinsurance ceded											
d. Net	14,290			12,170				2,120			

*Including matured endowments (but not guaranteed annual pure endowments) amounting to $........ in Line 1a, $........ in Line 1d, $........ in Line 6a and $........ in Line 6d.

**Including matured endowments (but not guaranteed annual pure endowments) amounting to $........ in Line 1a, $........ in Line 1d, $........ in Line 6a and $........ in Line 6d.

***Including matured endowments (but not guaranteed annual pure endowments) amounting to $........ in Line 1a, $........ in Line 1d, $........ in Line 6a and $........ in Line 6d.

†Equals sum of Exhibit 12, Lines 16.1, 16.2, 17, 22.1 and 22.2. Includes $........ premiums waived under total and permanent disability benefits.

*Business not exceeding 120 months duration.

12A

EXHIBIT 12 — RECONCILIATION OF LEDGER ASSETS

INCREASES IN LEDGER ASSETS

1. Premiums on life policies and annuity considerations
1A. Annuity and other fund deposits
2. Accident and health cash premiums, including $........ policy, membership and other fees (Schedule T, Line 98, Col. 5)
3. Considerations for supplementary contracts with life contingencies
4. Considerations for supplementary contracts without life contingencies, including $........ disability
5. Dividends left with the company to accumulate at interest
5A. Co ons* left with the company to accumulate at interest
6. Gr investment income (Exhibit 3, Line 10, Col. 1)
7. Increase of paid up capital during the year
8. From other sources (give items and amounts):
   8.1 ....
   8.2 ....
   8.3 ....
9. Borrowed money gross $........, less amount repaid $........
10. Commissions and expense allowances on reinsurance ceded
10A. Reserve adjustments on reinsurance ceded
11. ....
12. ....
13. From sale or maturity of ledger assets (Exhibit 4, Line 10, Column 2)
14. By adjustment in book value of ledger assets (Exhibit 4, Line 10, Column 1)
15. TOTAL INCREASES IN LEDGER ASSETS (Lines 1 through 14)

DECREASES IN LEDGER ASSETS

Details Omitted

16. Policy and contract claims (Exhibit 11, Part 2):
   16.1 Life
   16.2 Accident and health
17. For annuities with life contingencies, excluding payments on supplementary contracts (including cash refund payments)
18. Premium notes and liens voided by lapse, less $........ restorations
19. Surrender values
19A. Group conversions
19B. Interest on policy or contract funds
20. Dividends to policyholders:
   20.1 Life insurance and annuities (Exhibit 7, Line 9, Col. 1)
   20.2 Accident and health (Exhibit 7, Line 9, Col. 2)
20A. Coupons, guaranteed annual pure endowments and similar benefits (Exhibit 7, Line 9, Cols. 3 + 4)
21. TOTAL PAID POLICYHOLDERS
22. Paid for claims on supplementary contracts:
   22.1 With life contingencies
   22.2 Without life contingencies
23. Dividends and interest thereon held on deposit disbursed during the year
23A. Coupons* and interest thereon held on deposit disbursed during the year
24. ....
25. ....
26. Commissions to agents (direct business only):
   26.1 Life insurance and annuities, including $........ commuted commissions
   26.2 Accident and health, including $........ commuted commissions
   26.3 Policy, membership and other fees retained by agents
26A. Commissions and expense allowances on reinsurance assumed
27. General expenses (Exhibit 5, Line 13, Col. 4)
28.1 Taxes, licenses and fees, excluding federal income taxes (Exhibit 6, Line 10, Col. 4)
28.2 Federal income taxes, including $........ on capital gains
29. Decrease of paid up capital during the year
30. Paid stockholders for dividends (cash $........, stock $........)
31. Borrowed money repaid gross $........ less amount borrowed $........
32. Interest on borrowed money
32A. Net transfers to (+) or from (—) Separate Accounts (excluding Variable Life Insurance)
32B. Net transfers to (+) or from (—) Variable Life Insurance Separate Accounts
33. ....
34. ....
35. ....
36. From sale or maturity of ledger assets (Exhibit 4, Line 10, Column 4)
37. By adjustment in book value of ledger assets (Exhibit 4, Line 10, Column 3 and Exhibit 2, Line 4)
38. TOTAL DECREASES IN LEDGER ASSETS (Lines 16 through 37)

RECONCILIATION BETWEEN YEARS

39. Amount of ledger assets December 31st of previous year
40. Increase (+) or decrease (−) in ledger assets during the year (Line 15 minus Line 38)
41. TOTAL = LEDGER ASSETS DECEMBER 31ST OF CURRENT YEAR (Exhibit 13, Line 26, Col. 1)

*Includes coupons, guaranteed annual pure endowments and similar benefits.

EXHIBIT 13—ASSETS

(000 omitted)

	(1) LEDGER ASSETS	(2) NON-LEDGER ASSETS	(3) ASSETS NOT ADMITTED	(4) NET ADMITTED ASSETS (Cols. 1 + 2 − 3)
Bonds (Schedule D, Part 1)	480,590		160	480,430
Stocks:				
2.1 Preferred stocks (Schedule D, Part 2, Section 1)	2,860			2,860
2.2 Common stocks (Schedule D, Part 2, Section 2)	23,964	1,690		25,654
Mortgage loans on real estate (Schedule B, Part 1, Sec. 1):				
3.1 First liens	27,270			27,270
3.2 Other than first liens				
Real estate (Schedule A, Part 1):				
4.1 Properties occupied by the company (less $........ encumbrances)	8,690			8,690
4.2 Properties acquired in satisfaction of debt (less $........ encumbrances)				
4.3 Investment real estate (less $........ encumbrances)				
Policy loans	95,642			95,642
Premium notes, including $........ for first year premiums				
Collateral loans (Schedule C, Part 1)				
Cash on hand and on deposit:				
Cash in company's office				
Cash on deposit (Schedule E)	370			370
Short-term investments (Schedule DA, Part 1)	25,273			25,273
....				
Other invested assets (Schedule BA, Part 1)	830			830
Reinsurance ceded:				
.1 Amounts recoverable from reinsurers (Schedule S, Part 1)		8,002		8,002
.2 Commissions and expense allowances due		210		210
.3 Experience rating and other refunds due		2,731		2,731
.4				
Other assets (give items and amounts):				
.1 Agents' balances (gross debit $ 2,830 less $........ for doubtful accounts less $ 370 credit balances)	2,460		2,460	-0-
.2 Bills receivable				-0-
.3 Furniture and equipment	962		962	-0-
.4 Cash advanced to or in hands of officers or agents	730		730	-0-
.5 Loans on personal security, endorsed or not				-0-
.6				
Electronic data processing equipment	3,210			3,210
Federal income tax recoverable				
....				
....				
Life insurance premiums and annuity considerations deferred and uncollected on in force Dec. 31st of current year (less premiums on reinsurance ceded and less $........ loading)		6,045		6,045
Accident and health premiums due and unpaid		115	10	105
Investment income due and accrued		7,152	170	6,982
Net adjustment in assets and liabilities due to foreign exchange rates				
....				
TOTALS (Lines 1 to 25)	672,851	25,945	4,492	694,304
From Separate Accounts Statement				
From Variable Life Insurance Separate Accounts Statement				205,408
GRAND TOTAL (Lines 26 to 27B)				899,712

EXHIBIT 14—ANALYSIS OF NON-ADMITTED ASSETS AND RELATED ITEMS (Excluding Investment Adjustments Not Listed)

(000 omitted)

	(1) END OF PREVIOUS YEAR	(2) END OF CURRENT YEAR	(3) CHANGES FOR YEAR INCREASE (—) OR DECREASE (+)
Loans on company's stock			
Supplies, stationery, printed matter			
Furniture and equipment	942	962	20
Advanced commissions			XXX
Agents' balances (net)	3,630	2,460	(1,170)
Cash advanced to or in the hands of officers or agents	820	730	(90)
Loans on personal security, endorsed or not			
Bills receivable			
Premium notes, etc., in excess of net value and other policy liabilities on individual policies			XXX
Accident and health premiums due and unpaid			
Other assets not admitted (itemize):			
....			
....			
....			
Agents' credit balances (Page 3, Item 19 inside)			
TOTAL CHANGE	XXX	XXX	(1,240)

(To Item 36, Page 4)

Name

FIVE-YEAR HISTORICAL DATA

All Figures Taken From or Developed From Annual Statements of Corresponding Years

Show amounts in whole dollars only, no cents. Items from prior years should be included only if they are available from prior year's statements.

	(1) 19	(2) 19	(3) 19	(4) 19	(5) 19
Life Insurance in Force (Page 15)					
1. Ordinary—Whole Life and Endowment (Line 31D)					
2. Ordinary—Term (Line 22, Col. 4, less Line 31D, Col. 4)					
3. Credit Life (Line 22, Col. 6)					
4. Group, excluding FEGLI/SGLI (Line 22, Col. 9 less Lines 38 & 39, Col. 4)					
5. Industrial (Line 22, Col. 2)					
6. FEGLI/SGLI (Lines 38 & 39, Col. 4)					
7. Total (Line 22, Col. 10)					
New Business Issued (Page 15)					
8. Ordinary—Whole Life and Endowment (Line 31D)			DETAILS OMITTED		
9. Ordinary—Term (Line 2, Col. 4, less Line 31D)					
10. Credit Life (Line 2, Col. 6)					
11. Group (Line 2, Col. 9)					
12. Industrial (Line 2, Col. 2)					
13. Total (Line 2, Col. 10)					
Premium Income (Exhibit 1—Part 1)					
14. Ordinary and Industrial Life—First Year (Line 9d, Cols. 2 & 3)					
15. Ordinary and Industrial Life—Single and Renewal (Line 10d, Line 19d, Cols. 2 & 3)					
16. Other Life (Line 20d, Cols. 5 & 6)					
17. Annuity (Line 20d, Cols. 4 & 7)					
18. A & H (Line 20d, Cols. 8, 9 and 10)					
19. Total (Line 20d, Col. 1)					
Balance Sheet Items (Pages 2 & 3)					
20. Total admitted Assets Excluding Separate Account Business (Page 2, Item 26)					
21. Total Liabilities Excluding Separate Account Business (Page 3, Item 26 less Items 25A & 25B)					
22. Aggregate Life Reserves (Page 3, Item 1)					
23. Aggregate A & H Reserves (Page 3, Item 2)					
24. Mandatory Securities Valuation Reserve (Page 3, Item 25.1)					
25. Capital (Page 3, Item 27A)					
26. Surplus (Page 3, Item 29D)					
Percentage Distribution of Assets					
(Page 2) (Item No. ÷ Page 2, Item 10A) × 100.0					
27. Bonds (Item 1)					
28. Stocks (Items 2.1 and 2.2)					
29. Mortgage Loans on Real Estate (Item 3)					
30. Real Estate (Items 4.1, 4.2 and 4.3)					
31. Policy Loans (Item 5)					
32. Premium Notes (Item 6)					
33. Collateral Loans (Item 7)					
34. Cash and Short-term Investments (Items 8.1 and 8.2) (1981 and prior, Item 8)					
35. Other Invested Assets (Item 10)					
36. Cash and Invested Assets (Item 10A)	100.0	100.0	100.0	100.0	

FIVE-YEAR HISTORICAL DATA
(Continued)

	(1) 19	(2) 19	(3) 19	(4) 19	(5) 19
Investments in Parent, Subsidiaries and Affiliates					
37. Bonds (Page 29, Line 29, Col. 6)					
38. Preferred Stocks (Page 29, Line 47, Col. 3)					
39. Common Stocks (Page 29, Line 65, Col. 3)					
40. Short-term Investments (Schedule DA, Part 1, Col. 10)					
41. Total of above Lines 37 to 40					
Total Non-admitted and Admitted Assets					
42. Total Non-admitted Assets (Page 14, Line 26, Col. 3)					
43. Total Admitted Assets (Page 14, Line 28, Col. 4)					
Investment Data (Page 8)					
44. Ratio of Net Investment Income to Mean Assets (Exhibit 2, Line 8) (To 2 decimal places)	DETAILS OMITTED				
45. Net Investment Income (Exhibit 2, Line 7)					
46. Realized Capital Gains (Losses) (Exhibit 4, Line 11, Col. 6)					
47. Unrealized Capital Gains (Losses) (Exhibit 4, Line 12, Col. 6)					
48. Total of above Lines 45, 46 & 47					
Benefits and Reserve Increases (Page 5)					
9. Total Policy Benefits — Life (Items 8, 9, 10, 11, 11A & 12, Col. 1, less Items 11 & 11A, Cols. 9, 10 & 11)					
0. Total Policy Benefits — A & H (Items 11 & 11A, Cols. 9, 10 & 11)					
1. Increase in Life Reserves — Other than Group and Annuities (Item 17, Cols. 2 and 3)					
2. Increase in A & H Reserves (Item 17, Cols. 9, 10 & 11)					
3. Dividends to Policyholders (Item 28, Col. 1)					
Operating Ratios					
Insurance Expense Ratio (Page 5, Col. 1, Items 21, 21A & 22 less Item 5) ÷ (Page 5, Col. 1, Item 1 plus group annuity contribution funds) × 100					
Lapse Ratio (Ordinary Only) [(Page 15, Col. 4, Lines 14 & 15) × 100 ÷ ½ (Lines 1 & 22)]					
A & H Loss Ratio (Schedule H, Part 1, Lines 3 and 4, Col. 1, %)					
A & H Expense Ratio (Schedule H, Part 1, Line 8, Col. 1, %)					
A & H Claim Reserve Adequacy					
Incurred Losses on Prior Years' Claims — Group Health (Schedule H, Part 3, Line 3a, Col. 2)					
Prior Years' Claim Liability and Reserve — Group Health (Schedule H, Part 3, Line 3b, Col. 2)					
Incurred Losses on Prior Years' Claims — Health other than Group (Schedule H, Part 3, Line 3a, Col. 1 less Col. 2)					
Prior Years' Claim Liability and Reserve — Health other than Group (Schedule H, Part 3, Line 3b, Col. 1 less Col. 2)					
Net Gains From Operations After Federal Income Taxes by Lines of Business (Page 5, Item 31)					
Industrial Life (Col. 2)					
Ordinary—Life (Col. 3)					
Ordinary—Individual Annuities (Col. 4)					
Ordinary—Supp. Contracts (Col. 5)					
Credit Life (Col. 6)					
Group Life (Col. 7)					
Group Annuities (Col. 8)					
A & H—Group (Col. 9)					
A & H—Credit (Col. 10)					
A & H—Other (Col. 11)					
Total (Col. 1) (Page 5, Item 31, Col. 1)					

EXHIBIT OF LIFE INSURANCE

**Amounts of life insurance in this Exhibit shall be shown in thousands (omit 000)*

	INDUSTRIAL		ORDINARY		CREDIT LIFE[a] (GROUP AND INDIVIDUAL)		GROUP			(10)
	(1) NUMBER OF POLICIES	(2) AMOUNT OF INSURANCE*	(3) NUMBER OF POLICIES	(4) AMOUNT OF INSURANCE*	(5) NUMBER OF INDIVIDUAL POLICIES AND GROUP CERTIFICATES	(6) AMOUNT OF INSURANCE*	NUMBER OF (7) POLICIES	NUMBER OF (8) CERTIFICATES	(9) AMOUNT OF INSURANCE*	TOTAL AMOUNT OF INSURANCE
1. In force end of previous year										
2. Issued during year										
3. Reinsurance assumed										
4. Revived during year										
5. Increased during year (net)				DETAILS OMITTED						
5A. Subtotals, Lines 2 to 5										
6. Additions by dividends during year	XX		XX		XX		XX	XX		
7.										
8.										
9. Totals, (Lines 1 & 5A to 8)										
DEDUCTIONS DURING YEAR:										
10. Death							XX			
11. Maturity							XX			
12. Disability							XX			
13. Expiry										
14. Surrender										
15. Lapse										
16. Conversion							XX	XX	XX	
17. Decreased (net)										
18. Reinsurance										
19.										
20.										
21. Totals, Lines 10 to 20										
22. In force end of year, Line 9 minus Line 21										
23. Reinsurance ceded end of year	XX		XX		XX		XX	XX		
24. Line 22 minus Line 23	XX		XX		XX	†	XX	XX		

ADDITIONAL INFORMATION ON INSURANCE IN FORCE END OF YEAR

	INDUSTRIAL		ORDINARY	
	(1) NUMBER OF POLICIES	(2) AMOUNT OF INSURANCE*	(3) NUMBER OF POLICIES	(4) AMOUNT OF INSURANCE*
25. Additions by dividends	XX		XX	
26. Other paid-up insurance				
27. Debit ordinary insurance	XX	XX		

ADDITIONAL INFORMATION ON ORDINARY INSURANCE

	ISSUED DURING YEAR (Included in Line 2)		IN FORCE END OF YEAR (Included in Line 22)	
Term Insurance Excluding Extended Term Insurance and Term Additions:	(1) NUMBER OF POLICIES	(2) AMOUNT OF INSURANCE*	(3) NUMBER OF POLICIES	(4) AMOUNT OF INSURANCE*
28. Term policies—decreasing				
29. Term policies—other				
30. Other term insurance—decreasing	XX		XX	
31. Other term insurance	XX		XX	
31A. Totals, Lines 28 to 31				
Reconciliation to Lines 2 and 22:				
31B. Term additions	XX	XX	XX	
31C. Totals, extended term insurance	XX	XX		
31D. Totals, whole life and endowment				
31E. Totals, Lines 31A to 31D				

CLASSIFICATION OF AMOUNT OF INSURANCE* BY PARTICIPATING STATUS

	ISSUED DURING YEAR (Included in Line 2)		IN FORCE END OF YEAR (Included in Line 22)	
	(1) NON-PARTICIPATING	(2) PARTICIPATING	(3) NON-PARTICIPATING	(4) PARTICIPATING
32. Industrial				
33. Ordinary				
33A. Credit Life (Group and Individual)[a]				
34. Group				
35. Totals (Lines 32 to 34)				

ADDITIONAL INFORMATION ON CREDIT LIFE AND GROUP INSURANCE

	CREDIT LIFE[a]		GROUP	
	(1) NUMBER OF INDIVIDUAL POLICIES AND GROUP CERTIFICATES	(2) AMOUNT OF INSURANCE*	(3) NUMBER OF CERTIFICATES	(4) AMOUNT OF INSURANCE*
36. Amount of insurance included in Line 2 ceded to other companies	XX		XX	
37. Number in force end of year if the number under shared groups is counted on a pro-rata basis		XX		XX
38. Federal Employees' Group Life Insurance included in Line 22				
39. Servicemen's Group Life Insurance included in Line 22				
40. Group Permanent Insurance included in Line 22				

ADDITIONAL ACCIDENTAL DEATH BENEFITS

41. Amount of additional accidental death benefits in force end of year under ordinary policies* ....

BASIS OF CALCULATION OF ORDINARY TERM INSURANCE

42. State basis of calculation of (i) decreasing term insurance contained in Family Income, Mortgage Protection, etc., policies and riders and of (ii) term insurance on wife and children under Family, Parent and Children, etc., policies and riders included above.
(i)
(ii)

[a]Business not exceeding 120 months duration. †Group $ .... ; Individual $ ....

Form 1

ANNUAL STATEMENT FOR THE YEAR 19 OF THE LIFE INSURANCE COMPANY
Name

EXHIBITS OF ANNUITIES (PAID-FOR BASIS) AND SUPPLEMENTARY CONTRACTS WITH LIFE CONTINGENCIES

CLASSIFICATION	INDIVIDUAL ANNUITIES*		GROUP ANNUITIES			SUPPLEMENTARY CONTRACTS	
	(1) NO.	(2) ANNUAL INCOME	(3) CONTRACTS	(4) CERTIFICATES	(5) ANNUAL INCOME	(6) NO.	(7) ANNUAL INCOME
1. Outstanding at end of previous year							
2. Issued during year						X X X	X X X
3. Transferred from insurance account during year	X X X	X X X	X X X	X X X	X X X		
4. Totals							
5. Other net changes during year							
6. Outstanding at end of current year							

DETAILS OMITTED

CLASSIFICATION OF ANNUITIES AND SUPPLEMENTARY CONTRACTS WITH LIFE CONTINGENCIES OUTSTANDING AT THE END OF THE YEAR

CLASSIFICATION	INDIVIDUAL ANNUITIES*		GROUP ANNUITIES			SUPPLEMENTARY CONTRACTS		TOTAL	
	(1) NO.	(2) ANNUAL INCOME	(3)	(4) CERTIFICATES	(5) ANNUAL INCOME	(6) NO.	(7) ANNUAL INCOME	(8) NO.	(9) ANNUAL INCOME
7. Income now payable			X X X						
8. Deferred; fully paid			X X X						
9. Deferred; not fully paid			X X X						
10. Totals			X X X						

DETAILS OMITTED

*Individual Annuities. Include here all survivorship annuities and deferred annuities, including contracts providing for deferred annuities purchased by accumulations during deferred period and which provide for a death benefit during the period of deferment substantially equal to the value of the non-forfeiture benefit available on lapse.

SUPPLEMENTARY INFORMATION

GENERAL INTERROGATORIES

1. Have all the transactions of the company of which notice was received at the home office on or before the close of business December 31, been truthfully and accurately entered on its books? ANSWER: ....
2. Except as shown in the next succeeding question, does this statement show the condition of the company as shown by the books, records, and data at the home office at the close of business December 31? ANSWER: ....
3. Have there been included in this statement proper reserves to cover liabilities which may have been actually incurred on or before December 31, but of which no notice was received at the home office until subsequently? ANSWER: ....
4. In all cases where the company has assumed accident and health risks from another company, provision should be made in this statement on account of such reinsurances for a reserve equal to that which the original company would have been required to establish had it retained the risks. Has this been done? ANSWER: ....
5. Is the business of the company conducted upon the mutual, mixed or strictly proprietary plan? ANSWER: ....
6. Is the company a member of an insurance Holding Company System consisting of two or more affiliated persons, one or more of which is an insurer? ANSWER: ....
7. If the answer to General Interrogatory 6 is yes, did the company register and file with its domiciliary State Insurance Commissioner, Director or Superintendent, or with such regulatory official of the state of domicile of the principal insurer in the Holding Company System, a registration statement providing disclosure substantially similar to the standards adopted by the National Association of Insurance Commissioners in its Model Insurance Holding Company System Regulatory Act and model regulations pertaining thereto, or is the company subject to standards and disclosure requriements substantially similiar to those required by such Act and regulations? ANSWER: .... State regulating..........
8. Total amount paid in by stockholders since organization of the company as surplus funds (Stock Companies only). $ ....
9. Total dividends paid stockholders since organization of the company, cash $..........; stock, $..........
10. What interest, direct or indirect, has this company in the capital stock of any other insurance company? ANSWER: ....

10A. Are personnel or facilities of this company used by another company or companies or are personnel or facilities of another company or companies used by this company (except for activities such as administration of jointly underwritten group contracts and joint mortality or morbidity studies)? ANSWER: ....Net reimbursement of such expenses between companies; paid $.......... received $..........

11. CAPITAL STOCK OF THIS COMPANY

CLASS	NUMBER SHARES AUTHORIZED	NUMBER SHARES OUTSTANDING	PAR VALUE PER SHARE	REDEMPTION PRICE IF STOCK IS CALLABLE	IS DIVIDEND RATE LIMITED?	ARE DIVIDENDS CUMULATIVE?
Preferred.						
Common				X X X X	X X X X	X X X X

12. Does the company own any securities of a real estate holding company or otherwise hold real estate indirectly? ANSWER: ....If so, explain..........

    Name of real estate holding company .... No. of parcels involved..........Total book value $..........
13. Did any person while an officer, director or trustee of the company receive directly or indirectly, during the period covered by this statement, any commission on the business transactions of the company? ANSWER: ....
14. Has the company an established procedure for disclosure to its board of directors or trustees of any material interest or affiliation on the part of any of its officers, directors, trustees, or responsible employees which is in or is likely to conflict with the official duties of such person? ANSWER: ....
15. Amount of compensation, if any, received during the year by any representative, officer, trustee or director of the company for services rendered as a member of any bondholders' or stockholders' reorganization or protective committee with which the company has deposited any securities. ANSWER: $ ....
16. Amount of such compensation retained by the representative. ANSWER: $ ....
17. Total amount loaned during the year to directors or other officers $.........., to stockholders not officers $.......... Total amount of loans outstanding at end of year to directors or other officers $.........., to stockholders not officers $.......... (exclusive of policy loans).
18. Have the future loadings on the premiums, or any part thereof, been assigned or hypothecated in any way? If so, give full information. ANSWER: ....

18A. Except for retirement plans generally applicable to its staff employees, has the company any agreement with any person, other than contracts with its agents for the payment of commissions whereby it agrees that for any service rendered or to be rendered, he shall receive directly or indirectly, any salary, compensation or emolument that will extend beyond a period of 12 months from the date of the agreement? ANSWER: ....

19. What proportion of premiums on policies issued by the company may be taken in notes, or other form of lien, on the policies? ANSWER: ....
20. Were all the stocks, bonds and other securities owned December 31 of current year, in the actual possession of the company on said date, except as shown by the Schedules of Special and Other Deposits? ANSWER: .... If not, give full and complete information relating thereto ....

20A. Does the company own any investments in letter stock or other restricted securities? ANSWER: .... If yes, are they identified by appropriate symbol or otherwise in Schedule D? ANSWER: ....

20B. Have all private placement investments which were the subject of renegotiation or modification of their terms during the year been disclosed to the Valuation of Securities office of the NAIC, with full details as to the provisions renegotiated or modified? ANSWER: ....

20C. Have filings been made with the Valuation of Securities office of the NAIC in connection with acquisition and disposition of securities as required by Section 8 of the Valuation Procedures and Instructions for Bonds and Stocks? ANSWER: ....

21. Were any of the stocks, bonds or other assets of the company loaned, placed under option agreement, or otherwise made available for use by another person during the year covered by the statement? ANSWER: .... If yes, give full and complete information relating thereto..........

    Show all information if any securities were involved under a reverse repurchase agreement ....
22. State as of what date the latest financial examination of the company was made or is being made, and by what department or departments. ANSWER: ....
23. Has any change been made during the year of this statement in the charter, by-laws, articles of incorporation, or deed of settlement of the company? ANSWER: .... If so, when? .... If not previously filed, furnish herewith a certified copy of the instrument as amended.

    (Only United States branches of alien companies need answer 24).
24. What changes have been made during the year in the United States Manager or the United States Trustees of the company? ANSWER: ....

    Does this statement contain all business transacted for the company through its United States Branch on risks wherever located? ANSWER: ....
    Have there been any changes made to any of the trust indentures during the year? ANSWER: .... If yes, has the domiciliary or entry state approved the changes? ANSWER: ....
25. What officials and heads of departments of the company supervised the making of this report? ANSWER: ....
26. Has any direct new business been solicited or written in any state where the company was not licensed? ANSWER: Yes..........No..........If answer is "yes," explain
27. Is the purchase or sale of all investments of the company passed upon either by the Board of Directors or a subordinate committee thereof? ANSWER: ....
28. Does the company keep a complete permanent record of the proceedings of its Board of Directors and all subordinate committees thereof? ANSWER: ....
29. Have the instructions for completing the blank required by this department been followed in every detail? ANSWER: ....
30. Does this company have Separate Accounts? ANSWER:.......... If so, has Separate Account Statement been filed with this Department? ANSWER:.......... State the authority under which Separate Accounts are maintained. ANSWER: ....
31. During the period covered by this statement, did (a) any agent, general agent, broker, sales representative, non-affiliated sales/service organization, or any combination thereof under common control (other than salaried employees of the company), (b) any sales/service organization owned in whole or in part by the company or an affiliate, receive credit or commissions for or control a substantial part (more than 20 percent of any major line of business measured on direct premiums) of (i) sales of new business? (ii) renewals? ANSWER: (a) (i).......... (ii).......... (b) (i).......... (ii)..........

(000 Omitted)

NOTES TO FINANCIAL STATEMENTS

asis of Presentation.

he accompanying financial statements of the Company have been pre- and in conformity with accounting practices prescribed or permitted e National Association of Insurance Commissioner and the of ____________.

asis of Valuation of Invested Assets.

. Assets values are generally stated as follows: Bonds at amortized preferred stock at cost; common stocks at market; real estate at ciated cost. Other investments on the equity basis. Mortgage loans olicy loans at the aggregate balance. The maximum and minimum lending for mortgage loans during the year were 13% and 12% for all loans. age loans are made up to 75% of the value and fire insurance is red on all mortgaged property.

. The Company uses straight line depreciation on real estate.

ivestment Income.

. Due and accrued income was excluded from investment income for of Bond interest where collection of interest is uncertain.

The Company uses the investment year method for allocation of net ment income to lines of business which method was approved by the of _________ on March 1, 19XX.

tirement Plan.

e Company has a noncontributory pension plan covering substantially iployees and certain agents. Pension costs are funded as they and vested benefits are fully funded.

pital and Surplus and Shareholders Dividend Restrictions.

The maximum amount of dividends which can be paid during 19XX by of ________insurance company shareholders without prior approval of surance Commissioner is $21,980. 19XX dividend payment to share- s totaled $2,500.

The Company has no preferred stock outstanding.

rrowed Money.

e Company has outstanding $2,960 of 10% debentures due in 19XX, t to the Companies right to accelerate the call date after 19XX.

fe and Annuities Actuarial Resources.

The Company waives deduction of deferred fractional premiums eath of the insured and returns any portion of premiums paid beyond te of death.

As of December 31, 19XX the Company had $67,240 of insurance in for which the gross premiums are less than net premiums according to andard valuation set by the state of ________. Reserves to cover ove insurance totaled $1,530 at year end and are reported in t 8 with aggregate reserves.

emiums and Annuity Considerations Deferred and Uncollected.

ferred and uncollected amounts at December 31, 19XX were as follows:

	Gross	Net
Ordinary new business	$ 2,190	$ 1,511
Ordinary renewal	4,497	3,688
Group new business	437	302
Group renewal	663	544
	$ 7,787	$ 6,045

ases.

e Company does not have any material lease obligations at this time.

Note.—In case the following schedules do not afford sufficient space, companies may furnish them on separate forms, provided the same are upon paper of like size and arrangements and contain the information asked for herein and have the name of the company printed or stamped at the top thereof.

SPECIAL DEPOSIT SCHEDULE

Showing all deposits or investments NOT held for the protection of ALL the policyholders of the Company

(1) WHERE DEPOSITED	(2) DESCRIPTION AND PURPOSE OF DEPOSIT (Indicating literal form of registration of Securities)	(3) PAR VALUE	(4) STATEMENT VALUE	(5) MARKET VALUE
	DETAILS OMITTED			
	Totals			

SCHEDULE OF ALL OTHER DEPOSITS

Showing all deposits made with any Government, Province, State, District, County, Municipality, Corporation, firm or individual, except those shown in Schedule E, and those shown in "Special Deposit Schedule" above

(1) WHERE DEPOSITED	(2) DESCRIPTION AND PURPOSE OF DEPOSIT (Indicating literal form of registration of Securities)	(3) PAR VALUE	(4) STATEMENT VALUE	(5) MARKET VALUE
	DETAILS OMITTED			
	Totals			

SCHEDULE OF EXAMINATION FEES AND EXPENSES

(1) TYPE OF EXAM (a)	(2) STATE INITIATING EXAM (b)	(3) STATES PARTICIPATING (b)	(4) DATE BEGUN	(5) DATE COMPLETED	(6) DATE REPORT PUBLISHED	FEES AND EXPENSES INCURRED IN CURRENT YEAR (7) AMOUNT (c)	(8) STATE (b)	(9) OFFSETTING CREDITS, IF ANY
		DETAILS OMITTED						
					Totals		XXX	

M" for marketing conduct, "F" for financial condition, describe others
se 2 digit post office abbreviation
ow amount paid to each state (or representatives thereof) separately. The total amount plus $ .... for other state insurance department
enses and fees should agree with Page 9, Exhibit 6, Column 4, Line 2 in this statement plus the Separate Account business statement, if any.

Form 1

ANNUAL STATEMENT FOR THE YEAR 19 OF THE LIFE INSURANCE COMPANY

Name

SCHEDULE A—PART 1

Showing all Real Estate OWNED December 31 of Current Year, the Cost, Book and Market Value thereof, the Nature and Amount of all Liens and Encumbrances thereon, Including Interest Due and Accrued, etc.

REPORT INDIVIDUALLY EACH PROPERTY OWNED, EXCEPT THAT IN SUBDIVISIONS (a) AND (c) ITEMS WITH A BOOK VALUE UP TO $100,000 OR ONE TENTH OF ONE PERCENT OF TOTAL ADMITTED ASSETS AT END OF PRECEDING YEAR, WHICHEVER IS LESS, MAY BE SUMMARIZED.

(000 OMITTED)

NO.	(1) LOCATION AND DESCRIPTION OF PROPERTY (Nature of encumbrances, if any, including interest due and accrued. State if occupied or leased by company or by a parent, subsidiary or affiliate.)	(2) *DATE ACQUIRED	(3) YEAR OF LAST AP-PRAISAL	(4) NAME OF VENDOR	(5) AMOUNT OF ENCUMBRANCES	(6) **COST TO COMPANY	(7) BOOK VALUE LESS ENCUMBRANCES	(8) ††MARKET VALUE LESS ENCUMBRANCES	(9) INCREASE BY ADJUSTMENT IN BOOK VALUE DURING YEAR	(10) DECREASE BY ADJUSTMENT IN BOOK VALUE DURING YEAR	(11) †EXPENDED FOR ADDITIONS AND PERMANENT IMPROVEMENTS DURING YEAR	(12) ‡AMOUNTS RECEIVED DURING YEAR FOR SALES OF RIGHTS OR PRIVILEGES	(13) GROSS INCOME LESS INTEREST ON ENCUMBRANCES ***	(14) EXPENDED FOR TAXES, REPAIRS AND EXPENSES	(15) NET INCOME	(16)	(17)	(18)	(19)
(a) Acquired prior to current year and owned at end of current year (but not then under contract of sale)																			
						DETAILS OMITTED													
X X X	Summary—Items of less than $25,000 (No.)	X X X	X X X	X X X															
X X X	(See Note) Items from $25,000 to $49,999 (No.)	X X X	X X X	X X X															
X X X	Items from $50,000 to $99,999 (No.)	X X X	X X X	X X X															
				Totals, Part 1 (a)		12,780	8,690	8,690		957	1,307		1,890	810	1,060				
(b) Acquired during current year and owned at end of current year (but not then under contract of sale)																			
								NONE											
				Totals, Part 1 (b)															
				Totals, Part 1 (a) and (b)												X X X	X X X	X X X	
(c) Acquired prior to current year and owned under contract of sale at end of current year																CONTRACT SALE PRICE			
																TOTAL	DUE TO DATE UNDER CONTRACT	ACTUALLY PAID TO DATE	DUE CURRENT YEAR AND UNPAID
								NONE											
X X X	Summary—Items of less than $25,000 (No.)	X X X	X X X	X X X															
X X X	(See Note) Items from $25,000 to $49,999 (No)	X X X	X X X	X X X															
X X X	Items from $50,000 to $99,999 (No)	X X X	X X X	X X X															
				Totals, Part 1 (c)															
(d) Acquired during current year and owned under contract of sale at end of current year																			
								NONE											
				Totals, Part 1 (d)															
				Totals, Part 1 (c) and (d)												X X X	X X X	X X X	
				Grand Totals, Part 1												X X X	X X X	X X X	

*Under Parts (b) and (d) omit date acquired but indicate how acquired, by: f, foreclosure; p, purchase; t, trade.

**Include cost of acquiring title and all amounts expended for additions and permanent improvements to end of current year, less all amounts received for sales up to end of current year. If acquired by foreclosure, include all amounts expended for taxes, repairs and improvements in excess of the income of the property other than interest, prior to the date of acquiring title.

†Report only those amounts expended after acquiring title, including reductions in encumbrances.

‡Include any increases in encumbrances.

††State basis on which market value was determined

***State rent received for space occupied by Company (give items and amounts)

CLASSIFICATION

Showing the total amount of Real Estate owned in each State and Foreign Country

STATE	MARKET VALUE		STATE	MARKET VALUE		STATE	MARKET VALUE		FOREIGN COUNTRY	MARKET VALUE	
	FARM PROPERTIES	OTHER THAN FARM PROPERTIES		FARM PROPERTIES	OTHER THAN FARM PROPERTIES		FARM PROPERTIES	OTHER THAN FARM PROPERTIES		FARM PROPERTIES	OTHER THAN FARM PROPERTIES
Totals											

SCHEDULE A – PART 2

Showing all Real Estate SOLD during the Year, including Payments during the Year on "Sales under Contract"

REPORT INDIVIDUALLY EACH PROPERTY SOLD EXCEPT AS INDICATED BELOW

NO.	(1) LOCATION AND DESCRIPTION OF PROPERTY OR NATURE OF ADDITIONS AND IMPROVEMENTS (Nature of encumbrances, if any, including interest due and accrued)	(2) *DATE PURCHASED	(3) NAME OF VENDOR	(4) DATE SOLD	(5) NAME OF PURCHASER	(6) **COST TO COMPANY	(7) INCREASE BY ADJUSTMENT IN BOOK VALUE DURING YEAR	(8) DECREASE BY ADJUSTMENT IN BOOK VALUE DURING YEAR	(9) †EXPENDED FOR ADDITIONS AND PERMANENT IMPROVEMENTS DURING YEAR	(10) ††BOOK VALUE AT DATE OF SALE LESS ENCUMBRANCES	(11) ‡AMOUNTS RECEIVED DURING YEAR FOR SALES OF RIGHTS OR PRIVILEGES	(12) §ALL OTHER AMOUNTS RECEIVED INCLUDING PAYMENTS ON SALES UNDER CONTRACT	(13) PROFIT ON SALE	(14) LOSS ON SALE	(15) GROSS INCOME DURING YEAR LESS INTEREST ON ENCUMBRANCES	(16) EXPENDED FOR TAXES, REPAIRS AND EXPENSES DURING YEAR
	(a) Sold during current year but acquired prior to current year															
		X X X X	X X X X			NONE										
		X X X X	X X X X													
		X X X X	X X X X													
		X X X X	X X X X													
		X X X X	X X X X													
		X X X X	X X X X													
		X X X X	X X X X													
X X X X	Summary—Payments during the year under sales under contract	X X X X	X X X X													
		X X X X	X X X X		Totals, Part 2 (a)											
	(b) Sold during current year, acquired during current year															
						NONE										
X X X X	Summary—Payments during the year under sales under contract	X X X X	X X X X	X X X X	X X X X											
					Totals, Part 2 (b)											
					Grand Totals, Part 2											

*Under part (b) indicate how acquired, by: f, foreclosure; p, purchase; t, trade.
**Include cost of acquiring title and all amounts expended for additions and permanent improvements to end of current year, less all amounts received for sales up to end of current year. If acquired by foreclosure, include all amounts expended for taxes, repairs and improvements prior to the date of acquiring title. In reporting Sales under Contract, include payments received during the current year only.
†Report only those amounts expended after acquiring title, including reductions in encumbrances.
††In case of Sales under Contract, include payments received during current year only, until Book Value per Part 1 is exhausted.

‡Include any increases in encumbrances. §Indicate payments on "Sales under Contracts" by inserting the letter "P" after the number of the parcel.
Rates of interest under contracts of sale of real estate? Maximum .... Minimum ....
State amount of commissions paid for sale of real estate $........ and column in which the same is included........

SCHEDULE A — Verification Between Years

1. Book value, December 31, previous year (Exhibit 13, Item 4, Col. 1)
2. Increase, by adjustment: (a) Grand total, Part 1, Col. 9
   (b) Grand total, Part 2, Col. 7
   (c) Total increase (Exhibit 4, Item 4, Col. 1)
3. Cost of acquired: (a) Part 1 (b), Col. 6 net of encumbrances
   (b) Part 1 (d), Col. 6 net of encumbrances
   (c) Part 2 (b), Col. 6 net of encumbrances
   (d) Total acquired
4. Cost of permanent improvements: (a) Part 1 (a), Col. 11
   (b) Part 1 (c), Col. 11
   (c) Part 2 (a), Col. 9
   (d) Total improvements
5. Profit on sales, Grand total, Part 2, Col. 13 (Exhibit 4, Item 4, Col. 2)
6. Total
7. Decrease, by adjustment: (a) Grand total, Part 1, Col. 10
   (b) Grand total, Part 2, Col. 8
   (c) Total decrease (Exhibit 4, Item 4, Col. 3 plus **footnote amount for depreciation on real estate)
8. Received on sales: (a) Part 1 (a), Col. 12
   (b) Part 1 (c), Col. 12
   (c) Part 2 (a), Col. 11
   (d) Grand total, Part 2, Col. 12
   (e) Total received
9. Loss on sales, Grand total, Part 2, Col. 14 (Exhibit 4, Item 4, Col. 4)
10. Book value, December 31, current year (Exhibit 13, Item 4, Col. 1)

DETAILS OMITTED

*ANALYSIS OF BOOK VALUE OF REAL ESTATE ACQUIRED IN SATISFACTION OF MORTGAGE INDEBTEDNESS

	REAL ESTATE NOT UNDER CONTRACT OF SALE	%	REAL ESTATE UNDER CONTRACT OF SALE	%	TOTAL	%
1. Amount of mortgages at time of acquisition as real estate						
2. Taxes, foreclosure costs and other expenses capitalized and included in book value at time of acquisition as real estate						
3. Past due and accrued interest capitalized and included in book value	DETAILS OMITTED					
4. Capitalized expenditures for additions and permanent improvements						
5. Gross increases by adjustment in book value						
6. Other increases (specify):						
7.						
8.						
9. Subtotals		X X X X		X X X X		X X X X
DEDUCT:						
10. Gross decreases by adjustment in book value						
11. Payments received on contracts of sale	X X X X X X X X	X X X X				
12. Amounts received for sales of rights or privileges						
13. Net increases in encumbrances						
14. Other decreases (specify):						
15.						
16.						
17. Total deductions		X X X X		X X X X		X X X X
18. Book value, at end of current year, of real estate acquired in satisfaction of mortgage indebtedness		100%		100%		100%
19. Book value, at end of current year, of home office real estate						
20. Book value, at end of current year, of other real estate						
21. Grand totals (Exhibit 13, Line 4, Col. 1)						

*Only real estate acquired in satisfaction of mortgage indebtedness shall be included on Lines 1 through 17.

SCHEDULE B - Part 1 — Section 1

Summary of Long-term Mortgage Loans (including foreclosed liens subject to redemption) owned at December 31 of Current Year and changes therein during the year (000 OMITTED)

	FARM MORTGAGES		OTHER THAN FARM MORTGAGES			
	(1) Purchase Money**	(2) Other	(3) Insured or Guaranteed under F.H.A., N.H.A. or V.A.	(4) Purchase Money**	(5) All Other	(6) TOTAL
1. Book value of mortgages owned, December 31st of previous year			5,490	9,810	10,990	26,290
2. Loans in cash or granted on disposal of real estate			700	800	1,000	2,500
3. Cost of mortgages, insured and other, purchased						
4. Additional cash loaned on $.............. of refunded mortgages*						
5. Interest covered by increase in, or refunding of, mortgages						
6. Taxes covered by increase in, or refunding of, mortgages						
7. Other items covered by increase in, or refunding of, mortgages						
8. Accrual of discount on mortgages purchased						
9. Transfers						
10.						
11.						
12. TOTALS			6,190	10,610	11,990	28,790
13. Payments on principal including cash on mortgages refunded			190	610	720	1,520
14. Mortgages foreclosed and transferred to real estate						
15. Mortgages on properties acquired by deed, in lieu of foreclosure, and transferred to real estate						
16. Decrease in book value of mortgages refunded or by adjustment in book value of mortgages						
17. Amortization of premium on mortgages purchased						
18. Transfers						
19.						
20.						
21. TOTAL DEDUCTIONS			190	610	720	1,520
22.						
23. Book value of mortgages owned, end of year, per Exhibit 13, Line 3, Col. 1			6,000	10,000	11,270	27,270

*Where refunding or extension involves the advance of no additional cash, no entries should be made.

SCHEDULE B - Part 1 — Section 2

Summary of Long-term Mortgage Loans (including foreclosed liens subject to redemption) owned at December 31 of Current Year in each State and Foreign Country (000 OMITTED)

(1) STATE OR FOREIGN COUNTRY	FARM MORTGAGES						OTHER THAN FARM MORTGAGES										(10) GRAND TOTAL	
	(2) Purchase Money**		(3) Other		(4) Total Farm		(5) Insured or Guaranteed by Federal Housing Administration or under National Housing Act (Canada)		(6) Insured or Guaranteed by Veterans Administration (exclusive of any portion insured by F. H. A.)		(7) Purchase Money**		(8) All Other		(9) Total Other than Farm			
	No.	Amount	No.	Amount	No.	Amount	No.	Amount	No.	Amount	No.	Amount	No.	Amount	No.	Amount	No.	Amount
ARIZONA							12	1,000			3	800	4	750			19	2,550
	DETAILS OMITTED																	
TOTALS							22	6,000			42	10,000	91	11,270			281	27,270

**A purchase money mortgage is understood to be one which represents a part of the consideration received on sale of property owned by the company (Mortgagee).

GENERAL INTERROGATORY

1. Are any investments other than mortgage loans, such as ground rents, included in Schedule B? Answer: No

SCHEDULE B - Part 2 — Section 1

Long-term Mortgages owned at December 31 of Current Year upon which interest is not overdue more than three months, which are not in process of foreclosure or in course of voluntary conveyance to the Company. Show individually those which exceed $1,000,000 or 1/2% of admitted assets December 31 preceding year, whichever is smaller, and others upon which taxes, assessments or other liens are delinquent more than one year, and, with appropriate comment, those where mortgagor is an officer, director, parent, subsidiary or affiliate, classified by States in each sub-section. All others may be summarized.

(1) NUMBER	(2) STATE AND COUNTY OR CITY	(3) YEAR GIVEN	(4) AMOUNT OF PRINCIPAL INDEBTEDNESS AT END OF YEAR	(5) BOOK VALUE	(6) INCREASE BY ADJUSTMENT IN BOOK VALUE DURING YEAR	(7) DECREASE BY ADJUSTMENT IN BOOK VALUE DURING YEAR	(8) INTEREST DUE AND UNPAID**	(9) UNPAID TAXES*	(10) VALUE OF LAND AND BUILDINGS	(11) COMMENT
				NONE						

*Report *ALL* taxes unpaid by mortgagor, if any taxes are unpaid more than one year from date when penalty attaches.

**Show grand total only.

ANNUAL STATEMENT FOR THE YEAR 19 OF THE LIFE INSURANCE COMPANY
Name

SCHEDULE B - Part 2 — Section 2

Long-term Mortgages owned at December 31 of Current Year upon which interest is overdue more than three months, which are not in process of foreclosure or in course of voluntary conveyance to the Company. Mortgages upon which interest is overdue more than one year or upon which taxes or other liens are delinquent more than one year or which exceed $100,000 or 1/5% of admitted assets or, where mortgagor is an officer, director, parent, subsidiary or affiliate (with appropriate comment) shall be listed individually, classified by States in each sub-section. All others may be summarized.

(1) NUMBER	(2) STATE AND COUNTY OR CITY	(3) YEAR GIVEN	(4) AMOUNT OF PRINCIPAL INDEBTEDNESS AT END OF YEAR	(5) BOOK VALUE	(6) INCREASE BY ADJUSTMENT IN BOOK VALUE DURING YEAR	(7) DECREASE BY ADJUSTMENT IN BOOK VALUE DURING YEAR	(8) INTEREST DUE AND UNPAID	(9) UNPAID TAXES*	(10) YEAR OF LAST APPRAISAL OR VALUATION	(11) VALUE OF LAND AND BUILDINGS	(12) COMMENT
				NONE							

Form 1

ANNUAL STATEMENT FOR THE YEAR 19 OF THE LIFE INSURANCE COMPANY

Name

SCHEDULE B - Part 2 — Section 3

All Long-term Mortgages owned at December 31 of Current Year in process of foreclosure (including those in which transfer of legal title is awaiting expiration of redemption or moratorium period) and including those where properties are in course of voluntary conveyance to the Company. Classify by States and list all items. State if mortgagor is an officer, director, parent, subsidiary or affiliate.

(1) NUMBER	(2) STATE AND COUNTY OR CITY	(3) YEAR GIVEN	(4) AMOUNT OF PRINCIPAL INDEBTEDNESS AT END OF YEAR	(5) BOOK VALUE†	(6) INCREASE BY ADJUSTMENT IN BOOK VALUE DURING YEAR	(7) DECREASE BY ADJUSTMENT IN BOOK VALUE DURING YEAR	(8) INTEREST DUE AND UNPAID	(9) UNPAID TAXES*	(10) YEAR OF LAST APPRAISAL OR VALUATION	(11) VALUE OF LAND AND BUILDINGS	(12) COMMENT
				NONE							

*Report ALL taxes unpaid by mortgagor, if any taxes are unpaid more than one year from date when penalty attaches.

†Identify by dagger each foreclosed lien subject to redemption.

ANNUAL STATEMENT FOR THE YEAR 19 OF THE LIFE INSURANCE COMPANY

SCHEDULE B — Part 3

Long-term Mortgages foreclosed, properties transferred to real estate during the year, including properties acquired by voluntary conveyance to the Company. Classify by States and list all items.

(1) NUMBER	(2) STATE	(3) YEAR GIVEN	(4) BOOK VALUE OF MORTGAGE AT END OF PREVIOUS YEAR	ITEMS CAPITALIZED DURING YEAR					(10) PAYMENTS ON ACCOUNT OF PRINCIPAL RECEIVED DURING YEAR	(11) INCREASE BY ADJUSTMENT IN BOOK VALUE DURING YEAR	(12) DECREASE BY ADJUSTMENT IN BOOK VALUE DURING YEAR	(13) VALUE TRANSFERRED TO REAL ESTATE	(14) REAL ESTATE NUMBER
				(5) INTEREST	(6) TAXES	(7) FORECLOSURE COSTS	(8) OTHER	(9) TOTAL					
						NONE							

Form 1

ANNUAL STATEMENT FOR THE YEAR 19 OF THE LIFE INSURANCE COMPANY
Name

SCHEDULE B A–PART 1

Showing Other Long-term Invested Assets OWNED December 31, Current Year
(000 OMITTED)

(1) NUMBER OF UNITS AND DESCRIPTION*	(2) YEAR ACQUIRED	(3) LESSEE OR LOCATION	(4) AMOUNT OF ENCUMBRANCES	(5) COST TO COMPANY	(6) BOOK VALUE AT DECEMBER 31, LESS ENCUMBRANCES	(7) STATEMENT VALUE AT DECEMBER 31	(8) MARKET OR INVESTMENT VALUE AT DECEMBER 31, LESS ENCUMBRANCES	(9) ADDITIONS TO (+) OR REDUCTIONS IN (—) INVESTMENT†	(10) DECREASE (—) OR INCREASE (+) BY ADJUSTMENT IN BOOK VALUE DURING YEAR‡	(11) GROSS INCOME RECEIVED DURING YEAR	(12) NET INCOME RECEIVED DURING YEAR §	(13) AMOUNTS ACCRUED AT DECEMBER 31 §§	(14) AMOUNTS PAST DUE AT DECEMBER 31 §§
APARTMENT #76	19XX	XYZ		410	360	360	360	18		36	36		
DETAILS OMITTED													
Grand Totals				1,020	830	830	830	86	30	80	80		

*Give detailed description of investment and of underlying security (Footnotes may be used to describe leases for each class in the aggregate). Indicate statutory category of investment, i.e., real estate, mortgage, security, or other. Include in this Schedule, showing subtotals by class and grand total for all classes: (1) All loans on or investments in oil and gas production payments except those listed in Schedule D, Part 1 or Schedule DA; (2) All Transportation Equipment; (3) Timber Deeds; (4) Mineral Rights carried as admitted assets; (5) Motor Vehicle Trust Certificates; (6) Any other class of admitted investment not clearly includable in other statement schedules.

†Include additional investments made, or portion of investment repaid.
‡Include depreciation on real estate and transportation equipment, etc., amortization of preimum and accrual of discount if applicable.
§After appropriate reduction for interest paid to manufacturer during year and depletion and amortization of mineral rights.
§§After appropriate reduction for due and accrued interest payable to manufacturers.

SCHEDULE B A–VERIFICATION BETWEEN YEARS

1. Book value of other invested assets (Exhibit 13, Line 10, previous year) 774
2. Cost of acquisitions during year:
   - (a) Column 5, Part 2 . . . .
   - (b) Column 9, Part 1 . . . .
   - (c) Column 7, Part 3 . . . .
3. Increase by adjustment during year:
   - (a) Column 10, Part 1 86
   - (b) Column 8, Part 3 86
4. Profit on disposition, Column 9, Part 3 . . . .
5. Total . . . .
6. Deduct consideration on disposition, Column 5, Part 3 . . . .
7. Reductions in investment during year:°
   - (a) Column 9, Part 1 . . . .
   - (b) Column 7, Part 3 . . . .
8. Decrease by adjustment during year:
   - (a) Column 10, Part 1 30
   - (b) Column 8, Part 3 30
9. Loss on disposition, Column 10, Part 3 . . . .
10. Book value of other invested assets (Exhibit 13, Line 10, current year) 830

°Cash payments on account of capital, e.g., depletion and amortization of mineral rights.

ANNUAL STATEMENT FOR THE YEAR 19 OF THE LIFE INSURANCE COMPANY
Name

SCHEDULE B A – PART 2

Showing Other Long-term Invested Assets ACQUIRED During Current Year

(1) NUMBER OF UNITS AND DESCRIPTION*	(2) DATE ACQUIRED	(3) LESSEE OR LOCATION	(4) COST TO COMPANY	(5) CONSIDERATION PAID DURING CURRENT YEAR	(6) NAME OF VENDOR
		NONE			
Grand Totals					

SCHEDULE B A – PART 3

Showing Other Long-term Invested Assets DISPOSED OF During Current Year

(1) NUMBER OF UNITS AND DESCRIPTION*	(2) DATE DISPOSED OF	(3) LESSEE OR LOCATION	(4) NAME OF PURCHASER OR NATURE OF DISPOSITION	(5) CONSIDERATION	(6) BOOK VALUE AT DATE OF SALE	(7) ADDITIONS TO (+) OR REDUCTIONS IN (—) INVESTMENT	(8) DECREASE (—) OR INCREASE (+) BY ADJUSTMENT IN BOOK VALUE DURING YEAR	(9) PROFIT ON SALE	(10) LOSS ON SALE	(11) NET INCOME
			NONE							
Grand Totals										

* Include in this Schedule, showing subtotals by class and grand total for all classes (1) All loans on or investments in oil and gas production payments except those listed in Schedule D, Part 1 or Schedule DA. (2) All Transportation Equipment. (3) Timber Deeds. (4) Mineral Rights carried as admitted assets. (5) Motor Vehicle Trust Certificates. (6) Any other class of admitted investment not clearly includable in other statement schedules.

SCHEDULE C — Part 1

Showing All Long-term Collateral Loans IN FORCE December 31 of Current Year

(1) NO.	(2) DESCRIPTION OF SECURITIES HELD AS COLLATERAL DECEMBER 31 OF CURRENT YEAR (Give in this column the number of shares of each block of stock and rate of interest and year of maturity of each bond held as collateral)	(3) PAR VALUE	(4) RATE USED TO OBTAIN MARKET VALUE	(5) MARKET VALUE DEC. 31 OF CURRENT YEAR	(6) AMOUNT LOANED THEREON	(7) DATE OF LOAN	(8) MATURITY OF LOAN	INTEREST (9) Rate on Loan	INTEREST (10) Amount Past Due Dec. 31 of Current Year	INTEREST (11) Amount Accrued Dec. 31 of Current Year	INTEREST (12) Amount Received During Year	(13) NAME OF ACTUAL BORROWER (State if the borrower is a parent, subsidiary, affiliate, officer or director)
					NONE							
	Totals		XXX			XXX	XXX	XXX				

SCHEDULE C — Part 2

Showing All Long-term Collateral Loans MADE During the Year

(1) NO	(2) DESCRIPTION OF SECURITY ACCEPTED AS COLLATERAL WHEN LOAN WAS MADE	(3) PAR VALUE	(4) RATE USED TO OBTAIN MARKET VALUE	(5) MARKET VALUE AT DATE OF LOAN	(6) AMOUNT LOANED THEREON	(7) DATE OF LOAN	(8) MATURITY OF LOAN	(9) RATE OF INTEREST ON LOAN	(10) NAME OF ACTUAL BORROWER (State if the borrower is a parent, subsidiary, affiliate, officer or director)
				NONE					
	Totals		XXX			XXX	XXX	XXX	

ANNUAL STATEMENT FOR THE YEAR 19 OF THE LIFE INSURANCE COMPANY
Name

SCHEDULE C — Part 3

Showing All Long-term Collateral Loans DISCHARGED in Whole or in Part During the Year

(1) NO. Indicate partial payments by the letter P	(2) DESCRIPTION OF COLLATERAL RELEASED WHEN LOAN WAS DISCHARGED (In case of partial payments enter collateral released only)	(3) PAR VALUE	(4) RATE USED TO OBTAIN MARKET VALUE	(5) MARKET VALUE AT DATE OF DISCHARGE	(6) AMOUNT OF LOAN REPAID	(7) DATE OF LOAN	(8) DATE OF REPAYMENT	INTEREST (9) Rate on Loan	INTEREST (10) Amount Received During Year	(11) NAME OF ACTUAL BORROWER (State if the borrower is a parent, subsidiary affiliate, officer or director)
				NONE						
	Totals		XXX			XXX	XXX	XXX		

SCHEDULE C — Part 4

Showing All Substitutions of Collateral During the Year

(1) NO. (To Correspond with No. Shown in Parts 1, 2 and 3)	(2) AMOUNT OF LOAN Col. (6) of Parts 1, 2 or 3	COLLATERAL SUBSTITUTED (3) Description	COLLATERAL SUBSTITUTED (4) Date	COLLATERAL SUBSTITUTED (5) Par Value	COLLATERAL SUBSTITUTED (6) Market Value	COLLATERAL RELEASED (7) Description	COLLATERAL RELEASED (8) Date	COLLATERAL RELEASED (9) Par Value	COLLATERAL RELEASED (10) Market Value
				NONE					
Totals		XXX	XXX			XXX	XXX		

SCHEDULE D—SUMMARY BY COUNTRY

Long-term Bonds and Stocks OWNED December 31 of Current Year

(000 OMITTED)

(1) DESCRIPTION		(2) BOOK VALUE	(3) †MARKET VALUE (Excluding accrued interest)	(4) ACTUAL COST (Excluding accrued interest)	(5) PAR VALUE OF BONDS	(6) *AMORTIZED OR INVESTMENT VALUE
BONDS	1. United States	24,010	23,600	23,910	24,240	24,010
Governments (Including all obligations guaranteed by governments)	2. Canada					
	3. Other Countries					
	4. Totals	24,010	23,600	23,910	24,240	24,010
States, Territories and Possessions (Direct and guaranteed)	5. United States	7,270	7,270	7,720	7,860	7,740
	6. Canada					
	7. Other Countries					
	8. Totals	7,270	7,270	7,720	7,860	7,740
Political Subdivisions of States, Territories and Possessions (Direct and guaranteed)	9. United States	1,900	1,900	2,100	2,090	2,000
	10. Canada					
	11. Other Countries					
	12. Totals	1,900	1,900	2,100	2,090	2,000
Special revenue and special assessment obligations and all non-guaranteed obligations of agencies and authorities of governments and their political subdivisions	13. United States	4,000	3,720	3,970	4,070	4,000
	14. Canada					
	15. Other Countries					
	16. Totals	4,000	3,720	3,970	4,070	4,000
Railroads (unaffiliated)	17. United States					
	18. Canada					
	19. Other Countries					
	20. Totals					
Public Utilities (unaffiliated)	21. United States					
	22. Canada					
	23. Other Countries					
	24. Totals					
Industrial and Miscellaneous (unaffiliated)	25. United States	443,390	437,750	440,400	458,980	442,680
	26. Canada					
	27. Other Countries					
	28. Totals	443,390	437,750	440,400	458,980	442,680
Parent, Subsidiaries and Affiliates	29. Totals					
	30. **Total Bonds**	480,570	474,240	478,100	497,240	480,430
PREFERRED STOCKS	31. United States					
Railroads (unaffiliated)	32. Canada					
	33. Other Countries					
	34. Totals					
Public Utilities (unaffiliated)	35. United States	2,860	2,160	2,860		
	36. Canada					
	37. Other Countries					
	38. Totals	2,860	2,160	2,860		
Banks, Trust and Insurance Companies (unaffiliated)	39. United States					
	40. Canada					
	41. Other Countries					
	42. Totals					
Industrial and Miscellaneous (unaffiliated)	43. United States					
	44. Canada					
	45. Other Countries					
	46. Totals					
Parent, Subsidiaries and Affiliates	47. Totals					
	48. **Total Preferred Stocks**	2,860	2,160	2,860		
COMMON STOCKS	49. United States					
Railroads (unaffiliated)	50. Canada					
	51. Other Countries					
	52. Totals					
Public Utilities (unaffiliated)	53. United States	5,000	5,000	5,000		
	54. Canada					
	55. Other Countries					
	56. Totals	5,000	5,000	5,000		
Banks, Trust and Insurance Companies (unaffiliated)	57. United States					
	58. Canada					
	59. Other Countries					
	60. Totals					
Industrial and Miscellaneous (unaffiliated)	61. United States	18,964	20,654	18,964		
	62. Canada					
	63. Other Countries					
	64. Totals	18,964	20,654	18,964		
Parent, Subsidiaries and Affiliates	65. Totals					
	66. **Total Common Stocks**	23,964	25,654	23,964		
	67. **Total Stocks**	26,824	28,514	26,824		
	68. **Total Bonds and Stocks**	507,394	502,754	504,924		

†...ment value for Preferred Stocks. For certain bonds, values other than actual market may appear in this column (See Schedule D, Part 1, for details). *Companies, societies, and associations which do not amortize their bonds should leave this column blank.

The aggregate value of bonds which are valued at other than actual market is $ ....

SCHEDULE D—Verification Between Years

1. Book value of bonds and stocks, per Items 1 and 2, Col. 1, Exhibit 13, previous year . . . . ________
2. Cost of bonds and stocks acquired, Col. 5, Part 3 . . . ________
3. Increase by adjustment in book value: DETAILS OMITTED
   - (a) Col. 10, Part 1 . . . . ________
   - (b) Col. 9, Part 2, Sec. 1 . ________
   - (c) Col. 8, Part 2, Sec. 2 . ________
   - (d) Col. 9, Part 4 . . . . ________ ________
4. Profit on disposal of bonds and stocks, Col. 11, Part 4 ________
5. Total . . . . ________
6. Deduct consideration for bonds and stocks disposed of, Col. 5, Part 4 . . . . ________
7. Decrease by adjustment in book value:
   - (a) Col. 11, Part 1 . . . . ________
   - (b) Col. 10, Part 2, Sec. 1 . ________
   - (c) Col. 9, Part 2, Sec. 2 . ________
   - (d) Col. 10, Part 4 . . . . ________ ________
8. Loss on disposal of bonds and stocks, Col. 12, Part 4 . . . . ________
9. Book value of bonds and stocks, per Items 1 and 2, Col. 1, Exhibit 13, current year . . . . ________

FORM FOR CALCULATING MANDATORY SECURITIES VALUATION RESERVE
(Section 5(D) of NAIC's Valuation of Securities Procedures and Instructions for Bonds and Stocks)
DATA FROM ANNUAL STATEMENT OF BONDS AND STOCKS OWNED
(000 OMITTED)

Bond and Preferred Stock Reserve Component

Bond and Preferred Stock Component as of December 31 of preceding year (RESTATED) .... 6,124 A

Maximum Bond and Preferred Stock Component as of December 31 of preceding year 9,720 A.1

Ratio of component to maximum component (Line A ÷ Line A.1, carried to three decimals) .... .630 A.2

Maximum and annual increment for current year:

	(a) Statement Value	Maximum (b) Reserve Factor	Maximum (c) Amount		Annual Increment (d) Reserve Factor	Annual Increment (e) Amount (a) x (d)	
Bonds in 2% maximum reserve class	448,140	.02	8,963		.001	448	B.1
Bonds in 10% maximum reserve class	4,280	.10	428		.005	21	B.2
Bonds in 20% maximum reserve class	3,970	.20	794		.020	79	B.3
Preferred stocks in 5% maximum reserve class	2,860	.05	14		.0025	7	B.4
Preferred stocks in 20% maximum reserve class		.20			.010		B.5
Totals	459,250		10,199	B6.1		555	B.6

Annual accumulation factor (See Section 5(C)(a) for limitations on companies in business less than five years) .... 1.0 C

If Ratio On Line A.2 is	Accumulation Factor
0 — .249	3.0
.250 — .499	2.0
.500 — .749	1.0
.750 — .999	.5
1.000 or more	0

Required annual accumulation for the year (Line B.6 times Line C) .... 555 D

Net current year realized and unrealized capital gains (losses) permitted in the Bond and Preferred Stock Reserve Component (See Section 5(A)(b) Paragraphs (1-4) for limitations) .... 110 E

Voluntary additions for the current year (See Section 5(A)(c) for limitations). Do not include any amount which would make component greater than maximum:

Transferred from the common stock component F.1

Other voluntary additions F.2

Total voluntary additions to the Bond and Preferred Stock component (F.1 + F.2) F.3

Preliminary reserve component (Line A plus Line D plus Line E plus Line F.3) .... 6,789 G

Minus adjustment (down to maximum) (if Line G is greater than Line B6.1, enter the difference; otherwise enter "None") .... H

Bond and Preferred Stock Reserve Component, December 31 of current year (Line G minus Line H; if negative enter "None") .... 6,789 I

Common Stock Reserve Component

Common Stock Reserve Component as of December 31 of preceding year .... 176 J

Maximum Common Stock Reserve Component as of December 31 of preceding year 8,320 J.1

Ratio of component to maximum component (Line J ÷ Line J.1, carried to three decimals) .... .021 J.2

Statement value of common stocks (including $______, statement value of shares of controlled or affiliated companies valued under Section 4(B), but excluding $______, statement value of shares of certain wholly owned life insurance subsidiaries—see Section 5(B)) .... 25,654 K

Maximum Common Stock Reserve Component as of December 31 of current year (Maximum is 20% of shares of subsidiary, controlled or affiliated companies valued under Section 4(B)(a)(i) or 4(B)(a)(iii), included in Line K above, plus 33⅓% of the balance of common stocks included in Line K above) .... 8,551 L

Required annual accumulation for the year (.01 × Line K) .... 256 M

Net capital gains (See Section 5(B)(6)(i) and (ii)):

Net current year realized capital gains 1,272 N.1

Net current year unrealized capital gains N.2

(If company has net realized or net unrealized capital losses, report "None" on Lines N.1 or N.2 respectively and report such capital losses on Line P.)

Excess capital losses not yet restored as of December 31 of preceding year N.3

Total (Line N.1 plus Line N.2 less Line N.3, if negative, report "None") 1,272 N.4

Optional net realized capital gains transfers (See Section 5(B)(b)(i)(iii)):

Transferred to the bond and preferred stock component O.1

Transferred to surplus O.2

Total net realized capital gains transfers (Line O.1 plus Line O.2) O.3

Net current year realized and unrealized capital loss (Enter net loss as a positive number. If company has net realized and unrealized capital gain, report "None" here and report the net capital gains on Line N.1 or Line N.2) .... P

Voluntary addition for the current year (See Section 5(B)(c) for limitation). Do not include any amount which would make the component greater than the maximum .... Q

Preliminary reserve component (Line J plus Line M plus Line N.4 plus Line Q less Line O.3 less Line P) .... 1,704 R

Adjustment down to maximum (if Line R is greater than Line L, enter the difference) .... S

Common Stock Reserve Component (Line R minus Line S) as of December 31 of current year .... 1,704 T

Excess capital losses not yet restored as of December 31 of current year (Line N.3 minus Line N.1 plus Line N.2) (if negative, report "None") U.1

Absolute value of Line R, if negative; (if positive, report "None") U.2

Sum of Lines U.1 and U.2 .... U.3

Recapitulation of Reserve Components

Bond and Preferred Stock Reserve Component (Line I above) 6,789

Common Stock Reserve Component (Line T above) 1,704

Total Mandatory Securities Valuation Reserve as of December 31 of current year (Page 3, Item 25.1 of Annual Statement) 8,493

ANNUAL STATEMENT FOR THE YEAR 19 OF THE LIFE INSURANCE COMPANY
Name

SCHEDULE D — PART 1A

Maturity Distribution of Long-term Bonds Owned December 31, Current Year at Statement Values

(1) MATURITY	(2) GOVERNMENTS SCHEDULE D (Group 1)	(3) POLITICAL SUBDIVISIONS, GOVERNMENTAL AGENCIES AND AUTHORITIES (Groups 2, 3 & 4)	(4) OTHER (Unaffiliated) (Groups 5, 6 & 7)	(5) PARENT, SUBSIDIARIES AND AFFILIATES (Group 8)	(6) TOTAL BONDS
1. 1 year or less					
2. Over 1 year through 3 years		DETAILS OMITTED			
3. Over 3 years through 5 years					
4. Over 5 years through 10 years					
5. Over 10 years through 15 years					
6. Over 15 years through 20 years					
7. Over 20 years					
8. Totals					

Bonds to be grouped in the following manner and each group arranged alphabetically
(The listing in Groups 2, 3 and 4 should be alphabetical by State.) Show sub-totals for each group.

Form 1249

1. Governments (including all obligations guaranteed by governments).
2. States, Territories and Possessions (direct and guaranteed).
3. Political Subdivisions of States, Territories and Possessions (direct and guaranteed).
4. Special revenue and special assessment obligations and all non-guaranteed obligations of agencies and authorities of governments and their political subdivisions.
5. Railroads. (unaffiliated)
6. Public Utilities. (unaffiliated)
7. Industrial and Miscellaneous. (unaffiliated)
8. Parent, Subsidiaries and Affiliates.

ANNUAL STATEMENT FOR THE YEAR 19 OF THE LIFE INSURANCE COMPANY

Name

SCHEDULE D — Part 1

Showing all Long-term BONDS Owned December 31 of Current Year

(000 OMITTED)

Supplemental columns for data concerning Amortization. SEE NOTE

(1) **DESCRIPTION		(2) INTEREST		(3) DATE OF				(4)	(5)	(6)	(7)	(8)	INTEREST		(10)	(11)	(12)	(13)	(14)	(15)	(16)	(17)	(18)
				Maturity		††Option							(9.1)	(9.2)									
CUSIP Identification ***	Give complete and accurate description of all bonds owned, including the location of all street railway and miscellaneous companies. If bonds are "serial" issues give amount maturing each year.	Rate of	*How Paid	Year	Month	Year	Call Price	BOOK VALUE	PAR VALUE	Rate Used to Obtain Market Value	§§MARKET VALUE (excluding accrued interest)	ACTUAL COST (excluding accrued interest)	Amount Due and Accrued Dec. 31 of Current Year on bonds not in default	Gross Am't Received During Year	Increase by Adjustment in Book Value During Year	Decrease by Adjustment in Book Value During Year	Amount of Interest due and accrued Dec. 31, current year, on bonds in default as to principal or interest	§NAIC Designation	Year Acquired	Effective Rate of Interest at Which Purchase Was Made	†Amortized or Investment Value Dec. 31 of Current Year	‡Increase in Amortized Value During Year	‡Decrease in Amortized Value During Year
	GOVERNMENT																						
912810BL1	US TREASURY BOND	6.5	FA	20XX	JAN			4,060	4,100	99	4,059	4,090	30	266	5						4060		
	SUB-TOTAL GOVERNMENT							24,010	24,240		23,680	23,910	690	2,100	10						24,010		
	STATES, TERRITORIES, + POSSESSIONS																						
071170FT2	STATE OF X	5.0	MN	19XX	MAR			2,140	2,320	81	1,880	2,270	10	116	5						2,140		
	SUB-TOTAL STATES + TERRITORIES							7,270	7,860		7,270	7,7[illegible]2	210	792	20						7,740		
	POLITICAL SUBDIVISIONS																						
860845BF5	CITY X ELECTRIC	10.0	JD	19XX	JUN			740	750	95	712	740	5	75	5						745		
	SUB-TOTAL POLITICAL SUBDIVISION							1,900	2,090		1,900	2,100	40	121	5						2,000		
	SPECIAL REVENUE																						
129840BBT5	X INDUSTRIAL DEVELOPMENT	9.0	MN	19XX	MAR			500	500	Amort	500	500	4	45							500		
	SUB-TOTAL SPECIAL REVENUE							4,000	4,070		3,720	3,970	10	27	3						4,000		
	INDUSTRIAL + MISCELLANEOUS																						
058925106	ATLANTIC OIL CO.	9.5	JJ	19XX	JUL			495	500	91	455	490	22	47	2						495		
	SUB-TOTAL INDUSTRIAL + MISC.							443,390	458,980		437,750	440,400	5,052	41,583	1,740	49					442,680		
	TOTAL							480,570	497,240		474,240	478,100	6,002	44,623	1,780	49					480,430		

§§Where amortized value or any value other than the market value published in the NAIC Valuation of Securities Manual is entered in Column 7, insert a symbol alongside of the amount reported.

*Insert initial letters of months in which interest is payable.

**Where a bond is payable in a foreign currency the par value and purchase price in that currency should be included as a part of the description.

***From entry in the previous year's Annual Statement if owned at that time; from the purchase confirmation (or certificate) if purchased subsequently. Leave blank for private placements.

†Perpetual bonds, bonds in default as to principal or interest and bonds not amply secured, are to be entered in this column at market value.

‡Companies which use "Amortized Values" as "Book Values" may omit entering figures in these columns, and provide the following footnote: "The increases and decreases in amortized values are the same as those shown in columns for 'Increase and Decrease by Adjustment in Book Value,' excepting as otherwise indicated."

§Insert the NAIC designation for such security printed in the NAIC Valuation of Securities Manual.

NOTE—This supplemental information, required of all Companies which amortize their bonds, is not to be used as a substitute for the information required in the preceding columns but in addition thereto.

††Show year and call price pertaining to option, if any, on which amortization is based. On bonds purchased at a premium, the maturity date or call feature producing lowest amortized value should be used.

Banks, Trust and Insurance Companies (unaffiliated)
Industrial and Miscellaneous (unaffiliated)
Parent, Subsidiaries and Affiliates

Show sub-totals for each group.

SCHEDULE D – Part 2 – Section 1

Showing all PREFERRED STOCKS *Owned December 31 of Current Year*
(000 OMITTED)

CUSIP Identification ***	(1) DESCRIPTION Give complete and accurate description of all preferred stocks owned, including redeemable options, if any, and location of all street railway, bank, trust and miscellaneous companies.	(2) NO. OF SHARES	(3) PAR VALUE PER SHARE	(4) BOOK VALUE	(5) *RATE PER SHARE	(6) STATEMENT VALUE	(6A) RATE PER SHARE USED TO OBTAIN MARKET VALUE	(6B) MARKET VALUE	(7) ACTUAL COST	DIVIDENDS (8.1) DECLARED BUT UNPAID	DIVIDENDS (8.2) AMOUNT RECEIVED DURING YEAR	(9) INCREASE BY ADJUSTMENT IN BOOK VALUE DURING YEAR	(10) DECREASE BY ADJUSTMENT IN BOOK VALUE DURING YEAR	(11) §NAIC DESIG NATION	(12) YEAR ACQUIRED
	PUBLIC UTILITIES														
604219970	COUNTY ELECTRIC SERVICE	2,000	100	200	COST	200	49.5	99	200		17			4-S	19XX
	TOTAL PREFERRED			2,860		2,860		2,160	2,860	20	240				

*Insert the word "cost" for preferred stocks in good standing valued at cost. If the company elects to value stocks purchased prior to 1965 at 1964 Annual Statement Values, enter the rate shown in the 1964 Annual Statement with a symbol alongside the figure. Insert the market rate for preferred stocks not in good standing.

***From entry in the previous year's Annual Statement if owned at that time; from the purchase confirmation (or certificate) if purchased subsequently. Leave blank for private placements.

NOTES: Complete information must be furnished in connection with any holding of preferred or common stock on the statement date which is optioned or restricted in any way as to its sale by the insurer. Identify all such securities by the symbol "R" to be inserted beside the figure shown as the rate per share to obtain market value.
Transferable shares only, of Savings and Loan or Building and Loan Associations to be reported herein.
§Insert the NAIC designation for such security printed in the NAIC Valuation of Securities Manual.

Form 1349

Stocks to be grouped in following order and each group arranged alphabetically:
Railroads. (unaffiliated)
Public Utilities. (unaffiliated)
Banks, Trust and Insurance Companies. (unaffiliated)
Industrial and Miscellaneous. (unaffiliated)
Parent, Subsidiaries and Affiliates.

Show sub-totals for each group.

ANNUAL STATEMENT FOR THE YEAR 19 OF THE LIFE INSURANCE COMPANY

Name

30B

SCHEDULE D—Part 2—Section 2

Showing all COMMON STOCKS *Owned December 31 of Current Year*

(000 Omitted)

CUSIP Identification ***	(1) DESCRIPTION Give complete and accurate description of all common stocks owned, including redeemable options, if any, and addresses (City and State) of all street railway, banks, trust and insurance companies, savings and loan or building and loan associations and miscellaneous companies.	(2) NO. OF SHARES	(3) BOOK VALUE	(4) RATE PER SHARE USED TO OBTAIN MARKET VALUE	(5) MARKET VALUE	(6) ACTUAL COST	DIVIDENDS (7 1) DECLARED BUT UNPAID	DIVIDENDS (7 2) AMOUNT RECEIVED DURING YEAR	(8) INCREASE BY ADJUSTMENT IN BOOK VALUE DURING YEAR	(9) DECREASE BY ADJUSTMENT IN BOOK VALUE DURING YEAR	(10) §NAIC DESIG-NATION	(11) YEAR ACQUIRED
PUBLIC UTILITIES												
	ABC ELECTRIC	100,000	5,000	50	5,000	5,000						19XX
INDUSTRIAL AND MISCELLANEOUS												
003724890	ART INDUSTRIES	4000	101	30	120	101		6				19XX
	SUBTOTAL INDUSTRIAL AND MISC.		18.964		20.654	18.964		1.540				
	TOTAL COMMON		23.964		25.654	23.964		1.540				
	TOTAL PREFERRED AND COMMON		26.824		27.814	26.824	20	1.780				

NOTES: Complete information must be furnished in connection with any holding of preferred or common stock on the statement date which is optioned or restricted in any way as to its sale by the insurer.
Identify all such securities by the symbol "R" to be inserted beside the figure shown as the rate per share to obtain market value.

***From entry in the previous year's Annual Statement if owned at that time; from the purchase confirmation (or certificate) if purchased subsequently. Leave blank for private placements.
§Insert the NAIC designation for such security printed in the NAIC Valuation of Securities Manual

Form 1249

ANNUAL STATEMENT FOR THE YEAR 19 OF THE LIFE INSURANCE COMPANY

Name

Bonds, preferred stocks and common stocks to be grouped separately showing sub-totals for each group

SCHEDULE D — Part 3

Showing all Long-term Bonds and Stocks ACQUIRED During the Current Year

(000 OMITTED)

CUSIP Identification ***	(1) DESCRIPTION§ Give complete and accurate description of each bond and stock, including location of all street railway, bank, trust and miscellaneous companies.††	(2) DATE ACQUIRED*	(3) NAME OF VENDOR*	(4) NO. OF SHARES OF STOCK	(5) ACTUAL COST (Excluding Accrued Interest and Dividends)	(6) PAR VALUE OF BONDS	(7) PAID FOR ACCRUED INTEREST AND DIVIDENDS
	PREFERRED STOCK						
	DETAILS OMITTED						
					170	175	10

*The items with reference to each issue of bonds and stocks acquired at public offerings may be totaled in one line and the word "Various" inserted in Columns 2 and 3.
§Enter as a summary item the totals of Columns 6, 7 and 15 of Part 5. All bonds and stocks acquired and fully disposed of during the year are not to be itemized in this Part.

***From entry in the previous year's Annual Statement if owned at that time; from the purchase confirmation (or certificate) if purchased subsequently. Leave blank for private placements.
††If bonds are serial issues give amounts maturing each year. Securities acquired under a reverse repurchase agreement must be identified.

Form 1249

Bonds, preferred stocks and common stocks to be grouped separately showing sub-totals for each group.

ANNUAL STATEMENT FOR THE YEAR 19 OF THE LIFE INSURANCE COMPANY

Name

SCHEDULE D—Part 4

Showing all Long-term Bonds and Stocks SOLD, REDEEMED or Otherwise DISPOSED OF During the Current Year

(000 OMITTED)

(1) DESCRIPTION‡ CUSIP Identification ***	(1) DESCRIPTION‡ Give complete and accurate description of each bond and stock, including location of all street railway, bank, trust and miscellaneous companies.††	(2) DISPOSAL DATE**	(3) NAME OF PURCHASER (If matured or called under redemption option, so state and give price at which called.)	(4) NO. OF SHARES OF STOCK	(5) CONSIDERATION (Excluding Accrued Interest and Dividends)	(6) PAR VALUE OF BONDS	(7) ACTUAL COST (Excluding Accrued Interest and Dividends)	(8) BOOK VALUE AT DISPOSAL DATE	(9) INCREASE BY ADJUSTMENT IN BOOK VALUE DURING YEAR	(10) DECREASE BY ADJUSTMENT IN BOOK VALUE DURING YEAR	(11) PROFIT ON DISPOSAL	(12) LOSS ON DISPOSAL	(13) INTEREST ON BONDS RECEIVED DURING YEAR†	(14) DIVIDENDS ON STOCKS RECEIVED DURING YEAR†
BONDS														
		DETAILS	OMITTED											
					XXX	XXX	XXX	XXX	10	10	1,160	350	20	
PREFERRED STOCK														
		DETAILS	OMITTED											
					XXX		XXX	XXX	—	—	320	40		10
COMMON STOCK														
		DETAILS	OMITTED											
					XXX		XXX	XXX	—	—	1,920	260		

‡Enter as a summary item the totals of Columns 6 to 14 of Part 5. All bonds and stocks acquired and fully disposed of during the year are not to be itemized in this Part.
**Companies may at their option summarize all bonds of the same issue called, matured or redeemed during the year and omit disposal dates.
***From entry in the previous year's Annual Statement if owned at that time; from the purchase confirmation (or certificate) if purchased subsequently. Leave blank for private placements.

†Including accrued interest and dividends on bonds and stocks disposed of.
††If bonds are serial issues give amounts maturing each year.
Securities sold under a reverse repurchase agreement must be identified.

Form 1249

ANNUAL STATEMENT FOR THE YEAR 19 OF THE LIFE INSURANCE COMPANY

Name

Bonds, preferred stocks and common stocks to be grouped separately showing sub-totals for each group

SCHEDULE D – Part 5

Showing all Long-term Bonds and Stocks ACQUIRED During the Current Year and Fully DISPOSED OF During the Current Year

(1) DESCRIPTION		(2)	(3)	(4)	(5)	(6)	(7)	(8)	(9)	(10)	(11)	(12)	(13)	(14)	(15)
CUSIP Identification ***	Give complete and accurate description of each bond and stock, including location of all street railway, bank, trust and miscellaneous companies.††	DATE ACQUIRED*	NAME OF VENDOR*	DISPOSAL DATE**	NAME OF PURCHASER (If matured or called under redemption option, so state and give price at which called.)	PAR VALUE (BONDS) OR NUMBER OF SHARES (STOCKS)	COST TO COMPANY (Excluding Accrued Interest and Dividends)	CONSIDERATION (Excluding Accrued Interest and Dividends)	BOOK VALUE AT DISPOSAL DATE	INCREASE BY ADJUSTMENT IN BOOK VALUE DURING YEAR	DECREASE BY ADJUSTMENT IN BOOK VALUE DURING YEAR	PROFIT ON DISPOSAL	LOSS ON DISPOSAL	INTEREST AND DIVIDENDS RECEIVED DURING YEAR†	PAID FOR ACCRUED INTEREST AND DIVIDENDS
					NONE										

*The items with reference to each issue of bonds and stocks acquired at public offerings may be totaled in one line and the word "Various" inserted in Columns 2 and 3

**Companies may at their option summarize all bonds of the same issue called, matured or redeemed during the year and omit disposal dates

***From entry in the previous year's Annual Statement if owned at that time, from the purchase confirmation (or certificate) if purchased subsequently. Leave blank for private placements

†Including accrued interest and dividends on bonds and stocks disposed of

††If bonds are serial issues give amounts maturing each year

Securities acquired or disposed of under a reverse repurchase agreement must be identified

SCHEDULE D – PART 6 – Section 1

Questionnaire Relating to the Valuation of Shares of Certain Subsidiary, Controlled or Affiliated Companies

(1) Name of Subsidiary, Controlled or Affiliated Company	(2) Do Insurer's Admitted Assets Include Intangible Assets Connected with Holding of Such Company's Stock?	(3) If Yes, Amount of Such Intangible Assets	Common Stock of Such Compa[ny] Owned by Insurer on Statemen[t] Date	
			(4) No. of Shares	(5) % of Outsta[nding]
SUPPLEMENTARY INFORMATION				
	Total		X X X X	X X X

Amount of Insurer's Capital and Surplus (Page 3, Item 30 of previous year's statement filed by the insurer with its domiciliary insurance department): $

SCHEDULE D – PART 6 – Section 2

(1) Name of Lower-tier Company	(2) Name of Company Listed in Section 1 which controls Lower-tier Company	(3) Amount of Intangible Assets Included in Amount Shown in Column (3), Section 1	Common Stock of Lower-ti[er] Company Owned Indirectly [by] Insurer on Statement Dat[e]	
			(4) No. of Shares	(5) % of Outs[tanding]
SUPPLEMENTARY INFORMATION				
	Total		X X X X	X X

Form 1249

ANNUAL STATEMENT FOR THE YEAR 19 OF THE LIFE INSURANCE COMPANY
Name

SCHEDULE DA – PART 1

Showing All SHORT-TERM INVESTMENTS† *Owned December 31 of Current Year*

(000 OMITTED)

(1) DESCRIPTION**		(2)	(3)	(4) §INTEREST		(5) §DATE OF MATURITY		(6)	(7)	(8)	(9)	(10)	(11)	(12) INTEREST		(13)	(14)	(15)
CUSIP Identification ***	Give complete and accurate description of all investments owned, including identifying the kind of investment vehicle if other than short term bond.	§DATE ACQUIRED	§NAME OF VENDOR	Rate Of	*How Paid	Year	Month	BOOK VALUE	INCREASE (+) OR DECREASE (−) BY ADJUSTMENT IN BOOK VALUE DURING YEAR	PAR VALUE	RATE USED TO OBTAIN STATEMENT VALUE	STATEMENT VALUE (Excluding Accrued Interest)	ACTUAL COST (Excluding Accrued Interest)	Amount Due and Accrued Dec. 31 of Current Year on Bonds not in default	Gross Amount Received	PAID FOR ACCRUED INTEREST	NAIC DESIG NATION ††	EFFECTIVE RATE OF INTEREST AT WHICH PURCHASE WAS MADE §
			DETAILS OMITTED															
												25,273		310				
									†††									

* Insert initial letters of months in which interest is payable
** Where an investment is payable in a foreign currency, the par value and the purchase price in that currency should be included as a part of the description
*** From the purchase confirmation (or certificate). Leave blank for private placements
† Include all investments whose maturities (or repurchase dates under Repurchase Agreements) at time of acquisition were one year or less. Identify "Repos" and certificates of deposit in Column 1 and for "Repos", show repurchase date

†† Insert the NAIC designation for such security printed in the NAIC Valuation of Securities Manual
††† Includes $ other than accrual of discount and amortization of premium
§ Purchases of various issues of the same issuer of short term investments may be totalled on one line and the word "various" inserted in the columns

31B

Form 1249

ANNUAL STATEMENT FOR THE YEAR 19 OF THE LIFE INSURANCE COMPANY

Name

31C

SCHEDULE DA—PART 2

Verification of SHORT-TERM INVESTMENTS between Years

	(1) TOTAL*	(2) BONDS	(3) COLLATERAL LOANS	(4) MORTGAGE LOANS	(5) OTHER SHORT TERM INVESTMENT ASSETS**	(6) INVESTMENTS IN PARENT SUBSIDIARIES AND AFFILIATES
1. Book value, previous year						
2. Cost of short-term investments acquired						
3. Increase by adjustment in book value	DETAILS	OMITTED				
4. Profit on disposal of short-term investments						
5. Subtotals (Total of Items 2 to 4)						
6. Consideration received on disposal of short-term investments						
7. Decrease by adjustment in book value						
8. Loss on disposal of short-term investments						
9. Subtotals (Total of Items 6 to 8)						
10. Book value, current year						

*Column (1) amounts equal the sum of Columns (2) through (6); Column (1), Line 10 equals Part 1, Column (6), total

**Indicate the category of such assets, for example, joint ventures, transportation equipment

Form 1249

ANNUAL STATEMENT FOR THE YEAR 19 OF THE LIFE INSURANCE COMPANY
Name

Separate financial options into 2 groups, put options and call options; within each group, show separately fixed income, equity and other financial options. Show subtotals for each group and category.

SCHEDULE DB – PART A – Section 1

Showing All Financial Options Owned December 31 of Current Year

(1) DESCRIPTION OF ALL FINANCIAL OPTIONS OWNED INCLUDING DESCRIPTION OF UNDERLYING SECURITY(S) OR CONTRACT(S)	(2) EXPIRATION DATE	(3) EXERCISE PRICE	(4) INDICATION OF EXISTENCE OF HEDGE*	(5) DATE ACQUIRED	(6) ACTUAL COST	(7) INCREASE/DECREASE BY ADJUSTMENT IN BOOK VALUE	(8) BOOK VALUE	(9) MARKET VALUE	(10) STATEMENT VALUE	(11) GAIN/(LOSS)	
										(a) Recognized	(b) Deferred
					NONE						
Grand Totals	XXX	XXX	XXX	XXX							

SCHEDULE DB – PART A – Section 2

Showing All Financial Options Acquired During Current Year

(1) DESCRIPTION OF ALL FINANCIAL OPTIONS ACQUIRED INCLUDING DESCRIPTION OF UNDERLYING SECURITY(S) OR CONTRACT(S)	(2) EXPIRATION DATE	(3) EXERCISE PRICE	(4) INDICATION OF EXISTENCE OF HEDGE*	(5) NAME OF VENDOR	(6) DATE ACQUIRED	(7) ACTUAL COST
		NONE				
Grand Total	XXX	XXX	XXX	XXX	XXX	

*Has a comprehensive description of the hedge program been made available to the domiciliary state?
If not, attach a description with this statement.

Form 1249

ANNUAL STATEMENT FOR THE YEAR 19 OF THE LIFE INSURANCE COMPANY

Name

Separate financial options into 2 groups, put options and call options; within each group, show separately fixed income, equity and other financial options. Show subtotals for each group and category.

SCHEDULE DB – PART A – Section 3

Showing All Financial Options Terminated During Current Year

(1) Description of Financial Options Terminated, Including Description of Underlying Security(s) or Contract(s)	(2) Expiration Date	(3) Exercise Price	(4) Indicate Exercise Expiration or Sale	(5) Date Acquired	(6) Date Terminated	(7) Actual Cost	(8) Increase/Decrease by Adjustment in Book Value During Year	(9) Book Value at Termination Date	(10) Consideration Received on Termination	(11) Premiums Allocated to Purchase Cost or Sale Proceeds on Exercise	(12) Gain/(Loss) on Termination		
											(a) Deferred	(b) Recognized	(c) Used to adjust basis of hedge
						NONE							
Grand Totals	X X X	X X X	X X X	X X X	X X X								

SCHEDULE DB – PART A – Section 4

Verification Between Years of Book Value of Financial Options Owned

1. Book value of options owned, December 31, previous year (Sec. 4, Line 7, previous year) . . . . . . ________
2. Cost of options acquired (Sec. 2, Col. 7) . . . . . . ________
3. Increase/(decrease) by adjustment in book value of options (Sum of Sec. 1, Col. 7 and Sec. 3, Col. 8) . . . . . . ________
4. Deduct (gain)/loss on termination of options:
   - (a) deferred (Sec. 3, Col. 12a) . . . . . . ________
   - (b) recognized (Sec. 3, Col. 12b) . . . . . . ________
   - (c) used to adjust basis of hedge (Sec. 3, Col. 12c) . . . . . . ________ ________
5. Deduct consideration received on termination of options (Sec. 3, Col. 10) . . . . . . ________
6. Deduct premiums allocated to purchase cost or sale proceeds on exercise (Sec. 3, Col. 11) . . . . . . ________
7. Book value of options owned, December 31, current year (Sec. 1, Col. 8, current year) . . . . . . ________

Form 1249

Separate financial options into 2 groups, put options and call options; within each group, show separately fixed income, equity and other financial options. Show subtotals for each group and category.

ANNUAL STATEMENT FOR THE YEAR 19 OF THE LIFE INSURANCE COMPANY

Name

SCHEDULE DB – PART B – Section 1

Showing All Financial Options Written and in Force December 31 of Current Year

(1) Description of Financial Options Written and in Force, Including Description of Underlying Security(s) or Contract(s)	(2) XX	(3) Expiration Date	(4) Exercise Price	(5) Indication of Existence of Hedge*	(6) Date Issued	(7) Consideration Received	(8) Market Value	(9) Statement Value	(10) Gain(Loss) (a) Recognized	(10) Gain(Loss) (b) Deferred
				NONE						
Grand Totals	XXX	XXX	XXX	XXX	XXX					

SCHEDULE DB – PART B – Section 2

Showing All Financial Options Written During Current Year

(1) Description of All Financial Options Issued, Including Description of Underlying Security(s) or Contract(s)	(2) XX	(3) Expiration Date	(4) Exercise Price	(5) Indication of Existence of Hedge*	(6) Date Issued	(7) Consideration Received
			NONE			
Grand Total	XXX	XXX	XXX	XXX	XXX	

*Has a comprehensive description of the hedge program been made available to the domiciliary state? .... If not, attach a description with this statement.

XX If a call option, indicate "no" if the underlying investment was not owned at the time option was written; otherwise leave blank.

31F

Form 1249

ANNUAL STATEMENT FOR THE YEAR 19 OF THE LIFE INSURANCE COMPANY
Name

Separate financial options into 2 groups, put options and call options; within each group, show separately fixed income, equity and other financial options. Show subtotals for each group and category

SCHEDULE DB – PART B – Section 3

Showing All Financial Options Written That Were Terminated During Current Year

(1) DESCRIPTION OF ALL FINANCIAL OPTIONS TERMINATED INCLUDING DESCRIPTION OF UNDERLYING SECURITY(S) OR CONTRACT(S)	(2) EXPIRATION DATE	(3) EXERCISE PRICE	(4) DATE ISSUED	(5) DATE TERMINATED	(6) INDICATION OF EXERCISE, EXPIRATION OR CLOSING PURCHASE TRANSACTION	(7) CONSIDERATION RECEIVED	(8) COST OF TERMINATION	(9) PREMIUMS ALLOCATED TO PURCHASE COST OR SALE PROCEEDS ON EXERCISE	(10) GAIN/(LOSS) ON TERMINATION		
									(a) Deferred	(b) Recognized	(c) Used to adjust basis of hedge
					NONE						
Grand Totals $	XXX	XXX	XXX	XXX	XXX						

SCHEDULE DB – PART B – Section 4

Verification Between Years of Consideration Received for Financial Options Written

1. Consideration received for financial options written and outstanding, previous year (Sec. 4, Line 6, previous year) . . . . ________
2. Consideration received for options written during year (Sec. 2, Col. 7) . . . . ________
3. Deduct cost of terminating options by closing purchase transaction during year (Sec. 3, Col. 8) . . . . ________
4. Deduct gain/(loss) on termination:
   - (a) deferred (Sec. 3, Col. 10a) . . . . ________
   - (b) recognized (Sec. 3, Col. 10b) . . . . ________
   - (c) used to adjust basis of hedge (Sec. 3, Col. 10c) . . . . ________ ________
5. Deduct premiums allocated to purchase cost or sale proceeds on exercise (Sec. 3, Col. 9) . . . . ________
6. Consideration received for financial options written and outstanding, current year (Sec. 1, Col. 7, current year) . . . . ________

Separate financial futures contracts into 2 groups, long positions and short positions; within each group, show separately interest rate futures and other financial futures contracts. Show subtotals for each group and category.

ANNUAL STATEMENT FOR THE YEAR 19 OF THE *LIFE INSURANCE COMPANY*
Name

SCHEDULE DB – PART C – Section 1

Showing All Financial Futures Contracts Open December 31 of Current Year

(1) DESCRIPTION OF ALL FINANCIAL FUTURES CONTRACTS OPEN	(2) NUMBER OF CONTRACTS	(3) DATE OF MATURITY	(4) INDICATION OF EXISTENCE OF HEDGE*	(5) XX	(6) FUTURES CONTRACTS			(7) MARGIN INFORMATION		
									VARIANCE MARGIN	
					(a) Original Price	(b) Current Price	(c) Difference	(a) Initial Deposit Requirement	(b) Deferred Gain(Loss)	(c) Recognized Gain(Loss)
					NONE					
Grand Totals	XXX	XXX	XXX	XXX						

SCHEDULE DB – PART C – Section 2

Showing All Financial Futures Contracts Opened During Current Year

(1) DESCRIPTION OF EACH FINANCIAL FUTURES CONTRACT EXECUTED	(2) NUMBER OF CONTRACTS	(3) NAME OF VENDOR	(4) DATE OF OPENING POSITION	(5) DATE OF MATURITY	(6) XX	(7) INDICATION OF EXISTENCE OF HEDGE*	(8) ORIGINAL PRICE OF FUTURES CONTRACTS	(9) INITIAL MARGIN DEPOSIT REQUIREMENT
		NONE						
Grand Totals	XXX	XXX	XXX	XXX	XXX	XXX		

*Has a comprehensive description of the hedge program been made available to the domiciliary state? .... If not, attach a description with this statement.

XX If contract requires the company to deliver securities at the contract maturity date, indicate "no" if the underlying instruments were not owned at the time the futures contract was opened; otherwise leave blank.

Form 1249

Separate financial futures contracts into 2 groups, long positions and short positions, within each group, show separately interest rate futures and other financial futures contracts. Show subtotals for each group and category

ANNUAL STATEMENT FOR THE YEAR 19 OF THE LIFE INSURANCE COMPANY

Name

SCHEDULE DB – PART C – Section 3

Showing All Financial Futures Contracts That Were Terminated During Current Year

(1) DESCRIPTION OF EACH FINANCIAL FUTURES CONTRACT TERMINATED	(2) NUMBER OF CONTRACTS	(3) DATE OF TERMINATION	(4) INDICATION OF EXISTENCE OF HEDGE*	(5) FUTURES CONTRACTS (a) Original Price	(b) Closing Transaction Price	(c) Gain/(Loss) on Termination	(6) MARGIN INFORMATION (a) Gain/(Loss) Utilized to Adjust Basis of Hedge	(b) Gain/(Loss) Recognized in Current Year	(c) Gain/(Loss) Deferred Over Year End
				NONE					
Grand Totals	X X X	X X X	X X X						

*Has a comprehensive description of the hedge program been made available to the domiciliary state? ....
If not, attach a description with this statement.

SCHEDULE DB – PART C – Section 4

Verification Between Years of Deferred Gain/(Loss) on Financial Futures Contracts

1. Deferred gain/(loss), December 31, previous year (Sec. 4, Line 6, previous year) ....
2. Change in deferred gain/(loss) on open contracts (Difference between years – Sec. 1, Col. 7b) ....
3. a. Gain/(loss) on contracts terminated during the year (Sec. 3, Col. 5c) ....
   b. Less:
      (i) Gain/(loss) used to adjust basis of hedge (Sec. 3, Col. 6a) ....
      (ii) Gain/(loss) recognized in current year (Sec. 3, Col. 6b) ....
      (iii) Subtotal (Line 3b(i) plus 3b(ii)) ....
   c. Subtotal (Line 3a minus Line 3b(iii)) ....
4. Subtotal (Line 1 + Line 2 + Line 3c) ....
5. Less:
   Disposition of gain/(loss) on contracts terminated in prior years:
   (a) recognized ....
   (b) used to adjust basis of hedge ....
6. Deferred gain/(loss), December 31, current year (Line 4 minus Line 5) ....

Form 1

ANNUAL STATEMENT FOR THE YEAR 19 OF THE LIFE INSURANCE COMPANY
Name

SCHEDULE E

Showing all Banks, Trust Companies, Savings and Loan and Building and Loan Associations in which a deposit was maintained at any time during the year, with Balances, if any, at December 31 of Current Year (according to Company's records) and showing Largest Balance Carried in Each Month of the Current Year in Each Bank, Trust Company, Savings and Loan or Building and Loan Association in which the Largest Balance during the Year exceeded 1/40% of Admitted Assets, January 1, or $500,000, whichever is smaller. (Any other items to be shown where required by Statute.) Exclude balances represented by a negotiable instrument.

(1) DEPOSITORY* (Give Full Name and Location. State if depository is a parent, subsidiary or affiliate.) Show rate of interest and maturity date in the case of certificates of deposit or time deposits maturing more than one year from statement date.	(2) BALANCE December 31 of Current Year	(3) Rate of Interest	(4) Amount of Interest Received During Year	(5) Amount of Interest Accrued Dec. 31 of Current Year	(6) JANUARY	(7) FEBRUARY	(8) MARCH	(9) APRIL	(10) MAY	(11) JUNE	(12) JULY	(13) AUGUST	(14) SEPTEMBER	(15) OCTOBER	(16) NOVEMBER	(17) DECEMBER
OPEN DEPOSITORIES																
SUPPLEMENTARY INFORMATION																
Grand Totals		XXX			XXX	XXX	XXX	XXX	XXX	XXX	XXX	XXX	XXX	XXX	XXX	XXX

*In each case where the depository is not incorporated and subject to governmental supervision, the word "PRIVATE" in capitals and in parentheses, thus—(PRIVATE), should be inserted to the left of the name of the depository.
Any deposit in a suspended depository which is taken credit for should have a star placed opposite the amount in the schedule.
Deposits in federally insured depositories not exceeding $40,000 may be combined and reported in opposite the caption "Deposits in (insert number) depositories which do not exceed the $40,000 amount in any one depository".

Short-term certificates of deposit to be reported in Schedule DA.
Long-term negotiable certificates of deposit to be reported in Schedule D.

SCHEDULE F

**Showing all claims for death losses and all other policy claims resisted or compromised during the year, and all claims for death losses and all other policy claims resisted December 31 of current year*

(1) POLICY NUMBERS	(2) CLAIM NUMBERS	(3) STATE OF RESIDENCE OF CLAIMANT	(4) YEAR OF CLAIM FOR DEATH OR DISABILITY	(5) AMOUNT CLAIMED	(6) AMOUNT PAID DURING THE YEAR	(7) AMOUNT RESISTED DEC. 31 OF CURRENT YEAR	(8) WHY COMPROMISED OR RESISTED
		SUPPLEMENTARY INFORMATION					
			Totals				X X X

*Claims under Accident and Health policies need not be reported in this schedule. All other claims should be classified and reported in the following sub-divisions:
(a) Claims disposed of during current year. (b) Claims resisted. In each of the above sections, Death claims, Additional Accidental Death Benefit claims, Disability Benefit claims, Matured Endowment claims and Annuities with Life Contingencies claims, should be listed separately with sub-totals for each group. (c) Classify separately as between Ordinary, Credit, Group and Industrial.

SCHEDULE G

Showing (1) all payments in excess of $1,000 to each Trade Association, Service Organization, Statistical, Actuarial or Rating Bureau or Organization during the year; and (2) all salaries, compensation and emoluments, except bonafide commissions paid to or retained by agents, received in the current year by: (a) each director or trustee regardless of the amount thereof, (b) each of the ten officers or employees receiving the largest amounts, (Include in this schedule the aggregate amount received by the officer or employee attributable to his services to the reporting insurer whether paid directly by the insurer or by related or affiliated companies), and (c) any other person, firm or corporation if the amount received was in excess of $60,000 except for amounts included in Schedules I, J and K. (Any other amounts to be shown where required by statute.)

LIST ITEMS UNDER (1) AND (2) IN SEPARATE GROUPINGS

(1) TITLE	(2) NAME OF PAYEE	(3) LOCATION OF PAYEE	(4) AMOUNT PAID
	SUPPLEMENTARY INFORMATION		
		Total	

SCHEDULE H—ACCIDENT AND HEALTH EXHIBIT

	(1) TOTAL		(2) GROUP ACCIDENT AND HEALTH		(3) CREDIT* (Group and Individual)		(4) COLLECTIVELY RENEWABLE		OTHER INDIVIDUAL POLICIES									
									(5) NON-CANCELLABLE		(6) GUARANTEED RENEWABLE		(7) NON-RENEWABLE FOR STATED REASONS ONLY		(8) OTHER ACCIDENT ONLY		(9) ALL OTHER	
	Amount	%†	Amount	%†	Amount	%†	Amount	%†	Amount	%†	Amount	%†	Amount	%†	Amount	%†	Amount	%†
PART 1. ANALYSIS OF UNDERWRITING OPERATIONS																		
1 Premiums written																		
2. Premiums earned (see note b)																		
3. Incurred claims																		
4. Increase in policy reserves																		
5. Commissions*																		
6. General insurance expenses																		
7 Taxes, licenses and fees																		
8. Total expenses incurred																		
9. Gain from underwriting before dividends to policyholders																		
10 Dividends to policyholders																		
11 Gain from underwriting after dividends to policyholders																		
PART 2. RESERVES AND LIABILITIES																		
A. PREMIUM RESERVES:																		
1 Unearned premiums																		
2. Advance premiums																		
3 Reserve for rate credits																		
4. Total premium reserves, current year																		
5 Total premium reserves, previous year																		
6. Increase in total premium reserves																		
B. POLICY RESERVES:																		
1 Additional reserves																		
2 Reserve for future contingent benefits (deferred maternity and other similar benefits)**																		
3 Total policy reserves, current year																		
4. Total policy reserves, previous year																		
5 Increase in policy reserves																		
C. CLAIM RESERVES AND LIABILITIES:																		
1 Total current year																		
2 Total previous year																		
3 Increase																		
PART 3. TEST OF PREVIOUS YEAR'S CLAIM RESERVES AND LIABILITIES																		
1 CLAIMS PAID DURING THE YEAR:																		
a. On claims incurred prior to current year																		
b. On claims incurred during current year																		
2 CLAIM RESERVES AND LIABILITIES, DEC. 31, CURRENT YEAR:																		
a. On claims incurred prior to current year																		
b. On claims incurred during current year																		
3. TEST:																		
a. Line 1a and 2a																		
b. Claim reserves and liabilities, Dec. 31, previous year																		
c. Line a minus Line b																		
PART 4. REINSURANCE																		
A. REINSURANCE ASSUMED:																		
1. Premiums written																		
2. Premiums earned (see note b)																		
3. Incurred claims																		
4. Commissions																		
B. REINSURANCE CEDED:																		
1. Premiums written																		
2. Premiums earned (see note b)																		
3. Incurred claims																		
4 Commissions																		

DETAILS OMITTED

* Business not exceeding 120 months duration.
† In each column of Part 1, show the percentages of Line 2 for Lines 3 through 11 inclusive.

* Includes $............ reported as "Policy, membership and other fees retained by agents."
** If not included in claim reserves.
(b) Premiums earned are before adjustment for the increase in policy reserves which has been treated as a separate deduction.

SCHEDULE I

Showing all commissions and collection fees paid in connection with loans or properties during the year where the same amounted to more than $10,000 to any person, firm or corporation

PAYEE		WHAT ACQUIRED OR DISPOSED OF		(5) AMOUNT OF COMMISSION PAID
(1) NAME	(2) ADDRESS	(3) DESCRIPTION	(4) AMOUNT INVOLVED	
SUPPLEMENTARY INFORMATION				

SCHEDULE J

Showing in detail all legal expenses paid during the year (List individually all items of $5,000 or more)

PAYEE		(3) AMOUNT PAID	(4) OCCASION OF EXPENSE
(1) NAME	(2) ADDRESS		
SUPPLEMENTARY INFORMATION			
	Total of all other items		X X X X
	Grand Total		X X X X

SCHEDULE K

Showing all expenditures in connection with matters before legislative bodies, officers or departments of government during the year
(Items of less than $500 may be grouped unless prohibited by statute)

PAYEE		(3) AMOUNT PAID	(4) MEASURE OR PROCEEDING	(5) INTEREST OF THE COMPANY THEREIN
(1) NAME	(2) ADDRESS			
	Supplementary Information			
Total of all other items			X X X	X X X
Grand Total			X X X	X X X

SCHEDULE L

Proceedings at last annual election held on...

(1) NAME OF CANDIDATES FOR DIRECTOR OR TRUSTEE	NUMBER OF VOTES CAST FOR EACH CANDIDATE			(5) TOTAL VOTE
	(2) IN PERSON	(3) BY PROXY	(4) BY MAIL	
Supplementary Information				
Totals				

NOTE—Attach to this schedule a copy of the official minutes of annual meeting.

Name ....

SCHEDULE M – PART 1

Dividends Actually Paid On Policies Issued Twenty Years Prior To Year of Statement (Year of Issue 19........)

All Figures Per $1,000 Face Amount of Individual Life Insurance

(1) Description of Policy	(2) Age At Issue	(3) Amount *	Gross Premium** (4) Initial Premium	(5) Next Premium	(6) Ultimate Premium	Dividends Actually Paid In Policy Years (7) 1	(8) 2	(9) 3	(10) 4	(11) 5	(12) 6	(13) 7	(14) 8	(15) 9	(16) 10	(17) 11	(18) 12	(19) 13	(20) 14	(21) 15	(22) 16	(23) 17	(24) 18	(25) 19	(26) 20	(27) 20th Year Cash Value	(28) 20th Year Terminal Dividend *****	(29) 10th Year Cash Value	(30) 10th Year Terminal Dividend *****
Plans With Premiums Payable For Life																													
Ordinary Life	25																												
	35																												
	45																												
	55																												
***	25																												
	35																												
	45																												
	55																												
***	25																												
	35																												
	45																												
	55																												
Limited Payment Life Plans																													
Twenty Payment Life	25																												
	35																												
	45																												
	55																												
Life Paid Up at Age	25																												
	35																												
	45																												
	55																												
***	25																												
	35																												
	45																												
	55																												
***	25																												
	35																												
	45																												
	55																												
***	25																												
	35																												
	45																												
	55																												

DETAILS OMITTED

* When size bands, constant add-on factors or other methods of gradation by size of policy are used, show figures for both $10,000 and $25,000 policies and each such amount in this column followed by "G". Otherwise, show figures for policies issued for minimum amounts (if issued) and each such amount in this column followed by "M".

** Male premiums to be shown. Exclude charge for additional benefits. If such charge is not separable, attach description of the additional benefits included and list approximate yearly value of these for each plan and issue age. State adjustments for Female premiums.
For modified premium plans, indicate number of years each premium is payable in parentheses after the premium.
For level premium plans, enter premium in the "Ultimate Premium" column.

*** Information should be shown for any other plan with a volume (face amount of insurance) issued twenty years prior to statement year of 5% or more of total written business (individual policies) for year.

***** If terminal dividends are not payable until a policy year later than the 10th or 20th, enter amount of terminal dividend for earliest policy year payable and enter such policy year in parentheses after amount of terminal dividend.

NOTE: Attach to this schedule explanation showing precise methods by which dividends were calculated.

If no policies have been issued which are in their twentieth or succeeding policy years, data must be shown in this Schedule for policies issued less than twenty years for the maximum period such policies have been in force.

ANNUAL STATEMENT FOR THE YEAR 19 OF THE LIFE INSURANCE COMPANY
Name

SCHEDULE M—PART 1—(Continued)

Dividends Actually Paid On Policies Issued Twenty Years Prior To Year of Statement (Year of Issue 19.......)

All Figures Per $1,000 Face Amount of Individual Life Insurance

(1) Description of Policy	(2) Age At Issue	(3) Amount *	Gross Premium**			Dividends Actually Paid In Policy Years																				(27) 20th Year Cash Value	(28) 20th Year Terminal Dividend *****	(29) 10th Year Cash Value	(30) 10th Year Terminal Dividend *****
			(4) Initial Premium	(5) Next Premium	(6) Ultimate Premium	(7) 1	(8) 2	(9) 3	(10) 4	(11) 5	(12) 6	(13) 7	(14) 8	(15) 9	(16) 10	(17) 11	(18) 12	(19) 13	(20) 14	(21) 15	(22) 16	(23) 17	(24) 18	(25) 19	(26) 20				
Term Plans																													
....Year Term or Term To Age.... (cross out one)	25																												
	35																												
	45																												
	55																												
***........................	25																												
	35																												
	45																												
	55																												
Other Plans****																													
***........................	25																												
	35																												
	45																												
	55																												
***........................	25																												
	35																												
	45																												
	55																												
***........................	25																												
	35																												
	45																												
	55																												
***........................	25																												
	35																												
	45																												
	55																												
***........................	25																												
	35																												
	45																												
	55																												
***........................	25																												
	35																												
	45																												
	55																												

DETAILS OMITTED

* When size bands, constant add-on factors or other methods of gradation by size of policy are used, show figures for both $10,000 and $25,000 policies and each such amount in this column followed by "G". Otherwise, show figures for policies issued for minimum amounts (if issued) and each such amount in this column followed by "M".

** Male premiums to be shown. Exclude charge for additional benefits. If such charge is not separable, attach description of the additional benefits included and list approximate yearly value of these for each plan and issue age. State adjustments for Female premiums.............. [illegible] each premium is payable in parentheses after the premium.

*** Information should be shown for any other plan with a volume (face amount of insurance) issued twenty years prior to statement year of 5% or more of total written business (individual policies) for year.

**** Give descriptive title showing term of coverage and premium paying period.

***** If terminal dividends are not payable until a policy year later than the 10th or 20th, enter amount of terminal dividend for earliest policy year payable and enter such policy year in parentheses after amount of terminal dividend.

NOTE: Attach to this schedule explanation showing precise methods by which dividends were calculated.

ANNUAL STATEMENT FOR THE YEAR 19 OF THE LIFE INSURANCE COMPANY
Name

SCHEDULE M – PART 2

Illustrative Dividends For Policies Issued In Year of Statement Based Upon Dividend Scale In Effect For Year of Statement

All Figures Per $1,000 Face Amount of Individual Life Insurance

(1)	(2)	(3)	Gross Premium**			Current Dividend Scale For Policy Years																				(27)	(28)	(29)	(30)
Description of Policy	Age At Issue	Amount *	(4) Initial Premium	(5) Next Premium	(6) Ultimate Premium	(7) 1	(8) 2	(9) 3	(10) 4	(11) 5	(12) 6	(13) 7	(14) 8	(15) 9	(16) 10	(17) 11	(18) 12	(19) 13	(20) 14	(21) 15	(22) 16	(23) 17	(24) 18	(25) 19	(26) 20	20th Year Cash Value	20th Year Terminal Dividend *****	10th Year Cash Value	10th Year Terminal Dividend *****
Plans With Premiums Payable For Life																													
Ordinary Life	25																												
	35																												
	45																												
	55																												
***	25																												
	35																												
	45																												
	55																												
***	25																												
	35																												
	45																												
	55																												
Limited Payment Life Plans																													
Twenty Payment Life	25																												
	35																												
	45																												
	55																												
Life Paid Up at Age	25																												
	35																												
	45																												
	55																												
***	25																												
	35																												
	45																												
	55																												
***	25																												
	35																												
	45																												
	55																												
***	25																												
	35																												
	45																												
	55																												

DETAILS OMITTED

* When size bands, constant add-on factors or other methods of gradation by size of policy are used, show figures for both $10,000 and $25,000 policies and each such amount in this column followed by "G". Otherwise, show figures for policies issued for minimum amounts (if issued) and each such amount in this column followed by "M".

** Male premiums to be shown. Exclude charge for additional benefits. If such charge is not separable, attach description of the additional benefits included and list approximate yearly value of these for each plan and issue age. State adjustments for Female premiums ....
For modified premium plans, indicate number of years each premium is payable in parentheses after the premium.
For level premium plans, enter premium in the "Ultimate Premium" column.

*** Information should be shown for any other plan with a volume (face amount of insurance) issued during statement year of 5% or more of total written business (individual policies) for year

***** If terminal dividends are not payable until a policy year later than the 10th or 20th, enter amount of terminal dividend for earliest policy year payable and enter such policy year in parentheses after amount of terminal dividend.

NOTE: Attach to this schedule explanation showing precise methods by which dividends were calculated.

Form 1

ANNUAL STATEMENT FOR THE YEAR 19 OF THE LIFE INSURANCE COMPANY

Name

SCHEDULE M – PART 2 – (Continued)

Illustrative Dividends For Policies Issued In Year of Statement Based Upon Dividend Scale In Effect For Year of Statement

All Figures Per $1,000 Face Amount of Individual Life Insurance

			Gross Premium**			Current Dividend Scale For Policy Years																							
(1) Description of Policy	(2) Age At Issue	(3) Amount *	(4) Initial Premium	(5) Next Premium	(6) Ultimate Premium	(7) 1	(8) 2	(9) 3	(10) 4	(11) 5	(12) 6	(13) 7	(14) 8	(15) 9	(16) 10	(17) 11	(18) 12	(19) 13	(20) 14	(21) 15	(22) 16	(23) 17	(24) 18	(25) 19	(26) 20	(27) 20th Year Cash Value	(28) 20th Year Terminal Dividend *****	(29) 10th Year Cash Value	(30) 10th Year Terminal Dividend *****
Term Plans																													
....Year Term or Term To Age.... (cross out one)	25																												
	35																												
	45																												
	55																												
***..............	25																												
	35																												
	45																												
	55																												
Other Plans****																													
***..............	25																												
	35																												
	45																												
	55																												
***..............	25																												
	35																												
	45																												
	55																												
***..............	25																												
	35																												
	45																												
	55																												
***..............	25																												
	35																												
	45																												
	55																												
***..............	25																												
	35																												
	45																												
	55																												
***..............	25																												
	35																												
	45																												
	55																												

DETAILS OMITTED

* When size bands, constant add-on factors or other methods of gradation by size of policy are used, show figures for both $10,000 and $25,000 policies and each such amount in this column followed by "G". Otherwise, show figures for policies issued for minimum amounts (if issued) and each such amount in this column followed by "M".

** Male premiums to be shown. Exclude charge for additional benefits. If such charge is not separable, attach description of the additional benefits included and list approximate yearly value of these for each plan and issue age. State adjustments for Female premiums..............

For modified premium plans, indicate number of years each premium is payable in parentheses after the premium.

*** Information should be shown for any other plan with a volume (face amount of insurance) issued during statement year of 5% or more of total written business (individual policies) for year.

**** Give descriptive title showing term of coverage and premium paying period.

***** If terminal dividends are not payable until a policy year later than the 10th or 20th, enter amount of terminal dividend for earliest policy year payable and enter such policy year in parentheses after amount of terminal dividend.

NOTE: Attach to this schedule explanation showing precise methods by which dividends were calculated.

SCHEDULE O
Development of Incurred Losses
Non-Cancellable, Guaranteed Renewable, and Non-Renewable for Stated Reasons Only, Accident and Health Insurance

(1) YEARS IN WHICH LOSSES WERE INCURRED	SUM OF NET AMOUNT PAID POLICYHOLDERS AND CLAIM LIABILITY AND RESERVE OUTSTANDING AT END OF YEAR				
	(2) 1980	(3) 1981	(4) 1982	(5) 1983	(6) 1984
1980				X X X	X X X
1981	X X X				X X X
1982	X X X	X X X			
1983	X X X	X X X	X X X		
1984	X X X	X X X	X X X	X X X	•

•Equals the sum of Lines 1b and 2b, Columns 5, 6 and 7 of Schedule H, Part 3.

SCHEDULE S – Part 1
Showing Names and Locations of Companies and Amounts Recoverable on Paid and Unpaid Losses for all Reinsurance Ceded

(000 OMITTED)

(1) NAME OF COMPANY	NAIC COMPANY CODE	(2) ‡LOCATION	(3) PAID LOSSES	(4) UNPAID LOSSES
LIFE				
DETAILS OMITTED				
	X X X X	*Totals—Life*		
ACCIDENT AND HEALTH				
	X X X X	*Totals—Accident and Health*		
	X X X X	*Grand Totals—Life and Accident and Health*	8,002	

SCHEDULE S – Part 2†
Showing All Accident and Health Reinsurance Ceded as of December 31, Current Year

(000 OMITTED)

(1) NAME OF COMPANY	NAIC COMPANY CODE	(2) ‡LOCATION	(3) *TYPE	(4) UNEARNED PREMIUMS (estimated)	(5) RESERVE CREDIT TAKEN OTHER THAN FOR UNEARNED PREMIUMS
DETAILS OMITTED					
	X X X X	*Totals*	X X X X	40	180

(To agree with appropriate lines in Exh. 9)

†Include actual reinsurance ceded on group cases but exclude jointly underwritten group contracts.
‡Show also domiciliary state or country.
*Use the following abbreviations: GP (group business coinsured); GPO (group business reinsured on basis other than coinsurance); YRT (individual business reinsured on yearly renewable term plan); M (individual business reinsured on modified coinsurance plan); CO (individual business reinsured on coinsurance plan); OTH (other reinsurance of individual business). If more than one type in the same reinsuring company, show separate line for each type.

SCHEDULE S – Part 3A

(To be filed not later than April 1)

Showing Data on Reinsurance Ceded for ALL Life Insurance and Related Benefits†

(000 OMITTED)

(1) NAME OF COMPANY	NAIC COMPANY CODE	(2) ‡LOCATION	(3) *TYPE OF RE-INSURANCE CEDED	(4) #AMOUNT IN FORCE AT END OF YEAR	(5) RESERVE CREDIT TAKEN (a) Current Year	(5) RESERVE CREDIT TAKEN (b) Previous Year	(6) PREMIUM
DETAILS OMITTED							
		Totals	X X X	(To agree with Line 33, Page 15)	4,925 (To agree with appropriate lines in Exh. 8)	3,790	1,? (To agree Line 30c, Ex less Cols. 8,

†Include actual reinsurance ceded on group cases, but exclude jointly underwritten group contracts.
‡Show also domiciliary state or country.
*Use the following abbreviations: GP (group business coinsured); CAT (catastrophe reinsurance of group only, individual only, or group and individual combined); GPO (reinsurance of group business other than coinsurance or catastroph DIS (disability benefits included in individual policies); ADB (accidental death benefits included in individual policies); YRT (individual life reinsured on yearly renewable term plan); M (individual life reinsured on modified coinsura plan); CO (individual life reinsured on coinsurance plan); OTH (other reinsurance of individual life business). If more than one type in same reinsuring company, show separate line for each type.
#For catastrophe reinsurance (CAT), disability reinsurance (DIS) and accidental death benefit reinsurance (ADB) leave this column blank.

SCHEDULE S – Part 3B

Showing Data on Life and Accident and Health Reinsurance in Unauthorized Companies

(1) NAME OF REINSURER	NAIC COMPANY CODE	(2) RESERVE CREDIT TAKEN	(3) PAID AND UNPAID LOSSES RECOVERABLE (Debit)	(4) TOTAL COLS. (2) PLUS (3)	(5) DEPOSITS BY AND FUNDS WITHHELD FROM REINSURERS (Credit)	(6) MISCELLANEOUS BALANCES (Credit)	(7) SUM OF IT COLS. (5) A BUT NOT IN OF COL
LIFE							
		NONE					
	Totals—Life						
ACCIDENT AND HEALTH							
Totals—Accident and Health							
Grand Totals—Life and Accident and Health							

NOTES: Securities held on deposit should be valued in accordance with N.A.I.C. valuations. Letters of credit are to be included in Column (5) and indicated by an asterisk (*). Letters of credit are not to be inc in assets or liabilities on Pages 2 or 3 or supporting pages or exhibits.

SCHEDULE S – Part 3C – Section 1

(To be filed not later than April 1)

Showing Data on Reinsurance Assumed for Life Insurance and Related Benefits as of December 31, Current Year

(000 OMITTED)

(1) NAME OF REINSURED	NAIC COMPANY CODE	(2) †LOCATION	(3) *TYPE OF RE INSURANCE ASSUMED	(4) #AMOUNT IN FORCE AT END OF YEAR	(5) RESERVE	(6) PREMIUMS	(7) REINSURANCE PAYABLE ON PAID AND UNPAID LOSSES
		DETAILS OMITTED					
		Totals	XXXX		110	420 (To agree with Exh. 1, Part 1, Line 20b, Cols. 2 to 7)	130 (To agree with Exh. 11, Part 1, Line 4b, Cols. 2 to 8)

strophe reinsurance (CAT), disability reinsurance (DIS) and accidental death benefit reinsurance (ADB) leave this column blank.

SCHEDULE S – Part 3C – Section 2

(To be filed not later than April 1)

Showing Data on Reinsurance Assumed for Accident and Health as of December 31, Current Year

(1) NAME OF REINSURED	NAIC COMPANY CODE	(2) †LOCATION	(3) *TYPE OF RE INSURANCE ASSUMED	(4) PREMIUMS	(5) UNEARNED PREMIUMS	(6) RESERVE LIABILITY OTHER THAN FOR UN EARNED PREMIUMS	(7) REINSURANCE PAYABLE ON PAID AND UNPAID LOSSES
		NONE					
		Totals	XXXX	(To agree with Exh. 1, Part 1, Line 20b, Cols. 8 to 10)			(To agree with Exh. 11, Part 1, Line 4b, Cols. 9 to 11)

omiciliary state or country

owing abbreviations: GP (Group business coinsured), CAT (catastrophe reinsurance of group only, individual only, or group and individual combined), GPO (reinsurance of group business other than coinsurance or catastrophe) ty benefits included in individual policies), ADB (accidental death benefits included in individual policies), YRT (individual life reinsured on yearly renewable term plan), M (individual life reinsured on modified coinsurance ndividual life reinsured on coinsurance plan), OTH (other reinsurance of individual life business). If more than one type in same reinsuring company, show separate line for each type

GENERAL INTERROGATORIES

he company reported in this schedule the required data on all reinsurance ceded? ANSWER: ....

ny of the reinsurers listed in this schedule owned or controlled, either directly or indirectly, by the company, or by any representative, officer, trustee, or director company? ANSWER: .... If so, give full particulars ....

any policies issued by the company been reinsured with a company chartered in a country other than the United States (excluding U.S. Branches of such anies) which is owned or controlled directly or indirectly by the insured, the beneficiary, a creditor of the insured, or any other person not primarily engaged insurance business? ANSWER: ....

answer to Question 6 of Section 5, Schedule S – Part 4 on Page 43B 30% or more? ANSWER .... If so, has Schedule rt 4, Page 43B been completed and have the instructions contained therein relating to credit for ceded reinsurance been adhered to? ANSWER: ....

SCHEDULE S — Part 4

CEDED REINSURANCE REPORT

DETAILS OMITTED

(This schedule does not have to be completed unless the answer to the first question in General Interrogatory 4 on Page 43A is answered "yes".)

SECTION 1. Annual Report of Reinsurance Transactions

The company shall determine the answers to the questions set forth in Section 3 of this report as of the Annual Statement date. If the answer to any such question is "yes", the company shall then determine the answers to the questions set forth in Sections 4 and 5. If the answer to Question 6 of Section 5 is 30% or more, it shall report such fact in Question 1 of General Interrogatory 4 on Page 43A.

SECTION 2. Supplementary Report of Reinsurance Transactions

Whenever the company enters into a new reinsurance agreement or alters the terms of any existing reinsurance agreement, during the year following the date of this Annual Statement, it shall determine the answers to the questions as set forth in Sections 3, 4 and 5 as of the effective date of such agreement or alteration. If the answer to Question 6 of Section 5 shows a reduction in the then current surplus of 30% or more, it shall report such fact within fifteen days after the date of such new agreement or alteration to each Regulatory Authority with which this Annual Statement was filed.

SECTION 3. Ceded Reinsurance Report—Part A

"Ceded Reinsurance Report—Part A" shall consist of answers to the following questions:

1. Does the company have any reinsurance agreements in effect under which the reinsurer may unilaterally cancel any reinsurance for reasons other than nonpayment of reinsurance premiums? ANSWER: ....

2. Does the company have any reinsurance agreements in effect under which it is obligated to pay future aggregate reinsurance premiums minus reinsurance commissions, expense allowances and any premium tax reimbursements, which are in excess of 100% of the future aggregate gross premiums the company will collect on the reinsured portions of policies reinsured under such agreements less the amounts the company will pay as commissions and premium taxes or items similar to commissions? ANSWER: ....

3. Does the company have any reinsurance agreements in effect under which it may become obligated because of loss experience on the reinsurance to pay future aggregate reinsurance premiums minus reinsurance commissions, expense allowances and any premium tax reimbursements, which are in excess of 100% of the future aggregate gross premiums the company will collect on the reinsured portions of policies reinsured under such agreements less the amounts the company will pay as commissions and premium taxes or items similar to commissions? ANSWER: ....

SECTION 4. Ceded Reinsurance Report —Part B

"Ceded Reinsurance Report—Part B" shall consist of answers to the following questions concerning reinsurance agreements in effect for which the answer to Question 1 of Section 3 is "yes":

1. What is the amount of return commission which would have been due reinsurers if they had cancelled all of your company's reinsurance as of the end of the period covered by the accompanying Annual Statement? ANSWER: ....

2. What would be the amount of the reduction in surplus as shown in the accompanying Annual Statement if adjustments were made to reflect the full amount described in Question 1 of this Section and any additional reserves which would be required to be set up? ANSWER: ....

3. Have you established in the accompanying Annual Statement the full amount of liabilities for any additional reinsurance premiums which, on the basis of loss experience to date, would have been payable if the reinsurer had cancelled all of the reinsurance as of the end of the period covered by the accompanying Annual Statement? ANSWER: .... If not, what additional liabilities would have been required? ANSWER: ....

4. What would be the amount of the reduction in surplus (Page 3, Line 29D) as shown on the accompanying Annual Statement if adjustments were made to reflect the additional amount described in Question 3 of this Section? ANSWER: ....

5. What would be the percentage reduction in surplus (Page 3, Line 29D) as of the end of the period covered by the accompanying Annual Statement from the combined effects of the amounts described in Questions 2 and 4 of this Section? ANSWER: ....

SECTION 5. Ceded Reinsurance Report—Part C

"Ceded Reinsurance Report—Part C" shall consist of answers to the following questions concerning reinsurance agreements in effect for which the answer to Question 2 or Question 3 of Section 3 is "yes".

1. Do the future aggregate reinsurance premiums minus reinsurance commissions, expense allowances and any premium tax reimbursements, exceed the future gross premiums the company will collect on the reinsured portions of policies reinsured under such agreements less the amounts the company will pay as commissions and premium taxes or items similar to commissions? ANSWER: .... If so, by what amount? ANSWER: ....

2. What would be the amount of reduction in the company's surplus (Page 3, Line 29D) as shown on the accompanying Annual Statement if adjustments were made to reflect the additional amount described in Question 1 of this Section? ANSWER: ....

3. Do the future aggregate reinsurance premiums which may become payable based on loss experience of the reinsurance, minus reinsurance commissions, expense allowances and any premium tax reimbursements, exceed the future aggregate gross premiums the company will collect on the reinsured portions of policies reinsured under such agreements less the amounts the company will pay as commissions and premium taxes or items similar to commissions? ANSWER: .... If so, by what amount? ANSWER: ....

4. What would be the amount of reduction in the company's surplus (Page 3, Line 29D) as shown on the accompanying Annual Statement if adjustments were made to reflect the additional amounts described in Question 3 of this Section? ANSWER: ....

5. What would be the percentage reduction in surplus (Page 3, Line 29D) of the company as of the end of the period covered by the accompanying Annual Statement from the combined effects of the amounts described in Questions 2 and 4 of this Section? ANSWER: ....

6. What would be the percentage reduction in surplus (Page 3, Line 29D) of the company as of the end of the period covered by the accompanying Annual Statement from the combined effects of the amounts described in Questions 2 and 4 of this Section and Questions 2 and 4 of Section 4? ANSWER: ....

SECTION 6. Requirements for Reinsurance Credit

Whenever the answer to Question 6 of Section 5 shows a reduction in surplus (Page 3, Line 29D) of 30% or more, the company shall not take any credit under agreements for which the answer to any of the questions in Section 3 is "yes".

SECTION 7. Waiver of Requirements

Consistent with the purpose of this report, the Regulatory Authority (ies) may, in appropriate cases, waive one or more of the requirements of these instructions.

ANNUAL STATEMENT FOR THE YEAR 19 OF THE LIFE INSURANCE COMPANY
Name

SCHEDULE X – PART 1 – UNLISTED ASSETS

Showing all property owned by or in which the Company had any interest, on December 31 of current year, which is not entered on any other schedule and which is not included in the financial statement for the current year

(1) DESCRIPTION	(2) FROM WHOM ACQUIRED	(3) DATE WHEN ACQUIRED	(4) DATE WHEN CHARGED OFF FROM STATEMENT	(5) PAR VALUE	(6) ACTUAL COST	(7) BOOK VALUE WHEN CHARGED OFF	(8) MARKET VALUE DECEMBER 31 OF CURRENT YEAR	(9) GROSS INCOME THEREFROM DURING YEAR	(10) OUTLAYS MADE DURING YEAR	(11) REASONS FOR NOT CARRYING PROPERTY ON BOOKS
				NONE						
			Totals							XXXX

SCHEDULE X – PART 2

Showing all property acquired or transferred to Schedule X, Part 1, during the year except that shown in invested asset schedules and except furniture, fixtures and supplies

(1) DESCRIPTION	(2) DATE OF ACQUISITION	(3) FROM WHOM ACQUIRED	(4) PAR VALUE	(5) ACTUAL COST
	NONE			
		Totals		

SCHEDULE X – PART 3

Showing all property sold or transferred from Schedule X, Part 1, during the year except that shown in invested asset schedules

(1) DESCRIPTION	(2) DATE OF ACQUISITION	(3) FROM WHOM ACQUIRED	(4) PAR VALUE	(5) ACTUAL COST	(6) DATE OF SALE	(7) TO WHOM SOLD	(8) CONSIDERATION	(9) GROSS INCOME THEREFROM DURING YEAR	(10) OUTLAY THEREON DURING YEAR OTHER THAN COST
				NONE					
		Totals			XXX	XXX XXX XXX XXX XXX			

*Companies should limit entries in this schedule to items transferred from asset accounts.

SCHEDULE Y — ORGANIZATIONAL CHART

Attach a chart or listing presenting the identities of and interrelationships among all affiliated insurers and all other affiliates, identifying all insurers as such. No non-insurer affiliate need be shown if its total assets are less than ½ of 1% of the total assets of the largest affiliated insurer.

DETAILS OMITTED

NOTE: All members of a Holding Company Group shall prepare a common Schedule for inclusion in each of the individual annual statements and the consolidated Fire and Casualty Annual Statement of the Group.

SCHEDULE T — PREMIUMS AND ANNUITY CONSIDERATIONS
Allocated by States and Territories

(1) STATES, ETC.		(2) IS INSURER LICENSED? (Yes or No)	DIRECT BUSINESS ONLY		
			(3) LIFE INSURANCE PREMIUMS	(4) ANNUITY CONSIDERATIONS	(5) ACCIDENT AND HEALTH INSURANCE PREMIUMS, INCLUDING POLICY, MEMBERSHIP AND OTHER FEES
ibama	AL				
iska	AK				
zona	AZ				
kansas	AR				
ifornia	CA				
orado	CO				
nnecticut	CT				
aware	DE		DETAILS OMITTED		
t. Columbia	DC				
rida	FL				
orgia	GA				
waii	HI				
ho	ID				
nois	IL				
iana	IN				
a	IA				
nsas	KS				
ntucky	KY				
isiana	LA				
ne	ME				
ryland	MD				
ssachusetts	MA				
higan	MI				
nesota	MN				
ssissippi	MS				
souri	MO				
ntana	MT				
raska	NE				
ada	NV				
Hampshire	NH				
Jersey	NJ				
Mexico	NM				
York	NY				
Carolina	NC				
Dakota	ND				
o	OH				
ahoma	OK				
gon	OR				
nsylvania	PA				
de Island	RI				
Carolina	SC				
Dakota	SD				
nessee	TN				
as	TX				
h	UT				
mont	VT				
ginia	VA				
shington	WA				
t Virginia	WV				
consin	WI				
ming	WY				
erican Samoa	AS				
m	GU				
rto Rico	PR				
. Virgin Is.	VI				
ada	CN				
er alien (itemize)***	OT				
ny contributions for employee benefit plans		X X X			
ends applied to purchase paid-up ions and annuities		X X X			
ends applied to shorten endowment or ium-paying period		X X X			
nium or annuity considerations waived r disability or other contract provisions		X X X			
ALS (Direct Business)		X X X			
Reinsurance Assumed		X X X			
LS (All Business)		X X X			
Reinsurance Ceded		X X X			
tals (All Business) less Reinsurance Ceded		††			

Explanation of basis of allocation by states, etc., of premiums and annuity considerations

†Dividend accumulations used to purchase paid-up additions and annuities, or to shorten endowment or premium-paying period, should not be included in this item but should be included in Columns 3 and 4 and distributed by states for those states which allowed the dividends to be deducted in calculating premium taxes. For other states, separate totals similar to those for dividends so applied may be shown. Dividends applied to pay renewal premiums and consideration for annuities must also be included in Columns 3 and 4 and distributed by states.

*Premium or annuity considerations waived under disability or other contract provisions should be shown here in one sum and not included in the distribution by states.

**The sum of Columns 3 and 4 should balance with Exhibit 1, Lines 6d, 10d and 16d, Col. 1, less Cols. 8, 9 and 10. Column 5 should balance with Exhibit 1, Lines 6d, 10d and 16d, Cols. 8, 9 and 10, or with Schedule H, Part 1, Line 1; indicate which ……………

***All U.S. business must be allocated by state regardless of license status. ††Insert the number of yes responses except for Canada and Other alien.

SUPPLEMENTAL EXHIBITS AND SCHEDULES INTERROGATORIES

Details Omitted

The following supplemental reports are required to be filed as part of your annual statement filing. However, in the event that your company does not transact the type of business for which the special report must be filed, your response to the specific interrogatory will be accepted in lieu of filing a "NONE" report.

1. Will Schedule SIS (Stockholder Information Supplement) be filed with this Department by March 1? Answer (yes or no):............ If answer is "no," please explain:..............................

2. Will Schedule S, Part 3A and Part 3C (Sections 1 and 2) be filed with this Department by April 1? Answer (yes or no):............ If answer is "no," please explain:..............................

3. Will the Credit Life Insurance Statistical Report be filed with this Department by April 1? Answer (yes or no):............ If answer is "no," please explain:..............................

4. Will the Credit Life and Accident and Health Exhibit be filed with this Department by May 1? Answer (yes or no):............ If answer is "no," please explain:..............................

5. Will the Accident and Health Policy Experience Exhibit be filed with this Department by June 30? Answer (yes or no):............ If answer is "no," please explain:..............................

DIRECT BUSINESS IN THE STATE OF DURING THE YEAR

NAIC GROUP CODE: **LIFE INSURANCE** NAIC COMPANY CODE:

(1) ECT PREMIUMS AND ANNUITY CONSIDERATIONS (Excluding Reinsurance Accepted and without deduction of Reinsurance Ceded)	(2) ORDINARY	(3) CREDIT LIFE* (Group and Individual)	(4) GROUP	(5) INDUSTRIAL	(6) TOTAL
1. Life insurance					
2. Annuity considerations					
3.					
4. Totals					
4.1 Annuity and other fund deposits			X X X		X X X
DIRECT DIVIDENDS TO POLICYHOLDERS (Excluding Reinsurance Accepted and without deduction of Reinsurance Ceded)		DETAILS OMITTED			
Life insurance:					
5.1 Paid in cash or left on deposit					
5.2 Applied to pay renewal premiums					
5.3 Applied to provide paid-up additions or shorten the endowment or premium paying period					
5.4 Other					
5.5 Totals (Sum of 5.1 to 5.4)					
Annuities:					
6.1 Paid in cash or left on deposit					
6.2 Applied to provide paid-up annuities					
6.3 Other					
6.4 Totals (Sum of 6.1 to 6.3)					
7. Grand Totals (Lines 5.5 plus 6.4)					
DIRECT CLAIMS AND BENEFITS PAID (Excluding Reinsurance Accepted and without deduction of Reinsurance Ceded)					
8. Death benefits					
9. Matured endowments					
0. Annuity benefits					
1. Surrender values					
2.					
3. All other benefits, except Accident and Health					
4. Totals					

DIRECT DEATH BENEFITS AND MATURED ENDOWMENTS INCURRED (Excluding Reinsurance Accepted and without deduction of Reinsurance Ceded)	ORDINARY		CREDIT LIFE* (Group and Individual)		GROUP		INDUSTRIAL		TOTAL	
	No.	Amount	No. of Ind. Pols. & Gr. Certifs.	Amount	No. of Certifs.	Amount	No.	Amount	No.	Amount
. Unpaid December 31, previous year										
. Incurred during current year										
ttled during current year:										
.1 By payment in full										
.2 By payment on compromised claims										
.3 Totals paid										
.4 Reduction by compromise										
.5 Amount rejected										
.6 Total settlements										
. Unpaid Dec. 31, current year (15 + 16—17.6)										
POLICY EXHIBIT (Excluding Reinsurance Accepted and without deduction of Reinsurance Ceded)					No. of Policies					
In force December 31, previous year										
Issued during year										
Ceased to be in force during year (Net)										
In force December 31 of current year										

cludes Individual Credit Life Insurance: previous year $........; current year $........

cludes Group Credit Life Insurance: Loans less than or equal 60 months at issue, previous year $........; current year $........

ans greater than 60 months at issue BUT NOT GREATER THAN 120 MONTHS previous year $........; current year $........

NOTE: This company's participations in the FEGLI and SGLI policies are shown in this Policy Exhibit as direct business.

ACCIDENT AND HEALTH INSURANCE

(1)	(2) DIRECT PREMIUMS (Excluding Reinsurance Accepted and without deduction of Reinsurance Ceded)	(3) DIRECT PREMIUMS EARNED	(4) DIVIDENDS PAID OR CREDITED ON DIRECT BUSINESS	(5) DIRECT LOSSES PAID	(6) DIRECT LOSSES INCURRED
. Group Policies					
.1 Credit (Group and Individual)*					
.2 Collectively Renewable Policies					
her Individual Policies:					
.1 Non-cancellable					
.2 Guaranteed renewable					
.3 Non-renewable for stated reasons only					
.4 Other accident only					
.5 All other					
.6 Totals (Sum of 24.1 to 24.5)					
Totals (Lines 23 + 23.1 + 23.2 + 24.6)					

CREDIT LIFE AND ACCIDENT AND HEALTH INSURANCE
(Included in the above schedules)

(1)	(2) DIRECT PREMIUMS (Excluding Reinsurance Accepted and without deduction of Reinsurance Ceded)	(3) DIRECT PREMIUMS EARNED* (prior to Dividends and Retrospective Rate Credits Paid or Credited)	(4) DIVIDENDS AND RETROSPECTIVE RATE CREDITS PAID OR CREDITED ON DIRECT BUSINESS*	(5) DIRECT LOSSES PAID	(6) DIRECT LOSSES INCURRED*
Individual life policies					
Group life policies—loans OF 60 OR LESS months' duration					
Group life policies—loans OF GREATER THAN 60 MONTHS' DURATION BUT NOT GREATER THAN 120 MONTHS					
Totals (Lines 26 + 27.1 + 27.2)					
Group A & H policies—loans of 60 OR LESS months' duration					
Group A & H policies—loans of GREATER THAN 60 MONTHS' DURATION BUT NOT GREATER THAN 120 MONTHS					
Other A & H policies					
Totals (Lines 29.1 + 29.2 + 30)					
Totals (Lines 28 + 31)					

*The figures shown in these columns should be consistent with the corresponding figures in the Credit Life and Accident and Health Exhibit.
*Business not exceeding 120 months duration.

Date of filing: This exhibit is required to be filed not later than June 30

ACCIDENT AND HEALTH POLICY EXPERIENCE EXHIBIT FOR YEAR 19........

47 Form 12 MADE BY LIFE INSURANCE COMPANY
Name

(1) POLICY FORM NUMBER	(1) FIRST YEAR ISSUED	(2) NAME OF POLICY	(3) PREMIUMS EARNED (see note a)	INCURRED CLAIMS AND INCREASE IN POLICY RESERVES (4) AMOUNT	INCURRED CLAIMS AND INCREASE IN POLICY RESERVES (5) PERCENT OF PREMIUMS EARNED	(6) COMMISSIONS INCURRED	(7) RATE OF COMMISSION AND EXPENSE ALLOWANCE	(8) DIVIDENDS TO POLICYHOLDERS INCURRED
		DETAILS OMITTED						
		Total Direct Business						
		Reinsurance Assumed less Ceded						
		TOTALS (to agree with annual statement)						

Number of Accident and Health Policies in Force at End of Year: Group Certificates..........; Collectively Renewable..........; Non-Cancellable..........; Guaranteed Renewable..........; Non-Renewable for Stated Reasons Only..........; Other Accident Only..........; All Other..........

(a) Premiums earned are before adjustment for the increase in policy reserves which has been treated as a separate deduction.

Form 12

CREDIT LIFE AND ACCIDENT AND HEALTH EXHIBIT

Supplement to the December 31, 19 ...... Annual Statement of the LIFE INSURANCE COMPANY

To Be Filed on or Before May 1

PART 1—CREDIT LIFE INSURANCE

CLASSIFICATION (Accrual Basis)	GROUP POLICIES			INDIVIDUAL POLICIES			
	Direct	Reinsurance		Level Amount Direct	Decreasing Amount Direct	Reinsurance	
		ASSUMED	CEDED			ASSUMED	CEDED
1. Gross premiums							
2. Less return premiums on cancelled policies							
3. Line 1 minus line 2							
4.* Increase in reserve liability							
5. Line 3 minus line 4		NONE					
6. Losses (a) Death benefits							
(b) Other benefits							
7. Loss expense							
8. Commissions							
9. General insurance expense							
10. Taxes, licenses and fees							
11.							
12. Total (lines 6-11 inclusive)							
13. Net gain from operations before dividends and retrospective rate credits (line 5 minus line 12)							
14. Dividends and retrospective rate credits							
15. Net gain from operations after dividends and retrospective rate credits (line 13 minus line 14)							
16. Amount of insurance in force, December 31, previous year							
17. Amount of insurance in force, December 31, current year							

*State reserve basis, including valuation standards, used

PART 2—CREDIT ACCIDENT AND HEALTH INSURANCE

CLASSIFICATION (Accrual Basis)	GROUP POLICIES			INDIVIDUAL POLICIES		
	Direct	Reinsurance		Direct	Reinsurance	
		ASSUMED	CEDED		ASSUMED	CEDED
1. Gross premiums						
2. Less return premiums on cancelled policies						
3. Line 1 minus line 2		NONE				
4. Increase in unearned premium reserve						
5. Earned premiums (line 3 minus line 4)						
6. Losses						
7. Loss expense						
8. Commissions						
9. General insurance expense						
10. Taxes, licenses and fees						
11. Other reserve increase						
12. Total (lines 6-11 inclusive)						
13. Net gain from operations before dividends and retrospective rate credits (line 5 minus line 12)						
14. Dividends and retrospective rate credits						
15. Net gain from operations after dividends and retrospective rate credits (line 13 minus line 14)						

SPECIAL INSTRUCTIONS

Credit life insurance is defined as that form of insurance under which the life of a borrower of money or purchaser of goods is insured in connection with a specific loan or credit transaction. Credit Accident and Health insurance is that form of insurance under which a borrower of money or a purchaser of goods is indemnified in connection with a specific loan or credit transaction against loss of time resulting from accident or sickness. If a single insurance contract combines both Life and Accident and Health coverage, proper allocation should be made to the appropriate Parts of this Exhibit. These definitions shall not include Life insurance or Accident and Health insurance in connection with loans of more than 120 months' duration.

This Exhibit should be completed on the accrual, i.e., earned and incurred basis. Certain items may be either positive or negative, and should be entered accordingly.

"Direct" means that reinsurance ceded has not been deducted and reinsurance assumed is excluded.

LINE 1—GROSS PREMIUMS—Amounts should be reported before (a) dividends and retrospective rate credits, (b) returned premiums on cancelled policies, and (c) adjustment for unearned premium reserves, but should include membership and policy fees and any other charge made in connection with insurance policies or certificates.

LINE 6—LOSSES—Losses should include only actual benefits incurred during the year to beneficiaries or assignees in accordance with the policy provisions.

LINE 8—COMMISSIONS—Commissions should include policy, membership and other fees retained by agents.

LINES 16 AND 17—AMOUNTS OF INSURANCE IN FORCE, DECEMBER 31 PREVIOUS AND CURRENT YEARS—The amounts of insurance in force should be based on actual amounts of insured outstanding indebtedness, rather than on original amounts of loans.

NOTES

INDEX

ABOUT THE AUTHORS

CLAIR J. GALLOWAY, C.P.A., has served as an independent auditor, tax consultant, and business adviser with both large and small insurance companies for 25 years. His experience includes assistance with public stock offerings, acquisition of new companies, strategic planning programs, executive recruitment, income tax strategies, and reorganization plans. He has appeared before the Securities and Exchange Commission and the National Office of the Internal Revenue Service on matters of insurance accounting and as an expert witness on cases brought before the U.S. Tax and District Courts. His articles have appeared in several publications, including *The Management Accountant* and *The Best Review*. A former partner of Ernst & Whinney, Clair Galloway is president of the Galloway Company.

JOSEPH M. GALLOWAY, C.P.A., C.L.U., J.D., has been a tax consultant, auditor, and adviser with medium-sized and small life and property liability insurance companies for ten years. His experience includes working with reinsurance programs and the coordination of insurance commissioners' financial examinations. He is a chartered life underwriter and the author of numerous articles as well as the book *The Unrelated Business Income Tax*. Joseph Galloway is a praticing accountant and attorney and is president of Joseph M. Galloway P.C.